W9-CDK-036

ABH 3.95N

1508

POLITICAL REPRESENTATION IN ENGLAND AND THE ORIGINS OF THE AMERICAN REPUBLIC

POLITICAL REPRESENTATION IN ENGLAND AND THE ORIGINS OF THE AMERICAN REPUBLIC

J. R. POLE

READER IN AMERICAN HISTORY AND GOVERNMENT
IN THE UNIVERSITY OF CAMBRIDGE AND
FELLOW OF CHURCHILL COLLEGE

University of California Press
Berkeley, Los Angeles, and London

Originally published by
Macmillan and Company Limited
and St Martin's Press Inc.

© J. R. Pole 1966

California Paperback Edition 1971

University of California Press
Berkeley and Los Angeles

University of California Press Limited
London, England

Library of Congress Catalog Card Number 75–145792
International Standard Book Number: 0–520–01903–2

Printed in the United States of America

TO THE MEMORY OF

SUSAN ISAACS

Part Four

INTEREST REPRESENTATION IN BRITAIN
AND THE SLOW BIRTH OF THE
POLITICAL INDIVIDUAL

Part Five

THE COMPARATIVE DIMENSION

List of Maps

Preface

WHEN American spokesmen worked out their arguments against parliamentary taxation, though by no means of one mind on all questions, they were agreed in maintaining two contradictory propositions. They affirmed that they were British subjects, entitled to all the rights of Englishmen; yet they denied that they were represented in Parliament. But according to constitutional theory this was impossible: all British subjects were represented in Parliament. The American assertion compelled British parliamentarians to reconsider the relationship of Parliament to the colonies and to bring forth the specious doctrine of 'virtual representation'.

Virtual representation had a predecessor in Locke's doctrine of 'tacit consent'. The many British subjects at home who had no personal suffrage were supposed to have given their consent to live under the government by the mere fact that they lived under it, and to be represented in Parliament by sharing the interests of their wealthier neighbours who had votes or were eligible for seats. Parliament stood for the general interest of the whole nation, in which all were concerned; and by extension it was also the Parliament of the whole Empire. Virtual representation could thus become an instrument for the defence of existing political institutions, not only against rebellious colonists but against reformers who wanted to put political representation on a wider and more personal basis. Oddly enough, it could also be applied, if in somewhat diluted form, to explain some features of the domestic arrangements of the American states.

Americans, because they were British-born subjects, well knew that they were entitled to representation and could not be lawfully taxed except by an assembly elected by themselves. Such assemblies had long existed in the colonies. The nature of the argument with Britain naturally trained all their attention, their energies, and their dialectical skill towards the by no means simple problem of their true relationship with the mother country. Very little time or interest was left over for the hardly less complex problems of the meaning of representation in the colonial assemblies themselves.

Virtual representation, as a system of empire, died soon after being discovered. It had lasted only so long as it escaped detection and definition. This book does not concern itself with the problems of the relationship between the colonies and Parliament, which are already the subject of an extensive literature. The Americans had immediately to face and resolve the problems of representation for themselves, and to do so in a context in which all government had suddenly become in some form representative government. It is the internal problems of representation that were brought to a head on both sides of the Atlantic by the Declaration and War of Independence which form the subject matter of this study. The Revolution period takes a central place in the argument both because of the richness of the materials flung up by the making of American constitutions and by the British movements for parliamentary reform, and because of its obvious influence in forcing these things into the open. I have traced these issues to their earlier sources in each of the five areas of sovereignty, of independent assembly or parliamentary government, to which this study has been directed. In each of these five areas I have brought the story forward to a point — slightly different in each case — at which the older problems had been, in some substantial measure, absorbed and redefined, and when new forces were beginning to apply their transforming pressure to institutions that were already old.

The Americans and their British contemporaries were in a strong sense fellow-citizens of a great republic of Whig ideas. John Adams of Massachusetts or James Madison of Virginia could have entered British politics, and Charles Grey, Charles Fox — even Lord North! — could have entered American politics with a great deal more chance of being understood than Sieyès or Robespierre could have done in England, and with a great deal more physical safety than Tom Paine experienced in France.

The choice of five particular states requires some explanation. That of Great Britain, which was the source of American government, and which has the advantage of a single Parliament, is self-explanatory. The case for taking up the theme of representation as it affected the American continent, first through the study of the Continental Congress and later in the Constitutional Convention, is equally clear. But before coming to the Continental level I have made detailed analyses of representation on the smaller scale of three American provincial governments. These lesser units have been carefully chosen. Massachusetts was generally agreed to be the most influential of the New England provinces, and its domestic institutions bore a close enough resemblance to those of its neighbours to give it a roughly representative character. Variations found in other parts of New England appear to be variations of detail rather than kind. Pennsylvania had a character of its own because of the highly articulate republican theory that went into its foundation; its subsequent history made it in some ways a precursor of much more general American experience. Virginia is selected to stand for the

South in the same way as Massachusetts stands here for New England. Actually there were marked differences in local history between all of the Southern provinces; and it may be added that similar studies of New York, New Jersey, and Maryland would greatly enrich the texture of the story. I do not believe that the inclusion of additional sections on these or other provinces would alter any fundamental principle of the argument, though such studies would certainly add valuable and interesting variations of detail; I have concluded that more was to be gained by a thorough examination of three outstandingly important sovereignties than by a cursory study of a larger number.

This work has been conceived and developed as a study of political representation; but representation can be understood only in the relationship it bears to the political system as a whole, and I found myself unavoidably committed to some consideration of the theory of the state. For this reason I have given rather more extended attention to the views of those seventeenth-century English Whig writers who influenced both English and American development, than might have been expected if the work had been more narrowly focused on representation alone.

From these views there emerge certain themes, notably that of the supremacy of the 'legislative power', which are then transferred to and followed out in the selected American colonies. When this leading Whig theme has been satisfactorily settled and established in the colonies — assimilated, so to speak, as one of the 'rights' to which Americans were both accustomed and entitled — then the other major themes begin to develop and are grouped together in Part III. Americans had their own problems to work out in the relationship of social orders to political structure; 'interests', pressing for political recognition or advantage, became a natural part of the legislative process, and in due course of the representative system; and, most important of all, the idea of the political prevalence of the numerical majority struggled into existence. But these themes developed separately in the different states, not only at a different pace, but even with certain differences of quality and character depending on differences of regional history. I have, therefore, given careful attention to the development of these themes within the texture of the political and legislative histories of the separate states. I have risked a certain amount of repetition in order to gain in the conviction and firmness with which the conclusions may be said to stand in relation to the political issues as they presented themselves at the time. I have resolved on this method as the surest way of maintaining clarity and coherence in what was actually a very complex series of events.

A word of explanation about the noun 'Republic', which, as used in the title, bears two meanings: first, it refers specifically to the foundation of the new nation, the Republic known as the United States of America; but secondly, by using it I also imply an intention to analyse the concept of a 'republican form of government', which in American usage means representative government under a rule of law; in British usage, by contrast, a republic is merely a state whose head is elected rather than hereditary.

The book concludes with a chapter on the Comparative Dimension — a chapter which, without some self-discipline on the author's part, might easily have grown until it threatened to wag the book. I have kept it within a brief compass in the hope that the reader will treat the whole work, as I have tried to write it, as a comparative study in which the history and meaning of political representation in each of these closely related states will be deepened and illuminated by comparisons and cross-references that spring out from the separate sections.

This work explores the borderland between political ideas and the history of politics and if it is successful it will help to show, in the given historical situation, how and within what limits ideas may be said to make politics. I have tried to use the methods of a historian in arriving at conclusions that belong equally to the conceptual order of the political scientist; but I have not begun with preconceived notions of that conceptual order, nor have I forced the historical sources to concur in any single, unified conclusion. History is not like that; and even after the rise of the more generally recognised principles of modern democracy, representation was to remain a muddle of high principles and inherited practices.

The irregular spellings, punctuation, and capitalisation of old printed documents have, wherever safely possible, been rendered uniform; those of manuscript sources have in some cases been modified but where they do not interfere with legibility, have been allowed to stand.

Different sections of the manuscript have been submitted to the scrutiny of my friends and colleagues on both sides of the Atlantic. I am grateful to Professor Carl Bridenbaugh for advice given at a formative stage of my research. Chapters on the American side have also gained from the comments of Dr Richard S. Dunn, Mrs Mary Dunn, Professor Douglass Adair, and Professor Richard P. McCormick; Professor Jacob Viner gave me about two hours of advice that were worth several months of research. On the English side, Dr J. H. Burns (on Locke) and Dr John A. Woods (on Burke) offered me advice and criticism, and Mr H. L. Beales allowed me to draw freely on his large collection of rare political tracts. I want also to express an affectionate debt of gratitude for the help of Professor H. C. Allen and Dr F. M. L. Thompson.

The researches on which this book has been built were undertaken while I held the lectureship in American History at University College London. My prolonged visits to American archives were made possible, in the first place, by generous leaves of absence granted by University College. They were supported by grants made successively by the Commonwealth Foundation, the American Philosophical Society and the Rockefeller Foundation. Microfilms of early American newspapers were purchased through a grant from the Central Research Funds of the University of London. Dr Edward Leonard went to much personal trouble to supply me with photo-copies of other newspapers.

Among the many librarians and archivists who have given so much courteous attention to my investigations I would like particularly to mention Mr Leo Flaherty, guardian and deliverer of the State Archives in Boston, who often seems to have fought single-handed to keep me supplied with information; and Mr Steven T. Riley, Director of the Massachusetts Historical Society, who always does so much to make me at home there.

J. R. P.

Cambridge
4 *July* 1964

1. No Parliament without Representation

The struggle for power in seventeenth-century England required the major contestants to think about the nation as a whole. By the time of the Glorious Revolution, and still more by that of the Act of Settlement, the upheavals of a very full lifetime had brought about a marked clarification in constitutional ideas.

Parliamentary leaders and kings might from time to time have been willing to settle for power and forgo the theory of the state. But the logic of the argument in which systematic political thinkers chose to engage required them to go further. The more searching and significant arguments did indeed go further in a geographical as well as an intellectual sense: they were carried across the Atlantic to exert their influence on American constitutions even after they had faded out of active debate in England.

Three thinkers stand out from the English seventeenth century by reason of this dual influence, at home and, after their deaths, in America. James Harrington conceived of the community as a whole, to be regulated, in the common interest, from the centre. Algernon Sidney and John Locke received from their predecessors and transmitted to their political heirs the Whig doctrine of the supremacy of the legislative power. But where did that power lie? Together with all good Whigs they maintained that it lay ultimately in the people; both accepted the representative branch of government as the sole legitimate and normal instrument of the will of the people. But neither of them was anxious to scrutinise too closely the actual ability of Parliament to fulfil its representative function.

Both Locke and Sidney hinted at, but neither of them developed, the idea that a distinction might be drawn between the permanent or constitutional law of the land and the alterable statute law of Parliament. The doctrines of Locke, which eventually were to prove the more pervasive (perhaps because they were the more ambiguous) contained the seeds of majority rule. However, he could also be interpreted as the defender of the vested rights of minorities, and after the American Revolution, the Americans came to prefer him in the latter manifestation.

All of these ideas were to be tested in the century after Locke's death. It might have surprised him to know that the American continent was to be the proving ground.

IDEAS of representation are engrained in the history of Parliament. The High Court of Parliament, of course, could go on meeting for centuries without giving rise to a system of representative government; but there could be no Parliament without representation.

The idea was implied in the Roman law dictum, adopted by Bracton, that the law to bind all should be approved by all. Despite occasional changes in the practice, and distantly related reformulations of the concept, traces of the medieval heritage survived into the nineteenth century. Communities in different parts of the kingdom had originally been required to select reliable persons, to whom they would depute the power to treat with the king and commit their communities to grants of taxes. Property could not be legally seized but must be given; this required an authority to give which was procedurally, as well as legally, consistent with authority to treat on other matters. But the initiative always came from the king, an initiative that included the basic decision to call a parliament, the purposes in view, the scope and limits of discussion, and the termination of the meeting.

The history of representation proceeds at the same time on two levels. At one level it is the history of the gradual transfer of this initial fundamental responsibility from the Crown to the representatives of the communities. But while this was being worked out in the course of generations of constitutional struggle, the character of representation was also questioned, which introduces the second level. Precisely which of the common people were represented, and how? Did the fact that the shires and certain select boroughs sent representatives to the parliament entitle them to decide matters for the whole nation? In the eighteenth century, an age of political sophistication and of newspapers, these questions were to open up the fascinating but difficult problem of the relationship between public opinion and legislation.

Though parliaments owed their lawful powers to the fact of their summons by the Crown rather than to their claim to represent any form of public opinion, it was clear, long before the upheavals of the seventeenth century, that they also required the moral sanction implied by the idea, however nominal, that every individual had some voice in the proceedings which ruled him. The point was most clearly made in a much-quoted passage of Sir Thomas Smith, writing in 1572. Parliament, he explained 'representeth and hath the power of the whole realm both head and body. For every Englishman is intended to be there present, either in person or by procuration and attorneys, of what pre-eminence, state, dignity, or quality so ever he be, from the prince (be he King or Queen) to the lowest person of

England.'[1] This passage no doubt owes its popularity to the fact that statements about the representative character of Parliament in this extensive sense were unusual; another author, a generation later, made the same point more briefly when he said 'The Prince hath no authority to make laws nor to dispose of the Crowne, that must be done by the general consent of all in parliament. . . .'[2] Smith expounded a theory of direct consent. The people were present in Parliament 'by procuration and attorneys',[3] which made their relationship to their members that of clients with powers of instruction. This appears to have been the correct Elizabethan view. Much weight rests on the 'taken' in the statement that the consent of Parliament 'is taken to be every man's consent'. There was no examination here of the idea of consent, no suggestion that the gathering of these consents might involve any problems of political philosophy.

By the eighteenth century the publication of a survey of the institutions of the realm had become an annual affair with Chamberlayne's *Present State of Great Britain*. This work's account of representation went over the conventional ground about the wide suffrage before the statute of Henry VI, the decline in the value of currency since the discovery of America, and the consequent unintentional extension of the suffrage. When the compiler came to the existing property qualifications, he remarked that the exclusion of copyholders was a 'Defect or Absurdity', adding the somewhat cautiously republican observation that 'All Englishmen, who have considerable Estates, ought not to be taxed without their own Consent in Parliament, by themselves, or by their Representatives'.[4] By that time, then, it was no longer axiomatic that the House of Commons corresponded in any direct sense with the composition of the people outside. A great deal had happened in the history of representation between this statement and those of Smith and Wilson.

The English Constitution required that the decisive law-making power be exercised on a stretch of ground which in theory was held jointly between the Crown and the Houses of Parliament. This was not a no-man's-land; it rather resembled a territory under joint administration by two authorities. The success of the system postulated a consensus between these authorities

[1] Sir Thomas Smith, *De Republica Anglorum* (Cambridge, 1906), 46.

[2] F. J. Fisher (ed.), Thomas Wilson, *The State of England*, A.D. *1600* (Camden Misc., London, 1936).

[3] 'Procuration' is a technical term meaning the management by an agent of a client's legal affairs.

[4] Chamberlayne's *Present State of Great Britain* (London, 1735), 86.

as to the fundamental interests of the kingdom. The great achievement of the House of Commons in 'the winning of the initiative' was to gain an important sector of this common ground from the Crown. If the Crown accepted this result, though it would continue to share the territory in theory, it would in fact be reduced to giving its assent to the will of the Commons. What the Commons discovered, as a result of their progress, was that for the early Stuarts, and particularly for Charles I, the consensus was a mere legal fiction. Charles set out to show in his period of rule without Parliament, which was his own attempt to regain the initiative recently won by the Commons, that the theory of consent was not only a legal fiction but a sham contributing nothing to the lawful authority of his government. The House of Commons resumed its initiative under Pym; and in that phase it occupied the whole of the ground previously shared with the Crown, until it had dispensed not only with the Crown but even with the House of Lords, in giving laws to the nation.

The Civil Wars threw up the most extreme assertions of republican doctrine yet heard in England, but it is significant that the emergence of the Levellers and the other doctrinaires of the period was a result, not a cause, of the Revolution. The famous Putney debates of 1647 sprang up not in either Parliament or the constituencies but in the army.[1]

It would have been a happy thing for Oliver Cromwell if he had been able to find in the constituencies a common will, devoid of local or economic interests and agreed on the necessary strength of the government — the old royal prerogative, in fact. Cromwell, in his successive attempts to rationalise the basis of representation by reforming the distribution of parliamentary seats, was not seeking an ideal of pure or direct representation for its own sake. To later reformers, it looked as though that or something surprisingly like it had been his object. But Cromwell's idea of representation had its own prescriptive purpose — to secure a parliament based solidly on the independent country gentry of England. This effort effected a measure of parliamentary reform for the very substantial reason that a gentry parliament would in the nature of the case be more representative at least of the landed property and country population of the state than the existing arrangement,

---

[1] P. A. Gibbons, *Ideas of Representation in Parliament 1651–1832* (Oxford, 1914), 12–13. The point made here, however, is that it was the state of the army, not of the country, that produced these ideas of representation: but this does not quite conclude the matter, for the army was itself capable of being converted into an institution of representation much closer to the needs and desires of the common people than the Parliament. The army reflected the demands of a part of the country not properly represented in Parliament.

already hundreds of years outgrown. Cromwell's disappointments and the failure of his schemes were not due to their being intrinsically unworkable; they were essentially political failures, due to his refusal to recognise the need to organise a party either in the Commons or in the country. Thus in the central institution which he wished to make worthy of exercising the power he would confide to it, he was frustrated by the determination and abilities of the old Republicans — the leaders of the Rump who had pushed through the Navigation Act and led the country into aggressive anti-Dutch and mercantile policies.[1] But these were not the leaders of civic or mercantile wealth. The City of London and other ports were victimised by the new arrangements, and London was forced to appeal for fuller representation on the ground of its payment of taxes as well as its population.

The Restoration made republican ideas subversive to the state and dangerous to the holder. It also made them academic. But the Interregnum had produced some of the deepest investigations of political obligation ever published in England. The greatest of them, Hobbes's *Leviathan*, was based on the idea that the representation of the people by the sovereign was so complete as to amount to a virtual substitution; thus it abolished all need for representative institutions or elections; and this is one reason why it was also the least influential. The Commonwealthmen and their later disciples, on the other hand, attempted to distil the republican essence from the history of the period and to hand it down until in the fullness of time it should resume its rightful power in the Constitution.

I. JAMES HARRINGTON

James Harrington was the founder and acknowledged leader of the Commonwealthmen or, as they fondly styled themselves, True, or Old Whigs. There was much in common between his views and Cromwell's, though

---

[1] The suffrage franchise of 1653 was subject to severe property qualifications belying any suggestion that Cromwell was seeking out the will of the people in a popular sense. 'All and every person and persons seized or possessed to his own use of any estate, real or personal, to the value of £200 . . . shall be capable to elect members to serve in Parliament for counties.' (The Instrument of Government, December 1653.) Quoted in Christopher Hill and Edmund Dell, *The Good Old Cause* (London, 1949), 445. H. R. Trevor-Roper, 'Oliver Cromwell and his Parliaments', in Richard Pares and A. J. P. Taylor (eds.), *Essays Presented to Sir Lewis Namier* (London, 1956), 1–48. Trevor-Roper's analysis shows Cromwell's intentions (taken over from Major-General Lambert) with statistical clarity: the county representation was quadrupled, that of the boroughs cut by half.

Cromwell was not addicted to systematic thought. Harrington's thought was both systematic and extremely detailed, sometimes to the point of being quaint. His famous Commonwealth of Oceana was the happy result of a cautious application of Aristotelian principles to English society.

The influence of Aristotle is pervasive.[1] In accordance with the conventions of a classical education, Harrington adopted the Aristotelian classifications of government, and proceeded to the enunciation of the principle which made his fame and which his disciple Toland claimed for him as an original discovery: 'Such . . . as is the proportion or balance of Dominion or Property in Land, such is the nature of the Empire'.[2] He seems not to have been much impressed by the growth of mercantile and city wealth and constantly argued that real power in the state depended on real wealth, which was in land. In an extensive country, such as England or Spain, money could never come to overbalance land; money, it seems, would buy land — and land would still give the power. The basic reason for this was baldly stated in another famous phrase: 'An army is a beast with a great belly'. The lord of large enough estates could therefore feed an army to overpower the rest and could make subjects dependent on himself rather than on the republic.[3]

Safety and justice both lay in an equal distribution of land. Harrington was evoking the ideal of a republic based on the landed gentry[4] — on whom Cromwell would have liked to base his parliament under the Instrument of Government. But he did not mean literal equality; rather what concerned

[1] Though oddly enough it is not noticed by C. B. Macpherson, *The Political Theory of Possessive Individualism* (Oxford, 1962). See, however, Charles Blitzer, *An Immortal Commonwealth: The Political Theory of James Harrington* (New Haven, 1960), 289.

[2] John Toland (ed.), James Harrington, *Works* (London, 1700), *Oceana*, 38–39. All references to Harrington's works are taken from this edition. A variation appears, p. 101: 'such as is the Balance of Dominion in a Nation such is the Nature of its Empire' — where 'Dominion' means property and 'Empire' means protection or power.

[3] Harrington, *The Prerogative of Popular Government*, 245–9. J. G. A. Pocock, *The Ancient Constitution and the Feudal Law* (Cambridge, 1957), 143; the argument of this absorbing study is here taken too far, however, in stating that the whole of Harrington's case about the connection between land and power is that the distribution of land determines whether the soldier shall fight as a citizen of the public or as a dependent of his lord. Harrington does not develop this connection sufficiently to justify this assertion, and he makes a number of other references to the unequal distribution of property as a cause of sedition or unrest, which derive from Aristotle, whom he cites as his authority (*Politics*, v. 3), ibid., 295.

[4] *Oceana*, 56, 'There is something first in the making of a Commonwealth, then in the governing of it, and last of all in the leading of its Armys; which . . . seems to be peculiar only to the Genius of a Gentleman' (as opposed to clergy, lawyers and professions).

him was to prevent the development of dangerous inequalities through large accumulations. The instrument of this great purpose was to be the Agrarian Law, so fundamental to the state that its adjective thenceforward became a noun, and it was called simply Agrarian. By this power the state was to control the distribution of landed property and to forbid the addition by purchase to any estates worth £2,000 a year; while primogeniture was forbidden, to prevent family accumulations by descent.[1] Harrington had no thought of abolishing the nobility, whom he regarded as the wisdom of the commonwealth and vitally necessary to its counsels: when nobility and gentry were properly balanced, they gave life and soul to popular government — wrongly balanced, they were its destruction.[2]

Harrington's disciples have generally held that he stood for a high degree of equality: but elsewhere he dropped hints that his idea of an equal commonwealth could not only tolerate great economic inequalities, but require them as a safeguard for propertied interests; thus in discussing the Constitution of livery companies he stated that aldermen should be worth the enormous sum of £10,000.[3]

In one fundamental Harrington agreed with Hobbes in a view profoundly at variance with that which was canonized in the later Whig tradition. He rejected the belief that property derived from nature. Property, he declared, derived her being from law. The empire — the actual locus of power in the state — must therefore follow the balance of property established by the laws, not its natural state. Harrington attacked the doctrine that property could be held by anyone by 'a native right' which originated before the law; instead he asserted the bold alternative that the whole community shared a common interest which must prevail over the private interests of individual members.[4] This common interest was served and maintained by the Agrarian, and because the Agrarian prevented the rise of over-mighty estates it secured the commonwealth against sedition. Critics of Oceana, declared Harrington in a later commentary, had 'failed to find any inequality in it'. The Agrarian was no temporary expedient, but the enduring foundation of the state — it was intended to make the balance of

---

[1] *Oceana*, 54 ff.; *Prerogative of Popular Government*, 303; *Art of Lawgiving*, 456.

[2] *Oceana*, 42.

[3] *Oceana*, 170.

[4] *Prerogative of Popular Government*, 297–8. His supposititious 'Critic' in the dialogue argues here that government is to be fitted to property, and not property to the government. It is in reply to this that Harrington states that property derives from law. He goes on a little later (303) to forbid primogeniture and the inheritance by the eldest son of more than £2,000 in land.

government fixed and unalterable.[1] It seems clear that in Oceana justice itself flowed from the common interest. Harrington was willing to call his state a democracy,[2] and also 'an equal Commonwealth', but it was to be one in which the nobility should 'hold an underbalance to the People; in which case they are not only safe, but necessary to the natural mixture of a well-ord'd Commonwealth'.[3]

The elements of this natural mixture were the different orders of society — the social and economic groups regulating the role and identifying the interests of the individual members for whose interests they stood as spokesmen in politics.

Harrington's government comprised three branches; the Senate, the people in Assembly, and the magistracy. The Senate represented the wisdom of the Commonwealth, the Assembly represented the common interest: both the Senate and the magistracy were to be elective, and elaborate procedures were prescribed to ensure fair elections, but from what had already been said about the importance of the nobility there could be little room for doubt that the upper classes were likely to end up in these senior positions. This despite the avowal that the Senate would not be 'bound to a distinct order'. The people were not allowed to propose laws; 'invention is solitary', as he later explained;[4] but no law could pass without their assent. The magistracy was what came to be called the 'executive', consisting not of a single head of state, but of a series of departments charged with the duties of enforcing the laws; it was in effect a Civil Service. The interests of the whole were sustained by the fact that the right of supreme judicial determination lay in the people — without which, he declared, there could be no popular government.[5]

The idea of civil justice which sustained Harrington in working out his *Oceana* was inseparable from this concept of the common interest. Against the identification of natural with civil law, he argued that law proceeds from will; that will must have a mover, and its mover is interest — and it was from the definition of a commonwealth that its law proceeded, as must be

---

[1] *Prerogative of Popular Government*, 234–91.

[2] 'But for my part, where the People have the election of the Senat, not bound to a distinct order, and the Result, which is the Sovereign Power, I hold them to have that share in the Government [the Senate not being for life] whereof, with the safety of the Commonwealth, they are capable in nature; and such a Government, for that cause, to be a Democracy . . .' (Archon's speech, *Oceana*, 138).

[3] *Oceana*, 134–5, 55.

[4] *Prerogative of Popular Government*, 230–1.

[5] *Oceana*, 156–60.

the interest of the whole people.[1] The aristocracy, which he called the 'wisdom' of the Commonwealth, was not set against, but was included with that 'interest' which was the whole.[2] This insistence on a single common interest which determines the extent of property, regulates individual acquisitions, and gives the laws is Harrington's real advance on the more pragmatic thesis of his master Aristotle, and anticipates (though it does not reach) Rousseau's theory of the general will. Nowhere did Harrington anticipate the later Whig concept that the state owed its existence to a variety of voluntary acts of consent, or the still later and far more developed idea of the state as a community of participating interests, for which by the conditions of its existence it is required to find institutions of representation. It is possible that he hinted at the idea in his concept of 'orders', a term which he did not clearly define in *Oceana* but which he used in *The Art of Lawgiving* to mean 'the frame and model' of the Constitution; but he never implied that the orders existed before the government or that the Constitution came into existence by any act of the orders.[3] He recognised that the aristocracy might develop an interest of their own and that they might attempt to undermine the common interest; but he met this threat by saying that if this happened the majority would discern the danger and oppose it. The very detailed, almost loving attention he gave to the procedure for elections shows that Harrington was aware of the dangers of influence and corruption; yet he persistently ignored the problems of parliamentary politics and wrote as though there were no such thing as constituency organisation. His reason arose from the necessities of his thesis: he wanted to pre-empt all the ground of politics for his 'general interest', and thereby preclude parties from forcing their way into the government. This view, in essentials, anticipated that of Washington as first President of the United States. Harrington's studious aversion from political realities at this point became a serious theoretical weakness. He refused to see that if the aristocracy — or, more plausibly, members of the aristocracy — wanted to gain influence over the Assembly, they would do so by seeking individual supporters and dividing the populace into factions.

It is highly unlikely that Harrington influenced the opinions of Washington, despite their similarity, but it is clear that he exerted a definite influence on Washington's Vice-President and successor, John Adams. Adams, before reaching those great offices, had already concerned himself

[1] *Prerogative of Popular Government*, 240–1: '. . . therefore in a Commonwealth, law must be the Interest of the whole People'.

[2] *Oceana*, 47–48.   [3] *The Art of Lawgiving*, 160.

deeply with the dangers to be feared from aristocratic influence on the plebeians, and went so far as to advocate a separate, upper chamber to represent the aristocracy in politics, not in their own interests but in order to keep their hands off the representatives of the common people. He called it 'ostracism'. Adams was an admirer of Harrington's work and despite having greater political experience he followed him in failing to see (or refusing to admit) that an aristocracy sitting in an upper chamber would have the means to reach the commons, by whom they were in any case to be elected.

Harrington's scheme depended upon a complete system of representation. Under the influence of the Gothic myth, he prescribed a Saxon division of the republic into equal wards or hundreds, and took from Roman precedent the idea of secret ballot and rotation in office. It was essential that the representation should achieve the highest purity; that the men entrusted with power should exercise it exactly as their constituents would wish, that they should in no way develop a separate interest through the tenure of office and that they should expect to return to ordinary status after a short time. This concept of full and free representation seems to have been limited by the establishment of the orders; the popular Assembly, though not representative of any one order of society, was treated as though it became an order by its mere existence, and in that capacity it was never to overstep its bounds or subvert the authority of the Senate. On the danger from this cause Harrington again showed himself unrealistic about politics.

He also revealed that his thought contained an element of addiction to the property rights of the aristocracy, hardly acknowledged in his explicit theory. What safeguard had they against the levelling propensities of a majority 'entrusted with the vote, and keeping a sword'? He put the question into the mouth of a critic of *Oceana* — but it was to be asked again and again in England and America by men with more experience of popular majorities than Harrington. He replied with another question: 'What security is there that the People shall not cast themselves into the sea?' 'A Prince,' argued Harrington, 'may be mad and do so, but the People are naturally incapable of such madness.' A reassurance of which we all stand in very great need. Here he showed that faith in the fundamental capacity of the people to know their own best interest, which was later to inform much of the democratic thought of America. This faith was rendered more formidable by the certainty that the self-interest of the community, as determined by the majority, was itself coextensive with political morality.

He did not fear that the people would be jealous of the aristocracy, because he believed that under the Agrarian they would already possess all they needed; and, by inference, they also needed the wisdom of the aristocracy, and as reasonable beings with experience of the benefits of that wisdom, they could be depended upon to conserve their own interests by conserving the entire system. The people would never do anything demonstrably unreasonable. 'As Reason is Experience in the root,' he observed, 'so Experience is Reason in the branch.'[1]

Harrington is a lonelier thinker than has sometimes been supposed by his admirers. His views of property and social obligation do not lead to those of Locke, while his view of the state, with its general interest and Agrarian Law given by the will which represented that interest, is only of indirect consequence for the eighteenth-century whiggish parliamentary reformers. He stands closer to the Radicals of the later period. His insistence on the regulation of property in the public interest, coupled with his ordering of ranks within that regulated system, would have induced both a discipline and a rigidity which they would not have enjoyed for long. It must be admitted, however, that James Mill used arguments similar to Harrington's when rebutting the charge that universal suffrage would cause the downfall of the middle classes.

Harrington's most direct impact was more immediate and of greater importance than these far-ranging and shadowy influences. It was not only that he was absorbed by John Adams; in his own century, perhaps in his own lifetime, he or his school gave political and institutional forms to the ideals of William Penn. Penn's early plans closely resemble Harrington's model. Thus the republican stream irrigated the green country town of Penn's Quaker commonwealth and flowed out into the American continent.

II. ALGERNON SIDNEY

Harrington was persecuted for his beliefs; Sidney was put to death for his. His martyrdom alone would have secured attention for the posthumous publication of his political writings, but their contents showed developments in the analysis of republican institutions and responsibilities which were to secure them a place in the advance — not merely the handing down — of the tradition.

Political thought is particularly subject to the problems of the time, and Sidney's views on representation were controlled by his primary interest in

[1] *Prerogative of Popular Government,* 264–6.

asserting popular rights against those of the Crown. Sidney's contemporary, James II, demonstrated — like his father — that divine right will not go far without divine inspiration. One result of his reign was to concentrate Whig thinking on the question of legitimacy and to strengthen the idea of compact between ruler and subjects. Whatever institutions stood on the popular side tended to be accepted as legitimate. Thus Sidney did not think it necessary to look closely into the internal composition of representative institutions but was content in general to take their representative character for granted.[1]

Sidney never doubted the cardinal principle that power lay originally in the people and must be exercised through representation. Pure democracy he condemned as impracticable except in small towns. It is not certain that Sidney or his Whig contemporaries would actually have liked pure democracy if they had had to live with it; but England was not a small town, and therefore the virtue of pure democracy could be assumed without discussion.[2] In fact Sidney at once proceeded to treat mixed governments as equivalent to, almost synonymous with, purely popular ones. In his version of mixed governments, however, the existing estates were duly represented; they were popular governments because he conceived that all the regular orders would and did really enjoy representation through their estates. If he had chosen to apply his ideas to a direct democracy or city state he would have been obliged to notice that different orders would normally exist there too; Aristotle, the prevailing classical authority, did not advocate equality of property or the abolition of social classes. Sidney and other republican thinkers evaded a legitimate question when they dismissed direct democracy as irrelevant to their problem, for they usually revealed at some point a preference for the weighting of aristocratic votes or for giving institutional security to aristocratic authority. Pure democracy was unlikely to produce favourable conditions for political privilege.

Representation, for Sidney, did not develop as a mere technical modification of the communal gathering of the whole people; yet he came very close to this view once he had made allowance for the superior types who exercised natural leadership. His own version of Gothic history included an account of the origins of representation. The nobility of the northern nations, he explained, was composed entirely of fighting men, who were the gentlemen; in Denmark and Sweden 'noblemen' and 'gentlemen' were the same thing. This was the nobility of the northern nations and 'the true baronage of

[1] Algernon Sidney, *Discourses Concerning Government* (London, 1704), 217–19.
[2] Sidney, *Discourses*, 115.

England' — a nasty blow for the Normans (unless they too could be rescued because of their northern descent!) 'The inconveniences of calling them all together appear'd to be so great, that in time they chose to meet rather by Representatives, than every one in his own person. The power therefore remaining in them, it matters not what method they observed in the execution. . .'[1] This was an argument for the original and continuing superiority of the electorate over the legislature, but was very far from being a manifesto for popular rule. Evidently Sidney, sharply at variance with most later parliamentary reformers who accepted the Gothic story, did not believe that the common people had held a place in the constitutional arrangements of Saxon England; elsewhere he equated these gentlemen with the freeholders, saying that it was they who deputed representatives in Saxon times. And he was satisfied with the existing freehold suffrage in the counties.[2] This was safe Whig ground which would hardly have been disputed by any Tory.

Yet Sidney strongly affirmed a much more radical point: the right of individual assent to the government. Tacit consent, or failure to oppose a government, did not, he asserted, imply consent if freedom to dissent was not given. The point is particularly noteworthy because it answers in advance Locke's argument on the same issue — that 'tacit consent' (Locke used the phrase) was implied by the mere acceptance of government. Sidney's statement was probably prompted by the need to oppose tyranny; but the argument that government required for its legitimacy the express consent given, or the absence of dissent under conditions of free choice, on the part of all the individuals upon whom it was to act, would have deep implications when the time came for a republican society to make new governments. The time did come, across the Atlantic, less than a century in the future.

Sidney, like Locke, embraced the Whig tradition when he identified the fundamental power in the state as the legislative power, but he was less willing than Locke to let it go out of the hands of the people. It could not, he said, be conferred by the writ of summons to Parliament, but 'must be essentially and radically in the people, from whom the delegates and representatives have all that they have'.[3] But, while he held that rightful power lay ineradicably in the people, Sidney was actually willing to confer a great deal of discretion on Parliament, as he showed in discussing the crucial question of instructions and the relation between constituents and members. He attacked Filmer's view that representatives were chosen 'to do as they list',

---

[1] Sidney, *Discourses*, 353.
[2] Sidney, *Discourses*, 384–5. [3] Sidney, *Discourses*, 409–10.

and affirmed the power of the people to regulate their servants, to hold them to account and to reject them at the next election if they defied their electors' known will. This electoral control, together with a certain rather vague moral authority, was the full extent of the power of regulation. Sidney held along with this a strong view of the general interest, not only consistent with Harrington's but anticipatory of Burke's. Every county, he declared, did not make a distinct sovereign body, but was a member of the great body which comprehended the whole nation. It was fit that the legislators should listen to the opinions of the electors, yet, surprisingly, they were not strictly obliged to give an account of their actions to any. Therefore Sidney rejected the claim of a right to bind members of Parliament with previous instructions. That doctrine led to danger and confusion, for neither the electors nor their representatives could know what would be raised when Parliament met, and instructions would be given by those who knew nothing of the matters in question. Sidney saw beyond this practical point to a larger view of the national interest. Electors in their districts retained a right to tell their members what they thought and to reject them for failure to comply, yet the national assembly of representatives must by its nature be something more than a mere national meeting of isolated constituencies. The national interest might be visible from the standpoint of the national assembly but obscured from the sight of some of the constituencies, and Parliament alone could be entrusted with the power to take such decisions as were necessary to maintain that national interest.[1]

In legislation, Parliament emerged with sovereign powers — but it could never be superior to the people from whom it drew those powers. Sidney made a point of fundamental importance in the theory of representation, and one indispensable to later Whig doctrine when he said that legislative power was not to be trusted in the hands of any who were not bound to obey the laws they made.[2] The point was later to be taken up by James Otis of Massachusetts Bay, and it was one of the best, though not the best used, of the arguments in the American armoury.

The problem of the relationship between popular and parliamentary powers was not fully resolved by Sidney, who remained preoccupied with the assumption that Parliament was already as fully representative as need be. Yet his discussion of instruction showed that he was aware of the problem. Sidney believed that legislative power was the virtual definition of

---

[1] Sidney, *Discourses*, 410–13. It would surely be ironical but reasonable to argue that the case of ship-money was an example of national against local interests.

[2] Sidney, *Discourses*, 414.

sovereignty, a view that looked back to the medieval idea that the power of making laws is rather that of discovering than of creating law. Subsequent history, particularly in America, teaches us to look for a distinction here, between legislation on the one hand, and the permanent or constitutional power on the other. Sidney was groping towards this distinction, but it had not fully emerged in his time. It came out more clearly in the preliminaries to the American Revolution, when the Americans claimed constitutional rights against parliamentary legislation. This distinction was developed in America and was later embodied in the American Constitution.

III. JOHN LOCKE

Generations of scholars have discovered the spirit of Locke brooding, like the deity of the Pantheists, in the woods of America. But was he really there? Very little evidence exists to suggest that Locke exerted any effective influence on the political thought of the colonists until Thomas Jefferson came to draft the Declaration of Independence.[1] Yet Locke epitomised certain doctrines, without which the American revolutionaries would have found it difficult to explain their activities either to the opinions of mankind or even to themselves. The active doctrine was that of the social compact because in certain circumstances it justified rebellion, but behind the idea of such a compact lay three principles which gave it meaning. First, Locke both assumed and summarised the grand Whig principle of the supremacy of the 'legislative power'; secondly, in order to justify this power, he committed himself to statements from which it is logically possible to infer an advanced doctrine of majority rule; and thirdly, the necessity of government arose in the origins of society from the special value of private property. All of these views were present in the Whig tradition and each helped to inform the debates conducted by the Americans when they drafted new and independent constitutions. To say this is to justify continued attention to the arguments which Locke expounded and codified; what has not been established is that the doctrines of Locke's *Second Treatise* were specifically translated into institutional form; and an analysis will show that the majoritarian implications could be so translated only by doing violence to

[1] Carl L. Becker, *The Declaration of Independence* (New York, 1922; reprinted New York, 1959), chap. ii; H. Trevor Colbourn, 'Thomas Jefferson's Use of the Past', *William and Mary Quarterly*, January 1958, 56–70.

My views on the question of Locke's influence in America have been clarified by a conversation with Mr John Dunn, whose findings will be published in due course.

those which assumed the sanctity of property. Yet it was to the latter that the American constitutionalists attached the greater importance.

Most of his major work on politics, *Two Treatises of Civil Government*, was written in the reign of Charles II, under the stimulus of the need to make a Whig reply to the republication of Sir Robert Filmer's *Patriarcha*. Not only was Locke's work contemporaneous with Sidney's, but it had the same occasion.[1] This occasion accounts for the emphasis on those Whig principles which oppose the royal prerogative and patriarchal authority. In much of his most effective work Locke did not originate but consolidate, arguing his thesis with such cogency and finality that he achieved the ambiguous but by no means accidental distinction of imposing upon his political heirs a new type of authority to replace the old.

Effective and systematic political representation was as indispensable to Locke's as to any Whig view of government. He saw his primary task as that of establishing beyond question the right of the majority to originate the legislative power, the fundamental power in society. The object of this establishment was to protect property — but the right to property existed before society, and before government; government had therefore no rights of its own superior to those of the individual, consenting members of society. Political representation was assumed; but it was nowhere closely examined. The crucial problems of the succeeding century grew up in the interstices of Lockian theory.

Although the nature of legislative power is implied in earlier chapters of Locke's *Treatise* it is not fully developed until the eleventh chapter, after the author has already dealt with the fundamental problem of property, with other types of power, with the state of nature, and with the character and beginning of political societies. When he arrives at the appropriate point he is ready to make a full and extreme assertion: the legislative power is the supreme power of the commonwealth. At the beginning of the chapter, he gropes towards a distinction, as Sidney was doing, between fundamental or constitutional law on the one hand, and the power to govern by legislation on the other. 'The *first and fundamental positive Law* of all Commonwealths, *is the establishing of the Legislative* Power; as the *first and fundamental natural Law*, which is to govern even the Legislative itself, *is the preservation of the Society*, and (as far as will consist with the publick good) of every person in it.'[2] As the establishing of the legislature is a law in

[1] Peter Laslett (ed.), *Locke's Two Treatises of Government* (Cambridge, 1964), 51.

[2] *Second Treatise*, section 134. All quotations are taken from Laslett's edition; original spelling preserved.

itself — a law promulgated, it seems, by the community — there must be a distinction between the two types of law, the first being fundamental. But in Locke, this first law is never called back into action unless the government itself turns into a tyrant and has to be overthrown by the people or is otherwise dissolved. The function of this first law is to bring into being a permanent institution — not to declare principles to govern the conduct of that institution. That has to be attained through the legislators' own knowledge of the natural law which supplies the purpose of their existence; so that Locke's introduction of the incipient distinction between a constitutional law and a statute-making legislature remains very far short of the constitution-making developments in America a century later.

Affirmations of the supremacy of the legislative power were neither novel nor daring until one decided precisely where that power was to lodge. The Levellers had lodged it with the economically self-supporting section of the population whom they defined as 'the people', and insisted on the derivative nature of the law-making body;[1] Harrington had divided it carefully, giving to the popular assembly only the right to resolve, not to initiate or debate; Sidney accepted existing institutions but insisted on the continuing supremacy of the people; but Locke did not place the supreme power in the hands of the people. The people had the initial right to establish it; but once founded, the legislative power assumed an independent authority, untrammelled by institutional control. It was 'sacred and unalterable in the hands where the Community have once placed it'. A whiggish reader might well have expected that a Whig author expounding the principles of this awful power would feel strongly obliged to hedge it with some necessary restraints. How was society to prevent the power from being abused? What security was provided that representation should be full and free, elections pure? Sidney showed himself aware of such problems though he did not address himself to them in detail; Harrington thought them immensely important. Locke knew that all was not well; for when in a later section he criticised the state of representation in England he found himself at last facing the question of whether his own theories offered the possibility of reform, and admitted that as no inferior power could alter the legislature, and as the people themselves had '*no Power* to act as long as the Government

---

[1] 'The only and sole legislative law-making power is originally inherent in the people, and derivately in their commissions chosen by themselves by common consent, and no other. In which the poorest that lives hath as true a right to give a vote as well as the richest and greatest.' Lilburne, December 1646, Hill and Dell, *Good Old Cause*, 332; Macpherson, *Political Theory*, 107–59.

stands; this inconvenience is thought incapable of a remedy'.[1] And though this answer was not very satisfactory he did not use his system to develop a remedy.

The saving element in Locke's system lies not in institutions but in the laws of nature which govern all men, including legislators. They cannot pass laws which transgress the purposes for which society was brought into existence, nor rule by arbitrary decrees. Emphasis is placed on standing laws, and rights determined by 'known Authoris'd Judges'. The legislature for similar reasons cannot take away property without consent. With Locke, as with Sidney, an important safeguard lies in the fact that the legislators must themselves be subject to the laws they make. In the last resort, under arbitrary tyranny, the majority have a right to rebel — but no machinery for ascertaining the opinions or even the existence of a majority is suggested.[2]

Locke's indifference to detail becomes a general source of weakness when it covers imprecision of thought in matters of principle: but there was a positive side to all this. Although he deplored the abuses in the state of representation in England, he plainly did not think that the resulting composition of the House of Commons seriously distorted the popular will. A better constituted system would presumably have been both safer and more satisfactory, but it would not have produced radically different major policies. After the Glorious Revolution had been engineered by the Lords and Commons of the parliamentary system, Locke may well have felt that his confidence in the basic soundness of that system had been well founded. His writing belonged to a period when it was possible to suppose a homogeneity of interest among the different orders and communities of the realm, a condition which must have gone far to strengthen his conviction that the rights of individuals or minorities would be protected by that natural political virtue which itself sprang from man's knowledge of natural law and experience of social life.[3] But above all, that sense of homogeneity of interest in the community was promoted by the antithesis between the community and the Crown.

In Locke's view society was founded when any number of individuals contracted together to form '*one Community* or Government', whereupon

---

[1] *Second Treatise*, sections 134, 157, 158. He recognised the justice of electoral reform in the last section.

[2] *Second Treatise*, sections 134–42, 168.

[3] Laslett considers the development of the implications of this doctrine of natural political virtue to be 'the main theme of Locke's book'. *Two Treatises*, 116.

they were at once incorporated into a single body politic 'wherein the *Majority* have a Right to act and conclude the rest'.[1]

Once society and government — the terms are at first used interchangeably — have been founded, majority rule immediately comes into force as the fundamental principle of legislation; Locke's reasons are quite clear:

For [he says] that which acts any Community, being only the consent of the individuals of it, and it being necessary to that which is one body to move one way; it is necessary the Body should move that way whither the greater force carries it, which is the consent of the majority: else it is impossible it should act or continue one Body, *one Community*, which the consent of every individual, that united into it, agreed that it should; and so every one is bound by the consent to be concluded by the *majority*.[2]

Elsewhere Locke applied the principle to taxation. The consent of the majority or their representatives 'chosen by them' stood for the consent of each individual to the grant of taxes touching his own property. It was convenient at this point in the argument that English institutions provided a normal channel for the gathering of consent to taxation, which, allowing for Locke's unwillingness to scrutinise the system of representation, harmonised with his views on majority rule, without violating his doctrine of property rights.[3]

Majority rule, even when used by Locke, is not a self-explanatory term. He uses it in at least two senses. The first and underlying sense is that of principle. To agree to enter into society is to submit to the determinations of that society considered as a whole body, and at the same time to delegate to the majority the right to pronounce for the whole. In this sense the majority, once voices have been heard, expresses the collective interest; though Locke does not seem drawn towards ideas of a general will if they can be avoided. In a second and perhaps more active sense, majority rule is employed as an indispensable rule of procedure. A society which rejects majority rule will do so at the risk of dissolution. The rule of procedure here involves the question of principle, however. If people enter voluntarily into a society and by that act agree to submit to majority decisions, then any disregard for those majority decisions will be a violation of the understanding on which they entered into the society.

Locke regarded the fact of voluntary entry into society as equivalent to

---

[1] *Second Treatise*, section 95.
[2] *Second Treatise*, section 96.   [3] See Laslett, *Two Treatises*, 380 n.

the establishment of the majority rule principle. He looked no further. However, societies have been known to abandon democracy or representation and continue to exist as societies; the point would have been better made if he had said that, if the decisions of the majority (after due deliberation) were rejected, then legislation could proceed without representation. It would then be a different kind of society.[1]

The two senses of majority rule, then, are those of principle and expediency. But it is applied in two connections: those of the internal regulations of the legislature, already discussed in regard to practice; and secondly the popular vote by which the legislature is constituted. It is clear that the legislature must be elected by a majority, but once again Locke leaves us in doubt on points of detail which actually involve questions of principle. Ideally it might have been desirable that all the electors should vote for a single slate of candidates so that each member of Parliament would be elected by a majority of the whole electorate. (That plan was in fact adopted in certain American states, such as Virginia in 1799, but with the object of obtaining a preconceived result.) Obviously it could not apply to England, and Locke offered no hope for the reform of the prevailing distribution of seats in the constituencies. Allowing, for a moment, the hypothesis or legal fiction that this electorate really stood for 'the people', the supposition is that each member represents the majority of his own constituents, and therefore that each act he assents to commits all his constituents.

The rule of majority procedure inside the assembly thus directly corresponds to the sanction of the majority which has established the assembly. In Locke's mind the relationship was so close that he could put the community and the assembly into a single paragraph because they were both examples of the same majority principle.[2] The problem of instruction and the complex of problems in the relationship between representatives and their constituents were ignored.

In brief, Locke's concept of the voluntary character of society and the responsibility of government involved a necessary commitment to some form of majority rule. To achieve the fundamental objects of society it was essential that each individual should agree to be bound by the 'will and determination' of the majority. Every individual who votes thus gives his consent to every act of the legislature and assents to its exercise of lawful powers even when he happens to disagree with its acts.

[1] See the illuminating commentary of Willmoore Kendall, *John Locke and the Doctrine of Majority Rule*, Illinois Studies in the Social Sciences, xxvi. 2 (Urbana, Ill., 1941), 112–18.
[2] *Second Treatise*, section 96.

The legislature was invested with immense powers. Institutionally there was practically no restraint on it; the restraints lay rather in the assurance that the members of the assembly would not, because they could not, go against the basic purposes for which the society to which they belonged had been formed: nor could they exempt themselves from the laws. Locke actually granted the assembly great powers over property, and he never withdrew an assertion he made in 1667 that the magistrate can appoint ways of transferring properties from one man to another, and make what property laws he likes, provided they are equitable.[1] In the trust which Locke showed in the judicious exercise of the supreme legislative power and in his views on natural political virtue as a governing force, he revealed himself as a political optimist. Unlike the American heirs of his doctrines — or some of them — he does not seem to have feared that 'power is always running away from the many to the few'; he had none of the foreboding of a Harrington or a Madison or a John Adams or an Acton that the mere tenure and exercise of power would tend to corrupt the holder. This represents a significant difference in outlook from most of those who claimed in later generations to be acting under his authority. When he considered concrete institutions Locke took note of those prevailing in England; but his general theory did not lay down that these or any other specific institutions were indispensable, and even implied that the virtuous qualities which brought society and government into existence might suffice to maintain them.

What is political consent, and how is it obtained or known? This was a problem that Locke could not escape. 'It is to be considered', he acknowledged, 'what shall be understood to be a *sufficient declaration of* a Mans *Consent*, to make him subject to the Laws of any Government.' Obviously no problem arose in cases of express consent, but these were embarrassingly rare; and it was here that Locke introduced the conception of 'tacit consent', an expression which anticipated the whole doctrine of 'virtual representation'. Tacit consent was implied by any enjoyment of the protection of the laws of the government; even by walking freely on the public highway; even by having one's being within the territory ruled by that government.[2] After attaching great importance to voluntary consent he reduced it to a level not much above the conventional legal fiction: but slightly above it, perhaps; for he conceded that any persons who dwelt under a government to which they had not yielded their express consent remained free to withdraw their persons and their property and attach themselves to another. But those who had given express consent were never free to alienate themselves from

---

[1] The statement is Laslett's, *Two Treatises*, 104.   [2] *Second Treatise*, sections 119–22.

government or society (unless of course the government transgressed and alienated itself from the people — but in that case, though the people might change the government, they might not change the society).

It was obvious to Locke that when people came voluntarily into society under government, they brought with them their landed and moveable property, as well as the 'property' they had in their own persons and abilities, since the prime purpose of forming society was the protection of all these properties; the society to which they belonged had been formed simply by the coming together of consenting individuals. Elections were conducted by gathering individual votes. These points are of great theoretical importance, for Locke's views contained diverse implications. Locke said nothing to suggest that the external property which people brought with them ought itself to be weighed with them in the scale which measured political rights. Possession of such property was itself a fundamental right and properly constituted government would never fail in its duty to respect it; but properly constituted government was based on the consent of the individuals, and these individuals continued in society to enjoy the natural equality which Locke insisted on so strenuously as their condition in the state of nature. This must be maintained as the foundation of his argument about the beginnings of political society, despite the fact that at considerable risk of self-contradiction he later observed that certain inequalities were compatible with the natural and civil condition of equality; and despite his acceptance of the convention that persons in certain completely dependent positions — such as servants — were excluded from all political competence, though they might be included in the personal interest of their masters. What he maintained was that no type of inequality could justify subordination or the dominion of one man over another.[1] It follows that on the basis of Lockian society individuals mix together as pure political equals — but it is the individual, not his property, that counts. It is significant that the 'greater force' which moves a community 'one way' is made by the majority, entirely without reference to the 'force' supplied by the ownership of property. The argument leads straight to the counting of individuals in apportioning political representation.

---

[1] *Second Treatise*, sections 4–5, 54. Age, virtue, excellence, or birth might justify certain precedency or observance. This appears inconsistent; a person who is *obliged* by birth to pay any kind of observance to another can hardly be said to enjoy complete freedom from being subjected to 'the Will or Authority of any other Man' (Locke's words, section 54). What if he refuses to pay the observance? Would not the superior man's enforcement show the difference between them — an inequality?

To that extremity Thomas Jefferson of Virginia was prepared to follow it; further than Locke himself would in all likelihood have been willing to go. For Locke also spoke of the representation of corporations and of places, a style clearly reflecting the existing English structure, though he observed the justice of redistributing the apportionment of seats according to realities of population.[1]

Throughout the *Second Treatise* he placed the highest emphasis on property. The definition of property was complex; it included all the attributes of the person, his abilities, his labour, his liberty as well as the things to which he was entitled by having mixed his labour with them.[2] He stated repeatedly that the preservation of property was the original object of society, not always making clear whether he referred to material possessions or the more general attributes — one might at times say values — of which a person was possessed. The subtlety of this definition eluded Locke's successors. His own first definition, given in his chapter on the subject, lent itself to the belief that his main concern was with material objects and land; and his account of the origin of society planted in the minds of his American readers a very clear and simple picture of persons bringing their property with them and contracting together for its preservation. Thus it became easy to argue, when new Constitutions had to be made, that as persons and property were separate entities, and as persons had brought with them differing amounts of property, they were entitled to representation in the government in proportion to the size of the stake they had in society. This doctrine permeated the political discourse of the early constitutional period in America, giving tremendous authority to arguments against individual representation and in favour of the permanent establishment of separate houses of legislation, differing property qualifications, or other devices for the distinct purpose of institutionalising the representation of property. It may be remarked also that government was held to extend over land; Locke says so, and shows that when a tacit-consent landowner sells or quits, in quitting his land he

---

[1] *Second Treatise*, section 158. Laslett points out that Shaftesbury and the Whigs under Charles II introduced a Bill for the reform of the franchise and electoral distribution in 1679, and that Locke here joins up theory with English politics. Locke's view presupposed the tenure of property and in practice he would probably not have felt that they committed him to suffrage for persons with virtually no property of their own.

[2] *Second Treatise*, sections 5–51 ff.; Introduction, 101–6. This view was presumably conventional. See *Hamlet*, Act II, Scene ii:

> . . . no, not for a king
> Upon whose property and most dear life
> A damn'd defeat was made.

relinquishes the protection of the government;[1] at times, as Namier has said, the land rather than the people of England has seemed to be represented in Parliament.[2] To American constitution-makers it was clear that possession of property in general, but land in particular, gave the owner that stake in society which entitled him to representation in the government.

Truly Locke's political heirs were numerous, and of varying persuasions.

The very reasons for the existence of Whig thought in the seventeenth century directed that the main purpose of that thought should be to establish the right of popular power. This right, at its most advanced, was asserted to mean full and final legislative power as opposed to that of the prerogative. A distinction between permanent constitutional law and legislation by occasional statutes had begun to emerge in more mature form than that of the old and somewhat doubtful variety implied by Coke under James I; but proposals for the strengthening of the legislative authority were seldom thought to imply any questioning of the social relationships that prevailed under the existing political order. Yet these arguments unavoidably raised theoretical problems about the place of persons in the representative system. They opened a door to a path which, if followed, could lead to the discovery of the political identity of the individual; but the path was not followed, only surveyed from the terrace of the political country-house in which the debate took place. It was necessary to have a memorandum in the book, but it would have been dangerous to put the subject on the political agenda.

[1] *Second Treatise*, sections 120–1.
[2] Sir Lewis Namier, *England in the Age of the American Revolution* (London, 1961), 22.

PART TWO

America:
The Assertion of the
Legislative Power

THE original English Whigs defined the doctrine of legislative supremacy in the era in which the American colonies were being settled and their governments established. In England this supreme power was exercised by the full Parliament of Crown, Lords, and Commons. After the resolution of the conflicts of the seventeenth century the issue died out of English politics; the supremacy of the legislative power came very gradually, and without further violent controversy, to imply the primacy of Parliament without the Crown, and eventually, in the nineteenth century, the primacy of the House of Commons.

The Americans took up the issue at the point where the English had let it drop. As colonial legislatures were faced with the problems of local policy, the colonists soon sought a definition of legislative power that would place its centre of gravity firmly in the colonies themselves. The structure of colonial government, with its Governor, Council, and Assembly, appeared as a replica of that of the mother country; but a bare description of this structure did not give a full account of the question, nor could it satisfy the full demands of the colonists. Colonial laws could not be determined in the colonies, since all their legislation had to be submitted for approval by the Privy Council in London. Moreover the Governor, whether royal or proprietary, stood not only as the 'executive' in a 'mixed' form of government but represented an interest and a point of view that were not based in the colony in which he held his appointment.

The assertion, by the American colonies, of the colonial right to control the legislative power in the true Whig sense of the term was a theme with different variations in different provinces. In each case it was accompanied by two subordinate but necessary

developments. One of these was the gradual but certain triumph
of the Assembly over the Council as the repository and representative of the collective sense of a colonial 'interest'. The other was
the emergence of an American electorate whose feelings and
interests were generally, in the more important matters, harmonious with those of the colonial leadership.

Colonial Councils and Assemblies were both composed of
colonists and were therefore representative in some measure of
genuinely colonial, not British, interests. The colonial Council
was an indigenous growth, but it was one that corresponded to the
needs of a mixed government, a theory which the colonists had
received from England. In the early stages of the explicit demand
for legislative power the colonial leaders were not concerned to
assert the superiority of either chamber over the other ; what they
wanted to do was to establish the authority of their own, the
colonial, element in the form of mixed government that they
practiced. It was not until the eighteenth century that the
Assemblies began to upset the 'balance' of colonial governments
by obtaining a decisive leadership over both the colonial Councils
and the British Governors. The process had been completed in
Pennsylvania as early as 1701. In Virginia it began to emerge
clearly in the 1720s and 1730s. In Massachusetts, where the
Council was elected by the House of Representatives, and was
therefore never a strong arm of executive influence, it was virtually
complete by 1766.

The Assembly was by definition the representative element in a
mixed government. In Britain the same element, the House of
Commons, was often called 'the representation'. The electorates
on which these Assemblies were based reached deep into the
population. In general the voters respected the conventions of
leadership and authority which conferred the right to govern on
those who had attained or inherited social and economic eminence ;
but once in a while they would indulge in an eruption of protest.
These occasions might be infrequent (they occurred most often in
Pennsylvania) but they came as suggestions that here, in the
American colonies, a new kind of electorate might be in the

making — an electorate that was no respecter of persons and would want to be shown the record rather than the family name of the candidate.

Colonial electors, like English ones, were qualified primarily by property. The laws did not make these qualifications very steep. Exclusion from voting was only rarely a political issue in itself. Yet the property qualifications carried a very serious significance, for property was itself considered as a necessary attribute of any man who was both politically responsible and politically free. The retention of a theory of property in politics would have an effect on the character of government when the time came for American colonists to make their own constitutions.

The gradually increasing authority of the Assemblies in the eighteenth century certainly owed much to general harmony of interests expressed by the system of representation. The Assemblies adopted for themselves the theory of the British House of Commons and modelled themselves on its precedents and procedures ; in nearly all the matters that directly touched the people of the colonies, the Assemblies really acted as representatives and really governed. Although colonial taxation was light, the Assemblies laid the taxes, thus establishing their own normal ability to exercise this basic parliamentary power. They received petitions and made laws on innumerable local and provincial issues, session after session and generation after generation. They even devised means of circumventing the veto of the Privy Council. This accumulation of the habits of effective self-government taught the Americans self-reliance and helped to make them strong enough to seek their independence. The Americans laid the foundations for their later democracy by their long experience in the exercise of a more limited but very effective kind of political capability.

The rise of the Assemblies belongs to the domestic constitutional history of the American colonies but was significant for the Empire. They anticipated the course that 'mixed' government would eventually take, even in Britain. The truth was that a generally accepted theory of mixed government was being undermined in the colonies by facts that much more closely resembled the Old Whig model for a republic or commonwealth. It was because of the predominance and initiative which the Assemblies had gained by about the middle of the eighteenth century that they were able to take the lead in asserting, within the colonies, the traditional Whig doctrine of the supremacy of the legislative power. Assembly leadership converged with colonial legislative supremacy. The American Revolution was a result of this convergence, which in turn it helped to complete.

Section I

REPRESENTATION
IN MASSACHUSETTS

Introduction

T H E first step towards self-government in Massachusetts was also the biggest. It was based on the decision, taken by the General Court of the Massachusetts Bay Company in August 1629, and carried out early in 1630 under the governorship of John Winthrop, to take their royal Charter with them when they sailed for Massachusetts.

By this singular act of independence the founders of the Bay Colony seized their heaven-sent opportunity to build a new City of God — no place of shelter, but a city set on a hill to be a sign to the rest of the world. It also gave them the opportunity to effect the transition, from the company organisation given by the Charter, to a civil and ecclesiastical government as required for permanent settlement, with unusual rapidity and completeness; and allowed that government to make itself master of an almost complete legislative power.

Such an effective transfer of power was not to be expected in the early history of colonisation, but it was made possible largely by accident and inadvertence. Neither the government of Charles I nor that of the Commonwealth was strongly placed to enforce detailed obedience on a distant colony; and when contrasted with the immense preoccupations of domestic government and foreign policy, the affair of Massachusetts Bay was on so small a scale and affected so few people as to appear of minor importance. There was practically no early administrative supervision for the colonies and the development of an imperial policy was effectively begun only with the Navigation Act of 1651. But these attentions of the home government were destined to be continued after the Restoration.

The early settlers thus gained a great deal of ground in the direction of self-government in an almost deceptively easy manner. Much of this ground had to be fought for again in the eighteenth century; for the legislative power, assumed under the original Charter, was placed under more conventional limits by the second Charter of 1691. In that later process, the assertion of the colonial claim to legislative power over their own territory merged with the advance, within the province, of representative institutions. The leaders of opposition to British measures were able, through a wider suffrage franchise, to enlist an impressive bulk of popular support. It is tempting to picture these two developments as related strands in a single popular movement leading inevitably to the American Revolution; but the temptation is a deception. This confluence of the interests of self-government and of popular government was a potent reality in the eighteenth century, but it was not a necessity. Either could have gone forward without the other, or even against it; and that in fact had happened at an earlier period, coming to a head in the movement for suffrage extension of 1647.

From 1630 to 1634 the Bay Colony was ruled by a General Court made up solely of the Governor, Deputy-Governor and assistants — in effect the Company's board of managers. The assistants themselves were required to be annually elected by the freemen, but after agreeing to admit rather more than 100 additional freemen in 1630, the Court at the same session ordained that no one was in future to be admitted as a freeman unless he were a church member, which meant a communicant. Thus the politically competent community was confined to members of the congregationally-based Puritan Church. Four years later, deputies elected by the freemen obtained a valuable glimpse of the Charter, through which they were able to insist on their legitimate claim to sit as members of the General Court. A representative form of government had been inaugurated.

That representation should be confined to the faithful seemed perfectly consistent with the aims of a theocratic state. Within that state it was equally natural that authority should lie with the magistrates, a term used interchangeably with 'assistants'. This select group, which claimed a right to negative the votes of the deputies, also formed a court of appeal; thus sharing in all the activities of government. The voice that expounded the scripture, deducing from revealed truth both religion and law, was the voice of a customary magistracy with authority both ecclesiastical and civil. As John Winthrop remarked, 'In all times some must be rich some poor, some high and eminent in power and dignity; others mean and in subjection.'

The Puritan religion as revealed to this magistracy had been developed along paths illuminated by ideas of contract. Its exponents might have been considered the lawyers of theology, taking professional delight in explaining in great detail the legalistic nature of God's covenant with man. The theological significance of this lay in the fact that it bound men to God by their own act: when they broke God's law they broke a covenant to which they had voluntarily acceded. It was all the more important that in civil matters they should obey the magistrate who was authorised to interpret God's law on earth.

This theory of authority, in which the deity appeared to combine the legislative, judicial, and executive powers, transferred itself to earth in the form of a political theory of contemporary utility. The Puritan idea of contract could be applied to the obligations existing between the royal government of Charles I and his subjects. But the Puritan leaders had never conceived that, once their true theocracy had been set up, any further questions of the same sort might arise. Once free of all subjection to an English government, the Puritan magistracy was free to exert its full and unfettered authority in New England. That — if anything — was the meaning of freedom. It certainly did not mean personal liberty; service to the community of God was liberty enough, and John Winthrop never envisaged the private interest of the individual as a rival to the purpose of the community. Yet ideas of contract were inclined to develop a political life of their own; they gave rise to the possibility that the old, shadowy, English legal notion of an individual consent to the laws might actually be translated, under favourable conditions, into political practice.

The question of the right to participate in government was settled, for church members only, in 1634. They took advantage of it, more than once, to unseat Winthrop from the governorship, but never failed to assure him a place among the assistants and eventually restored him to power. In general they remained content to live under the rule of their habitual leaders. The annual elections, provided for as a business procedure in the Charter, served as an effective check on the government when translated to political affairs; beyond that, the freemen only occasionally felt the need to intervene in the running of the province. It was from outside their ranks that the protest began to grow.

The exclusion of non-churchmen was a safeguard which seemed reasonable enough to the defenders of a theocratic society. But it had the odd effect of excluding from any role in government a number of the men whose economic and social position entitled them to be regarded as members of the customary ruling *élite*. The document known as the Body of Liberties, published in 1641, proved inadequate to the demands of the politically disabled; and it was one of this class, Dr Robert Child (though himself a comparatively recent arrival in the colony), who in 1647 led the sharpest movement for reform.

Child's Remonstrance, which blamed on the colony's management all its recent misfortunes in economic affairs and even in public health, expressed alarm at the danger of arbitrary government; laws were inadequate to make life, liberty, and estate safe; the form of government was not settled according to the laws of England. The Remonstrance went on to demand civil liberty and the right to vote for the thousands of righteous and peaceable taxpayers, all Englishmen, who were excluded because they belonged to the Church of England.

It was a well-judged blow in the light of the struggle then waging in England. Well judged, in particular, because Child proposed, if rejected in Massachusetts, to take his cause to Parliament. To demand English intervention in the colonial government amounted to treason, and Child, after being heavily fined, was expelled; but his movement was not without effect, and though Parliament did not see fit (and hardly had the means) to answer the Remonstrance, an extension of political privileges was granted in 1647 by the General Court.

Already, in 1644, the assistants had withdrawn from the body of the deputies to sit as a separate House. The ingredients of an articulated system of government were established; and the formalisation of social relationships in an expanding colony led in 1658 to the adoption of a property qualification for voting in town meetings.

After the Restoration the royal government began to take a more protective interest in the rights of Englishmen in the colony. The exclusion of Anglicans was no longer tolerable; and after a royal commission of enquiry had visited Massachusetts, the colony was instructed to allow the suffrage franchise to all persons of 'competent estates', of orthodox religion, and not vicious in conversation.

The grudging compliance offered by the General Court did not satisfy the English authorities. In the first place, Church members were enabled to become freemen without reference to their economic position, so that non-churchmen, even when they qualified, did so on sufferance; in the second place, non-churchmen were required to be twenty-four years of age, which in a young population set them at a marked, if minor, disadvantage; in the third, a property qualification, from which churchmen were free, was imposed on Anglicans.[1] But England was occupied once again with matters of greater immediate importance than the details of voting in distant Massachusetts; and no further intervention followed until the rule of Andros.

The General Court defended its principles against the English government with a high-toned vindication of ecclesiastical authority; and in spite of the emergence of economic qualifications for voting, economic rivalries were not the main issues at stake in disputes about the proper bounds of the political community. But even within the colony, the ecclesiasts were going on to the defensive; and after the zeal of the first generation had cooled, the main trend of New England life for the remainder of the century was its gradual, irresistible secularisation.

As early as 1662 the General Court, by agreeing to the 'Half-Way Covenant', eased the way to freemanship for Church members who were not full communicants. This step both recognised and helped forward that dissociation of Church and State which led, before the end of the century, to the disappearance of the system of conferences between magistrates and clergy which until then had made Massachusetts so distinctively theocratic.[2] The secularisation of society helped in turn to give political meaning to those contractual ideas which descended into the meeting house by the ladder of Puritan theology.

The whole basis of government as built up in Massachusetts was attacked by Governor Andros (1686–9), who went to its root by forbidding the town meeting. His rule brought the people into the harmony of rebellion; and in due course the Revolution in England gloriously vindicated the doctrine of the social, or political, contract.

The franchise had been creeping forward. In 1681 the General Court permitted its extension to townsmen who had proved their worth in local affairs. And in 1690, when forty of the fifty-four towns supported the Court in demanding a return to the Charter of 1629, the Court prudently modified the requirements for the admission of freemen. Property qualifications were reduced (not abolished) and the certificates of character were to be replaced

[1] Scholars are not entirely agreed on the extent of the disfranchisement effected. What remains clear is that the law was intended to put Anglicans at a disadvantage. B. Katherine Brown, 'Freemanship in Puritan Massachusetts', *American Historical Review*, July 1954, 865–83; Richard C. Simmons, 'Freemanship in Early Massachusetts: Some Suggestions and a Case Study', *William and Mary Quarterly*, July 1962, 422–8.

[2] H. L. Osgood, *The American Colonies in the Eighteenth Century*, 4 vols. (New York, 1924–5; reprinted Gloucester, Mass., 1958), i, 301–2 (hereafter referred to as *American Colonies*).

by a simple certificate from the selectmen[1] that the candidate for freemanship was 'not vicious in life'.

Sixty years of largely independent government had taught the people of New England self-confidence; much of what they would later have to fight for was already implicit in their political life. Yet in all this sturdy independence there was an element of self-flattering illusion. They were not really as independent as they seemed. In a world of rival Empires they could not hope to stand alone; and it was precisely because they enjoyed the implicit, unquestioned protection of the English system that they were so free to develop their own institutions, their own liberties.

The true nature of the relationship was therefore somewhat more faithfully reflected in the Charter of 1691 which converted Massachusetts into a royal province and imposed a royal governor. Yet this Charter, which also gave a substantial measure of control to the legislature, proved an instrument of its own ultimate subversion; it was a building which provided the colonists with ample floor space and corridors leading to most of the seats of power; within its walls they were able gradually to recapture the legislative power which they had once so easily gained but so lightly held.

The General Court, though standing at the centre, was no longer the true focus of the loyalty of the people. The diffusion of the population had led to the quiet growth of the town. Civic life was locally organised. The town and its town meeting were the basis not only of communal life but of the representative government of the province.

1. The Town

There is a particular reason for taking the town as the starting-point for the examination of both the concept and the practical working of political representation in Massachusetts and in all New England. The towns were the political constituencies of the provincial Assemblies. Moreover, the town was to New England what the corporation was to the British parliamentary system; and the

---

[1] The selectmen were the annually elected town committee.

townspeople of New England loved their towns far more than they loved their provinces. The town, both in its social and political life, maintained a strong sense of corporate identity. In order to understand representation in the province it is first essential to appreciate the character of this corporate life in the towns.

THE New England town was the *polis* of America. Like that of an earlier time, it was, in reality, neither politically as independent nor socially as self-contained as it seems from the outline it has projected upon the screen of history. Both in the actual order of events and in constitutional authority the town was preceded by the Great and General Court, which consisted of the Assembly of elected representatives from the towns, the Council elected by the Assembly, and the Governor appointed by the Crown.

Towns were legally incorporated by act of the General Court. It was their government; and it sometimes intervened to settle their internal disputes. For long periods in the town life of the eighteenth century it was easy to lose sight of this government, but its authority, though distant, was never absent and was of great prospective importance.

The first comers to the town were the first owners of the land on which it lay; these original proprietors were the grantees of pieces of territory received under the authority of the General Court. Such men were not engaged in private or speculative enterprise: that came later. The plan for a township was the plan for a community, and involved making provision for residence, religion, local government, schooling, the apportionment of lots, and the protection of common rights. The original proprietors had a special responsibility for making these provisions, but the administrative responsibility for running the town soon passed from their hands to those of the settlers collectively. What the town proprietors retained was not so much a responsibility as a special interest.

By the end of the seventeenth century this special interest in the ownership of the land had clearly come to stand out as being separate from that of the inhabitants, more particularly because proprietorship itself became separated from residence. The town grew more populous and pressed against the undisposed property of the proprietors; proprietors sought to make gains from the increasing price of their remaining lands and claimed rights to the common land for private sale. Disputes arose in which the townsmen and proprietors stood for opposed interests in the same land. Sometimes they had to go for adjudication to the General Court. When this happened, the General Court showed a tendency to respect the claims of the proprietors, which is interesting because the Assembly itself consisted of town representatives. It suggests that the wealthier and socially more eminent people who were usually elected as representatives had sympathies and interests in common with those of the proprietors, and it is easier to explain if one remembers that although these disputes were dramatic they were not the general rule; the town interest in such cases was not identified with a general anti-proprietary interest through the province.[1]

At an even earlier point, the New England town had begun to lose the controlling inspiration of its religious purpose. It is doubtful whether this force, in its early intensity, survived the generation whom it impelled to the early migrations. But the clergy did not relinquish their influence on social conduct or, in certain respects, government policy. The Sabbatarian discipline which regulated the domestic arrangements of the townsmen was reinforced by the political energy of the clergy in the American Revolution and as late as the election campaign of 1800. In Connecticut, the ecclesiastical arm was generally believed to exert a virtual control of the state until disestablishment was effected in 1818; in Massachusetts, the rather looser authority of the recognised Church was not finally disavowed until 1833.

The responsibility for maintaining the moral and political economy of town life was assumed by the laymen who managed town affairs, but that economy continued through much of the eighteenth century to be applied with a humourless and pettifogging severity. Perhaps the pecuniary aspects of this discipline pressed upon the selectmen with greater urgency. Town records tell of many times when strangers who had come into the town without permission were warned to leave; when householders were rebuked for entertaining strangers without permission and ordered to dismiss them. The governing fear was that such people might, without visible means of support, become charges on the town.

No general statement is likely to bring home the effect of this system on

---

[1] For the town proprietors and their place in the development of the politics of the town see R. H. Akagi, *The Town Proprietors of the New England Colonies* (Philadelphia, 1924) (hereafter referred to as *Town Proprietors*). The remarks about the general characteristics of town government are based also on: J. F. Sly, *Town Government in Massachusetts, 1620–1930* (Cambridge, Mass., 1930) (hereafter referred to as *Town Government*); E. S. Griffith, *History of American City Government, Colonial Period* (New York, 1938) (hereafter referred to as *American City Government*); G. E. Howard, *Introduction to the Local Constitutional History of the United States* vol. i (Baltimore, 1889); Edward Channing, *Town and County Government in the English Colonies of North America* in Johns Hopkins University Studies in History and Political Science, 2nd series, no. x (Baltimore, 1889) (hereafter referred to as *Introduction . . . Local Constitutional History*).

everyday life as closely as the records themselves. In 1674, the selectmen of Dedham were informed that certain children of John Littlefield were staying with persons in the town. What had become of the father we do not know; but the town had no intention of being responsible for the children, with the result that:

Ser Auery and Ser Ric Elic are desired: to giue all persons notice: that non of them are alowed to remayne in the Towne unles they have particular: alowance from the select men.[1]

The selectmen lived up to their trust. In 1680, John Eaton and Peter Woodward, on information given that they entertained strangers contrary to town orders, were given notice to forbear; earlier, a townsman who had made proper application was refused permission to have a journeyman living with him. In 1701 there was another outbreak of hospitality, this time none the better for being fraternal. 'John Starr an Impotent person' was entertained 'in our Town' and might become a town charge. The constable was to tell him to quit and 'his brother Comfort Starr disallowed to entertain said John Starr'.[2] Small comfort for John. Examples could be multiplied from other towns. In 1758 the selectmen of Dudley are reported as having given notice to the constable to order six families to leave the town, with which order the constable soon reported that he had complied. More families were warned to leave town the next year.[3]

The corollary to this exclusive and jealous attitude towards strangers was a strong sense of collective responsibility for the spiritual and economic welfare of the community together with care for its own members in distress. The attention given by Dedham to the question of Abigail Littlefield provides an illustration. In January 1684 John Hunting, who had employed Abigail as a servant, told the town that her time with him was over and asked the town to provide for her. The town answered that as he took her into his family against the 'minds and concurrence' of the selectmen, 'as by the record doe appear', the charge fell legally on him. Nevertheless the town, on consideration of the case, was ready to do as much or more than was incumbent on it, and voted that Abigail should remain with her master John Hunting another year and that it would allow him 'four pounds in current country pay' for his care and charge that year. Two years

[1] D. G. Hill (ed.), *The Early Records of the Town of Dedham, Massachusetts, 1602–1706* (Dedham, 1819), 18.

[2] *Dedham Town Records*, 68, 106, 207.

[3] *Town Records of Dudley, Massachusetts, 1732–1794* (Pawtucket, R.I., 1893), 34–35, 42. *Watertown Records*, vols. v and vi (Newton, Mass., 1928), 277, 284, 287, 315.

later, Abigail was again a town problem; she was under 'great affliction by extraordinary burning'. It was agreed to give Hunting twenty-four shillings towards her cure and also five pounds for the ensuing year. 'This vote not for Abigail an inhabitant but given to her master considering that before her burning she was a burden to him.' But four men, listed below the minute, declared that they would pay none of this money.[1] Nothing was done to admit that Abigail herself had a claim which might let her in as an inhabitant.

The same community, about the same time, exercised its competence over local economic development. It appeared that the town needed a fulling mill. Two men desired the liberty to erect a mill, and the selectmen called a general town meeting to make a decision. The general meeting set up a committee of three to consider whether it would be beneficial to the town and if so, to whom to grant permission; and two weeks later the privilege was granted to James Draper, a partner, and their heirs. But the town made the conditions. A date, some eighteen months later, was set for completion, and it was provided if the grantees did not improve the stream and the land granted to them to the satisfaction of the town, or if they let their mill lie unserviceable for more than six months, the whole property would return to the town. More: if the town decided to set up a corn mill on the same place they might do so, unless the persons in the agreement did it at their own charge and to the town's content. The right to the mill was not to be alienated without the town's consent.[2]

No responsibility was more important than that of the provision of a meeting house. The furnishing of pews, making alterations, and generally maintaining the building as well as providing for the accommodation of its users were continual problems, noted repeatedly in town records. The town had also to support a minister, and as it grew more comfortable it also wanted a schoolmaster. The increase of population brought in the eighteenth century a marked increase in the diversity of occupations. The strict control over personal movements, however, had a restrictive effect on economic development, as indeed did the general supervision of activities by the selectmen and the town meeting: but by the middle of the eighteenth century municipal control was losing its effect. The boundaries of the town itself were becoming indistinct. The area of authority, comprehending much countryside and farmland, was too large to police; while a large part of the population was simply less willing to be controlled. Economic diversity and occupational

[1] *Dedham Town Records*, 165, 183.
[2] *Dedham Town Records*, 133–4, 140.

mobility began to weaken the detailed grip in which the community had held its members.[1]

The predominance of the town as a political unit tends to give an unduly urban idea of the township. It may well be that the importance of inland commerce, riverborne and by road, is under-estimated in conventional accounts, and that activities proper to the town, such as storekeeping, law practice, and other professions, really played an influential part in the economy of the provinces; but the fact remains that, away from the seaports, New England life was farm life, whose rhythm was controlled by the seasons, whose people worked the soil or lived by its product. The township extended to include the farm land within the area of the town's legal incorporation, and the inhabitants and freeholders of the town were members of a political corporation but not necessarily townsmen in the domestic sense of the word.

This community was governed by that most famous of all New England institutions, the town meeting. This had originally been simply a meeting of the proprietors, who had a common interest in the administration of the land. As the running of the town fell into the hands of the inhabitants, however, the proprietors went on meeting to discuss their special interests and in particular to regulate the common land. Where the proprietors were absentees, they plainly had no voice in the town meeting; but where they remained in the town, they had, by the eighteenth century, fallen into a small minority as against the numerous freemen and other inhabitants who had no share of the original grant.[2] The proprietors played a gradually diminishing part in the political life of the town, as the questions connected with land titles and common rights were gradually settled. There was nothing more for them to discuss. The full authority devolved upon the town meeting. But as late as the Revolution, a long dispute in Pittsfield between absentee proprietors and inhabitants ended with most of the proprietors going Tory and most of the inhabitants going Whig.[3]

The first generations of settlers moved tentatively towards the institution of some limited form of permanent town government by the delegation of powers to a standing committee. By 1634 Dorchester, Cambridge, and Watertown had each taken the step of electing a sort of executive committee to order the civil affairs of the towns, and these selectmen were soon given

---

[1] Griffith, *American City Government*, 141–3.

[2] Akagi, *Town Proprietors*, 44–49, 64, 73.

[3] Robert J. Taylor, *Western Massachusetts in the Revolution* (Providence, 1954), 43–44 (hereafter referred to as *Western Massachusetts*). Most absentee landlords went Tory: L. N. Newcomer, *The Embattled Farmers* (New York, 1953), 17.

power to determine local tax rates and to act as the town's legal representatives.[1]

The town was a civic community. But the civic community was coterminous with that of the church; and nothing could have better symbolised the connection than the meeting house itself; both place of worship and seat of government — symbol and fact united in one. Despite the gradual dissociation between town and church which is the history of the towns in the seventeenth century, and the related extension of the privilege of participating in town meetings to an increasing proportion of inhabitants, the strong sense of authority which had sustained New England Puritanism was active in town affairs. 'The powers that be are ordained of God' remained throughout the eighteenth century the most popular text for election sermons.[2]

Church membership did not depend primarily on those economic and social characteristics which established an Englishman as a member of the gentry. Election was essentially a matter of worth; and a good and godly character might be borne as well by a poor man as by a rich one. In the closely-knit New England towns, the moral vigilance of the community was directed to the conduct and character of the individuals. With the growing secularisations of society there came a greater formality, a more clearly understood set of social distinctions; to which was attached the appropriate degree of political weight. The original equality of souls — though it certainly never struck John Winthrop as a right foundation for political power — had imparted to Massachusetts town life a freshness and moral fibre whose traces were deeply absorbed into its political being. In these conditions, order, even a measure of imposed authority, did not breed subservience; they were compatible with a high degree of self-respect.

Yet order was also convention. The New England town accepted about as full a measure of differentiation in social rank and station as it was possible to establish in the conditions of settlement. The people who joined to plant a town were not of equal wealth, and their inequalities were reflected in the first divisions of the town lands.[3] Each town of any wealth or amenities was able to sustain a recognised class of gentry, who lived in houses of superior size and furnishings, tended to occupy the leading positions in local govern-

[1] Sly, *Town Government*, 30–37.

[2] Many New England sermons are preserved in the Houghton Library, Harvard.

[3] Carl Bridenbaugh, 'The New England Town: A Way of Life', *Proceedings* of the American Antiquarian Society, vol. 56, April 1946 (Worcester, Mass., 1947), 19–48 (hereafter referred to as 'New England Town').

ment, and sat in the best pews in the meeting house, generally elevated above the level of the rest. Until 1768 at Yale and 1769 at Harvard, students were officially 'placed' according to the social rank of their parents.[1] It must have seemed perfectly natural to the people of Dudley, Massachusetts, that a distinguished pew should be set aside for their patron, the honourable Colonel Dudley, should he desire to have it. There seems, however, to have been an anticipated *quid pro quo*, for Colonel Dudley declined, upon which the pew was voted to Mr Samuel Morris and his heirs 'on their paying what is behind towards the charges of the meeting house according to what another has paid that has a pew of like dignity'; and also on condition that they paid towards the finishing of the meeting house and the minister's rate: and if they refused, the pew should return to the town again. Mr Morris evidently did not command the universal respect accorded to the Dudleys, for seven voters dissented from this offer.[2] In the same session, the town conferred specified pews on fourteen other town dignitaries. The extreme economy common to the mind of New England townsmen must have found these arrangements congenial. The practice may perhaps be likened to the sale of public honours in Britain; a convenient form of public (or party) revenue, but to be applied only in respect of people who have established some more general claim to recognition. (It must, of course, be admitted that not all British Prime Ministers have observed these proprieties.)

Dudley town awarded the leading pew not only to Samuel Morris, but also to his heirs, provided that they continued to deserve the honour by keeping up their payments. It was not to be a title of nobility, but it was to be a hereditary distinction, given by a sort of civic contract, to lapse if the recipient's heirs failed on their part. Americans, for no single reason, were generally inclined to apply the more republican implications of Whig political thought to their own colonial situation and to repudiate the very notion of inherited patents of nobility. The Revolution did not produce this state of mind; but the Revolution certainly advanced it and gave it new strength.

American colonists had no mission to repeal the order of nature, and that order, translated into human institutions, meant the greatest possible measure of stability and permanence in social rank. What the American experience gave distinctively to this concept was the conviction that such rank, to be maintained, had always to be earned anew.

[1] Griffith, *American City Government*, 189–91. S. E. Morison, *Three Centuries of Harvard, 1636–1936* (Cambridge, Mass., 1942), 104–5.

[2] *Dudley Town Records*, 67–71 (1738–9).

This deferential order of society did not, on the whole, give occasion for great internal strife or dissatisfaction. It is true that the New England townsman valued the independence which was so much part of his life, but he saw no reason to feel that this independence was in any way curtailed by according to his social superiors the respect associated with their station in life. It might, on the contrary, have been thought of as an affirmation of his own position, a voluntary expression of self-respect. It is probably because the offer of social deference has seemed to be inseparable from submission and servility to later generations of Americans that they have had so much difficulty in comprehending the fact that in the eighteenth century it was compatible with a very vigorous notion of one's own importance.

The interests of the New England town gentry did not require, nor did the social order suggest, anything in the nature of a rigid hierarchy of power. There were potent equalising forces in the life of the majority of country towns, not least being the nearness of all to the agricultural sources of sustenance, the absence of a large force of cheap labour, the community of worship in the meeting house, and the community of entertainment in the tavern. The social order, which was quietly acknowledged and visible most clearly in the seating arrangements of the meeting houses themselves, did much to facilitate the orderly working of government. It was by no means necessary, and it would be an absurd reduction of the system to geometrical design to suppose, that the top men simply planted themselves in the top posts. What was necessary was that town government should be run with a view to securing the permanent and weighty interests of the town, the most permanent and weightiest being property. It was a property happily and on the whole widely diffused. It was secured by a general tendency to select for leading positions men of substance, generally ranking in the upper half of the rating lists though not exclusively representing a dominant class.[1]

It cannot always have been easy to find enough men who were willing to give the time to the increasingly numerous tasks of a voluntary but indispensable system of self-government. In 1702 Cambridge recorded the election for the ensuing year of three constables, five selectmen, three

[1] *Dedham Town Records*, 7 (1673), 28 (1674), 104–6 (1680). Bridenhaugh, 'New England Town'; Robert E. Brown, *Middle-Class Democracy and the Revolution in Massachusetts* (Ithaca, 1955), 98. None of these works offers exhaustive evidence on the subject of the exact relationship between economic substance and eligibility to office. The purpose of Brown's work is to show that town government represented a fair cross-section of a generally property-holding community; his treatment of the suffrage stands as his main contribution, and the examination of town officers is cursory by comparison.

assessors, a town clerk and treasurer, four highway surveyors, fourteen 'tything men', eight fence viewers, four haywards, a sealer of leather, a sealer of weights and measures, thirteen inspectors of the yoking and ringing of swine, three assistants in the making of the minister's rate and two men 'to take care of the great bridge over the Charles River'.[1]

With the exception of the clerk, and possibly in larger towns the treasurer, these jobs were unpaid. It was a very detailed application to New England conditions of the principle of the unpaid Justices of the Peace who meant so much to the development of local self-government in England under the Tudors. In the seventeenth century the gentry were more willing to give their time to serve the community in humble offices than in the revolutionary era, and there were those who, at different periods, were willing to pay fines in lieu of duty. Of course many of these tasks were humble but they were nonetheless needful; they taught the townsmen how to govern themselves. The senior posts became difficult to fill because of the need for men of higher calibre, who were sometimes unwilling to serve.[2]

In 1664 the General Court had adopted an economic definition of civic competence with the object of disfranchising Anglicans. By the eighteenth century the concept of economic qualifications for the exercise of civic functions was firmly established in principle and in practice. It was formally introduced on the remodelling of Massachusetts under the Charter of 1691 given by William and Mary. This move was controlled by the general strategic purposes of William's anti-French policies, which gave the English government an interest in unifying Protestant sentiment in the colonies.[3] The religious tests were redefined to include Protestants and to exclude Catholics, while the right to participate in political life was determined by a uniform property qualification. The suffrage franchise for elections to the General Court was extended to holders of freehold property worth 40s. per annum, and to non-freeholders owning £40 worth of property, whether real, personal, or mixed. The figure of £40 was arrived at, not by a nice calculation of the exact level at which pecuniary worth could be translated into political power, but by an error of transcription — the original charter read '£50'; the copy brought to Massachusetts said '£40'. Even Hutchinson,

---

[1] *Cambridge Town Records*, 343–4.

[2] Clifford K. Shipton, *Sibley's Harvard Graduates* (Cambridge, Mass., 1933), iv. 5; Sly, *Town Government*, 101–2, n. 3; Griffith, *American City Government*, 175–6, 381. This fact alone would be enough to correct any inference about town government which depended solely on tax lists.

[3] G. H. Haynes, *Representation and Suffrage in Massachusetts, 1620–1891* (Baltimore, 1894), 80–82.

however, does not claim that this accidental concession to mob rule altered for the worse the subsequent history of the province.[1]

Despite this inconsequential error, the intentions behind these qualifications were not merely haphazard, as appears from the curious fact that the qualifications for voting in town meetings were generally maintained at a different level from those for the General Court. Throughout the eighteenth century a town inhabitant was required to possess £20 of rateable estate in the town in order to vote in town meetings; in 1701 it was laid down that he must be officially admitted as an inhabitant by the selectmen; while in 1720 a further statute added that freeholders wishing to vote must also possess this minimum of property — a clarification of the law which suggests that some freeholders failed to qualify for the town franchise, and that some non-freeholders may have succeeded.[2]

The 40s. freehold for the provincial suffrage was, of course, simply the old English county franchise. The £40 provision for others represented some attempt to set up a standard applicable to local conditions. Forty pounds, on the face of the matter, looks twice the size of twenty and suggests that the vote for the General Court was twice as important as that in the town: but unfortunately the rateable estate required to qualify a voter in town meetings was not valued in the same monetary notation as that which applied to elections in the General Court. Not only were there two permanent currencies, but they frequently fluctuated in value, with the result that qualifications for town voting were now lower, now higher, than for provincial voting. The figure of £20 is itself deceptive, since an estate rateable at £20 would in actual market value be worth a very much higher figure. The problem is to find out the real intentions behind the qualifications. When the whole situation was reviewed and stabilised in 1750, the town qualification was made the higher of the two. From that time forth, the freehold qualification for town voting was 66s. 8d.; for provincial voting 53s. 4d.[3]

These are not accidental figures. The difference between them is 13s. 4d., which happens to be one-quarter of the provincial voting qualification of 53s. 4d. Not perhaps a great difference, but obviously a calculated one. The

[1] Francis Newton Thorpe, *Federal and State Constitutions, Colonial Charters and Other Organic Laws*, 7 vols. (Washington, D.C., 1909), iii. 1878-9 (hereafter referred to as *Federal and State Constitutions*). *Acts and Resolves of the Province of Massachusetts Bay* (Boston, 1869-1922), i. 363 (hereafter referred to as *Acts and Resolves*).

[2] *Acts and Resolves*, i. 451; x. 45; iii. 47-48.

[3] Brown, *Middle-Class Democracy*, 78-88. Mr. Brown has here untangled the different currencies and explained their varying values with admirable lucidity.

members of the General Court may well have felt that in their capacity as the representatives of the people — the commons' House — they ought to make the provincial suffrage as wide as was thought to be compatible with the safety of the state — to justify as far as possible their claim to be representatives, not merely of a congeries of individual towns, but of Massachusetts Bay as a political whole. As representatives of individual towns they remained responsible for securing the government and property of the towns. The town was the primary political unit. The affairs which bore most directly on the people were town affairs, and a voice in town government called for some assurance of a tangible and personal stake in local interests — something to lose if things went wrong. If continental or provincial affairs were of more general interest, justifying a wider suffrage, they were also of far more distant concern to the majority of townsmen.

The towns stood directly under the General Court for political purposes, but not in matters of justice, administration, or even in all matters of taxation. Massachusetts was also divided into counties; and these counties were administered by the courts of quarter sessions. The judges, who owed their appointments to the Governor, had extensive powers over county administration and controlled taxation for county purposes. Their powers represented a pronounced limitation on the self-governing, self-taxing liberties of the towns.

It would be impossible to read the records of the New England towns without getting a lively, sometimes an affectionate, sense of the vitality of the community. A warrant is sent out for a town meeting, 'to see whether the Town will consider hiring a minester for a year to preach the Gospel to them'. A warrant is issued 'to see whether the Town will hire a schoolmaster'. It is voted 'to a number of young men in the South West corner of our meeting house over the men's stairs for to build them a pew at their own cost' — a pew later taken away from them, we do not know why. It is voted 'to culour our pulpit the canopee and the brest work of our gallerys'.[1] Gradually the style becomes slightly more formal and mention of those qualified to attend becomes more exact, but the record always abounds with questions about 'our meeting house', 'our school', 'our pulpit', 'our highway', and 'our town'. There is nothing in the least sentimental about this. It was their town, and no one else's.

The people of Massachusetts were strongly attached to their towns. The feeling is manifest as early as 1644, when in their town meetings they

[1] *Dudley Town Records* 7, 73, 38–39, 41, 69.

rejected a proposal from the General Court that, as the increase in the number of towns had led to a burdensome increase in the number of deputies, the town should be replaced by the shires as the unit of representation.[1] And it was not until as late as 1857 that the town was finally abandoned as the political constituency of the General Court.[2]

Massachusetts, then, was a province and later a state, composed of towns. Each town owed its legal status to an Act of Incorporation by the General Court, and as population grew and new settlements sprouted from old ones these Acts were granted only when the new group had reached an appropriate size. When the time came to make a state Constitution in 1779 there was to be a sharp debate about the exact number of inhabitants entitled to be incorporated into a town. Being incorporated, the town conducted its affairs through the town meeting, duly summoned on a warrant issued by the selectmen; and only those subjects named in the warrant were to be discussed, though additional matter might be placed on the agenda if ten signatures were presented. The election of a representative in the General Court was technically supposed to be held at a different meeting; though in practice it appears that the two functions were often performed in a single meeting, and under conditions in which it must have been difficult to tell the difference between the legal voters for town officers and for representatives, or indeed between the legal voters and the rest. The correspondence of the Crown officers from the time of the Stamp Act onwards contains much evidence of the uproar on these occasions. One of the most vivid descriptions came from Hutchinson in 1772.[3]

the meetings of that town [Boston] [wrote Hutchinson to the Earl of Hillsborough] being constituted of the lowest class of the people under the influence of a few of a higher class but of intemperate and furious dispositions and desperate fortunes. Men of property and of the best character have deserted these meetings where they are sure of being affronted. By the constitution forty pounds sterl. — which they say may be in cloaths household furniture or any sort of property is a qualification and even into that there is scarce ever any enquiry and anything with the appearance of a man is admitted without scrutiny.

No doubt it would be tendentious to suggest that Boston was typical; but common sense and a little experience of public meetings will also suggest that it must often have been difficult to enforce the distinction between different types of citizens when votes were taken in a crowded meeting house.

[1] Howard, *Introduction . . . Local Constitutional History*, 355.
[2] Thorpe, *Federal and State Constitutions*, iii. 1916–23.
[3] Brown, *Middle-Class Democracy*, 60.

The qualifications of representatives in the colonial period were no different from those of their electors. This significant distinction was introduced for the first time in the independent Constitution of 1780. What a man needed, apart from the economic competence implied by his quantum of property, was the respect of his fellow citizens. In quiet towns of steady habits, shrewd calculations, and traditional loyalties, the citizens sought a man who would be truly representative because he was truly one of them and who at the same time stood out sufficiently to command a general respect.

Nothing could be more telling than the observations of New England life upon which John Adams drew to illustrate human nature:

Go into every village of New England, and you will find that the office of justice of the peace, and even the place of representative, which has ever depended only on the freest election of the people, have generally descended from generation to generation, in three or four families at most.[1]

Deference to men of this standing was a mark, not of subservience, but of confidence.

Such respect could be augmented by thrift, since the towns were obliged to meet the expenses of their representatives. In 1750 Cambridge voted to send two representatives to the General Court if they undertook to serve gratis. Two representatives were duly chosen and re-elected the next year. In 1752 one of them refused the conditions and a substitute was found; but the practice was soon dropped.[2]

Unless the General Court was to discuss matters which touched the town directly, there was a strong temptation to leave the whole business alone. The town meetings frequently decided not to send a representative, a decision which was often unanimous. This neglect was an offence against constitutional duty, and could be punished by the General Court with a fine.

In 1768 the warrant and record of the Chelsea town meeting mentioned, 'To see, if they would send a Representative. Passed in the Negative by a great Majority'. But in 1770 Chelsea was find £7 for neglect — remitted the following June 'by reason of the smallness of the town and the poverty of the inhabitants'.[3]

[1] John Adams, *Defence of the Constitutions of the United States*, 3 vols. (Philadelphia, 1797), i. 110–11.

[2] Lucius R. Paige, *A History of Cambridge, Massachusetts, 1630–1877* (New York, 1883), 133.

[3] Mellen Chamberlain, *A Documentary History of Chelsea* [*Massachusetts*] *1624–1824*, 2 vols. (Boston, 1908), 537.

The towns, therefore, were the constituencies whose representatives formed the General Court. This constituent character was the fundamental ingredient of the system of representation in the Assembly in the new constitutions of Massachusetts; both the defeated proposals of the General Court of 1778 and the adopted Constitution of 1780. Some of the towns, in discussing these instruments, put into their reports a clear statement of this condition, particularly when arguing for the maintenance of the highest attainable degree of equality between the towns as separate corporations.

This State [said the town of Lincoln]

is constituted of a great number of Distinct and very unequal Corporations which Corporations are the Immediate Constituent part of the State and the individuals are only the Remote parts in many respects — in all acts of the legislature which Respect particular Corporations each Corporation has a distinct and separate interest Clashing with the Interest of all the rest and so long as Human Nature remains the same it now is Each Representative will be under an undue bias in favour of the Corporation he Represents. Therefore Large Corporations having a Large Number of Representatives will have a Large and Undue Influence in determining any Question in their own favour.[1]

Under the Constitution of 1780, the apportionment of representatives among the towns was based on a numerical scale of population, and it was this principle of numbers, worked out and applied in detail, which seemed to threaten the corporate identity of some of the towns. Thus the corporation idea was not expressed for the satisfaction of enunciating general principles. Its application to the issue was put plainly by the town of Ware:

We look upon the great Disproportion in the matter of representation between the greater & less Towns meerly on account of numbers to be pregnant with dangerous Consequences with regard to some very important matters — therefore we could heartily wish that representation could be weigh'd by Towns rather than by number of polls, which would be similar to the proceedings of the Honble Congress and some neighbouring well regulated States that have been attended with wholsome Effects....[2]

The town of Sunderland observed that 'each Town has Rights, Liberties and Priviledges peculiar to the same, and as dear to them as those of any other and which they have as just a right as any others to have guarded and protected'.[3]

---

[1] Massachusetts Archives: Town meeting returns on the Constitution of 1780: vol. 277, 17.

[2] Mass. Archives, 277, 116.   [3] Mass. Archives, 276, 67.

The sense in which the spokesmen of these towns defended the concept of equality seems almost elaborately archaic; but in their own time it was a sense that everyone could understand. It was grounded in the history and daily life of the people. This conviction of the essential equality of the towns was no longer strictly tenable in the increasingly complex and variegated politics of the state. Yet it arose from the deep sense of attachment which Massachusetts townspeople felt for their own communities, a feeling which is also communicated in a sympathetic and intimate way by the records of the town meetings — already going back nearly a century and a half.

From the point of view of a Hutchinson, preoccupied with the decline of traditional authority, the appalling thing about town meetings was their air of brazen equality — the unification of all interests into one mass, or mob, all level on the floor: what he and his peers were inclined to call 'an absolute democracy'. But Hutchinson also observed the disintegration of central authority, arising from a basic disrespect for any authority that transcended that of the town.[1]

The attitude which Hutchinson noticed was due to cause the new state of Massachusetts a great deal of trouble. Many of the western towns were so pleased with the decline of central control, and so hostile to the pretensions of Boston, that they maintained an attitude ranging from insubordination to virtual self-rule from the early days of the Revolution until 1780.

This sense of community was undoubtedly one of the most important of the constant factors of local life; it was also important in forming the feelings of the townspeople towards their own political representation. Through much of the colonial period, carefully drawn property qualifications had excluded a certain proportion of the able and adult men from the privilege of voting in elections for their own representative in the General Court; and instead of being swept away in a whirlwind of indignation, these restrictions were retained, actually in a slightly raised form, in the new Constitution of the state. This cannot be explained entirely by reference to town habits, but there is reason to suppose that the integrity of the town gave to its members a strong and valuable feeling of identity and of membership in a lively and self-conscious community. This community's right of representation was one of its rights as a corporate body.[2]

---

[1] T. Hutchinson to Richard Jackson, 19 November, 1767; T. Hutchinson Letterbooks, xxv. 215–19, Massachusetts Historical Society.

[2] This point influenced the Justices of the Supreme Judicial Court when in 1815–16 they had to decide whether the dissenting minority could proceed to an election of a representative after the majority had decided not to do so. The right of the town to elect

There may not have been any public doctrine of 'virtual representation' in America, and had one been propounded about this time it would probably have had a short life; but virtual representation was a fact widely practised without protest. The Massachusetts town meeting probably came closer than anything else in Britain or America to making such a concept into an acceptable reality in which even the humblest members of the town felt that their interests, involved with those of their town, were included in its representation. The affirmative sense of membership was likely to matter more than the negative sense of humiliation through exclusion from the suffrage. In this way the town, with its own meetings, interests, and separate character, contributed materially to the complex texture of a political life that could be called 'Whig' — in contrast to monarchy on one side and democracy on the other.

2. The Triumph of the Legislative Power
1691–1775

The rise of the legislative power in Massachusetts was an extremely lengthy and complicated process. It took place, bit by bit, as the result of a series of piecemeal encounters between elected representatives and royal governors; and it was not easy to see the significance of these events in their fullness and unity until the entire development had nearly reached its end. Representatives saw the constitutional implications of particular struggles but they did not plan the process as a whole. It was only as late as 1766 that the Assembly gained definitive leadership over the Council, but in the intervening years the leading interests of the mercantile seaboard had gradually come to dominate the Assembly. The advance of the controversy between the province and Great Britain facilitated a rapprochement between the seaboard leadership and the towns of the interior,

was held to be a Corporate right; the action of the majority bound the whole body, even though it might deprive them of representation, or of electing the number to which they were entitled. Luther S. Cushing, Charles W. Storey, and Lewis Josselyn, *Reports of Controverted Elections in the House of Representatives in the Commonwealth of Massachusetts from 1780 to 1852* (Boston, 1853), 198–200 (hereafter referred to as *Controverted Elections*).

with striking effects on the character of political representation. The Assembly relied on the support of the towns, erected a gallery for visitors, and rallied the people in defence of their local liberties. The effect of all this was a marked advance in the idea of popular sovereignty.

I N spite of everything that can be said of the primacy of the town in the political life of Massachusetts, the constitutional supremacy belonged to the General Court. Its legislative powers included not only that of incorporating new towns, which involved the right of representation, but also the normal legislative control of the suffrage and elections.

Since the grant of the Charter of 1691, the full General Court had comprised the royally appointed Governor, the Council, and the Assembly. Since the members of the Council were elected annually by the Assembly sitting with the Council of the previous year, both of the legislative chambers were composed of members who owed their political existence to the towns. The influence of the Governor, as far as actual membership went, entered the Council through his power to veto the choice of individuals; and it became something of a byword in the province that a negatived councilman made a good representative.

The new order that came about when Massachusetts ceased to be a chartered corporation and became a Crown province brought certain distinct changes in the bases of political power. Formerly — except for the interval of the rule of Andros, which may be regarded as abnormal — the Governor owed his appointment to the General Court and was therefore a representative of the province. After 1691 being appointed by the Crown — though he might be (and often was) a Massachusetts man — he got his instructions from, and owed obedience to, an authority outside the province. On the other hand, the Board of Assistants, who had sat formerly as an upper House and as the nominal representatives of the company, had stood for a separate order, a special interest in the constitution; and when they disappeared it remained to the Council to carry forward a somewhat attenuated idea of a separate constitutional interest, without actually standing on a separate political basis. It does not appear surprising that effective power was quickly seized by the Assembly and that after 1691 the Assembly dictated the course of provincial political development.

The appearance of the new Charter also brought into permanent form in Massachusetts the principle of the economic determination of political rights. When the property qualification had been adopted at the Restoration, it was rather a device to keep down the Anglicans than as a permanent principle.

But the various redefinitions of the actual property quotient in the assessment of political responsibility which followed through the eighteenth century all took their source from the introduction of property qualifications in the Charter of 1691.[1]

I. THE ASSERTION OF LEGISLATIVE POWER

Differences among the people — economic differences, which in town life meant clearly understood and deeply felt distinctions of social rank — were thus imported into the political constitution of the province; an expedient became a principle and a habit. Whether the actual structure of the General Court in the eighteenth century was at all different as a result of these qualifications from what it would have been without them, is a question which is perhaps worth asking even though it cannot be answered. It was after, not before, the Revolution, that the Court pursued policies which culminated in a rebellion. The Court was liable, of course, to reflect differences of interest between towns or economic groups, and it has been noticed that in disputes between towns and proprietors the Assembly generally tended to side with the latter. Even when the Court clashed with the Governor, it did not necessarily speak for the whole province: but its composition put it in a strong position when it clashed with the Governor on specifically constitutional issues. Precisely because it exercised so large a proportion of the internal authority, it viewed the means by which it operated as a matter of essential right, and fiercely resisted the slightest encroachment.

The encroachments came in matters of finance. It is not difficult, though it is certainly quite misleading, to read the history of colonial Assemblies as one long, repeated struggle with royal or proprietary Governors over the question of the Governors' salaries. Whenever the matter came up, the Assemblies naturally fought the Governors by means of their power over salaries; and owing to the unwillingness of the British authorities to put colonial Governors on the Civil List, the Assemblies eventually got the upper hand. When the matter did not come up, as most of the time it did not, the contests of colonial politics did not normally arrange themselves in the form of a confrontation between Assembly and Governor. On the contrary, the conflicting intentions of various groups, 'rings', or leaders, often connected with land purchase and speculation, were likely to be reflected in the

1 See above, pp. 47–48.

contests between Assembly factions, an internal struggle in which the Governor might become involved because of his own extensive patronage and power. The authority which resided in the mother country was normally to be considered, not as an enemy, but as a possible ally in such contests. This was nowhere clearer than in the great controversy over royal government in Pennsylvania, where the anti-proprietaries actually aimed to return the province to royal authority in order to defeat their domestic rivals.

This is not to say, however, that in questions of the effective source of control of internal matters, the Assembly would ever cede what it assumed to be its rights. There were two important issues of financial control which brought it into open and often bitter conflict with the royal authorities. Of these central issues, one concerned the control of appropriations and expenditure, the other the question of the Governor's salary. In 1721, the Massachusetts Assembly began a practice of voting money grants by resolution, a procedure which escaped the revision of the Privy Council — whose discretion extended only to the acts, not to the resolves, of the provincial legislature. The Privy Council condemned the practice in 1729,[1] but did not thereby extinguish the interest of local legislators in determining this obviously important aspect of their own fortunes. The matter came up again when the Assembly began to claim a power to audit muster rolls and payment warrants issued by the Council in its executive capacity.

Soon afterwards the House tried to control disbursements by voting that when funds were raised by a vote of the House the provincial treasurer was to pay them out only on warrants issued by the House; but Governor Belcher refused to sign warrants under this form, and as the burden of debt on the province soon became intolerable, by 1733 the House was forced to recede.

Nevertheless, under a new set of royal instructions to the Governor, the Assembly made certain important gains. It retained the right, which it had claimed, to audit the treasurer's accounts after payments had been made, and to enter complaints against warrants passed by the Council. It succeeded, moreover, in asserting the right to detail the purposes for which the Council might issue pay warrants.[2]

The power to complain of grievances against the provincial treasurer after payments had been made might seem to be a technical, rather than a substantial, gain. But behind this lay the fact that the treasurer was elected

---

[1] Osgood, *American Colonies*, iii. 165, 185.

[2] Henry Russell Spencer, *Constitutional Conflict in Provincial Massachusetts* (Columbus, Ohio, 1905), 112–14 (hereafter referred to as *Constitutional Conflict*).

annually in joint session with the Council, while the Council itself was in large measure elected by the Assembly. On the whole, viewing the rights confirmed under these instructions in the light of the existing distribution of power within the province, the General Court had emerged with a gratifying measure of real control. It alone possessed the power to raise public monies at home by taxation, and over the disbursement of these monies it had achieved a degree of control which, if not altogether commensurate with its claims to a form of internal parliamentary sovereignty, was real enough to meet the practical interests of the General Court as the representative body of the province.

Over the salary question, the final struggle lasted from about 1728 to 1735. The basic position taken by the British authorities was simply that the Governor's salary should be raised by a permanent appropriation, passed by the General Court at the beginning of a new governorship. This would make the Governor independent of the Assembly in any disputes that might arise, especially touching matters of power; and it was in this light, of course, that it was understood by the representatives. The Board of Trade was faced with the untiring persistence of the Massachusetts Assemblies in refusing to grant their Governors' salaries by any other method than an annual appropriation, and by the fact that the administration was never willing to go to either the expense or the political risks inherent in granting a Civil List salary. In 1731 the Board began to weaken when it permitted Governor Belcher to accept a grant from the Assembly, differing in form from that required in his instructions. The form was to be an annual, instead of a permanent, appropriation; and the explanation offered was that this concession would avert the hardship which would otherwise fall on the Governor and his family. Like all steps which begin a long line of retreat, the concession was accompanied by a firm warning that it was not to be considered as a precedent. As such it was repeated year after year, until in 1735 general permission was given for the passage of an annual Act, and it was no longer necessary to secure the consent of the home government.[1]

The process may be considered, as it was by the home government, a relentless advance by the colonial Assembly into the domain of the imperial prerogative. Governor Shute had asserted, in a memorial to the king, that the Massachusetts representatives had much greater powers than the British Commons, as they controlled the whole legislative power and also much of the executive through their influence over the expenditure of the revenues. 'By the artifice of a few leaders and the insinuations of some people in

[1] Spencer, *Constitutional Conflict*, 93; Osgood, *American Colonies*, iii. 322–3.

Boston,' he wrote, 'the whole country was made to believe that the house was barely supporting the privileges of the people, when it was really invading the rights of the crown.'[1]

He then adverted to those accusations of 'Levelling' which were to become a familiar ingredient in the complaints of British agents against the political character of the people of Massachusetts. But the Assembly could not have everything its own way. In 1726 it was obliged to accept what was designated an 'Explanatory Charter',[2] issued by the Crown in the previous year, which confirmed the Governor's right to veto the House's choice of speaker, and further curtailed the privileges of the House by denying it the right to adjourn its own sessions for more than two days.

Although these disputes may not have represented the normal tenor of political life, there is no escaping the fact that the issues they raised were fundamental; each point, gained or lost by either side, meant a gain or a loss in effective constitutional power. They had the effect of giving a peculiarly sharp definition to the conventional language in which political institutions were discussed. Thus Governor Burnet, in his opening speech to the General Court in 1728 emphasised the parallel between the 'due balance' which formed the excellence of the British Constitution and the corresponding distribution of power in the province;[3] and when the House clashed with Burnet over the salary question, their dispute flared into an argument on the nature of precisely this matter of the 'balance of the constitution'. Faced with an executive who owed his appointment to an extraneous authority the legislators, while accepting the convention of balance, were really demanding legislative power. In reply to Burnet, they drafted a statement known as the 'Advice', which reviewed the history of the salary question, and asserted both that their position was based on Magna Carta and that to agree to a diminution of their control over money taxation would lessen the freedom and dignity of the House, which would not be a proper method of preserving the balance between the three branches of the legislature.[4] The separateness of the branches, on which the Governor insisted, lodged in the executive section a firm control of legislative policies.

The circumstances of the dispute conduced to a close liaison between legislators and their constituents. Shute remarked that the house was

---

[1] Osgood, *American Colonies*, iii, 174–5.

[2] *Massachusetts Charter, Laws and Resolves* (Boston, 1726), 12–13.

[3] *A Collection of the Proceedings of the Great and General Court on the Salary Question* (Boston, 1729), 40.

[4] *Collection of the Proceedings*, 61–65.

composed of men 'of small fortunes and mean education'; Burnet, observing the intimacy between the Boston members and the citizenry, adjourned the General Court to Salem. It was the Boston members, in his opinion, who were always trying to pervert the country members on the salary question.[1] This discovery was made in his turn by Governor Belcher; the Boston members were firm, when many country representatives would have been willing to yield.[2] It is clear that in this crisis the Governor would have liked to see a change in the membership of the House resulting from the elections of 1729, and that the general continuity of membership resulting from those elections represented a serious disappointment. The Boston town meeting had instructed its representatives to vote against a permanent salary.[3]

Leadership in Boston politics, as in Pennsylvania, was capable of being related to issues. The House leaders who formed the stand against successive Governors on the salary question regarded the support of the towns as important; the reason given for the adoption of the 'Advice' of 1728 was: 'To prevent any misrepresentation that may be made to the several towns'. The members claimed that they wanted 'to know the minds of their principals', but it is still more likely that they desired their 'principals' to know the minds of their leaders.[4] The politicians of Massachusetts did not want to make life unbearable for their Governors or to be constantly at war with them. According to Hutchinson, the two parties 'which had long subsisted in the government, were vying, with each other, in measures for an expedient or an accommodation' with Belcher on his arrival: but Hutchinson could not attribute all the trouble to mischief made in the Assembly, and went on to remark that 'the major part of the house were very desirous of giving satisfaction to the governor and to their constituents both, but that' he concludes, 'could not be'.[5]

These observations do not make it easy to determine the exact source of Assembly policy, or to say whether the impulse rose from the towns, or whether the Assembly steered ahead with its policies while spreading its sails to catch the support of the towns — but it is of some significance that Burnet should have hoped to improve the position by the simple expedient of removing the General Court from Boston, even though the experiment failed. It is also of significance that one of the long-standing Assembly

---

[1] Spencer, *Constitutional Conflict*, 62, 81.

[2] J. S. Barry, *History of Massachusetts*, 3 vols. (Boston, 1855, –6, –7), ii. 130.

[3] Osgood, *American Colonies*, iii. 181–2, 184.   [4] Spencer, *Constitutional Conflict*, 80.

[5] L. S. Mayo (ed.), William Hutchinson, *History of Massachusetts Bay*, 3 vols. (Cambridge, Mass., 1936), ii. 284–5 (hereafter referred to as *Massachusetts Bay*).

leaders, Elisha Cooke the younger, himself the son of a distinguished assemblyman, should have lost his popularity, and eventually his seat, from Boston as a result of his endeavours to keep on good terms with the Governor.[1]

These events helped to determine the meaning of representation. The House, owing its election directly to the towns, was by definition the representative branch of government in Massachusetts, a definition with which no constitutional lawyer would have quarrelled; and the conflict with the Governors served to distinguish with a clarity as unmistakable to the province as it was unwelcome to the Governors themselves, the meaning that inhered in the distinction between the legislative branch of government and the executive. It is of vast importance for American development that this distinction, which lingered in the British Constitution only in the changeable forms of a cloudy historical convention, was in the colonies and provinces driven into the institutional channels of the struggle for power.

The Assembly could claim with reason to be representative in more than constitutional form. Its members were far closer to their constituents than were most members of the House of Commons. But, more than this, except for the royal Governor the whole of the General Court came, either directly or — in the case of the Council — indirectly within the compass of the elective system.

In their quarrels with the Governors the representatives forcefully asserted their representative character. Under the stress of the economic difficulties of the 1730s they applied that character to matters of policy; in their search for remedies they pressed their powers to the limit and in the process discovered where the limit lay.

The idea of meeting the shortage of credit and currency by founding a provincial bank was not new when Belcher became Governor. A 'Bank of Credit' with securities based on land had been projected some twenty years earlier, giving rise to a small-scale pamphlet controversy.[2] But the British policy, which showed a habitual preference for extreme caution in the relief of distant distresses, became systematically restrictive after the collapse of the

---

[1] Hutchinson, *Massachusetts Bay*, ii. 286–7. In 1733 he won by one or two votes out of six or seven hundred. Later he was defeated. Ibid., ii, 337.

[2] Paul Dudley, *Objections to the Bank of Credit Lately Projected at Boston* (Boston, 1714), Samuel Lynde and others, *A Vindication of the Bank of Credit Lately Projected at Boston* (Boston, 1714). Anon., *The Present Melancholy Circumstances of the Province Considered, and Methods for Redress Humbly Proposed* (Boston, 1719). Anon., *The Distressed State of the Town of Boston once more Considered . . . with a Scheme for a Land Bank Laid Down* (Boston, 1720).

South Sea Bubble in 1720. It was not applied with absolute consistency, and occasional paper issues were permitted under conditions of immediate need; but when such an issue was sanctioned in 1733 the condition was attached that nearly all the outstanding bills of credit were to be called in, not later than 1742. Thus in the later 1730s the province moved towards a deep and predictable financial crisis. The currency and credit available were already insufficient to provide for the existing terms of trade, and wholly failed to take notice of the expansion of population. A policy of contraction could not fail to impress upon the province the remoteness of their own problems from British concern and at the same time to stimulate them to invent their own remedies.

The revival of the Land Bank scheme, under the leadership of John Coleman, was received with widespread support throughout the province. Although, according to Hutchinson, 'the needy part of the province in general favored the scheme',[1] the leadership came from Boston. Belcher had already been fighting the Assembly about paper money for some years, but found the elections going against him. By 1740 he was faced with what Hutchinson called 'the land bank house', which proceeded to establish that institution. There were some 800 subscribers, including a large proportion of the representatives; bills, based on real estate mortgages and not liable to be redeemed for twenty years — and even then payable in commodities — were issued as the medium of exchange; there was no specie capital, or, as Osgood more cryptically remarks, 'no capital'.[2] The economics of the project alarmed some of the merchants, who countered with a 'Silver Scheme' whose subscribers promised to redeem notes in silver and agreed to redeem other notes only at a discount.

These events brought about a head-on collision between Governor Belcher and the House of Representatives, a collision between branches of the system of government over a major issue of policy. It cannot be said that the province stood on one side against the royal executive on the other; the province was divided. But, as Hutchinson grimly observed, one of the votes of the needy would go as far in popular elections as one of the most opulent, and there could be no doubt as to which were the more numerous.[3] Governor Belcher denounced the Land Bank in a proclamation, but the fact was that the Bank could not be crushed by the forces available in Massachusetts.

---

[1] Hutchinson, *Massachusetts Bay*, iii. 299–300.   [2] Osgood, *American Colonies*, iii. 354.
[3] Hutchinson, *Massachusetts Bay*, iii. 299–300. But this majority seems to have been sectional; the western part of Massachusetts appears to have been indifferent to larger political questions or hostile to Boston. Taylor, *Western Massachusetts*, 52–54.

Parliament had to be called in. By an Act of 1741, to become effective in the same year, the 'Bubble Act' which prohibited speculative corporations and was interpreted to apply to the Land Bank was extended to the colonies:[1] but not before the Governor had done everything to destroy the Bank with his own powers, using the patronage at his disposal and dissolving the House elected in 1740 in the hope of improvement. The electoral system did him no service. The new House was equally favourable to the Land Bank. Nothing could have more clearly demonstrated the relationship between the electoral system and the constituencies, or the contrast between the constituencies and the executive power.

II. THE EMERGENCE OF INTERESTS

The victory of the Assembly on the salary question had the effect of a constitutional reform, since it brought a permanent modification in practice; but there was no modification of the constitutional structure from that time until the amendment of the law of representation, in 1775. This does not mean there was no development; it means that development took place as a result of shifts in the location of power within the existing framework. One such development, advised by the Board of Trade,[2] was the creation of new districts without the privilege of representation in the General Court. This was not the policy of the Assembly. Many new towns were given representation, increasing the number of members of the House, while the Council remained stationary, to the consternation of both Bernard and Hutchinson: but many new towns also were denied representation, as a direct application of restrictions by the home government.[3] This practice strengthened the representation of the Eastern seaboard; and in general, where new unrepresented districts lay in the interior, the effect was to give a relative addition to the East.

The most striking development in this period, especially in the years antecedent to the Revolution, was the seizing of provincial leadership by the House of Representatives. But the leadership inside that House had a history of its own. Despite the fact that the populations of the seaboard counties of Essex and Suffolk were chronically under-represented, and that Boston was entitled under the Charter to only four members, the seaboard towns rose in

[1] Osgood, *American Colonies*, iii. 358–9.

[2] Harry A. Cushing, *The Transition in Massachusetts from Province to Commonwealth*, Columbia University Studies vii, i; (New York, 1896), 22. Hereafter referred to as *Transition in Mass.*

[3] Hutchinson, *Massachusetts Bay*, iii. 39–40. Cushing, Storey, and Josselyn, *Contraverted Elections*, 23–27.

some thirty years before 1766 from comparative ineffectiveness to an ascendancy over the House of Representatives that was an indispensable condition of the movement for Independence. The rise of Boston and its neighbours was in part that of a strong centre of population, but not of an over-all majority. The real character of the process was that of the emergence, through a complex of social forces, of a major economic interest. The interest, stated generally, was that of the seaboard merchants; and the development in Massachusetts politics of a rudimentary but powerful form of interest representation was in due course to pose problems which separation from Britain alone would not solve. The new state inherited as its colonial legacy a complex of interests competing within the recognised order of representation and competing for control of that order. The political manifestation of these interests, though less extensive and subtle, was not in principle very different from that to be observed in the mother country.

Boston had long been forward in the struggles against the prerogative. During the salary disputes, as has been seen, the Boston members were the most pertinacious.[1] Boston members took an active part in the Land Bank business.[2] This position was not easy to maintain; and the economic troubles which the Land Bank scheme had been meant to alleviate, coupled with the rise of rival ports and shipbuilding centres, caused a serious decline in the prosperity, confidence, and influence of the capital.[3]

The renewal of Bostonian influence was not because of any single factor. The return of prosperity, which not only quickened the pride and restored the self-confidence of the citizens but also extended their credit and commercial power over other sections, was the indispensable basic force; but in the growth of a general seaboard 'interest', Boston found herself in alliance with her immediate neighbouring rivals; more so when this interest, under merchant leadership, confronted the threats posed by the policies of Grenville.

The political power of the seaboard interest is traceable in the election to the key position in the House of Representatives, that of the Speaker. From the period of the Boston revival in the 1730s the Speaker was a representative either of Boston itself or of one of the neighbouring towns of the related seaboard area (Braintree, Ipswich, Taunton, Barnstaple, Plymouth, Salem) right through to the Revolution; with the exceptions of elections from Worcester County in 1749, 1762, and 1763.[4]

---

[1] See p. 60.   [2] See p. 62.

[3] Carl Bridenbaugh, *Cities in Revolt* (New York, 1955), 47–48. 'Boston was the only city not to experience an increase in population and commercial expansion before 1760.'

[4] *Journals of the House of Representatives.*

The trend was noted by Hutchinson, who thought it became 'conspicuous', when James Otis the younger entered the House as a Boston member, in 1761.[1] The elder Otis had always sat for Barnstaple, which was traditionally jealous of Boston; but when the son came into the House for Boston, the father — who had quarrelled bitterly with Governor Bernard — threw his weight behind Boston, and with it much local influence.

A reader of Hutchinson might get the impression that the American Revolution was the direct result of the feud of the Otis family with the royal government of Massachusetts Bay. The disappointment of the elder Otis in his expectation of being made Chief Justice was undoubtedly the source of much personal animosity.[2] But whatever the personal animus, the forensic talents of James Otis, as exhibited in the case of the writs of assistance and in the Stamp Act crisis, gave a powerful lead against British policy.

The merchants saw trouble coming when the British administration prepared to introduce the Sugar Act of 1764. As early as April 1763 they founded the Society for Encouraging Trade and Commerce within the Province of Massachusetts Bay; and for five years they concerted their efforts to convince the British authorities that the Trade Acts were a burden both to the colonies and to Britain itself.[3]

---

[1] Hutchinson, *Massachusetts Bay*, iii. 120, 69.

Hutchinson says: 'For thirty or forty years after the charter, the members of the town of Boston had less weight in the house than many of the members from the country towns; and there was a jealousy lest the town should obtain too great influence.' He concludes that the influence of the Boston members, which had been increasing for several years, reached its height in the Stamp Act controversy. These statements are confusing. 'Thirty or forty years after the charter' was the period of Boston ascendancy between 1720 and 1730; yet in the same sentence the author leaps to 1766. It is true that there was a phase of Boston leadership under Shute, Burnet, and Belcher, but, as has been seen, it was followed by a deep decline. The period Hutchinson discusses here was that of the 1760s, but he seems to run the two together.

[2] John Adams is not often found in such close agreement with Hutchinson, but in June, 1762, he writes: 'I have him [Otis, presumably junior] in the utmost contempt. I have the utmost contempt of him. I had as lief say it to him as not. I have the utmost contempt of him. . . . The origin of all this bustle is very well known. I heard a gentleman say he would give his oath, that Otis said to him if his father was not made a Judge, he would thro the Province into flames if it cost him his Life.' L. H. Butterfield (ed.), *Diary and Autobiography of John Adams*, 4 vols. (Cambridge, Mass., 1961), i. 225–6.

[3] C. M. Andrews, 'The Boston Merchants and the Non-Importation Movement', Colonial Society of Massachusetts *Publications*, 1916–17 (Cambridge, Mass., 1917), 161–8. It is interesting to observe that Hutchinson saw the whole issue quite clearly and was quick to spot the fallacy of any distinction between 'internal' and 'external' taxation. If Parliament began with 'internal' taxes 'I know not where any line can be drawn. If it be

The principal Boston merchants, organised under the patronage of James Bowdoin and John Rowe, were far more immediately affected by British policies than were the inland towns. But with the Stamp Act the British administration played into their hands. What was involved was by then a general colonial 'interest'; and Bostonian leaders reaped the advantage of their prominent and patriotic position.

It was not until as late as 1774, and then after prolonged and assiduous efforts by Sam Adams, that the western districts, particularly Berkshire and Hampshire, adhered firmly to the leadership of Boston in opposition to Britain. It was by exciting a fear that quit-rents would be levied and farms seized by the British for the reward of favourites that Adams succeeded in bringing the British danger home to the western farmers. The resolves of the seaboard merchants, and attempts to enforce the wearing of home-made goods had met with very little sympathy from the West during the renewed phase of conflict over the Townshend duties in the later 1760s.[1] In February 1768 Sam Adams was instrumental in calling a provincial Convention whose membership bore a marked resemblance to that of the General Court which Governor Bernard had recently dissolved. This was one of the earliest exercises in the practice of summoning shadow parliaments, and is more important as an example than it proved in action. For the Convention proved to be so cautious and moderate in its conduct that Adams himself withdrew for the time being from the radical position. He found himself lacking in any extensive degree of popular support.[2]

In domestic policy Boston was still more liable to meet with opposition from country towns. In 1761, the capital encountered difficulty in reconciling its recent — but none the less ostentatious — prosperity with its pleas of poverty for purposes of taxation.

John Adams's diary gives a comic account of the dilemma. Country representatives, invited to town for entertainments 'were scarcely able to walk the streets, for the Multitude of Chariots, or hear themselves speak for the rapid rattling of Hoofs and Wheels'. But in response to the enquiries of

said there is none but their discretion we are in danger of unequal distressing burdens which finally must affect the Nation as much as the colonies themselves.' — the same point as that of the merchants — to Wm. Bollan, 7 November 1764. It was, he pointed out, a fallacy to suppose that duties on trade were imposed for the purpose of regulating trade 'whereas the professed design of the late Act is to raise a revenue. The consumer pays, whether the product is taxed at port or the tax is paid by a licensed inland vendor.' — to Ebenezer Silliman, 9 November 1764. Hutchinson Papers, transcripts, M.H.S.

[1] Taylor, *Western Massachusetts*, 52, 57–62.

[2] John C. Miller, *Sam Adams, Pioneer in Propaganda* (Boston, 1936), 151–65.

the country gentlemen, no better method of assessing the wealth of the city was found than the Valuation Act passed in January 1761 — to which, 'What we cry? We obliged to tell upon Oath how much we are worth? must not we drink Madeira, eat in silver and China? Ride in our Chariots? Go to Concerts and assemblies? and let our sons and Daughters spend a few Guineas a Week at Cards without telling the assessors, and having it recorded that we are in debt for all this, and £10,000 worse than nothing. Oh these vile shoe string Representatives'.[1]

Boston again encountered resistance over the question of paying compensation to Hutchinson and the other victims of the riot of 28 August 1765. Despite a widespread feeling that Hutchinson ought to be compensated, the country towns denied responsibility and urged that a special tax be laid on Boston.[2]

The influence that Boston could exert on questions of provincial interest was due in part to its least agreeable features. Several members of the Assembly of 1766 who had followed Sam Adams and Otis on the Stamp Act, though duly elected by their towns were prevented from taking their seats, while others were intimidated, by the Boston mobs. The election of 1766 in Boston itself was dominated by the threat and fear of mob violence; and the resulting victory of the Sam Adams–Otis party, or 'Whigs', can hardly be considered an unforced expression of public opinion in a free election.[3]

The roughnecks who commanded the Boston mobs and terrorised their enemies with fire and stones while emitting their war-whoop, 'Liberty and Property', might not have sought or expected a place in the history of the concept of representation. But the mob was highly organised in a semi-military formation: different commands, made up of differing levels of citizenry, responded to their given authorities; and a link with the legitimate political organisation of the city was provided by Sam Adams. Control of city policy was exercised in its town meeting, and through that the Adams–Otis party urged their policies on the Assembly of the General Court.[4]

---

[1] John Adams, *Diary and Autobiography*, i. 213–14. In 1775, Boston instructed its representatives to secure a just valuation of rateable estates. Boston groaned under an unequal tax burden affecting 'Every Rank of Men among us'. — Bowdoin-Temple Papers, M.H.S.

[2] Adams, *Diary and Autobiography*, i. 325–6; Hutchinson to Wm. Bollan, 22 November 1766, Hutchinson Letterbooks.

[3] Miller, *Sam Adams*, 105.

[4] The command system under Sam Adams's generalship is described by Miller, *Sam Adams*, 69–70. Hutchinson gave a bitter but not inaccurate account of the way things

The system by which Boston town meetings were directed was not the invention of Sam Adams. Private meetings of the Boston 'Caucus Club' had been going on for years — possibly for a generation — before their procedure was discovered by John Adams and noted in a diary entry which has become deservedly famous and in the present context deserves full reproduction:

Boston Feby 1763. This day I learned that the Caucas Clubb meets at certain Times in the Garret of Tom Daws, the Adjutant of the Boston Regiment. He has a large House, and he has a moveable Partition in his Garret, which he takes down, and the whole Clubb meets in one Room. There they smoke tobacco till you cannot see from one End of the Garret to the other. There they drink Phlip I suppose, and there they choose a Moderator, who puts Questions to the Vote regularly, and select Men, Assessors, Collectors, Wardens, Fire Wards and Representatives are Regularly chosen before they are chosen in the Town. Uncle Fairfield, Story, Ruddock, [Sam] Adams, Cooper and a rudis indigestaque Moles of others are Members. They send Committees to wait on the Merchants Clubb and to propose, and join, in the Choice of Men and Measures. Captn. Cunningham says they have often solicited him to go to these Caucas, they have assured him Benefit in his Business, &c.[1]

Among the more eminent Whigs, a sense of collective interest was consolidated both by economic interests and by ties of family. The creation of a board of customs commissioners, whose most notorious act was the seizure of John Hancock's sloop *Liberty* in June 1768, struck at both the incomes and the importance of some of the leading merchants. The advance of British policies, made visible by the presence of British officials and British

were run, in a mock description of 'the model of government among us', beginning with the 'lowest branch partly legislative partly executive'. This consisted of the rabble led by Alexander Mackintosh, whose main job was to pull down houses and hang effigies; but 'since government has been brought to a system they are somewhat controlled by a superior set consisting of the master masons carpenters &c of the town of Boston'. Matters of more importance, such as opening a custom house, were directed by a committee of merchants under Mr Rowe, but affairs of a general nature were reserved for general meetings of the inhabitants 'where Otis with his most high eloquence prevails in every motion and the town first determine that it is necessary to be done and then apply either to the Governor and council or resolve it is necessary the general court should meet and it would be a very extraordinary resolve indeed that is not carried into execution'. Hutchinson to Pownall, 8 March 1766. Hutchinson Letterbooks.

[1] John Adams, *Diary and Autobiography*, i. 238 and notes. Dawes was a bricklayer and a militia officer. The levelling propensities of Boston society could hardly have been more evident. Though he was obviously a prototype of the later ward boss, and to have owned a large house must have risen in his trade, it was a humble enough calling. The caucus described by John Adams here was not the only one in town but was the South End caucus. Note the reference to business benefits from membership.

troops, solidified among the Americans their sense of a separate political identity. This identity was expressed, especially after 1765, in the House of Representatives.

The General Court was thus used as an agency for the dynamic purposes of the Whig party. But the leaders of this party, in the process of exploiting the Court as the chief agency of the cause which came, step by step, to be distinctively the American cause, wrought a profound transformation in the relationship of the Court to the people.

This transformation was demonstrated by the decision of the House of Representatives to build a public gallery. It was only one of several departures taken by the Assembly, tending to publicise its proceedings and by so doing to strengthen the bonds holding the colonists together — holding the representatives who were engaged in the exalting business of defying the Crown to their electors in scattered home towns. The move was suggested by the town of Cambridge in its instructions to its representatives in May, 1766; the reason given was to enable anyone to see that nothing was passed which was not to the real benefit and advantage of the constituents.[1] Speeches addressed to the gallery were often, as Hutchinson cryptically remarked, 'of more service to the cause of liberty' than they would have been if confined to the members of the House.[2]

This was a dramatic step, both symbolically and practically, at once expressing and advancing the representative character of the House. But it was not difficult to take, and it was far from being the first manifestation of its kind. The controversies of the past had several times evoked the warning that voters should examine the records of their representatives: as early as 1729, Governor Burnet had tried to beat a recalcitrant General Court by means of an election only to find himself faced with the same men over again,[3] an incident clearly showing that a deliberate stand was taken by the returning members. The Land Bank episode brought a similar result, the House of 1740 being an outstanding example of an eighteenth-century legislature elected on a major public issue and returned with what was virtually a mandate — and much more obviously so than the mandates claimed by many a modern party. In 1749 an election pamphleteer attacked the record of the House for failing to accept this sort of public responsibility; a petition had reached the House requesting that the application in the province of the recent parliamentary grant (of repayment to Massachusetts

[1] Paige, *History of Cambridge*, 140.
[2] Hutchinson, *Massachusetts Bay*, iii. 120.　　　　[3] See p. 60.

for expenses in the capture of Louisburg) be made public for some time before being enacted. 'This modest and reasonable petition', complained the author, 'was contemptuously rejected and its writers described as tinkers and taylors.' He then listed the members who had objected and suggested that the voters reject them at the polls.[1] The appeal to the electors made in this case shows that the idea was somewhat new. The members did not consider it necessary to consult the electorate, even in so important a matter as the disbursement of funds for the whole province; but the members were not beyond reach. They came closer as the General Court turned its attention increasingly to matters affecting the fate of the province. A broadside of 1760 makes it clear that an electoral ticket — here called a list — was circulating, and objected to several of the names on it; yet, although the records of the men in question were alluded to, they were not mentioned by name. That had been done in 1749, but it was still evidently a daring step, perhaps not yet admitted as proper election tactics. The voters, of course, were not expected to have any difficulty in seeing who was meant.[2]

What the House did in 1766 when it erected a gallery was to publicise the special relationship that had always been understood to exist between the representative and his constituents. The representative was sometimes called a delegate. A complaint in the 1760 broadside was that one of the men on the list had 'lately refused to follow the instructions of his constituents'. Nothing could be more to the point. The relationship between the representative and his town was essentially a private matter, in which the voters claimed the right to issue instructions on matters especially affecting them, but usually left their man free to make up his own mind on all other questions. This privacy was in turn transferred to the deliberations of the Court. Not only were its proceedings held in private, but they were not made public except through the printing of the laws and resolves. The freedom of members to speak their minds was the freedom of the inmates of a club.

By exposing its debates to the public, the Assembly offered itself to the people as an agent of public opinion far more direct and immediate than could have normally been the case before. But its action also proceeded in the reverse direction — towards the public. The publicity of debates excited interest and accentuated the sense of crisis. The members, while framing their bold policies of resistance, challenged the people to support them.

The immediate public was that of Boston: and this was of no small

---

[1] A New-England Man, *Letter to the Freeholders and Qualified Voters relating to the Ensuing Election* (Boston, 1749).
[2] *To the Freeholders of the Town of Boston* (Boston, 1760).

significance, since it was the Boston mob which executed the most provocative acts of violence and resistance, which could terrorise reluctant representatives from country towns, and whose hearts and minds could so effectively be stirred to mutiny and rage. The close liaison between the private meetings of politicians in their caucuses, the merchants in their clubs, the leaders of Boston in the town meetings, and the same, or nearly the same, men in the House, this was the unofficial system of resistance.

It was a characteristic development of this method, that when the House framed a Bill for compensation to the victims of the Stamp Act riots, it had it printed and circulated to the towns for their deliberation.[1] More important was the use of the Press. Otis used the threat of printing the names of members who opposed his measures as a means of pressure. The newspapers were kept supplied with 'speculations and compositions' in the service of the Whig cause by the Assembly leaders.[2] These methods were applied relentlessly to the members of the Council. As early as 1762, in a division on the question of the provincial agent in London, the majority of the upper body were prevailed on to concur with the House by what Hutchinson graphically called 'the terror of Election'.[3] But the turning point in the history of the Council came in the election after the Stamp Act — and before the expected news of its repeal had reached the province. Five of the most consistent supporters of prerogative were dropped. Governor Bernard was intensely displeased and indicated to the House that its action deprived the government of some of its ablest servants; to which that Assembly retorted that the gentlemen in question, being also judges, would be freed from their legislative duties to advance their knowledge of the law. The places remained vacant, and the Council, from that time forth led by James Bowdoin, became the ally of the House in matters of imperial policy. As late as 1769 Hutchinson, defending the general conduct of the Council, gave it as his opinion that they had disapproved of the most exceptionable parts of the proceedings of the House until that year. Despite the manner of their election, which deprived them of the freedom and independence they ought to have had, they had served the purpose of a second chamber by preventing undue advances by the other two branches, for seventy or eighty years.[4] But the effectiveness

---

[1] Hutchinson, *Massachusetts Bay*, iii. 114.

[2] Hutchinson to Pownall, 8 March 1766. Hutchinson Letterbooks. Hutchinson, *Massachusetts Bay*, iii. 120–1.

[3] Hutchinson to Wm. Bollan, 24 April 1762. Hutchinson Letterbooks.

[4] Barry, *History of Massachusetts*, ii. 322–3; Hutchinson to ?, 16 February 1769. Hutchinson Letterbooks.

of the pressure of the Assembly and of the public beyond was most candidly admitted by the councillor who acknowledged to Governor Bernard, in a moment of relaxed conversation, that though he no longer entered the chamber with the free mind he had once had, since he did not choose to quit his place he must be content to hold it on such terms as he could.[1]

The transformation in the General Court was reflected in the insistence of the towns on using their right of instruction. Instruction, which was yet to have a complex and disputatious history in American representative government, was in Massachusetts a singularly non-controversial subject. It does not seem to have appeared much before 1740; in 1742 one election pamphleteer advised his readers that prints from England showed that it was common for towns and corporations to give their representatives instructions in extraordinary cases, while Boston had done the same on the salary question in Burnet's time.[2] When a new state Constitution came to be written, the right of instruction was expressly declared. But it is doubtful whether there would have been many to dispute it. It seemed natural and obvious to the New England townsmen that in deputing a member of their own body to speak for them in the General Court, they were entitled to tell him what to say. The constitutional complexities of this simple position were not apparent to the political mind of the towns. Hutchinson saw the problem all too clearly since his riot compensation was at stake. 'For towns when any important point is in agitation', he remarked, 'to let their representative know the general opinion of their constituents upon such point may be well enough but, upon a bill consisting of serious matters to require the opinion of each town and to hold each representative to vote according to the opinion of his town is unconstitutional and contradicts the very idea of a parliament the members whereof are supposed to debate and argue in order to convince and be convinced.'[3] The conception of an intrinsic right to instruct was deeply involved in the corporate character of town life. The main activity of the town meeting was that of making rules and electing officials for town government; the concerns of the General Court often seemed too remote to call for any representation at all — when a delegate was sent it seemed obvious that he would be bound by the sovereign authority of his own community.

The Stamp Act began to call forth instructions on general policy; and the

[1] Bernard to Hillsborough, 12 November 1768; Bowdoin-Temple Papers.

[2] Anon., *A Letter to the Freeholders and other Inhabitants . . . qualified to vote . . .* (Boston, 1742).

[3] Hutchinson to Wm. Bollan, 22 November 1766, Hutchinson Letterbooks.

renewal of the crisis in relations with Britain on repeated occasions aroused the towns to make it a regular practice to look beyond town interests and instruct their representatives how to conduct themselves in defence of American liberties.[1]

These events had one institutional tendency and one ideological consequence, both of which were to be of lasting importance. Ideologically, the rise of town opinion as the determinant of the policy of the whole province (though it may often have been stimulated and led by the Assembly itself) gave an irresistible force to the idea of the sovereignty of popular will. Naturally, since 1689 — if not earlier — the sovereignty of the people had been held to be the rightful foundation of government; and the resistance of the General Court to encroaching royal instructions as well as the encroachments of the Court on the prerogative were all founded on this cardinal doctrine. The advancing crisis with Britain aroused the towns as never before to affirm their views about their constitutional rights; and if they could do this with impunity, then it followed that they would be entitled in due course to declare themselves on whatever new form of government was to be adopted. If the dismissal of royal authority threw them back — or half-way back, for the exact condition was ambiguous — into a state of nature, then it was the people in their towns who would proceed to establish among themselves the contract of government. The doctrine was not perfectly clear, and in 1777 many of the towns appeared willing to let the General Court draw up a new constitution; but that frame of government had to be submitted to the towns, by whom in 1778 it was decisively rejected. And in 1779 the choice of delegates to the new constitutional Convention was opened to every free adult male in the state.

The institutional tendency was a clear and steady concentration of power in the House of Representatives. The House was that part of the legislature in which the people through their representatives exerted their share in the legislative power; it was not the whole of that power, nor did the theory of mixed government, once transplanted to American soil, permit the notion that a single institution could rightfully control the whole of the legislature. The constitution, urged an anti-prerogative pamphleteer in 1739, was an epitome of mixed monarchy, under which the Governor had every right to protect and defend, no right to injure or oppress, the subject. 'You have a large share in the Legislature,' the writer told the voters, 'you

---

[1] 1765, Dedham instructed its representative on the duty of resisting the Stamp Act — and maintained the town's right to give instructions. The practice was clearly unusual. *Historical Records of Dedham, 1635–1847* (Dedham, 1847), 30.

have the sole power over your purses. . . .' He advised them to choose 'uncourtly people'.[1] The true American view, which never lay far beneath the surface of the numerous expostulations and remonstrances of Assemblies to royal or proprietary governors, was that all rightful legislative power was in the people: a view which had the effect of separating the executive most distinctly from the legislature in the theory and practice of government in America, since the executive could never be put into commission, as the English Whigs hoped to do with the monarchy in 1688.[2]

The decline of the Council — in Massachusetts particularly after 1766 — was only a symptom of the engrossment of power by the House. 'Mixed' government was in fact breaking down, but mainly because mixed government was itself an implement of British authority. It never disappeared from the institutional thought of the American Whig leadership, and it was restored to a place not merely of honour but of great political importance in the new state Constitutions. Meanwhile, however, it was the House of Representatives which collected the common sense of the people.

This legislative power was in no way reversed when, in the course of British assaults on the self-government of the province, the town meetings were declared illegal and the General Court dissolved. On the contrary, British action united the colonists behind their own institutions. A provincial Congress, erected on the same foundations as the Assembly, in effect seized power. The last session of the legislature convened by the Governor was dissolved by him in June 1774. Early in October, representatives elected by the towns met at Salem and formally awaited the recognition of Governor Gage. When this was not forthcoming, they proceeded to act as a constitutional legislative body and exercised the only effective central power over Massachusetts; until in response to advice which had been sought from the Continental Congress the Charter of 1691 was declared to have been 'resumed', and the form of government prescribed by it was reinstated. New elections, held in the towns in the old manner, returned a new Assembly in July 1775; a Council was formally elected; and in this close imitation of the charter form of government — differing in that the executive function had perforce to be exercised by a legislative committee — the province declared

---

[1] Americanus, *A Letter to the Freeholders, and other Inhabitants, qualified by Law to vote in the Election of Representatives* (Boston, 1739).

[2] See also Gershom Bulkeley, *Will and Doom, The Miseries of Connecticut . . .* (1692) (Hartford, 1806, reprinted 1895), which attacks the Connecticut General Court for 'engrossing the legislative power to themselves'.

itself to be a state and conducted its business until the final ratification of the Constitution of 1780.

Resistance was organised and independence achieved through the voluntary action of innumerable towns, meeting in the traditional manner but extending their authority to cover the varied exigencies of the crisis. They lacked only the sanction of royal writ; and that was something they were well able to do without. The committees of correspondence, the town meetings, the county Conventions, the provincial Congresses, were all founded on a long experience of local self-government operating through representative institutions. The Revolution had but begun, indeed independence had not yet been declared, when these institutions were subjected to the strain of internal controversy. The crisis had momentarily thrown the House of Representatives, and its successor the Provincial Congress, into high relief as supreme organs of the people's united voice; but the House was a complex body, in which conflicting interests and conflicting ideas of the basic purposes of representation were contained. The outcome of these conflicts was to be of vital importance for the future of the state. They did not long remain concealed.

Section 2

THE FIRST CYCLE OF
PENNSYLVANIA HISTORY

Introduction

THE half-century which elapsed between the granting of the first Massachusetts Charter and the founding of Pennsylvania was a period of revolution, restoration, and of fundamental thinking in England. Penn and his associates, in devising a frame of government, were able to draw on the republican theory of the Old Whigs or Commonwealthmen. The result was a Constitution closely resembling that of Oceana. The Pennsylvanian government recognised the interest of property, but also gave specific advantages to the Penn family as proprietors. To Penn's dismay, the people were not grateful. Penn's weakness was due to the fact that the forces of the larger landowners were outnumbered by the property-holding majority. So that the combination of numbers and property, which was to break through the barrier of corporate representation in Massachusetts in 1776, achieved its decisive gains in Pennsylvania in the first twenty years.

The question of legislative power was also posed in the early years, the Council first taking the lead rather than the Assembly. The Charter of 1701 vested nearly all power in the Assembly, and Pennsylvania came close to having a unicameral legislature. The upholders of the legislative power of the province continued to contest the issue with the Penn family and with their supporters in Pennsylvania long after William Penn's death. Meanwhile, immigration and settlement began to alter the early character of the province. Germans and Scotch-Irish formed distinct groups of increasing political importance. A bitter conflict developed between the old Quaker interest and that of the proprietors; and the Quakers, who regarded themselves as holding the basic interest in the whole province, were alarmed to see the proprietary party working to enlist immigrant support. Pennsylvanian politics thus developed an early sophistication which in many ways anticipated the character of American experience in the nineteenth century.

A radical element emerged in the midst of these conflicts. Shortly before the onset of the Revolution, the Quakers actually tried to persuade the Crown to resume possession of the province in order to take it away from the Penns. The imperial crisis, however, presented the Radicals with a splendid opportunity: forcing the hand of the Assembly, they contrived to make the conflict with Britain into a means of gaining power in Pennsylvania, and then to make a new Constitution for the state. In social and economic terms it was much the most 'radical' or genuinely democratic instrument of the Revolution but, as an instrument of representation, it was flawed by the exclusion of the Radicals' political enemies. In 1790 Pennsylvania reverted to the more conventional form of American government — Whig rather than Radical.

3. William Penn: High Ideals against Local Power

William Penn aspired to found a Harringtonian commonwealth but he failed to observe the most important of Harrington's precepts: he made no attempt to establish an Agrarian Law to enforce equality in the ownership of land. At the end of less than twenty unhappy years of dissension and experiment, Penn was compelled to grant the province a new Charter. That instrument placed the main domestic power in the hands of the Assembly; the Council was enfeebled, leaving the interest of the proprietors vested in the person and office of the Governor. Much of Penn's political weakness resulted directly from the fact that his republican doctrines had worked only too well. Power really had been distributed among the ordinary owners of property and the proprietary position had been outflanked without a battle. One consequence of Penn's constitutional arrangements was that Assembly and Executive embodied different and potentially rival political interests.

POLITICAL philosophers of idealist leanings have been tempted to express their ambitions in fantasy. Plato had his Republic; More his Utopia; Harrington his Oceana; William Penn, unluckier than these, had Pennsylvania. In his desire to found a province whose polity would be just, tolerant, and pacific, Penn was deeply sincere; but he was wholly unable to see that his equally compelling desire to make of that province a patrimony that would provide both a fortune and a right of government for himself and his family must entail conflicts with the settlers whose gratitude he regarded as his personal due. Even in the drafts towards a Constitution for Pennsylvania and the first Frame of Government as it was adopted, incipient difficulties foreshadowed later divisions. Within twenty years the settlers had gained from Penn a charter which gave them the balance of power; and almost within his own lifetime, Pennsylvania was ruled by men who knew him not.

In the history of his government in Pennsylvania, whether in person or by deputy, Penn's political philosophy can never be separated from his interest as proprietor — elements between which Penn himself discerned no implication of conflict. But this philosophy had two main and distinct sources.

Undoubtedly the foremost of these in the immediacy of personal experience was his Quaker religion, by which he knew the meaning of religious intolerance and persecution. Quakers, more than any other of the sects which had sprung to life since the English Reformation, believed in the direct relationship of the individual, and therefore of the responsibility of the individual, to Christ. The innumerable distinctions of society were, to their eyes, levelled in the light of this direct relationship; and this levelling, with its consequent simplicity and refusal of worldly affectation, was the distinctive outward feature of their religious and communal life. Although this outlook was not hard to reconcile with a reading of the Gospels, it put the Quakers violently at odds with the prevailing assumptions of an intricate hierarchy. Some aspects of Quaker belief and procedure can be regarded as irrelevant to politics and having no political consequence; but two were bound to involve them in far-reaching political responsibilities. One of these was their pacifism, which was eventually to weaken their hold in Pennsylvania; the other was their devotion to the worth of the individual. It was this valuation of the individual that put government to the test.

Not that it was a simple test. Its complexities were implicit in the second principal source of Penn's philosophy, which was in the Whig doctrines of his own times. No one who believed on principle in toleration and had seen anything of the turmoil of the English Revolution could have failed to be impressed by the efforts of the Old Whigs, or 'Commonwealthmen', to work out some system of government which, without jeopardising the stability of the state, would secure the subject in the enjoyment of everything that he rightfully owned — his life, his liberty, his private conscience, and his property. Penn's debt to these ideas is general: his plans for Pennsylvania are suffused with the desire to establish a just commonwealth based on individual consent. 'Peace', he wrote in 1693, 'is maintained by justice, which is a fruit of government, as government is from society, and society from consent.'[1] Thus consent was at the beginning of everything; it was consent which brought society into existence, and society which contracted for the establishment of government. A moment later he involved himself in confusion, if not flat contradiction, by observing that government was at first 'patrimonial'; the eldest son or male kin succeeded the father in authority. Other claims then developed, 'as hard to trace to its original as are the copies we have of the first writings of sacred and civil matters. It is certain that the most natural and human is that of consent, for that binds freely (as I may say), when men hold their liberty by true obedience to rules of their own making.' Unable to affirm that this was the historical origin of government, he defended it as 'the most natural and human'. Consent had become an abstraction; but when institutions existed through which governments ruled by consent then justice would be 'a fruit of government'.

If consent could not be proved in the origin of government, it could be obtained through such institutions. To run no risks, he took the strict view that representation was to be a matter of pure delegacy:

Every Representative in the World, is the *creature of the people*; for the people make them, and to them they owe their being. Here is no transessentiating or transsubstantiating of being from *people* to *representative*, no more than there is an absolute transferring of *title* in a letter of attorney; the very term Representative is enough to the contrary.[2]

Penn's first Charter from Charles II gave him authority to rule with the consent of the freemen — though he might govern without it in an emergency.[3] Penn clearly took a very practical view of this doctrine of consent, which he implemented when drafting the first Constitution by the

---

[1] William Penn, *An Essay Towards the Present and Future Peace of Europe* (1693) (Philadelphia, 1944). He refers here to the maintenance of peace by the scheme of European government propounded in the essay.

[2] William Penn, *England's Present Interest Discover'd* (London, 1675).

[3] Edwin B. Bronner, *William Penn's 'Holy Experiment'* (New York, 1962), 23 (hereafter referred to as *Penn's 'Holy Experiment'*).

safeguards of instruction and the ballot, which was even to be used for votes
in the Assembly. He desired that the freeholders should annually elect two
representatives to the Assembly by ballot; and that each member should come
to the Assembly armed with the instructions of his constituents. But as early
as 1696 the ballot was cast aside (in a Council election) by the freemen of
Philadelphia County themselves, and it disappeared from the Charter of
1701. Penn lamented the loss, which he attributed to the influence of David
Lloyd, an early but long-lived legislative opponent of proprietary interests,
and warned the settlers against 'throwing away the use of the ballot which
their children, as I told them, will have, perhaps, cause sufficient to repent
at their folly therein'.[1]

Penn's emphasis on consent and his unusually explicit assertion of the right
of constituents to instruct their delegates were not taken to mean that men
could, merely by withholding their consent, free themselves from their
obligations under government. Whatever might be said about the voluntary
origin of society, God had instituted law and government to restrain man
from evil. In the preface to his first Frame of Government Penn quoted the
author of Romans 13:

The powers that be are ordained of God. Whosoever therefore resisteth the power,
resisteth the ordinance of God. This [Penn continued] settles the divine right of
government beyond exception, and that for two ends; first, to terrify evil-doers;
secondly, to cherish those that do well; which gives a government a life beyond
corruption, and makes it as durable in the world, as good men shall be. So that
government seems to me a part of religion itself, a thing sacred in its institution and
end.[2]

That doctrine could not, in Penn's view, be used to defend unjust government, and the strict whiggism of his political ideas was shored up by a
somewhat dulcified version of the dark folk-lore of the Gothic myth. In one
of his English election pamphlets he affirmed that the free men of England
had been present at the signing of Magna Carta, and that representation
had been instituted at a later date to solve the problem of numbers; but
looking further back, the Saxons had in their time brought no change to the
country because they already enjoyed government by consent, and even
William the Conqueror had agreed to accept Saxon laws and become king

---

[1] W. R. Shepherd, *History of Proprietary Government in Pennsylvania* (New York,
1896), 230, 232–3, 266, 292 (hereafter referred to as *Proprietary Government*), *Penn and
Logan Correspondence* (Philadelphia, 1872), ii. 18. Thorpe, *Federal and State Constitutions*,
v. 3078.

[2] Bronner, *Penn's 'Holy Experiment'*, 11.

'by leave'. Penn pushed matters even further: Caesar had said that British cities elected their generals; and if in war, why not in peace?[1]

The mere problem of numbers, then, was supposed to have been the primary reason for substituting representation of the commons for the elemental form of a general meeting; but on closer analysis even this purest form of the ancient Constitution appeared to have had other values. In a further pamphlet, addressed to the electors in 1679,[2] Penn returned to the lessons of history:

> Before Henry the Third's time, your ancestors, the Freemen of England, met in their own persons, but their numbers much increasing, the vastness of them, and the confusion that must needs attend them, making such assemblies not practicable for business, this way of Representatives was first pitch'd upon as an expedient, both to maintain the Commons Right, and to avoid the confusion of those mighty numbers. So that now, as well as then, *No Law can be made, no money levied . . . without your own consent*: then which, tell me, what can be freer, or more secure to any people?

In this account, the maintenance of the commons' right preceded the problem of numbers; so that, by implication, other rights than those of the commons were present even in earliest times; there were other estates of the realm. But the innocent felicity enjoyed by the Saxons in their political arrangements becomes further clouded when one notices that Penn made no differentiation between government by consent in those times and in his own: 'now, as well as then . . .' — an impression greatly strengthened by returning to the pamphlet of 1675, which begins with a eulogy of the British Constitution, which he calls 'impartially free and just'. The birthright of every Englishman included the ownership of property and 'a voting of every law that is made, whereby the ownership or propriety may be maintained'. Penn was not addressing the people of England, but the electors, a small minority; no doubt he had reason to urge them to live up to their responsibilities, but he could hardly have written in these terms if he considered the system of representation itself to be gravely defective. The concept of delegacy, which seemed to Penn so clear and which he undoubtedly meant with all sincerity, did not take him so far from the more orthodox ideas of political differentiation as might appear when it is emphasised in isolation, because it did not mean the direct and unlimited control of the commons over the whole process of government. The point is implied, again, in one of his clearest affirmations of the principle of free government:

[1] Penn, *England's Present Interest.*
[2] William Penn, *England's Great Interest in the Choice of this New Parliament* (London, 1679).

Any government is free to the people under it, (whatever be the frame) where the laws rule, and the people are a party to those laws; and more than this is tyranny, oligarchy, and confusion.[1]

It is one thing to be 'a party' to the laws, and another to be the sole maker of them. The point of view is essentially legal. The people have an interest, expressed through their agents or attorneys, the representatives. It needs only the faintest sense of political procedure to realise that this representation will hardly amount to a power of veto unless the representatives achieve a remarkable degree of unity. They speak for their clients to the other parties in the government.

When Penn's profound and obvious concern that government should be established by the consent, and confirmed by the loyalty, of the people at large is honestly weighed, these complications fall to minor proportions. Minor, but not insignificant: for despite this concern, the fact was that Pennsylvania did from the beginning contain more elements, more 'estates' than those of the undifferentiated commons; and that, before long, the interest of the Penn family as proprietors was to lead them into bitter conflict with that of a large and powerful body of the people.

The conflict was made all the worse by the fact that Penn was unable to believe in the existence of any difference of interests between governor and governed; yet the preliminary drafts towards a first Constitution show the presence, among some of Penn's associates in the enterprise, of a potent demand for awarding superior political powers to the greater landed interests. One of the drafts actually proposed to establish a hereditary upper House based on the ownership of 5,000 acres purchased from the proprietor; and the dignity was to be relinquished by any holder whose estates might shrink to less than 2,000 acres.[2] Penn's own preferred plan was an almost classically simple form of representative government. There was to be no distinction between the functions of his two legislative Houses, or of the qualifications of members, since the Council was to be chosen by the Assembly from among its own members. The representatives were to be those 'of the best repute for virtue, wisdom and integrity'. Bills passed by the legislative bodies were to be presented to the Governor for his approval; and they were not to conflict with 'the rights of the proprietor, either in his just share in the government or his property'. Even such innocently good-natured arrangements as these would soon have produced dissension altogether beyond Penn's power to imagine; for the proprietary property was immense, and

[1] Bronner, *Penn's 'Holy Experiment'*, 11.
[2] This account is based on Shepherd, *Proprietary Government*, chap. iv.

purchase from the proprietor was to be the chief source of landed wealth. In some of the drafts for the First Frame, the upper House was called 'the House of Proprietors'; the lower one, that of the freemen. It would hardly have needed exceptional prescience even at that period to see that the more ambitious land-grabbers and merchants would soon develop a special interest in the economy and that they would use the extensive liberties of representation as an agency of their aims.

Their influence was felt so early that Penn was not even able to have his own way with the original Frame of Government, but accepted a more conventional scheme. More conventional, but in a distinctly Old Whiggish sense. The design of the first Frame of Government appears to reflect the ideas of Harrington. Under this Frame, the Council was charged with the duty of preparing laws, which were submitted to the popular Assembly for debate and resolution. Legislation, in other words, was not to be initiated in the lower House. This procedure is explicit in *Oceana*. It is true that members of the Council, like those of the Assembly, were to be elected by the freemen: but it is equally clear that the Council was to be the superior body, the Assembly subordinate; and that the Council was intended to put the real direction of government into the hands of the more substantial owners of landed property. The seventy-two councillors were to be men 'most noted for wisdom, virtue and ability'. The difference between this expression and Penn's 'virtue, wisdom and integrity' is a difference of intention, for 'ability' meant property. In later times, these differences had to be defined in amounts of property; it is noteworthy that as American society became more complex and sophisticated its law-makers took increasing pains to translate social position into political prescription; their efforts culminated in the early state constitutions, several of which made elaborate attempts to determine a scale of relationships between economic respectability and political competence; but in Penn's day these refinements would have seemed beside the point. It was not until 1710 that the British House of Commons adopted a membership qualification of landed property. The difference between the men who were qualified to lead and those who were not must have seemed too obvious to require special safeguards; these would come later, and when they came it might indeed be because the differences were no longer so obvious.[1]

---

[1] Shepherd, *Proprietary Government*, 238, remarks that as the Council was elected by the people, it represented them as truly as did the Assembly. This observation overlooks his own point that 'ability' was understood to mean 'wealth'. On p. 237, n. 1, he states that all the preliminary schemes of government except Penn's own provided that the Council should consist of large landowners.

The Harringtonian scheme was followed in the Constitution. Members of the Council were to retire in rotation; the principle of representation was to apply to the ordinary freemen only after the first year; during that time, the Assembly was literally to be a general assembly of the whole body. After a year, the Assembly would be composed of 200 (or up to 500) freemen, 'eminent, honest, and fit for government'.

The suffrage franchise was reserved for the freeman, who was defined as any inhabitant,

that is or shall be a purchaser of one hundred acres of land, or upwards, his heirs or assigns, and every person who shall have paid his passage, and taken up one hundred acres of land, at one penny an acre, and have cultivated ten acres thereof, and every person, that hath been a servant, or bondsman, and is free by his service, that shall have taken up his fifty acres of land, and cultivated twenty thereof, and every inhabitant, artificer, or other resident in the said province, that pays scot and lot to the said government.

The last and lowest term in this definition is that of the payer of scot and lot, or in effect a house tax. So that the suffrage was a householder suffrage. Not only the indentured servant and slave, but also the farm labourer not owning land and living with his employer, the journeyman or apprentice or artisan lodging with his master, or lodging elsewhere, and the grown-up sons of householders were incapable of electing or being elected (until, in the latter case, they acquired separate houses, presumably on marriage). The care with which this basic franchise of political privilege was delineated is itself worthy of notice.

The suffrage basis was the same for Council and Assembly; and if the Council had stood for nothing other than administrative continuity, Penn's conception of an identity of interests might have lasted a little longer; but when it was given all the effective power, and its membership weighted with men of the greatest economic substance, friction was bound to develop between it and the Assembly of the freemen. This instability is reflected in the basic inconsistency with which the principles of Harrington were applied to the province. For Harrington's *Oceana* is little if it is not a scheme for social stability. Justice was to be secured, not only by the rigid details of procedure in elections and representation, but in the limits placed on the ownership by individuals of private landed property. Harrington well recognised the ungovernable nature of private economic power. His scheme of government, therefore, was a total scheme, providing in all the necessary detail for the distribution of property, for political rights and duties and procedures, for national defence, and for education. Oceana might well have satisfied Man's aspirations towards security but hardly his ambitions. It would have been a better place to retire to after making one's fortune than to make one's fortune in. No restraint of this sort hemmed in the ambitions of the settlers of Pennsylvania, and it may be doubted whether many of them would have given their support to the plantation if they had not been granted, in the Council, the powers they thought necessary to maintain their interests.[1]

Despite his greater liberalism, which arose from greater confidence in the goodwill that was to prevail in his commonwealth, Penn's position was not dissimilar. He secured in the first Frame of Government a clause which gave him, and his proprietary heirs, three votes in the Council; and when a Friend, Jasper Yeates, took him to task, Penn in a flash of self-revealing anger made an unusually plain statement of the interest he had in Pennsylvania:[2]

What civil right has any man in government besides property? Is it not men's freehold that entitles them to choose and be chosen a member to make laws about right and property? Wilt thou not allow me and my heirs as much as three fifty-acre men have in the government, that have fifty hundred times more property? No, Jasper, thy conceit is neither religious, politic, nor equal, and, without high words, I disregard it as meddling, intruding, and presumptuous.

Yet Penn was to concede this very point once he was engaged in the work of government in the province. The threefold vote disappeared from the second Frame of Government, agreed by Penn with the Council and Assembly in April 1683. It is possible that he made this concession in the mood of early optimism promoted by faith in his 'holy experiment'; he may even at that time have doubted whether he could retain a power of veto, but if so his doubts left him; for he alluded to his veto in 1689 and exercised it in 1698. That Penn in 1683 was in a mood of benign optimism about both his own interests and the future of the province is certainly suggested by his agreement to a clause providing that the Governor was to perform public acts only 'by and with the advice and consent of the Provincial Council'.[3]

This mood quickly evaporated. The two years that Penn spent in this first spell in Pennsylvania, before returning to England in 1684, revealed the origins of the bitter political disputes that were to rend the province

---

[1] Shepherd, *Proprietary Government*, 237, n. 1.

[2] *Pennsylvania Magazine of History and Biography*, vi. 471, quoted by Shepherd, *Proprietary Government*, 249–50, n. 3.

[3] Bronner, *Penn's 'Holy Experiment'*, 41–42.

during his ensuing absence. It is not without significance that before his departure Penn had seen the passage of a law which protected him and his government against subversion 'by writing, publishing or uttering contemptuous or malicious things to stir up hatred or dislike of the Governor'.[1] Had this law been enforceable the history of Pennsylvania would have contained more than one rebellion.

Two separate but related conflicts lay concealed in the folds of Penn's dual interest in Pennsylvania. The first to appear — and that very quickly — was a conflict both of interest and, to some extent, of dignity, between the two designated Houses of the legislature, the Council and the Assembly.

It was clear in the first Frame of Government that the Council was to be much more important than the Assembly. The prototype of Lords and Commons had been transmuted; the smaller, weightier, and superior chamber was now to hand down laws for acceptance or rejection by the delegates of the people. But no sooner had the first Assembly met, and busied itself with drawing up rules of procedure, than it established a committee to prepare Bills and agreed that any member might introduce Bills on his own initiative. It was the second legislative session, held in March 1683, which agreed to the new or second Frame of Government. Although this Charter was superseded by a period of royal government, 1692–4, Penn himself held it to be operative until it was returned to him in 1700. It set up a Council of eighteen members and an Assembly of thirty-six, and confirmed the superior privileges of the Council. At once the Assembly heard resolutions claiming for it the power to initiate legislation, only to be sharply reprimanded for infringing on the Governor's royalties and privileges and for seeming to render 'ingratitude for his goodness towards the people'. Penn himself rejected the demand; but the struggle for power between Council and Assembly continued unabated after his departure, and when the upper chamber refused to yield, a deadlock lasting two years prevented the passing of any legislation. In 1688 Penn showed that he had not conceded a jot of the Assembly's claim:[2]

The Assembly, as they call themselves, [he wrote] is not so, without Gov'r & P[rovincial] Council, & that no speaker, clark or book belong to them; that the people have their representatives in the Pro. council to prepare and the Assembly as it is called, has only the power of Aye or no, yea or nay. If they turn debator, or judges, or complainers you overthrow your Charter . . . one prepares and promotes, the

---

[1] Bronner, *Penn's 'Holy Experiment'*, 38. *Pennsylvania Archives*, 8th series (Harrisburg, 1931–35), i. 52–53 (hereafter *Pa. Archives*). The Bill was subject to considerable debate and amendment.   [2] Bronner, *Penn's 'Holy Experiment'*, 39–43, 93.

other assents or denies — the Negative voice ... is not a debating, amending, altering, but an accepting or rejecting pow'r. Mind I entreate you that all now fall to pieces.

Penn saw the Assembly as a constituent body; it was, as nearly as representation could make it, the whole people. So that representation was working on two levels. The Council, consisting of men of property and distinction, though an elective body, clearly stood much closer to the Governor than did the members of the Assembly. In 1689 Penn, having heard that objections were raised against any man who was on his side — or 'in the proprietor's interest' — being chosen for the Council, instructed the Secretary of the province to take the matter up. He considered these objections an 'invasion and oppression' and asked, 'Is my interest already rendered so opposite to the country's, that I and those employed by me become such ill men, that it is impossible they can serve the country and me together?'[1] The Council was based on representation for purposes of selection: to get the right men into authority. The Assembly, on the other hand, was representative for purposes of mere convenience — in the same way that Penn imagined the House of Commons to have been invented, 'to avoid the confusion of those mighty numbers'. It was supposed to be the People in miniature. Though the population was in fact small, and the interests of the province not yet grown great or diverse, the prospective significance of these divisions was as great as the vast prospective growth of the country.

The second conflict, though partly concealed by the first, was also quick to emerge and was implicit in much of the dispute between Council and Assembly. Penn himself had plainly seen it by 1689, when he asked resentfully whether his interest was now 'rendered so opposite to the country's?' It was nothing less than the conflict between the Penn family as proprietors and governors, as the greatest landowners and as the executive branch of government, and the interests of the people of Pennsylvania. These two conflicts were contemporaneous; but the latter was of far greater importance and would last down to the assumption of Independence. Once having won the substance of the struggle against the Council, the Assembly itself became the centre for the assertion of the interests of the settlers as against those of the proprietors; it was then, unhappily enough, the Quakers against the Penns.

In December 1688 John Blackwell arrived as Penn's Lieutenant Governor, to encounter stubborn resistance from the Council. The issue at

[1] Shepherd, *Proprietary Government*, 270.

stake in Blackwell's comfortless administration was really that of self-government, the Council rather than the Assembly being, at this period, the branch of the provincial representation most capable of putting up resistance. Although the Council majority was careful to advertise its devotion to Penn's interests, his name was in reality only an instrument in their deeper strategy. Partly due to Penn's own tactical ineptitude and his unfair treatment of Blackwell himself, the Council came through it all acting in the end as a collective governing group under Penn's own commission.

Penn had shown no willingness to concede more power to the Assembly. This decisive shift was achieved, however, as soon as the province was resumed by the Crown. In 1693 Governor Fletcher, acting under royal command, permitted the Assembly the right to initiate legislation; a move that was perhaps to be balanced by the new provision that the Council was to be appointed by the Governor instead of being elected by the voters. Of Fletcher's Council of twelve, only four were Quakers.[1] The Assembly quickly advanced its claims, proceeding in 1694 to allocate the moneys obtained by a Supply Bill. Fletcher informed them that they had no right to control the distribution; all money raised was for the Crown; to which the Assembly retorted with a Remonstrance declaring that they could appropriate money as they saw fit. They did not complete the process of control of supply until 1723, but their recent gains were consolidated under Fletcher's successor, William Markham, who came to act for Penn after the restoration to him of the proprietorship of the province.

The Assembly greeted Markham by telling him that he could have no supply without a new Constitution. After the dissolution of this Assembly and the holding of new elections Markham reorganised the government by offering the settlers what became known as 'Markham's Frame', adopted — for practical purposes, since its strict legitimacy remained in some doubt — in 1696. Two trends seem visible. The first was the clear confirmation of the strength of the Assembly, which was now at least the equal of the Council; the second was a stiffening of what may be called a gentry and merchant control. In the rural areas the property qualification for the suffrage was reduced from 100 acres to the fifty prescribed by Penn, ten acres of which were to be 'cleared and seated'; but in the town districts the former payment of scot and lot — mere local taxes which fell on all householders — ceased to be a qualification and the requirement was raised to

---

[1] Bronner, *Penn's 'Holy Experiment'*, 157, 163–4. Of these four, some were Keithians, a sect which was denouncing the main body of Quakers in Pennsylvania as being untrue to the precepts of the Friends.

ownership of property worth £50 lawful money clear estate — that is, clear of debts. Residence was fixed at two years, 'within this government' previous to the election. That this move meant a narrowing of the suffrage was attested by a petition of protest signed by over 100 persons in March 1697; the process of social and economic differentiation, advancing with the success of the province, was bringing its normal consequence in the distribution of political power.[1] The principle, already recognised, that membership of the legislature ought to be compensated as a public service was strengthened by an increase in the remuneration of members.

Penn, who at last came back to his province in 1699, could not easily reconcile himself to these constitutional changes. In 1700 he was still insisting that the Council and Assembly, though two bodies, were 'but one power; the one prepares and the other consents'. But he found the colonists deeply discontented about the confused and doubtful state of their land titles and expectations, about conflicts over various commercial and administrative questions, and the inadequacy of the judicial system. There were thus many matters to be settled and the existing confusion strengthened the hand of the Assembly in its demand for a new Charter of Government, extracted from Penn in 1701.[2]

Under this new Frame of Government, which was to endure until 1776, the Assembly acquired the parliamentary privileges that were dear to all colonial assemblies: it was to choose its own Speaker, clerk, and other officers; appoint its own committees, prepare Bills, impeach criminals, be the judge of the qualifications of its own members and determine disputed elections; redress the grievances of its constituents; and to decide on its own adjournment. As the Council was maintained merely to advise the Governor, the Assembly became the sole effective branch of the legislature; viewing the Council — now appointive — as a residual Privy Council rather than an upper chamber, the Assembly thenceforth regarded itself as the legislative body of a unicameral system. But the proprietors' practice of sending instructions to their governors acted as a restraint on the effective power of Assemblies and tended to blur the edges of their constitutional advantage; the assumption, though commonly made, that Pennsylvania had a purely unicameral legislature through the remainder of its colonial history must be qualified by the consideration that, until 1763, all governors were instructed by the proprietors that the consent of the Council was necessary to their own part in legislation. The Charter incorporated the suffrage qualifications of a

[1] Bronner, *Penn's 'Holy Experiment'*, 175–9.
[2] Shepherd, *Proprietary Government*, 286.

law of 1700 which had confirmed those of Markham's Frame; but cleared
or improved acreage was raised from ten to twelve, and qualifications of
citizenship by birth or naturalisation were laid down.[1]

The crucial issue was the location of legislative power. So long as the
Penn family maintained its connection with the provincial government this
question could never be settled with finality. For what the Penns had was
an estate, and it is of the utmost significance that Penn had refused in 1701
to concede the most important claim of the settlers who, under the leadership
of David Lloyd, demanded a new charter of landed rights; and had insisted
instead on maintaining his family's vast proprietary stake in the domain of
Pennsylvania.[2] Thus, in spite of the broad Whig principles which Penn had
so optimistically planted in his settlement, the claims of his family really
amounted to a classic case of the privileges of the hereditary nobilities of
Europe, which in his case included the exemption of the proprietary estates
from taxation. These privileges were of the kind which were soon to
cause Montesquieu to observe that because they were odious in themselves,
the nobility must be allowed to defend them in a separate legislative
chamber.

But the Penns, though a principal estate of the realm of Pennsylvania,
did not have to themselves an upper chamber. What they controlled instead
was the executive.

Legislative power had plainly passed to the Assembly, much against
Penn's wishes, in 1701 : and the powerful Assembly element under Lloyd's
leadership quickly grasped the fact that the presence of the Penn family as a
controlling branch of government was not in itself a necessity intrinsic to the
effective government of the province. The Assembly duly proceeded from
legislative towards executive ambitions; a point grimly perceived by Penn
himself when in 1710 he wrote that the claim being advanced by Lloyd's
party on behalf of the Assembly, 'to a power, to meet, at all times during the
year, without the Governor's concurrence, would be to distort government,
to break the due proportion of the parts of it, to establish confusion in the
place of necessary order, and to make the legislative the executive part of
government'.[3] It is small wonder that Penn and all those associated with the

---

[1] The statute was repealed by the Queen in Council, 7 February 1705. Thorpe, *Federal
and State Constitutions*, v. 3037, 3048, 3050, 3055, 3058, 3060, 3066–7, 3071–3, 3078.
Statutes at Large of Pennsylvania (N.P., 1896), ii. 24–27. Shepherd, *Proprietary Government*, chap. v.

[2] Roy N. Lokken, *David Lloyd, Colonial Lawmaker* (Seattle, 1959), chap. ix (hereafter
referred to as *David Lloyd*).

[3] Lokken, *David Lloyd*, 185–6.

proprietary interest wanted a strong Council as a makeweight to the Assembly. The issues before the legislature were not of the theoretical preference of one system to another; they were issues of vital importance, involving the rights to massive areas of property and opportunities to make massive amounts of wealth. Nor was it to be long before they were issues of peace and war.

The constitutional argument was periodically resumed. The free air of Pennsylvania had early made for disputatious tempers but it appeared also to make for longevity, and in 1725 the principals of the early period, James Logan for the proprietary interest (with which he had long been connected), and David Lloyd were still locked in articulate antagonism.

This time the proprietrix, Mrs Hannah Penn — William's widow — had issued instructions limiting the authority of the Governor, Sir William Keith, by requiring him to act only with the consent of the Council. In a controversy that involved the question whether a deputy may be restrained by his principal, or whether on the other hand the deputy, once commissioned, might do all that the principal might do, the question of substance turned once more on the powers of the Assembly. Lloyd not only denied any power to the Council in this debate; he attacked the authority of the proprietor, arguing that the legislature derived its rights from the Charter given by Charles II in 1681. In this document Lloyd discerned the gift from the King to his people of the legislative power. That Charter was therefore the fundamental law in Pennsylvania; by contrast the Charter of 1701 was merely the constitution of government — that is, the establishment of institutions, an act done in conformity with the fundamental law but not to be mistaken for it. Logan on the other side maintained the convention of an analogy between colonial institutions and those of England, by which means he defended the Council, as resembling the House of Lords. This analogy Lloyd had completely rejected, arguing that the only elements of the British Constitution reproduced in Pennsylvania were the King and the Commons; thus the Lords had withered away leaving nothing but an advisory replica of the Privy Council.[1]

Since in Lloyd's view the King had given the people of Pennsylvania the gift of legislative power, and the presence of the proprietors as a branch of government was wholly irrelevant, the implication was of profound importance for all colonial history. For the argument meant that the legislative

[1] Lokken, *David Lloyd*, 214–16; David Lloyd, *A Vindication of the Legislative Power* (Philadelphia, 1725); James Logan, *The Antidote: Some Remarks on a Paper of David Lloyd's* (Philadelphia, 1725).

power was entirely contained within the province. Legislative power, the nub of the debate, was coextensive with colonial self-government.

Charles II would hardly have wished to have been made a witness to that brief.

In other provinces, as in Britain, the numerical principle of representation emerged in the process of the clash of other interests. But in Pennsylvania there was an important sense in which that battle was won from the beginning; for it is reasonable to suppose that in assigning equal numbers of representatives to each county the early charters assumed that population would be about equally distributed among them — a purpose conforming to the explicit intention of Penn's 1682 Charter of Liberties.[1] For a true believer in the Gothic lore it was a natural, if rather unsophisticated, method to adopt. It remains as a tribute both to Penn's sincerity and to his political simplicity that he should have supposed that the deep material interest of himself and his heirs could be sufficiently secured, first by a threefold Council vote, but also by the mere goodwill and gratitude of the people. The fact that this major issue was decided in the first twenty years without rebellion or the threat of force should not be taken to mean that it was of minor importance. On the contrary, it was precisely because Penn had ceded political power through the basic structure of the Assembly to such an obvious and overwhelming majority that the reforms leading up to and incorporated in the Charter of 1701 were secured with such ease.

The self-evident character of this majority may also tend to conceal the related influence which was in fact of fully equal importance — that of property. The power that established effective Assembly rule was the combined power of numbers and of property — the latter already moving with deliberation towards the exclusion of the lower ranks of society from participation in politics. Though the influence of numbers was particularly evident in the founding period, it was never of greater consequence than the interest of property. The theme of the rights of property would run its thread through the whole colonial history of the province; and by the middle of the century, references to the factors to be weighed in the measurement of representation were to reveal that wealth was normally a consideration of, if anything, higher importance than mere heads.

The principle of representation had throughout been of cardinal importance. Penn believed in it because he was an Old Whig; and the form he

[1] Thorpe, *Federal and State Constitutions*, v. 3050, 3060, 3064, 3078.

granted, though it was intended to include the people in giving consent to, rather than in making, the laws proved susceptible to very rapid extension. The need to attract settlers would of course have necessitated some form of representative government just as it did in other plantations, but it did not dictate the precise form or timing of the grant. Representation at once took root and soon became the natural means of political expression and action.

Once again, the smoothness of the process tended to conceal problems that were bound to arise, not out of the mere perversity which Penn so often and aggrievedly attributed to his colonists, but from the nature of conflicting realities.

Penn's plans for his republic were based on the assumption of a harmony of interests. When the Quakers, who habitually regarded the province as their own by a right previous to and better than that of all other comers, established themselves as the governing element they assumed that their own interest must remain essentially at one with that of the province as a whole. They supposed the whole polity of Pennsylvania to be based on a pervasive political consensus, made safe by the expectation that immigrants of other religions, other origins and other ambitions would perpetually entrust the Quakers with authority. Yet the founding and development of Pennsylvania necessarily anticipated the accretion of the population, which was no mere accident of later fortune; so that when in due course the interests and ambitions of the newcomers began to conflict with the Quaker hegemony, the consensus was exposed to a challenge which in the end it could not survive.

The greatest gift of Penn and the first founders of the province was that which ensured that representation would be the machinery of these ensuing conflicts. It was an irony which William Penn would hardly have appreciated that his heirs, lacking a sufficient following among the Quakers, turned to the settlers from Northern Ireland for the votes to maintain their interest, and learnt to rival the famous Quaker Party with a Proprietary party of their own.

4. The Discovery of the Electorate and the Assertion of Legislative Power

Pennsylvania began its new life under the Charter of 1701 with a wide and politically experienced electorate. That electorate was capable of exercising a high degree of independence, and in the course of the political struggle of the next half-century, rival factions developed the techniques of election campaigning. In Philadelphia it was not unusual for pamphlets to appeal to the voters on specific issues — a very advanced procedure for the period.

The Assembly was subject to factional and personal rivalries but for many years these rivalries were generally contained within the Quaker hegemony over provincial politics. The Assembly, however, was also engaged periodically in a more serious struggle with the governors, who represented the proprietary interest. This intermittent struggle between Assembly and governors was the struggle for the assertion of the legislative power within the province. The conflict had an economic aspect. The Quakers stood for the settled merchant interests of the east: the proprietors made headway among the new Scotch-Irish settlers in the west, whose interest lay in the land. The proprietors, however, found it difficult to make their cause popular, and the chief danger to the freedom of representative government arose from the Governor's powers of patronage. These powers were augmented in the wars of the 1740s, and the Quakers never ceased to warn the voters of the resulting danger to their liberties. Was representation to be subjected to a new form of prerogative power? The republican aspect of the government was at stake in these contests. Quaker electoral successes gave them reassurance in the early 1740s. Meanwhile the immigration of Germans and Scotch-Irish brought new forces and unfamiliar problems into political life. For a number of years, however, the Quakers succeeded in keeping the Germans on their side. It could not last for ever.

AN active electorate, responsive to issues, extensive in its relation to the whole population, and broadly united in interest and outlook, was the natural base for the operation of the Assembly in its disputes with the proprietors. And it was precisely for this factor that Penn's original plans, with their insistence on the right of instruction, the Quaker experience of many of the early settlers, and the conditions of political life in Pennsylvania's first generation specially provided. Yet after Penn's final departure in 1701 it was all that could be needed to complete his gloom or Lloyd's buoyancy.

In the course of his weary disputes with Lloyd's Assembly majority in the first few years of the century Penn became deeply grieved by the fact that his opponents could command electoral support against his governors and his supporters, chief of whom was Logan. 'I confess', wrote Logan to Penn in 1705, 'were this Province in general truly represented by some of the chief leaders in Assembly, I think that not only the Queen's Government, but anything that's human would be good enough for us; but there are great numbers of honest, tho' careless, people here, who author these proceedings, and at another election would not, I believe, be so imposed upon.'[1] The dispute referred to by Logan took place in 1704. It was no mere faction fight, for it involved the basic right of the Governor to summon, prorogue, and dissolve Assemblies. Lloyd, acting in the Assembly's name, sent home a remonstrance which the members had not seen and whose contents were so insulting to Penn as to offend the loyalties of the electorate. After the message had been made public, several of Lloyd's adherents lost their seats — an early example of an electoral response to a specific point of conduct.[2]

This electoral rebuke might have been unremarkable if it had remained an isolated occurrence. But in 1710 Penn himself gained a sweet and glorious vindication in an election which must in certain respects be considered the most extraordinary in American colonial history.

Lloyd, who remained leader of the Assembly and its Speaker, had tried to complete the passage of legislation for the reorganisation of the judiciary; but the opposition of two successive Governors, Evans and then Gookin, supported in each case by the Council, had brought matters to an impasse. In September 1709 Lloyd and his men submitted to Gookin a remonstrance against proprietary instructions, blaming Logan for many of their difficulties because of his advice to Penn. Logan replied with a public 'Justification' which gave great offence to the Assembly. It is interesting to note that Logan, who occupied the position of Secretary of the province, accused Lloyd of having submitted his remonstrance with the intention of influencing the forthcoming election. Lloyd and the Assembly went so far as to try to prevent Logan from carrying the case to England, by placing him under arrest, a step that was thwarted by the Governor and Council; and though Lloyd had carried the election of 1709, Logan, after visiting England, was

[1] *Penn and Logan Correspondence*, ii. 5th 2nd mo. 1705.
[2] Shepherd, *Proprietary Government*, 306.

able to return with a letter from Penn, giving him a personal exoneration, severely criticising the subservience of the Assembly to Lloyd, and asking the colonists to signify, 'in fair election', whether they were for him or against him.

The tide was now running against Lloyd. Economic conditions were bad and getting worse; trade with Maryland and Virginia was bringing in poor returns, while ordinary but necessary civic improvements, requiring legislative sanction, were held up by the inability of the Assembly under Lloyd's leadership to work in conjunction with the governors. The Assembly's poor record of accomplished business in recent years was blamed on the obstructiveness of the Lloydian faction by Isaac Norris, who addressed himself to the voters in a new pamphlet, *Friendly Advice to the Inhabitants of Pennsylvania*.[1] The peculiar feature of the situation in Pennsylvania was that this appeal to the verdict of the whole electorate was a reality. The whole community was so small that it was still arranged in only four constituencies — the City of Philadelphia and the counties of Philadelphia, Bucks, and Chester: the counties sent eight delegates each to the Assembly, the City two, making a representative body of twenty-six, capable of meeting in a large drawing-room; which, to accommodate a member disabled by lameness, they were later known to do.[2] It is unmistakably evident that the electorate behind this body was conscious of its powers and equal to the demand for a verdict. If Lloyd and his party had hoped to establish themselves as a legislative corps exercising a kind of avuncular authority to which their constituents gave a merely obedient consent, they received in 1710 a shock which ought to reverberate through the pages of the history of representative government, for in the election of that year every single member of the previous Assembly was turned out of his seat.[3]

It was a personal triumph for William Penn, who had asked for such an expression of confidence — one of the very last triumphs he was to enjoy before his powers gave way. It was also a triumph for something more; for the principle which Penn had planted in his province, a principle inherent in the combination of Old Whig doctrines and Quaker faith which had inspired the original Frame of Government. That principle had indeed been pushed considerably further than can have been expected by the framers. The choice of 1710 was a verdict of 'no confidence' in a whole Assembly of

---

[1] Lokken, *David Lloyd*, 185–7.

[2] Isaac Norris to Sampson Lloyd, 31 March 1760. Isaac Norris Letterbooks, Historical Society of Pennsylvania.

[3] *Pa. Archives*, 8th series, ii. 911, 937.

legislators. Basically, the electorate was to have been the body reserving an ultimate power of consent or dissent; but events had given it a more substantive authority.

The intense internecine strife which marked the early period of the settlement, and of which Pennsylvania was seldom for long to be relieved, tends to obscure from view the underlying unity which gave to the politics of the colony a distinctive character. The politics of faction, even of deadly antagonism between proprietors and assemblymen, were also the politics of a certain basic homogeneity. To this extent the Quakers and Penn himself had been right in assuming a political consensus. It derived from the sources of population, still largely English and Welsh Quakers of modest social origins; from the custom of the Quaker meeting; from the smallness of the province and the domestic character which still attached to its political life. The lines from the Assembly ran straight back into the constituencies. Constituents knew their candidates and their representatives, and what is more they did not hold them in awe. They were prepared to judge men on their records, and though pamphleteering was as yet a rare device, it was already understood to be an appropriate method of influencing the outcome of an election. As this homogeneity was lost in the welter of subsequent immigration, the character of politics experienced a subtle but far-reaching change.

The electoral system in Pennsylvania, however, had not only been tested but had developed some of the refinements of later campaigning long before these major demographic changes had begun to alter the character of the province. This priority of the effectiveness of the representative process was to be of profound importance. The fact that its influence was in a sense negative, by permitting the gradual assimilation of new social ingredients into an already workable and adaptable procedure, has perhaps made it appear undramatic and even uninterestingly normal; but this appearance can best be measured in contrast to the possibilities of political oppression, violence, or even secession on the part of discontented elements, which would have been a more likely character of political life if there had been no effective electoral machine at work.

In the controversies involving Governor Sir William Keith and later Andrew Hamilton, as in all of the major disputes to which the Assembly was a party, the strivings of personal ambition affected the balance of constitutional power. The Quakers as a political party with control of the

Assembly never allowed the electorate to lose sight of the ultimate character of these sometimes local and merely factional conflicts. It was quite clear to the Quaker leaders that, if their proprietary enemies succeeded not only in building up a party which could challenge them for Assembly power, but in developing a province-wide system of patronage which would capture the loyalties of men who had influence over electoral communities, then the original liberties of Pennsylvania would be subverted. They watched for this subversion in every dangerous proprietary move throughout the complex period that embraced the rise of German and Scotch-Irish immigration and the outbreak of wars first between Britain and Spain, later between Britain and France, and therefore involving the safety of the American continent and of the outlying settlements of Pennsylvania itself. They perceived the proprietary plot to destroy the liberties of the province in corrupt or violent elections as well as in alliances with the Presbyterians. In the end — long after they had ceased to be predominantly Quaker in religion — the party of that name turned in desperation to the Crown in a last attempt to destroy the power of the proprietors.

The governorship of Sir William Keith (1717–26) was distinguished by an almost implausible degree of amiability between executive and Assembly. In 1723 the Governor backed the Assembly, which was still under the leadership of Lloyd, in legislation for the issue of paper money that was desperately needed by the economy of the province; a measure that was opposed by the Penn interests — taken over in 1724 by Mrs Hannah Penn, still counselled and supported by Logan. In the course of the ensuing dispute, Mrs Penn instructed Keith to take no legislative action connected in any way with the Assembly without first having the consent of the Council.[1] It was this instruction which led to the constitutional debate which brought forth Lloyd's *Vindication of the Legislative Power* and Logan's *Antidote* as well as a number of other occasional pieces. Keith's deposition from the governorship by the Penns in 1726 did not end his ambitions in Pennsylvania. It was alleged by his enemies, with corroboratory evidence from two of his former adherents, that he had intended to gain control of a party in the Assembly and to make matters so intolerable for the Penns that they would be forced to turn the government over to the Crown, through which procedure Keith hoped to gain political domination over the province. After his removal from the governorship, Keith continued his attempt to win

[1] Lokken, *David Lloyd*, 212.

control of the Assembly, at last parting company with Lloyd, who became his enemy.

Keith's proceedings suggest baronial ambitions, adapted within not very modest limits to the exigencies of parliamentary conventions. He won a seat in the Assembly with the aid of political clubs which he had organised for the purpose. Determined to assert his authority by winning election to the Speakership, he rode into Philadelphia accompanied by eighty horsemen, while guns were fired to assist the deliberations of the Assembly. The members, however, did not take kindly to these tactics, and instead elected Lloyd, who had been returned for Chester county.[1] Keith seems to have been convinced by this failure that he could not expect to gain power in the Assembly, and without formally resigning his seat he departed for England. His followers decided to fill the vacancy by electing his nephew; but the Assembly, under Lloyd's leadership, refused to allow the Speaker to issue a new writ, and instead of a by-election they merely excused Sir William from attendance. The majority did, however, order the issue of a new writ to fill a vacancy caused by the death of another member. Keith's party concluded that the Lloydians were deliberately discriminating against them with the object of keeping down their representation, and registered their protest by withdrawing from the session, thus depleting the Assembly of its quorum. They refused to comply with the Governor's summons to attend a new session.[2] The remaining members resolved to proceed with business. These events prepared the ground for the contest in the election of 1727.

The voters of Pennsylvania had already, from earlier elections, gained experience of the practice of partisan electioneering.[3] The election broadside was not a novelty, and had already been developed as an instrument of undoubted purpose and of some precision. If by later standards it lacked refinement, it must be remembered that later refinements would not have served the purposes of earlier campaigning conditions. The constitutional implications of the conduct of the Keithian group were brought to the notice of the electors:

In other Colonies, [said a Lloydian broadside] the Governour can call an Assembly when he pleases; but it is otherwise here: therefore if the people ruin their own Assembly, and the Governour cannot call another, all men must own this is such a

[1] Lokken, *David Lloyd*, 226–7. *Pa. Archives*, 8th series, iii. 1787.

[2] Charles P. Keith, *Chronicles of Pennsylvania* (Philadelphia, 1917), 711–12.

[3] But the practice had been going on for over seventy years before the word 'electioneering' came into use. The earliest usage found was in 1778 — Robert L. Brunhouse, *Counter-Revolution in Pennsylvania 1776–1790* (Harrisburg, 1942), 54.

breach on the very being of an *English* Government, that either the Proprietor, or the Crown, might think it necessary to take Notice of it as a Forfeiture....[1]

One of the tactics adopted by Keith's men was to circulate an alarm that the prevailing party had designs against the paper money of the province. The Lloydian broadside found it necessary to rebut this charge, and denounced their opponents for a campaign 'of shams and falsehoods'. 'The last refuge' was to 'renew the cry about paper money'. But the country realised the benefit of that currency, which now had no opponents. It was pointedly stated that no candidate for representative opposed it. This and another sheet developed an attack on the political pretensions of the Keithians, which no doubt had special reference to the political clubs. Voters were urged to mind the need for representatives bearing charter qualifications (which included wisdom) and without private views or interests.

But we find [declared another broadside]

a particular *set* amongst us, have from year to year, and now openly and avowedly, as if they were incorporated for that purpose, taken upon themselves to say who shall *represent* us, who shall be our *Commissioners* and *Assessors*, and who shall fill every *post* or *place* that depends on the choice of the people.[2]

This great concern of elections [said another broadside] (in order to choose men of integrity in our Assemblies) is become too important to be dallied with, and 'tis necessary that all who are interested [meaning all who were affected] should become fully acquainted with their rights.

The writer hoped that those hinted at would mend their ways.[3]

When the date of these campaign sheets is considered they develop an interest that goes somewhat beyond the light they shed on the subject matter of Pennsylvanian politics at that time. They not only carry their story of personal ambitions, of constitutional dangers, of political tactics and campaign innuendoes. They show that these issues were brought before the voters; that the voters, or a considerable portion of them, were expected to be literate — no light assumption, and one which makes a vast difference to the possibilities of propaganda; that they were, moreover, deemed fully capable of deliberation and of decision between rival candidates on their records as representatives and their claims to recognition. These matters were brought forward in very clear style — a style which promised to have a

[1] Anon., *To the Freeholders and Freemen Electors of Representatives for the County and City of Philadelphia* (1727). Historical Society of Pennsylvania, 1727–10.

[2] Anon., *To the Freeholders and Freemen. A Further Information* (2 October 1727). H.S.P., 1727–4.

[3] 'J.H.', *To the Freeholders, to Prevent Mistakes* (Philadelphia, 1727). H.S.P. 1727–3.

flourishing future. It is equally important to recall the limits of the methods then employed. In the first place the campaign appears to have been conducted principally in the City and County of Philadelphia, affecting ten seats at the most. Although the past conduct of members was held up, there was no offer of legislative action. Neither was any rival candidate commended by name to the voters (who could be expected, however, to know which was which). The general appeal for men of integrity was, of course, less disinterested than it appears. The Quakers had a long-standing claim to represent the general and normal interests of the province, a claim which derived both from their social preponderance and their championship of the 'popular' interest against the encroachments of the proprietors. The charge that Logan had given mischievous counsel to Mrs Penn could still be trotted out for this purpose.[1] The Keithian faction could be isolated as a 'party', a group with 'private views or interests', and thus made to stand out against the benevolent normality of steady Quaker domination. The Quakers in this situation may be likened to the great Whig families in England when their long ascendancy was disturbed by the injection of new forces into parliamentary power after the accession of George III. But the analogy was to become more pointed in later years and in more dangerous controversies.

Throughout the long period of Quaker hegemony, the Quakers regarded themselves as the natural spokesmen for the common people. It had to be admitted that certain distinguished public men — Logan and Andrew Hamilton for example — were not Quakers: but this very fact helped the Quakers to appreciate clearly the view of Pennsylvania life which they had long assumed; that men who rose up to advise and counsel the proprietors, to speak for them in the Assembly or Council, or to form factions in the constituencies and in the legislature, were not simply against the Quakers, but were anti-people; they were discordant elements jarring against the people as a whole. And the people as a whole, speaking in either their religious or their political capacity, were one with the Quakers. The point could hardly have been put more tartly than in the Assembly assertion to Governor Thomas that since Pennsylvania had been given to a Quaker for benefit of Quakers, all who did not like their system of government might go elsewhere.[2] It is in this light that one must view the common practice in the Quaker meeting which would have been known somewhat later as that of a

---

[1] 'J.H.', . . . *to Prevent Mistakes.*
[2] Shepherd, *Proprietary Government*, 525.

caucus. For it was in the annual meeting that the candidates for forthcoming Assembly elections were decided on.[1] Since Pennsylvania had been founded as a Quaker colony, and since the annual meeting was the representative general meeting of the Quaker community, there is no reason why they should have seen anything invidious in using the occasion to settle the question of their political representation. It would only be when Pennsylvania ceased to be a Quaker colony and the Quakers, ceasing to be synonymous with the whole community, imperceptibly became themselves a party, that the practice of nomination in the meeting would look to outsiders like an unwarranted engrossment of power; the earliest case, perhaps, of the closed primary.

Every dispute between the Assembly and the proprietary power, whatever the issue, was fraught with unavoidable constitutional implications. Where the Constitution was itself a matter of disagreement this was bound to be so; and when interests of vast prospective importance might be affected by the exertion of power, or the gaining of an advantage, in a particular case, it is not to be wondered at that the Quakers took seriously the problem of maintaining their preponderance in the Assembly. The most persistent source of dispute was the paper money question; and since the Penns tended to the orthodox British conservatism, and so instructed their deputy Governors, the question of their power to instruct the Governor lay close behind. But after the outbreak of the British war with Spain in 1739 matters took a sharp turn for the worse.

Governor Thomas ordered or permitted the enlistment, for overseas service in the West Indies, of indentured servants in the province; an act which embroiled him in bitter controversy with the Quaker leaders, who took the position that it was illegal to enlist servants without the masters' consent. It was not a question of the rights of the servants or the terms of their contracts but a violation of the masters' rights of property.[2] But this was far from all. For it was in the frontier troubles, arising from the wars of this period, that the Quaker policy of pacifism began to cut across the positive necessity of military defence. The Governor could not induce the

---

[1] Theodore Thayer, *Pennsylvania Politics and the Growth of Democracy, 1740–1766* (Harrisburg, 1953), 16 (hereafter referred to as *Pennsylvania Politics*). Thayer states that this was done in 1740 and was the usual practice. Also attributed to *c.* 1740 by William Smith, *A Brief State of the Province of Pennsylvania* (London, 1755).

[2] It appears that this practice dated back as far as 1711. Shepherd, *Proprietary Government*, 523.

Assembly to make legislative provision for militia; and the unprotected condition of the western settlements, the plight of Governor Thomas in trying to comply with royal command while securing compliance from a stubborn but constitutionally effective majority, led to sarcastic recriminations, petitions and appeals to the Board of Trade, threats to appeal to the king, and in the constituencies of Pennsylvania to hotly contested elections.

The failure of Keith to form a party capable of coming to power in the Assembly opened the way to a decade of relative tranquillity. The main source of political faction, before the new round of disputes that descended on Governor Thomas, arose from the ambitions of Andrew Hamilton. Hamilton, whose fame in history results from his intervention in the Zenger case involving the freedom of the Press in New York, was a forceful, if erratic figure in Pennsylvanian politics. He was influential enough to become Speaker of the Assembly: and at times he appeared as spokesman for the proprietary interest; but his exact relationship to the proprietors is not easy to determine. He was often consulted by them; but this did not prevent him from criticising them in public.[1] Probably the truth is that his politics were largely personal, and that he aspired to command in the Assembly a personal following influential enough to make him one of the arbiters of the destiny of the province. Isaac Norris, the Quaker leader whose correspondence tells much of the political strife of the period, regarded Hamilton as the leader of the opposing party; and his reports show that Hamilton was an energetic practitioner of the techniques of constituency campaigning. In 1740 Hamilton spent a fortnight working on electors in Lancaster County, but 'after using his utmost still he has failed . . . prodigiously thro' the whole Prove. . . . The Old Ticket', Norris added with satisfaction, 'was carried by a great majority'.[2]

The 'ticket' may have been old; but the expression appears to have been new. One does not find it in political discussion before this time, and as the adoption of a convenient term may be associated with the recognition of a convenient practice, it is likely that the formal agreement of the Quaker meeting to its nominees for Assembly was now admitted to be a political decision taken in face of a political opposition. When Hamilton died, in 1741, Norris remarked cryptically that the opposing party would fall into

[1] Andrew Hamilton in *Dictionary of American Biography*.

[2] Isaac Norris to Dr Charles, Philadelphia, 11 October 1740. Isaac Norris Letterbooks H.S.P. Some 970 votes were cast in this election.

confusion;[1] but his optimism was due to be tested by new forces of opposition.

These forces were no longer those of the personal politics of Hamilton's type. The proprietors were gathering to their support those elements whose growth would later threaten the stability of Quaker power. It has been observed that not all the great men were Quakers; but in addition to the former Quakers who were prepared to go into political opposition, there was a growing Anglican group, strengthened after the retirement of Logan by the fact that the office of Secretary of the province was assumed by the Rev. Richard Peters, a clergyman of the Church of England. The proprietors were also working to bring the newer settlers, German Reformed, Lutherans, and by this time a few Presbyterians, into a political alliance.[2]

Defence was not the only issue. In fact, though on occasion by somewhat evasive devices, the Quaker majorities in the Assembly authorised the raising of substantial sums that were used for military purposes.[3] With advancing prospects of western development, however, the fundamental difference between the Quaker faith in forbearance, peace, and goodwill between white men and Indians, and the ambitions of speculators and settlers became increasingly manifest in the politics of Pennsylvania. The whole question of the future of Pennsylvania, the possibilities of enrichment from the development of its landed resources, was at stake and in these prospects the interests of the proprietors were deeply involved. So also were those of the newer settlers. Thus there came into existence the foundation for a political alliance which was to grow stronger as the Scotch-Irish immigration began to reach significant proportions after 1744.[4]

[1] Norris to Charles, 10 August 1741. Norris Letterbooks. Though he was not prepared to give Hamilton much credit as an opponent and added that even had he lived his party would have been 'too weak to be dangerous'.

[2] Frederick B. Tolles, *Meeting House and Counting House* (Chapel Hill, 1948), 21 (hereafter referred to as *Meeting House*).

[3] Tolles, *Meeting House*, 21–22. Shepherd, *Proprietary Government*, 528–9. In 1745 the Assembly refused the request of Governor Thomas for powder; but it authorised £4,000 to be spent by him on 'bread, beef, pork, flour, wheat or other grain'. Thomas proved equal to the equivocation and took 'other grain' to mean gunpowder, which he bought without opposition from the Assembly. Professor Tolles argues that historians who have persistently regarded the Quakers' refusal to raise money for defence as the main issue of the period have overlooked the fact that defence funds were in fact raised. But it is surely important to ask what confidence the western settlers would be likely to place in the attitude towards their own interests of an Assembly which incessantly quibbled and equivocated about matters which, on the frontier, were matters of life and death.

[4] Weyland F. Dunaway, *The Scotch-Irish of Colonial Pennsylvania* (Chapel Hill, 1944), 119.

This political conflict can be posed in economic terms. The Quakers, whose preponderance in the eastern counties gave them a habitual domination of the Assembly, had made their fortunes in trade. The great Quaker families were, on the whole, merchant families. These families took the lead in eastern society, and received the deference that, in conformity with conventions to which even the Quaker community had early lost its imperviousness, was held to be due to social distinction — to rank. But this leadership did not look primarily to the development of western settlement. It did not depend on the west for its profits; while the profits to be made from the rise in land values accrued to their proprietary rivals.

The contrast in economic interests was compounded by political and, in a broad sense, social attitudes. The recent settlers had no ties of kinship or religious association with the Quakers; they had different ambitions; they would, in the long run, change the character of the land.

It was not until the time of the French and Indian wars that the Scotch-Irish immigration became large enough to alter the balance in the national and sectarian composition of the province; and when this happened, they soon became the main element in the political opposition to the Quakers; an opposition which had the satisfaction of seeing the Quakers unseated from their domination of the Assembly — without, however, enjoying the reward of political power for itself. When these things happened, the politics of the province were reflecting the changing structure of its society; the Quakers were no longer, by any stretch of the imagination, the whole people. They had become instead the most deeply entrenched, the most experienced, and the wealthiest of a variety of interest groups, whose characters were to be found in their national origins and their sectarian alignments, as well as in their ambitions and methods of self-advancement. The Quaker hegemony was over.

It was this profound change in the character of politics which began to confront the Quaker leaders in their bitter strife with the Governor and the proprietors after 1739. It would be a mistake to argue that this was the origin of factional politics in the province;[1] factional politics had been at

[1] Professor Tolles observes that the Quaker historian, Robert Proud, is 'apparently forgetful of the earlier strife between rival Quaker factions' when he attributes the 'formation and increase of party' to the 1740s. Tolles, *Meeting House*, 21. Robert Proud, *The History of Pennsylvania* (Philadelphia, 1797), ii. 228–9 (hereafter referred to as *History*). Proud's treatment of this expresses the genuine Quaker feeling that the previous rivalries were, so to speak, mere family matters, whereas the formation of rival political groups with designs on the legislature, based on the great sectional and sectarian divisions, was the real beginning of 'faction'. The important thing is that for Quakers there was a distinction in character between the two types of political faction.

work from the beginning, and had led on occasions to a definite struggle for leadership in the Assembly, conducted by means of intense and sophisticated election contests. When Logan and Hamilton spoke for the proprietors or led a personal opposition, they stood out against a background of prevalent Quaker coloration; when it was the Penns against the Quakers, the similarity of interest between the Quakers and the settlers of Pennsylvania as a whole was made all the clearer.

Both sides were acutely aware of the importance of controlling the Assembly. The representative branch of government was all the more important because of the wide range of appointments within the gift of the proprietors and the ease with which proprietary influence, by means of patronage, could penetrate the legislature itself. The constitutional arrangements of Pennsylvania made very little provision for a separation of the different branches of government. The judicial Courts naturally sat as distinct bodies from the legislature; but nothing in the Frame of Government restrained a judge from taking his seat as an elected legislator. David Lloyd, for example, had been a member of the Assembly while sitting as Chief Justice of the Supreme Court, using his powers to frame a Bill to bring Pennsylvanian judicial practice closer to that of England.[1] In the war situation of the 1740s, there was an increasing danger of extension of executive appointments, particularly in the field of commissions in the militia. The struggle for the Assembly came to a head in 1742 when the proprietary interest tried to have its way by the use of mob violence. A gang of sailors, who were said to have been 'kept hot and near drunk for the purpose',[2] was loosed upon the voters, and neither side seems to have been innocent of the use of violence. The incident aroused great indignation in the Assembly, in which the Quakers retained their majority despite the best efforts of their opponents. An investigation was set on foot, only to be obstructed by the Governor. It all did the proprietary interest no good. The Quakers gained ground steadily between 1740 and 1743, after which the Governor appears to have given up his efforts in disappointment.[3]

Yet while the Quakers had occasion to rejoice over their electoral successes they could not relax their efforts, in view of the danger posed by the executive power of appointment. Isaac Norris, giving an account of the

---

[1] Lokken, *David Lloyd*, 198–201.

[2] Norris to Charles, 21 November 1742. Norris Letterbooks. Shepherd *Proprietary Government*, 526. Proud, *History*, ii. 229.

[3] Norris to Charles, 11 October 1740, 31 March and 3 May 1741, 10 August 1741, 1 October 1743. Norris Letterbooks.

elections of 1741, indicated how representation might be offset by appointment:

The elections thro the whole prov. have this year turned out against the Govr. more than last[.] not only the Assem but the sheriffs and every other officer in the election of the people are obtained in direct opposition to his measures and inclinations but to be revenged fully he bends all his power to support himself by putting all offices in his gift into such hands as have no rule but his will and pleasure.[1]

By 1743, while Norris was writing with some complacency about the lack of opposition to 'the old ticket',[2] a Quaker pamphlet set the matter in a more alarming light by warning the voters once again of the Governor's encroachments, lamenting the loss of 'irrecoverable rights' — for power would never give up what it had once acquired — and urging them to hold on to what was left:

Let us [it continued] therefore trust NO ONE who is under the shadow and influence of [the power of the Governor], and least of all those judges and magistrates to whom the interpretation and execution of the laws are committed, and who hold their places at the will of the Governor. Should a majority composed of such get into the Assembly, as is now attempted, the Legislative and Executive Power would be in the same hands, which is the very essence and definition of tyranny.[3]

The issue raised was that of the independence of the Assembly. The statement alleged that the proprietor and Governor believed that the Assembly should not be allowed to sit on its own adjournment — a privilege which was peculiar to Pennsylvania — or to have the sole disposition of the public money. An Assembly majority in the proprietary interest would endanger these fundamental liberties. Voters were also warned in the same breath that the power of choosing the inspectors of elections and of judging the qualifications of electors 'might be transferr'd to the Governor's creatures, under the specious pretence of preventing tumults, as was formerly attempted, and so we shall all be legally ruin'd and undone'.[4]

The basic reason why the Quakers were able to keep the upper hand in

---

[1] Norris to Charles, 26 October 1741. Norris Letterbooks.

[2] Norris to Charles, 1 October 1743. Norris Letterbooks.

[3] Anon., *To the Freeholders of the Province of Pennsylvania* (1743). John Carter Brown Library, copy in H.S.P., 1743-2.

[4] It seems, however, that an accommodation with the Governor had already been reached in the previous June, when Norris wrote: 'Revolutions of an uncommon size[.] the Govr and Ass. are reconciled our bills are passed and our Speaker is made C. Judge of Sup. Court'. Norris to Charles, 22 June 1743. Norris Letterbooks. Perhaps the Quakers were not prepared to trust the Governor on election day.

politics, apart from the strong combination of tradition and experience, was the lack of any nucleus or programme for a rival party. The proprietors themselves might have good reasons for wanting to challenge Quaker power in the Assembly, and might be able at any time to count on the support of a few socially influential men who held proprietary offices; but it was difficult to see what the proprietors could offer to the people. Yet, despite their electoral successes, and the surface tranquillity which reflected steady control of the Assembly and, at least, working arrangements with the Governor,[1] the Quakers held a gradually loosening grip on the province as a whole. Their protestations of willingness to act for purposes of defence were seldom sufficient to convince any but themselves. When, in 1747 and 1748, the Assembly failed to take adequate measures to meet the danger from the French, Benjamin Franklin organised a military association consisting of militia units which elected their own officers up to the rank of colonel; this plan extended to the convening of a general military council, to be elected annually at a meeting of deputies representing the units in each county. The association was a great success. Franklin, and others aspiring to popular leadership, were elected to military commands. Not surprisingly, political leaders who were not involved saw this strange enterprise in amateur soldiering as the basis of a potentially dangerous political movement. The scheme was not persisted with after the end of the war in 1748, when the Quakers reinforced their position by backing a new paper money movement.[2]

Although the pacifism of the Quakers weakened their claims to the loyalty of the province in time of war, the same conditions did much to sharpen the animosity between the tax-paying population and the proprietors. The dispute arose between the Assembly and the Governor, who was compelled to carry the political burden of the proprietary policy of refusing to permit the taxation of proprietary estates. Since defence costs rose in war time the inequality was then most strongly felt. The enlistment of servants was another measure of military policy which caused great unpopularity to the executive as long as war beset the colonies. The proprietors, as a political interest of Pennsylvania, were thus confronted by their own difficulties in trying to lay any sort of claim to popular support.

[1] By 1746 Norris reported elections 'pretty quiet', and remarked on his own reluctance to accept re-election. Norris to Richard Partridge, 15 October 1746. Norris Letterbooks.

[2] Thayer, *Pennsylvania Politics*, 21–23.

5. The End of the Quaker System

Long after the Quaker party had ceased to be distinctively Quaker, its leaders continued to assert that both in fact and by right they alone represented the general interest of the Province against the predatory and unconstitutional designs of the proprietors. Proprietary pamphlets accused the Quakers of trying to subvert the 'mixed' form of government and convert it into a 'democracy'. Quakers denied the charge and accused the proprietors of attacking the right of representation. In fact the 'Quaker' majority in the Assembly was using the language of mixed government but what it really wanted to do was to get its own way. In claiming to stand for the whole people it significantly denied being a 'party' and attached to the proprietors the odium for dividing the province into factions. But the Quakers, like their rivals, had now to compete for votes.

FROM early in the 1740s popular support had to be found, not merely in the old Quaker and Anglican settlements, but in the increasing bodies of German immigrants. In this the Quakers were notably more successful. The German sects included Quietists, to whose pacifism the Quakers were able to appeal for support. Quaker influence over the Germans was maintained by the management of John Kinsey, who combined the positions of Chief Justice of the province and Speaker of the Assembly. Kinsey posed as a patron of the Germans, on one occasion permitting a gang of German coiners who were prosecuted in the Supreme Court to get away with a light fine in order to avoid antagonising their compatriots.[1] Kinsey also had charge of the loan office of the province, which he ran in such a way as to consolidate his political alliances. To the older inhabitants, the tide of German immigration presented alarming uncertainties. The Germans appeared to them to consist of a large, extremely homogeneous mass, addicted to strange customs, ruled by their own religious and political leaders. The language barrier was surmountable only for a few individuals on each side. The truth was that this monolithic appearance was an illusion, sustained by the lack of intercourse

---

[1] Governor Hamilton to Thos. Penn, 14 September 1750. Quoted by Dietmar Rothermund, 'The German Problem of Colonial Pennsylvania' (hereafter referred to as 'German Problem'), *Pennsylvania Magazine of History and Biography* lxxxiv. no. 1, January 1960, 7–8, n. 12.

between the national groups.[1] The Germans were actually in the throes of the Moravian revivalist movement, which caused internal upheavals enough to hold back any effective intervention of the Germans in Pennsylvanian politics for several years. The Quaker technique was to establish confident relationships with a few respected German leaders, who in turn were to marshal their followers behind the Quaker ticket.

The system worked well enough to cause great irritation to the proprietary party, but it was not without anxiety for the Quakers, especially after the death of Kinsey in 1750. They evidently felt unsure of their continuing power of control, and offered no opposition when the Governor's party introduced an early, but by no means unsophisticated, measure to gerrymander the counties. A proprietary councillor, Dr Thomas Graeme, reported to Thomas Penn an interview with Governor Hamilton in which he had pointed out to the Governor

that the legislature in erecting the two late countys, allow'd them only two members each, and that upon the division of the countys of Phila & Bucks, which was also much wanting, if they brought the division line 16 or 18 miles to the southward of Reading, and that of Bucks as far to the Southward of the Forks, and to each county two members, they would by this division comprehend to a trifle the whole body of the Dutch and consequently forever exclude them from becoming a majority in the assembly, for allow Lancaster, York and the two not yet appointed Countys to send all Dutch it would make but ten members in 38, and to this if the assembly would be induc'd to add two more to the City of Philada it would still strengthen this scheme.[2]

This scheme caused some of the German leaders to perceive the untrustworthy self-interest of the Assembly, but no protest against the unfair distribution of representation made headway until the crisis of the Revolution was far advanced. The Quakers, who had acquiesced in this measure when they could easily have rejected it, had themselves to thank for the distrust with which they came to be regarded by those whom they did not directly represent.

The Germans brought to Pennsylvania what may well be considered to have been the earliest major problem of multi-national relationships caused by mass immigration. To the Anglo-Pennsylvanians this problem presented itself as that of preventing an imminent German majority from taking over the province; of maintaining the fundamentally English character of law, institutions, and language; of breaking down the apparent solidity of the German mass. To the Germans it might present itself in different ways.

[1] These remarks are based on Rothermund, 'German Problem'.
[2] Rothermund, 'German Problem', 9.

Leaders of opinion such as Christopher Sauer, Conrad Weiser, Michael Schlatter, and H. M. Muhlenburg moved, through different processes and with distinctly varying degrees of success, in directions which would eventually bring the Germans into a normal and conventional participation in political life. Other sects preferred, and still prefer, retreat, isolation from the world, and the preservation of an ancient mode of life. Proposals to establish restrictions on the franchise, to induce assimilation by compulsory use of English in all official documents and by setting up English schools, and to restrict immigration, were all seriously considered by prominent Anglo-Pennsylvanians — including Franklin. In 1755 a House Bill to restrict German immigration was amended by the Governor.[1] By 1764 Germans were taking opposite sides in a hotly contested election and a German-Pennsylvanian, Heinrich Keppele, was elected to the Assembly. A distinctive German social element continued to figure in Pennsylvanian life for generations; but the Germans were no longer feared as a powerful and foreign menace by those of British descent.[2]

The alarm caused by the German problem is not in the least surprising, for the immigration was so sudden and voluminous that by the middle-fifties the Germans were believed to be the largest single group. William Smith estimated the German population at 220,000, nearly half the inhabitants;[3] Isaac Norris, Speaker of the Assembly, giving an account to his friend Charles in England, observed that the Germans were far more numerous than either the Presbyterians or the Quakers though they did not equal all the others together.[4]

In the same letter, Norris remarked on the 'great importations from Ireland, and their Encrease', by which he meant that the Presbyterians had come to exceed the Quakers. The Irish were of course the Scotch-Irish, whose arrivals began in the 1740s but became so heavy in the 1750s and 1760s as to people the back-country and give to Western Pennsylvania a character utterly different from that of the Quaker or Anglican sections.

[1] Wm. Smith, *A Brief State*. Also Franklin in Penn Papers, Official Correspondence viii. 287, cited by Rothermund, 'German Problem', 11–12: Norris to Charles, 20 June 1755. Norris Letterbooks.

[2] It is somewhat previous to say that this famous election 'definitely marked the end of Pennsylvania's German problem' — Rothermund, 'German Problem', 19. No doubt the problem assumed an entirely different character; but as late as 1817 the elections for Governor were fought in part on the emotional issue of 'German' feelings. P. S. Klein, *Pennsylvania Politics: 1817–1832: A Game without Rules* (Philadelphia, 1940), 93–96.

[3] Wm. Smith, *Brief State*.

[4] Norris to Charles, 29 April 1755. Norris Letterbooks.

The Scotch-Irish were, by general consent, forceful and ambitious. The fact of their relative proximity to the Indians might alone have caused tension; but the newer settlers lacked the tact and goodwill which had always distinguished Quaker policy in Indian affairs, and the mutual antipathy frequently erupted into violence on both sides. The Scotch-Irish are generally referred to in the correspondence of the period as the Presbyterians. Their social and their religious organisations seem to have been closely connected through the synod and the leadership of the elders. They were brought into politics chiefly by two factors, one arising directly from their own interests, the other from their obvious usefulness against the Quaker party. In the first place, it was soon clear that the Scotch-Irish intended to develop their land claims with an aggressiveness which would result in clashes with the Indians and would soon call for a far more positive and assertive, if not militant policy, than any the Quakers had offered. Secondly the proprietors began to cultivate them as political allies. The climax came in the election of 1764.

By that time, however, the Quaker party had ceased to be Quaker. The events of the protracted French and Indian Wars resurrected all the old and bitter quarrels between settlers (now divided into numerous groups and interests) and proprietors, and produced military contingencies in which Quaker pacifism could no longer represent the general interest of the community. The Quakers, as long as they could, affirmed their ability to serve the province and denied that their religious scruples amounted to an incapacity.[1] Yet as early as 1741 their indifference to the defence of the province provoked a remonstrance from eighty-five 'Gentlemen, Merchants and others of Philadelphia', which the Assembly denounced as a high insult and menace and a breach of privilege.[2]

The Assembly's increasing loss of touch with the people led directly, in 1756, to the admission that the representation of the people had broken down. In face of mounting criticism that their party could not defend the province in time of war, six Quaker members of the Assembly resigned their seats. Technically this may not have destroyed the majority with Quaker sympathies, but it left the Assembly under the control of politicians who acknowledged little or no debt to the ancient ideal of a Quaker society. Their

---

[1] 'Philadelphus', *To the Freemen of Pennsylvania, and more especially those of the City and County of Philadelphia* 1755. Historical Society of Pennsylvania. This answers essays charging that the Quakers are incapable, from religious principles, of doing anything in time of danger, and defends the Quaker record in the Assembly. It counters with the charge that the point at issue is whether they were or were not to be governed by instructions of the proprietors.

[2] *Pa. Archives*, 8th series, iii. 2680–4.

party continued to bear the name of Quaker in common parlance. It continued to count on its former sources of support, the Quakers and, in all probability, the great majority of the inhabitants of English stock. It went on fighting the proprietors over the conscription of servants, over proprietary instructions, over taxation and the exemption of proprietary estates, and over the respective powers of Governor and Assembly. Its supporters insistently defended its record as being that of a party with an unbroken history of government.[1]

Between the Assembly and the party of the proprietors, the antipathy continued unabated. The problem of the land tax was only the most immediate aspect of the general problem of land policy. It was the insistent complaint of the proprietors' rivals that the proprietors held a monopolistic advantage which they meant to use to overturn the constitutional balance of power. This advantage derived from their exclusive right to purchase land from the Indians; and their abuse of this right was also blamed for the inadequate state of the frontier defences of the province. In a pamphlet written to answer Smith's *Brief State*, Joseph Galloway[2] attacked the law forbidding anyone but the proprietor from purchasing from the Indians, which meant that all others had to purchase from the proprietor. Instead of large purchases made at once on the frontier in order to fortify the province, small tracts were bought by the proprietor or his officers 'in order to jobb, and parcel them out at extravagant rates'.[3] It is not necessary to suppose that the complaints of the opposition were wholly disinterested, when rising western land values were coming to compete with commerce as a principal source of wealth in the province. The proprietary policy from the viewpoint of the Assembly threatened not only to accumulate an overwhelming economic advantage, but by the distribution of offices and by the obedience of the Governor to secret instructions, to displace the ultimate authority of the Assembly itself.[4] The whole course of the disputes thus swung back inevitably to the nature of constitutional government in Pennsylvania.

The progress of constitutional history has given to the American colonial period a susceptibility to the Whig interpretation which has become — if

[1] Documents relating to the resignation of the six members appear in *Pa. Archives*, 8th series, v. 4245–50. The hostility of the Governor to the Quakers and his use of the incident is described by Isaac Norris, to Charles, 16 June 1756. Norris Letterbooks.

[2] The attribution was made by William Franklin. Thayer, *Pennsylvania Politics*, 40.

[3] Joseph Galloway, *An Answer to an Invidious Pamphlet, intituled, A Brief State . . .* (London, 1755), 24.

[4] Address to Governor Denny by the Assembly. *Pa. Archives*, 8th series, vi. 4638–45. 1757.

possible — even more difficult to resist than its English counterpart. Yet in the mid-eighteenth century it was by no means obvious that this view either would be, or ought to be, the wave of the future. The Penn family took the view that, Pennsylvania being theirs by royal grant, their possessions in the province were as clearly and legally exempt from taxation as were Crown lands at home. Nor did it appear to them as right or natural that any tendency in the constitution should be in the direction of increasing the power of the Assembly. The publications of the Assembly constantly laid stress on the sinister designs of the Governor and his creatures, but it is at least worth noting that, from the standpoint of the proprietors, the designs of the Assembly might seem equally sinister, equally tending to the subversion of the legitimate balance of power.

In this connection, the proprietary spokesman, William Smith, in his *Brief State*, made a full statement of the charges against the Assemblies, and set them in the frame of an interesting view of constitutional legitimacy. The wrong trend in Pennsylvania he traced to a law of 1723 giving the Assembly the sole disposal of all public money, an expression of 'manifest contempt' for all proprietary instructions which rendered all governors dependent on the Assembly. Since that time, the Assemblies had gained from the governors the nomination of a great many officers holding the most lucrative posts — provincial treasurer, loan office trustees, collector of excise, brander of flour, of beef and pork, etc. From the proprietary standpoint, this concentration of power in the popular branch of government was a thoroughgoing subversion of the intention of the original royal grant and an invasion of the inheritance of the Penn family.

To take this view did not imply any intention to destroy the rights of representation; it did imply that representation was only one element in a mixed frame of government conceived in the conventions of Whig political ideas. Smith explained that infant settlements flourished fastest under governments 'leaning to Republican or popular forms', because such a government immediately interested every individual in the common prosperity. The people were few, the public offices gave small profit. Government could therefore be administered without the factiousness usual with popular government. He was perhaps wise not to investigate the early history of the province, or the circumstances leading to the Charter of 1701.

But [he went on] in proportion as a country grows rich and populous, more checks are wanted to the power of the people; and the Government, by nice gradations, should verge more and more from the popular to the mixed frame.

But the Quakers' successors had held on to power; the people, instead of being subject to more checks, were under fewer than at first. With numbers and riches their power was increasing while that of the Governor declined; the consequence was that the government was now 'more a *pure republic*, than when there were not ten thousand souls in it'.

To this proprietary apologist, then, the leaning of the early system towards a popular form was part of the Founder's intention. What he missed was the fact that all the ingredients of a mixed system, in so far as those ingredients consisted of actual vested economic and political interests, were present in the claims of the proprietors at the beginning, but that these had been whittled down by the effective local strength of the popular element — which was also the representative of rival property interests — in the Assembly. If he had been right in saying, without qualification, that the early form was popular, then he would have had to claim that the proprietors themselves wanted to develop, subsequently, a mixed system; and he admitted to this view by saying that more checks were wanted, that the government should verge towards mixed forms, as the country grew rich and populous. It was a weak argument, since there was no more reason why the proprietors should have a right to change the Constitution than the Assembly. He blamed the Assembly for enlarging its powers while claiming the same right for the proprietors.

Since the author had earlier stated that nearly one half of the population was made up of Germans, and that the Quakers were not quite two-fifths of the residue, his equation of the Quakers with the people was as flattering as the Quakers themselves could have wished it to be. But it was of course true that the Quakers had proved astute political managers of the German population. The gravamen of Smith's indictment was that the Assembly was establishing an unmixed government, a government lacking the necessary safeguards for the other leading interests, particularly in this case the fundamental interest of the proprietors. Though he did not call it a 'democracy', his reference to a 'pure Republic' carried this damaging implication. And damaging it was certainly felt to be. For when Joseph Galloway published a reply four years later,[1] he denied the charge that the tendency of the government of Pennsylvania was to grow more popular. 'This Government,' he said, 'in its first Establishment, and under our present Charters, does not incline more to a *popular* than *monarchical* form.' It was a charter government ruled by persons 'no ways connected with its Interest

[1] Anon., [Joseph Galloway] *A True and Impartial State of the Province of Pennsylvania* (Philadelphia, 1759). Dedicated to the Rt. Hon. Wm. Pitt.

and Property', and was 'as near the mix'd Form, as Wisdom and Prudence could direct'.[1] The author refused to admit the special claims of the Penns, whom he accused of undermining the Charter by sending secret instructions. Since the Charter could not, by its own terms, be changed without the consent of the Governor and six-sevenths of the Assembly, instructions limiting the power of the Governor over legislation were always held by the Assemblies to be unconstitutional. These invasions of the rights of the subject were enlarged, according to the pamphleteer, when the Governor altered money bills from the Assembly and claimed other powers over the disposal of funds raised within the province. The author adverted to the danger from great riches in the hands of private subjects. Great riches placed subjects on too near a level with their sovereign, and (he added) 'destroy among the Commons the balance of property and power which is necessary to a Democracy or democratical part of any government'.[2] The meaning of this point was clear in the context of Whig discourse, though it could easily be misunderstood from the standpoint of later democratic ideology.

The share of the democracy, or democratic part of a mixed government, was maintained by its 'balance of property'. That balance would be threatened by an accumulation of property in the hands of any subject — it was just such aggrandisement which led to the historic problem of the 'over-mighty subject'. In Whig doctrine the whole argument descended from Harrington; though Pennsylvania seemed, at least since the thwarting of Keith, to have averted the risk of baronial armies which had alarmed Harrington. The proprietors, however, were just such over-mighty subjects.

This argument of course disregarded the fact that the proprietors were not subjects in the proper sense but were hereditary rulers. The Quaker party followed up the implications of that point when at length they turned to the Crown to depose the Penns and resume the province.

Once the proprietors were out of the way, what would be left, what 'interest' would remain, to check the popular power which the author called the 'Democracy'? It is difficult to see how the remaining institutional structure would have lent itself to mixed government, despite the fact that he claimed to be defending the interest only of the 'democratical *part*'. What his argument quietly assumed was that discord would disappear because the Assembly represented a single, harmonious, undifferentiated society. It was a specious contention.

From the period as early as Markham's Frame the Assembly leadership

[1] *True . . . State*, 9.   [2] *True . . . State*, 38.

had been occupied with the interests of property. Lloyd's unsuccessful pressure on Penn in 1701 was directed to securing the interests of land-owners; property remained throughout the colonial period as a leading concern of all Assembly policy and later evidence was to suggest that when the apportionment of representation was in question, property stood before persons among the interests to be weighed. The owners of property of course already enjoyed personal liberty, and liberty in any case was generally under-stood to mean liberty to have and dispose of one's property. That liberty by good fortune extended to most of the inhabitants. But it did not extend to all; and the *principle* on which it was extended to most was fully compatible with the denial of liberty to minorities. The Assembly made this point plain by reiterating their charge relating to the enlistment of indentured servants; they declared that their action in withholding supplies until such violations of property were redressed, must be approved by

Whoever well considers the nature of our indented servants, that they are our pro-perty, purchased under the sanction of Acts of Parliament, and a positive law of this Colony; that they are considered by our Courts of Justice, as personal chattels, and go to the executors of persons deceased, for payment of debts, in common with their other effects; that upon them the cultivation of our land, our trade and commerce chiefly depend.[1]

The Assembly wanted to gain the highest possible measure of self-government, whether it was called mixed or democratic, provided only that within that self-government the existing majority could have things their own way.

That the Quakers and their Assembly allies feared the rise of executive power, both from the creation of new offices in the gift of the Governor, and from the intervention of the Governor acting under secret proprietary instructions in the ordinary exercise of legislative duties, was affirmed by both sides. The *Brief State* sneered at this anxiety; the *True and Impartial State*, in line with other broadsides and pronouncements, accused the pro-prietors of aiming by these methods to subvert the Charter. Galloway denounced the Governor in his *Answer to . . . A Brief State* for making conditions before signing a money Bill. The executive case was that the Bill which contained a grudging agreement to raise money for defence, was drawn up in a way which the Governor was bound to reject. Immediately behind this dispute, waged while the frontier settlements were exposed to

[1] *Pa. Archives*, 8th series, iii. 2601, begins long and acrimonious disputes on enlistment of servants. Also *Pa. Archives*, 8th series, v. 4187–9.

attack, lay the bitterness of the Assembly over the non-taxation of proprietary estates, which were to benefit from the appropriations for defence. He also argued that in England, though members of the House of Lords did not vote for members of the Commons, the Lords continually submitted their estates to be taxed by that House.[1] This was true; and it was also true that the Lords were not supposed to alter money Bills. But the great difference was that the Lords constituted one of the Houses of legislature in Britain and enjoyed, through the structure of society, an inordinate influence over the affairs of the Commons. The Penn family, the greatest landowners in Pennsylvania, and also the lawful governors of the province, had only the executive office through which to defend their rights, or advance their ambitions.

In the face of these ambitions it was inevitable that the normal agencies of government in Pennsylvania should become not merely the instruments of policy but the substantive subject matter of political conflict. The Quaker Party thus insisted, year after year, in election broadsides, in Assembly statements, and in the private correspondence of its adherents, that the fate of the Charter was at stake. The whole tenor of Quaker party argument was to warn the electors of the province that the proprietors were out to seize power by encroaching on the constitutional representation of the people and by establishing a vast system of patronage. The elections of the early 1740s came to play an important part in the Quaker view of the development of this scheme, and voters were reminded of the methods by which the Governor had tried to force an electoral advantage by intimidation and violence.[2]

The Quakers on the other hand represented themselves as the upholders of the basic constitutional liberties of the people. They were the defenders of the Charter, and, by means of the Charter, of the right of popular government. The Assembly majority lost few opportunities of putting the case, in the most forcible addresses to the governors, or reports on their conduct. From these statements there emerge not only polemics but much of the Quaker view of the proper nature of Pennsylvanian government. In September 1757 — only a few days before the annual election — the Assembly, in a formal statement, complained of Governor Denny's rejection of, and attempts to amend, Bills; it criticised the Governor for wanting complete power of nomination of all military officers without recommendations by the people, and went on to attack

[1] *True . . . State*, 137.

[2] *Answer to Brief State*, 66. *To the Freeholders of the County of Philadelphia*, signed 'Pennsylvanicus', 1757–4, Historical Society of Pennsylvania.

Designs of a party, which they have been weak and wicked enough to publish to the world in their *Brief State*. The plan the Governor recommends to us, is the plan they wish for. They declare, they expect it will 'alter the face of affairs, by creating a vast number of new relations, dependencies and subordinations in government: the militia will vote for Members of Assembly, and being dependent on their officers, would probably be influenced by them'; and the officers being recommended by the proprietary creatures, and commissioned by their deputy, would be directed by them, and thus our proprietaries would be vested with the appointment of both branches of the legislature. Under their extensive influence, added to that which will ever attend the immense property of the proprietaries, can any liberty, that the people are entitled to, be safe? The freedom of elections and of Parliament will be violated and destroyed. The balance of power between Governor and people, so wisely established by the royal and proprietary Charters, and Laws of the Province, will be totally subverted, and our present Constitution be transformed into a Government the most despotic and arbitrary....[1]

It may be noted that although the Assembly so plainly felt that the constitutional balance was perfectly safe if nearly all the weight lay on their own side, they found it necessary at least formally to subscribe to the doctrine that the proper structure of the government, established by royal and proprietorial charter, was still that of balance. Like the English Whigs a few years later, they objected to an enlargement of the effective powers of the executive tending, in their opinion, to destroy the normal and correct constitutional balance, and without doubt tending to weaken their own power. They themselves (they added) could have no views but to the good of the province, no motive but the good of the people and the preservation of their country. For confirmation they turned to the basic institution of republican government:

But [they concluded] should our constituents think otherwise, the day of our anniversary election is at hand, and we shall soon again mix with the people; and if our late conduct has been inconsistent with their sentiments, they will no doubt supply our places with such as they conceive will accede to your Honour's measures, and give up those rights which we have thought, and ever shall think, it our indespensable duty to support and maintain.

That the election was at hand was a point not lost on Governor Denny, who remarked in reply that the assemblymen had put off their answer to him, to make sure of their own ends, until two days before the election day.[2] It was thus not merely a defence of the Charter but an election manifesto. Again in the locally notorious case of an action to remove William Moore, an enemy

---

[1] *Pa. Archives*, 8th series, vi. 4638 ff.   [2] *Pa. Archives*, 8th series, vi. 4650.

of the Quakers who was accused of oppressive conduct in his capacity as a magistrate, the Assembly committee on the question denounced the Governor and Council for failing to uphold the impeachment of the House. The case had its own complexities, but the committee found the explanation of the outcome in

An apparent design to overthrow the Constitution, and enslave the people, by depriving the representatives of their most essential rights, powers and privileges, and particularly that of redressing the aggrievances of the subject.[1]

In a further argument on the same case, when the Governor had objected to assuming the power to determine on the impeachment of the Assembly, that body made a poignant affirmation of the incorruptibility of a representative institution:

A sheriff may be corrupted, a jury packed, a court who hold their commissions during pleasure may be influenced; but it is unnatural to assume that the representative body of the people should be partial, corrupted, or do injustice.[2]

Isaac Norris, whose independence had not always conformed to Quaker party wishes, reflects very clearly in his correspondence the hostility of the Assembly to the attitude of the executive. The element which the representatives found intolerable above all was that of secret instructions. The inevitable outcome, in Norris's opinion, which shows the direction of Quaker party plans, would be a rupture with the proprietors. The tendency of the instructions, some of which had come to light, was

to throw both the Executive and Legislative part of our Constitution into the hands of a mere Council of State put in and turned out at the pleasure of their master three thousand miles distant from us. . . .

This letter bore the news that the Quaker party had decided to try for relief by asking the Crown to resume the proprietorship of the province of Pennsylvania.[3] The London Quakers, through Dr Charles, had every opportunity of knowing the sufferings of Pennsylvania. The debts incurred in defence, the unfair exemption of proprietary estates from taxation, the tyranny of secret and arbitrary instructions, were reported to have produced economic decline and to have resulted in emigration from the back counties towards the south.[4]

---

[1] *Pa. Archives*, 8th series, vi. 4838–40.   [2] *Pa. Archives*, 8th series, vi. 4696–703.
[3] Norris to Charles, 4 April 1757. Norris Letterbooks.
[4] Norris to Charles, 19 January 1757, 28 April 1758, February 1758. Norris Letterbooks.

Benjamin Franklin, who had become the leading member of the Quaker party in the Assembly about 1755 — a development which signalised the eclipse of any distinctively Quaker character in that party — was sent to England in 1757 to oppose the proprietors. The unpopularity of Quaker reticence in matters of defence was offset — especially after the resignation of the six Quaker members and the emergence of a new leadership — by the extreme odium incurred by the proprietors through their claims for exemptions. Yet the whole force of the reiterated Quaker party claims on behalf of the Charter and representative government depended upon one vital postulate. It was essential for them to maintain that it was they who truly represented the people as a whole. It was essential to sustain the tradition that Quaker party leadership was truly a leadership for the united and undifferentiated interest of the whole community of the province. This was the significance of the expression used by the Assembly in 1757, which condemned the 'Designs of a party which they have been weak and wicked enough to publish to the world in their *Brief State*'. The statement denied, by intent, the notion that the Assembly was itself led by a party. On the contrary, it was the opposition, the Governor and his ring of office-holding hirelings, who were designated a 'party'. The Assembly, and the point was central to the Quaker view of political life in the province, were the direct representatives of the whole people. This was what made possible the affirmation that it was 'unnatural to assume that the representative body of the people should be partial, corrupted, or do injustice'. The concept was from a very pure strain of republican principle. For it derived from the electorate not only political authority but, in the last analysis, political right. It placed the greatest responsibility upon the institution of political representation.

The underlying weakness of the Quaker position was precisely that this very concept of a Quaker leadership responsible for, and accepted by the whole community was losing its application to reality. What if the Quakers should cease to have the assent of the people to their mode of government? What would become of all their passionate asseverations of republican principle? They were not unaware of the question; they were not unaware of the disturbing implication that some other, more fundamental ground for Quaker ascendancy might have to be found. The problem was actually discussed by Galloway in his *Answer to . . . A Brief State*. One of the questions raised was that of how Quakers were continually chosen to the Assembly, and Galloway, in answering it, went into a justification of Quaker motives in Pennsylvanian politics. The land, he declared, was their birthright and possession; justice belonged to them. They could not be blamed for using their endeavours to keep possession, and to hinder others from reaping the fruits of their labours. For two reasons, prudence and justice evinced the obligation, and even the necessity, of returning the Quakers to the Assembly: because they had been the first settlers; and because by good government they had shown themselves fit persons to run the colony.[1]

The statement was less than full of comfort; for if at any time the Quakers ceased to run the colony well, their priority as settlers would hardly be countenanced by others as a ground for continuing to monopolise the representation. And it was this very charge that, in the crisis of French advances in the Ohio Valley and Indian activity on the frontier, of back-country settlement and internal dissension, the Quakers were obliged to rebut. 'I am sensible', wrote Norris in 1755, 'and always was, that the popular clamour would be against us, if we did not give liberally, and in due time, both of which I think we have done, and to the entire satisfaction of our constituents.' And after animadverting on proprietary methods, he concluded:

I look upon the Quaker System in Pennsyla in a political view which if overturned, at least at present, would introduce violent convulsion in this prov. unless we are to be a Govt of meer force.[2]

'The Quaker system.' It is a serviceable phrase. Undoubtedly it was a system; undoubtedly it was run not merely by men eminent in the Quaker meeting (that aspect indeed was beginning to weaken), but also on the basis of an undenied prior authority in the realm of government. It was specifically in the process of representation that this authority was to be exercised. The Assemblies' dauntless expressions of willingness to stand or fall by the determination of their constituents reflected a genuine sense of confidence in the effectiveness of the republican principles by which they stood; though it must be admitted that, despite the exigencies of war, no Assembly of this period feared any such disaster as had overtaken their predecessors in the amazing election of 1710. The Quakers, even after 1756, continued to think of themselves as the natural guardians of the political interests of the province. At least until the rise of sectarian animosities[3] they were still capable of commanding a remarkable degree of loyalty among other sects.

[1] *Answer to . . . A Brief State*, 64–66.

[2] Norris to Charles, 24 May 1755. Norris Letterbooks.

[3] Noted by Thayer, *Pennsylvania Politics*, 42, as the period at which the Quakers ceased to have a big following in the west.

Thus in a report on the election of 1755, Norris was able to tell his correspondent that all the country members had been re-elected except for a few who had declined, and to observe

It is remarkable ... that the frontier county of Lancaster, composed of all sorts of Presbyterians and Independents, and all sorts of Germans, & some Church of England Electors, have chosen all their representatives out of the Quakers, tho' there are scarcely one hundred of that profession in the whole county, and they have made the returns without the least solicitation on the part of the present members that I know.[1]

The letters of Norris, which keep up a most informative commentary on the electoral history of the province, are alive with references to consultations with constituents, and in one case contain a positive demand for instruction on their wants.[2]

It was obvious that the spread and increase of sects placed the Quaker management under a strain. And in view of these rapid changes in the population, it is significant that political interests were thought of in direct relation to sects and nationalities; the prevalent type of definition is sectarian. In an optimistic letter of 1755, Norris undertook to tell Dr Charles of the state of 'our parties here, if they can be called such, for I think I may say, the Province was never more united ... than at present'.[3] He went on to speak of the Church of England (very few), the numerous Quakers, the now more numerous Presbyterians ('by the great importations from Ireland'), the Germans, outnumbering any other one sect though by no means equal to them altogether, the few Anabaptists and Moravians. He noted the need for the Church of England to keep in with the Quakers politically, and the internal animosities of the Presbyterians. 'The Church of England & Quakers continue on very strong terms of Union for the interest of the whole, and themselves in particular' — a candid touch! — 'without any formal cabals for that purpose. And the Dutch joyn them in a dread of arbitry [sic] govt. — So it seems absolutely necessary to keep the Quakers as a balance here,' he concluded, coming up with another justification for 'the system'.

But the German, or 'Dutch' monolith was cracking, making it possible for parties or factions to cut into the German community and seek electoral

[1] Norris to Charles, 5 October 1755. Norris Letterbooks.
[2] Norris to Jas. Wright, 15 February 1753. Norris Letterbooks.
[3] Norris to Charles, 29 April 1755. Norris Letterbooks.

support from diverse elements;[1] and when the proprietary party began to enlist the aggrieved Scotch-Irish of the back-country, the Quakers lost the foundations of their concept of an essentially complacent community under Quaker leadership. Political husbandry could no longer conceal the transformation of a grand design into a disintegrated patchwork quilt.

[1] Rothermund, 'German Problem'.

LEGISLATIVE POWER AND HOME RULE IN VIRGINIA

Introduction

OF the three American provinces examined in this book, Virginia bore the most significant resemblance to England, and the application of Whig principles in Virginia provided the most illuminating test of their meaning in practice.

In England, the landed interest was generally recognised as the most permanent and important in the kingdom. Virginia had a much more predominantly landed economy, supporting a gentry whose pretensions were comparable (within appropriate limits) to those of the English aristocracy. In Virginia, as in other colonies, the Council led in the struggle to assert the local supremacy of the legislative power; but, as happened elsewhere, the Assembly superseded the Council and became the representative instrument of the leading colonial interests.

The Assembly, although based on a wide franchise, was dominated by the deeply entrenched gentry of the counties. No attempt to understand the character of representation in Virginia can succeed without taking account of the system of government in the counties. The county court, a co-optive and oligarchic body, was controlled by the local gentry and was never open to the same pressures which could rage in the New England town meeting. The Assembly gradually came to represent a sort of federation of county oligarchies, in principle not unlike the House of Commons.

The extension of the suffrage could go forward under this system as long as it did not conflict with the interests of the gentry. All of the leading men were Whigs and many of them held views which closely corresponded to those of the Yorkshire movement for parliamentary reform in England. A franchise based on property could be liberal when property was widespread. These principles could also lead to the exclusion of large numbers when property was not widespread; and demands for further enfranchisement became insistent a generation after the Revolution, after about 1812. The spread of the population into new areas of the state also brought a demand for the redistribution of seats. The demands for suffrage and for reapportionment joined forces in an uneasy alliance.

Reform in Virginia was a slow business. A major Convention was finally held in 1829–30 — its timing only just anticipating that of parliamentary reform in England. A similar combination of forces was at work in both countries: demands for seats in the legislature, proceeding from new areas of wealth, together with demands for suffrage from the lower as well as the middle classes.

The agricultural nature of Virginian society affected its politics. Reform always came more quickly under pressure from the cities. When reform was debated, conservatives adapted the theories of Locke and Madison to an American version of interest representation, while reformers followed the lines laid down by Jefferson in the direction of political individualism and majority rule.

6. The Identification of Legislative Power

Virginians quickly proved themselves adept in self-government. The tribulations of England in the seventeenth century gave them opportunities of which they took such good advantage that by the end of the century the House of Burgesses had made itself a sophisticated legislative body. This, however, did not settle the question of legislative power. Virginians knew that if they could establish the location of the legislative power they could give themselves the authority for effective home rule. The Council early showed itself equal to the task of government. But in the first quarter of the eighteenth century, the power shifted gradually into the hands of the Assembly. The issues were joined when a strong Governor, Alexander Spotswood, attempted to build up his own party in the House. His failure proved two things. First, that local forces could use the electoral system to defeat the royally appointed executive; and secondly that the elected representatives were stronger than the appointed councillors.

PARLIAMENTARY institutions took root in Virginia at the time of their tribulation in England. They were begun in 1619 when Governor Yeardley, under the instructions of the Virginia Company, called the first Assembly ever to meet on American soil; and it was significant that the commercial purposes of the Company so quickly and so naturally called for the kind of consultation which could best be provided by a procedure that had about it the essential attributes of a civil form of government. After the dissolution of the Company in 1624 the royal government managed the affairs of the colony for four years without the benefit of an elected assembly; and to all appearances the first phase of representative government had also been the last. But the plantation could never survive as a mere business organisation; to meet its urgent needs in defence and trade, the royal government in turn found that it required the co-operation of the planters in an assembly, which was accordingly summoned in 1628.

The expansion of the settlements and the gradual development of diverse and local interests called for steps to put these institutions on a permanent basis. In 1634 Virginia was divided into eight counties, within which local government was to be conducted under county courts on the English model. Each county became a constituency of the House of Burgesses; but this new county representation was not at first the only system, for the practice, started in 1619, by which any community or parish within a county was allowed to send a burgess to the Assembly provided it was prepared to pay his expenses, was continued alongside it for several years.[1]

The planters who participated, both as voters and representatives, learnt the methods of self-government by personal experience; from which they learnt also that government by participation could thrive in a new plantation even when it was threatened by prerogative power at home.

At first the Council and Assembly sat together with the Governor in a single chamber. The genuine collectiveness of the interests of all dwellers in Virginia in their own immediate survival gave their political arrangements a touch of familiarity of far greater importance than any separate interests that might tend to divide them. Yet Virginians, no less than other colonists, would develop an early appetite for local power — an appetite that grew with

[1] Wesley Frank Craven, *The Southern Colonies in the Seventeenth Century, 1607–1689* (Baton Rouge, 1949), 169, 172 (hereafter referred to as *Southern Colonies*). G. E. Howard, *Introduction to the Local Constitutional History of the United States* (Baltimore, 1889), 124.

tasting; and although Virginians remained formally loyal to the Crown for
as long as possible during the Civil Wars and Interregnum, the prolonged
slackening of central control gave them time to gain confidence in their
powers of self-government.

Self-government went exceptionally far in so new a colony when, during
the Interregnum, the burgesses actually appointed both their Governor and
the Council. So independent was the character of the burgesses that by the
end of that period they had taken to sitting as a separate House — a House
made up of the selected spokesmen of the county magistracies, who by this
time were firmly seated in the control of their respective counties.[1] The
House soon distinguished itself by the adroitness and skill with which it
developed its committee system for the management of business. That
business included the major issues of internal affairs, and instead of appointing
ad hoc committees to tackle specific problems in separate sessions, the House
resourcefully anticipated its needs by creating standing committees which by
taking up petitions and considering Bills and other business, entered into the
normal procedure of legislation. These House committees formed themselves
into organs of government.[2] The Stuart monarchy might be restored, but
chips off the prerogative of government were flying away across the Atlantic.

Order, which in America meant the unquestioned authority of royal
government, was restored by the Restoration. The legislature of Virginia
was a good example of what would later be acclaimed as the best of all
possible forms of government — the 'mixed' kind — having a strong royal
Governor, an appointed Council of great men of weight and property, and
an Assembly drawn mainly from the more substantial elements of the local
communities. After the temporary upheaval of Bacon's Rebellion in 1676,
the government was consolidated and the main lines of an enduring system
were laid down. Governor and Council continued to be the centre of power
and the source of policy; the elected Assembly participated in debate,
gradually establishing its control over the raising and disbursement of money,
and deliberately modelling its procedures and claims to constitutional power
on those of the House of Commons.[3]

[1] Craven, *Southern Colonies*, 288–91.

[2] Ralph V. Harlow, *History of Legislative Methods before 1825* (New Haven, Conn.,
1917), 10–17.

[3] Jack P. Greene, *The Quest for Power: The Lower Houses of Assembly in the Southern
Royal Colonies, 1689–1776* (Chapel Hill, 1963), 66–7, 80–1, 85–6, 101–4, 185–9, 204. The
House of Burgesses as early as 1691 gained the power to appoint the provincial Treasurer.
— ibid., 243.

The first interest of Virginians was to grasp the legislative power firmly in their own hands. To do this, however, did not necessarily mean exalting the Assembly. For half a century after the Restoration the drive for local authority — in so far as the tendency was positive enough to be called a drive — was mainly manifest in accretions to the power of the Council. Only later did a secondary movement, an undercurrent of this conciliar period, emerge in the ambitions of the Assembly; and it did so when the balance was tipped by the energy of a royal Governor attempting to gain Assembly support in rallying his own policies. Between 1720 and 1730, legislative power came to be defined to the satisfaction of Virginians to mean that of the two chambers without specific reference to the Governor; and between those two, the elective House had by that time gained an ascendancy from which it could never be dislodged.

The passage of increasingly complex Navigation laws, the mapping out of more positive colonial policies as implied by the founding of the Board of Trade, and the issuing of instructions to royal Governors tending to strengthen the prerogative, brought about a painful need to examine the true standing of the colonies in regard to their own affairs. A writer, probably Robert Beverley, raised the problem in public in 1701:

Of late years [he wrote] great doubts have been raised, how far the Legislative Authority is in the Assemblies of the several Colonies; whether they have the power to make certain acts or ordinances in the nature of byelaws only; or, whether they can make acts of attainder, naturalisation, for settling or disposing of titles to lands within their jurisdiction, or other things of the like nature; and where necessity requires, make such acts as best suit the circumstances and constitution of the country, even tho' in some particulars, they plainly differ from the Laws of *England.*[1]

The phrase 'Legislative Authority' was here used in its full sense, and the 'great doubts' were no mere debating points: the mention of them manifested a strong sense of grievance that any doubt should exist at all.

The author of the *Essay* had stated the outline of the problem of American self-government as it was to develop for three-quarters of a century. But he had not addressed himself to the question of the distribution, between the branches of domestic government, of these powers to make Acts which might 'plainly differ from the Laws of *England*'. At the time of his writing it

[1] Louis B. Wright (ed.), *An Essay upon the Government of the English Plantations on the Continent of America* (London, 1701; San Marino, 1945), 23. The question of authorship is discussed in the Introduction.

would have been difficult to anticipate that within twenty or thirty years the Council would have dwindled to relative insignificance; in the struggle which was then opening, the Council was the dominant local force. But this does not mean that the Council, in the later American sense, was a 'patriotic' influence: it means rather that the councillors were determined to use their constitutional powers for their own advantage, if necessary against those of both Governor and Assembly.

The keen struggle that developed over Governor Nicholson's policies in the first few years of the new century involved matters too complex to be explained simply by rivalry between home government and colony. Nicholson, who took up his duties as Governor for a second term in 1699, was guided by instructions the purport of which was to limit land sales to actual settlers and to prevent encroachments by the colonial branches of government — particularly the Council — on the royal prerogative. Though Nicholson's conduct made many enemies, his land policy was acceptable to the smaller planters, while it incurred the hostility of the greater landowners whose plans for family aggrandisement turned on the opportunities for expansion and speculation in the west. These men dominated the Council. The public controversies of Nicholson's rule, which were complicated and embittered by conflicts of personality and disappointment in love, set the Council, embodying the great planter interest, against not only the Crown but also the Assembly, in which the middling and smaller men managed to retain a measure of influence.[1] It was the Council which worked to grasp the power of making policy and thus to advance the cause of self-government; but, as happened more than half a century later in Pennsylvania, self-government was not an object in itself but an instrument in the struggle for more immediate and more tangible aims.

After the recall of Nicholson and the early death of his appointed successor, Edward Nott, an interval of four years elapsed before the arrival of a new Governor. It was a significant period. The position of head of the government devolved upon Edward Jennings, as President of the Council. The interlude of conciliar power was not wasted. In 1706 the Council had taken advantage of the opportunity, presented by a violation of instructions concerning the exempting of English liquors from import duties, to amend an Assembly money Bill; from 1706 until 1710 the Council governed altogether without the Assembly; and succeeded in defeating the Board of

---

[1] Osgood, *American Colonies*, ii. 161. David Alan Williams, 'Political Alignments in Colonial Virginia 1698–1750' (Ph.D. thesis, Northwestern University 1959), 4–21, 36–37, 48–50, 70–76 (hereafter referred to as 'Political Alignments').

Trade's land-distribution restriction plans which had formed an important part of Nicholson's permanent policy.[1]

The conciliar period ended with the arrival of Governor Alexander Spotswood and the issue of writs for new Assembly elections. Nicholson had been able to secure a measure of support from his Assemblies because the land policies he was instructed to pursue found sympathy among the county voters. Spotswood, whose policies were far more energetic but not so easily submitted to, embarked on the course of controlling the Assembly by the distribution of patronage.

He sought to build up a party through which he could exert continuous and personal control. The inauguration of a systematically enforced inspection of tobacco with destruction of inferior crops, though badly needed in the long-term interests of the economy, was extremely unpopular with the lesser planters, who could ill afford the effects on their livelihood. The posts of tobacco inspectors, being within the Governor's gift, provided him with the means he required, and in the session of 1713–14 he conferred this distinction on no fewer than twenty-five members of the House of Burgesses.[2]

In 1715 the electors gave him their answer in one of the most remarkable of colonial landslides. The campaign resulted in the defeat of all except one of the burgesses holding inspectorships, and the return of thirty-seven new members in a House of fifty-two; it was comparable — though on entirely different issues — with the Pennsylvanian result of 1710. After a short and unproductive session, the Governor, who was not given to generosity about the merits of his political opponents, delivered a diatribe against both the petitions for redress which had come up with the new House, and the ignorance, incompetence, and illiteracy of the members. He then dissolved the House.[3]

Spotswood's extensive plans for the reform of the administration of Virginia included not only the economy but the judicial system, and it was here that he suffered his most striking defeat. The Council, with the assistance of some prudent fee-placing in London on the part of its agent William Byrd, reversed the Governor's project for altering the composition of the court of oyer and terminer, of which the councillors claimed the sole right of membership.[4] The details of this dispute were of constitutional

---

[1] Osgood, *American Colonies*, ii. 182–3. Williams, 'Political Alignments', 84–5.

[2] Williams, 'Political Alignments', 149.

[3] Osgood, *American Colonies*, ii. 236–8; Williams, 'Political Alignments', 163–4; Leonidas Dodson, *Alexander Spotswood* (Philadelphia, 1932), chap. vi.

[4] Williams, 'Political Alignments', 172–9.

significance only to the extent that the councillors sensed, in the recon-struction of the courts, an invasion of their rights by the prerogative. In this affair, as in the matter of the Governor's attempt to build a party of place-men, the reaction of the interested colonial leaders was directed against the development, within the province, of political power depending on the Governor. It did not mean the rejection of specific proposals for colonial improvement. The tobacco inspection plan, despite early diffi-culties and set-backs, was applied with increasing vigour as the more power-ful planters became convinced of its necessity for their own economic strength.

The separation of the administration of this scheme from the influence of the Governor forms a significant comment on the advancing political authority of the colonists in their own institutions. The issue was not closed until long after Spotswood's rule had come to an end; but in 1736 tobacco inspectors were disqualified from serving as members of the House of Bur-gesses or from participating in elections. In 1738 the appointment of these officials was taken from the Governor and placed in the hands of the county courts. Since these courts were virtual committees of the leading planters of the several counties, the effect of these steps was to consolidate power more firmly in their hands. The advance of the power of the legislative institutions of the province was itself both a manifestation and consolidation of the domestic authority of the great slave-owners and landowners who dominated Virginia.[1]

Within the legislative system, the rising power and competence of the House of Burgesses helped to induce the concomitant decline of the Council. But this was not a matter of weights and pulleys; the House did not rise on the incline of the rope whose descending half drew the Council down.

The Council had from the beginning stood as a house of legislation. The London Company gave it this position as early as 1618, a grant confirmed by royal authority in 1628. After the Restoration, the powers of the Council were increased by British policy, and there were periods in the late seventeenth and early eighteenth centuries, especially that of the conciliar interlude of 1706–10, when the Council emerged as the strongest single institution in the province. Legislation did not proceed upward from the burgesses. It was, on the contrary, decided on by the Governor with the Council's possible

---

[1] Williams, 'Political Alignments', 274–5. W. W. Hening (ed.), *The Statutes at Large: Being a Collection of all the Laws of Virginia, 1619–1792* 13 vols. (Richmond, 1809–23), iv. 481–2 (hereafter referred to as *Statutes*).

assistance and passed down to the House. The Council was powerful enough, as has been seen, to thwart Governor Nicholson and it was able to interfere with the plans of other governors, including the forceful Spotswood.[1]

The contemporary view of the existing balance of power in the legislative structure was indicated by certain turns of phrase. The pamphleteer of the *Essay*[2] of 1701 had referred to recent doubts 'how far the legislative authority is in the Assemblies of the several Colonies'. But Beverley, probably the same author, left little room for doubt that Virginians expected policy to spring from the executive, attributing it personally to the Governor. Lord Culpeper was thus credited with having divided the Council from the burgesses over the question of appeals;[3] Andros, apparently by his own authority as Governor, and as President of the Council in its capacity of the highest court of the province, applied all English statutes as law in the Virginia courts.[4] Equally significant was the statement: 'In his first Assembly, Lieutenant-Governor Nicholson pass'd acts for encouragement both of the linen manufacture, and to promote the leather trade, by tanning, currying, and shoe-making'.[5] This is much more than the formal ascription of legislation to the reign in which it occurred; no one would have said that King William founded the Bank of England or that King George I passed the Bubble Act. The Governor evidently had a share — which in the case of vigorous men like Spotswood was a dominant share — in passing legislation: but the Governor did not work unaided on the problems which involved the provincial economy, and the councillors as great men, if not the Council as a constitutional body, must have exerted substantial influence. Moreover, though the Council itself originated no legislation, it was empowered to advise the Governor on the calling, proroguing, and dissolution of the Assembly; and its assent, with that of the Governor, was necessary to make Acts of the Assembly into law.

British governments had undoubtedly hoped that an appointive Council of provincial dignitaries would act as a check to the pressure of an Assembly whose interests were more distant from those of Britain. Until Bacon's Rebellion, members of the Council were exempted from all public taxes in addition to being awarded an honorarium for their attendance. The tax

---

[1] Percy Scott Flippin, *The Royal Government in Virginia, 1624–1775* (New York, 1919), 167–70 (hereafter referred to as *Royal Government*).

[2] See p. 129.

[3] Robert Beverley, *The History and Present State of Virginia* (London, 1705), (ed. Louis B. Wright), (Chapel Hill, 1947), 92–93 (hereafter referred to as *History*).

[4] Beverley, *History*, 101.   [5] Ibid., 100.

exemption was dropped in 1676, but the remuneration was substantially increased. Until the end of the seventeenth century, they enjoyed the lucrative advantage of appointments as customs collectors and naval officers in their several districts. But this privilege was taken away on orders from the British government in 1698.[1]

It was only very gradually, and more especially after the retirement of Spotswood in 1722, that the decline of the Council became apparent. Spotswood himself was in some degree responsible. When he determined to inaugurate a forceful policy he turned his back on the possibilities — which at that period must have been promising ones — of gaining the confidence and collaboration of the Council, although the tobacco inspection programme was in fact more likely to prove attractive to the bigger planters than to the lesser. Instead he tried to work through patronage and the Assembly. His mistake may well have been due to misguided dependence on English experience. His failure not only set back the influence of the Council but rejuvenated that of the Assembly. The House of Burgesses had begun its advance to the centre of colonial power.

Plain practical difficulties also contributed to the decline of the Council. Its meetings were held in Williamsburg, where it had to perform judicial duties extending far beyond the demands made on assemblymen for the sessions of the legislature; consequently it was essential that its members should live within easy reach of the capital, and it became increasingly difficult to find men of sufficient substance who could meet the demands of attendance. The expansion of the province meant that the typical great men of whom the Council was to be composed were scattered in widely distributed sections of Virginia, making it, to an increasing degree, unrepresentative — even of the upper class. Composed as it was of native Virginians, who were usually closely related to the leading members of the House of Burgesses, the Council came gradually to have less sense of identification with the interests of the Governor.

This is not to say that it sank into insignificance or disrepute. The Council was capable of holding its own in domestic disputes with the House. In 1749, after a sharp exchange occasioned by the demand of the House to search the record of the Council's proceedings, the upper chamber went so far as to take its case to the public by ordering the *Virginia Gazette* to publish a statement which it had drawn up in its own vindication. The obedience of the printer brought a severe reprimand from the House, to which the

[1] Philip Alexander Bruce, *The Institutional History of Virginia in the Seventeenth Century* 2 vols. (New York, 1910), ii. 376–83 (hereafter referred to as *Institutional History*).

Council replied with an affirmation of its full responsibility.[1] Election broadsides and pamphlets were already familiar, but the publication of a defence of policy in a legislative dispute was a highly unusual experiment, though the public opinion to be influenced would not have extended far beyond the gentry in the neighbourhood of Williamsburg.

Neither should the decline of the Council's separate influence be thought to represent the disappearance from Virginia of the English principle of the bicameral legislature. Virginians retained an upper chamber when they made their own constitution in 1776; and so radical a revolutionary as Richard Henry Lee, in discussing with approval John Adams's *Thoughts on Government*, remarked that the term of the upper House should be longer than that of the lower, 'in order to answer the purpose of an independent middle power'.[2] But as the House of Burgesses came to be filled by the leading men of each county, and to be dominated by the great families of Virginia, the two chambers lost their distinctness of social character — a feature which had in any case seldom been very pronounced.[3] It is worth noting that in this respect the history of the two Houses resembled that of their prototypes in Britain. The House of Lords after the Glorious Revolution did not experience a history of continuous decline, even though it had lost much of its weight and initiative by the time that Walpole, translated into the Earl of Orford, sardonically remarked upon his diminished significance.

Within some twenty or thirty years of the publication of the *Essay on the Government of the English Plantations*, the question how far the legislative power lay in the colonies had, so far as Virginia was concerned, been effectively answered. It was hardly surprising that in 1776 the leading Virginians, who had grounded themselves in the lessons of the seventeenth century, should have fortified themselves with the doctrines of Locke. For Locke not only vindicated them in affirming the supremacy of the legislative power; he also confirmed their impression that this power was justly exercised only when it was based on a representation of the people. And in Virginia the people, whatever shades of discrimination might be imposed through the laws governing elections and representation, could only be Virginians.

[1] Osgood, *American Colonies*, iv. 104–5.
[2] James Curtis Ballagh (ed.), *The Letters of Richard Henry Lee*, 2 vols. (New York, 1912), i. 179.
[3] Osgood, *American Colonies*, iv. 231–2.

7. The Character of the Electorate

The suffrage in Virginia was based on laws closely similar to those of Great Britain. Religious qualifications were enacted at the end of the seventeenth century. The distribution of land, and the permissive way in which sheriffs applied the law, actually produced a wide franchise. So long as the interests of the gentry were parallel to those of their tenants and the lesser planters, there was no internal conflict, and the House of Burgesses could approve measures (subsequently disallowed by the Crown) to extend the suffrage. A generation after the Revolution, when incipient conflicts of interest began to emerge, this harmony disappeared and the House steadily resisted reform.

ELECTIONS presuppose an electorate. As early settlement turned into permanent society, Virginian political life assumed the normal characteristics, found in the English counties, which by the end of the seventeenth century had emerged in their conventional form to include qualifications of property and religion for the exercise of the suffrage; to these Virginia added the requirement of residence. The dominant characteristic of the electorate as an element of society was political responsibility defined by the possession of property — in most cases landed property. This fact, in Virginia as in other provinces, was of fundamental importance for the whole further development of American politics. Owing to the availability of cheap land and the shortage of labour, a high proportion of the adult population of white men might reasonably hope to acquire enough to win them the right to vote; but no such right existed as a mere condition of their membership of, and obedience to, society. The conception laid down in Virginia after the Restoration was prescriptive: men who by birth or fortune found themselves outside the political pale might work their way into it, by toil or chance, or they might remain outside. Political values were so permeated with the idea of property that the laws made it appear that property by itself, as though it had a life of its own, was entitled to representation. If the people below the property-line became so numerous that their very numbers held the danger of alterations in the basic character of society, then political society, so far from meeting them in their needs, would reaffirm its own prescriptive character and defend its frontiers against them.

Suffrage restrictions, however, were not consistently maintained. After the French and Indian Wars the ruling elements themselves encouraged a broad movement for suffrage extension, which was in their own interests; and as many as fifty per cent of the adult white males appear occasionally to have exercised the franchise; but after a short phase of flexibility, the basic principles which had helped to form the institutions of the province were rewritten into the Constitution of the State. These principles permitted the passage of a reforming and codifying statute in 1785. Thereafter, demands for reform and extension of the suffrage met with determined and prolonged resistance from the entrenched gentry of Virginia.

All freemen in Virginia appear to have enjoyed the right to vote until 1654. In that year it was restricted to 'housekeepers', whether freeholders, leaseholders, or tenants; the restriction lasted only one year, and was repealed on the equitable ground that 'we conceive it something hard and unagreeable to reason that any persons shall pay equal taxes and yet have no vote in elections'. All freemen were readmitted to the suffrage: but the condition was added that votes must be given 'by subscription and not in a tumultuous way'.[1]

Early Virginia, like other settlements, had of necessity a certain primal homogeneity; its founding settlers were not, so far as they knew, engaged in the experiment of a kind of primitive democracy of the city-state type transplanted to agrarian conditions, but were developing a new community, with the object of making large commercial profits, under acute difficulties. The Indian massacres of 1622 and 1644 were enough to show how grave those difficulties truly were. Yet Virginian society advanced. With growing security there was also a growing proportion of servants, as well as agricultural wage earners who though freemen were not freeholders. The re-emergence under American conditions of distinctions which prevailed in England was an indication of American growth; and John Winthrop's affirmation, given in Massachusetts in 1630, certainly held equally firmly for Virginia: it was the intent of God that in all times some must be rich and some poor, some 'highe and eminent in power and dignitie; others meane and in subieccion'.[2] Until the adoption of statutes of primogeniture and entail early in the eighteenth century, the law of inheritance in Virginia was governed by the principle of partible descent; but consciousness of social class, leading to the

---

[1] Hening, *Statutes*, i. 403.

[2] Bernard Bailyn, 'Politics and Social Structure in Virginia', in James M. Smith (ed.), *Seventeenth Century America* (Chapel Hill, 1959), 91, 106.

imitation of the older forms of land usage, was increasing in the latter part of the seventeenth century.[1] A property qualification for the suffrage was a conventional part of the process. A forty shilling freehold standard had, after all, been in force in England since 1430; and Virginians were English.

In 1663 the new royal Governor, Sir William Berkeley, proposed to the Assembly that taxes should be imposed on land rather than on polls; but the Assembly, observing that this would enable landowners alone to claim the right of election, declared that the remainder of the freemen — a majority in number — would rather pay their taxes than lose the privilege of voting. But by 1670 this same Assembly — there had been no intervening election — had changed its mind. The burgesses, deeply seated in what now seemed an almost timeless privilege and perhaps sensing some rivalry for a share of control from the smaller farmers, restricted the franchise to freemen who owned property or houses. Though in itself a modest step, it signified that the burgesses, who now represented a local ruling class, were aware of the political implications of their social position. The reasons they gave were the need to prevent tumults at elections, and conformity with the laws of England; and they could both have been valid, for electoral riots were certainly compatible with lower-class discontent.[2]

This statute contained the first formulation of the concept that was to prescribe the nature of political right in Virginia:

... The laws of England grant a voice in such election [it explained] only to such as by their estates real or personal have interest enough to tie them to the endeavour of the public good.

More than a century later the same basic principle would be reformulated by George Mason in the Virginia Declaration of Rights.

The ageing Assembly was at length succeeded by new elections in 1676. By this time, discontent over a variety of problems — fanned by the irascible and impetuous Nathaniel Bacon — looked so threatening that Governor Berkeley himself extended the suffrage to all the freemen. The legislation passed by the Assembly of June 1676, while Bacon was rampaging about the country in his role of General in a war against the more defenceless of the local Indians, clearly indicates that the smaller planters felt aggrieved by the earlier suffrage restrictions; the law of 1670 was repealed. Most of the Acts

[1] Craven, *Southern Colonies,* 404–5.
[2] Wilcomb E. Washburn, *The Governor and the Rebel* (Chapel Hill, 1957), 49–50. Craven, *Southern Colonies,* 296. Hening, *Statutes,* ii. 280.

of the rebellious June Assembly were carried again after the suppression of Bacon's rebellion and the holding of new elections; but the one which had extended the suffrage was dropped. From 1677 Virginia settled to a normal condition in which property qualifications were incorporated into the electoral system.

It seems probable that such restrictions would in any case have been re-imposed before long by the men who were coming to power in the counties and whose property in land and slaves made them leaders of the province. If any opposition survived it remained incoherent. The significant fact was that although the short-lived Act of 1676 might recall the idea of a freemen suffrage, it was not supported by, and did not belong to, any corpus of opposition principles. There was never a rival philosophy of government to oppose the combined (if not always harmonious) authority of the burgesses and the Council. What happened instead was the firm establishment and the gradual absorption into the texture of political philosophy of the principle that any man who wanted to enjoy the privilege (not the right) of suffrage must qualify himself by possessing a stake in the community. This cardinal principle underlying the composition of the electorate was confirmed again in the Constitution of 1776.

The bitter religious intolerance, which afflicted English life after the Restoration and even before the rise of a Roman Catholic menace in the concrete form of French expansion, was transported to Virginia at the end of the century. In 1699 a new election law[1] barred the class known as recusants convict both from voting and holding office. Recusants, being those who failed to attend their parish church, might have been held to include Protestant Nonconformists as well as Roman Catholics. In England, Dissenters were, of course, subject to penalties, but they were not usually described as 'recusants',[2] and the intentions of the Virginian legislators were certainly directed against Catholics. Quakers were permitted to vote about the beginning of the century,[3] which confirms the acceptance of Pro-testantism as the main religious principle.

Catholics continued under these disabilities, at least in law, until the

---

[1] Hening, *Statutes*, iii. 172–5.

[2] The word 'recusant' was not used as a description of Dissenters in the repressive legislation against them in England under Charles II. Sir Charles Grant Robertson, *Select Statutes, Cases and Documents* (London, 1947), 32–53, 67–74 (hereafter referred to as *Select Statutes*).

[3] Flippin, *Royal Government*, 191.

Revolution. The Constitution of 1776 offered them no explicit relief; and as late as 1784 Madison expressed doubts about their rights. But the religious disability was dropped in the comprehensive revision of the election laws passed in 1785.[1]

Long before the end of the seventeenth century the legislators had been confronted with the problems of framing distinctive laws for that special class of servants whose fate was irremediable slavery; and for the intermediate class of free Negroes and their mulatto relations — who were, of course, not less clearly the relations of the whites. It was not until 1723 that Negroes, mulattoes, and also Indians were excluded by law from the polls; but this measure gave legal form to long-standing custom.[2]

The rise in the power of the House of Burgesses dating from Spotswood's régime gave a sharp edge to the competition for seats, leading eventually to a revision of the election laws which affected the right of suffrage. Political competition led to abuses and the need for further regulation; a problem that was complicated in 1735 by an election campaign which centred once again on the issue of tobacco regulation. The renewal of the unpopular inspection law had been passed in 1734, and the smaller planters, who were those most threatened by the practice of destroying the inferior product, appear to have exacted from their candidates promises to vote for repeal.[3]

Some of the abuses of the election of 1735 were recounted in the preamble to the election law of the following year. Candidates had made fraudulent conveyances in order to qualify their non-freeholding supporters as voters. With the aim of preventing this practice, the law contained the rather vague expression that the qualifying land must have been in the possession of the freeholder 'for a term of years'.[4] The suffrage franchise was defined with a new and limiting precision: it included all freeholders owning either twenty-five acres with a plantation — meaning cultivated land — and a house, or one hundred acres with no settlement; and also freeholders in the towns.

It was under this law that Virginia offered a remarkable fractional vote to joint owners. Provided that their joint freehold was big enough to qualify,

---

[1] A. E. McKinley, *The Suffrage Franchise in the Thirteen American Colonies* (Philadelphia, 1903), 35 (hereafter referred to as *Suffrage Franchise*); James Madison, *Writings*, ed. Gaillard Hunt, 9 vols. (New York, 1910), ii. 54 n. Hening, *Statutes*, xii. 120.

[2] Hening, *Statutes*, iv. 133–4; J. A. C. Chandler, *History of Suffrage in Virginia* (Baltimore, 1901), 12; Craven, *Southern Colonies*, 402–3.

[3] Williams, 'Political Alignments', 281–3.   [4] Hening, *Statutes*, iv. 475–8.

and that they could agree with each other, they might unite to cast a single vote for their freehold. Land seemed to have acquired a right of representation apart from people.[1]

One of the most significant innovations made in this law altered the previous requirements of residence. The original provision, that each settlement was to send representatives to the Assembly, had been so perfectly natural to the circumstances that no other plan would have suggested itself; nor did the development of the county as the Assembly's normal constituency make any difference to the basic idea that the residents of that constituency should elect one of their own number as representative. The expectation that the voter should be a resident of the county in which he voted was confirmed in an election law of 1705.[2] But the requirement of the law fell behind the pace of social development, in this case through the accumulation of landed property. It was no longer unusual for landowners to hold property in more than one county. The reform introduced by the Assembly of 1736 was significant of the interests and composition of that body. The requirement of residence, as such, was dropped, and the landowner was thenceforth allowed to vote in each county in which he owned sufficient land to meet the property qualification. As elections usually lasted several days plural voting became a practical possibility.

Lesser planters, whose holdings happened to lie across a county boundary, might also benefit from this move. But it must be remembered that the amount remained, in each county, twenty-five acres planted and with a house, or one hundred acres without. This meant that the law-makers had no reservations about giving one man more than one vote. It is a revealing measure. For it demonstrates once again the profound permeation of political ideas by the concept of property — or property as a social entity, requiring representation, so to speak, through its owner. This provision was wholly acceptable to prevailing ideas of social justice. If a landowner held property in counties A and B, then the acts of the Assembly in regard to county A would affect his interest there, and its acts in regard to county B would equally affect him as a landowner in B. As much legislation did in fact touch local government, such a line of argument was reasonable. Needless to add, the power of the greater men was commensurately increased. A man's property became the measure of his political influence. Virginia was a single province, and its Assembly was a single legislature, claiming to be a provincial parliament. A man whose local interests entitled him to representation in

[1] McKinley believed this to have been a unique provision. *Suffrage Franchise*, 40.
[2] Hening, *Statutes*, iii. 238.

two counties, or more, became by the same token a man with two or more votes in the election of this General Assembly; whatever the local interest, when his rights were seen from the provincial point of view, they were raised by his property above the level of his fellow subjects.

To this was attached the old and enduring idea that a genuine interest in the locality was determined by time. A year's possession of the property directly before the election was a condition of the qualification. But here again, property itself had in certain cases the power to transform its master, for those who had the good fortune to acquire their lands by inheritance or by marriage gained from their touch an immediate right to vote.

The growth of towns in Virginia long remained more notable in prospect than achievement. Charters often represented the intention to build a town rather than its existence, which makes it easy to infer from the legal records the development of a widespread town life which in fact did not exist. In the few towns which undoubtedly did exist, the suffrage was defined by their charters of incorporation. It was soon obvious that the ordinary freehold idea of a property qualification would not give an adequate representation to the equivalent interests of trade and manufacture. Moreover, a more generous idea of the kind of personal independence expected in the voter prevailed in regard to the towns, perhaps partly in order to encourage their growth. In Williamsburg and Norfolk, a freehold plot bearing a house 'in tenantable repair', and of the modest dimensions of twelve feet square, was enough to qualify the owner to vote; and would do so whether held in single or in joint tenancy, joint tenants being entitled to a single vote between them. Even a non-freeholder of twelve months' residence could vote if he possessed a 'visible estate' worth fifty pounds in current money. The liberty extended to those whose training confirmed them as artisans, provided they showed their commitment to the extent of being 'housekeepers' as well as inhabitants; when such men had been apprenticed for five years to a trade within the city, and had obtained a certificate to that effect from the court of hustings, they too were entitled to vote. But indentured servants were excluded.[1]

Although the Act of 1736 remained until the Revolution as the definitive election law of the province, it later ceased to represent the will of the House of Burgesses — a point which invites some scepticism as to its influence in determining the conduct of elections. By 1762 the burgesses had decided that the process of making the General Assembly conform to the practices of the House of Commons should be taken to the stage of establishing a regular seven-year term of office. This view probably arose from the repeated

[1] Hening, *Statutes* (May 1742), v. 206, for Assembly.

clashes between the claims of the House and the prerogative of the Governor, which had increased in acerbity since Governor Dinwiddie in 1752 imposed a fee unknown since William III of one pistole[1] for each grant of land issued under his seal. The French and Indian wars exacerbated the problem of authority. In 1754 the House refused to send a delegation to the Albany Congress, and it later went so far as to interfere with the Governor's control of military operations by detailing the uses to which military appropriations were to be put.[2]

The Act of 1762 was a comprehensive measure, designed to deal with all the problems in the character of the House of Burgesses that had arisen since the earlier legislation. The power of the Governor, with the advice of the Council, to determine the time and length of all Assembly sessions, must have seemed increasingly dangerous to the burgesses as experience multiplied the examples of clashes of will which often seemed to correspond to clashes of interest. The most important feature of the new measure was the limitation of the life of an Assembly to seven years, with the provision that a new one was to be called not more than three years after the dissolution of the old.[3]

This proposed statute also embodied an attempt to extend the suffrage. By a new provision, the area of freehold land, without house or plantation, to be held in order to qualify the holder to vote for burgesses was reduced from 100 to 50 acres. The preamble contained no indication of the motive for this change. The House, however, had by this time begun the practice of maintaining an agent in London for the purpose of representing its interests with the Board of Trade, and the House Committee of Correspondence, writing to the agent, dwelt mainly on the question of the length of the legislative term. 'The Reasons for the several other amendments', it said, 'will readily occur to you by comparing this Act with those that are repealed by it.'[4]

Although no explicit reasons were advanced, it is not difficult to see why the intended reform of the suffrage should have been generally acceptable and why, therefore, they would 'readily occur' to the agent when he compared this with former acts. One effect of the reduction of the required amount of uncleared land from 100 to 50 acres would have been to increase the voting power of the larger landowner. The absence of a residence

[1] One pistole was worth about 16s. 8d. in sterling at contemporary rates. Richard L. Morton, *Colonial Virginia*, 2 vols. (Chapel Hill, 1960), ii. 632.

[2] Flippin, *Royal Government*, 210–11.

[3] Hening, *Statutes* (November, 1762), vii, 517–30.

[4] *Virginia Magazine of History and Biography* (Richmond, 1893–), xi. 133–5.

requirement was already an advantage to those owning land in more than one county; the number of such beneficiaries would undoubtedly be increased.[1] But another and no less significant effect, especially in the back-country of the west, would be an increase in the number of qualified voters among the pioneer and poorer farmers. It would take these settlers some years to bring their first twenty-five acres under cultivation. The reform thus rendered the west more attractive to settlers, an object itself to be desired by the great speculative interests ambitiously engaged in the promotion of western land values. The rivalry between these groups of speculators called forth, in 1770, an anonymous charge that the Governor and Council had made immoderate grants of land west of the Alleghanies; to which William Nelson, who as President of the Council was senior official in the interim between Governors, replied that these grants, which had been made before 1763, were made to 'men of consequence who were most likely to be able to procure settlers'.[2] The price of land mentioned by Nelson was only three pounds (Virginian) for a hundred acres.

The interests of the many Tidewater planters who were engaged in land speculation were in this period not at variance with those of the settlers, who could be expected to want the right of political participation. But this common interest did not long survive the Revolution.

Another advantage of this reform to the larger landowners as a class was that it would enable them to enfranchise their sons by conveying land to them. No objection was raised in Britain to this proposal to extend the suffrage. There is a strong indication in a letter from Robert Carter that although other portions of the Act were unacceptable because they infringed the royal prerogative, the section on the qualifications of voters, if passed again, would meet with approval.[3]

The infringement of the prerogative, however, occurred in the main section, establishing the length of the terms of the Assembly. No colonial legislature under royal government was supposed to enjoy this right, a matter of which the Virginia House Committee of Correspondence showed some appreciation when, writing to Edward Montague, their London agent, they protested the Assembly's innocence of any such intention.[4] Governor

---

[1] Sydnor considered this to be the probable motive for the measure. Charles S. Sydnor, *Gentlemen Freeholders: Political Practices in Washington's Virginia* (Chapel Hill, 1952), 164.

[2] Nelson to Board of Trade, 18 October, 1770; CO 5, 1372/125-37.

[3] Carter wrote after attending a meeting of the Assembly committee of correspondence at which its London agent's letters on the subject were read. Robert Carter to Landon Carter, 21 January 1764, Landon Carter Papers, University of Virginia Library.

[4] *Virginia Magazine of History and Biography*, xi. 133-5.

Fauquier shared the burgesses' opinions about the reasonableness of the legislation, but added that it was his duty to draw the attention of the Board of Trade to the possibility of an infringement of the prerogative.[1] This proved to be a point of which their lordships had no need to be reminded. The measure was duly condemned by the Board's counsel, Sir Matthew Lamb; and the Board, noting that the statute contained the appropriate suspending clause, agreed to await further argument from the colony's agent. No further discussion is recorded in the Board's journal, however, and the Act failed to receive the royal assent.[2]

Most of the provisions of the rejected law of 1762 were re-enacted in a new Act of the session of 1769. The same extension of the suffrage was proposed, and the period of required previous tenure was reduced to six months, evidently a concession to new settlers, but although no objection appears to have been raised on points of major importance, the Act again failed of approval.[3]

It would however be risky to suppose that because an Act approved by the burgesses was disallowed for comparatively trivial reasons in England, it was therefore disused. The conduct of elections in each county was really controlled by the sheriff: and the evidence presented in cases of disputed elections, which appear in the pages of the *Journal of the House of Burgesses*, constantly revealed the wide measure of local discretion which the sheriffs exercised. It is hard to believe that an extension of the suffrage, which was already known to be the desire of the House, and was clearly desired by many of the people, could have been kept in restraint at the court houses of the counties. In the circumstances the House Committee on Elections would probably have proved unsympathetic to complaints of voting by freeholders whose lands met the measure set by the House itself. Half a century later, when the suffrage established in the Revolutionary period was under attack

---

[1] Fauquier to Board of Trade, 20 March 1763, CO 5, 1330/395-7.

[2] *Journal of the Commissioners of Trade and Plantations*, 1759-63 (London, 1935), 369 (hereafter referred to as *JCTP*).

[3] *JCTP*, 1768-75 and 1775-83 (London, 1937 and 1938) *passim*. The disapprobation of this measure was based on the exclusion of sheriffs and under-sheriffs from the House of Burgesses both during and for two years after their tenure of office. These officers were added, by the Acts of 1762 and 1769, to the list of excluded placemen, which already contained the tobacco inspectors. The board seems only to have queried the continuation of the exclusion for the two years after office. An adequate, and in fact an interesting, explanation was received from Lord Dunmore in October 1773. Board of Trade to Dunmore, 11 March 1773, CO 5, 1369/323-5; Dunmore to Board of Trade, 9 July 1773, CO 5, 1372/252-3.

from reformers, one of the leading defenders of the existing order drew the Act of 1769 into his argument. The Constitution of 1776 left the franchise unchanged; but, according to Benjamin Watkins Leigh, the makers of the Constitution knew that the disallowed Act of 1769 was really in effect. The phrase 'as at present exercised' would therefore mean as under that Act — giving an extensive suffrage.[1] Leigh was arguing a case, and arguing it from a time before his own, but probabilities support him.[2]

It is clear that the suffrage was often exercised in fact by persons to whom it did not belong as a right under the law. Virginians themselves both then and later had great difficulty in ascertaining, and remained uncertain of the extent of the suffrage either in fact or law. The scarcity of continuous series of tax lists or of voting lists makes definite statements precarious, but enough materials survive to establish a strong trend of probabilities.

Thomas Jefferson, when compiling his *Notes on Virginia*, looked into the suffrage question and came to the gloomy conclusion that the majority of men in the state who paid taxes and fought did not possess the right to vote. Estimates — not of voters, but of tithables and of freeholders paying quit-rents — had been drawn up and transmitted at earlier dates by Governor Dinwiddie (1756) and Auditor-General John Blair (1773) as information for the Board of Trade. To these surveys must now be added the much more detailed evidence of the distribution of property and of the actual exercise of the suffrage disclosed by the assiduous researches of Professor and Mrs Brown. The effect is certainly to make Jefferson's findings appear excessively gloomy.[3]

The character of a suffrage franchise based on property will obviously be affected by economic opportunity. The prevailing factors of cheap land, a population that grew without growing faster than the resources of the

[1] Benjamin Watkins Leigh, *Substitute Intended to be Offered to the Next Meeting of the Citizens of Richmond on the Subject of a Convention, in lieu of the Report of the Committee* (Richmond, 1824), 18. (Copy in Library of Congress.)

[2] The same view was expressed by an opponent of Leigh on reform: 'Before the Revolution [the non-freeholders] generally held the right of suffrage; after the Revolution, they are denied the right of suffrage. They are taxed without their consent.' 'Solon' in *Richmond Enquirer*, 24 December 1824.

[3] Thomas Jefferson, *Works*, ed. Worthington Chauncy Ford (New York, 1894), iii. 222. 'Tithables' in Virginia were all persons subject to the basic poll-tax. Masters were responsible for paying the poll-tax due on servants. Bruce, *Institutional History*, ii. 548–55. Robert E. Brown and B. Katherine Brown, *Virginia 1705–1786: Democracy or Aristocracy?* (East Lansing, Mich., 1964) (hereafter referred to as *Virginia*). For an early study, pointing in the same direction, see J. Franklin Jameson, 'Virginia Voting in the Colonial Period, 1744–1774', *The Nation*, lvi. 27 April 1893.

economy, and the all-important basis of a labour force of slavery and indentured servitude, combined to liberate a high proportion of the white
population to the extent of becoming owners of freehold or leasehold property
in land. The effect, taken together with the laxity and uncertainty in the
enforcement of the election laws from place to place, was to yield an effective
voting force which could rise to over sixty per cent of the white male population of adults and which under pressure could be pushed considerably
higher. When elections were closely contested the candidates, who themselves were always members of the gentry, showed a keener interest in
swelling their support by agreeing to a liberal interpretation of the franchise
than in a strict insistence on the letter of the law: at least until the election
was lost. The bitterness of defeat often led disappointed candidates to
challenge the return and dispute the election before the House of Burgesses.

The House Committee on Elections made a habit of examining the tax
rolls when hearing the evidence in disputed elections. The factor that extended the suffrage beyond the limits implied by freehold ownerships was the
agreement to treat tenants for life and tenants of long leases as freeholders
for purposes of voting. It is clear that a variety of practices was tolerated under
different sheriffs provided that, by local agreement, certain ground rules were
observed by both sides, and one may suspect that it was when these rules were
broken that the other side disputed the return. The House Committee faithfully maintained the landed qualification (except, of course, in cases of town
suffrage where it was not required) and the most frequent single ground of
objection to a voter was recorded as 'no freehold'.[1] Tenants could hardly
have expected to vote as a matter of right, and might either be turned away
by the sheriff or have their votes cancelled by the House of Burgesses.[2]

The evidence of suffrage practices in different counties under varying
local interpretations of the law is bound to be inconclusive. Men who acquired
enough property to enable them to vote may often have spent a fair portion of
their lives getting it. Given the basic condition that the economy was built
on the backs of a vast, unenfranchised labour force, the most important thing
to grasp is the trend rather than specific local conditions. 'By common
consent and contrary to law', concludes the most distinguished historian of
the subject, 'a local movement toward universal manhood suffrage was on
foot.'[3] It was a period of ambitious activity, involving men of all ranks in

---

[1] Sydnor, *Gentlemen Freeholders*, 20–21. Brown, *Virginia*, chaps. i and vii.

[2] *Journals of the House of Burgesses*, ed. H. R. McIlwaine (Richmond, 1909), record
details of evidence in election disputes throughout the period.

[3] Sydnor, *Gentlemen Freeholders*, 20–21.

prospects of enrichment in the west. The gentry of Virginia, who were not a European aristocracy, strove with some success to emulate the character of an eighteenth-century oligarchy: but it was not one of ancient and effete families clinging to power against the tide — on the contrary, it was vigorous, furiously ambitious, and tolerably open to recruitment. The 'open' side of this society did not long survive the American Revolution; and without the Revolution it is at least possible that its mood might have been reversed even sooner. The facts that property was widespread and relatively easy to acquire did nothing to liberalise the legislators towards those who fell outside the circle of property owners, or who might do so at some future period. The law based on property could be and often was permissively administered. But a marked and effective restriction could be brought about by a mere change in the mood of the administration, without any change in the principle of the law. In fact, no new restrictions had been enacted in Virginia when, even before Jefferson's Republican Party had won a national election, bitter complaints against suffrage restriction began to reach the House. Universal suffrage was assuredly not the basis of Virginian political society when Jefferson led his party to victory in the Federal government in 1800; and that party did nothing to make the suffrage more liberal in his own state.

8. Between Members and Constituents: What did Elections decide?

Elections in Virginia were enormously enjoyable public entertainments which temporarily brought the gentry down to the common level. On certain occasions, even in the first half of the eighteenth century, the electorate used an Assembly election to express their feelings on specific issues; but the ordinary course was to leave the running of the Province to the larger owners of its land. The same sense of deference and hierarchy was reflected in the organisation of the House of Burgesses. In each county the court was the centre of the electoral system — the men who controlled local government were those from whose numbers the representatives were chosen. Strict conventions of propriety governed the conduct of elections, and 'electioneering' was frowned on. Yet these conventions came under a very great strain when competition grew keen. The growth of political parties, in the 1790s, began to shake the older proprieties and to cause an acute tension between the old order of politics and the new.

THE jocular familiarity of elections in Virginia both before and after the Revolution, the occasionally large turnout of voters and the keen competition between candidates give its politics an attractive air of republican vitality. In fact, however, this appearance can be deeply deceptive. The role of the electorate was extremely circumscribed. The voters were called into action to elect a new House of Burgesses in the colonial period about once every three years;[1] they knew little of issues, had practically no opportunity to read political debates, and were very rarely called on to make decisions that would determine between alternative policies. They formed an essentially deferential electorate who willingly acknowledged the leadership and authority of the gentry. Membership of the gentry was a condition which conferred the right to participate in politics; an attempt to participate might be an ambitious man's test of whether his social standing was recognised by his county neighbours. In face of keen competition, the laws and conventions which precluded active advocacy of one's own cause began to break down; the disgraceful practice of 'electioneering' gradually became a painful necessity — and never ceased, for its beneficiaries, to be a feast of entertainment. If the suffrage was fairly wide shortly before the Revolution, it was a suffrage that did not threaten the existing social leadership; and long afterwards, in the era of the Republican Party, the politics of Virginia continued in large measure to be dominated by a recognised upper class; the Republican Party of Virginia represented the mobilisation of that leadership in the interest of capturing the Federal government.

The key to this Republican leadership after the emergence of the national issues on which political parties were built up, was the continued claim of the Republican gentry to the loyalty and support of the freeholders. When personal competition, which had begun to open the system, gave place to competition on divisive issues such as Jay's Treaty of 1794, it became all the more important for Republican leaders to stand together, and to maintain the unity of that social fabric of which they had always stood as the recognised heads. Their success in this enterprise enabled them to withstand the pressure for a more democratic suffrage and for a reapportionment of seats in the

---

[1] Lucille Blanche Griffith, 'The Virginia House of Burgesses, 1750–1774' (Ph.D. thesis, Brown University 1957), 73 (hereafter referred to as 'House of Burgesses').

Assembly for another generation. For heirs and bearers of the amateur tradition, it was no mean political achievement.

The crucial event in any system of representation is the election itself. The procedure changed very little in Virginia throughout the eighteenth century and its main features could still be recognised in the days of Jackson. For all concerned an election was an important and exciting event. The poll was not movable, and voters had to come up for the day, often passing a night on the journey accommodated by one of the candidates or his supporters. To open the proceedings in the court house the sheriff, after reading aloud the writ, took his place behind the long table, at each end of which sat the candidates. If, as usually happened, a poll was required because the result could not be decided by shout, the electors filed up, one by one, announced their votes and were then, as a rule, entitled to be thanked by the gentleman of their choice. 'Sir, I shall treasure that vote as long as I live'; 'Sir, may you live a thousand years', were acceptable epithets from a grateful recipient. The elections often lasted all day, and might go on for two or three, but when the sheriff was satisfied that all the votes had been taken he might close the poll at his own discretion. Before doing so he was expected to give public warning lest any intending voters remained outside. The sheriff's return was transmitted to the House of Burgesses and would serve to certify the claim of the elected candidates to their seats. Before this, however, the effects of the rum, of which prodigious quantities were available in the taverns and the houses of the candidates' supporters, had usually begun to make themselves known. An election without a fight would have been almost as rare as a western movie without a shooting bout.[1]

The records of voting in the colonial period do not yield any continuous series by which to establish the proportion of participants. But groups of returns from several counties, in 1755 and in 1771, together with a number of other more isolated cases, show that between 30 and 40 per cent of the adult white males frequently made their way to the polls, the proportion sometimes reaching up to 60 per cent.[2] These are high figures. Track roads, fords, and freshets often made the going difficult; and the casting of a vote for one gentleman or the other could hardly seem much inducement to such exertions. But elections were social events. The rivalry between backers of different candidates was often of the sporting kind, like that of football

[1] The most attractive account of Virginia elections is, and will probably remain, that of Charles Sydnor, *Gentlemen Freeholders*, chap. 4.
[2] Jameson, 'Virginia Voting'; Griffith, 'House of Burgesses', 89–93. Brown, *Virginia*, ch. vii.

teams, excited but inconsequential. Meanwhile the election was a hilarious county reunion, and best of all it was a time when the mighty were forced to show fellowship with the common freeholders amid much back-slapping, rum tippling, and protestation of political reticence.

Representation in Virginia was not based on the assumption that conflicting interests called for conflicting spokesmen. Each county was supposed to have its own homogeneity of character,[1] deriving no doubt from the earliest settlements, and the county would naturally want to be represented by its most distinguished citizen. It was no small part of communal pride. That was the nature of his distinction. In the Assembly he would be expected to confront, on equal terms, the weightiest men of other communities. Such gentlemen were not expected to vulgarise themselves by making crude promises of material betterment. Only men striving for advancement adopted such ungentlemanly methods.

Virginia counties, especially those in the Tidewater and Piedmont, were politically dominated by their magnates. Issues seldom entered elections, and even when they did it was often agreed that the natural leaders were the best men to entrust with the decisions. There could be no more striking instance than the fact that even in the elections to the Virginia ratifying Convention for the Federal Constitution, many districts were content to elect their two leading men regardless of the fact that they were of opposite opinions on the Constitution, while eight delegates voted contrary to the wishes of their constituents without any apparent loss of popularity.[2]

Early organisers of the Republican Party both noticed and made use of the leading factor of personal influence. 'The elections in Virginia', Madison informed James Monroe, who was in Paris, 'are over and in part known. The only two districts in which the election turned on *political* rather than *personal* considerations, were those in which Alexandria and Winchester stand.'[3] And it is significant that these were city, not country, districts. John Randolph, reporting Federalist successes eight years later, remarked that the elections had been governed by 'personal and local, rather than political, considerations', which he repeated with emphasis to another correspondent. He was not of course anxious to admit Republican defeats, but was probably

[1] J. A. C. Chandler, writing a history of representation in 1895, still maintained this view. *History of Representation in Virginia* (Baltimore, 1896), 83.

[2] Jay B. Hubbell and Douglass Adair (eds.), Colonel Robert Munford, *The Candidates: or, the Humours of a Virginia Election* (Williamsburg, 1948), Introduction, 10. R. A. Brock (ed.), Hugh Blair Grigsby, *History of the Virginia Federal Convention of 1788*, 2 vols. (Richmond, 1890–1), i. 34.

[3] Madison to Monroe, 27 March 1795; Madison Papers, Library of Congress.

justified in declaring, in 1803, that Virginia 'was never more united in opinion than at this time'.[1]

These remarks only represented a continuation of old tradition. In an agrarian commonwealth, great landed property naturally induced political power, and in view of the chronic shortage of white labour, the larger slave-owner became a virtual lord of his neighbourhood.

The authority of the leadership of Virginia was demonstrated in moments of crisis. It had even been at work in subtle form in 1735, when the bigger planters had gone up to the Assembly with a virtual mandate to reverse the tobacco inspection laws, but after manfully failing in the attempt, had nevertheless succeeded in keeping control firmly in their own hands.[2]

In the Revolution there were few defections from that leadership, though it is probable that admissions to it had begun to broaden a little since the death of Robinson in 1766. But the hardships of the war grated on the poor, some of whom began to suspect the gentry of indulging desires for independence for selfish purposes. The militia became disobedient; soldiers agreed secretly to oppose any order to march them out of the State. 'I fear', wrote John Augustine Washington to Richard Henry Lee, 'we have among us some designing dangerous characters who misrepresent to ignorant, uninformed people, the situation of our affairs and the nature of the contest, making them believe it is a war produced by the wantonness of the gentlemen, and that the poor are very little if any interested. . . .'[3] The effects of unpopular measures by the gentry and at the same time the necessity for gentry leadership to rally the country, were both brought out in the anxiety which followed from the election of Colonel Harrison, 'an aristocratical gentleman', as Speaker of the House in 1778. 'Our friend Mr Jefferson was greatly out-voted', wrote another of Lee's informants, explaining that the majority of members present were from the lower counties on the James and York rivers. 'Pray inform our republican friends the true cause of that appointment, that they may not for a moment entertain the thought that we are lapsing into aristocracy. . . . We have many true Whigs, and they are upon their guard.' He added the revealing observation, 'The spark of liberty is not yet extinct among our people, & if properly faned [sic] by the gentn. of influence, will, I make no doubt, burst out again into a flame.'[4]

---

[1] John Randolph to James Monroe, 15 June 1803; to Nicholson, 14 June 1803; Bruce Randolph Collection, i. 141, 144, Virginia State Library.

[2] Williams, 'Political Alignments', 285–9.

[3] 20 June 1778; Lee Papers, University of Virginia.

[4] Mann Page to R. H. Lee, 15 May 1778; Lee Papers.

Exactly the same type of sentiment recurred, though the crisis was very different, when the Virginia Republicans rallied support in the election of 1800. 'The present crisis', wrote one of Madison's correspondents, 'loudly demands the patronage and exertions of influential gentlemen; and it appears to me that our liberties and happiness can be supported only by their coalition.'[1] The Republicans of Pennsylvania depended on the same type of social organisation. 'We rely on the activity of all the men of property and influence in the Republican interest', wrote Alexander Dallas in 1799.[2] This tendency for political leadership to fall to the propertied gentry and merchants was so strong that even in Kentucky, whose Constitution (with that of Vermont) was the first to adopt universal white manhood suffrage, the old Virginian George Nicholas feared it would prove irresistible. 'The wealthy', he told Madison, 'will nineteen times out of twenty be chosen. The House of Representatives will therefore always have a majority at least of its members men of property. The Senate will be composed altogether of that class. I will give up my opinion as soon as I see a man in rags chosen to that body.' He remarked sourly that he knew Madison would not approve of the total disregard for property qualifications both in electors and elected; but, said Nicholas, 'Exclude any particular class of citizens and sooner or later they will be oppressed. . . .'[3] And in that sentence he cut through Madison's Whig conventions to state a precept of democracy.

The insistent tendency of Virginian society to form itself on lines of rank and eminence reappeared to determine the character of the House of Burgesses before the Revolution. On a close analysis, however, it would certainly prove that many of the men who got into the House of Burgesses were neither great planters nor men of any particular distinction. Spotswood's contemptuous remarks in 1715 about the low character and abilities of the burgesses, though obviously prejudiced, cannot have been without substance. In 1758 one of Richard Henry Lee's correspondents told him of the election of two new burgesses because he 'knew no better way to support the independence of the legislature and guard the liberty of the subject than by now and then shifting the representatives of the people, especially those who have neither natural nor acquired parts to recommend them'.[4] But the elected

[1] Charles Polk to James Madison, 20 June 1800; Madison Papers.
[2] Stephen G. Kurtz, *The Presidency of John Adams* (Philadelphia, 1957), 385–6 (hereafter referred to as *John Adams*).
[3] George Nicholas to Madison, 2 May 1792; Madison Papers.
[4] Alexander White to R. H. Lee, 1758; Lee Papers, University of Virginia.

gentry recognised their own upper class, to whom they accorded a respect and leadership in the all-important committee system of the House. Although the general elections of the eighteenth century often resulted in fairly extensive alterations in membership, they seldom unsettled the leaders. In 1756, for example, no fewer than forty-one new members came into a House numbering 105, but the leadership remained in much the same hands.[1] The central pillar of this establishment was Speaker John Robinson, first elected to that office in 1735, and thereafter both Speaker and Treasurer till his death in 1766. It was the Speaker who made most of the appointments to committees and through whose good offices the great families exercised their traditional control of the legislative process. He was in this both their good servant and their representative.

The proceedings of the House were continuously dominated by a select few. Between 1720 and 1776, out of 630 who sat throughout that period, these few numbered only 110. Only some twenty members continually took a leading part in its activities, and most of the leaders were actually provided by three families — the Robinsons, the Randolphs, and the Lees.[2]

It is likely that the incursion into Williamsburg of Patrick Henry, and the weaknesses exposed by the notorious scandal of John Robinson's estate, which revealed to the world the fact that many of the leading men of the province had relied on secret loans out of public funds,[3] probably helped to loosen the system. Robinson's successor as Speaker, Peyton Randolph, offered committee assignments to more members than before;[4] but even this may have been a manoeuvre rather than a gesture, for inner groups never have much difficulty in controlling large committees.

This Virginia leadership was regarded by its contemporaries — and particularly by its opponents — as an aristocracy. Supporters of Jefferson would call its principles 'aristocratic', a term of opprobrium opposite but similar to

[1] Griffith, 'House of Burgesses,' 70; *Journals of the House of Burgesses,* 1752–5 and 1756–8, Introduction, xxv.

[2] Jack P. Greene, 'Foundations of Political Power in the Virginia House of Burgesses, 1720–1766', *William and Mary Quarterly* (October 1959), 485–6. Robert LeRoy Hilldrup, 'The Virginia Convention of 1776' (Ph.D. thesis, University of Virginia), 1935, 9–10.

[3] Robinson lent to the heavily indebted planters of the Tidewater the paper money which, under British law, was supposed to have been called in, but which as Treasurer he was able to dispose of. When exposed after his death it caused the greatest financial scandal of the whole of American history, up to that time. See the masterly analysis by David J. Mays, *Edmund Pendleton, 1721–1803* (Cambridge, Mass., 1952), esp. i, chap. 2.

[4] Greene, 'Political Power', 486.

'democratic' when used of good republican Whigs — who were not democrats. Such designations must be kept in a due proportion. The great Virginia
landowners did not make large incomes out of rent rolls; the social and
economic equivalent lay in their slaves. Their mansions would have served
as gatehouses on the estates of European noblemen. They were in fact
gentry. Virginia had its fair share of Squire Westerns; and the cultural
distinctions of the Virginians of this class belong rather to the realm of
historical piety than of probable fact.[1] In areas of recent settlement any
serious degree of educational depth was almost unattainable. Conditions in
the Valley during the revolutionary period were alarmingly primitive; when
Jefferson and Madison tried to spread the gospel of their Republican Party
they were dismayed by the limited circulation and reading of newspapers,
which were almost unknown in the West and were very little read outside
the Tidewater and the towns.[2] Yet even in the Valley the social tendency
was in the same direction: nearly all the Valley's political leaders in the
Revolution were themselves the proprietors of the larger estates.[3] Representation in Virginia was a process of social selection. It was in fact the
American version of the very unpopular theory of virtual representation.
That definition was actually adopted by a later Virginian conservative in an
open defence of the system.[4]

But an upper class is defined, realistically, in relation to its subordinates.
The system which the county magnates of Virginia built up in the generation after Bacon's Rebellion was not a tightly closed one. The ordinary voter
stood much closer to his representative in Virginia than he was likely to do
in England; it was easier for men of ability, such as Edmund Pendleton, to
rise through the ranks — though Pendleton had the patronage of a great
family. A process of appraisal and selection, of prudent recruitment from
the ranks, was conducted by the local magnates in their own counties.

The agency of this process was the county court. Although the county
court in no way resembled the New England town meeting, and did not
nominate or elect representatives, it played an indispensable part in the
representative system, and the government of Virginia would have been unworkable without it. Bearing far more directly on the lives of the people

[1] On which see Carl Bridenbaugh, *Myths and Realities: Societies of the Colonial South*
(Baton Rouge, 1952), chap. 1.

[2] F. H. Hart, *The Valley of Virginia in the American Revolution* (Chapel Hill, 1942), 26;
Jefferson to Madison, 5 February 1795; Madison to Jefferson, 5 May 1798; Madison Papers.

[3] Hart, 58.

[4] Benjamin Watkins Leigh, *Substitute . . . proposed by Mr Leigh, of Dinwiddie . . . on the
. . . Right to Instruct . . . Senators* (n.p., n.d. [1812]).

than the remote and occasional meetings of the legislature in Williamsburg — and after the Revolution in Richmond — the county court held in its hands all the reins of local government. It was modelled on that of Elizabethan England. In addition to dispensing justice in criminal, common law, and equity cases, it determined the tax rate for the year, appointed local assessors, licensed ordinaries, and fixed the prices of liquor, provender, lodging, stabling, and fodder, decided on the making and maintenance of public buildings, roads, and bridges, and appointed certain county officers. The justices sent up each year to the Governor's Council three names chosen from their own number for selection as sheriff — the most lucrative post in the county. Entirely untrammelled by responsibility to the voters, the county magistrates filled vacancies among themselves virtually by co-option, since it was customary for the Governor and Council to make new appointments from nominations supplied by the court.

The county court did not itself nominate candidates for the Assembly; but elections were conducted in the court house, by the sheriff. So closely was the court knit into the process by which the county itself was represented in the House of Burgesses that the sheriff was required to publish, at every church and chapel in the county, a notice inviting people to present 'Propositions and grievances and the public claims' to a special session of the court, called for the purpose of hearing them. These, duly certified by the clerk of the court, were handed over to the burgesses. Thus the court system was the channel for the representation of the needs of the county to the burgesses, who in turn would take its problems to the Assembly.[1]

The House of Burgesses had powers superior to those of the courts; but one of the ways in which it resembled the House of Commons was in representing a kind of federation of county oligarchies.

Conflicts within the leadership of Virginia's deeply deferential electorate were usually conflicts of personal ambition. It was not only improper, but illegal, to advance these ambitions by making promises to the voters: such promises were classed as bribes and therefore fell under the designation of corrupt practices. The election laws merely reflected the conventional proprieties. As early as 1705 these had expressly forbidden candidates either to treat prospective candidates with food or drink or to solicit their votes in

---

[1] Mays, *Pendleton*, 42–61. An admirable account of the court also appears in Charles S. Sydnor, *The Development of Southern Sectionalism* (Baton Rouge, 1948), chap. ii, which makes an interestingly close comparison with that on the county court in J. D. Black, *The Reign of Queen Elizabeth* ('Oxford History of England' (Oxford, 1959)).

return for promises.[1] These conventions soon collapsed in face of the will to succeed; but personal bribery was tolerated for a long time before the making of more general political or economic offers for the advantage of the voters came to be permitted. All of such advances were held to intrude on the freedom of the elector to make up his own mind; they offended against that cherished liberty, his independence.

Yet offers to work in the interest of the public, however immoral, were not unknown. The elections of 1715 and 1735 did in fact turn in large measure on actual issues of policy. What was despised and repudiated was the endeavour of an individual — particularly if he happened to be unpopular — to win himself a seat by some kind of personal policy. An offender of this kind — an old contender called Matthew Marrable — was unseated after an election in 1758 in Lunenburg County. Marrable was alleged to have promised in writing 'to do something extraordinary for the freeholders of the Upper Settlement, or to forfeit a large sum of money, in order to gain their votes'. The something extraordinary proved to be a proposed division of the county so as to give the upper section independent county status. Marrable was elected by an expectant majority, after 'a large number of freeholders came to Mr Marrable's and were genteelly entertained', and, in fact, after no fewer than thirty gallons of rum had been expended; but on hearing of these improprieties the House decided that Marrable had been unduly elected and deprived him of his seat.[2]

In the later era of 'internal improvements' Marrable's programme would have struck everyone as not only reasonable but modest. This kind of claim would soon be a perfectly legitimate local election issue. The people of the county were directly affected; demands for the creation of new counties by the division of old ones were frequent and in fact were frequently agreed to when they came up to the legislature in the form of petitions. It was a real need when counties were so large that a visit to the court house involved a day's journey and a night's lodging — often with the expense of ferriage.

In view of the familiarity of the burgesses with the practice of election 'treating' it seems possible that they were actuated by personal prejudice against Marrable. 'Swilling the planters with bumbo' — the local term for rum — was an ordinary election procedure in the Virginia in which George Washington grew up. Treating at elections seems to have been even heavier and more costly in Virginia at this period than it was in the English counties shortly before the Reform Act.[3] But the dislike of open vote-seeking long

[1] Hening, *Statutes*, iii. 243.   [2] *Journal of the House of Burgesses* (1758–61), 14, 83–84.
[3] Norman Gash, *Politics in the Age of Peel* (London, 1953), 119.

continued to be deeply engrained. Things changed slowly in Virginia, and the convention was still serious enough to cause an acute dilemma in the career of James Madison when he sought election to Congress in 1788.

Writing from Philadelphia, Madison explained his reluctance to return to Virginia to counteract the machinations against his election to the House of Representatives, saying, 'It will have an electioneering appearance which I always despised and wished to shun. . . .' Nevertheless, he was given severely practical advice: 'Upon the whole, the Baptist interest seems everywhere to prevail. . . . I think upon such an occasion, I wd. even solicit their interest, thro some friends or in some proper manner.' 'I know', wrote another correspondent, urging him to return for the election, 'this has not been your usual practice, and am certain that it will be very irksome to you, but your friends hope that you will make some sacrifices however disagreeable they may be. . . .' Madison summed up his anxieties in a letter to Washington which gives pitiful expression to a not uncommon dilemma:

But I am pressed much in several quarters [he wrote] to try the effect of presence on the district into which I fall, for electing a Representative; and am much apprehensive that an omission of that expedient, may eventually expose me to blame. At the same time I have an extreme distaste to steps having an electioneering appearance, altho' they should lead to an appointment in which I am disposed to serve the public; and am very dubious moreover whether any step which might seem to denote a solicitude on my part would not be as likely to operate against as in favor of my pretensions. . . .[1]

A candidate convinced that service to the public and his own career are identical objects seldom fails to find the practical solution. Madison did go back, and was elected.

At the time of Madison's election to the House of Representatives, it was still unusual for a public man to enter politics for political reasons. Though political life engrossed a large proportion of the time and care of many of Madison's eminent contemporaries, it was not a career in itself, but the consequence — the duty incurred in consequence — of a superior station in life. Men entered the House of Burgesses (after 1776, the House of Delegates) for similar reasons to those adduced by Namier in his famous account of why men went into Parliament.[2] Energy and self-esteem combined to

[1] Madison to Edmund Randolph, 23 November 1788; Burgess Ball to Madison, 8 December 1788; Hardin Burnley to Madison, 16 December 1788; Madison to Washington, 2 December 1788. Madison Papers.

[2] L. B. Namier, *The Structure of Politics at the Accession of George III*, 2 vols. (London, 1929), i, chap. i.

spur men to seek this, the most dignified and celebrated form of public recognition.

But the transition from the older and more settled way, under which actual canvassing was deprecated and the making of promises was technically equated with the offering of bribes, to the more modern style of aggressive stump campaigning, marks a profound change in the concept of political representation. For a long time, the two attitudes persisted side by side; and both candidates seeking votes, and constituents seeking assurances, disclaimed any intention of advancing the practice of deliberate electioneering.

Election ambitions were closely allied to social position. 'In this part of the state, and from hence back,' wrote an informed observer in Charlotte County, in 1807, 'there are no persons honoured by the confidence of the public, except in this way, and hence it is that every decent man is striving to get a seat in the legislature.'[1] 'Every decent man'; but evidently some others, for he went on:

There are violent contests everywhere that I have seen, to the great anoyance [*sic*] of old John Barleycorn, who suffers greatly in the fray. It is remarkable what a mania pervades the bar on this subject. There is hardly a county where some man who thinks highly of his own pretensions (and often with good reason) does not appear to make it the height of his ambition to be associated with some popular blackguard, and in his endeavour to attain this, to be willing to take the risque of a defeat at the hands of some still greater blackguard.

The association of worthy with doubtful characters in the pursuit of electoral ambitions was illustrated by a leading Virginia planter of the older generation in an early comedy, *The Candidates*, written in 1770.[2] This piece, said to be one of the earliest extant American comedies, shows the struggle that takes place after the announced retirement from politics of the local magnate, a personage of suffocating stateliness called Worthy. Three new men, Sir John Toddy, Mr Strutabout and Mr Smallhopes vie for his place; the blessing of Mr Wou'dbe, who is less great than Worthy but superior to the rest, is sought by the competitors as a valuable aid to election. But the dangers that threaten the county from such ignoble representation bring Worthy back to duty, and in association with Wou'dbe, he is elected with acclamation.

The Candidates is as keen a commentary on its subject as could be found

[1] Nathaniel Beverley Tucker to St. George Tucker, 25 April 1807; Tucker-Coleman Papers, Colonial Williamsburg.
[2] Colonel Robert Munford, *The Candidates*.

in any treatise.[1] Despite their conflicting claims, the most significant distinction between the candidates — for Sir John, Strutabout, and Smallhopes rely more on their vanity and promises than on their social standing — is implied but never even expressed. The fact emerges that Worthy not only does not have to canvass, but is not expected to make any sort of statement of his intentions at all. If he were to do so he would not be Worthy.

Some good republicans hoped that the Revolution would purify American politics.

[1] The disintegration of the old prohibition on promises is brought out with vigour:

Wou'dbe: . . . I'll make it a point of duty to dispatch the business, and my study to promote the good of my county.

Guzzle: Yes, Damn it, you all promise mighty fair, but the devil a bit do you perform; there's Strutabout, now, he'll promise to move mountains. He'll make the rivers navigable, and bring the tide over the tops of the hills, for a vote.

And further:

Twist: Moreover, I've heard a 'sponsible man say, he could prove you were the cause of these new taxes.

Wou'dbe: Do you believe that too? or can you believe that it's in the power of any individual to make a law himself? If a law is enacted that is displeasing to the people, it has the concurrence of the whole legislative body, and my vote, for, or against it, is of little consequence.

Guzzle: And what the devil good do you do then?

Wou'dbe: As much as I have abilities to do.

Guzzle: Suppose, Mr Wou'dbe, we were to want to get the price of rum lower'd — wou'd you do it?

Wou'dbe: I cou'd not.

Guzzle: Huzza for Sir John! he has promised to do it, huzza for Sir John!

Twist: Suppose, Mr Wou'dbe, we should want this tax taken off — cou'd you do it?

Wou'dbe: I could not.

Twist: Huzza for Mr Strutabout! he's damn'd, if he don't. Huzza for Mr Strutabout!

Stern: Suppose, Mr Wou'dbe, we that live over the river, should want to come to church on this side, is it not very hard we should pay ferryage; when we pay as much to the church as you do?

Wou'dbe: Very hard.

Stern: Suppose we were to petition the assembly could you get us clear of that expence?

Wou'dbe: I believe it to be just; and make no doubt but it would pass into a law.

Stern: Will you do it?

Wou'dbe: I will endeavour to do it.

Stern: Huzza for Mr Wou'dbe! Wou'dbe forever!

A minor feature of the small talk of the freeholders is the deference shown for persons of 'larning'. It was a popular belief that reading improved the mind and so was good preparation for public responsibility; but reading was also supposed to be a characteristic of the greater planter, who had some leisure and a library. (*Wou'dbe*: [to his servant] I'm going into my library, and if any gentleman calls, you may introduce him to me there.)

I had hoped [wrote Edmund Pendleton in 1785] that our annual elections would have put a stop to every species of bribery, and restored perfect freedom in our choice of representatives in General Assembly, but I am sorry to find myself disappointed. In a neighbouring county ... three candidates have employed as many months in canvassing, not only from house to house, but at frequent and expensive treats; a species of bribery, the more dangerous, since it is masqued, and appears not in its plain shape as an offered piece of gold would. In our County, a new declaring candidate at the last Court, made a sacrifice of much wine, bottles and glasses to the fortunate Deities.

But Pendleton was not ready to admit the failure of annual elections. They must wait patiently for the good effects which, with the aid of honest if simple republican sentiment would, though slow, be 'certain and permanent'.[1]

In the Federalist era, for perhaps ten years, political parties and national issues intruded into Virginian politics. A two-party system hardly took root in the state; but the party contest helped to splinter the fences of the old régime. It encroached on the personal character of the relationship between representative and electors by introducing considerations of general and impersonal policy.

Electors began to meet to inform their representatives of their opinions of their performance; and, an equally unusual departure, representatives began to report the proceedings of the session to their constituents. During John Adams's presidency, John Clopton and Samuel J. Cabell, Virginia members of Congress, distributed printed circular letters about congressional proceedings, a practice that gave rise to an instructive controversy. A Federalist grand jury in Richmond 'presented' this practice as an evil requiring attention, to which Clopton's constituents returned the compliment by re-electing him; a gesture he acknowledged with another circular.[2] Meanwhile the Republican Party, fearlessly mobilising public opinion as a force to influence events, developed a technique of carefully organised county meetings on political issues.[3]

The aims of parties encroached not only on the former privacy of the relationship between electors and representatives but, in a subtle way, on the tradition against campaign promises. If a candidate could be called on — even instructed — to throw his vote and influence on certain prescribed lines,

---

[1] To R. H. Lee, 14 March 1785; Lee Papers.

[2] J. Dawson to Madison, 25 February 1794, Madison Papers. Circulars in John Clopton Papers, Duke University Library; John Clopton broadside letter to his constituents, June 1797.

[3] Harry Ammon, 'The Republican Party in Virginia, 1789–1824' (Ph.D. thesis, University of Virginia, 1948), 172–3.

it might be argued that, by agreeing or offering to do so, he was making a corrupt promise. The tension between the older ideas and newer needs was exposed in an interesting letter from the citizens of Norfolk to their state representative, Littleton W. Tazewell, later to be a leading figure in Virginian politics. 'We hope never to see the day', they began, 'when the principle of representation, the soul of our republic, shall be abused, polluted, and corrupted by the adoption of those electioneering arts which give the brazen and hollow sycophant the advantage over the man of modesty, virtue and talents. . . .' He had, therefore, a right to abstain from canvassing; but they on their side had a right to get his answer to several very pointed questions about his principles, which were suspected of being Federalist, and about his recent conduct in public office.[1]

In face of the demand for election pledges the reign of Worthy could not last much longer. Such demands implied another right, of which much has been heard in New England but very little in Virginia: that of instruction. Yet there is evidence that it was used at least once as early as 1754. Landon Carter's *Diary* refers to debates on

whether a representative was obliged to follow the directions of his constituents against his own reason and conscience or to be governed by his conscience. The arguments for implicit obedience were that the first institution of a representative was for avoiding the confusion of a multitude in assembly. He, therefore, ought to collect the sentiments of his constituents and whatever the majority willed ought to be the rule of his vote. Thus argued the favourers of popularity, who were all headed by the Speaker, [Robinson] for these were nearly his own words. The admirers of reason and liberty of conscience [to whom Carter obviously belonged] distinguished upon it and said, where the matter related particularly to the interest of the constituents alone, there implicit obedience ought to govern, but, where it was to affect the whole community, reason and good conscience should direct, for it must be absurd to suppose one part of the community could be apprized of the good of the whole without consulting the whole. For that part, therefore, to order an implicit vote must be absurd and the representative acting accordingly could only augment the absurdity because he must suppose his people so perverse as not to be moved by reasons ever so good that might be advanced by other parts of the community. . . .[2]

Carter had succinctly stated the argument against instruction. At the time of the Revolution he saw through another use of that doctrine. Representa-

---

[1] Citizens of Norfolk to L. W. Tazewell, 9 March 1805, Goldsborough-Wirt Papers Southern Historical Collection, University of North Carolina.

[2] Landon Carter Diary, 1754. I am indebted to Dr Jack P. Greene for drawing my attention to this passage, which is published by permission of the trustees of the Carter Papers.

tives could induce their constituents to 'instruct' them in favour of policies on which they were already determined, and though Carter believed Independence to be inevitable he questioned the advisability of circulating papers 'for poor ignorant creatures to sign as directions to their Delegates to endeavour at an Independency'.[1] In 1785, when the question of public support for religion was under discussion, counties with Presbyterian majorities instructed their delegates.[2] Both Republicans and Federalists discovered that instruction might have its uses — but also its embarrassments — during the controversy over Jay's Treaty. John Marshall, having called a big meeting in Richmond with the intention of getting instructions in favour of implementing the Treaty for transmission to the Virginia members of the House of Representatives, rapidly changed his plans when he found that he might be outvoted. Instead, said a hostile report, 'he betook himself to a petition, in which he said, all the inhabitants of Richmond, though not freeholders, might join'.[3]

When, in 1811, the United States Senators from Virginia denied their obligation to obey instructions voted by the state legislature which had elected them — the issue was the renewal of the Charter of the Bank of the United States — the doctrine was exposed to a searching public re-examination. Benjamin Watkins Leigh, who was later to lead the fight against reform of the state Constitution, published a pamphlet arguing the right of instruction from republican first principles. The debate was thus transferred to the national level, and the first question at issue was whether the United States made up a 'community' with that kind of collective interest which belonged to a single state. The debate, which was prolific in pamphlet literature but meagre in new political ideas, was renewed every time a United States Senator dared to differ from his state Assembly.[4]

But in the domestic politics of Virginia, and in the heyday of the undivided leadership of the gentry, the question seldom arose, for the simple reason that few counties would have had the effrontery to instruct their leading citizens in their legislative duties. Instruction was hardly compatible with deference.

The traditional antipathy to electioneering had crumbled by the time

[1] *Tyler's Quarterly Magazine*, xiii. 248–51, quoted by Hilldrup, 'Virginia Convention', 137.

[2] 'The delegates from those counties, in which the majority is of their persuasion, are affected with full and pointed instructions. . . .' Edmund Randolph to Arthur Lee, 24 September 1785; Lee Papers.

[3] Edmund Randolph to Madison, 25 April 1796; Madison Papers. Albert Beveridge, *Life of John Marshall* (Boston, 1916), ii. 150–3; Kurtz, *John Adams*, 56–7.

[4] Benjamin Watkins Leigh, *Substitute . . . on the . . . Right to instruct.*

political warfare was renewed in the 1820s. In 1827 a resident New Englander witnessed election scenes that would have dismayed the contemporaries of Washington. The road from his lodgings, he reported,

was alive with cavalcades of planters and country folk going to the raree show [i.e. the election]. A stranger would be forcibly struck with the perfect familiarity with which all ranks were mingling in conversation, as they moved along on their ... horses. Indeed, this sort of equality exists to a greater degree here than in any other country [i.e. any other part of the United States] with which I am acquainted.

When I came near the village, I observed hundreds of horses tied to the trees of a neighbouring grove, and further on could descry an immense and noisy multitude covering the space around the court-house. In one quarter, near the taverns, were collected the mob, whose chief errand is to drink and quarrel. In another was exhibited a fair of all kinds of vendibles, stalls of mechanics and tradesmen, eatables and drinkables, with a long line of Yankee wagons, which are never wanting on these occasions. The loud cries of salesmen vending wares at public auction, were mixed with the vociferation of a stump orator, who in the midst of a countless crowd was advancing his claims as a candidate for the House of Delegates. I threaded my way into this living mass, for the purpose of hearing the oration. A grey-headed man was discoursing on the necessity of amending the State constitution, and defending the propriety of calling a convention. His ... arguments [were] plausible, especially when he dwelt upon the very unequal representation in Virginia. This, however, happens to be the unpopular side of the question in our region, and the populace, while they respected the age and talents of the man, showed but faint signs of acquiescence. The candidate ... was followed by a rival, who is well known as his standing opponent. The latter kept the people in a roar of laughter by a kind of dry humour which is peculiar to himself. Although far inferior to the other in abilities and learning, he excels him in those qualities which go to form the character of a demagogue. .... We proceeded (or rather as many as *could* proceeded) to the court-house, where the polls were opened. The candidates, six in number, were seated upon the Justices' bench, the clerks were seated below, and the election began *viva voce*. The throng and confusion were great, and the result was that Mr Randolph [who was absent through illness] was elected for Congress, Col. Wyatt for the [state] Senate, and the two former members to the Legislature of the State. After the election sundry petty squabbles took place among the persons who had been opposing one another in the contest. Towards night a scene of unspeakable riot took place; drinking and fighting drove away all thoughts of politics, and many a man was put to bed disabled by wounds and drunkenness.[1]

Not all of the changes would have struck an eighteenth-century visitor as improvements. The air of social equality was more forthright than of old

[1] John Hall, D.D. (ed.), *Forty Years Familiar Letters of James W. Alexander* (New York, 1870), 160.

and seems to have been more demonstrative — though this appearance was somewhat deceptive: for elections were traditional scenes of good fellowship; the appearance of so many trade stalls, including Yankee wagons 'never wanting on these occasions', was a development from the simpler festivities of earlier days. The open electioneering of the candidates would certainly have struck anyone bred in the habits of the eighteenth century as a debasement of the dignity of the legislature and a corruption of the freedom and purity of elections.

These transformations came about over the long and crowded period of the Revolution and its aftermath in the rise of national political parties. They did not represent a complete change in the character of Virginian society or politics; though the composition of the leadership underwent subtle modifications, leaning more to alliances with law, business, and the Press, that leadership defended the forms of the eighteenth-century political structure against wave after wave of reformist assault. The base on which the conservatives stood had been laid in the Revolution — and in their view it needed no further reform.

PART THREE

Revolution in America:

Orders, Interests, and the Beginnings of

Majority Rule

Introduction

W HEN philosophically minded Americans before the Revolution tried to explain their form of government, they became uneasily aware that something was missing. The form might be that of 'mixed' government and the separate chambers might truly perform the prescribed functions; but the social order that lay behind the legislatures did not in itself necessitate or justify the forms in which the colonists habitually affirmed their belief. The rise of the Assemblies had not, of course, meant the levelling of society; but it did at least mean that, for reasons internal to the colonies, the dominant men in colonial society found it safer and easier to exert their political power through the Assemblies than through the governors' Councils.

The old terms, the language of 'estates', and 'orders', did not fit. Colonial thinkers were groping towards the idea that was soon to be successfully formulated in the theory of 'interests'. The very looseness and flexibility of this concept made it particularly adaptable to American use. Conflicts of interest might arise between rich and poor, between the great planter and the tenant farmer (similar things were happening in England); or they might arise between equals. The broadest and most widely seen distinction of this sort was that of the landed and the commercial interests. In Massachusetts, with the emergence of Boston and the prosperous seaboard towns, such a distinction became manifest about the middle of the eighteenth century. Philadelphia, in its overbearing relationship to the back-country of Pennsylvania, enforced by its grip of political power, showed a corresponding development.

Perhaps the angriest clashes of interest were those between rival religious sects. Certainly these, because of their multiplicity and because of the intense but limited type of demand they made on government, justified the idea that conflicts between interests rather than between regions or economic classes were appearing as the characteristic style in American politics.

Political rights, however, were generally conceived of and practised as a function of the rights of property. Property was a complex thing which included property in one's own person ; but for political purposes, colonial law tended to concentrate on property in the form of physical possessions. Neither individuals nor towns nor other voting formations were thought of as being separate from the property they owned.

The early experience of Pennsylvania, however, suggested that a political distinction between persons and property might one day emerge. In Massachusetts, during the Revolution, a decisive breach with the past made this very distinction into a cardinal doctrine of American ideology. Persons and property were henceforth explained as the separate entities under government ; property was thus established as a sort of substitute for the faded and inadequate idea of the separate 'estate' of an aristocracy with a right to separate representation. This clarification accompanied one of the greatest departures in the origins of modern and democratic government.

Under the Constitution of 1780, the allocation of seats in the Massachusetts legislature was based simply on the populations of constituencies : the numerical majority was at last on its way to power. However, it did not get there on its own strength. This decisive advance in constitutional practice was made possible by the fact that the leading mercantile interests, with their great concentrations of city property, could best maintain their influence through the use of the numerical principle.

By extension, a similar alliance of forces worked towards the same results in the government of the Continent and also, in due course, in the Constitution of Virginia. But the principle of majority rule was not established completely ; it issued from these debates with strong claims to logical pre-eminence, but with an ambiguous constitutional authority. It was not until 1964 that the process of the argument was completed, and then by the Supreme Court.

Americans in the Revolutionary era drew so heavily on John Locke and the older English Whig theorists that they seem, at times, to have owed more to them than did the British Constitution itself. Yet, by the time when an American Constitution had been formed, much that was most significant in this heritage, including the great theory of legislative supremacy, had at last been outgrown and rejected.

Section I

MASSACHUSETTS DISCOVERS THE MAJORITY PRINCIPLE

1. The Men of Property open a Side Door to the Majority

Under the Charter of 1691, all the towns in Massachusetts, except Boston, had equal representation in the Assembly. In view of the differences of population, this equality of towns meant great inequalities among the people. The crisis of the Revolution led the Assembly to increase the representation of the interior towns; but this step caused an outcry from the seaboard merchant gentry of Essex county, who felt their own security threatened by the new arrangements. The outcome of this clash was a new departure in New England constitutional policy. From 1776 the towns were represented on a scale determined strictly by population. This development, which was made possible by the alliance of seaboard merchant property with city populations, thenceforth became a permanent principle. The conflict of interests continued to give rise to much debate. In 1778 the towns rejected a draft Constitution proposed by the General Court. The gentry of Essex, once more engaged in political argument, met to draft a statement of principles. In a pamphlet, known as The Essex Result, *they laid down the doctrine that government acts separately on the two entities of persons and property; therefore, they concluded, these two entities must be safeguarded in separate houses of the legislature. What the memorialists had achieved was to formulate the American view of the rights of property, which had been developed as a defence against Britain, into a principle to determine the internal structure of American government. Their statement was a brilliant success which had lasting effects on American constitutional thought.*

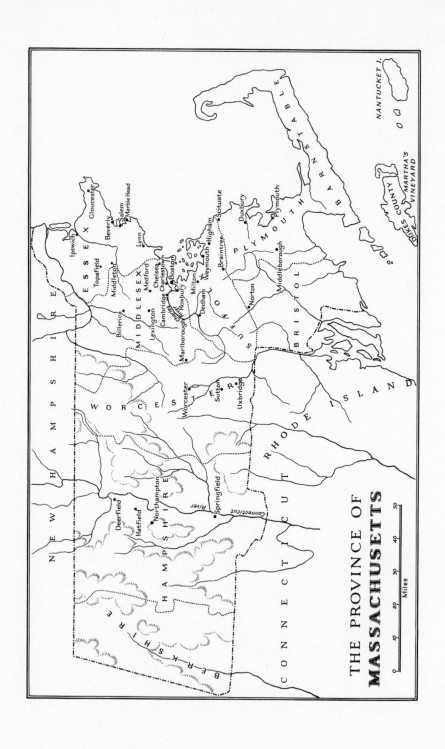

THE PROVINCE OF
MASSACHUSETTS

NANTUCKET I.

MARTHA'S VINEYARD

DUKES COUNTY

BARNSTABLE

PLYMOUTH

BRISTOL

RHODE ISLAND

CONNECTICUT

NEW HAMPSHIRE

ESSEX

Gloucester
Beverly
Marble Head
Salem
Lynn
Ipswich
Topsfield
Middleton

MIDDLESEX

Medford
Chelsea
Charlestown
Cambridge
Roxbury
Boston
Milton
Dedham
Billerica
Lexington
Marlborough

SUFFOLK

Hingham
Weymouth
Braintree
Scituate
Duxbury
Plymouth
Norton
Middleborough

WORCESTER

Worcester
Sutton
Uxbridge

HAMPSHIRE

Deerfield
Hatfield
Northampton
Springfield
Connecticut River

BERKSHIRE

Miles
0   10   20   30   40   50

I. 'NUMBERS, OR PROPERTY, OR BOTH'

THE success of the Eastern political leadership, particularly after the accomplishment of the difficult task of winning the support of the Western counties in 1774, showed how much could be done by organising within the existing provincial framework. The seaboard was not imposing its own policy on an unwilling province. Its spokesmen, by persistent propaganda and exertion, assisted by what seemed a monolithic hostility in all branches of the British government, stirred the interior towns to agreement on the imperial question. Seaboard leadership, in fact, depended to a large extent on the genuine and increasing primacy of the imperial question over all domestic issues. But that agreement did not extend to the question of authority at home. Even while western towns were protesting their determination to defend their liberties against Britain, they remained acutely suspicious of the intentions of the dominant group in the Assembly.

Representation in the Assembly was not the only issue. Much feeling was aroused by the distribution of patronage, a matter which tended to merge, at the level of institutional theory, into the more general question of the relationship of different branches of government: the separation of powers. But representation was the basic problem, and the Assembly juggled furiously with it in the crucial year before Independence was declared. The subject was regulated twice, in divergent senses, by Acts of August 1775 and May 1776.[1]

Unluckily the military emergency reduced the output of newspapers and there is little information to be had about these measures from other sources.

The first Act, that of August 1775, was intended to correct the injustice which had developed gradually as a result of British insistence on the practice of incorporating new towns without granting them the right of representation. This was the Massachusetts equivalent to the deliberate underrepresentation of the newer settlements practised on their own initiative by the older counties in Pennsylvania. It was less effective, because Boston itself was restricted to four members by the Charter; but the intention should not be mistaken. The new Act granted the right of sending one representative to every town or district of thirty or more qualified voters — which meant approximately 150 inhabitants. Towns of 120 voters were to send two;

---

[1] *Acts and Resolves*, v, 1775–6, 1st session, chap. 3, 419–20; chap. 26. 502–3.

Boston alone was entitled to four. Every district which had been invested with the rights and privileges of a town was declared to be a town for the purpose of representation; but only towns and recognised 'districts' could be represented, so that unincorporated plantations or settlements still lacked this constitutional privilege.

The result of this restoration of the position of 1691 was a great increase in the number of representatives from towns in the interior. The obvious inference is that the measure was intended to rally support throughout the province — to give the townspeople a sense of attachment to their Assembly. If it achieved this, however, it also succeeded in producing great consternation on the seaboard.

The rejoinder came from Essex County, where a Convention held in April 1776 presented the legislature with a memorial in which the new basis of representation was held out as a major grievance.[1] The memorialists declared that they would be satisfied with 'equality or representation, whether it has respect to numbers, or property, or both'. The argument closely resembled that of Philadelphia in similar plight.[2] A single town in Essex, it was urged, paid more taxes than thirty other towns and districts; while under the new distribution, a majority of the General Court could be obtained from towns which did not pay one-fourth of the total taxes. Essex paid one-sixth of the taxes but sent only one-tenth of the representatives.[3]

Numbers, or property, or both: the Essex claim deserves attention. It was the first public challenge to the venerable tradition of town representation. The basic interest at stake, as the tax statement makes clear, was that of the great concentration of mercantile and city property on the seaboard; and this wealth was allied to the higher concentration of population. Thus a numerical scale could be introduced to undermine the principle of corporate representation. And, after all, was not the connection between taxation and representation the crux of the American case against Britain? To the memorialists of Essex, the principle seemed clear cut; a plain matter of equality.

The tactical problem was how to get the basis of representation changed

---

[1] *Acts and Resolves*, v. 542–3. Cushing, *Transition in Mass.*, 202.

[2] And of London in 1649. Vernon F. Snow, 'Parliamentary Reapportionment Proposals in the Puritan Revolution', *English Historical Review*, July 1959, 423.

[3] This claim is substantiated by the tax lists published in the *Province Laws*. Essex was assessed for £8,687 out of a total province assessment of £46,000. *Acts and Resolves*, chap. 6, 432–3.

by an Assembly elected under the very Act that was to be attacked. The accomplishment of this task showed much understanding of the management of representative bodies. The memorial appeared at the end of the session. It is clear from subsequent criticisms that the majority of the members from interior towns had already gone home when, in response to the petition, the new Bill for reapportionment was introduced; the measure was propelled through its three readings in a single day.[1]

The preamble of this new Act stated that the representation in the colony was 'not as equal as it ought to be'. The reform was drastic. Each town of 220 freeholders was thenceforth to be entitled to no fewer than three representatives, while each additional hundred freeholders gave one additional member. Moreover, the measure was to come into force at once, in time for the coming elections.

This last procedural provision aroused as much protest as the substance of the Act. In the short interval before the election, the law was not properly circulated; one writer alleged that there were towns within twenty miles of the Court that had never heard of it — while others scorned to act on it, holding the measure to be illegal.[2] A county convention held a year later in Worcester declared that the Act, passed 'in a very thin house, at the close of the Session, when the members in general were returned home, expecting no further business of importance would be attended to, and even after writs were issued for a new choice', was contrary to the general sentiments of the people; and ended by recommending the towns to instruct their representatives to vote for repeal.[3] Two towns later used the unsatisfactory basis introduced by this Act as a reason for holding the General Court unqualified to draw up a new Constitution for the state.[4]

However, the composition of the new House, in consequence of the new basis, was highly satisfactory to the defenders of property. The representation of Suffolk increased by 23 members; of Essex by 25, of Middlesex by 10, and of Plymouth by 7; while the failure of the prescripts to reach the West was reflected in the fact that Worcester's members dropped from 37 to 34, those of Hampshire rising by 2 and rebellious Berkshire by 4. The number of members at the session of May 1776 rose from 201 to 266, the increase from the seaboard being enough to account for the whole of the difference.[5]

[1] *House Journal*, session 1775–6, 235, 242.
[2] *Massachusetts Spy*, 16 January 1777.
[3] *Mass. Spy*, 24 April 1777.
[4] Returns of Ashby and Topsfield; Mass. Archives 156/83, 184.
[5] Cushing, *Transition in Mass.*, 203, n. 2.

The representation of Boston immediately went up from the traditional 4 to 12.[1]

One effect of this Act was to produce a House of unwieldy size. A Boston member even gave it as his opinion that the object was to produce a period of confusion, after which the leading men of property would be left in charge.[2] The principal result was to give the advantage in the making of legislative policies to the commercial interests of the Eastern section.

From the seaboard view, the need for efficient legislative power was urgent. The non-importation agreements, the closure of the port of Boston and the threat of war had produced most serious hardships; the Boston Port Act had in fact called forth aid to Boston from other colonies and it was a well-recognised fact that Boston had stood the brunt of the recriminatory actions of the British government. By contrast the position of the farmers was relatively comfortable. The commercial and city interests wanted to use the government to impose economic regulation, particularly with regard to the prices of agricultural produce, and to keep a firm control of monetary policy. The policy of currency retraction was begun as early as 1777; and although it proved difficult to hold on to a steady economic policy, the Assembly continued to attack the same types of problem, and to develop an increasingly regulatory attitude to economic affairs. In 1779, Massachusetts joined New York and other New England states in a convention at Hartford directed towards the general question of controlling prices and wages;[3] and in pursuit of this policy a scale of currency depreciation was worked out and published by 1780.

The debate about the basis of representation was not a high-minded debate about forms of government. It was the constitutional expression of a vigorous struggle to command effective legislative powers. This point was as clear to the agricultural section as it was to the commercial. The convention in

---

[1] Alden Bradford, *History of Massachusetts from 1775 to 1789* (Boston, 1825), 107 (hereafter referred to as *History*). Boston, as Mr Brown remarks (*Middle-Class Democracy*, 48), does not seem to have known how many members it was entitled to.

[2] 'Mr. Best [?] will tell you what an Enormous number of Reps we are to have this year. The last Genl. Court made the Act 10 ch has raised the number, I suppose to 5 or 600 in imitation of the first Caos, expecting they would sit but a little time before they will annihilate themselves, and reduse the Number of Reps to a good Hundar'd of Estates of freehold Especially. The Idea is good but what Creature of the making of G*D or man ever annihilated itself, that a better might succeed.' Benjamin Kent to Samuel Adams, Boston, 24 May 1776; Samuel Adams Papers, New York Public Library. If the number did not reach '5 or 600' it was probably because many towns did not send.

[3] Oscar and Mary Handlin, 'Revolutionary Economic Policy in Massachusetts', *William and Mary Quarterly*, January 1947. *Acts and Resolves* (1779–80), xii, chap. 765, 351–2.

Worcester County in 1777 complained, in one of its resolves, that the new representation law tended

to fix an Object of contention and opposition between the Landed and Mercantile interest in this State whereby it is to be feared great difficulties distress and confusion will be brought upon the people hereof.[1]

When the Essex gentry and their associates in Boston declaimed so stridently about 'property', they did not exclusively mean ships, workshops, and warehouses. Land itself was, of course, far more valuable in the city areas, and was assessed with 'personal' property for taxation. But such land ownership was an adjunct of mercantile wealth. The 'interest' involved was essentially that of the merchants, traders, sailors, fishermen, and the numerous skilled and busy artisans, clerks, teachers, preachers, and lawyers who were associated with the life of the seaboard and dependent on each other's labours. By pre-empting the term 'property' to describe their interest, they gathered to themselves a flattering constitutional respectability at some risk of clouding the issues. The implication was that the opposed interests were unpropertied, and hence reckless of property values and not to be relied on in legislation.

The opposed interests were really very varied. In the Connecticut River Valley the great landowners dominated the life of their section to such effect that they were known as 'river gods'. Such towns as Pittsfield, Springfield, and Northampton in the west supported a respectable gentry. Some of these men walked into the Whig leadership and into the jobs offered by the new government. The western towns themselves were in part the creations of commercial enterprise and credit, supporting the trades and professions upon which the farmers depended. The broad differentiation between the landed and the commercial interests cannot be regarded by the historian as a conclusive guide to the alignment of forces on particular issues; and each interest was likely to be infiltrated by strands attaching it to others.

Nevertheless, it was a distinction which satisfied the representatives of the towns of Worcester County and was understood, if not stated in so many words, by those of Essex on the other side. It is surely of some significance that at this moment of crisis in the history of America, immediately before the elections that would lead to Independence, the gentry of Essex County should have produced a memorial in which nothing was said of the grievances of America against Britain, but everything of the grievances — the prospective grievances, at that — of 'property' against the representatives of the

[1] *Mass. Spy*, 24 April 1777.

countryside. In another two years, the same group was to distinguish for purposes of representation between property and persons — but not in such a way as to weaken the influence of property in the House of Representatives; rather to secure its special protection in the Senate. In contrast with most of the interior, both property and persons were tremendously concentrated in the seaboard towns. The intense and calculated struggle over representation was fought out in face of the danger of an almost indefinite diffusion of representation among smaller towns, many of them in regions which had shown prolonged resistance to Bostonian leadership.

In a practical sense, therefore, a commercial and a landed interest had emerged within the representative system, conscious of conflicting claims and jealous of each other's powers and ambitions. The seaboard merchants had claimed the weighty distinction of standing for 'property'; by which means they misled both contemporaries and historians into imagining that the landed elements who held a different kind of property belonged mainly to the rural poor. Contemporaries who accepted this argument were persuaded that the constitutional powers of those rural elements ought to be carefully circumscribed; and historians later went so far as to infer, from the supposed lack of property, that the landed interest must in fact have been virtually unenfranchised. Such influence over the opinions of both their contemporaries and their descendants, gained largely in defiance of the facts, must be reckoned a considerable achievement for the seaboard propagandists.

II. REPRESENTATION IN THE REJECTED CONSTITUTION OF 1778

The Declaration of Independence was not thought to have created a vacancy for the office of king of Massachusetts, and the new state did not advertise for a successor. More discomfiture was felt about the lack of a Governor, whose place was taken by an executive Council appointed by the Assembly. The royal Charter, moreover, could no longer be considered to derive its authority from its original source; and although the New England states of Connecticut and Rhode Island were content to go on with the charters which they claimed to have defended against illegal encroachments, there was little or no opposition in Massachusetts to the seemingly obvious view that an independent and sovereign state must have its own Constitution.

The legislature of 1776, before its dissolution, advised the towns that the next set of representatives should be elected with a view to forming a constitution; and after the April elections, the new Assembly deemed itself authorised to join with the Council in carrying out this work. A committee of twelve was formed in June 1777 and in January 1778 the draft Constitution was approved by the General Court and submitted to the people in their town meetings — who rejected it by an overwhelming majority.

If evolutionary analogies could be applied with any accuracy to the historical process, this rejected Constitution might be considered a most important example of the missing link; and the returns of the towns give the reasons why it perished. History, perhaps unfortunately, does not yield itself to this method; or rather, if subjected to this method it does not yield the truth. The Constitution accepted in 1780 may not have been in every way preferable, but by 1780 the need for a Constitution was more urgent; and that of 1778 was rejected, not only because of its content, but because of the manner of its adoption.[1]

In respect of representation, the draft of 1778 did not differ from the Constitution of 1780 in any point that would have been likely to cause its rejection. The suffrage franchise was to be extended to all adult male tax-payers having one year's residence in the town in which they voted, provided that they were white; but this provision, an extension on the provincial franchise, was to apply only in voting for the House of Representatives. To vote for Governor, Lieutenant Governor, or Senators, the qualified inhabitant must also be worth 'sixty pounds clear of all charges thereon'.[2] The phrase 'worth' so much money, which was also used in New Jersey,[3] was legally, not to say morally, ambiguous; and the failure to define the type of currency in which the money was to be valued would quickly have resulted in the inflationary collapse of all property qualifications. This was obviously not intended. The interest of these plans lies not in any originality but rather in their type. They were characteristic of the thinking of contemporary American constitution makers in the concept of a graduated scale of participation in politics, arising from a broad base to a narrow pinnacle in the person and office of the Governor.[4] Similar systems were introduced, with

---

[1] John Adams was frankly puzzled by the rejection of the draft Constitution; he thought it imperfect but better than nothing. He also noted that only 12,000 people voted and that 120 towns made no return. He regarded the influence of Boston (which voted unanimously) as decisive. Charles Francis Adams, (ed.), *Works of John Adams*, Boston, 1851), iv. 214.

[2] The draft Constitution of 1778 is printed as an appendix to Bradford, *History*, 349–62.

[3] *New Jersey Session Laws* (Trenton, 1776–1845) 21 session, 2nd sitting, 174.

[4] Qualifications for office under the draft of 1778 were: for Governor and Lieutenant Governor, five years' residence; and respectively £1,000 worth of estate, £500 being real

variations of detail, in a number of other states in the Revolutionary era; and although the scale adopted in Massachusetts in 1780 was different, the principle was the same.

The clause governing the representation of towns gave to every incorporated town, no matter how small, at least one representative; and two representatives to those with 300 voters — a figure which, on general grounds, may be held to have stood for about 1,500 inhabitants. A sort of compound scale then came into the reckoning. The next step, to three representatives, was taken by an addition of 220 voters, to a total of 520; the next, by an addition of 240, to 760; and so on, each time adding 20 to the previous number of increase. The inhabitants of two or more towns, not wanting to send a representative for each, were to be allowed to join in the choice of one. There was no upper limit.

These arrangements made no attempt to provide for the fairly large number of inhabitants who lived in unincorporated villages. There would not have been much technical difficulty in doing so: but to draw up some form of electoral district would have struck at the primacy of the town as a constituency, and although a small number of suggestions of this sort were in fact made by towns commenting on this draft,[1] it was a step for which the people would have been almost entirely unprepared. It may even have been felt by the public men of the General Court that the people who chose to dwell in habitations which had not been granted incorporation by that body, were in a sense lacking in the qualities of citizenship. Not all such villages could necessarily expect to attain charters. It was a form of political non-existence, relieved by the privilege of tax payment.

The town thus remained the primary unit, which gave to its members their political status; but beyond this, one is at once struck by the earnestness of the attempt to work out a scale of representation according to numbers. The notion that a larger number of voters was not entitled to an allocation of representatives in exact proportion to a lesser number, but that their entitlement should be diminished on a compound scale, suggests a compromise between two concepts: the first, that representation should be strictly proportional to numbers as would be the case if one member were allotted for every hundred, or every two or three hundred, voters; and the second, that

estate; and £500, £250 being real estate, both held within the State. For Senator, £400, of which £200 was to be real estate lying within the district he represented. For Representative, £200, of which £100 was to be real estate within the town he represented. Senators and Representatives to have been residents of their districts at least for the year previous to their election. Bradford, *History*, 351–2.

[1] Sutton, Beverly, Upton; Mass. Archives 156/347, 389, 429.

people living in towns really had a collective interest which could be as well represented by a given number of members as by an exact numerical proportion. And this system had two further advantages: it would help to limit the total size of the House of Representatives (though not very effectively); and it would help to protect the smaller towns against the danger of being swamped by the voting power of the larger ones. Here again, the corporate interest of the town remained a factor in the state. But it was not, in the opinion of some, a strong enough factor. Williamstown, in rejecting the draft by seventy-seven votes to one, declared that no town should be allowed to send more than two representatives to the General Court, and Sandisfield, instructing its delegate to the Convention of 1779, stated that the business of representation which made it most necessary was 'the Preventing the several Bodies Corporate from which the great whole is formed, from Encroaching in the Privilege and interest of each other, therefore it is necessary, that each Body Corporate within this State, shall be authorised to send one representative to the Genl Court Excepting the town of Boston, which shall be authorised to send Two . . .'.[1] This afforded the capital no opportunity for undue preferment.

For representation in the Senate, the counties were to be grouped into districts and the members allocated according to population, the distribution being subject to periodic revision under the authority of the legislature. The population basis would assure the seaboard a comfortable majority; but the upper class character of the Senate was meant to rest on the property qualification for Senate voters. This purpose was not lost sight of in 1780, when the Senate representation was put on the basis of taxes paid in each county.

It was not universally agreed that the General Court had acted within its powers in constituting itself a Convention to frame a Constitution for the state. The objection was particularly strong in Boston, which voted overwhelmingly in town meeting to reject the draft. But there were several other objections pertaining to matters of substance rather than manner. The document contained no Bill of Rights, although Virginia had set a notable example; there was no clear provision for the separation of powers; the basis of representation was held to be unequal, though not always on the same grounds. It was also feared that members of the legislature would have a corrupt interest in the places created in a new constitution framed by themselves. This was one of Boston's strongest objections. The dissatisfaction of the people, manifested in a vote of some 10,000 against 2,000, could hardly

[1] Mass. Archives 156/344, 160/255. See statement of the corporate character of the town, above, p. 52.

have been more pronounced.[1] Some of the towns objected on grounds which held with equal force against the Constitution of 1780, such as the existence of a property qualification for the suffrage; the requirements that towns pay the expenses of their own representatives, and the bicameral legislature; some thought the towns were made too much equal to each other, others the reverse. But the surviving returns are few: and it is not to be forgotten that in Berkshire and other western parts, the people seemed to thrive on the absence of a Constitution in general and courts in particular.[2]

The submission of this draft Constitution to the towns gave rise to some earnest discussion of principles. In formulating objections, the people affirmed their beliefs — perhaps in some cases discovered them. Nowhere did the debate have more weight or significance than in Essex County, the centre of perhaps the most active group of political minds next to Boston. A convention of town delegates, meeting in Ipswich to consider the draft, concluded by publishing a pamphlet giving the result of their deliberations and known ever since as *The Essex Result*. The authorship is traditionally awarded to Theophilus Parsons. And it is perhaps no great exaggeration to state that this document summarised the institutional ideas of the Whig-republicans when applying themselves to the domestic problems of constitutional government, no less effectively — if much less poetically — than did the Declaration of Independence on the problem of the Empire.

III. PERSONS AND PROPERTY: 'THE ESSEX RESULT' ON THE PRINCIPLES OF REPRESENTATION

The Essex Result is fired throughout with the spirit of an exceedingly temperate republicanism. It is a pity that an earlier Mr Dooley was not present to expound its principles by declaiming: 'On the one hand, the voice of the people is the voice of God; but on the ither hand, not so fast.' It proceeds

---

[1] Bradford, *History*, 157–8. William Gordon in Boston *Independent Chronicle*, 2, 16 April 1778. The influential comments of Gordon had much in common with the position taken by the gentry of Essex in the *Essex Result*, and by Boston town meeting on the same issue. The representation provided was disproportionate both with regard to wealth, as measured by ten payments, and numbers of population.

[2] Mass. Archives 156/344, 347, 366, 368, 393, 407, 414, 419, 426, 429. Taylor, *Western Mass.*, 89, shows that Berkshire towns opposed the Constitution by twelve to five, Hampshire towns by twenty-six to four. The draft constitution of 1778 provoked some protests by excluding Negroes and Indians from the suffrage, a restriction that was omitted from the Constitution of 1780

from the conventional whiggish assumptions about the origins of society and of government, and applies these to the American situation in such a way as to produce a constitutional justification for the special protection of the rights and privileges of property.

The belief that all men are created equal had no place in this argument; it was more moderately and more cryptically affirmed that 'the rights possessed at birth are equal and of the same kind'.[1] The steps by which men were supposed in the seventeenth-century whig theory to have come together to form a civil society still seemed to belong to a single process:

When men form themselves into society, and erect a body politic or State, they are considered as one moral whole, which is in possession of the supreme power of the State. This supreme power is composed of the powers of each individual collected together, and VOLUNTARILY parted with by him. No individual, in this case, parts with his unalienable rights, the supreme power, therefore, cannot control them; and even of his alienable rights the individual surrenders control only when the good of the whole requires it.

It would be difficult to find a clearer exposition of the essential Whig concept of the voluntary nature of both civil and political society — an idea that, so long as contract theories of government persisted, was to have a pervasive influence on the idea of the nature of the state. The pamphlet then went on to affirm that the supreme power could act legitimately only for the good of the whole and that political liberty rested on consent to the laws. No man could be considered as consenting to a law enacted by a minority.[2] These arguments were not sustained by a philosophical exposition. The question in what sense a man may be said to consent to a law which he has opposed was simply not raised. It appeared that any law enacted by the majority for the good of the whole, enjoyed the consent of the whole; and the concept of 'the good of the whole' was also adopted without enquiry.

From these first principles, discovered in the origin of society, it was necessary to cross to Massachusetts in 1778, and the road led clearly to the destination aimed at by the gentry of Essex. Directions were now indicated not by *a priori* principles but by experience, which taught that the elements of aristocracy and of democracy were both fraught with the virtues necessary to a republic; and more particularly was this so when the democracy applied its honesty and probity with regard to the good of the whole to the virtue of

---

[1] Theophilus Parsons, *Result of the Convention of Delegates Holden at Ipswich in the County of Essex* . . . (Newburyport, Mass., 1778), 13 (hereafter referred to as *E.R.*).
[2] *E.R.*, 14.

being led by the wisdom, firmness, learning, and consistency of character exhibited by the aristocracy.[1]

The *Result* accepted all the fundamentals of the Whig-republican view of political society and developed them in ways which were to become characteristically American. Thus there was no attempt to deny that the suffrage ought to be placed on a broad basis — to be extended to every adult male 'with a will of his own'. This particular qualification may have owed something to the influence of Blackstone, who had argued the need for property qualifications on the ground that unpropertied voters could be bought up by men of wealth;[2] but with or without Blackstone, there would have been little or no possibility that the members of the Essex Convention would have demanded the total abolition of property qualifications for voters. There followed a vigorous denunciation of slavery, which came more easily to republicans in New England than in Virginia.

When the pamphlet came directly to the role of representatives, it propounded the doctrine that lay at the centre of old whiggism: representatives should think, feel, and act like the people, 'and in fine be an exact miniature of their constituents'. The representative body was to be simply the whole body politic on a reduced scale. The underlying thought, though not here drawn out in detail, had been repeated over and over in the arguments both of the English Old Whigs and the American new ones. Representation had become necessary simply because numbers had made a general assembly of the people impracticable, but the representative Assembly must be merely a small-scale replica of the whole people, drawn directly from it and reproducing it without the slightest distortion.

The importance of this argument lay in its entire lack of originality; the writers of the *Result* had something important to say about the political rights of special interests, and they adopted the traditional language of Whig thought with which to say it. It would be possible to accuse them of disingenuousness, since their doctrine seemed to go far towards assimilating all interests in the state into a single 'whole', a community resembling that of

---

[1] *E.R.*, 18–20.

[1] Sir William Blackstone, *Commentaries on the Laws of England*, 4 vols. (Oxford, 1765), i. 165; *E.R.*, 28–29. But an earlier statement was given by Montesquieu: All citizens should have a vote for representation except those who were in such a low condition as to have 'no will of their own'.

De l'Esprit des lois, livre xi, 266, in *Œuvres complètes* (Paris, 1835). But elsewhere he condemns the secret ballot and says that popular suffrage must be public because 'the lesser people must be enlightened by the principles and held in check by the gravity of certain personages' (26). Is this having a will of one's own?

Rousseau, coming close to the contemporary idea of a 'democracy'. But the accusation would be unjust. There were logical weaknesses in the case, but logical weaknesses are fortunately not proof of insincerity; and the existence of special and important rights in personal property, which it was the particular duty of government to protect, was a matter of universal agreement. The great strength of the argument lay in the fact that it produced an institutional defence of these rights on traditional republican grounds.

The next step was taken without a break in the paragraphs. Equal interests among the people, it was said, should have equal interests in the body of representatives.[1] Hence every law affecting property should have the support of the majority of those with property.

The relationship between the interests comprising the state and the institutions of government was not taken up at this point but was developed later in the pamphlet. It even seems as though the writers' thought developed in the course of writing. The need for two legislative Houses was at first argued on the general ground that one House was too liable to the influence of an individual, was subject to ambition and avarice, and needed the restraint of a revising chamber.[2] But later a much more important reason was advanced: and despite a gap of some thirty pages, this followed from the first statement about persons and property, which said:

The only objects of legislation are the person and property of the individuals which compose the state. If the law affects only the persons of the members, the consent of a majority of any members is sufficient. If the law affects the property only, the consent of those who hold a majority of the property is enough. If it affects, (as it will very frequently, if not always,) both the persons and property, the consent of a majority of the members, and of those members also, who hold a majority of the property is necessary.[3]

What this means in terms of counting votes is not very clear. But a basic principle had been expounded: government operates only on two objects — on the person and the property of individuals. It was from this notion that the difference between the two legislative Houses was later explained. For towards the end, Parsons stated that the first House was to represent persons, not property, and was to be called the House of Representatives: and the other House, or Senate, was to represent property.[4]

For the election of the House, a scheme of indirect election by county conventions of delegates drawn from the towns was proposed, and it is likely

[1] *E.R.*, 29–30.   [2] *E.R.*, 33–34.   [3] *E.R.*, 22.
[4] *E.R.*, 49–52. Cf. Penn to Jasper Yates, 1683, in defence of the Governor's three votes in the Council for Pennsylvania, above, p. 85.

that this plan concealed the hope that the indirectness itself would somehow separate the purer elements from the grosser ones churned up by a popular election. Nevertheless, the representatives were to be exactly proportioned to the population in each county and any tax-payer of two years' standing in his county was to be eligible as a representative. There need be no property qualification for the voter, it was explained, precisely because the House was to be representative of persons. The suffrage for the Senate, on the other hand, was to be based on the state tax on the freeman's estate, which could be relied on to bear a 'just relation to the normal value of money'. The Senators should be apportioned by counties on the basis of the taxes paid by the counties — a plan that was in fact to be adopted in 1780. They were to be elected by a state convention, composed of delegates from the towns, themselves elected on a property suffrage.

The Essex convention did not include John Adams, who was in France, but Adams influenced its deliberations. The phraseology of the assertions that the Assembly should resemble the people and that equal interests among the people should have equal interests in the Assembly, reflected statements in Adams's recent 'Thoughts on Government'.[1] But in that paper Adams did not go on to create legislative Houses out of the interest of persons and property. This development of the argument seems to have originated in the *Essex Result* and was to be of great consequence. It was adopted as the official explanation of the bicameral system in the Massachusetts Constitution of 1780, and it was rapidly accepted as a normal tenet of political thought.

This point is due to reappear, when it assumes slightly different forms in altered contexts; for the ideas of the 'persons and property' concept were related to somewhat more complex views about the estates, or, to use the word of which John Adams was fond, 'orders', of which political society was supposed to be constituted. The author of the *Essex Result* propounded the basic argument, and this he had developed from the Whig postulate of the voluntary nature of political society.

In the structure of this system, the idea of this original 'voluntarism' was indissolubly connected with other controlling concepts of equality and rights, or rather of equality in rights. And it is essential to bear in mind that the rights in question, being natural rights, precede the formation of society: it was precisely in order to give them the most effective possible safeguard that free individuals were supposed to have agreed on the forms of both society and government.

[1] John Adams, 'Thoughts on Government' in *Works*, iv. 195.

The right to acquire and hold property was a natural right. This view was a blend of Old Whig and vintage Locke, aged in American bottles and uncorked in considerable profusion before and during the American Revolution. The problem of political society, then, was not to secure equality of property — it was to maintain equality of rights. Individuals, entering voluntarily into society under government, parted only with those alienable rights which had to be given up so that government could function, 'for the good of the whole'. They did not, and in fact could not, part with their rights to property because those were by nature inalienable.

It might have been better from the point of view of theoretical exposition if Parsons had maintained a distinction between 'powers' and 'rights'. This at least would have been clearer than 'alienable' and 'inalienable' rights. For the argument then went on to lay it down — and the point is fundamental — that actual rights over property had been 'parted with' in order to secure the benefits of protection. The individual who had parted with certain rights, or powers of control, over his own property, must therefore in justice retain a share in the government commensurate with the sacrifice. To maintain this equality in rights it was essential to establish an inequality of political influence. Equal influence for each member without regard to property would give to some greater benefits and powers than to others, compared with the rights parted with to purchase them.[1]

The strength of this argument, as has been remarked, lay in its obviousness; it had all the appearance of being a mere continuation of the principles of American resistance to Britain. In Massachusetts in 1778 its weaknesses were not easy to see, though they would become apparent to critics holding a different view of the desirable nature of the social order. Other sections of the *Result* also appealed strongly to public opinion by offering rather an advanced form of the doctrine of the separation of powers, and by criticising the draft Constitution of 1778 for the omission of a Bill of Rights.[2]

The writers of the *Essex Result* maintained the legalistic myth of an

[1] *E.R.*, 22–23. But it is difficult to exonerate the author from the suspicion of special pleading. Each qualified voter for the Senate would also qualify to vote for the House; but House voters would not help to elect the Senate. Some were more equal than others. The interests of property, moreover, were strengthened by the power of veto over legislation in the Governor and Council — a safeguard for 'property' supplementary to that of legislative representation. See the acute discussion of these points in E. P. Douglass, *Rebels and Democrats* (Chapel Hill, 1953), 182.

[2] *E.R.*, 4. These were important integral parts of the pamphlet and are not treated here only because they have no direct bearing on the concepts of representation as they occur in the *Result*.

original, voluntary compact which, whether it was believed literally or regarded as allegorical, gave moral support to the sanctity of private property. Differences in private wealth had long existed in the colonies, and were increasing. Yet, in a situation where political rights were enjoyed widely and where some form of legislative supremacy was likely to succeed the royal government, even the obvious rights of private property might seem to be threatened with the invidious distinction of being considered special, even privileged interests. It was a powerful stroke of political strategy to bring the leading tenets of the colonial constitutional argument into the defence of these interests.

One of the problems which the theorists of Essex did not examine, however, was that of the relationship between the original contractors of the social order to the interests of their own day. The wealth held by individuals in Massachusetts in 1778 was not the same wealth, nor were the individuals the same people, who were imagined to have founded society; unless a state of nature was thought to have been restored by the abrogation of the royal government. Some people, in Berkshire County,[1] did think so; but they were of precisely the opposite political tendencies to the gentry of Essex. The gap is bridgeable. It could be held that there was some sort of continuous contract, renewed by each generation or each individual. More tenably, they could argue that the original purpose of defending the natural rights of private property still held with equal force, so that government had invariably the same duty in that regard as it had at its first founding. Of course, government had for ages taken private property. It did so by taxation for the general purposes of government, and in war-time by the impressment of goods, servants, and subjects; but all this could be explained if it were for the common good. Since property was at stake, the exact interpretation of the common good would be safe only in the hands of the representatives of property: but whose property? And was not every man of private property likely to act at least partially in his private interest? There might soon be many different views of the meaning of the common good.

Since the first founding of society, even of American society, a good deal of property had changed hands. One of the features of the stream of institutional thought which demanded the special protection of the rights of property was a consistent tendency to regard the interests in question as having a high degree of homogeneity — a kind of institutional fiction which constantly broke down in political life. Yet this belief, which was manifest in

[1] J. E. A. Smith, *History of Pittsfield Massachusetts*, 2 vols. (Boston, 1869 and 1876), i. 347.

the *Essex Result*, and which left its imprint on much of the constitutional history of the Revolution period, must obviously bear very important indications of the preoccupations of the time. It was assumed that there existed a permanent, visible, and politically separable propertied interest, so distinct from that of mere persons that its representatives could be given specific institutional recognition. This led to the erection of carefully calculated property qualifications for suffrage and for office; and it was expounded further in justification of the institution of separate houses of legislation.

It can be objected that all these men were really doing was finding satisfying reasons for keeping in being the political institutions to which they were accustomed; the states which had always had two legislative Houses kept two, Pennsylvania and Georgia carried on with only one: but the issue was fiercely contested in Pennsylvania, where the Revolutionary Constitution was a party document, ultimately to be supplanted in favour of the more usual form; while what is equally significant, in other states including Massachusetts, is that such potent elements could everywhere see their interests as best secured by the retention of the traditional forms. It is hardly good enough to explain that this was conservatism, the force of mere tradition or resistance to innovation. The point is rather that there were interests at stake which bicameral institutions were intended to conserve.

It is a defect, however, of the reasoning in the *Essex Result*, that the organisation of the legislature in the bicameral form does not follow logically from the stated original purposes of social organisation. Amounts of private property varied immensely; and practically no one was without property at all. The fact — or notion — that society was founded to protect the rights of property does not lead by necessity to any specific form of government; the protection of property at certain levels could presumably have been just as well safeguarded by various other types of arrangement. Moreover, the argument from original purposes failed to provide any clear or logical guide to political action, even when the interests of property were directly involved — as was discovered with painful speed in the bitter disputes about paper money. The *Result* succeeded by establishing a frame of thought in which the purposes it had in mind were seen to be worthy purposes in conformity with expressed American ideals; it went on to adapt a familiar institutional system to these purposes. More, for the moment, could hardly be expected; it had done much.

2. The Constitution of 1780

A new Convention met in 1779 and drafted a Constitution which was completed and adopted in 1780. The Convention circulated the document to the towns, together with an 'Address' by way of explanation. As the Address made clear, the distinction between persons and property had been systematically applied to the structure of government. Seats in the House of Representatives were placed on a numerical basis to represent persons; seats in the Senate were apportioned on the basis of taxes paid up by the counties. A hierarchy of economic qualifications was introduced into the control of eligibility for participation in politics, all the way from the Governor down to the electors. Property qualifications for the suffrage were raised, but honest men earning an independent livelihood could usually expect to have the right to vote.

However, the records show that much disagreement flared up in the Convention over the meaning of that elusive notion 'equality'. The new Constitution adopted the numerical idea which recognised the equality of persons as the permanent law of the state; but it did so in a manner that still recognised the town as a basic political unit.

THE rejection of the draft in 1778 left the independent State of Massachusetts without a Constitution; the manner of that rejection expressly repudiated the General Court's claim to act for the people as a constituent assembly. There were parts of the state, particularly the thinly populated rural county of Berkshire, where the disadvantages of being without a formal Constitution seemed for a time to be outweighed by the advantages, which included the suspension of the courts of quarter sessions. The good people of Berkshire, ruling themselves by means of directly elected local committees, seemed to be putting the most straightforward construction on Old Whig doctrine; and though it could not last indefinitely, and the demand for a central government gradually regained influence, the Berkshire example reinforced the feeling that any new constitution must arise, as directly as possible, from the will of the people. This feeling was already strong. It had behind it the history of the town meeting as a school of self-government. And in recent years it had been expounded and developed in a prolonged spate of articles and letters in newspapers, and of pamphlets.

Public opinion was permeated with the contractual nature of government and the doctrine of consent; and the converging of the stream of New England local history with the theory of contract made that consent, for the first time, a series of personal affirmations.[1]

When the time came for the election of a special Convention, the ground was exceptionally well prepared for that return to first principles which dictated the abandonment of all property qualifications in the election of delegates. In the call to the Convention, every free man of twenty-one years, an inhabitant of a town, was to have the right to vote, while the Convention was left free to determine the method of ratification. The procedure decided upon was that the draft Constitution should be submitted to the towns during an adjournment of the Convention. The towns might, if they wished, send new delegates to the resumed sitting of that body, which would consider the votes of the towns and would declare the Constitution adopted if it proved to have been ratified by two-thirds of the votes cast. Not only did this plan extend the call to the Convention to a wider electorate than that which supported the existing government of the state,[2] but it placed the Convention on a wider basis of representation than the government established under the new Constitution itself.

I. THE CONSTITUTION AND ITS MAKING

The Convention duly met in Cambridge in September 1779, and with little delay resolved that it had sufficient authority from the people to frame a 'new Constitution of Government'. A committee of thirty-one was soon appointed to prepare a draft Constitution and the full Convention then adjourned to wait for the committee's report. The detailed work of preparation was further delegated to a sub-committee of three — James Bowdoin, Samuel Adams, and John Adams — while John Adams was also entrusted with the drawing up of a Bill of Rights. These tasks completed, the Convention met again, debated for about a fortnight, and then adjourned until January. The winter proved extremely hard — some thought it the worst for half a century — and delegates could not make their way through the

[1] J. E. A. Smith, *History of Pittsfield* i, chap. xviii; Taylor, *Western Mass.*, 92, 96, 100; Cushing, *Transition in Mass.*, chap. xvii; Douglass, *Rebels and Democrats*, chaps. 9 and 10; files of *The Independent Chronicle* and *The Massachusetts Spy* for these years.

[2] As noted by S. E. Morison, 'The Struggle over the Adoption of the Constitution of Massachusetts of 1780', *Proceedings* of the Massachusetts Historical Society, vol. 50, 1916–17.

snows to perform their duties. Attendance became sparse and irregular. When regular meetings were resumed, on 17 January 1780, only sixty members were present, from forty-two towns. The Convention completed its work at the beginning of March and ordered the Constitution to be printed and circulated to the towns for ratification. In June the Convention reassembled, somewhat changed in composition, and after about a month's delay and deliberation declared the Constitution duly ratified.[1]

The Constitution that emerged from these proceedings was a lengthy document, in which the different obligations, powers, and limits of government were allocated, separated, and established far more systematically than in any previous instrument of the American Revolution.[2] The leading part in both the Bill of Rights and the Constitution was undoubtedly that of John Adams, who could not stay to see the work through because, after but a few months on American soil, he was sent to Paris by the Continental Congress as one of the United States commissioners for the treaty of peace.

In a sense the whole problem of the Constitution was the problem of representation. After the extinction of royal power, there remained no external interest in the government, and within the community there existed no hereditary interest. Since no power in the government arose from either hereditary rights or property rights vested in office, all power was admitted to arise from the people; all power was, in the last resort, elective. There was no good government, John Adams had written, but what was republican; but he was careful to add the Aristotelian dictum that it must be a government of laws and not of men.[3] When he said further that the only valuable part of the British Constitution was republican, he probably referred to the elective system in the House of Commons, though he may also have meant to include the independence of the judges and the common law. Adams saw that this only began the quest for good government. The possible variety of republics was as inexhaustible as the innumerable variations in the combinations of the powers of society. The problem was to make rules for representation.

Certain sections of the Constitution were the direct product of the search, not only for rules, but for governing principles of representation. Other sections were reflections of representation only in the sense that Adams and his colleagues were themselves acting under the mandate from the people, by whom their work would have to be ratified.

[1] Cushing, *Transition of Mass.*, chap. viii.
[2] The Constitution is printed in Thorpe, *Federal and State Constitutions*, iii.
[3] Adams, 'Thoughts on Government', *Works*, iv. 194.

Two branches of government sprang directly from representation: the legislative and the executive. The judiciary was to be appointed by the Governor acting with the Council. The executive power was treated in a separate chapter, which significantly came after the legislative power.

The General Court, then, no longer included the Governor or Lieutenant Governor, but comprised only the two elective Houses of legislation. That there were two such Houses conformed to the tradition of the province, but was not altogether to be taken for granted. Several towns made it clear (at different times) that they saw no need of two Houses; if the people were to rule, what need was there to introduce different principles into the legislative structure?[1] John Adams was strongly in favour of a bicameral legislature but the matter appears to have occasioned some debate before his plan was adopted.[2] Each house was to have a power to negative the other. This arrangement could be defended as serving the commonsense purpose of checking hasty measures; but as the two houses were expressly supposed to represent separate interests, the mutual check had a deeper political purpose.

The House of Representatives was to be the branch of government representing the towns. In pursuit of the doctrine of 'persons and property', as laid down in the *Essex Result*, it was also intended to represent the persons of the Commonwealth. These two conceptions deserve to be set side by side in this manner, not to indicate confusion, but rather the element of imprecision, that attended the attempt to define the idea of a constituency. If the House were truly to represent persons, then its constituency was the whole state, and the method of division would have become a mere matter of administrative convenience. The truth was, however, that the House continued to be made up of members representing town constituencies; the town, as a corporation, remained the basic unit to be represented. The method of reconciling these two ideas was the old one of a numerical scale.

Every town already incorporated was to continue to enjoy the right of representation. But the state was growing; and in providing for the future, the Convention decided that no town should be entitled to a representative until — or unless — it contained 150 rateable polls. A town with 150 rateable polls, which meant males over the age of sixteen, would, as the population was then composed, have numbered some 600 inhabitants; so that in a state with numerous minor settlements, the disfranchisement of all

---

[1] Such opinions were expressed either in commenting on the draft of 1778, or in instructions to delegates, or in returns on the Constitution of 1780. See Mass. Archives 156/366, 160/288, 276/69 and 71, 277/54, 83 and 91 part 2 — in the last case, a minority opinion.

[2] Cushing, *Transition of Mass.*, 239 and n. 5.

communities below this total was not trivial. The 'mean increasing number' as it was called — the additional number giving entitlement to each additional representative — was set at 225.

The Senate was to have a new and fundamentally different basis. Throughout the provincial history of Massachusetts, the upper House had been elected by the lower House sitting in conjunction with the former Council, and had thus stood between the representatives of the towns and the Governor, who held a power of veto over appointments. This was a flimsy foundation to support a royal or an aristocratic interest and in the 1760s it practically collapsed. But the same mistake was not to be made again. The new Senate was separated from the towns and put on a basis of districts, which coincided with counties. No county was to be entitled to more than six senators and the total was not to rise above forty. But the key to the intended character of the Senate lay in the provision for apportionment: senators were to distributed among the county districts, not on the basis of population, but of public taxes paid in the county. By this provision it was intended to make the Senate represent the property, while the House represented the persons, of the Commonwealth.

Property qualifications for office were established in accordance with the conception of economic and social hierarchy that governed orthodox Whig institutional thinking. At the top of the scale stood the Governor, who must have been an inhabitant of the state for the previous seven years, and be the owner of a freehold in the state worth £1,000, and be of the Christian religion. The same qualifications applied to the Lieutenant Governor. Next came the senators, qualified by being inhabitants of the State for the five preceding years, residents of their districts and owners of either a £300 freehold in the state or £600 worth of mixed, real, and personal estate. It was not required that this property should be held in the constituency, a point of some importance — since many wealthy men would probably own property in more than one place. It was easier to qualify as a representative: one preceding year's residence, with ownership in the town of £100 or of rateable estate valued at £200. At the bottom of the scale came the ordinary voter, owning a freehold at an annual value of £3, or any estate valued at £60. He had to be a male aged twenty-one years; in the case of the Senate suffrage, owning his property in the state; for the House, owning his £3 estate in the town — of which he must have been a resident for one year.

In these severely practical arrangements, these numerical equations of property with political responsibility, lay the system of representation in

Massachusetts under the Constitution of 1780. In their explanation lies an understanding of the meaning of representation, and through it the meaning of republican government. How, then, were they reached?

II. THE OFFICIAL DEFENCE: THE RE-DEFINITION OF A CONSTITUENCY

Whatever the intrinsic merits of the Constitution, the Convention did not entirely trust them to speak for themselves. A small committee was therefore delegated to draft a defence. The resulting paper, called the *Address*, appears to have been written by Samuel Adams, though in the opinion of his first biographer it was undoubtedly revised by James Sullivan.[1] The *Address* was printed and circulated among the towns with the Constitution. Since the Constitution itself was the product of months of debate upon the plan drawn up by John Adams, who had long since departed[2] and had taken no part in the main discussions, there is an element of fiction in calling the *Address* the philosophy of the Constitution. It might today be called the official handout. Its importance lies not only in what it seeks to explain but in the fact that it appeals to the voters in terms they were expected to understand.

Before government was reached, part of the paper was taken up with explaining the arrangements which had been made for the maintenance of religion; which, in view of the furious outcry from a large number of the towns, stood in most need of defence.[3] Then the bicameral system was described. Departments of government, it was claimed, had been kept down to the number absolutely necessary — which happens to have been the same number as before. 'The House of Representatives is intended as the representative of the persons, the Senate of the property, of the Commonwealth.' Thus was succinctly stated the central principle of the system. It had evidently made such progress since the *Essex Result* as to need no further

[1] W. V. Wells, *The Life and Public Services of Samuel Adams,* 3 vols. (Boston, 1865), iii. 89 (hereafter referred to as *Samuel Adams*); Wells prints the *Address,* ibid., 90–96. A copy is placed with the Constitution in Mass. Archives, vol. 276.

[2] To the loss of the State, in the opinion of James Bowdoin; who wrote to Adams, 'What was done after you left was not all for the better'. Bowdoin to Adams, 11 January 1781. Jas. Bowdoin papers, M.H.S.

[3] At least fifty-nine towns objected to the third article of the Bill of Rights, which gave the legislature the duty of requiring the towns to provide from their own funds for the support of public worship, and placed dissenting denominations at a certain disadvantage as opposed to the Congregationalists.

justification. Each House was to be annually chosen and was to have a check on the other; and the two Houses were together vested with powers of legislation.

The *Address* then came, in the same paragraph, to explain the principles of the suffrage.

> Your delegates [it said] considered that persons who are twenty-one years of age and have no property are either those who live upon part of a paternal estate, expecting the fee thereof, who are but just entering into business, or those whose idleness of life and profligacy of manners will forever bar them from possessing property. And we will submit it to the former class, whether they would not think it safer for them to have their right of voting for a representative suspended for a small space of time than forever hereafter to have their privileges liable to the control of men who will pay less regard to the rights of property because they will have nothing to lose.

The grounds on which these property qualifications were explained were thoroughly familiar. What the *Address* demanded essentially was that the participating citizen should possess a stake in society, something closely akin to George Mason's 'permanent common interest with and attachment to the community'. The exclusion of certain classes, who were undoubtedly bound by laws to which they had given only the most tacit whisper of implied consent, could be defended by the argument that it was open to them to earn enough money to meet the qualifications; the condition assigned to those 'just entering into business'. But it was not necessarily an earned right: it could be acquired by inheritance or by marriage. The cardinal fact was that the state gave protection to property; the economic system, however, was expected to make the acquisition of property a continued practical possibility. This being so, the makers of the Constitution did not have to face the question whether their principles would have led them to condone the exclusion of much larger numbers if property, under the existing condition of affairs, had happened to be differently distributed. But this question was implicit in the doctrine which underlay their system, and was not long to lie dormant.

In a kindred field, the silence of the *Address* is of unusual interest, approaching that of the dog in the night. For although it was thought necessary to explain the property qualifications for the suffrage, not a word was said about those for legislators and Governor. This silence can be a path to understanding. The American thinking of the period was far more deeply permeated with the strain which in England was called radicalism than was English political thought in general; in institutional terms it contained elements that would rapidly become democratic in a more modern sense of the word than was common at that time. Men were fully convinced that the people were sovereign and that only the people or their representatives could rightly wield the legislative power. It is exceedingly easy, and has sometimes proved equally tempting, to misread these signs and proceed by them to take a short cut into the nineteenth or twentieth centuries. But it is not only the provisions in the Constitution of 1780 that bar this road; it is the attitude to those provisions of the men who had made them, and those who were free to reject them. Had the erection of an elaborate system of property qualifications in the legislature which was to make laws to bind all and the executive that was to enforce them been regarded in any way as an unrepublican or anti-popular device, cutting across public opinion or diminishing the sovereignty of the people, it would assuredly have called forth a vindication at least as careful as that which was given to the suffrage. Instead, there was no vindication, no mention of the matter at all. The truth is that no one — or anyhow no one of any political consequence — was expected to question for a moment the propriety of the general plan.

The other matter of representation dealt with by the *Address* was the constituency of the town. The wording in which the system was explained was itself symptomatic of the developing conflict of ideas about the true nature of a constituency.

You will observe [stated the *Address*] that we have resolved that representation ought to be founded upon the principle of equality, but it cannot be understood thereby that each town in the Commonwealth shall have a weight and importance in a just proportion to its numbers and property. An exact representation would be impossible, even in a system arising from a state of nature, and much more so in a state already divided into nearly three hundred corporations. But we have agreed that each town having one hundred and fifty ratable polls shall be entitled to send one member; and, to prevent an advantage arising to the greater towns by their numbers, have agreed that no town shall send two, unless it hath three hundred and seventy-five ratable polls; and then the still larger towns are to send one member for every two hundred and twenty-five ratable polls over and above three hundred and seventy-five. This method of calculation will give a more exact representation when applied to all the towns in the State than any other we could fix upon.[1]

The phrase 'exact representation', in this text means having 'a just proportion to ... numbers and property'. But what unit should have this relation? In principle the constituency, the electoral division; but in fact the town. The opening expression establishes that 'equality' was already under-

[1] Wells, *Samuel Adams*, 94.

stood to mean equality of numbers, in some way weighted with their property. But it was recognised as a concurrent principle that 'equality' also referred to towns themselves. The advantage which would accrue to greater towns 'by their numbers' (i.e. by their populations) was obviously considered by some to be an unfair advantage. The numerical scale had the effect of placing representation upon a strict numerical basis; but the respect paid to the integrity of the town suggested that a compromise had been reached between divergent principles, both of which remained present in the idea of the state.

The Constitution of 1780, so far as its provisions involved political representation, and the defence offered in the Convention's official work of apology, were laid before the people of Massachusetts in their town meetings in the spring of that year. This frame of government was devised by one of the most learned and clear political minds of the era, and was then subjected, first to debate in the Convention, and later to extensive debate in the towns. It did not emerge into the light of political existence without a series of struggles.

III. EQUALITY AGREED: BUT WHO IS EQUAL TO WHOM?

Of the debates in the Convention there remain only fragmentary reports.[1] An important fragment, happily, touches on the question of corporate representation, and consists of a memorandum jotted down by one of the members of the committee of thirty-one. This was William Cushing, already prominent in Massachusetts politics and later to be a justice of the Supreme Court of the United States.

Cushing's memorandum[2] shows the central place of the struggle between individual and town representation. It shows also that the abandonment of town constituencies in favour of electoral districts was advanced at least twice, on the second occasion receiving some support in debate. The idea of drawing election districts *ab initio* on a pure population basis was not entirely new; about half a dozen towns advocated some similar plan between 1778 and 1780, and Chelsea instructed its delegate that as it was impossible to found representation merely on property he should try for an equal representation estimated from numbers 'esteeming it righteous that the same

[1] Apart from the *Journal of the Convention* (Boston, 1832), which does not record the debates.
[2] Commissions, Cushing papers, M.H.S.

given number in any part of the State should have equal Voice with the same number in another part'.[1] The Convention, however, rejected the proposal, and in view of the extent and depth of town sentiment it was right to do so. The battle was then pitched between small and large towns. The large towns wanted representation according to numbers, Samuel Adams advocating a basis of rateable polls.[2] The spokesmen for the smaller towns did not necessarily oppose a scale of apportionment, giving more members to large populations, but they did insist upon allowing every town at least one representative. And this demand was not based on the individual representation of the inhabitants of those towns, but on the corporate interests of the smaller towns themselves. The committee's view was that smaller towns could secure the representation they needed by uniting with neighbouring towns in order to make up the number entitling them to send a representative, but one member replied that Brookline had not 150 polls and if joined with Boston would have 'as good as no voice at all'. Samuel Adams here denied that Brookline would thus be deprived of its voice of citizenship. What it might lose was its present corporate right, and this ought to be given up for the general good.

There were repeated and insistent arguments for small town representation. James Sullivan[3] moved that every town had a right to send a representative, a position defended by at least nine members in debate, and he pointed out that no fewer than forty-seven towns had not 150 polls. John Lowell, of Suffolk, opposed representation for towns below 150 polls, to be saracastically answered by a 'Gent from Stow' who remarked that if Mr Lowell would make out that 149 polls had no right to a voice in choosing a representative, he would give up his point.[4]

Several towns, when their turn came to consider these provisions, noticed a connected point of considerable prospective importance. This was the size of the quorum in the House of Representatives, which was to be set at sixty members. Some fifteen town meetings had the foresight to raise objections against permitting so small a number to make a quorum when attendance from country districts was likely to be dangerously thin.[5] The first House

[1] Mellen Chamberlain papers, vol. vi. 133, M.H.S.

[2] The reference is to 'Adams'; but John had left by the time of this discussion. Dr L. H. Butterfield established this identification.

[3] Governor of Massachusetts, 1807. Barry, *History of Mass.* iii. 349.

[4] However, the figure of 150 is an amendment made by the convention on that of 200 in John Adams's original draft. John Adams, *Works*, iv. 239.

[5] Mass. Archives, 277, 276/47, 115, 112, 106, 104, 99, 92, 91, 90, 87, 76, 66, 63, 62, 60, 48, 15, 14.

under the new Constitution actually contained 228 seats, of which 82 were left vacant, most of the vacancies belonging to the outlying counties.[1] In anticipating this situation, the towns making the protest looked to the effects of the system of representation on government policies. The seaboard had long dominated the General Court, and that domination had been made possible by the management of the system, not by the strict working of its principles. By raising the quorum these interior towns hoped to ensure that some of their members were always present, to counter the danger that a small minority from the eastern towns might push through special interest legislation — something that had been done on the apportionment of representatives itself in the rushed Act of May 1776.

The debate on town representation in the Convention was really only a continuation of a struggle that had been going on at least since the apportionment Act of August 1775; and the debate was to be renewed in the town meetings. No principle was more universally agreed than that which proclaimed the great republican doctrine of equality. Representation must be equal. The only problem which remained to bedevil the State was that of deciding precisely who was to be equal to whom.

The course of the debate brought out the development of a new tension between the corporate unit, embodied in the town, and the individual citizen. The corporate principle, so trenchantly expressed by such towns as Lincoln and Ware,[2] was giving way before the novel but attractive notion that the state was really composed of all its individual members; that the equality of rights, about which much had lately been heard, was not merely a theoretical dictum of use to lawyers, but a fact of political life which the state was bound to recognise and maintain.

Yet the traditionalists had on their side much more than the theory of corporate interest — they had a large part of the habitual affections of the people. What perhaps mattered most to the inhabitants was their strong sense of town identity — it was the town which gave them their political existence; and this sense persisted long after the town had ceased to have much relevance to the making of policy. When questions of economic policy arose, it was the representation of the interior towns which collected the sense and interest of the farmers of the Commonwealth. Thus the agricultural interest found itself in a natural alliance with the corporation interest that was so deeply felt in the smaller towns; and the significance of this alliance, with regard to the making of policy, was precisely what was perceived with such apprehension by the gentry of Essex. They, in their Convention of April

[1] *Acts and Resolves*, 1780.　　　　[2] See p. 52.

1776, chose to call their own interest that of 'property'. They meant, perhaps, to imply that the opposition was slightly less reputable, but certainly Essex represented the greater concentrated accumulation of property. But property of a different type: 'personal' as opposed to 'real'. The immediate danger was taxation. Taxes levied on polls, which were traditional, fell equally on all individuals; the more effectively the expenses of the State could be met by poll taxes, the less the merchants and gentry had to fear from assessments on property.

Assessments on property would affect the substantial farmer no less than the merchant; so that a poll tax is a tax touching the rich lightly and bearing on the poor. A situation of this sort began to develop when hard times hit the whole farming community after the war. Then, the poor farmer as an individual, the poor labourer, and the poor artisan found themselves together with many more substantial farmers as victims of the depression, exacerbated by the debtor laws. In this situation, the poll tax of 1783 struck like an engine of oppression and was indeed an instrument of property as opposed to persons. But this was not the case during the war. Farmers and artisans were doing well. Property, as well as polls, was of course to be taxed, and the vital question was that of how the assessments were to be made. And here, the degree of control exerted by the interests of agriculture and of commerce would be of crucial importance. The mechanism of representation thus cuts right into the formation of policies — policies that would make or spoil fortunes and affect the course of the State.

The question of how such assessments were to be made, how land and agricultural produce were to be judged against personal property and the produce of trade, was precisely the question which reintroduced the interests. Under the disadvantages and hardships of non-importation and war — a war against the great source of commercial supply, at that — the seaboard felt acutely threatened by the power of the farmers, already doing well out of shortages and now offering to flood the General Court with representatives from innumerable minor settlements.

The reply of the seaboard, emerging from the Essex meeting of April 1776, was double-barrelled. The act of May 4 restricted representation to towns of 220 freeholders, and then gave an extra member for each hundred.[1] The effect, as has been seen, was to produce an unmanageable multitude of members; but also, if only by indirection, to reintroduce eastern domination. The opportunity was not wasted. As early as 1777 the General Court began the policies of currency retraction which became the conspicuous feature of

[1] See p. 175

Massachusetts economic policy until Shays's Rebellion in 1786. The effects were not seriously felt within the state, owing to the flood of continental dollars, until the retirement of the continentals was begun in 1780.[1] It is significant, however, that these policies did not have to wait for the Constitution of 1780, but could be enacted on the strength of the apportionment given by the Act of May 1776.

In the light of this domestic struggle, which was fought with much recrimination and many charges of unpatriotic conduct, it becomes a great deal easier to see the reasons for the outraged protests of Boston against the provisions of the proposed Constitution of 1778. The committee which the town meeting entrusted with the task of drafting instructions to the delegates in the Assembly reported two weighty objections to that draft. The first in order was against the drawing up of a Constitution by the legislative body. The importance of the distinction between the legislative and the constituent power was a practical matter; the legislators were suspected of making jobs for their own subsequent employment. But although this point came first and no doubt was expected to have a state-wide appeal, the most violent language was reserved for the section on representation.

This passage is worth quoting in spite of its verbose sarcasm:

But [stated the report] was it unexceptionable in all its parts, except that of Representation, that alone would be sufficient with every one possessed of the least idea of justice, or with the smallest knowledge of the *Rights* of Human Nature, to reject with disdain, a proposal so diametrically opposite to *both*. — Representation ought to be conformable to some Rule, either *Property* or *Numbers*, or *both*; but in the present no regard is had to either, and *Reason*, *Justice*, and common sense, must be tortured to a great degree, to accept that representation, as equal, which may be as *Ten* or *Twenty* to *One*.

The offending clause was here quoted, giving to every incorporated town the right to send one member, while no town with under 300 inhabitants was to send more than one.

If this is equal, [continued the report] if this is just, all the Rules of Arithmetic, which have been in use since the formation of figures, must be done away; but until this *new Rule* of calculation received the Stamp of Authority, we cannot consent to it, for we are possessed of that *antiquated Notion*, that two and two are always equal to four. . . .

Finally the delegates were instructed, should the Constitution unfortunately

[1] Oscar and Mary Handlin 'Revolutionary Economic Policy in Massachusetts' *William and Mary Quarterly* January 1947.

be adopted, '*to enter your solemn Protest against the Glaring Injustice of the Representation*'.[1]

Two and two might be equal to four, but two and two what? It was here that the indignant committee foreclosed the argument. For they meant persons: but the whole point of the small-town case was that the towns were themselves the units of representation. Inequality occurred when preponderance of numbers was used as a base for increased representation.

The numerical concept was not a complete stranger, however, even to the interior towns. Though not wholly welcome, it was not warned to leave, like a member of the itinerant poor. In general the towns which insisted on representation for each corporation were willing to concede that the larger ones had some right to more members, and Boston was admitted to occupy a special position.[2] Where very great disparities of population were involved, the idea of numerical representation would thus come into play as a counterweight, but not as a first principle. A few of the towns made returns suggesting a new start. The inhabitants of Beverly thought that the best method of securing an equal representation without risking an unwieldy House would be to lay aside the distinction of towns and adopt a representation by counties; each county would be divided into districts containing equal numbers of freemen.[3]

But the individual had not divested himself of the other attributes of political personality which inhered in property. The claim for representation by numbers was frequently associated with a demand for the weighing of taxes or valuations. A lengthy statement by the town of Upton on the draft of 1778 showed that the idea of dividing the state into equal electoral districts was fully compatible with the inclusion of property with individuals in the apportionment of representatives:

We are confident that we shall never have a court to the satisfaction of the People till this matter is remedied about the Representation, and there be a rational number concluded upon for the House, & the whole state divided into so many representative

---

[1] Boston Town Records, 1778–83, in *Report of the Record Commissioners of the City of Boston* (Boston, 1895), 22–24. An intriguing question remains open: why was a scheme so objectionable to Boston drafted by a General Court based on the representation of 1776?

[2] Mass. Archives, 276/53, 54, 55, 13, 67, 277/60, 102.

[3] This suggestion was made in 1778. Mass. Archives, 156/429. Upton in the same year suggested dividing the state into districts to be equally proportioned every twenty years 'either by valuation or polls'. The towns were 'so unequal and numerous in this large increasing State'. Mass. Archives, 156/389.

districts; as near as may be according to the Numbers, Freehold and Invoice at large....[1]

The Constitution of 1780 retained the town as the constituency but superimposed upon it the numerical scale in apportionment of representatives. By the exclusion of future towns below 150 rateable polls, the instrument reduced the danger of a flood of delegates from newly settled areas. At the same time it served the important purpose of keeping the House membership within practical limits.

The smaller towns insisted on their rights, but they were willing to concede the primacy to the state in the matter of the payment of members. The Cushing memorandum shows that the question of payment was discussed at least twice in the Convention. The Constitution as drafted and adopted provided that each town should pay the expenses of its own representatives incurred in attending the session. Their travel expenses for one journey each way were to be payable by the state treasury. Some sixteen towns advocated the payment of full expenses. Worcester town associated this demand with a philosophy of representation acceptable to Burke: 'Because we apprehend that each member of the said House is the Representative of the whole State and not merely of the corporation by which he is elected'.[2]

The point about payment was of very great consequence and of greater practical significance, in all probability, than the question of the precise basis of representation. Interior towns, especially those at more than a day's journey from Boston, very frequently failed to send a member at all. The cost of maintaining a representative in the capital through the legislative session was a heavy burden to which the frugal farmers saw little reason to subject themselves: were it necessary to be represented, in order to put the town's view in some dispute, a single member would be cheaper than two. For the seaboard towns the capital was relatively accessible. Their greater wealth also made it easier for them to maintain representatives. All the normal circumstances of economic and political life therefore tended to give the advantages to the east coast. Eastern members, moreover, could come and go with greater ease; attendance was less likely to involve the neglect of business.

[1] Mass. Archives, 156/347.   [2] Mass. Archives, 277/120.

3. Suffrage and the Political Individual

The Address which accompanied the draft of the new Constitution carefully explained the principles which governed the franchise. The only people to be excluded were young men starting in business and 'the idle and profligate'. The rejected draft of 1778 had offered a wider franchise, but had been equally true to prevailing conventions by proposing higher qualifications for voters in elections for the Senate. In each case the guiding principle was that which prevailed in British theory and was declared also in Virginia : that the individual must have some property to lose — 'a stake in society'. Yet the political identity of the individual had already been proclaimed by the numerical or majority basis of seats in the House. In terms of property distribution the suffrage had always been widespread and remained so. The mass of the city populations contained many of these political individuals.

In any theory of representation, the question 'How?' is preceded logically by the question 'Who?' or perhaps, 'Whom?'; and whatever system may be worked out, a place of fundamental importance belongs to the suffrage franchise. To be fundamentally important is not to be all-important. Suffrage restrictions do not necessarily cause discontent, while an extensive franchise may be manipulated or abused. The American gerrymander emerged before the abolition of the English rotten borough. But without suffrage there can be no representation, and without representation there can be no republic.

The provincial suffrage of Massachusetts was firmly grounded in the concept of property. The idea had been introduced in order to place Anglicans at a disadvantage in 1664, had been established by the Charter of 1691, and had become engrained in the habits of political thought. This tendency was probably strengthened by the legal and constitutional literature of justification produced in the struggle over the Stamp Act and afterwards. All of the American arguments presupposed the sanctity of private property, and the notion that the state bore a very special responsibility to the institution of private property was translated with almost irresistible facility into the argument that the possession of private property was a necessary qualification of those who were to participate in the affairs of the state.

Private property was, in any case, widely diffused. The scarcity factors in the colonial economy were labour and money. But the evidence of the distribution of goods tends to confirm the widely-held contemporary opinion that a high proportion of the people enjoyed a satisfactory measure of economic independence. There could hardly be a more eloquent voice than that of the perceptive and tenacious Thomas Hutchinson, chief justice and later Governor of the province. 'To restore the tranquility of the Colonies,' he wrote in discussing the Townshend duties in 1767,

and at the same time preserve a just dependence on great-britain hic labor, hoc opus est. Property is more equally distributed in the Colonies, especially those to the Northward of Maryland than in any Nation in Europe. In some Towns you see scarce any man destitute of a Competency to make him easy. They may have as high notions of Liberty as any part of the Globe, but then they are as tender of their property and see the Importance of enjoying their Estates in quiet. I find no arguments so successful as urging them that under the notion of obtaining their Liberty they are pursuing measures which will deprive them of their property as well as Liberty or render it of Little Value.[1]

The actual distribution of property, when examined in relation to other evidence of numbers of qualified voters, helps to establish the observed fact that, under provincial laws, the enjoyment of the suffrage franchise was a normal expectation of a majority of adult men. Though the proportions varied from one town to another, it was normal for two adult white men out of three, or even three out of four, to exercise the franchise by legal right; sometimes the figures were slightly higher, sometimes lower.[2]

While the legally qualified voters were extensive, the enforcement of the law was sometimes latitudinarian. Hutchinson here is an informed, though also a sarcastically critical observer.

All matters [he wrote of the New England corporations] are determined by the majority of voices and altho' the Province Law provides that a man who does not pay a small tax shall not be deemed a qualified voter yet it is not one time in 20 that any scrutiny is made 5 or 6 hundred are upon the floor together upon a level to all intents and purposes one only excepted who pro. hac vice only is raised above the rest to put to vote such questions as are called for. The town of Boston is an absolute Democracy. ... Every man in the Government being a Legislator in his town thinks it hard to be

---

[1] Hutchinson to Richard Jackson, 20 October 1767. Hutchinson Letterbooks typed transcript, vol. 25, 183. M.H.S.

[2] Brown, *Middle Class Democracy*, 49–50. The figure for Boston is only 56 per cent, which Mr Brown considers so low as to be 'far out of line' with the rest. See also John Cary, 'Statistical Method and the Brown Thesis on Colonial Democracy', *William and Mary Quarterly*, April 1963, 251–64; and Mr Brown's 'Rebuttal', 265–76.

obliged to submit to laws which he does not like and which were made by a House of Representatives consisting of 100 men for one or two only of which he could give his vote....[1]

These conditions in the conduct of elections were only a manifestation of an equalitarian or 'levelling' spirit for which Massachusetts had long been suspect, but which seemed to surge up with especial vitality when the country rallied against the Stamp Act. 'A Spirit of Levillism Seems to go through the Country and Very little distinction between the highest and lowest in office', wrote a dismayed correspondent of Hutchinson in 1766.[2] A British officer, travelling in 1765, observed 'that ancient, rugged spirit of levelling, early imported from home, and too successfully nursed, and cherished ...'.[3]

Many of these comments are hostile, emanating from Tories or servants of the royal Government; they tend to pick out the elements of disorderliness, disrespect for authority, and the influence of the lower classes in determining political decisions. As early as 1749 Hutchinson, after an election defeat, could write: 'You have heard my Fate. I could make but about 200 votes in near 700. They were the principal inhabitants but you know we are govern'd not by Weight but by Numbers.'[4] The picture these and other similar comments offer is one-sided, because in their resentment and anger the commentators portray their opponents as being dominated by the mob. They do not in general make it their business to analyse or explain the structure of the opposition, the character of its leadership nor the methods by which 'Numbers' as opposed to 'Weight' could be exploited or manipulated.[5] The evidence they give of a widely exercised suffrage can be considered only as one ingredient, though very important, in a complex economic and geographical distribution of power.

The task of making a new constitution made it necessary to try to work out a suffrage formula that would reaffirm the American Whig concepts of political competence, both as a matter of principle, and as a practical foundation for government. There was more than one way in which this might be attempted. The legislators who drafted the Constitution of 1778 adopted a

[1] Hutchinson to Jackson, 19 November 1767, Hutchinson Letterbooks, vol. 25, 215–19.
[2] John Cushing to Hutchinson, 15 December 1766. Hutchinson Letterbooks, vol. 25, 119.
[3] 'Journal of an Officer ... 1765', quoted by Brown, *Middle Class Democracy*, 57.
[4] Hutchinson to Israel Williams, 19 May 1749, Israel Williams Letterbooks, M.H.S.
[5] An important exception [discussed elsewhere, p. 67 n. 4] is a draft letter by the discerning Hutchinson, addressed, but apparently not sent, to Thomas Pownall, 8 March 1766, in Hutchinson Letterbooks, vol. 26, 393.

different plan from that of 1780, though each was a fair expression of Whig-republican principles. In the 1778 draft, the suffrage was to be extended in the election of representatives to all adult white male tax-payers, subject to a one year's residence qualification. Persons who were by law excused tax payment were to retain the right to vote. This then was the system of tax-payer suffrage which seemed to be justified by the doctrines of the Revolution. But it was not to apply to the higher offices. Voters for Governor, Lieutenant Governor, and Senators must be worth sixty pounds 'clear of all charges' — that is, unencumbered by debt.[1] All the voting was to be by ballot.

The plan of a differential qualification to distinguish voters for the different houses was that actually adopted in New York and North Carolina. It was as logical a method of obtaining a separate representation for persons and property as the one eventually adopted, under which apportionment of senators was based on taxes paid in the county. It was included as part of a scheme which also gave a higher degree of representation to the country towns than was acceptable in Boston. Despite the 'levelling spirit' of which so much had been heard, the town meeting which denounced the scheme of representation had nothing to say against the differential voting qualifications. Perhaps the constitution makers hoped that the one would offset the other.

The 1778 plan would probably have given Massachusetts as extensive an Assembly suffrage as any other state. Too extensive, it would seem, for John Adams, whose draft based the suffrage on a much more solid property qualification. But the solidity was partly that of conservatism, for his own new model was actually much less novel than that of 1778.[2]

Under the Charter, the Assembly suffrage belonged to men owning a freehold property worth 40s. per annum, and to non-freeholders who owned £40 worth of property, whether real, personal, or mixed.

The Constitution of 1780 cannot be understood without reference to the monetary notation of Massachusetts currency. At the time of the grant of the Charter, the end of the seventeenth century, silver was minted in England at 5s. 2d. per ounce, and the monetary values in the Charter were stated in sterling. But Massachusetts money then stood towards English money in a ratio of 137 to 100. The sterling value was thus appreciably difficult to get, and in Massachusetts the value of silver seems to have been rated at 6s. 8d. per ounce. This rate was named by the General Court of 1741 as the value at which all contracts were to be payable.[3] That it was a standard rate in Massa-

---

[1] Bradford, *History*, 352.   [2] Thorpe, *Federal and State Constitutions*, iii. 1898.
[3] Hutchinson, *Mass. Bay*, ii. 306. The Act was passed in the aftermath of the Land Bank affair.

chusetts is suggested by the fact that the new State Constitution expressly declared it to be the value of silver.[1] Thus in order merely to maintain the existing levels of property qualifications, the Charter rates of 40s. and £40 in sterling would have to be raised to the new level of Massachusetts silver.

Under the new Constitution, a qualified voter was to possess either a freehold bearing an annual value of £3, or other property to the value of £60. The £3 rate is to be contrasted, however, not with the Charter 40s. but with the legal qualification of 53s. 4d. established by the General Court in 1750. The difference of 6s. 8d. is one-eighth of the previous amount. This is less than the nominal difference between the earlier English silver rate of 5s. 2d. and the Massachusetts rate of 6s. 8d., but as the Massachusetts rate was actually in force, the translation from the Charter rate is merely a matter of form. It is the alteration from the 1750 rate that counts.

The suffrage qualifications were thus raised, in practice, 12·5 per cent over those under the existing law. This is not a great increase, but it is conspicuous in the light of the fact that the people of Massachusetts were engaged in a struggle for their political independence in the course of which much had been said about equality. The best explanation is probably that the new figures were simple round figures — £3 and £60 — which were both close to the old values and convenient to use. The adoption of these restrictions was undoubtedly intended to produce some disfranchisement. The intention was in fact proclaimed in the *Address*.

In justice to all concerned, it is only right to distinguish between the intentions of the framers and the effects of their work. Such disfranchisement as was intended by the Constitution of 1780 soon proved to be insignificant in practice. Within a very few years, the property qualifications were ignored and it appeared to be the custom to allow every man who had a settled residence and paid a poll tax to vote. In 1786 it was noted that 'estate to the value of sixty pounds, or the yearly value of three pounds' was commonly construed to mean any man who could earn £3 a year.[2] Thus, soon after the adoption of the Constitution, conditions resembled those described with such scorn by Hutchinson before the Revolution.

It is not easy to know exactly what line of division the framers had in

[1] Curtis P. Nettels, *The Money Supply of the American Colonies before 1720* (University of Wisconsin Studies, no. 20) (Madison, 1934), 180–1. Thorpe, *Federal and State Constitutions,* iii. 1910.

[2] Samuel Eliot Morison, *The Life and Letters of Harrison Gray Otis, Federalist, 1765– 1848* (Boston, 1913), ii. 235 n. 24.

mind. The farmer, however modest his holding, and the artisan who owned his shop and tools, fell within the class of those having a 'stake in society', and without doubt they were intended to be voters. It was the common labourer, the journeyman who worked for others and did not own his own premises or tools, who must presumably have been intentionally excluded. As a matter of fact, however, every common labourer must have earned £3 a year, even when reckoned in the revalued currency of 1780, and of course much more than that in current money.[1]

A curious gap remains, if not in the political privileges of the population, then certainly in the minds of the framers. If the distribution of wealth and of economic opportunity made it possible for every hard-working man to earn himself the qualifications to vote, then the residue should have been small and insignificant; they were dismissed in the *Address* as 'the idle and profligate'. It seems an invidious expression to have come from Sam Adams, whose sympathies had been traditionally with the underdog and who had always proved himself an extraordinarily idle and incompetent business man. But if this class were really so small as to be insignificant, one may ask why the *Address* took such an alarming view as to warn the others that their own privileges might be 'liable to the control' of such men. By what means could the outnumbered dregs of a strong and prosperous republic be expected to seize control?

There is no particular reason to treat this question as merely one of theory. The framers of the 1778 draft had dispensed with anything beyond whiteness and tax payment as qualifications for the House suffrage — but had safeguarded the interests of property by a higher qualification for the Senate suffrage; the decision in 1780 to retain the old franchise, rounding it off upwards rather than down, was deliberate. And there is good reason to suppose that

---

[1] The price-fixing convention which met in Hartford in 1779, representing the states of New England and New York, set up a wage scale which gave house carpenters 72s. a day along with ship joiners and riggers; at the bottom of the scale were common labourers, 'finding themselves' — which presumably means finding their own food and clothing — at 48s. Employment was in general high in this period, and criticisms of exorbitant labour demands imply a strong bargaining position (Richard B. Morris, *Government and Labor in Early America* (New York, 1946), 127). These figures represent a grossly inflated currency; by January 1780 the mean rate of depreciation was officially declared to have reached 32–5 to one (*Acts and Resolves* 1779–80, xxi, chap. 765, 351–2), but when these fluctuations are taken into account, it remains clear that labour wages would easily have met the suffrage qualifications in terms of income. Whether they would have done so if reckoned strictly in terms of ownership, is a much more difficult question. The ratio of property value to income would have varied from one man to another; but it seems probable that it was along this line that the framers intended to draw the qualification for the suffrage.

the men of property who sat in that Convention knew who they meant by 'the idle and profligate'. No instrument had been more terrifyingly powerful in the not infrequent moments of crisis under late British rule than the Boston mob. On certain well-remembered occasions it had perhaps done its job to satisfaction. But the performance was not to be repeated. To have enfranchised this class would not have been to risk any sort of 'class war'; the danger which presented itself to men of this period was that a mass of promiscuous voters could fall under the influence of some demagogue — 'designing men', they were usually called — or of some large-scale employer of labour who could control their votes.

The draft of 1778 would probably have proved more popular in its suffrage provisions than that of 1780, whose property qualifications excited much discussion and were the subject of the fourth largest number of objections to the Constitution. The returns preserved in the Massachusetts Archives number rather more than 200. Of these, 46 carry objections to the property qualifications for the suffrage, of which 29 were from interior counties, 17 from seaboard counties. Forty-six amounts to between one-fourth and one-fifth of the recorded returns, as compared with 70 objections to the failure of the Constitution to require that the Governor of the state must be a Protestant; 59 objections to the third article of the Bill of Rights for imposing an obligation on the citizen to support some form of public worship; 68 against the failure of the Constitution to require absolutely (instead of merely permitting) the holding of a future convention; 30 against the tenure of judges (during good behaviour) and their method of appointment; 17 against the property qualifications for the legislature.[1]

Some of the objecting towns merely recorded their dissent; others entered statements of opinion. Belcherstown feared that some would 'be deprived of having any share in Legislation — nay denied that Liberty and Freedom which we are this day contending for'. Dorchester gave an interesting indication of at least one possible view of the economic trend — a trend which would leave more, rather than fewer, people outside the bounds of privilege:

... the Article as proposed by the Convention, infringes on the Rights and Liberties of a number of useful and respectable members of Society; which number we believe is daily increasing and possibly may increase in such proportion that one half of the People of this Commonwealth will have no Choice in any Branch of the General Court, and who are at the same time liable ... to pay such a proportion of the

[1] Mass. Archives, 276, 277.

Publick Taxes as they [i.e. the General Court] shall judge reasonable; and the members of the said Court being men of Considerable Property, may be induced to lay too great a proportion upon the Polls, & by that means ease their Estates, and bring a heavy burden upon those who have no power to remove it. — And being fully convinced that Taxation and Representation ought to be inseparable, and that the Property and Estates of the People will be sufficiently guarded by the Senate who represent the same, we see no reason of sufficient weight to Debar any Person Qualified as in the article amended provides [i.e. without property qualifications] from Voting in the Choice of Representatives.[1]

This is a valuable statement, because it looks beyond principles to the anticipated effects of the new Constitution; and the fear about the poll tax proved to be only too well founded. It also reminds us that it was possible to take the view that the increase of population would lead to a widening of the gap between rich and poor; so that the establishment of property qualifications at a moment of relative prosperity could lead, without further legislative action, to a state of much sharper discrimination in political privileges.

All the more so, in fact, because the new Constitution conferred on the legislature the power to increase the qualifications required of persons elected to office. Against this provision — which lay in an inconspicuous place near the end of the document, in the clause about the valuation rate of silver — 21 towns entered their protests.

The town of Mansfield also became eloquent on the suffrage.

Doubtless [it said] there are, and ever will be some in the commonwealth who pay little regard to the rights of property . . . this we readily grant, but on the other hand, how many young men neither Profligates nor idle persons, for some years must be debard that privilege? how many sensable, honest, and naturly Industerouss men, by numberless misfortins never Acquire and possess propperty of the value of sixty pounds? and how many thousands of good honest men, and Good members of Society, who are at this day possessed of a complete Interest, which before publick debts of the commonwealth are discharged, will not be possessed of a sufficiency to qualify them to vote for Representatives if this article takes place as it now stands . . . shall it be . . . argued, that thousands of honest Good members of society shall be subjected to laws fram'd by Legislators, the Election of whom, they could have no voice in? Shall a subject of a free Commonwealth, be obliged to contribute his share to publick expenses, or give his personal service . . . see bill of Rights page 10th and be excluded from voting for a Representative; This appears to us in some degree, slavery.[2]

Northampton 'strongly disapproved' the qualifications as 'rescinding the

---

[1] Mass. Archives, 276/40 and 67.   [2] Mass. Archives, 276/33.

natural, essential and unalienable rights of many persons inhabitants of this Commonwealth'.[1]

Energetic, loquacious, and sometimes bitter as these complaints are, they represented a minority. The great majority were prepared to acquiesce in a Constitution by which an uncertain but appreciable portion of the people were meant to be disfranchised.[2] These townsmen were not afraid of stating their opinions; the majority were already privileged, and for the majority that appears to have been good enough — as it usually is.

The basic principle that was involved, and which was struggling to emerge, from these protracted debates over the suffrage, was that of the political responsibility of the individual. Its philosophical ancestry was both long and respectable, and on Massachusetts soil it had experienced a robust upbringing, culminating in the forcing house of the revolutionary argument. But political individualism gained a great addition of strength from one place — Boston. It was the strategy of the debate on representation which turned the corner. For Boston and its lesser seaboard neighbours, though not great cities by imperial standards, stood as great cities in relation to the scattered villages which were the ordinary towns.

It was Boston which insisted on the new meaning of 'equality'. The older view — whose ancestry was the better in New England — had maintained the corporate integrity of the towns; and it was between the towns that equality was to be kept up. Such concessions as were made to the populations of Boston and other larger places were grudging and did not by any means concede the principle of a rational numerical scale. But the Boston town meeting brought the equality of individuals firmly into the centre of the

[1] Mass. Archives, 276/58.

[2] It was shown in an early study of the Constitution that the ratification was achieved only with the help of a certain amount of juggled arithmetic (Morison, 'Adoption of the Constitution', 353–411). But the voting on the suffrage did not need to be rigged. That problem applied to the third article of the Bill of Rights. There is no ground for suggesting that opposition to the suffrage clause deprived it of the necessary two-thirds vote. Douglass, *Rebels and Democrats*, gives as his own estimate that 'there was something approximating an even split on the question' [of suffrage], 204. To demonstrate this point, Douglass needs to show that the voters in 45 towns which opposed, equalled those in some 140 towns which agreed. Actually, so far as details about numerical voting can be supplied from inspection of the town returns — many of which did not separate their votes on different articles — it can be stated that at least 6,900 Massachusetts townsmen accepted the property qualifications and at least 2,100 opposed them. However, 25 towns approved without recorded dissent; only 5 rejected the Constitution without recorded division. On a rough computation the unknown voting strength of some 20 towns must be added to the figure of 6,900 given for individual approvals; the figure is probably nearer 8,000.

argument, aligning its interests in the State with the doctrines of individual rights, springing from nature and the Constitution, which had for many years held an honoured and invincible position in the case for America. It was the strategic marriage of this doctrine with the political interest of Boston, the greatest single concentration of numbers, by which political individualism made its decisive advance to constitutional recognition. When numerical representation came to the top, it was because Boston was the town whose corporate interest happened to be best served by the use of a numerical scale of calculation. The individual triumphed in the mass which hid him.[1]

4. Bicameralism and the Social Order

Under its new Constitution, Massachusetts retained the old bicameral structure in the legislature. This decision was not the result of mere habit; it represented an attempt to provide an American equivalent to the 'estates' which were believed to divide English society and to be present in the two Houses of Parliament. The chief intellectual influence on these arrangements in Massachusetts was John Adams — who in turn had been influenced by Harrington. Some of the towns held contrary opinions; but they were in a small minority. The idea that 'orders' in government should correspond to ranks in society was coming under great pressure, especially in New England; but it had not collapsed.

BY the time of the Revolution, the practice of dividing the legislative body into two Houses had become one of those longstanding habits of political life which no longer seem to require theoretical justification. Wherever the bicameral system was instituted, one principle was constant. The Council

---

[1] The process was not complete until 1840, when rateable polls ceased to be enumerated as the basis for representation and a pure population census was substituted. Smaller towns were only entitled to occasional representation, ascertained in accordance with their numbers. C. F. Adams considered that this amendment had the effect of favouring property over numbers. John Adams, *Works* iv. 240, 243, n. 1. He meant the kind of property that was concentrated in larger towns; and he implies that this interest still dominated the Town elections.

was invariably composed of men of great estate, who were usually connected by ties of interest, of property, and of social rank with the Governor. The same interests, often cemented by marriage, connected them with each other.[1] The Assemblies, on the other hand, were accessible to men of moderate estate who either directly or indirectly represented the whole of the rest of the community.

The popular rage against the Stamp Act swept through the Assembly of Massachusetts Bay and disturbed every corner of public life. The leading councillors of British sympathies lost their seats, while the effect on the conduct of others is clearly portrayed in one of Governor Bernard's letters to the Earl of Hillsborough:

These two conferences with the Council [he wrote] passed with good Humour and in the course of them I had opportunity to observe and lament the Servility, in regard to the people, with which the Business of Council was now done in comparison with what it used to be. This was not denied, and one Gentleman said, that he did not now enter the Council chamber with the free mind that he used to have. But he liked to be concerned in public Business and did not chuse to quit his place in the Council, and therefore must be content to hold it on such terms as he could. So fair a confession deserves not to be passed unnoticed.[2]

Though the Council became little more than a sort of dignified ante-chamber which both Assembly and Governor tried to occupy at the same time, it did not cease to exist — it did not cease to symbolise the personal presence of a chosen upper class in the representative system; and if the existence of two chambers had become a habit, it was one for which some theoretical justification had to be discovered when Massachusetts became a State.

Peers of the realm — with certain under-privileged exceptions — were entitled to be summoned personally to Parliament. Members of colonial Councils, owing their appointments to the Governor's nomination, held a somewhat analogous position in the colonial legislative system; as it happened, the elective procedure of Massachusetts precluded this flattering analogy, but despite this disadvantage a distinct, if pallid, resemblance to the British upper House survived. In Parliament, each House represented an order, an estate of the realm. The upper House, in fact, represented two: the peers spiritual, always named first, and the peers temporal. The rest were commons. To have argued that the British state was actually composed of

[1] Leonard W. Labaree, *Conservatism in Early America* (New Haven, 1948).

[2] Bernard to Hillsborough, 12 November 1768, Bowdoin–Temple papers. The letter adds that the need is for the king to have the Council chamber in his own hands.

estates, distinct in themselves and as distinct in their parliamentary representation, would have required a pious exercise in what might be called constitutional imagination, supported by a lively ignorance of contemporary politics. The influence of the peers was powerful in the Commons, while commoners were often translated into peers. But institutions can mummify the ideas which once gave them their life's blood. The mere continuing existence of a House of Lords helped to sustain the notion that the peers of England were a sort of classical 'aristocracy', in a sense close to that which educated Americans read of in their texts. Especially so when English life was viewed at a great distance, which tended to reveal the constitutional outlines rather than the political details.

There were very strong reasons for seeing it in this light. They lay in the presuppositions which Americans insisted on in their own defence; the great merit of the English Constitution was held to be its mixture of the three main elements, monarchy, aristocracy, and democracy. It was a balanced form of government; what was imperfect was due to imperfections in this classical balance. This deeply inculcated conception required that aristocracy should be a recognised element. Not surprisingly, colonists succeeded in recognising it. With administrations formed by dukes and marquesses and manned by earls and viscounts, they were greatly assisted in perceiving in it everything except, perhaps, the superior wisdom and loftier motives of the high nobility.

To have resisted the idea that society was composed of orders, or some form of estates, would have required a certain boldness of mind. In truth, the American colonies, particularly (as Hutchinson remarked) north of Maryland, gave some ground for such boldness. By the time John Adams came to write his *Defence of the Constitutions* he felt able to state the matter in explicit terms:

In America, [he wrote] the balance is nine tenths on the side of the people. Indeed, there is but one order; and our senators have influence chiefly by the principles of authority, and very little by those of power. . . .[1]

It is significant that Adams was here discussing Harrington, who was concerned at this point with the political effects of the different ways in which power might be distributed among the estates. In America, said Adams, there was but one order, or estate. He agreed with Hutchinson that property was so widely diffused as to dispose of any problem arising from the conflicting

[1] John Adams, *A Defence of the Constitutions of Government of the United States* (1787) in *Works*, iv. 434 (hereafter referred to as *Defence*).

interests of different estates of the American realm. (Both men, of course, wrote with a personal experience mainly of the north-eastern region.) Yet this is one of the few places in Adams's writings where an unambiguous assertion of this kind may be found. Numerous passages in the *Defence* indicate a preoccupation with the problem of aristocracy in a republic. These, without being defences of aristocracy, confronted the question of how the aristocracy was to be prevented from exercising an undue influence. They plainly could not have had the slightest relevance or meaning if Adams had not firmly believed that a social and economic order of the aristocratic type did exist in America, even in New England, which would inevitably use its advantages to wield an undue proportion of political power.

Since John Adams was the author of the first draft of the Constitution of 1780, the importance of this phase of his thought can hardly be overestimated; the more so because the arrangements for a bicameral legislature and the different bases on which they were founded, were among those which were not subsequently amended by the Convention.[1]

It is not easy to distinguish Adams's descriptive comments on aristocracy from his opinions — and is more difficult still when his opinions seem tinged with a touch of half-acknowledged admiration. That a hereditary aristocracy could not take root and would be grotesquely out of place in America, he made perfectly clear in his autobiographical comment on 'the Weissenstein Affair', an episode in which a person of that name acted as bearer of a message to Benjamin Franklin in Paris, proposing the establishment of such an order as one of the conditions of reconciliation between Britain and the Colonies.

Whether the Design was to seduce Us Commissioners, [remarked Adams] or whether it was thought We should send the Project to Congress and that they might be tempted by it, or that disputes might be excited among the People, I know not. In either case it was very weak and absurd, and betrayed a gross Ignorance of the Genius of the American People. An Aristocracy of American Peers! hereditary Peers I suppose were meant, but whether hereditary or for Life, nothing could be more aborrent to the general Sense of America at that time, which was for making every Magistrate and every Legislator eligible and that annually at least.[2]

Adams did not believe that a hereditary peerage was the only form in which aristocracy could present itself, or that the improbability of such a phenomenon as a product of domestic conditions would eliminate the advantages

---

[1] See the draft, with editorial notes, in *Works*, iv. 219–67.

[2] John Adams, *Diary*, iv. 152 and n. 4. The incident occurred in 1778. Franklin believed the proposal came from King George III.

conferred by birth. A long passage in the section of the *Defence* on the opinions of Franklin is devoted to the political significance of inequality. Although there were no 'artificial inequalities or legal distinctions ... no established marks, as stars, garters, crosses or ribbons', there were neverthe-less 'inequalities of great moment in the consideration of a legislator, because they have a natural and inevitable influence in society'.[1] The first was of wealth, whether acquired by descent or by superior skill. Here Adams noted the influence of rich manufacturers over the men in their employ, a point which has been discussed in connection with the property qualifications for the suffrage. The paragraph ends with an observation that is both perceptive and, perhaps, revealing:

Nay, farther it will not be denied, that among the wisest people that live, there is a degree of admiration, abstracted from all dependence, obligation, expectation, or even acquaintance, which accompanies splendid wealth, insures some respect, and bestows some influence. Let no man be surprised that this species of inequality is introduced here. Let the page of history be quoted, where any nation, ancient or modern, civilized or savage, is mentioned, among whom no difference was made, between the citizens, on account of their extraction. The truth is, that more influence is allowed to this advantage in free republics than in despotic governments, or would be allowed to it in simple monarchies, if severe laws had not been made from age to age to secure it. The children of illustrious families have generally greater advantages of education, and earlier opportunities to be acquainted with public characters, and informed of public affairs, than those of meaner ones, or even than those in middle life; and what is more than all, an habitual national veneration for their names, and the characters of their ancestors, described in history, or coming down by tradition, removes them farther from vulgar jealousy and popular envy, and secures them in some degree the favour, the affection, the respect of the public. Will any man pretend that the name of Andros, and that of Winthrop, are heard with the same sensations in any village of New England? Is not gratitude the sentiment that attends the latter? And disgust the feeling excited by the former? In the Massachusetts, then, there are persons descended from some of their ancient governors, counsellors, judges, whose fathers, grandfathers, and great-grandfathers, are remembered with esteem by many living, and who are mentioned in history with applause as benefactors to the country, while there are others who have no such advantage. May we go a step further, — Know thyself is as useful a precept to nations as to men. Go into every village in New England, and you will find that the office of justice of the peace, and even the place of representative, which has ever depended only on the freest election of the people, have generally descended, from generation to generation, in three or four families at most.[2]

[1] *Defence* in *Works*, iv. 392 ff.
[2] John Adams, *Defence*, 110–11.

Soon afterwards, Adams gives an account of what is presumably an imaginary argument in a tavern — though it may have drawn upon arguments heard many times — in which one disputant affirms that as the man he upholds has been a good governor, so he and his heirs should 'rule over us for ever'. He is at once caught out by his interlocutor, who asks what has become of his republican principles? And the first speaker has to admit that the sentiment he has just uttered is out of harmony with his own claim on that subject.[1]

The next inequality he discussed was that of birth.

The natural propensity of the people to the adulation of great men and great families struck Adams as a sort of corollary to the dangerous influence of such men by their wealth and their connections.

There are [he said again] and always have been, in every state, numbers possessed of some degree of family pride, who have been invariably encouraged, if not flattered in it, by the people. These have most acquaintance, esteem and friendship with each other, and mutually aid each other's schemes of interest, convenience, and ambition. Fortune, it is true, has more influence than birth. A rich man, of an ordinary family and common decorum of conduct, may have greater weight than any family merit commonly confers without it.[2]

There was, in Adams's opinion, a natural aristocracy which would appear in any society, arising from the combination of birth, wealth, and personal qualities; and the advantages of birth and wealth would of themselves serve to strengthen, both in the public eye and in personal ability, those qualities which made for leadership.[3]

The purpose of this discussion was to argue that the aristocracy could not be trusted with legislative power in a single chamber. The reason why it

[1] 'For the future the question can never be, How *long* has anyone governed, but *how* does he govern?' Article in *The Worcester Magazine* (Worcester, Mass.), 319–23, 1st week October 1787.

[2] *Works*, iv. 396–7.

[3] Other statements of this view appear, *Defence*, 290, 397, 399, and 414, where the author says: 'If there is, then, in society such a natural aristocracy . . . as all history and experience demonstrate, formed partly by genius, partly by birth and partly by riches, how shall the legislator avail himself of their influence for the benefit of the public? and how, on the other hand, shall he prevent them from disturbing the public happiness? I answer, by arranging them all, or at least the most conspicuous of them, together in one assembly, by the name of a senate; by separating them from all pretensions to executive power, and by controlling in the legislative their ambition and avarice, by an assembly of representatives on one side, and by the executive authority on the other. Thus you will have the benefit of their wisdom, without the fear of their passions.'

came into the section devoted to Franklin is that Franklin was believed to favour a single, supreme legislative House, such as had been established with the aid of his guidance in Pennsylvania — where in any case it was traditional. In his *Thoughts on Government*, Adams treated the second chamber under the general problem of preventing an engrossment of power in the Assembly. He suggested that as in Massachusetts the Council be elected by the Assembly.[1] But he did not enter into the question of orders or of the special protection of property. By 1779 he had had more time to reflect; and to observe the formation of bitter social divisions over the issues between merchants, artisans, and farmers; between town and country in general; between lawyers and the victims of litigation; between creditors and debtors.

The conclusion of his argument in the *Defence* was that, as the aristocracy's advantages would be certain to procure them seats in the Assembly, in which body they could be counted on to form factions and followings, the only safe course was that of creating a separate chamber in which they would be contained. The honour of sitting there would apparently be enough to satisfy their ambition; while the representatives of the people could debate without risk of corruption in the Assembly. The seclusion of the aristocracy in the Senate he called 'an ostracism'.[2]

One definite contribution Adams made in this discourse was his insistence on the effectiveness of the executive. In the draft which Adams left with the Massachusetts Convention, the Governor was given an absolute power of veto over legislative acts, and the modification of this provision by the Convention was a substantial departure from Adams's intentions. Adams, deeply mistrustful of the aristocracy, was determined to set up a power that could check them;[3] but he was concerned to do more than this. He wanted to

---

[1] *Works*, iv. 195–6.

[2] *Works*, iv. 290. This conclusion is actually stated in the preface but is logically connected with the remarks on Franklin.

[3] In which he appears to have been influenced by Delolme; but Adams insisted on the point more strongly. (R. R. Palmer, *The Age of the Democratic Revolution : 1, The Challenge* (Princeton, 1959), (hereafter referred to as *Democratic Revolution*), 272–3.) Professor Palmer argues persuasively that the character of Adams's thought is anti-aristocratic, in that he is much occupied with the problems of safeguards against the abuses to be expected from aristocracy. In later life Adams wrote to Jefferson: 'Your *aristoi* are the most difficult animals to manage in the whole theory and practice of government. They will not suffer themselves to be governed'. (Palmer, ibid., 273, n. 52.) But I suspect that despite all this, Adams shared a trace of the admiration for aristocracy that he described so well. It will be recalled that the natural aristocracy in Adams's view of society did not consist simply of the people of the best natural endowments; but rather of those who combined high abilities with high birth, advantageous wealth, and a general superiority of up-

reproduce in America, in perfect and uncorrupted form, those virtues of balance which were the ideal (not the actual or contemporary) merit of the British Constitution. For these ideal virtues Adams shared all the enthusiasm that Burke poured out on the British Constitution in its capacity as a venerable pile. A bicameral legislature was a central part of the edifice. And this was Adams's opinion in 1776, before he had developed his fears of aristocratic domination. His *Thoughts on Government* copied the provincial practice of election for the upper chamber, and gave different reasons from those which were to follow in 1779 and 1786; but the two chambers were already firmly planted in his scheme.

These passages contain valuable observations of American political life, but the reasoning which Adams applied to them was curiously weak, and in turn reflects on the quality of some other of his observations.

There is absolutely no reason to suppose that an aristocracy which possessed the influence and the ambitions attributed to it by Adams could be effectively contained or caged in its separate chamber. The leading men would control parties or factions in the lower House; and indeed there would be nothing to prevent such leading men from securing seats for themselves in the Assembly rather than the Senate. But, Adams replies, 'When a senate exists, the most powerful man in the state may be safely admitted into the house of representatives, because the people have it in their power to remove him into the senate as soon as his influence becomes dangerous.'[1] The most

bringing and training. It was 'this natural aristocracy' which formed 'a body of men which contains the greatest collection of virtues and abilities in a free government, is the brightest ornament and glory of the nation, and may always be made the greatest blessing of society, if it be judiciously managed in the constitution. But [he adds] if this be not done, it is always the most dangerous; nay, it may be added, it never fails to be the destruction of the commonwealth' (*Works*, iv. 397). Adams believed that the growth of some such class was inevitable; and his language suggests that he would have been willing to add that a society which failed to produce an aristocracy would have been that much poorer. The problem, then, was to harness or contain them. It would be a little singular if John Adams, who had by this time done the state some service, had met all the important men in the United States, and many in Europe; who was yet to be President of the United States; who had a son for whom he was ambitious and of whom he was proudly fond, and who could not have failed to be aware of the advantages that his position conferred on that son; who was himself proud, shrewd, and vastly the superior of most of his colleagues — and who was the first great member of the most distinguished of the 'great families' of recent history — a little singular if John Adams had really harboured no latent respect for the qualities of aristocracy. Even a little superhuman. Adams, moreover, had a tremendous respect for the attainments of the nobilities of Europe. Edward Handler, *America and Europe in the Political Thought of John Adams* (Cambridge, Mass., 1964), 143–6.

[1] *Works*, iv. 291.

powerful man in the state would be unusually deficient in political ability if he could not use his power to place himself in whichever House he wanted. By whom would the people be informed, or led, in removing him? The Senate, he says, 'becomes the great object of ambition; the richest and the most sagacious wish to merit an advancement to it by services to the public in the house.' But obviously, if the richest and most sagacious were also the most ambitious they would not seek to be kicked upstairs. And if they were also the most powerful they would certainly control the elections in their constituencies.

What is all the more strange is that Adams wrote these passages in London, after having plenty of opportunity to observe English political realities. And in reality the House of Lords did not stand for any distinctive interest in the realm. Still less did it 'contain' or restrain a bevy of over-mighty subjects. British administrations were formed from both Houses, and Prime Ministers could be found in either. The Marquess of Rockingham was a peer; Lord North, for parliamentary purposes at least, was a commoner. The Earl of Shelburne sat in the Lords; Fox in the Commons — and so on. Interests, of the most complex and inter-penetrating kind, were represented in both Houses, and especially in the Commons; but a great and classical division between an aristocracy and a democracy would have been one of the most unlikely deductions to be drawn by an uninstructed observer of the English scene. John Adams unfortunately was far from uninstructed. He was deeply versed, not only in the ancient classics, but in the modern commentators. When he looked at the English situation he experienced a sort of double vision. He was quite capable of noting that the House of Commons needed reform, but he thought this necessary in order to give the Commons their due weight against the corrupting influence of the Crown and the peers. The fact that Parliament had completely ceased, in practice, to represent the ancient estates of the realm and had come to represent the infinitely more varied complex of interests seems to have escaped him. He was thinking of a great design. One is tempted to say that he missed the trees for the wood, but the truth is that the wood itself had changed shape.

It is a clue to John Adams's temperament that he should have occupied himself with the problem of an over-mighty aristocracy at a period when more of his contemporaries were alarmed by the dangers of an over-mighty democracy. To say that Adams willed the aristocracy into existence in order to shut them up in the Senate would be unfair to him, and unjust to the pretensions of the very formidable core of great merchants, planters, and patrons whose influence shaped political life; but it would not be unfair to say that life for Adams would have been very flat if there had been no incipient aristocracy to worry about.

A combination of familiar conditions, governing the settlement and growth of American life — the shortage of labour, the community of the town, the rise and character of the city, cheap land and the opportunities for acquiring it — tended repeatedly to undermine the formation, and detract from the stability, of a permanent upper class. These factors, however, were slow to undermine the notion that society normally was and ought to be ordered into its various estates, ranks, and degrees. Americans learned from Locke that society had been formed by voluntary compact. This compact was between individuals, not between existing estates. Between the association of individuals and that of social orders lay a gap that was bridged better in imagination than in either fact or theory. There was no logical link to connect these aspects of the contractual character of social relations, other than Locke's specious attempt to argue that individuals by agreeing to use money had 'consented' to inequalities of wealth in a manner analogous to their 'consent' to government.[1] Yet, given the existence of society from time immemorial — a point admitted by Locke but not admitted by him to detract from the plausibility of a real original compact — Adams and his contemporaries were content to allow the two streams, from individual consent and from the association of orders, to flow together into the same pool of social contract.

Although Adams was deeply impressed by the writings of Harrington, that influence had practical limits. It would be hard to imagine John Adams of Massachusetts submitting to a scheme under which the representatives of the people sat listening to the debates of their seniors on subjects which they themselves had no share in propounding, with no further power than that of a final vote. What did influence him was the powerful argument that the distribution of landed property was the final determinant of political power, and the concept of a state organised into political order which bore some correspondence to the orders of society.[2]

There was a further factor which, despite the persistent erosive force of American conditions, helped to keep in being the idea of a basic ordering of

[1] Locke, *Second Treatise*, sections 48, 49, 50.
[2] Cf. R. R. Livingston in New York, who said in 1799 that he still favoured the bicameral principle and a balanced form of government, a form which recognised different orders in society 'as necessary to a steady government'. Chilton Williamson, *American Suffrage from Property to Democracy* (Princeton, 1960), 151.

society represented in political institutions. This was the actual existence of
these institutions. Every province had its Council — even Pennsylvania had
one. Although, in the revolution crisis, the Governor's circle and the Council
tended to reveal a higher ratio of Tory sympathies than did any other
institution, the Council had not always stood on the side of the Crown and
was a branch of government in which some of the most influential of the
colonists had habitually sat. Nor was it an extraneous or a superimposed
institution; it was a native development of American colonial politics. It
served to establish as a normal fact of colonial political life the presence of an
élite at the seat of government. Only those few Americans who had already
developed positively levelling ideas were disposed to do away with the
Council altogether.

When Theophilus Parsons formulated the views of the Essex gentry in
the *Essex Result* in 1778, the two elements which he identified as the objects
of government action were persons and property. Persons were supposed to
have brought their property, for protection, into society under the auspices
of government. It was a short step from this reasoning to the belief that
society was made up of 'estates', or orders. The more so when such orders
had, to everyone's knowledge, always existed; and when the orders were
reduced to such elemental forms as were expressed in the 'persons and
property' formula.

The *Address* of 1780, which adopted the concept of persons and property,
made clear that these traditional views had determined the basic form of
government. The House of Representatives was stated to be 'intended as the
representatives of the Persons, the Senate of the Property, of the Commonwealth'.[1] This separation was also, by implication, one formulation of the
separation of powers; it prevented the concentration of all legislative power
in one House, which would overthrow the necessary balance in the machinery
— or the building, for an architectural analogy was also used — and would
lead to tyranny. The two Houses would check each other.

As each House was conceived to represent a separate interest, it was
important to declare that the Governor was 'emphatically the Representative
of the whole People, being chosen not by one Town or County but by the
People at large'. For this reason he was given the power of revising bills
(though not of final veto) and was made Commander-in-Chief.

In some of the Massachusetts towns this concept was challenged. Wren-
tham adopted a report which took exception to the separate representation
of persons and property, 'which principal we utterly disclaim, we are of

[1] The *Address*, Mass. Archives, vol. 276.

Opinion that the representatives elected in each town ought to be the Representatives of the property as well as the persons'; and argued that as the people at large were not so well qualified to elect councillors or Senators, these ought to be elected by the House of Representatives. Interestingly, in view of the former sentiment, no attack was made on property qualifications; and it was even said that the property qualifications of members of Congress ought to be expressly stated.[1]

The lengthy and querulous document drawn up by Joseph Hawley for Northampton made the point that any distinction between a personal and a property representation must rest on a difference between the qualifications of the voters for the two Houses rather than on the basis provided; but it did not appear to call in question the idea of such differentiation.[2] Mansfield in Bristol County held that 'the Senate ought to represent persons as well as property, and that the Second Branch represents property as well as persons for sure both branches make but one Genl Court, and each Branch ought equally to consult the Safety, Prosperity and Happiness of the Whole' — and went on to declare that every adult male capable of managing the ordinary affairs of life should have the Senate franchise.[3]

The towns which quarrelled with the Constitution on grounds of personal equality did not necessarily object to the separation of persons from property in the principles of representation. Dorchester, in Suffolk, arguing for a more extensive franchise, made use of the differentiation: 'And being fully convinced that Taxation and Representation ought to be inseparable, and that the Property and Estates of the People will be sufficiently guarded by the Senate who represent the same, we see no reason of sufficient weight to debar any Person Qualified . . . from Voting in the Choice of Representatives'.[4]

The same point was made by three officers who resigned their commissions in protest against the property qualifications for the suffrage: all who were subject to taxation ought to have the free exercise of the right of representation 'at least in that branch of the legislature that more immediately represents Persons'.[5] Stoughton instructed its representatives that every free man and all the property in the state should be represented, and the legislature should consist of two branches accordingly; while Chelsea, in a very pronounced expression of the view of general, but graded, political responsibility which was common to Whig-republican thought, advocated universal suffrage for adult males satisfying a residence requirement and went on to

[1] Ibid., 277/9.   [2] Ibid., 276/58.   [3] Ibid., 276/33.   [4] Ibid., 277/67.
[5] Samuel Talbot to John Hancock, 16 November 1782; Hancock Papers, M.H.S.

insist that delegates to Congress should possess double the sum needed to qualify as a Senator.[1]

On the whole, the objections to the differentiation principle were few. Seventeen towns (of which five were in maritime counties) objected to the property qualifications for membership of the legislature; about half a dozen wanted a unicameral legislature. In general, the governing concept in the Convention carried the consent of the town meetings. The people were clearly not all satisfied with these provisions, and some argued that the principle of equality was offended by them. But the notion that 'equality' ought to mean an elemental equality between persons, regardless of their property or social position, and regardless of the corporate interests of towns or communities, though present in different forms, was neither clearly understood nor widely accepted. Where equality between persons was insisted on for one institution, it seemed quite proper to accept a different principle for another institution; thus safeguarding the integrity of different interests, a procedure which was generally accepted as just. And what was just could not be considered unequal.

5. Rebellion

In 1786 Massachusetts was shaken by a rebellion. How did this come about in a state which enjoyed all the obvious advantages of government by consent? The precipitating causes were economic; but the rebellion itself was an alternative to political opposition. Because the Constitution was supposed to embody the will of the people, the idea of organised opposition appeared faintly seditious. Political parties were yet unborn. Yet the legislative structure allowed the seaboard mercantile interests to continue to dominate politics with all the advantages and none of the odium attaching to a formal organisation. The opposition, deprived of this opportunity, resorted to county conventions reminiscent of revolutionary

[1] Mass. Archives, 160/266, 277/65. West Springfield gave an exemplary expression of the same convention: The qualifications of voters to be reduced; but the property to qualify Senators to be 'ratable' — to exclude Household furniture, etc. 'which ought not to qualify them for that station' — ibid., 276/71.

days; and eventually turned to violence. Yet the system was capable of taking the
strain. In the elections following the defeat of the rebellion, the forces of discontent
scored resounding successes.

A constitutional historian of Massachusetts, after bringing his subject safely
through the year 1780, might feel entitled to lay down his pen and contem-
plate a work well done. Few were disposed to deny that the Constitution had
been adopted with the general consent of the governed or that the annually
elected legislators conformed to the accepted notion of true representatives.
This impression of consent is made stronger by the tacit admission of the
rebels and malcontents who within a year had begun to challenge the General
Court by holding county conventions. Their numerous demands for constitutional revision were not advanced on the grounds that the ratification of
the Constitution had been a mere legal fiction; the justice of the Constitution
was impugned, but not its legality.

Within six years, longstanding discontent throughout much of the
Commonwealth had been fanned into organised riots, and these in turn
were raised, under the hesitant leadership of Captain Daniel Shays, into a
minor rebellion. The rebellion, a strangely disjointed, aimless affair, was
crushed with slight loss. The State Constitution not only emerged unshaken,
but proved itself capable of absorbing the impetus of discontent through the
normal elective system; at the ensuing elections, in April 1787, both
Governor James Bowdoin and a great majority of representatives lost their
seats. Within a few months, and particularly after the ratification of the
Federal Constitution, it was easy to believe that the whole episode had been
greatly over-rated; but before it was over it had given the legislators and
many substantial citizens, in Massachusetts and in other states, a severe
fright. If a truly republican government could not hold the allegiance of the
people, was the American experiment destined to fail?

The question gave rise to some of the animus against 'democracy' expressed in the opening days of the Philadelphia Convention. Shays's Rebellion
thus has a peculiar stature, much out of proportion to its local character. The
history of Europe is dotted with minor peasant revolts, local, wild, and
hopeless, which barely attract the attention of the historian; Richelieu
would have made short work of Shays and his friends. But the rising of 1786
demonstrated with cruel violence that something had gone wrong with the
very institutions of representation which the people of the Bay Colony had
fought to defend and had agreed, by conference, to maintain.

The grievances underlying the county conventions of 1786 and the rebellion itself were repeatedly expounded at the time. They may be summarised as economic distresses, arising from the aftermath of war and from legislative policies, administered through, and exacerbated by, the courts, the legal profession, and the county officials. The burden of taxation to meet State debts was compounded by the burden of private debt, and both were made terrifying by the practice, or the threat, of the imprisonment of debtors. The exorbitant expenses of court action often precluded the poorer victims from seeking relief through litigation, even when they had the better case. The petty tyrannies of sheriffs and constables aroused bitter hatred.

No administration could entirely have averted the post-war economic crisis; but the form it took in Massachusetts was in large measure a product of the policies of the General Court, a point firmly grasped by the more articulate and better informed spokesmen of the protest movements.

As early as 1777, the General Court had initiated the hard-money policy which it pursued, with much tacking and veering but with unwavering purpose, right down to the crisis. By Acts of 1780 and 1781, all legal tender except gold and silver was abolished and heavy taxes were imposed. Further measures in the following years constantly proclaimed the dedication of successive legislatures to the principle of redeeming the State's obligations to its creditors at whatever cost to the overburdened and the poor. And the poll tax, the most consistently used means of raising money, being levied at a flat rate, had a most unequal operation.[1]

It seemed by the early spring of 1786 that the hard struggles of the Revolutionary War were to produce, for those who had fought or endured them, nothing better than a dwindling lifetime of debt, poverty, and even imprisonment. What made this intolerable was that every officer of government was engaged as a matter of duty in forcing home the exactions, inflicting the hardships.

The General Court was not unaware of the plight of the country. Several towns instructed their representatives to procure remedies; a graphic statement coming from the town of Palmer, in which the removal of the General Court from Boston and the establishment of a 'bank of paper money' were asked for — 'Considering the great desperateness of the

---

[1] Oscar and Mary Handlin, 'Revolutionary Economic Policy in Massachusetts', *William and Mary Quarterly*, January 1947. Robert A. East, 'Massachusetts Conservatives in the Critical Period', in Richard B. Morris (ed.), *The Era of the American Revolution* (New York, 1939); Taylor, *Western Massachusetts*, 27–33, gives the best modern account of the court system, which is vividly described in J. E. A. Smith, *History of Pittsfield*, i, chap. 23.

Inhabitants of this commonwealth (and the said Town of Palmer in particular) labours under by reason of the great scarcity of surculating medeam'.[1]
A few measures of relief were passed in 1786, but in general the legislature
did not allow itself to be deflected from its main objectives either by the
evidence of economic crisis or by the fact that its own policies were not working. As late as January 1787 the import and excise were renewed for three
years and outstanding taxes ordered to be collected 'instantly'.[2]

When every allowance has been made for the imperfections of economic
science and the humanity of the legislators, their course on the one hand, and
on the other the county conventions and the outbreak of rebellion, raise
questions which cannot be answered by examining either economic statistics
or the provisions of the Constitution of 1780. The question is why a government consisting solely of duly elected representatives should have pursued a
policy capable of alienating a large section of the people and driving the
remnant to despair and revolt; the question is also why, under a representative government, the opposition should have been able to find no means
of attaining redress, both constitutional and effective.

It is clear that, despite occasional hesitations and tackings, the Assembly
majority did pursue a definable policy. It is also clear that this policy
conformed in general to the objectives of the leading economic interest of the
seaboard, and that it aroused heated and widespread opposition.

The appointment of representatives was still determined under the Act of
May 1776[3] which will be recalled as the first to depart from the pure
principle of the corporate equality of the towns.

The larger numbers of members from the eastern towns were, of course,
within much easier reach of the capital than their colleagues from the
interior; their attendance could therefore always be more regular. Their
position also gave them the opportunity of seeing each other and conferring
in ways denied to the interior. The county conventions so popular in the
west, though hotly denounced as unconstitutional and subversive, may
reasonably be considered an organised counterpart to this unofficial but
immensely useful seaboard advantage, which had originated so many years
before in the private caucus meetings in Boston.

The Speakers of the House continued to be Representatives either of
Boston or of other towns in the seaboard area, right through the war and the

[1] House documents, no. 2234, 4 February 1786, Mass. Archives.
[2] House Journal, 1786–7, vol. 7, 26 October 1786. *Acts and Resolves*, May session 1786,
chaps. 28, 29, 100, 113; January session 1787, chap. 29.
[3] See p. 175.

Confederation period, with the single and interesting exception of the critical year 1786–7 when the Speaker came from Shrewsbury in Worcester County. For most of the same period the clerk of the House was also a Boston man.

The significance of this unauthorised system was understood by the opposition. Few demands of the protest movement were more insistently repeated than that for the removal of the General Court out of Boston; and Massachusetts was a noteworthy exception to the general tendency to remove the capital in a westerly direction soon after the Revolution. This was frequently linked with demands for a reform in the basis of representation and, significantly, for the abolition of the Senate.[1] These three measures were aimed at the machinery by which the seaboard kept its grip; but it is doubtful whether they would ever have made a permanent difference without the aid of some standing political organisation.

Opposition demands for reform of the basis of representation were usually general, and failed to specify precisely what reform was desired. A clue seems to lie in a statement from the town of Greenwich, suggesting (in reply to a letter from Boston town meeting) that each town should send two members as of old, under the Charter.[2] This letter included another point of greater importance than seems to have been appreciated by many of the protesters: that members of the General Court should be paid from the state treasury since their service was to the whole community. Had this been adopted in the Constitution, the chronic non-representation of the poorer towns could have been remedied.[3]

The mere existence of the Senate was a grievance. The conservatism of that body consisted partly in its tendency to reject reforms emanating from the

[1] Resolutions of Worcester County Convention, 17 August 1786, *Worcester Magazine*, 4th week, August 1786; Resolutions of Hampshire County Convention, *Worcester Magazine*, 3rd week, September 1786; town instructions to Representatives, East Sudbury, May 1786, House Documents, no. 2305; Watertown (which itself was adjacent to Boston and probably jealous of its power), 29 May 1786, House Documents, no. 2281; Framingham, 22 September 1786, House Documents, no. 2279; Salisbury, 25 September 1786, House Documents, no. 2278; Freetown, 14 May 1787, House Documents, no. 2698; Mansfield, 14 May 1787, House Documents, no. 2706; Dracut, 16–26 May 1787, House Documents, no. 2709; Wendover, 28 May 1787, House Documents, no. 2708; Hardwick, 21 May 1787, House Documents, no. 2705; Douglass, 28 May 1787, House Documents, no. 2702; Harvard, 28 May 1787, House Documents, no. 2696; Watertown (again), 28 May 1787, House Documents, no. 2695 (Mass. Archives).

[2] *Worcester Magazine*, 4th week, November 1786.

[3] The provision in the Constitution was that the treasury should pay members their expenses but that their towns were then assessed for the amount in taxes.

House,[1] partly in the mere presence of a constitutional body based on property rather than persons. The election of James Bowdoin as Governor in 1785, which took place in the General Court owing to the lack of a popular majority for any candidate, was carried with the aid of a senatorial majority of commercial interests.[2] Economic distress and the policies of the General Court had begun to make this principle seem more objectionable than it had seemed in theory in 1780. The young John Quincy Adams noted in 1787 that the Senate had several times within the last eighteen months 'saved the commonwealth from complete anarchy, and perhaps from destruction'; but he observed with earnest exaggeration that its hands were tied, that the 'democratical branch' of the government was 'quite unrival'd'; and that the people were too generally disposed to abolish the Senate as 'a useless body'.[3]

The actual distribution of senators on the basis of taxes paid, rather than numbers, did not make a great difference.[4] Suffolk County, with Boston, had six senators instead of the four to which it would have been entitled on a numerical basis; the central and western counties were short by one or two senators; but it is a mistake to assess representation in merely arithmetical terms. All the senators, from whatever counties, were required to be men of substance; and it is important to note that because they represented counties, not towns, the senators were free from the restrictions imposed by the prevalent and very strongly held doctrine of the right of constituency instruction.[5] The senate, indeed, retained its character long after the fires of Shays's Rebellion had burned out and its political cast was generally Federalist in the 1790s.[6]

The better informed commentators who contributed essays on economic policy to the newspapers showed much understanding and often a fund of knowledge; but this was brought out only by the crisis and the usual situation

---

[1] As late as October 1786 the Senate rejected a committee report for simplifying legal procedure by requiring all original processes in civil cases to be opened before Justices of the Peace, and that in cases of default executions should issue without further delay. *Essex Journal*, 1 November 1786.

[2] Richard B. Morris, 'Insurrection in Massachusetts', in Daniel Aaron (ed.), *America in Crisis* (New York, 1952), 35.

[3] *Life in a New England Town: 1787, 1788* (Boston, 1903), 120. Being the Diary of John Quincy Adams. [4] Palmer, *Democratic Revolution*, 226.

[5] Taylor, *Western Massachusetts*, 140. Thus the senators were much less tied by local opinion than the representatives, and occupied a position analogous with that of the provincial councillors.

[6] Anson E. Morse, *The Federalist Party in Massachusetts to 1800* (Princeton, 1909), 64 (hereafter referred to as *Federalist Party*).

in the towns showed little change since the days before the Revolution. Newspapers very seldom reported Assembly debates — the *Hampshire Gazette* was roused to do so as late as November, 1786, and it did not become a habit.[1] The House itself did nothing to inform the people either of its measures or the reason for them; even when it had acted to redress grievances it failed to explain its actions.[2] A contributor sympathetic to the demonstrators pointed out that it would be well if the General Court would inform their constituents more particularly of the state of public affairs; especially of the state's part of the national debt, the amount of the domestic debt, the annual charge for the support of government, and the interest paid annually; the takings of the treasury by imposts, excise, licences and auctions, and taxes; and many other matters of political economy which were later to become the currency of political discussion.[3] Other glimpses of the curiously episodic state of information about public affairs are caught from the instructions of Douglass in May 1787, which remarked to the representative that as he would have better information in that capacity than the town he might make all reasonable alterations; a remark by the chief justice that the representatives were better informed than the towns, and a remark by another town that it 'believed' laws had been passed contrary to the peace treaty — plainly admitting to uncertainty about legislative history.[4]

These deficiencies were admitted by the General Court to be part of the reason for the prevailing dissatisfaction — or rather they were proclaimed on the ground that better information would have led to fairer appreciation of the efforts of the legislators. In October 1786 a committee of both branches of the legislature brought in a long report directly designed to answer recent complaints and to provide public information, and several measures of redress were ordained; one of which, the introduction of a new institution to take the place of the unpopular court of Common Pleas, was later rejected by the Senate.[5] Soon afterwards, a formal Address to the People by the General Court gave an account of public revenues, spending, expectations from land sales, and the state of the debt. This was necessary because, it was stated, discontent had arisen largely from misinformation.[6]

---

[1] *Hampshire Gazette*, 1 November 1786.   [2] Taylor, *Western Massachusetts*, 136.

[3] 'From a Friend . . .', *Hampshire Gazette*, 11 October 1786.

[4] House Documents, nos. 2702, 2705, Mass. Archives; *Hampshire Gazette*, 29 November 1786.

[5] *Hampshire Gazette*, 18 October 1786; *Essex Journal*, 1 November 1786.

[6] *Worcester Magazine*, November–December 1786; *Hampshire Gazette*, 13 December 1786.

The great increase in the numbers of newspapers that had taken place since before the Revolution might have been expected to alter this situation for the better. Yet the Press remained a medium for episodic and often disconnected information. Acts of the General Court were frequently reported, often being reproduced in full; at the end of the session the papers sometimes regaled their readers with a complete list of Acts passed. News from Europe was given great prominence as often as it arrived by the packet. But state and continental news came in for very inconsistent treatment; and it is probable that much that was known in the tavern was not thought worth reproducing in the Press. What, in general, this Press system represented, by contrast with the later development of the Press, was a lack of any organised news-gathering service, — something only vaguely felt by the printer-editors as they solicited news and contributions.

In constitutional theory the towns were represented through their right to instruct representatives. Through them the General Court would possess all the information it needed for legislative purposes. The difficulties experienced not only by Massachusetts but by the American economy after the end of the war might have been expected to provide the legislators with all the information they needed. Yet the months before the outbreak of violence in Western Massachusetts present a curiously mixed picture. On 2 June 1786 Governor Bowdoin addressed the legislature on matters requiring their attention. He remarked on the importance of paying the revenue due to Congress and observed that appropriate tax Acts would be necessary to raise the funds to meet the domestic debt; he alluded also to the question of the Commonwealth's boundary with New York and the need to support Harvard College. No one would have guessed from this speech that the western counties seethed with discontented elements on the point of revolt.[1]

Why, then, had not the afflicted areas themselves made better use of their constitutional rights to instruct their representatives and to apply for redress? If the instructions and petitions for relief lying in the state archives are grouped together the cries of distress sound insistent and impressive. None speaks clearer than the plea of Ludlow:

We humbly Conceve that your honours are well acquanted with the distresses of the people of this Commonwealth and are possesed of Bowels of pitty and tenderness.[2]

Not all these petitions agreed with each other. Most demanded paper

[1] *Acts and Resolves*, 1786–7, 2 June 1786.
[2] 6 February 1786, House Documents, no. 2033, Mass. Archives.

money, and a few denounced it:[1] but the curious thing is that, from the period January to June 1786, the total number surviving is 15 out of a total of instructions and petitions numbering some 220.[2] The other factor of great significance is the chronic non-representation of the smaller towns.

May 1786 began a session at which, in view of the growing discontent, a large delegation might have been expected from the western counties. In fact, of 314 towns entitled to representation no fewer than 145 failed to elect a member. The three western and central counties of Hampshire, Worcester, and Berkshire — entitled between them to 130 representatives — could send only 67. This figure probably represented a strenuous exertion, for it compared favourably with the percentage of the state as a whole. But where Hampshire, Worcester, and Berkshire achieved a representation of about 51 per cent against a state average of about 53, the eastern counties of Suffolk, Essex, and Middlesex sent delegations from 46 of their 78 towns — almost 60 per cent; and if the count is confined to Essex and Suffolk, which between them concentrated most of the seaboard population and mercantile property, the contrast becomes still more striking: 29 out of 40 towns, or 72 per cent.[3] When all the unofficial advantages of the seaboard are weighed in, and the lack of unity, previous consultation, or even uniformity of interest of the interior counties is considered, the political influence of the east becomes almost a tangible thing.

The basic reason for this non-representation was economic. The town records show again and again that when the cost of being assessed for the support of a member throughout the legislative sessions was considered by a community, the gains to be had from representation frequently did not seem worth the price. But the very factors which made representation urgent also made it more burdensome. The harder the times, the more inducement to the towns to cut their costs. That any one town's one or two representatives would be able to make an effective impression on the general policies of the

[1] Newburyport asked for a stronger Congress and support for agriculture, as well as drawing attention to unemployment in the shipbuilding industry. Paper money was rejected as a bad remedy. *Worcester Magazine*, 3rd week, June 1786.

[2] The serial numbers run from 2,009 to 2,231 for this period. But the arrangement of the documents does not make this a conclusive guide. Between late 1785 and early 1788 there appear to be some 5,000 petitions. The number of these bearing reference to economic distress is surprisingly small.

[3] *Acts and Resolves*, May 1786. The state average is computed with the omission of Duke's, Nantucket, and York, which for geographical reasons were untypical. The low representation of Middlesex County, in which only 17 of 38 towns sent delegates, is evidence of the difficulties of the times. It was not only in the west that these were felt.

Court or on the condition of the Commonwealth always seemed improbable. It was easier to risk the fine for non-representation and hope for the success of a plea of poverty. The worse the crisis, the worse the representation of the state as a whole at the seat of government; and this was a weakness that applied particularly to the areas of greatest distress. The times thus gave great force to the argument of Greenwich, that all representatives should be paid from the public chest — a view which only some dozen towns had thought worth advancing in their returns on the Constitution of 1780.

But the unwillingness of the dissatisfied towns to make an instrument of reform of the General Court is not fully explained by their poverty. It must be recognised that there occurred a dangerous breakdown of confidence between the General Court and a large body of citizens — a much larger body, to judge by the county conventions, than eventually took part in the disturbances. Against the strangely small number of petitions seeking redress from the legislature, the conventions brought together and gave vent to an impressive volume of indignation.

The link between the county conventions and the Shays disorders is obscure. The chief justice, William Cushing, charged that every county to have held a convention also produced a rebellion; the others had not.[1] Hostile critics heaped mountains of abuse on the conventions, repeating incessantly that they were unconstitutional bodies led by desperate men; it was also alleged that the leaders were old partisans of Britain, still acting under her guidance; and it was occasionally said that they aimed at complete levelling and the seizure and division of property. Whether or not the Convention leaders were possessed with the frenzy of class hatred and the purpose of class war, such motives were freely attributed to them by their enemies.[2]

Much of the frenzy was worked up by the 'conservatives', who convinced themselves that a new social revolution was in the making, although there is no evidence of rebel plans against the state government; it was on western ground that the rival forces met, and hardly anyone on either side was hurt.

Not all conventions were radical. During the strange earlier interlude of Berkshire's semi-independence, the conservatives, those who adhered to the central government and styled themselves 'friends of order', held a convention in Stockbridge;[3] on one occasion at least the legislature actually

---

[1] *Hampshire Gazette*, 29 November 1786.

[2] These attacks were carried widely in the newspapers through the summer and winter of 1786–7.

[3] Theodore Sedgwick to James Sullivan, 16 May 1779. Sedgwick Papers, M.H.S.

ordained a county convention in Berkshire, to settle a dispute about the site of a new county court house.[1] But it was of course perfectly true that the Convention movement which revived even before the end of the War and gathered momentum in the post-war crisis was a movement of protest.

The conventions were composed of delegates from the towns, regularly elected in town meetings. It was open to each town to decide whether or not to send a delegation, and those in which a majority — or the leading citizens — opposed the whole practice sometimes gave their reasons for declining. Thus Medford, refusing to attend the Worcester Convention of August 1786, declared it an unwarrantable attempt to take the public business out of the hands of those (i.e. the General Court) to whom the Constitution had confided it. The proper procedure was to lay grievances before the General Court through instructions to representatives; but the call did not specify any grievances. The Convention, this statement sharply added, was likely to create more grievances by making parties and counteracting the proceedings of the General Court. Medford believed the state debts to be debts of honour, the price of victory in war. If the states repudiated it, the prediction of their enemies that the Americans were incapable of governing themselves would be completely verified.[2]

The biggest gain from the conventions may well have been that by causing excitement and public debate they attracted attention to the widespread nature of the grievances which called them forth. But as a means of concerting opposition, they were not very effective. The complaints listed in the resolves of the conventions frequently reappeared in the instructions or petitions of the towns which had sent delegations. But the repetition of these demands made little impression on the General Court. As early as 1782, a Convention in Worcester County demanded that the treasury make out an annual account to be circulated among the towns, asked for the removal of the General Court from Boston, and attacked the problem of the jurisdiction of the civil courts.[3] The chief justice, in his comprehensive indictment delivered in 1786, charged the conventions, two or three years previously, with having drawn up a list of nominees recommended for election to the House and Senate;[4] and this is just the step that the conventions might be expected to have taken in view of the need for an organised opposition, representing the discontented elements in the country.

This step was taken after the defeat of Shays. A Convention in Worcester

[1] In September 1784. Smith, *History of Pittsfield*, i. 429.
[2] *Worcester Magazine*, last week, August 1786.
[3] *Massachusetts Spy*, 23 May 1782.   [4] *Hampshire Gazette*, 29 November 1786.

County then drew up and caused to be circulated a list of proposed senatorial candidates — a fact made public by the denunciation of the practice by a newspaper correspondent. It appeared that a town meeting, called by the malcontents, had written inviting other towns to send delegates to Patch's tavern in Worcester. 'Their ultimate dependence', said the writer, 'is on a new General Court; and their greatest wishes are, to have men of their own character and sentiments elected into the legislature, that they may have a pardon enacted for all their treasonable practices, and laws passed whereby they may be absolved from all obligations to pay their debts, or be allowed to cheat their creditors out of their dues, under sanction and colour of law.'[1] Another letter in the same number, by a correspondent who had caught wind of the scheme, hoped that the report was without foundation, asserting that every measure of that kind 'to INFLUENCE Elections, is a violation of the CONSTITUTION'. The news was confirmed one week later, however, by a letter calling for the meeting, and signed by the three committee members from the town of Lunenburg.[2]

The fate of this initiative is extremely interesting. Two letters in the same issue, one from the town of Athol and one from an individual, denounced the plan. The Constitution, said the Athol reply, had wisely provided that senators be chosen by the free suffrage of the people, 'and anything that gives an undue influence on the election of Senators is unconstitutional, and therefore criminal . . .'. So hostile was the response of the county that the chairman of the meeting at Patch's actually published, in the same issue, a notice stating that the lists being handed about had not emanated from his meeting; no person for senator or any other government office was agreed on; 'We thought it best not to do any business of that kind, and dispersed without doing any'.

This reaction was quite characteristic of the times. In Massachusetts, electioneering was still held in that sort of disfavour which makes a practice impossible to admit in public. But in other states this tradition was already crumbling and could not last long.

The attack on the plan to prepare lists was not a mere trick by the other side. The governing conception was that the election was an occasion on which every freeholder voted his own mind; and any attempt to influence him, by temptation or pressure, was an attempt to corrupt the essential freedom of the election. Massachusetts, before the rise of political parties, was on the whole singularly free from complaints of improper electoral

[1] *Worcester Magazine*, 3rd week, March 1787.
[2] *Worcester Magazine*, 4th week, March 1787.

tactics, and the tickets which had so long been prepared by the Quakers in Pennsylvania, the lavish treating in New York, and the gentlemanly canvassing, not by the candidates so much as by their hospitable friends in the South, would still, at this date, have seemed grossly corrupt in New England, except perhaps in Rhode Island.

It was the general policy of the conventions to correspond with each other on views, grievances, and remedies. Their meetings became more frequent as the crisis developed. It is not surprising that by early in the new year they should have begun to plan for the forthcoming elections. Their whole procedure, indeed their existence, was disagreeably reminiscent, in the opinion of their opponents, of the measures by which the province had been rallied against the Crown. Then, at least from about 1774, there had been a rising degree of unity; it could be argued that the Charter, under attack by the British, was being defended by the people. But once the Constitution of 1780 had gone into force, conventions challenged the legitimacy of the government of the state. It was therefore consistently argued by all their opponents that since the Constitution made no provision for them, but had provided adequate means of representation, they lay outside the Constitution and were illegal.

The charge of illegality can best be understood as an implied counter-assertion that the Constitution, having been established by the consent of the governed, comprehended all possible modes of legitimate political action. That instrument, as Chief Justice Cushing observed, had parcelled out all the power to be exercised under it; no delegated power remained to give to the county conventions, unless it were to counteract the General Court and compel or over-awe them. What then was to be done about real grievances? The answer was plain: follow the ancient usage by applying at regular town meetings to lawful representatives, either by petition or instruction. The Constitution expressly protected the right of instruction and the right of assembly.[1]

This counsel, however, ignored the core of the dissidents' problem. In legislative divisions the instructed members might simply be defeated. It was inherently unlikely that instructions could overturn set legislative policies unless the opposing members had had the opportunity of concerting their own measures. Here and there a specific mistake or grievance might be corrected; but that was not at all the same thing as reversing the entire direction of economic policy. Yet the whole system under which the General

[1] *Hampshire Gazette*, 29 November 1786.

Court operated tended to preclude such previous consultation; the country members came together from all over the state; and the very steps by which some co-ordinated policy might have been devised were denounced by all the agents and supporters of central government as unconstitutional. Within the formal constitution of government was an informal but no less powerful system by which the government was carried on. There was no lack of opportunity for concerting policy by the men who were always on the spot and who anyway held most of the strings of power and influence. The county conventions must be understood as the natural — indeed, the normal — response of the discontented elements to the effective exercise of power, through the control of the 'system', by their opponents.

The county convention, springing directly from the towns, upon particular occasions and derived from the popular resistance of revolutionary times, seemed to its supporters to be nearer to the people than did the General Court. The Court was of course made up of representatives, no one denied that; but they were chosen on a basis that was now found to be unsatisfactory, they were subject to the check of a Senate chosen on a different basis and free from the great control of instruction, and they were governed by detailed rules of procedure not the least significant of which — as some towns had noticed in 1780 — was the rule that only sixty members were required to make a quorum; this provision gave a standing advantage to the nearby coastal and eastern towns. The conventions seemed to claim to be an 'anti-Court' in the same way that the association which convened almost contemporaneously in England seemed to its opponents to be an 'anti-Parliament'; and they, too, denounced the body as unconstitutional.

The conventions, then, emerged as an old way of meeting new problems. They reflected not so much the power as the lack of effective instruments in the hands of a gravely discontented section of the people. It is this sense of lack which offers us a clearer view of them — though one that was not available to them. The conventions were the only mode of collective protest, of the concerting of policies, which the dissidents could hit on before the rise of the organised political party. Conventions disappeared when parties arose, until in due course the parties revived them for party purposes; but after this they acquired a national, and lost their local, character.

The upheaval of the spring elections of 1787 was all the more remarkable. It was reflected in the sheer scale of participation by the voters. In 1786, some 8,000 of them took part in the election for Governor, being about 11 per cent of the adult white males of the state; this, though slightly low, was not much below the average for such elections since 1780. But 1787 produced a turnout of over 24,000; about 32 per cent and nearly twice as high as any before.[1] The *Worcester Magazine* reported the election of sixteen new senators. The towns made an unprecedented effort to return representatives. No fewer than 228 made elections, leaving only 87 as absentees. (Next year an ebbing of this exertion was already to be noticed, with 108 towns unrepresented.) In Hampshire 41 of 59 towns, in Berkshire 21 of 25, and in Worcester, by a magnificent effort, every one of the 46 towns, returned representatives. Essex also achieved 100 per cent representation of its 18 towns, Suffolk 18 out of 22, and Middlesex 32 out of 38. An extraordinary proportion of the representatives were new; no fewer than 159 out of 253 were counted by the *Worcester Magazine*.[2]

The social composition of the House of Representatives had already begun to change by 1786, if the rank claimed by members can be considered as a guide. The dignity of an 'esquire' still told in such matters, but the 'esquires' had begun to yield place, particularly to members bearing a military rank dating from the Revolutionary War.[3] In policy, the results of the elections were felt more in relief of distress than in a fundamental change of direction. The former legislature had acted to suspend the collection of debts in specie, and this Act was periodically renewed; and a measure was passed for the relief of poor prisoners committed for debt. Acts were also passed postponing the payment of taxes.[4] The new legislature also showed notable leniency towards the Shaysites, who had been subjected to certain disabilities by the preceding body. To those who had been disfranchised, the suffrage franchise was restored in June 1787 after the disqualification had been in effect for only four months and had applied only to the election of April 1787.[5]

These measures do not disclose a basic reorientation of economic policy. The encouragement and protection of Massachusetts production and commerce, which was already legislative policy under the Confederation, was continued; but the new legislature did not initiate the paper money policy, or the establishment of a 'bank of paper money', which were demanded by so

---

[1] See Appendix II, p. 543.

[2] *Acts and Resolves*, May session 1787; May session 1788. *Worcester Magazine*, 1st week, June 1787.

[3] East, 'Massachusetts Conservatives', 358, 367.

[4] *Acts and Resolves*, May session 1787, chap. 6; October session 1787, chap. 20, chap. 29; February session 1788, chap. 53.

[5] *Acts and Resolves*, 1787, chap. 21, approved 15 June 1787.

many of the stricken towns.[1] It should be recognised that even at the height of discontent, the opposition to these measures was strong and highly articulate, even in the west. The articulateness, the grasp of political language of the economic conservatives, especially when combined with their social position, gave them an advantage that could not easily be outswayed. In the election which turned out the old General Court, even the insurgent county of Berkshire returned two of the staunchest conservatives in America: Henry Van Schaack and Theodore Sedgwick. The authority of men of their social pre-eminence outweighed adverse political opinions.

When the new legislature met, the Philadelphia Convention had already begun its sessions. In considering the course of state economic policy by that time, it is well to remember that the expectation of a new and stronger central government must have influenced all deliberations.[2]

The seaboard party of merchant leadership, the creditor interest which is generally — though somewhat mistakenly — described as 'conservative', was the party of Federalism. They supported the new Constitution and they immediately appeared as friends of the attitudes that would soon be identified with Hamilton. They no longer felt, after the elections of 1787, that they could be sure of controlling the state, but they took great comfort in the superior power of the Federal Congress. 'In my opinion', wrote one of them, 'we never had a worse House of Reps — I thank God that we have a federal Govt.' Another observed that the Massachusetts House was said to be the worse that had ever sat, and added pungently, 'I desire to thank God, it is not in their power to make paper money or to take many other disgraceful measures which we should undoubtedly be obliged to submit to but for that sovereign balm the Federal Constitution'.[3] Theodore Sedgwick, on his election to the state legislature in 1787, received the congratulations of

---

[1] A Bank of Massachusetts had been founded in 1784 (M. Jensen, *The New Nation* (New York, 1950), 232) but it was an enterprise of the Boston merchants and did not respond to the demands of the loose money interests.

[2] However, the General Court was still debating modes of paying the state debt as late as June 1789, though Federalists had reason to doubt whether the majority had any real intention of providing for it. Thomas Dwight to Theodore Sedgwick, 19 June 1789, Sedgwick papers.

[3] S. Henshaw to Sedgwick, 14 June 1789; Thomas Dwight to Sedgwick, 9 July 1789; Sedgwick Papers. As early as May 1788 Sedgwick, reporting on the new legislature, assured his friend Van Schaack that at least two-thirds of both Houses were 'federal'. Clearly the word had already been translated from its reference to the controversy over the Constitution, which had been ratified by Massachusetts but had not yet been adopted, to a description of interests represented by groups in the legislature. Sedgwick to Van Schaack, 29 May 1788, Sedgwick Papers.

Rufus King, who hoped there would be enough of his sentiments 'to check the madness of Democracy'.[1]

The year 1780 established the Constitution of Massachusetts but did not bring any change in the conduct of its politics. The province had long been used to political factions, to the struggle for prominence of energetic men, to the caucus and the manipulation of the town meeting; from about 1774, something like a united front was brought into being against British tyranny, but this front did not hold the government of the Bay Province together. When, soon after the adoption of the new state Constitution, the policy of the legislature began to provoke renewed discontent, the opposition resorted to the use of the county convention, the only form of effective organisation it knew.

Though effective as an expression of grievance, it was less useful for securing redress. The persistent weakness of the opposition was a phenomenon of some complexity. There were real difficulties about the working out of a satisfactory economic policy, and these difficulties were multiplied for those who, being in a permanent minority and not standing at the centre of information and authority, were never in a position to formulate a clear policy of their own. The merchant party did not handle the economic affairs of the state with great success, and were ready to permit modifications and to alleviate undue hardships when the need was pointed out to them: but they did in effect work as a political party. Their strategic position, their opportunities of mutual consultation, and the quorum rule in the House of Representatives gave them all the advantages of a party without the distasteful formality of organisation; nor were they required to face the extremely arduous task, which gave much trouble to later party organisers, of keeping the machinery of a party in existence between elections.

The organisation of opposition through committees of correspondence had worked splendidly during the Revolution because of the essential unity of purpose between the towns and the provincial Congress, which soon became the Assembly of the state; but it was a different matter when the opposition was to the policy of the state's own legislature. American politicians had not learned to differentiate between opposing the policy of the majority and opposing the Constitution itself; it was a distinction which

---

[1] Rufus King to Sedgwick, 10 June 1787, Sedgwick Papers. King, writing from Philadelphia, where he was a member of the Convention, remarked that he was precluded from communicating, *'even confidentially'*, any particular of the proceedings. One may wonder how many politicians could be relied on to observe such a pledge in the conditions of modern democracy.

until very lately had been delicate in Britain, where the idea of a 'formed' opposition was officially held to imply disloyalty to the Crown. Supporters of majority policies could easily denounce the efforts of their opponents as unconstitutional — as 'disloyal', in the American sense.

What the opposition needed, instead of a series of county conventions, was a state-wide political party. The need was urgent, a fact which can be seen very clearly in retrospect; but the idea was inchoate, and when it began to take shape it reeked of those signs of conspiracy, of dissent from the agreed will of the sovereign people, of the attempt to interfere with the elemental freedom of the choice made by the voter on the spot at the time of the election, which the managers of the system always found so easy to discern and denounce.

The amount of public information carried by the newspapers increased through the period; and during the Shays troubles they fairly groaned with political and economic argument; that none of them was sympathetic to the malcontents was a factor which diminished their utility as organs of a possible organised opposition; but some of them gave both sides a hearing, and they could always be used to announce meetings and to sound opinion.

After the recent excitements, and the struggle over the adoption of the Constitution, the townsmen watched their representatives with keen and suspicious attention. A particularly bad impression was created by the Act of the new Congress establishing the salaries of members. The husbandmen of Massachusetts were not prepared to acquiesce in letting politics become a remunerative career; and the Act caused great anxiety to the Federalists, who had the job of explaining and justifying the Congress to the electorate. 'The idea of making money out of the public *at this time*', wrote Van Schaack, from Pittsfield, to Sedgwick, now in Congress, 'ought to be expunged.' If the report of the committee on this matter were adopted it would lessen the confidence of 'a considerable number of the yeomanry of the country'.[1] The frugal people of New England were not impressed by the explanation that the Congress had to pay regard to the habits of Southern gentlemen; gentlemen and yeomen were unanimously against it.[2] A year later the defeat of a respected member was attributed to his support of this measure.[3]

Nothing could more persuasively demonstrate the system of personal influence by which the Federalists maintained their leadership than the

[1] Van Schaack to Sedgwick, 5 July 1789. Sedgwick Papers.
[2] Van Schaack to Sedgwick, 26 July 1789. Sedgwick Papers.
[3] Thomas Dwight to Theodore Sedgwick, 13 July 1790. Sedgwick Papers.

correspondence between Sedgwick, the leading Federalist of Western Massachusetts and one of the leaders in Congress, and his close associates at home. It was as a result of a militia matter that Van Schaack was able to confirm the accuracy of his impressions about the remuneration of federal representatives and officers of government; while Sedgwick was urged to tell other members of Congress to 'take every opportunity to write to their country friends' about every beneficial measure; no pains should be spared to make a favourable impression among the great body of people.[1]

The language of this correspondence is that of a network of distinguished men who, understanding each other well, expected to be able through the exercise of traditional influence to lead the yeomanry. These were the gentlemen, and they knew it; the yeomanry were expected to follow. To maintain their leadership by this time required hard work: it meant making sure that people attended town meetings, and even making sure that votes, once cast, were returned to the secretary of state's office within the proper time.

'I am persuaded by recent experience', wrote another of Sedgwick's friends, 'that we can do infinitely more by private Letters than by News paper publications'.[2]

This was the old system, and it was not played out yet. But in order to make it work, the Federalists would soon have to admit the necessity for a more permanent and even a more professional form of organisation; and it would not be long before they proclaimed — or admitted — themselves to be a political party.

6. The Rest is History

T H E system of representation which had been introduced by the Constitution of 1780 proved strong and supple enough to absorb the shocks of 1786 and 1787. The easing of difficulties that followed was produced in part by legislative policies, in part by more general improvements. The Whig frame

[1] Van Schaack to Sedgwick, 19 July 1789, 7 February 1790. Sedgwick Papers.
[2] S. Henshaw to Sedgwick, 15 April 1789. Sedgwick Papers.

of government was not intended to give way to formal democracy, and throughout the era of the 1790s the Senate remained generally Federalist.[1] But in practical politics the special representation of property did not long present a very effective opposition to the 'democratical' element, whose participation was manifest in the exercise of the suffrage.

The property qualifications placed little material restriction on the extent of the suffrage. The haphazard kind of enforcement which had been observed before the Revolution continued to prevail; so that although a proportion of the people were excluded by legal definition, they do not appear to have constituted that kind of aggrieved group or class whose demands make themselves felt in pressure on the legislature. The best evidence of this point is that of their silence. During the years of depression and strife after the end of the War, huge numbers of petitions were despatched to the General Court, giving a vivid and detailed account of the grievances of the inhabitants of different towns and sections; and the absence of demands for suffrage extension can best be interpreted to mean that suffrage restrictions were not felt to be a grievance.

The enforcement of the laws was largely a matter of local option on the part of the selectmen. Evidence adduced by official enquiries into disputed elections showed that a line of exclusion could be drawn, but that it was in general a very elastic line. Farm labourers and apprentices, for example, whose residential qualifications were called into question, might be admitted as voters without being submitted to questions about their property. Popular participation in elections never ran very high in Massachusetts until the time of Jefferson's Embargo in 1807. But when 68 per cent of the adult white men voted in the election for Governor in 1812 they established a record that was not to be beaten at any time in Jackson's presidency; it was not until the great leap of 1840 that as many as 66 per cent were to participate in voting for Governor, 65 per cent for President.[2]

No alteration in the laws seems materially to have affected these fluctuations. The Constitution was revised in 1820, when a male taxpayer's suffrage was introduced; but the statistics show that participation before this reform, at periods of political excitement, could run as high as at any later time. When reform was discussed in the Convention of 1820–1, the delegates well knew that very few men were effectively excluded. But there were still speakers in the old line of Whig thought who opposed any further extension, not in order to keep out the industrious worker, but to forestall the danger that employers of large masses of wholly dependent labour might

[1] Morse, *Federalist Party*, 64.   [2] See Appendix II, pp. 544–48.

march their men to the polls in droves. It was an echo, clearer now in the presence of nascent industrial power, of Madison's fears of 1787; and the demand for the personal economic independence of the voter descended from the Old Whig view (repeated by Blackstone) that the vote could not be entrusted to those who had 'no will of their own'. But these defensive arguments were not convincing enough to hold back the drive for an official extension of the suffrage to taxpayers. The right to vote was already widespread, but no doubt a good many of the votes cast in the heated contests between Federalists and Republicans were technically illegal.

The widespread suffrage in Massachusetts was therefore not constitutionally secure. To emphasise this point, the number of persons legally qualified to vote declined appreciably from 1807 to 1815 as a direct result of the hard times due to the Jeffersonian Embargo and the War of 1812.[1] In any case, people prefer to act by right rather than by the indulgence of the authorities, so that the large number of voters who were unsure of their rights could be expected to attach great importance to constitutional reform. When that reform came about it was no mere formality but a significant advance.[2]

These uncertainties existed within the framework of a suffrage which was already very extensive in practice. Consequently, when political parties began to emerge as the organising force in politics, they did not need to place suffrage extension on their agenda but were able to occupy themselves directly with the problem of leading a large electorate that was already politically free.

Property had been introduced into the Constitution in a manner that contributed to the new understanding of that ancient but indefinite concept, the electoral constituency. Representation in the Senate was to be apportioned among districts, depending on taxes paid by each district; and the legislature was enjoined to take the existing counties as senatorial 'districts' until the General Court should decide that it was necessary to alter the basis. The system required periodic redistribution on the basis of new valuations, but when in 1787 a House committee reported that representation in the Senate was already in need of readjustment, the recommendation was

[1] Benjamin W. Labaree, *Patriots and Partisans: The Merchants of Newburyport 1764–1815* (Cambridge, Mass., 1962), 200.

[2] Cushing, Storey, and Josslyn, *Controverted Elections*, 67–70, 85–90, 137–8. *Journal of Debates and Proceedings in the Convention . . . to Revise the Constitution of Massachusetts . . . 1820–1821* (Boston, 1853), 246–53.

ignored.[1] The basis was not in fact challenged until the managers of the Jeffersonian Republic Party thought they could gain an electoral advantage by changing it.

The administration of Elbridge Gerry, grasping at the possibility of engineering a majority for the future, made up its mind that the time to discard the county basis had at last arrived; it carried out a new property valuation, and by a not unduly subtle departure from the terms of the Constitution proceeded to apportion the Senate seats, not on the basis of taxes paid, but of taxes to be assessed for possible future payment.[2] The combination of Gerry's name and the striking resemblance of one of these newly contrived districts to the shape of a salamander, gave to the world of party politics a word which it no doubt richly deserved; but the joke did not please the electorate.

The protests of the outraged opposition reaffirmed the old principle of the representation of property. In this case the 'equality' to be respected was the equality of property. Yet equality of persons made its appearance even here. A petition from Brimfield asserted that the law served only to give an ascendancy to a political party 'over a majority of people, whose sentiments and property ought to be represented at the board of the Senate', another from a town in Essex protested that the law had given a minority of voters a very large majority of seats, while another pointed out that the division of Worcester had been the means of defeating two senators who were supported by a large majority of electors in that county.[3]

One of the habitual sentiments offended by this famous gerrymander law was that of community. Voters did not think of themselves as mere numbers; the petitions complained that old connections had been sundered by the new divisions. Genuine 'interests' had been divided. The only interest served was that of the party.

An electorate not yet hardened to the science of party politics had recourse to the old republican remedy and threw the administration out at the next election. Next year the Districting Act was repealed.[4] The Gerry administration by putting party before property had certainly demonstrated their respect for the technical advantages of numbers — for the tax assessment

---

[1] Senate Documents (1787), no. 796; Legislative Papers (House), no. 2152. House Journal, 1788–9, MS., vol. ix in Mass. Archives.

[2] *Acts and Resolves 1811*, chap. 97.

[3] *Acts and Resolves 1813*, chap. 65 original papers, Mass. Archives.

[4] House Journal, 1811–12, vol. xxxii, app. 10, 'Protest of the Minority . . .', *Acts and Resolves 1813*, chap. 65.

was merely a device, no longer a principle — but in doing so it had both advanced and subverted the principle of numerical representation in the same blow. The schoolmasters of the party system would one day teach the electorate to appreciate the advantages of political cynicism.

The county districts were to enjoy a long life. In the Convention of 1820–1, an amendment to the Constitution was adopted, proposing to restrict the advantages of the commercial and manufacturing eastern counties by imposing a limit of six senators for any one district. The members from Essex were 'most offended' by the arrangement; and the popular vote rejected it by a large majority.[1] The outcome is significant; for the point demonstrated was the power of the combined forces of property and numbers in the city areas of greatest concentration; a power which had helped to bring in the existing arrangement between 1775 and 1780.

The majority principle had to wait another twenty years, until 1840, the year of the Whig victory over the Jacksonian Democrats, for another significant advance. Although the existing senatorial districts were then declared to be permanent, a gesture towards redistribution was in fact made by the adoption of an amendment which required the Governor and Council to assign the number of senators to be chosen in each district on a basis of census returns of population. It was not until 1857 that a district system was adopted. In that year also the towns of Massachusetts at last ceased to be the formal constituencies of the House of Representatives.[2]

It was in 1840 that the property qualifications for membership of both the legislative Houses were finally discarded; but those for Governor were retained until 1892.

The Constitution of 1780 was made up of a judicious blend of the Anglo-American principles of the Whig Republic. Not least among these was a wise indistinctness about exact definitions. The political habits of the town and all its historical associations were retained; but the weight and importance of each town was defined, far more emphatically than ever before, by its population. That result was brought about, however, by the force of arguments based on the rights of property; and those rights were specifically represented in the Senate. The Governor, himself to be a man of great wealth, was set up as the single representative of the whole state.

The rise of political parties as the driving force of political life, combined

---

[1] Isaac Parker to Harrison Grey Otis, 10 January 1821, H. G. Otis Papers, box 7, M.H.S., *Journal of Debates*, 634.

[2] Thorpe, *Federal and State Constitutions*, iii, 1912, 1916–23.

with the growth of an industrial population to reinforce the mercantile one, brought gradual but deep changes in the earlier balance. That balance did not predetermine the direction of subsequent development: it could have given rise to more than one possible course. The rest was history.

REPRESENTATION AND THE STRUGGLE FOR POWER IN PENNSYLVANIA

7. Politics and Revolution, 1764—76

At the climax of the Quaker struggle against the proprietors, the Assembly, in which the Quaker party held a majority, tried to persuade the Crown to resume the province. The advent of the Stamp Act suddenly made this move look extremely foolish. But in the next election in 1764 the Quakers held their own against their rivals, the Presbyterian party, who were in league with the proprietors. The Quakers, however, were gradually losing touch with the province. The Assembly consistently refused to grant representation to new counties; and its members assumed the style of an oligarchy. In Philadelphia a new Radical movement formed of artisans sprang up to oppose the traditional leadership of the gentry. The result of this highly class-conscious development was a three-cornered struggle between the Quaker oligarchy, the Presbyterians plus proprietors, and the Radicals, in which the Radicals seized the initiative. They probably did not enjoy the support of an overall majority. But in driving for American independence they had the advantage that Philadelphia was the scene of the Continental Congress and that the trend of external events was on their side.

In this struggle for power, representative institutions served as an instrument for all parties, but the character of representation was itself one of the issues. Property had always been a factor in government, and until the appearance of the Radicals, no one on any side in Pennsylvania had proposed to separate property from persons in laying down the rules of representation. The new Constitution of 1776 was to show how far the Radicals could go.

I. A SUMMARY OF POLITICS

I F the decision of the Assembly majority to appeal to the Crown to resume authority over Pennsylvania was a dangerous threat to the proprietary interest it was also a sign of the difficulties, almost the desperation, of the old Quaker party. For they were now faced with a Proprietary party whose organisers had learnt to combine the influence of patronage with the skills required for the manipulation of the now mature system of representation. These opposing forces were to try their strengths in the election of 1764.

Only in the light of subsequent events did the appeal to the Crown to rescue the province from tyranny begin to appear a very paradoxical policy. But that light was already beginning to break, had Franklin and his cohorts been able to see it. Within a year, the dispute had been swallowed up by the Stamp Act crisis, and the failure of the Quaker party to foresee the violence of the revolt against the stamp tax was, to say the least, a lamentable lapse on the part of the very men who claimed to be better qualified to speak for the province than their opponents in domestic affairs. Franklin himself did not help matters by using his position in England to get his friend Hughes appointed to be a stamp distributor; his spokesmen actually had to deny the charge that he had promoted the Stamp Act, and to affirm that he had opposed it so warmly that his friends in England 'feared he would lose his influence in his other business by occasion of his opposition'. As for the appointment of Hughes: 'When the sun is setting on our liberties, ought we not to light tapers till it rise again?'[1]

The accusation that the Quaker party was prepared to hand the province over to royal authority at the very time when British policy threatened American liberties was powerfully made in the Assembly by John Dickinson, who warned the representatives of the danger to their religious liberties and to their representative government under the Charter of 1701; some of these privileges were contrary, he observed, to royal government and the prerogative.[2] It was not to be long before Dickinson, as the author of the *Letters of a Pennsylvania Farmer*, was to be one of the most celebrated publicists of the cause of American resistance. Yet Dickinson belonged to that large group whose chief desire was to preserve both existing American liberties and the

[1] *To the Freeholders and Other Electors of Assemblymen for Pennsylvania*, 1 October 1765, Library Company of Philadelphia.

[2] David L. Jacobson, 'John Dickinson and Joseph Galloway' (Ph.D. thesis, Princeton University, 1959), 38–44.

prevailing social order within the protection of the British Empire; as the pressure of radical secessionists confronted him with the choice of American Independence as the safest means of securing American liberties, he drew back and exerted all his influence for moderation.

The fact that Philadelphia was the greatest city in America made it the obvious choice for the meeting of the Continental Congress, and the Congress in turn enhanced the importance of Philadelphia. The conservatism and caution of opinion in the city caused constant anxiety to the Independents, notably to those active spirits John and Samuel Adams of Massachusetts. The politics of Pennsylvania thus became extremely complicated. Events in this period were closely packed, but the leading spirits in the struggle against Britain succeeded in bringing into existence a provincial Convention which met in the State House in January 1775 and soon claimed to rival the authority of the Assembly. The new Convention was made up of delegates from most of the counties, but the initiative had been taken in Philadelphia, where a series of public meetings had been held to support the afflicted people of Boston. The greatest, held on 18 June 1774, was said to have been attended by 8,000 people. It was then that a standing committee was formed; and the county committees of correspondence, apparently springing from this movement, appeared at the same time. As early as July 1774 a committee for the whole province had arrogated to itself the right to instruct the Assembly, which was about to meet.

The Assembly held its own for nearly another two years. It managed this partly by appointing to the Pennsylvania delegation to the Continental Congress only its own members and thus excluding two of the Committee leaders, James Wilson and the (at this stage) still radical Dickinson; but after being elected to the Assembly in October 1774 Dickinson was soon added to the delegation to Congress. The Provincial Convention was itself the scene of conflict between differing policies, and Dickinson, faced with the possibility that effective opposition to Britain would veer into separation from Britain, began at this phase his trend toward moderation. But in broad outline the difference between the Convention and the Assembly became the difference between radical opposition willing to opt for Independence, and a defence of American liberties that was not ready to go outside the Empire.

It would be a mistake to suppose that what happened as a result of the conservatism of the Assembly was that an incensed populace rose up to overthrow it and install a patriotic Convention in the seat of power. On the contrary, opinion was deeply and genuinely divided; as late as May 1776 the Whig candidates were defeated in Philadelphia. It is doubtful whether the Radicals would have succeeded in Pennsylvania but for the powerful influence of the Continental Congress whose most significant step, directed towards internal Pennsylvania politics, was a Resolution on 15 May 1776 recommending the several colonies to establish 'new forms of government' no longer derived from royal authority.

The Radicals, who counted heavily on support from the western section of the province, discovered a further reason for overturning the Assembly when that body belatedly granted reform in the apportionment of representatives in March 1776. Even with an addition of seats that left little ground for complaint, the west was still outnumbered and the Radicals were unable to gain a majority in the Assembly. Neither did the west show the expected signs of mass discontent which the Radicals had counted on; discontent may indeed have been assuaged by the granting of a fair representation.[1]

The Resolution of the Continental Congress, however, struck a severe blow at the authority of the Assembly, whose position was further undermined when on 27 May the news arrived that Virginia had instructed its delegation for Independence. The Independence members of the Assembly then proceeded to thwart its action by refusing to attend its sessions and thus depriving it of a quorum. Under these difficulties it gradually ceased to meet and was superseded by a new Convention, called on the insistence of the Radical Independents in Philadelphia with the object not only of declaring for Independence but of overthrowing the Charter and imposing an entirely new Constitution. Their power to carry through this *coup* was drawn from a combination of factors: from the pressure of the Continental Congress, the example of other provinces, and the energy of their own organisation backed by the Committee of Privates of the Pennsylvania forces, centred in Philadelphia but working assiduously through the back-country. In the last analysis they gained from British policy, which failed to offer American moderates the chance they so desperately needed to regain the initiative and prove that they had a policy which could save America.

[1] Theodore Thayer, 'The Quaker Party in Pennsylvania, 1755–1765', *P.M.H.B.* January 1947, 19–43, shows that the Proprietary party, when hoping to rally western support against the Quakers, would have been left in a minority by a full reform on a numerical basis. David Hawke, *In the Midst of a Revolution* (London, 1961), 83–84.

II. REPRESENTATION AS A MATTER OF PRINCIPLE BUT AN INSTRUMENT OF POLITICS

When Quaker spokesmen explained the idea of representation they had great and increasing difficulty in concealing the bosom of their desires beneath the plain garments of republican theory. They were reluctant to admit the extent to which their view of representation was prescriptive. But the multiplication of national and sectarian groups, and especially the immigration of the Germans and the Scotch-Irish, meant that Pennsylvania gradually ceased to be what once, to all intents and purposes, it had truly been — an essentially Quaker community, embarking on what one of its historians has called 'A Quaker Experiment in Government'.[1] Despite their adroitness in political management the Quakers were trying to keep control of an increasingly heterogeneous assortment. Nowhere did the prosperous, peaceful, and perhaps somewhat complacent, leaders of the merchant society of Philadelphia reveal themselves as being more dangerously out of touch with new developments than in connection with the claims and grievances of the frontiersmen, whose bitterness against Assembly policies of moderation towards the Indians was compounded by under-representation in that body.

It all came to a hideous climax in the massacre of a group of Indians living peaceably in the Conestoga Manor, a Christian reserve, in 1763, followed by the rebellious march of the men from Paxton, which threw Philadelphia into a fright. Governor Thomas Penn, quickly giving up any idea of making political capital out of back-country discontent, asked Franklin to form a military association. Franklin met the marchers at Germantown where, backed by a considerable show of military force, he persuaded them to go home. But, as if to underline the extent to which the ascendancy of the Quaker party was now maintained through the systematic and unremedied violation of the principles of republican government as understood in the Charter, a petition from the outlying county of Cumberland soon afterwards declared the belief that the influence of Quaker principles was prejudicial to the province in general and oppressive to the petitioners. This was almost exactly what the Quakers said of the proprietors. The petitioners added that 'the design and letter of the charter, the right of British subjects, reason and

[1] Isaac Sharpless, *A Quaker Experiment in Government* (Philadelphia, 1898).

common sense', combined to demand a more equitable representation of the frontier counties.[1]

When the Assembly, in its Session of 1763–4, finally resolved to try to oust the proprietors by petitioning the Crown,[2] their enemies, now under the personal leadership of Governor Thomas Penn, countered with a vigorous campaign aimed at unseating Franklin and weakening his party in the Assembly itself. Their respective efforts culminated in the famous election of 1764.

Both sides had recourse to groundwork in the constituencies. After a long contest over a supply Bill, the Assembly passed several resolutions of protest and then went into a brief adjournment 'in order to consult their constituents about applying to the King to take the government under his immediate care and protection'. The results of these consultations appeared in the form of petitions for the resumption, signed by 'great numbers of the inhabitants', and 'pretty generally by the members of our [i.e. the Quaker] Religious Society'. It was greatly feared that the proprietors would get the legislative as well as the executive part of the government into their hands; they had already gained this object in some counties.[3]

The note about consultation with constituents is significant. The form employed was that of seeking instructions by which the representatives would then be bound; but of course what was really happening was that the members were going back to inform, in effect to instruct, their electors. Good Old Whig theory was not without its practical applications.

Although the terms 'Quaker' and 'Proprietary' remained in use they were no longer hard and fast definitions of political formations; and the Proprietary group actually concentrated their attack on Franklin to an extent which, as one Quaker remarked with some relief, at least had the effect of drawing some of the fire away from the Quakers as a society.[4] The anti-Quaker organisation

[1] The Paxton episode, which caused virulent controversy, is the subject of a mass of literature. The present account, which is condensed to those aspects which bore essentially on Assembly representation, is derived primarily from Shepherd, *Proprietary Government*, 546–8, n. 3, and Brook Hindle, 'The March of the Paxton Boys', *William and Mary Quarterly*, October 1946, 461–86.

[2] Thayer, *Growth of Democracy*, 95.

[3] Stephenson to Samuel Fothergill, 13 June 1764, Pemberton papers, Historical Society of Pennsylvania. This letter ends with a note remarkable for other reasons: rumours had been heard of a stamp duty. 'A scheme of this kind', said Stephenson, 'in my opinion would not be burthensome or exceptionable'; but the experience of neighbouring governments suggested that it would not produce much revenue. As this opinion duplicates that of Benjamin Franklin one is tempted to feel that the Quaker party was not as close to the pulse of the people as it claimed to be!

[4] Stephenson to Fothergill, 3 September 1764.

was centred on Philadelphia under the leadership of John Dickinson.[1] Franklin's party, now sometimes called 'the Old Ticket', were accused of having enriched themselves by their control of Assembly-appointed offices; of dispossessing the Germans of their political representation; of aiming at the establishment of a king's government under which Franklin himself would become Governor and chancellor, and land cases of immense importance would be tried before him without a jury; while all important officers would be nominated by the Governor.[2] The Old Ticket on their side reminded voters of the 'knock-down election of 1742', warned them of plans to make all men bear arms without regard to conscience and accused the proprietors of having engrossed the best lands and driven poorer settlers away. As to a change of government, on which the New Ticket — the proprietors' men — denied having intentions hostile to the constitution, Franklin's side pointed out that neighbouring New Jersey, which had reverted to being a royal province, was 'happy under the immediate care of the most virtuous of kings'. They added that, from the different conditions of the two provinces, a foreigner would conclude that Pennsylvania and New Jersey were under different sovereigns.[3]

The campaign had much to commend it. In the first place it was carried to the voters with exceptional vigour by both sides. Although there was much appeal to prejudice and fear and much personal animosity,[4] there was also the assumption of a high degree of literacy. There can be no doubt that the lower classes were courted as never before, and the high turnout at the polls indicates that despite the property qualifications, the potential electorate was already extensive. Moreover, though the New Ticket did not gain power, it succeeded in defeating Franklin, an impressive achievement which Franklin angrily attributed to the work of a rabble, who perjured themselves in swearing to their voting qualifications.[5] All observers agreed as to the exceptional heat of the election and the size of the poll, which was said to number nearly 4,000.[6]

[1] Jacobson, 'Dickinson and Galloway', 56.

[2] *To the Freeholders and Electors of the City and County of Philadelphia*, 1764–4, H.S.P.

[3] Election broadsides 1764–4; 1764–5, H.S.P.; *Address to the Freeholders and Inhabitants of . . . Philadelphia, in answer to . . . the Plain Dealer*, Library Company of Philadelphia.

[4] Too much, according to old Isaac Norris, who was again elected Speaker but was in poor health and fatigued by the ordeal and so declined; in a letter after the election he mentions 'personal considerations and party views' but ignores the high principles claimed on each side. Norris to Charles, 7 October 1764, Norris Letterbooks.

[5] Jacobson, 'Dickinson and Galloway', 61.

[6] Thos. Stewardson, 'Extracts from the Letter-Book of Benjamin Marshall, 1763–1766',

The election of 1764, though it left the Quaker party with an Assembly majority, marked unmistakably the decline of the Quakers from their earlier ascendancy to a position in which they found themselves as one party among others, contesting for the supremacy in the legislature. The Quakers themselves were made anxious, as the campaign gathered force, by the activity and organisation of their opponents. Supporters of the Old Ticket accepted the view that the New Ticket was set up by the Presbyterians in their synods and was in effect dictated by the elders. A Church of England clergyman reported that the Presbyterian ministers, 'with some others, held synods about the election, turned their pulpits into Ecclesiastical drums for politics, and told their people to vote as they directed them at the peril of their damnation'.[1] A savage satire, put out in the form of a pretended report of a council of Presbyterian ministers and elders, told the voters that the Presbyterians expected the passage of laws favourable to themselves in return for laws exempting the proprietary lands from taxation forever. The kirk was to become the established Church; an annuity of £1,000 would be settled on succeeding governors; attendance at Presbyterian worship would be made compulsory, and laws would be passed to prohibit marital intimacies on Sundays.[2] There was clearly much to fear from a Presbyterian ascendancy. That the elders exerted some influence over the political inclination of their flock seems probable. Early in 1764 the Philadelphia Presbyterians sent out a circular against the petition for a change in the government. The Quaker party petition, on the other hand, did not emanate from the Quaker meeting; it was presumably the concoction of the Assembly members led by Franklin and Galloway. But the Presbyterian circular was signed by three Presbyterian ministers. The Presbyterian council derided by a hostile pamphleteer was in fact held on the last Tuesday in August, 1764, as indicated.[3] But it does not

---

P.M.H.B., no. 20, 1896, 204–12; Norris to Charles, 7 October 1764; Stephenson to Fothergill, 11 October 1764.

[1] Guy Soulliard Klett, *Presbyterians in Colonial Pennsylvania* (Philadelphia, 1937), 256 (hereafter referred to as *Presbyterians*).

[2]   When Gospel Trumpeter surrounded
        With long-ear'd rout, to battle sounded,
        And pulpit Drum ecclesiastic
        Was beat by fist instead of a stick
        Such Priests deserve to have their A–se kick'd. —

The Substance of a Council held at Lancaster August 28th 1764 by a Committee of Presbyterian Ministers and Elders deputed from all parts of Pennsylvania in order to settle the ensuing Election of Members for the Assembly.

[3] Klett, *Presbyterians*, 257, 258.

follow that the writer had accurate information of its proceedings, and it is as well to remember that nearly all the surviving information comes in the form of Quaker correspondence and Franklinian propaganda. We can say what the Quaker party believed, and what it wished the voters to fear, but it is more difficult to be certain whether it spoke the truth.

Neither side achieved its objective. The Presbyterian party gained only twelve of the thirty-six Assembly seats and failed to prevent the majority from voting to send Franklin to England to assist 'in soliciting and transacting the affairs of this Province in Great Britain'.[1] The Quaker party, however, never succeeded in persuading the British authorities to effect the change of ownership; in due course the American Revolution dispossessed the proprietors, while at the same time it divided and discredited the Quaker leaders.

The struggle for domestic power had repercussions of marked, if accidental, significance: for the electoral contest which brought out some 4,000 voters in Philadelphia in 1764 had stimulated extraordinary interest in politics, and had in the process provided some useful political education, while the parties, who had to flatter the people in the process of seeking votes — did not Franklin attribute his defeat to a 'rabble'? — were forced to learn where the votes were to be found.

It is quite possible, however, that the political education of the Philadelphian electorate may have had a different effect from that supposed by the American Whigs or Patriots, or by their ideological successors who have been inclined to regard democratic politics and American self-government as interchangeable terms. For even in the crisis of the spring and summer of 1776, despite the rousing propaganda of Paine's *Common Sense* and the energetic partisan activities of the Committee of Privates, these voters, who were long used to weighing the issues, showed that kind of maturity which finds it extremely difficult to reach unilateral decisions in complex situations. As late as May 1776 they refused to give the Whigs a majority in the Assembly, and three-quarters of the Philadelphia seats were held by known moderates.[2] There was in Philadelphia no mob to be whipped up like that of Boston, which was at the beck and call of Sam Adams. And a majority of Philadelphians seemed prepared to place their trust in their traditional, acknowledged leaders even when the loyalty of those leaders was impugned by revolutionary Radicals. It is highly significant that Dickinson, despite his

[1] *Pa. Archives*, 8th series, vii. 5690.
[2] Hawke, *Midst of Revolution*, 30.

earlier conservatism as to Independence, was soon elected President of the new Commonwealth of Pennsylvania.

The electoral excitements of these and ensuing years gave renewed importance to the question of the suffrage franchise, which never seems in itself to have been a centre of serious controversy since 1701. The qualification of £50 personal property for town residents did not prevent the mechanics, or independent artisans, of Philadelphia from taking some part in the election of 1764; in 1770 they helped to elect John Dickinson in a hotly contested campaign. Soon afterwards they formed a Patriotic Society for the advancement of their political interests, but six years later they could still claim with indignation that no mechanic was ever elected to the Assembly.[1]

That mechanics should aspire to be assemblymen was itself a sign of upheaval. They had not been in the habit of contending for public distinction against men like Galloway or Dickinson or Franklin — and Franklin, significantly, was constantly re-elected, for honour's sake, during his years in England. Whether a qualification measured in provincial currency, among a class who actually claimed that they owned half of the property in Philadelphia, disfranchised enough men to make an actual difference to the outcome of elections must remain hard to determine.[2] The property qualification was not the only limitation; a portion of the German population was excluded until the naturalisation laws had been satisfied.

Throughout the countryside the law restricted the vote for assemblymen to freeholders of fifty acres. Township tax officials were required to prepare lists of taxables to guide the county election officers in their duties. If the freehold qualification was strictly enforced then a substantial section of the adult male population was certainly without the franchise; available lists of freeholders for several counties suggest variations from less than fifty up to some seventy-five per cent of the population of adult males.[3] However, as

---

[1] Thayer, *Growth of Democracy*, 149–50.

[2] Williamson, *American Suffrage*, 57, 86–88. Professor Williamson notes a complaint that a law providing for the easy eviction of tenants would not have passed if mechanics had sat in the Assembly. Here is a genuine case of a political issue where the claim is made that a reform in the system of representation would produce a concrete difference in the social character of legislation.

[3] Williamson, *American Suffrage*, 33–34, 58. Professor Williamson thinks it 'highly probable that in practice the county electorate comprised the freeholders only' (p. 34). Yet it is he who later notes 'confusion as to whether freemen who were not freeholders in the counties could vote' (p. 58).

The records of voting in Pennsylvania have never been examined with the care that Professor Brown has given to Massachusetts and Virginia and Professor McCormick to

confusion sometimes arose about the claims of freemen who were not free-holders, and as the indications from comparable situations in other provinces generally suggests indulgent administration of the laws, one may suspect the higher figure to have been more general than would appear from the lists.

Discontent about the suffrage, which came to a head and strengthened Radical recruitment immediately before the crisis of Independence, was linked as an issue with the question of representation through the apportionment of seats in the Assembly; and both issues were pressed with great vigour in Philadelphia itself. Here, as in Massachusetts and later in Virginia, the suffrage did not give rise to a body of discontent that would expect to gain major reforms without the alliance of the forces that were victimised by the unequal distribution of seats. But suffrage was certainly an issue, and one that could be exploited by direct reference to the rights claimed by the colonists against Britain. The extent of actual disfranchisement may even have been exaggerated for purposes of propaganda. What really mattered, especially among a populace agitated by a revolutionary ferment about political rights, was that even in their own province, under their own laws, these rights remained both precarious and obscure. In these circumstances, the franchise was wide enough already to give the mechanics some political power and to add force to the advancing claims of the Pennsylvania Radicals. It was still narrow enough to inflame those claims with the anger of a genuine grievance, not least because the law made the right insecure. It was this margin of grievance that the Constitution of 1776 wiped away.

III. PROPERTY, RANK, AND PERSONS

Although distinctions of rank may not have entered into the community of the Quaker meeting, they were present from the beginning of the province in the distribution, by purchase, of vastly differing quantities of landed property. The Friends themselves allowed that some of their members were 'weighty Friends', a designation that attached to individuals for their sufferings in the cause, for their religious experience or for a seniority that would be gradually transmuted into a recognised social ascendancy.[1] When

New Jersey, but the statistics that have been produced for individual elections, together with the inferences about political life that can be drawn from the tenor of newspaper and pamphlet debate strongly suggest that the suffrage was widespread, though probably not as extensive as in the more democratic of the Massachusetts towns.

[1] Bronner, *Penn's 'Holy Experiment'*, 52; but these remarks represent an inference from Bronner's account, to which his own observations do not expressly commit him.

Markham appointed his Council in 1696 he told them that he had selected them for their loyalty to the king and to Penn and because they owned 'a plentiful portion' of real estates.[1] The property qualifications applying to the suffrage in the early period and extended, though slightly, under Markham's Frame, accorded with the normal sanctions of a society in which property was the principal 'interest' under the protection of government.

The success of the Philadelphia merchants in overseas trade enabled them to raise fortunes which provided for 'a structure of aristocratic living comparable to that of the Virginia planters, the landed gentry of the Hudson Valley, and the Puritan merchant princes of Boston'.[2] The distinctive features of an upper-class mode of life, superior education, a country place for the summer months, stylish carriages, and that significant characteristic of an *élite* status, the tendency to produce a network of interrelationships through marriage, had all developed to a high and conspicuous level. John Adams, when attending the Continental Congress, was struck by the grandeur of upper-class style: 'We adjourn, and go to dinner with some of the Nobles of Pensylvania [*sic*] at four O Clock and feast upon ten thousand Delicacies, and sitt drinking Madeira, Claret and Burgundy till six or seven. . . .'[3]

In domestic affairs, the achievements of the Assemblies dominated by this prosperous but eminently practical class of merchant-gentry had been worthy of respect. In many aspects of civic development, including education, hospital work, and civic administration in general they could boast an enlightened, progressive record. But their achievements centred mainly on the development of facilities in the eastern region. It is true that after the French and Indian wars the Assembly relaxed taxation for the benefit of the badly afflicted western counties and that evidences of attention to western problems can be found in the record of their legislation. But it was not a primary attention. One of the most alarming discoveries of the later 1760s was of the decline not merely of political following, but of commercial intercourse, between the port and City of Philadelphia and the western counties of Pennsylvania. Western farmers were sending their produce down to Baltimore, a route on which they found better and cheaper means of transport and, in their opinion, better treatment from the local

---

[1] Bronner, *Penn's 'Holy Experiment'*, 176: 'I know', said Markham, 'you are all men that are fastened to the country by visible estates, I mean such as the law calls real estates, of which each of you have a plentiful portion, and that's a great security you will study the interest of the country. . . .'

[2] Tolles, *Meeting House*, 109.

[3] *Adams Family Correspondence* (Cambridge, Mass., 1963), i. 164.

authorities.[1] It was a striking indication of loss of leadership by the provincial Assembly — of its decline as a genuinely representative institution.

This weakening of genuine representation was regarded by the western counties as being directly connected with the distribution of seats. In the election contest of 1764 Franklin claimed the support of the back counties in opposition to the proprietors and in answer to the charge of under-representation; but he admitted that more members might properly be awarded to those counties.[2] It was a curious feature of this imbalance that the great commercial city of Philadelphia was itself the chief victim. It continued to send only two representatives to the Assembly, though its population of some 40,000 made it one of the biggest cities in the British Empire.[3]

From the time of Penn's original Charter the arrangements for maintaining a fair distribution of representatives were supposed to be based primarily on the growth of population and were left in the hands of the Council and Assembly. The original 200 of the Assembly were to be enlarged up to 500,

The appointment and proportioning of which . . . in future times most equally to the division of the hundreds and the counties which the country shall hereafter be divided into shall be in the power of the Provincial Council to propose and the General Assembly to resolve.[4]

Although this formula was repeated in subsequent frames of government, the intention was disregarded when its application would have had some value. As the importance of property was understood from the beginning and was present in the qualifications for the suffrage, it might have seemed unnecessary to establish stronger institutional safeguards until the province began to grow; the constituencies of Pennsylvania could safely be drawn in equality with each other, each standing for approximately equal amounts of property and numbers; and this concept of the composition of Pennsylvania's political society having been laid down it was natural that the different constituencies should have been expected to remain equal to each other. The province was conceived as a whole, and the division into constituencies was a mechanical function designed to assure the inhabitants of a just representation. Massachusetts was constituted of corporations; Pennsylvania was subdivided into constituencies.

---

[1] Charles H. Lincoln, *The Revolutionary Movement in Pennsylvania, 1760–1776* (Philadelphia, 1901), 62–63.

[2] Benjamin Franklin, *Cool Thoughts on the Present Situation of our Public Affairs* (Philadelphia, 1764).

[3] Bridenbaugh, *Cities in Revolt* (New York, 1955), 217.

[4] Thorpe, *Federal and State Constitutions*, v. 3050.

Population, however, was never by itself regarded as the determinant of greatness — of 'weight' or that sort of importance that established the claim to representation. That claim was formed through a subtle connection between property and population, a connection which had been present in the foundation of Pennsylvania as in the other colonies and which nothing in the history of the province had yet tended to displace. The demand for an increase in members was put forward as early as 1752 by Philadelphia on the ground that the City together with the old eastern counties, being much the richest, paid by far the heaviest weight of taxes, giving them a right to a proportionately greater weight of representation. The increase of the trade, wealth, and population, commerce, and navigation of the City rendered the addition 'equitable and necessary', and would accord with the original intention of the Founder, which was to give to every part of the inhabitants a share in the legislative government 'agreeable to natural equity'.[1]

Natural equity plainly decreed that the interests and activities that went into the making of wealth were entitled to political representation for their own sake, because of their intrinsic importance, in which the numerical addition to the population remained only one of a variety of factors. The payment of taxes had already been mentioned. In the 1764 election the existing apportionment was defended in detail on the basis of the burden of taxation. Cumberland County, in the west, complained that its eight members were too few, remarked an Old Ticket broadside; very well, Cumberland paid a yearly tax of £911 7s. 9d.: but Philadelphia County [not the City] paid £12,000! The writer then attacked the New Ticket as being made up of the men who contended that 'without any proportion to their numbers, or proportion of the public tax they pay, each of the back counties should have as many members to represent them as either of the three old populous and wealthy counties of Philadelphia, Bucks and Chester...'.[2] There was a rumour that the Proprietary side would themselves appeal to the king for permission to give additional representation for the five back counties, possibly sending over a deputation. 'Should this scheme take effect,' remarked one of the Quakers in private correspondence with a (London) Friend, 'our politicians will feel it is a great point gained, and enable them to return a majority of their Presbyterian friends for Representatives, and the people of this City, and County, plead it as equitable that an additional

[1] *Pa. Archives,* 8th series, iv. 3486.
[2] Election broadsides nos. 1764/5, H.S.P.

number should be allowed them in proportion to the part they bear of the provincial taxes, which is reckoned one third of the whole.'[1]

The more recently formed counties used the same theme. In 1772 'a great number of the inhabitants of Northampton' complained that their single representative gave them 'a very partial and inadequate share of representation', and went on,

the petitioners conceive the basis, on which the principles of representation are founded, is the wealth and number of inhabitants,

by which Northampton could be seen to be deficient in representation by comparison with other counties. Other petitioners repeatedly mentioned their tax contributions when requesting increased representation.[2]

The principle that political power inhered in the combination of numbers with property was continuously illustrated in political life. Philadelphia, like Boston, could tolerate its own under-representation partly because it lay at the centre of a group of prosperous counties which collectively, and with a strong sense of collective interest, maintained an effective majority; partly because the City itself was the seat of every kind of power and influence.[3]

Philadelphia, with its (by colonial standards) enormous population, its commerce and manufacture, its thriving newspaper press and literate population, was at the same time the capital of the province and the centre from which the appointments and promotions, the major administrative decisions, and the legal system were controlled. Few points could illustrate more clearly the vital importance of opinion in Philadelphia than the fact that both the proprietary opposition to the Quakers, and later the Radical drive for Independence found it essential to make the City the base and centre of their operation, from which they might carry their work into the back country. 'Our situation', stated the Philadelphia Committee of Safety and Observation, in working to arouse the spirit of Independence in the back country, 'makes us a kind of sentinel for the safety of the Province.'[4]

Philadelphia was large enough to contain a variety of commercial and professional interests as well as different nationalities and religions. The

[1] Stephenson to Fothergill, 4 July 1764.

[2] *Pa. Archives*, 8th series, vi. 5419–20 and viii. 6779–80.

[3] From the time when additional counties were first formed, in 1738, the Speaker of the Assembly continued invariably to be chosen from one of the eastern counties until 1775. *Pa. Archives*, 8th series, iv–vii.

[4] Hawke, *Midst of Revolution*, 76–81; 144. Carl and Jessica Bridenbaugh, *Rebels and Gentlemen, Philadelphia in the Age of Franklin* (New York, 1942).

wide suffrage, whose extent was only really discovered during hotly contested elections — such as that of 1764 and some in the years preceding
Independence — made it essential for all 'tickets', though themselves composed of recognised gentry, to seek out the favour of the artisans. Paine,
writing in 1778 on the provincial £50 suffrage qualification, observed, 'The
only end this answered was, that of tempting men to forswear themselves.
Every man with a chest of tools, a few implements of husbandry, a few spare
clothes, a bed and few household utensils, a few articles for sale in a window,
or almost anything else he could call or even think his own, supposed himself
within the pale of an oath, and made no hesitation in taking it.'[1] The tax
books indicate that some 46 per cent of the adult males of Philadelphia were
genuinely qualified by their property; but Paine's statement, which adds to
the high probability that any form of property was considered, suggests that
some 75 per cent were recognised as voters.[2] The City's political character
somewhat resembled that of other vigorous and populous centres of imperial
commerce, not only those in America but in Britain too. A fairly broad,
robust, literate, and intelligent electorate, informed by newspapers and
pamphlets, enjoying a kind of jocose familiarity with the great men who
sought its support, was prepared to accept the leadership of those great — or
greater — men as a part of a perfectly legitimate order of society.

The strain to which the system was liable to be exposed by the internecine
conflicts in the province was revealed as early as 1759 when on the Proprietary
side 'gentlemen of the best fortune entered the houses of the lowest mechanics
to solicit their opposition' to the Franklinian military association. Franklin
himself angrily attributed his defeat of 1764 to a 'rabble' who had perjured
themselves as to their voting qualifications; and Dickinson, attacking the
petition for a change of government, sneered at the petitioners as 'a number
of *rash, ignorant* and *inconsiderate* people, and generally of a low rank'. To
which charge Galloway replied in the Assembly that they were truly not
Proprietary officers, dependants, or expectants, who were 'chiefly the people
of *high rank* among us; but they were otherwise generally men of the best
estates in the province, and men of reputation'.[3]

Both Galloway and Dickinson were committed to the kind of social order
that presupposed a recognition of 'rank'. In Galloway's view, the impulse

---

[1] Hawke, *Midst of Revolution*, 33–34.

[2] Williamson, *American Suffrage*, 23–34. In the counties the freeholders assessed for fifty
acres seem to have numbered about 60 per cent of the adult males.

[3] *True and Impartial State*, 60–61; *Speech of Joseph Galloway Esq. . . . in answer to John
Dickinson Esq., delivered in the House of Assembly May 24 1764* (Philadelphia, 1764).

of government came from its leadership, while the necessity to consult constituents acted as a check on the legislature; a check, but not a guide, still less a mandate. Galloway was soon to stand out as an American Tory. But only with regard to the question of self-government did his basic postulates sunder him decisively from the views of many a respectable American Whig. His early defence of American liberties was based on English constitutional principles. But the excellence of the parliamentary system arose, in his view, as much from the necessity of a supreme power in the land, able to order, direct, and regulate every member of it, as from its character as a representative body. What he believed the House of Commons represented was the landed interest, because it represented property, of which land was the most permanent and excellent kind. This prevented the House of Commons from becoming tyrannical and helped it to achieve the most important goal of any government. Representation of the propertied order was seen as the essence of the English Constitution.[1]

The protection of the landed interest — it was an unusual emphasis in a city whose prosperity was built so largely on trade — gave security to all other interests; it would protect property in general. These views were not dissimilar to those of George Mason and other great Whig patriots, particularly to the south of Pennsylvania, who saw the land as the basis of the stability of society. When it came to domestic government as distinct from Independence, John Adams was strong for the political installation of a propertied order. Galloway's outlook, however, was somewhat more authoritarian than those of his Whig compatriots; it dispensed with the voluntary aspect of social origins; society needed government, and that was enough to justify parliamentary power — at home, of course. That the *raison d'être* of such power was the legitimate protection of property was a concept held wholly in common under the Whig convention.

Galloway was not the sort of man to feel that his theories of government ought to stand or fall by the attitude of the lower classes. To the southward of Pennsylvania, those who expounded political ideas, or made constitutions, were generally free to postulate the tacit consent of their social inferiors without fear of contradiction; but Galloway and his contemporaries in Pennsylvania did not enjoy this luxury. Galloway himself soon began to feel the edge of lower-class resentment. The resistance to the Townshend duties seems to have given an impetus to the political consciousness of the artisans and tradesmen of Philadelphia.

[1] Jacobson, 'Dickinson and Galloway', 51–52, 181, quoting 'Arguments on both sides of the dispute', *New Jersey Archives*, 1st series, x. 478–92.

Consciousness became at once almost identical with dissatisfaction. Their grievances against the conduct of economic affairs by the bigger merchants quickly turned against an Assembly in which these men could get what they wanted in the form of legislative action. Not only did the legislature appear to be susceptible to the influence of the dominant merchants, but the processes of legal redress for the subject smelt of corruption. As the election approached in 1770, a number of tradesmen met and drew up a resolution of protest against the manner in which Assembly elections were limited in advance by the decision of a few leading men on their choice of candidates. For the first time, men claiming to speak expressly for the skilled worker and small trader demanded a voice in the making of nominations.[1] They lamented that 'greatness and opulency' had become qualifications for office when once it had been uprightness and stability; and the voters were warned of the danger of allowing political power to be combined with great wealth. In the same issue of the paper which carried this announcement was a notice calling on tradesmen, artificers, and mechanics to join to elect one of themselves to be a member for Philadelphia.

The organised mechanics of Philadelphia, mobilised by Charles Thomson,[2] had the satisfaction of contributing to the defeat of Galloway in his bid to represent Philadelphia. Galloway, still obsessed with the anti-proprietary theme, was losing touch with the issues. Franklin, in England, and the newer leaders in Pennsylvania, had grasped the need to put the imperial problem into the centre of politics. Meanwhile Dickinson, become famous by his authorship of the *Letters of a Farmer in Pennsylvania*, had moved towards an alliance with the opposition to parliamentary policy.

During these years the 'tradesmen and mechanics' became increasingly bitter about their systematic exclusion from the taking of political decisions and scornful of the affability shown to them, at election times only, by members of the gentry. It is clear that many of them were voters; but it is equally clear that many were somewhat arbitrarily excluded from the suffrage. In August 1772 the foundation was announced of a Patriotic Society on democratic principles, to resist violations of rights and privileges either in America or across the Atlantic — an expression of sympathy with the English radicals whose activities had sprung from the Wilkes case. A year later, a letter in the *Pennsylvania Gazette* began to identify tradesmen

[1] 'Brother Chip' letter in *Pennsylvania Gazette*, 27 September 1770. Quoted by Lincoln, *Revolutionary Movement*, 80–81, n. 1. Jacobson, 'Dickinson and Galloway', 153.

[2] John J. Zimmerman, 'Charles Thomson, the Sam Adams of Philadelphia', *Mississippi Valley Historical Review* December 1958, xlv. 3, 478–9.

candidates with the cause of resistance to the ministry, and warned voters against men 'who would be fond of representing you', who said,

it is time the tradesmen were checked — They take too much upon themselves. They ought not to intermeddle in state affairs. They ought to be kept low. They will become too powerful. When gentlemen of character and in office among us can dare to express themselves to this purport, men whose ancestors two generations ago were on an equality with the meanest of us, what may we expect? . . . Every election should be considered as voting in a new Assembly. The consideration that such or such a gentleman has represented us for several years is vague in itself. Let us consider what he has done (for it is vain to fill the house with ciphers).[1]

As the imperial crisis grew more intense, the movement for reform, both of suffrage and the distribution of representation in the Assembly, became more closely identified with American resistance and more dangerously hostile to the Assembly majority. In March 1776 the privates of the Military Association of the City and Liberties of Philadelphia petitioned for an extension of the suffrage, particularly to Germans, who were excluded. It was said — incorrectly — to be the practice of all countries, as well as being highly reasonable, to admit to the privileges of citizenship those who exposed their lives in defence of their country.[2] Another communication to the Press indicated, in a series of questions, the opinion held by mechanics and farmers of their own position in society:

Do not mechanicks and farmers constitute ninety-nine out of a hundred of the people of America? If these, by their occupations, are to be excluded from having any share in the choice of their rulers, or forms of government, would it not be best to acknowledge the jurisdiction of the British Parliament, which is composed entirely of GENTLEMEN? Is not half the property in the city of Philadelphia owned by men who wear LEATHERN APRONS? Does not the other half belong to men whose fathers or grandfathers wore LEATHERN APRONS?[3]

It was a curiosity of the internal politics of the province that the proprietors, whose privileges and exemptions had until recently been a genuine grievance among a people taxed for defence,[4] interested themselves in

---

[1] *Pennsylvania Gazette* 23 September 1773. Quoted by Lincoln, *Revolutionary Movement*, 92–93, n. 1.

[2] *Pennsylvania Packet* 4 March 1776.

[3] *Pennsylvania Packet* 18 March 1776. On the growth of an egalitarian spirit, especially in Philadelphia, see Bridenbaugh, *Gentlemen and Rebels*.

[4] The Penns reluctantly and ungraciously accepted tax liability in 1759. Thayer, *Growth of Democracy*, 72–73.

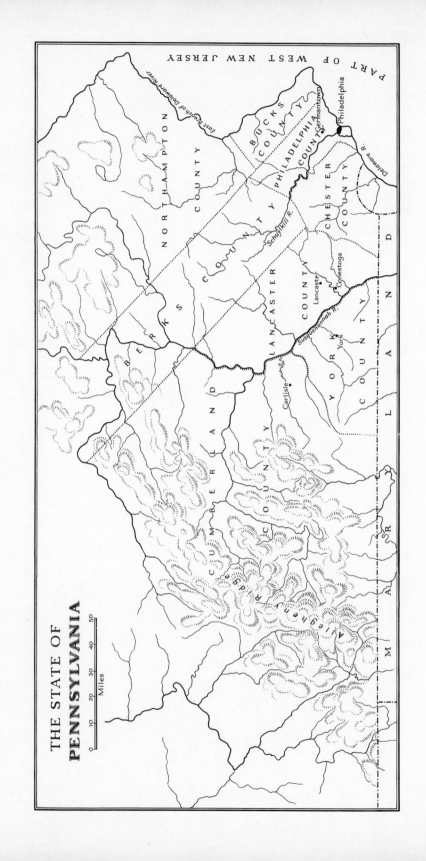

THE STATE OF
PENNSYLVANIA

Miles
0   10   20   30   40   50

PART OF WEST NEW JERSEY

Philadelphia
Germantown
BUCKS COUNTY
PHILADELPHIA COUNTY
CHESTER COUNTY
NORTHAMPTON COUNTY
BERKS COUNTY
Schuylkill R.
Lancaster
Conestoga
LANCASTER COUNTY
Susquehanna R.
York
YORK COUNTY
Carlisle
CUMBERLAND COUNTY
Allegheny Ridge
East Branch of Delaware River
Delaware R.
M A R Y L A N D

recruiting support among the Scotch-Irish Presbyterians, whose views did not on the whole lend themselves to the pretensions of aristocracy.

One of the most influential of all the Presbyterian elders of the late colonial period, the Reverend Francis Alison, told his congregations that farmers and mechanics were the sinews of a commonwealth — adding without much concession to the upper orders that 'gentlemen of superior abilities' should contrive to carry useful projects into execution, promoting agriculture and home manufacture; he broadened social into civil and political equality by affirming that all were equally entitled to protection and to reap the benefit of honest industry, and advocated equal access to public honours and places of profit and trust according to ability and to each one's quali-fications to serve the public: both rights and privileges on the one hand, and burdens on the other, should be equally distributed. In a later discussion of civil power Alison held that the end of all civil power was public happiness and that if civil power were abused, the people, who gave it, might abolish it. He sought the source of civil power by discussing the problem of the death of an elective king. The state did not dissolve, but reverted to a sort of simple democracy. 'And they may determine by a plurality of votes, of those, at least, who used to be concerned in civil affairs, what shall be their future plan of government, and who shall govern them. . . .' But Alison observed also that the highest honour and deference were due to good rulers and that subjects were not exempted from their duty by the faults or mistakes of governors.[1]

Doctrines of social, and of a considerable measure of political, equality could always turn for strength to the intentions of William Penn and to the provisions of the early frames of government. But in all probability the greatest single unifying force, charging these beliefs with the energy and fire of a social gospel, was Thomas Paine. Paine spent some two years in Philadelphia after his arrival in 1774, and by his blunt speech, unexpectedly sharp imagery, and power of energetic, direct reasoning both in talk and print, he incessantly pressed the influence of his ideas into the receptive minds of the already discontented leaders of artisan society. His famous essay, *Common Sense*, published in January 1776, was the epitome of the arguments he had already made familiar.

Paine associated closely with the men who were shortly to seize power and make a new constitution after their own ideas. These aspiring new leaders were James Cannon, Dr Benjamin Rush, Christopher Marshall, Timothy Matlack, and Thomas Young — all men who were in one or another way

[1] Francis Alison sermons, folder 5, vi (24 January 1756) Presbyterian Historical Society; *Of the Rights of the Supreme Power and the Methods of Acquiring it* (undated, 1760s).

of modest or disappointed fortunes, though Rush was to rise to great eminence in medicine. These men were political Radicals of a stamp closely corresponding to that of the Westminster sub-committee of the parliamentary reform Association that was formed soon afterwards in England. They paid less attention to history, however, and were more consciously dedicated to building a new future than to restoring a lost past. They wanted to convert their beliefs about civil equality into institutional realities that would thenceforth govern Pennsylvania.[1]

The Radical Independents used the Committee of Privates — of the Pennsylvania militia — as the instrument of their intentions; and as a result of the collapse of the Assembly they were able to assist in the calling of a new provincial Convention charged with the responsibility of drawing up a constitution that would conform to the dictum of the Continental Congress, in being wholly independent of British authority. These men did little to make the events which drove America towards Independence; but, seeing Independence as their only hope of power, they exerted themselves to convince the voters in the capital and from the capital throughout the back country, that separation from Britain was the only hope for American liberty. Aided by events beyond their control, their efforts were successful; and they used their success to draft for their new state a new and Radical constitution.

8. The Constitution of 1776:
A Badge of Lost Innocence?

The unicameral system made no provision for the separate representation of 'orders' or interests such as persons and property. The Radicals of Pennsylvania shared the official British doctrine that each voter must have economic independence; but they also shared the belief of the most advanced form of 'True

---

[1] Hawke, *Midst of Revolution*, 101–6, gives an interesting account of the members of this group and their influence on Pennsylvanian politics in the months leading to Independence. He discounts the role of George Bryan, who has usually been considered a leading maker of the 1776 Constitution.

Whig' thinking in England that the state was composed of individuals, not interests. Economic qualifications other than tax-payment were swept away. But unfortunately the Radicals found themselves forced to substitute a test of loyalty to their Constitution, which was equally proscriptive and aroused bitter animosity.

Their aim was to set up a system which would make representation as direct and clear a link between people and legislators as any Old Whig could desire. This led them to adopt the 'locality rule' requiring representatives to be residents of their constituencies. What the Constitution failed to do was to win the loyalty of the Radicals' political enemies in the State. It was therefore a reversion to the normal American Whig structure when, in 1790, Pennsylvania revised its Constitution and imitated the Federal Constitution by setting up a bicameral legislature.

I. THE RADICAL PLAN IN ACTION

The new Constitution was the most radical frame of government to emerge during the Revolution. It was not altogether new, however. The central institution of colonial Pennsylvania, the unicameral legislature, was retained; but the Radicals succeeded in converting it to their designs in a manner which actually made an old system serve a new political force.

Orthodox Whigs, in America no less than in Britain, regarded a bicameral system as an element essential to the balance of liberties in a properly regulated society. The unicameral principle made no provision for the special representation of different interests, a need which American Whigs were coming to define by the broad distinction between persons and property. All must find their voice within the single chamber; no House of Lords or any such replica as a provincial Council or state Senate could stand between the immediate, annually elected representatives of the people and the making of all law and policy. When, in the new Constitution, all legislative power was grasped by this single body, the concentration became alarming to special interests of a minority character, and the popular power very quickly looked to its opponents like a new tyranny. The septennial Council of Censors, intended to review legislation to determine whether the Constitution had been infringed, proved useless as a means of restraint and became an object of party strife.

The new Constitution did however establish a Council, which was connected with the executive and given extensive powers in appointments, to the judiciary, of naval and military officers, and of civil officers, such as did not fall to the Assembly. In the recess of the Assembly the Council was empowered to lay embargoes and prohibit exports. All this was to be done in conjunction with the President, who was to be elected by a joint ballot of Assembly and Council. The President and Council thus formed a plural executive with an important range of authority over the judicial system, the state patronage, and, within limits, over the economy. The Council was subject to popular election and was to consist of twelve members. Those local officers, the Justices of the Peace and the sheriffs, whose duties meant so much to the lives of local communities, were to be locally elected — a reform which met a widespread and popular demand.

Much the most striking advance of radical individualism came with the extension of the suffrage. The former property qualification was abolished and the suffrage extended to all tax-paying adult freemen who had satisfied a residence requirement of one year in their constituencies. The makers of the Constitution stated, in a slightly different connection but in the same document, that every freeman ought to have some 'profession, calling, trade or farm' in order to preserve his independence. This concept was in fact similar to that announced by Blackstone; the difference was simply that Pennsylvania, unlike Great Britain, was putting it into practice. The language used in stating the basic right of representation no doubt owed much to the recent Virginian Declaration of Rights:

That all elections ought to be free; and that all free men having a sufficient evident common interest with, and attachment to the community, have a right to elect officers, and be elected into office.

The principle was elaborated in the next clause:

That every member of society hath a right to be protected in the enjoyment of life, liberty and property, and therefore is bound to contribute his proportion towards the expence of that protection, and to yield his personal service when necessary, or an equivalent thereto: But no part of a man's property can be justly taken from him or applied to public uses without his own consent, or that of his legal representatives....[1]

A tax-payer suffrage is not the same thing as universal manhood suffrage. For one thing it is less extensive, and for another it is based on a different principle. It would even expose a community exempted from taxation as a result of economic distress — a relief which had been extended by the

[1] Thorpe, *Federal and State Constitutions*, v. 3081–92.

Assembly to parts of the west — to the technical possibility of being disfranchised (although this has probably never been done). But it could certainly be expected to disfranchise paupers and possibly anyone accepting public relief. Clearly these considerations were not forward in the minds of the constitution-makers, who stated that all ought to contribute, and in whose views the right to vote was earned by contribution. What their work did was to sweep away the basic economic presupposition that the ownership of a specified amount of property was an essential guarantee of political competence. This step alone was enough to horrify John Adams, who was to have a major share, only three and a half years later, in drafting the constitution of his own state.[1]

Nothing was said about the rights of unfree men — indentured servants or slaves. There was still such a thing as a 'political nation' which was distinctly less than coextensive with the whole. Disfranchisement was abruptly carried right across the community by the very Convention which, acting as an interim legislature before the meeting of the first Assembly, had made the Constitution. The Constitution was plainly not sustained by the loyalties of a damagingly large number of the old electorate. To obviate the serious danger that the new Assembly might actually have a substantial enough number of anti-constitutionalists to obstruct or undo their work, the framers imposed as a test on the voters an oath of loyalty to this Constitution.[2]

The exact extent of this disqualification has never been possible to determine. It is clear that it was meant to be extensive since it would otherwise have been a pointless exercise in repression. The oath was not uniformly administered, and the rising anti-constitutional strength in elections over the succeeding several years makes it perfectly clear that numerous opponents of the Constitution were prepared to risk the providential consequences of falsely taking an oath imposed by Radicals. The oath itself became one of the chief grievances against the Constitution and against the Radicals as a party,

[1] 'Depend upon it, Sir, it is dangerous to alter the qualifications of voters; . . . every man who has not a farthing, will demand an equal voice with any other, in all acts of state. It tends to confound and destroy all distinctions, and prostrate all ranks to one common level.' (Adams, *Works*, ix. 378, quoted by Hawke, *Midst of Revolution*, 174.)

[2] J. Paul Selsam, *The Pennsylvania Constitution of 1776* (Philadelphia, 1936) 221–2 (hereafter referred to as *Constitution*). The Constitution itself applied the oaths of loyalty only to officers of government, but on 26 September the Convention decreed that electors must take the same oath of loyalty before being allowed to vote. Article ten of the Constitution required members of the Assembly to submit to an oath of belief in one God and in the divine inspiration of the Old and New Testaments.

though new reasons were quickly added after a year or two of Radical administration.[1]

The imposition of an oath of allegiance was mitigated in the conventional style for the benefit of Quakers by adding the alternative of an 'affirmation'. But Quakers had often objected to affirmations as being merely oaths in disguise. A section of the community which had been in the habit of regarding the whole province as its own patrimony was bound to consider any requirement to a firm allegiance to a new Constitution for that province as not only a declaration by the Radicals of their determination to rule under their own Constitution, but as a calculated insult to themselves. The intense bitterness provoked by the oath persisted like a malignancy until the whole instrument was overturned and a new Constitution adopted in 1790.[2]

To complete the Radical plan for a republican frame of government it was essential to revise the basis of representation. The addition of seventeen new members to the Assembly in March 1776 had taken the wind out of Radical sails without giving them a majority. The increase in the representation of Philadelphia had actually led to a strengthening of the Moderate element after the May elections of 1776. The Radicals of Pennsylvania were the heirs to the purest strand of the Old Whig or Republican tradition — so pure that its progenitors would have hesitated to admit parentage — which regarded persons as the only factor in the character or composition of a constituency, and regarded property as merely a variable attribute of the persons who were to be represented.

It followed that the allocation of seats must be exactly proportioned to population. This plan was adopted after an interim arrangement lasting two years.

The Provincial Conference, called together by the various county committees of correspondence to meet on 18 June 1776, laid the plans for the succeeding Provincial Convention, to which it fell to draw up the new Constitution. The Conference provided for representation on a basis of county equality; the Convention, in turn, decided that for two years each county, and the City of Philadelphia, should have six representatives; but it went on to state the permanent principle, to take effect when lists of taxable persons had been completed:

Representation in proportion to the number of taxable inhabitants is the only prin-

---

[1] Selsam, *Constitution*, 221–6; Brunhouse, *Counter-Revolution*, 54–55. As late as 1785 a group of non-jurors whose religious scruples had already forbidden them to fight, had cause to complain that, as they were deprived of the franchise, they were being taxed without their own consent. *Assembly Journal*, 3 November 1785.

[2] See, in general, Brunhouse, *Counter-Revolution*, for the period 1776–90.

ciple which can at all times secure liberty, and make the voice of the majority of the people the law of the land.

The Assembly was charged with the duty of apportioning representatives in proportion to the number of taxables, the increase of population to be provided for by septennial reapportionments.[1]

The Council was not constituted on this basis: each county was to be represented by one member, each representative serving a fixed three-year term.[2] There was no provision here for alterations according to population. The Radicals were weakest in Philadelphia and the eastern counties, and on their own reckoning clearly regarded the more numerous and increasing back counties as a source of strength. The executive and patronage policy might therefore prove to be controlled by a body which was not only less responsive to popular developments than the Assembly, but less responsive if such developments swung to the disadvantage of the Radicals. This inference cannot be regarded as a clear deduction, however, for the Council, not being a legislative body, would not in any case have been based on precisely the same principles.

The central working principle of the *ancien régime* in American practice as in British theory was the representation of specific interests, primarily those of corporations and of the middle and upper ranges of property, within a system which recognised varying degrees of participation by a wider section of the ordinary people. The history of Massachusetts in the Revolution showed that the decisive combination needed to crack the walls of this old order was that of the interests of property with the force of numbers. The history of Virginia would later show the power of the same combination in a more diffused and gradual form; that of British parliamentary reform would do so in its own more limited and complex way. The same connection could be got to work in Pennsylvania only with a subtlety that failed the Radicals and thus forced them to try again. When the Assembly in March 1776 agreed to a large increase in the direction of numerical representation, the outcome was a defeat for the Independents less than two months later, and an unmistakable victory for the Moderate or Conservative forces in the vital stronghold of Philadelphia. The senior elements, those of traditional social leadership, which were loosely connected with the idea of special and propertied interests, still dominated the loyalties of more than half the voters; nor does the history of subsequent elections suggest that this political orientation was materially affected by the extension of the suffrage.

[1] Thorpe, *Federal and State Constitutions*, v. 3086. Selsam, *Constitution*, 129, 187–8.

[2] Thorpe, *Federal and State Constitutions*, v. 3086–7.

The shift towards the numerical basis therefore assisted the conservative forces, already prevalent in the Assembly, in maintaining their preponderance. It may have looked, and has looked to historians, as though they acted in desperation under extreme pressure; but if that were so, then it must be admitted that for men acting under pressure their timing was remarkably shrewd.

This step in Pennsylvania was tactical rather than strategic. It had not the importance of those of Massachusetts or Virginia or of other states going through similar upheavals.[1] The reason lies in Pennsylvania's own history and the fact that the decisive advance of this distinctive combination towards that particular disposition of political power had actually been achieved between 1693, when the Assembly first gained from the Crown the right to initiate legislation; and 1701, when the Charter confirmed the legislative power of the Assembly. All of this was achieved at a stage before the growth of the population had begun to carry far-reaching significance for the distribution of internal power; and before the emergence of those political formations known at the time as parties, which arranged the disparate ingredients and interests in Pennsylvanian politics with an unprecedented degree of order. In general the revolutionary implications of the combination between property and numbers had their greatest significance in states where parties were confined to parliamentary or Assembly politics and did not yet reach out among the people.

The principles guiding the makers of the Constitution of 1776 were those of the English Radical reformers of the same generation, owing much to the Old Whig tradition but also undoubtedly influenced by the Scottish democrats, notably Hutcheson. They saw the state as a whole, a collection of separate individuals, each supposed to be independent in a distinct economic sense, to be virtuous because of that independence, and for these reasons to be politically responsible. The state, being a single whole, would be moved by the decisions of the majority of these individuals. In this concept, it was not the business of the system of representation to prescribe patterns or formations or to predetermine the character of politics; the system was conceived as existing to find any such formations among the people and to translate them into decisions and policies.

The unity and wholeness of the state — for it was the modern state which these doctrines ushered into being; a state whose theory no longer recognised as political entities those undigested ingredients which orthodox Whigs regarded as the peculiar duty of government to protect — did, how-

[1] Notably New York, New Jersey, Maryland, and the Carolinas.

ever, presuppose the fundamental consent of the governed. It was here that the Radicals encountered the most baffling and painful irony in their system. In order to secure themselves the certainty of power to rule, they were obliged to impose a test that deliberately excluded their political opponents: they were required as one of their first acts of state to prescribe the character of politics.

II. BETWEEN CONSTITUENTS AND REPRESEN-TATIVES: AN INTIMATE RELATIONSHIP

The Assemblies of Pennsylvania had demanded from the beginning, and had very soon gained, the right to deal with questions of public policy. At a very early date, David Lloyd discovered the advantages of taking an issue to the voters. The choice between leading men was also a choice between different policies, or at least different attitudes. Early Pennsylvanian elections have an extraordinary air of precocity; and when rival parties, with their own political objects, began to proselytise among poorly assimilated immigrants for electoral support, the province assumed characteristics which may be said in some degree to have anticipated those which became more general in American politics a full century later. It is well to take note of the limits bounding the area of choice and the determination of policy.

Debates in the Assembly were private. The concept of Assembly proceedings as a sort of continuous public debate on public questions did not exist. When the policies of Franklin and Galloway were under fire in 1764 they resisted proposals that debates be made public, a move that would clearly have carried the controversy to the people. The Assembly refused to enter Dickinson's speech against royal government in its published proceedings, Franklin apparently remarking that it would 'encumber the minutes'. Galloway offered an elaborate defence, explaining that the publication of minority protests was the practice of the House of Lords — not the House of Commons, which was their model. There was no precedent for it. Representatives were accountable to their constituents, so that if minority reasons were advanced, the reasons of the majority would have to be printed, and the *Votes*, intended merely as a register of propositions and determinations, would be filled with the disputes of members with each other, and the public business 'would be greatly retarded'.[1]

---

[1] William Smith, *An Answer to Mr Franklin's Remarks on a Late Protest* (Philadelphia, 1764); *Speech of Joseph Galloway, Esq., in Answer to John Dickinson, Esq., delivered in the House of Assembly May 24 1764* (Philadelphia, 1764).

The responsibility of representatives to their constituents had clearly to be discharged first in the Assembly and secondly in the information which representatives could give to their electors at home. Issues might be taken to the electors to influence an election. But once the legislature met, its deliberations were as private as its right to settle disputed elections or to make its own rules of procedure.

It was not until 1770 that the Assembly resolved to admit strangers to hear debates, and only qualified electors were then to be admitted.[1] The cautious majority in the Assembly may well have feared, even when it was interested in rallying support for mercantile forms of resistance to Britain, that its own position could be weakened by throwing matters of state open to the public. Even when the public was admitted, however, the printers of the newspapers were slow to see the debates as matters of public interest, and it was not until 1776 that their pages began to record the debates, despite an ever-increasing burden of contributions on imperial and domestic policies. They did report some of the petitions that came before the Assembly and regularly recorded the results of elections.[2]

It was obviously the intention of the early frames of government that representatives should be residents of the constituencies for which they were elected. The counties would literally 'send' certain of their members to represent them. The principle of delegation which Penn had in mind does not, however, necessarily imply residence, and an attorney can be deputed to represent his client without any such connection. No residence law was in fact laid down in Pennsylvania, and by the time elections were hotly contested some of the party leaders were beginning to discover the advantages of a more flexible arrangement. In 1764, Franklin derided his enemy William Allen, who lived in Philadelphia, for being unable to get himself elected there and owing his seat to a remote frontier county; but an anti-Quaker sheet sneered at the Franklin party for putting Galloway himself up in two counties for this election.[3]

The incident shows that election in one's own county, though not legally required, was normal. A more important case occurred in 1770, when Galloway stood for election both in Philadelphia County and in Bucks, in both of which he owned property. In Philadelphia he was either defeated, or

---

[1] *Pa. Archives*, 8th series, vii. 6589.

[2] These remarks are based on examination of the files of the *Pennsylvania Packet* 1771–6, *Pennsylvania Chronicle* 1768–74, *Pennsylvania Gazette* 1768–76.

[3] *To the Freeholders and Electors of Pennsylvania*, 1764–4, H.S.P. Thayer, *Growth of Democracy*, 103.

possibly withdrew before the election. In Bucks he was elected as a result of last-minute substitution. The incident drew forth a bitter pamphlet attack by William Goddard, editor of the *Pennsylvania Chronicle*, in the following year.[1] In this it was made very clear that although there was no actual rule against the election of a non-resident, the step was resorted to only in desperation and was vulnerable to criticism on the grounds that the candidate in such a case was not known to his constituents. The whole point was that the people of Philadelphia County, who did know the man, had thrown him out. 'Shall we then', it was asked, 'receive the *Cain* of *Philadelphia* County? The wretch! Whose only pretension to residence among them [i.e. the people of Bucks] is a few possessions. . . .'

Galloway was intensely unpopular among his political opponents, and his election squarely raised the question of non-resident representatives. In these circumstances it is not uninteresting that the Assembly had discussed the question as early as January 1770, when a long debate occurred on an amendment to a Bill dealing with the counties of Berks and Northampton, by which it was to be declared that the representatives of the people in the provincial Assembly 'Shall be chosen from among the Inhabitants of the City or County respectively, for which they are elected'.[2] The amendment was carried only by the casting vote of the chairman. Three days later a Bill was introduced with the specific object of preventing non-resident representation, as well as to allow Berks and Northampton two representatives each. The Governor offered amendments, which the House rejected; with the result that the Bill failed to pass into law.[3] There was thus no legal barrier to the election of Galloway for Bucks later that year. The residence requirement, which came to be known generally as the 'locality rule', was included in the Constitution of 1776.

The locality question seems not to have excited any public discussion or legislative move before 1764 and 1770. If, then, there were any occasions on which a county, rather than going to the expense of representation by its

---

[1] *A True and Faithful Narrative of the Modes and Measures Pursued at the Anniversary Election . . . 1770; by a Bucks County Man* (Philadelphia, 1771). Copy in H.S.P. The attribution of authorship is made by Jacobson, 'Dickinson and Galloway', 152.

[2] *Pa. Archives*, 8th series, vii. 6487. Whether Galloway's case provoked this debate remains uncertain. If his Bucks election were a regular election, it would not have been until October 1770 and would not have occurred yet; but if it was in some way irregular, it might have been in 1769, for the session 1769–70. Goddard's pamphlet appears to relate to the election of 1770; but it may refer to elections for the 1769–70 session. If Galloway's case is not involved, we are still in the dark as to what started the debate.

[3] *Pa. Archives*, 8th series, vii. 6489, 6491, 6502.

own member, entrusted that duty to some responsible person already living in Philadelphia, the practice was rare enough to be uncontroversial. It seems significant that the practice itself should have come under fire at the time when elections were fought about fiercely controversial issues. The English system did not confine constituencies to the talents of their own inhabitants, and in the revolutionary period, in the absence of any definite rules, the English practice might have taken root in America. But a time of constitution making was a time for laying down rules of procedure; and the probability is that even though no law precluded non-resident representation, it was so unusual as to appear almost irregular. Custom would therefore suggest the new rule; it was an easy step to take when the only persons to have departed from the custom were politically unpopular.

The Charter of Pennsylvania had frequently been involved in the prolonged disputes between Quakers and proprietors. The cardinal failure of 1776 was that the makers of the new instrument failed to set constitutional issues at rest, but instead provided a frame which became a matter of contention in the ordinary politics of the state. The War, with its burdens of taxation and military administration, its problems of state finance and economic policy, placed heavy responsibilities on the Assembly, whose actions would at the easiest of times have been a source of some controversy. When the great questions turning on the Bank of North America became subject to party politics in an Assembly from whose vote there was no appeal to a second chamber, the Republican party, as the enemies of the Constitution had styled themselves, carried much conviction in their arguments for reform. They were unsuccessful in earlier attempts, but achieved their objective with remarkably little opposition in 1790. In this they were undoubtedly aided by the powerful example of the new Federal Constitution, itself framed in Philadelphia.

American thinking was deeply imbued with ideas of the separation of the different branches of government and the jarring elements of everyday political strife. Much recent state history seemed to reinforce these opinions. The principal reform of 1790 was a return to the bicameral system, to Pennsylvanians a thing unknown for a lifetime. But the practical principles of representative government were deeply grounded now in Pennsylvania soil. Political parties also had learnt from experience. Whig forms of government would not inhibit the hearty animosities of political warfare.

Section 3

THE WHIG REPUBLIC IN
VIRGINIA

9. The Constitution of 1776:
Republican Representation, Old Authority

The making of a new Constitution in 1776 was not allowed to interfere with the traditional system of government in Virginia. Good Old Whig principles were applied and the centrepiece of the new instrument was the declaration that the people who were to be entrusted with political responsibility must possess some tangible and permanent stake in society. Thomas Jefferson looked into the meaning of Whig doctrine and saw in it the principle of majority rule by politically equal individuals; but he did not carry any significant portion of followers with him. The suffrage was moderately extended in 1784, but that step completed the reforms begun in 1776 and led no further. Significantly, the system of county government was left untouched. Even Jefferson's proposals would have extended only to the free population; but the institution of slavery lay at the foundation both of the economy and of the political system.

THE immediate constitutional result of discarding all shadow of royal authority was to base the whole of the government on the authority of the people. Thus the fundamental objective, not only of American Whigs but of Old Whig philosophers, was achieved at one blow. The suddenness of this achievement in turn confronted these same American Whigs with the problem of constructing a form that would maintain the classical ideals of 'mixed' government. Because so large a part of political power was concentrated in the Assembly, the new Constitution struck some of the more conservative landowners as leaning alarmingly towards what they called the 'democratical' form; but influence remained in the hands of those, such as Mason, who believed that it was possible to combine radically Old Whig constitutional principles with a profoundly safe and traditional social order. That this arrangement should have been workable was a tribute to the stability of Virginia's social and political leadership, which retained effective control of the counties and thence the state government. By contrast, such states as Massachusetts and North Carolina, in which local affairs were liable to be swept by more egalitarian currents, found it necessary to establish more elaborate institutional safeguards in the forms of differential property qualifications; and even — in purpose if not with much effect — the outright representation of property.

The most distinctive feature of the Revolution in Virginia was the skill with which it was led. Viewed, so to speak, from the other side of the War, the Virginian gentry, breathing defiance in Assemblies — legal or illegal — and leading the people in arms, presented an appearance of almost monolithic authority. Yet the unity of this leadership on the question of Independence did not conceal, from an internal view, deep divisions of attitude about the kind of state Virginia should become. These were accentuated by some intense personal animosities.

At the earliest practical phase of the new government, Thomas Jefferson began the movement for the reform of the land laws which led ultimately to the abolition of primogeniture and entail; and it was Jefferson too who opened the hard struggle for the equality of religious sects which resulted in the final disestablishment of the Anglican Church and the separation of Church from State. The humane codification of the laws of Virginia, in which Edmund Pendleton — who had opposed him on the other issues — shared the labour with Jefferson, caused less dissension. On the major issues the leadership was divided; for there were many large landowners who found the entails on their estates a positive hindrance to plantation economy, primogeniture had not become a dominant social custom, and the Anglican gentry had begun to learn the necessity for political accommodation with the Dissenters. The social changes proved to be of an order to which most of the existing leadership could reconcile themselves, and which they could contain; the political results of Independence were duly incorporated into the state Constitution of 1776.

In the advance of the revolutionary crisis, in Virginia as in other provinces, the General Assembly gradually lost its grip. Its last meeting was from March to May 1776. But provincial conventions, based on county elections conducted in the usual manner and probably called by retiring members of the House of Burgesses, began to meet in August 1774; and before the end of the last session of the legal Assembly, the Virginia Convention had seized all effective power.[1]

The provincial conventions were little more than the House of Burgesses meeting under another name. The membership was substantially the same; the conventions were dominated by men of long legislative experience.[2] By April 1776, it was already known that the forthcoming Convention, for which elections were about to be held, would be likely to have to decide on the great issue of Independence. The elections were scenes of high excitement.

This time the contests were keen, and several distinguished public men were either defeated or subjected to the humiliation of winning their seats by narrow majorities. None of the private reports suggests that the contests turned on issues of political importance. Neither the question of Independence nor the direction of domestic policy appears from the records to have been put before the electorate.[3] The strenuousness of these elections, however, is not hard to understand. The members of the new Convention would have powers to instruct the Virginia delegates in Congress to vote for Independence; and after that they would proceed to make a new Constitution for the state. It was to be the most powerful body in the history of the province. It can hardly be surprising that ambitious men should have been eager for places, or that the appearance of this great opportunity should have excited new ambitions. One must also allow for the reasonable possibility that the freeholders in some districts may have felt a weariness of their traditions and a surge of unwonted desire to see new faces in public office. The outcome of all these excitements struck George Mason as worse than useless, and in view of the veneration which the defenders of the Constitution later bestowed on it, his opinion of the framing committee is in the best tradition:

We are now going upon the most important of all subjects — Government! The Committee appointed to prepare a plan is, according to custom, over-charged with useless members — you know our Convention — I need only say that it is not

---

[1] Charles R. Lingley, *The Transition in Virginia from Colony to Commonwealth* (New York, 1910), chaps. v and vi (hereafter referred to as *Transition*).

[2] Lingley, *Transition*, 111; 136. Hilldrup, 'Virginia Convention', 141–2.

[3] Josiah Parker to Landon Carter 14 April 1776; Landon Carter Papers. Robert Brent to R. H. Lee, 28 April; William Aylett to R. H. Lee, 20 April; Lee Papers. Robert Wormeley Carter Diary, Colonial Williamsburg. See on this point also Hilldrup, 'Virginia Convention', 141–2.

mended by the late elections — We shall, in all probability, have a thousand riciculous and impracticable proposals, and of course a plan form'd of hetrogeneous [*sic*] jarring and unintelligible ingredients; this can be prevented only by a few men of integrity & abilitys, whose country's interest lies next their hearts, undertaking this business and defending it ably through every stage of opposition. I need not tell you how much you will be wanted here on this occasion. . . . We cannot do without you.[1]

After this prognosis, the achievement of the Convention was something with which Mason could well be gratified, and which was due in no small part to his own great influence. The outlines of the three main institutions, Governor, upper and lower chambers, with a Council to assist the Governor, remained; but only at the cost of a decisive shift of the seat of power. The governorship was retained largely as a decorative and symbolic office, deprived of all power over the calling or dissolving of the Assembly, with no veto over its acts and little influence in appointments. The Governor was to be annually appointed by the Assembly. The upper House, now called the Senate, was to consist of twenty-four members, each elected from a separate district. The districts were to be formed by the grouping of existing counties, and elections would take place as usual in the court houses of each county. Senators were required to be freeholders and residents of their districts and were to be at least twenty-five years of age. The Senate was put on a system of rotation derived from the principles of the Old Whigs; six of the members were to retire each year.

This plan of senatorial districts meant that the whole of the legislature had been placed on a representative basis; the executive was the vestigial royal Governor — but it deprived him of even a trace of power over the composition of the legislature. The grouping of counties into districts represented an attempt to create an upper House that would be smaller than the Assembly while based broadly on the same representative principles; and — what was perhaps for practical purposes more important — on the same administrative base, already provided by the counties. Virginia did not adopt the property-based differentiation of the upper House used in New York, Massachusetts, and North Carolina; but its bicameral legislature, governed as it was by a particularly solid gentry, went as far to secure the blessings of mixed government as then seemed necessary to a body of representatives who fully intended to exert an effective monopoly of power. Only a few years were to pass before Jefferson complained that by their very

[1] George Mason to R. H. Lee, Lee Family Papers, 4, 209–12; Virginia Hist. Soc., 18 May 1776.

similarity the two Houses had begun to encroach on the liberty they were meant to defend.

The newly named House of Delegates was at last placed on the annual basis that stood as the republican cornerstone against tyranny. Each county was to send two representatives, who were to be freeholders and residents of their counties. Williamsburg and Norfolk were each to send one delegate, and each borough subsequently incorporated was to be allowed to have one member. A borough would lose the right of separate representation if for seven years its population was less than half that of any Virginia county.[1]

No distinction was drawn between voters and representatives: any man qualified to vote was deemed fit for election. Although the habitual deference of the electorate had recently shown some rather rude disturbances, it could reasonably be expected to resume its sway. Mason and his colleagues thought it neither necessary nor compatible with their republican principles to protect the elective offices by a special qualification; yet it seems likely that if social conflict in Virginia had threatened them they would have modified their principles, for like-minded men in several other states showed no hesitation about property qualifications for all members of the government.

The legislature continued the colonial practice of making provision for the payment of members from public funds. Colonial Virginia did not support the kind of aristocracy whose members could expect to leave their estates to the care of stewards while they maintained themselves in style for several months in the capital. The remuneration was intended to cover their expenses. From the earliest days the counties had been expected to provide travelling expenses, but in 1661 the legislature began to grant a salary. In 1723 this was converted from tobacco to current money at the rate of 10s. for every 100 lbs., which later became a regular 10s. a day. The treasurer paid out these sums on the Governor's order on receipt of a certificate from the speaker. The payments were frequently in arrears owing to delays in collecting duties and to capital expenses.

The sum of 10s. a day was payable, of course, only during sessions. If spread over a year it would have given burgesses about £180. When this figure is compared with other professional salaries such as that of the clerk of the House, who ranged from £50 to as high as £300 for a session but averaged some £125, it appears that the burgesses were comfortably able to meet their expenses away from home but were not freely indulged at public expense. There would have been no room for making a profit from politics. Moreover the habitual arrears of payment meant, in effect, that members must be able

---

[1] Hening, *Statutes*, ix. 112–19.

to bear the costs for upwards of a year. Men whose farms or businesses required their frequent personal attendance — those who had few or no slaves or subordinates — would not have been able to defray the additional costs occasioned by absence from home from the treasury salary.

The Constitution of 1776 was silent on the matter. But in 1779, in accordance with the express desire that fit men should be enabled to serve the public, the House voted a salary of the modest sum of 50 lbs. of tobacco a day plus 2 lbs. a day for mileage. The price inflation made a revision necessary, a task assigned to the grand jury. The depleted state of public funds in the past had often made it necessary to pay the members' expenses in arrears, and the treasury reverted to this dismal practice in 1783.[1]

Despite the irregularity of payments, the law in Virginia laid down a principle for effective and regular representation. In Massachusetts the liability fell on the towns, which frequently preferred non-representation to the expense of maintaining a member in Boston.

The provisions for the suffrage, which were to last with only slight modification until 1850 — a longer period than in any other state — were guided by the principle laid down by George Mason in a famous phrase of the Declaration of Rights:

That elections of members to serve as Representatives of the people in assembly, ought to be free; and that all men, having sufficient evidence of permanent common interest with, and attachment to the community, have the right of suffrage. . . .[2]

It was generally agreed in 1776 that the best evidence of this 'permanent common interest' lay in the freehold ownership of land.[3] But there was room for important differences in the definition of this evidence. The most advanced views in the Convention were those of Jefferson, who gave a general indication of his ideas in his own first draft for the Constitution. He there laid it down that the qualifications of electors should be such as proved 'a fixed purpose of residence'; but the precise terms remained indefinite —

---

[1] Thorpe, *Federal and State Constitutions*, vii. 3812–19; Hening, *Statutes*, May session 1779, chap. ix. 29; October session 1779, chap vi. 137; May 1783, chap. xxxiv. Flippin, *Royal Government*, 195–7; Anne Bezanson, *Prices and Inflation during the American Revolution: Pennsylvania 1770–1790* (Philadelphia, 1951), 249–55, 335–7.

[2] Thorpe, *Federal and State Constitutions*, vii. 3813.

[3] Compare: 'I think that no person has a right to an interest or share in the disposing of the affairs of the kingdom, and in determining or choosing those that shall determine what laws we shall be ruled by here — no person hath a right in this, that hath not a permanent fixed interest in this kingdom. . . . That is, the persons in whom all the land lies, and those in corporations in whom all trading lies. . . .' Commissioner-General Ireton, 29 October 1647. Hill and Dell, *Good Old Cause*, 355.

payment of scot and lot, or ownership of an unspecified number of acres, being suggested in brackets. His final draft required that voters be males of full age and of sound mind, owners of a quarter-acre freehold in the towns or twenty-five acres in the country; and all residents who had paid scot and lot to the government — a two-year period being suggested.[1] For Jefferson, then, a 'fixed purpose of residence' could be identified by a small property qualification, and this meant 'interest and attachment'; but he went further, and instead of taking the conventional course of confining such privileges to those who held existing freeholds, he advocated the policy of giving fifty acres to all men of full age who wanted the land. Through this early conception of the homestead policy, he would have proceeded to make of the Constitution itself an instrument for securing the attachment of the citizens.[2] The Government would not confine itself to allocating the rights or privileges of the people, but would go to them with its arms outstretched.

The opinions of Mason on the meaning of his own historic phrase were decidedly more conservative. Mason revealed some scepticism about the political reliablity of youth by advocating the age of twenty-four as the lower limit for the suffrage. The point may seem merely to be one of judgment about the political age of consent; but in a population so heavily weighted with youth as that of America in this period of rapid growth, the effect would have been to give an emphatic bias towards the parental generation. It was a bias which Mason underlined by offering to confer the suffrage on every father of a household with three children — a reasonable indication of an interest in the future of the community. In the absence of this connection, his notion of property requirements was much stiffer than Jefferson's ; Mason's men of twenty-four were to hold estates of inheritance worth £1,000 or leases in which there was an unexpired term of seven years.[3] For Jefferson, attachment might be prospective; for Mason it was to be already in substantial existence.

No less interesting were the differences between the two men on the basis of representation — the idea of what formed a constituency. Mason was successful in the Convention in contending for a fixed ratio of two members for each county, regardless of population.[4] This view was to be of great prospective importance; the back country of Virginia was filling up

---

[1] Julian P. Boyd and others (ed.), *The Papers of Thomas Jefferson* (Princeton, 1950), i. 341, 348, 358–9 (hereafter referred to as *Papers of Jefferson*).

[2] Dumas Malone, *Jefferson the Virginian* (Boston, 1948), 238.

[3] Boyd, *Papers of Jefferson*, i. 366–9. See the interesting discussion of Mason's proposals.

[4] Lingley, *Transition*, 171–2.

rapidly, and there could be no difficulty in anticipating the gradual shift in the centre of population which came about in the ensuing generation. But there was no written principle to declare that new counties must be equal in population to old ones, so that the Tidewater and the Northern Neck, in which Mason lived, could expect to keep their political predominance by holding fast to the equality of counties. Perhaps if Mason had been able to anticipate the future growth of population in Alexandria he would have looked more generously on the argument of Jefferson.

Constitution-makers are guided by the ideas of the society they want to see. Mason believed, with Jefferson, that elections should be frequent and free; he had no diffidence about consulting the people, but a letter written at the end of the war, and expressing his hopes from peace, gives an unmistakable sense of the dominant part to be played by the class to which he belonged. 'I hope', he said,

To see our great National Council, as well as our different assemblies, filled with men of honest Characters, and of independent Circumstances and principles : for until this shall be the case, our affairs can never go well.[2]

What really mattered here was the essential connection between independent circumstances and independent principles. Expressions such as this stood at the centre of Whig social thought: such men would never be swept into enthusiastic movements or allow themselves to be corrupted by party. If events unhappily made concerted action a necessity, as British policy had done, they would lead. There should thus be no change in their quietly authoritative position at home. But as popular movements would normally not rise from the demands of men of independent circumstances, it must be clear that independent principles would turn out under pressure to be the principles concerned with the maintenance of these circumstances.

The author of the affirmation that governments derived their just powers 'from the consent of the governed' had done some purposeful thinking about the meaning of consent. His work in the Convention showed that he had penetrated to the principle that if consent were to be obtained through a system of representation then it must be through the representation of individuals. The number of representatives for each county or borough was therefore, in Jefferson's drafts, to be proportioned to their numbers of qualified voters.[2] He also provided that the House of Representatives should make periodic adjustments when necessary. Jefferson's point of vantage for

---

[1] Mason to Arthur Lee, 25 March 1783. Lee Family Papers transcripts, vol. 4, V.H.S.
[2] Boyd, *Papers of Jefferson*, 348, 358–9.

formulating this concept was Albemarle, a large Piedmont county still sparsely peopled but capable of supporting a large population. He was not an immediate product of the Tidewater aristocracy; and, as he showed in the Declaration of Independence, he was keenly aware of the injustice of denying equal representation to the growing population of the west.[1] No doubt he was already suspicious of the tendency to the over-representation of the Tidewater which he later denounced in his *Notes on Virginia*. But he enjoyed the additional advantage of a mind singularly unencumbered by venerable but meaningless platitudes. Jefferson saw right through to the logic of numerical representation as the necessary consequence of the doctrines of equality to which his compatriots, through his agency, had so fully committed themselves. This was essentially an equality of persons; it could be no other kind.

What is at least equally significant is his failure to win any substantial support. We do not know whether he found any supporters in the committee. The problem of putting down a declaration that all men were born 'equally free and independent' caused acute difficulties in the Committee on the Declaration of Rights, where some of the conservatives — those whom the more radical Whigs called 'aristocrats' — apparently tried to hedge the pronouncement with qualifications;[2] Jefferson's radical views were evidently too daring for those who consented to the statement, as finally formed, that all men were born equally free and independent in rights; and he found himself in the odd position of being an advocate without clients — of offering to lead a popular movement without a popular following.

Jefferson's views on the suffrage and the numerical basis of representation make a coherent system. Had they been adopted, Virginia would have had a profoundly different history. It was the apportionment of representatives, rather than the suffrage, which formed the central issue in the great movement of protest that led to the Convention of 1829–30, and by the conjunction of reformers opened the way to the extension of the suffrage. But if a numerical scale apportionment had been adopted in 1776 without wider suffrage, the suffrage reform movement would certainly never have found strength to carry its point before the Civil War.

[1] By 1829, Albemarle was suffering worse under-representation even than the Trans-Alleghany West, since its (by then) large population was still confined to two representatives. Jefferson's anticipation was thus justified. *Proceedings and Debates of the Virginia State Convention of 1829–30* (Richmond, 1830), 673 (hereafter referred to as *Convention 1829*).

[2] Thomas Ludwell Lee to R. H. Lee, 1 June 1776; Lee Papers.

Ten years before the Revolution, Richard Henry Lee had criticised the constitution of Virginia on the grounds that two-thirds of the government was vested in the Crown. His explanation of the comparative merits of the British and the Virginian Constitutions, though entirely conventional, was so clear a statement of the prevalent concept of mixed government as to deserve full quotation:

Let us place the two [he wrote to his brother] in comparative points of view, and then the difference will be striking. In Britain the three simple forms of Monarchy, Aristocracy, and Democracy, are so finely blended; that the advantages resulting from each species separately, flow jointly from their admirable union. The King tho' possessing the executive power of government, with the third of the legislative, and the House of Commons representing the democratic interest, are each prevented from extending improperly prerogative or popular claims, by a powerful body of Nobles, independent in the material circumstances of hereditary succession to their titles and seats in the second bench of the Legislature. Thus you see of what essential importance is the House of Lords in the British constitution, and how happily their independence is secured. With us, the legislative power is lodged in a Governor, Council and House of Burgesses. The first two appointed by the crown, and their places held by the precarious tenure of pleasure only. That security which the constitution derives in Britain from the House of Lords, is here entirely wanting, and the just equilibrium totally destroyed by two parts out of three being in the same hands.[1]

Not the least notable aspect of this statement is the significant misconception, shared by Lee with almost all other Americans, of the ideal balance by which the British Constitution mixed the three basic forms. It was not long before Americans spotted the fact that the representative branch in Britain had been 'corrupted' by Crown patronage, but they never let go of the idea that the British Constitution embodied the best principles. Lee's picture of the Lords as an indispensable check on both the Crown and the Commons was subtly different from that of John Adams, who thought it essential to retain an upper House in order to prevent the aristocracy from exercising an undue influence on the representatives. Adams also wanted the executive to hold an absolute power of veto over the acts of both Houses. It is significant that both Adams and Lee, leading members of the revolutionary movement in the two greatest provinces, were firmly convinced of the importance of an upper House as essential to their idea of the Whig republic.

This conception appeared in Adams's *Thoughts on Government* (1776), in

[1] To Arthur Lee, 20 December 1766; Ballagh, *Letters of R. H. Lee*, i. 18–22.

commenting on which Lee drew attention to the importance of establishing an upper chamber with a longer term than that of the House 'in order to answer the purpose of an independant [*sic*] middle power'.[1] It remained for the Virginians to find a way of 'blending the three simple forms of Government in such a manner as to prevent the inordinate views of either from unduly affecting the others, which has never been the case in Engld., altho' it was the professed aim of that System'.[2] Certainly Lee was imbued with the belief that even if America lacked the hereditary nobility which gave to the English Constitution such reassuring strength, even if America had no 'great oaks', an independent Virginia needed the security of an upper House with entrenched safeguards for its independence.

The necessity arose from the simple fact that when royal authority had withdrawn, the whole of the system that remained rested on an elective base. This led Richard Henry Lee to observe of the new plan of government,

'Tis very much of the democratic kind, altho' a Governor and a second branch of legislation are admitted, for the former is not permitted voice in Legislation, he is in all things to be advised by his Privy Council, and both are by joint ballot of both houses to be chosen annually. . . . Both of the Houses of the Legislature are to be chosen by the whole body of the people. . . .[3]

Thus the imbalance of which Lee had complained in 1766 was suddenly reversed, and the new situation threatened to upset the 'blending of the simple forms of Government' with a preponderance on the popular side. It was a danger of which good Whigs like Richard Henry Lee and George Mason or John Adams were bound to take notice; but it was a cause of even greater anxiety to Carter Braxton, a great conservative planter whose whiggism was hardly the less orthodox for being distinctly less enamoured of popular rule. Braxton, writing to influence the deliberations of the Virginia Convention, noted the agreement among all writers that government was designed to promote and secure 'the happiness of every individual member of society' — a somewhat American reading of the history of political thought — and went on to discuss the different forms and the unhappy corruption of the English system which had begun with William III's funding system. But the triennial legislature, with the exclusion of placemen, was the best plan for securing the independence of the Commons and the dignity of the Lords. Virginia's problem was to adopt and perfect the English plan. Braxton

[1] To Patrick Henry, 20 April 1776; Ballagh, *Letters of R. H. Lee*, i. 176–80.
[2] To Edmund Pendleton, 12 May 1776; Ballagh, *Letters of R. H. Lee*, i. 190–2.
[3] To General Charles Lee, 29 June 1776; Ballagh, *Letters of R. H. Lee*, i. 203.

attacked the tumult and riot of simple democracies and the 'unjust attempts to maintain their idol equality by an equal division of property'. His proposals for Virginia went as far as possible to establish permanency in the executive. The Governor, to be elected by the representatives, was to continue in office during good behaviour, and in case of a vacancy the place was to be filled by a majority of the Council and the Assembly. Twenty-four men, chosen from the state at large by the representatives, were to form a Council of State and to serve for life; vacancies to be filled by the Assembly. The Governor was to have the assistance of a Privy Council to advise him. Neither these, nor any member of either House, except the treasurer, were to hold office in the government. The Governor and Privy Council would appoint judges, to serve during good behaviour. The Governor ought not to be at the mercy of elections as this would induce him to relax laws which might cause unpopularity. In cases of dispute between the Governor and the Assembly, the Council of State was to mediate, and it might also propose laws. Governor and Council of State were to keep out of the elections of representatives — except that, as citizens, they would have votes.[1]

Carter Braxton's personal views may not have been very important, but the pamphlet stands as one of the earlier statements in the Whig-Republican case for replacing the permanence and stability of royal power by introducing as large an ingredient of domestic permanence and stability as was compatible with representative government. State Constitutions in this period were loaded with institutional attempts to solve the same problem. Maryland devised the electoral college for the election of Senators; North Carolina and New York both hit on the device of higher property qualifications for the voters for the upper than for the lower House; Massachusetts put its Senate on a basis of paid-up assessments.

By contrast the form of government finally adopted in Virginia, with its resounding Declaration of Rights, was weighted on the popular side. Although the Declaration of Rights affirmed the great principle of the separation of powers, which had been learnt from the British theory about the exclusion of placement, and had been doctored a little by readings of Montesquieu's somewhat cursory remarks on the same subject, the truth was that Virginia emerged from the debris of royal government with a firm foundation of legislative power. No more, as under a Culpeper, a Nicholson, or a Spotswood, would it be possible, even nominally, to attribute legislative

---

[1] Carter Braxton, *An Address to the Convention of . . . Virginia on the Subject of Government in General, and recommending a Particular Form to their Consideration: By a Native of the Colony* (Philadelphia, 1776), copy in Library Company of Philadelphia.

action to executive authority. All the principal powers were gathered into the hands of the two Houses of the legislature, both of these were based on elections by freeholders, and the House of Delegates of course inherited the long matured experience of its predecessor in the administration of legislative business.

The electoral system was rounded off in 1785 when the legislature passed a comprehensive revision of the election laws.[1] The intentions of the disallowed laws of the 1760s were at last given full legal force; the amount of unimproved land required to qualify a voter was reduced to fifty acres; the suffrage was expressly restricted to white males, a limitation which had no doubt existed in custom though not in law, but the religious disability against Catholics was dropped. The law-makers attempted once again the somewhat doctrinaire requirement of compulsory voting; any qualified voter failing to give his vote was liable to a fine amounting to one quarter of his annual tax. Delinquents were to be presented by the Grand Juries.

Attempts to enforce the compulsory voting law, although very rare, were not entirely unknown. In 1793 the Mecklenburg County Grand Jury, seized with Jacobinic frenzy, suddenly presented no fewer than 570 persons for failing to vote in elections to Congress and to the House of Delegates. The victims, praying relief from their fines, explained that as planters and farmers they were too busy to vote and their horses were in use; others lived too far away and some did not even know of the elections. But significantly they also pointed out that the law had not previously been put into force and that no Grand Jury in any adjacent county had enforced it.[2]

The vestigial idea of compulsory voting deserves to be remembered as part of a total conception of the state. It had been on the books since 1705 yet had never had the slightest effective significance; it stood as a reminder that every subject had some part to play in the carefully designed machine of government, that a properly working commonwealth was thought to involve the participation of all its members.

The towns received separate attention. In Williamsburg and Norfolk the vote was conferred on owners of freehold houses — 'housekeepers' — of six months' residence and £50 worth of visible estate. Freeholders in these cities

---

[1] Hening, *Statutes*, xii. 120–9.

[2] *Calendar of Virginia State Papers*, vi. 419. In 1796 one Chaney Gatewood was fined £1 19*s*. 2½*d*., being one-fourth of his tax, plus costs, on presentment for not voting, by the Grand Jury of King and Queen County. This seems to be the only other case of which there is a printed record. ibid., viii. 382.

enjoyed the exceptional privilege of voting in both town and county polls in the same election, an advantage which must have been of particular interest to the planters who ran town businesses and which they did not lose until 1831, although by a statute of 1787 it was withheld from future incorporations.[1] In other cities, a man would become a qualified voter by virtue of having possessed a freehold lot for six months; but the right was immediate if the lot were held by descent, devise, or marriage; unearned property had not lost its magic. The laws governing municipal elections were various; but only in Norfolk and Williamsburg did the municipal electors have the right to vote by the same token in general elections. The Richmond Charter was so restrictive on this head that as late as 1852 it had to be amended to give the municipal vote to townsmen already enfranchised for state elections by the new State Constitution.[2]

The conduct of elections continued to be a matter of much local discretion. No attempt was made to work out a system of registration. If a candidate, or his agent, suspected that an intending voter lacked the required qualifications, it was his responsibility to challenge the man at the poll; not all voters who refused to affirm their right by giving an oath were necessarily disqualified, for it was quite easy not to know the exact extent of one's property and it might be safer to refuse an oath than to risk perjury. Such a voter might have his name entered in a separate book and if scrutiny of the deeds sustained his claim then his vote would be duly recorded. In principle, an oath was still enough to satisfy the law.

By these measures did the Whig founders of the Virginia Constitution apply their deeply held doctrines of government in the new making of the commonwealth. And although there were notes of alarm — accentuated by the hardships imposed on creditors by the war-time inflation — it was in these measures, especially in the Constitution of 1776, that they revealed the profound confidence which sustained them in their management of the affairs of the state. No reforms were made in the oligarchic government of the counties and little change appeared in the social texture of the leadership. It has been noticed that when Madison, Monroe, and Jefferson wanted to organise a national party, they relied on the great traditions of gentry leadership to gain the influence required among the freeholders. In Massachusetts, the Whig gentry went to the lengths of instituting a complex pyramid of privileges to safeguard the different interests involved in the government; but in Virginia, every elector was eligible for membership of either House.

[1] Hening, *Statutes*, xii. 642–3.
[2] J. A. C. Chandler, *History of Suffrage in Virginia*, 20.

The pre-eminence of the traditional leaders was secured in part by the equality of the counties, in part by legislative experience, but in the greatest degree by the unbroken traditions of authority and deference.

The making of a new Constitution gave Virginians the chance to lay down the principle that representatives ought to be residents of their constituencies. Before the Revolution it was common for members of the lower House to represent counties in which they held enough land to qualify as voters but did not reside; but this seemed to the Old Whigs of Virginia to be a departure from the basic intention that each community should elect one of its own men. The Constitution of 1776 required members of the House of Delegates to be residents of their districts, but in spite of this, the old practice did not immediately come to an end.[1] The question was reopened, however, by the Federal Constitution, under which members of Congress could come from any part of their state.

Madison himself was at the centre of the question. Patrick Henry, who was violently opposed to Madison owing to their antagonistic views of the Constitution, wielded enough power in the state legislature to deprive Madison of his expected seat in the United States Senate. Madison then began to look for a seat in the House. There are strong grounds for believing that Henry developed a plan to group Madison's county of Orange into a congressional district, with a majority of his opponents, to be led by James Monroe. The alarm of Madison's friends even led his father to suggest that he should stand for election in Williamsburg, of which he was not a resident. The legislature, under Henry's guidance, forestalled this move by passing a residence law to govern congressional candidates, plainly aimed against Madison; but his projected arrangement of the counties was frustrated and Madison was duly elected to Congress, where he soon began to defend those local interests which Henry professed to have at heart.[2]

Once again, as had happened in Massachusetts as early as 1694, and apparently in Pennsylvania in the case of Galloway, the rule of residence resulted from an attempt to keep out a particular man or men. But it was consonant with sound republican views and in principle it already enjoyed the approval of Madison himself. He had remarked in the Federal Convention that if state residence were not required of representatives, rich men might get themselves elected in neighbouring states after having failed in their own

[1] Sydnor, *Gentlemen Freeholders*, 70–71, 164.
[2] Edward Carrington to James Madison, 9, 15 November 1788; Madison to Jefferson, 8 December 1788; Burgess Ball to Madison, 8 December 1788; Madison Papers. Elmer C. Griffith, *The Rise and Development of the Gerrymander* (Chicago, 1907), 30 f.

— the practice, as he said, in the boroughs of England.[1] He failed to note that it was the way in which many of the best men got into Parliament without the support of a county.

10. Elective Despotism and Other Perils: Jefferson and Madison on the Shortcomings of the Constitution of 1776

The effect of the new system was to place all legislative power in the hands of the Assembly. Under the stress of war and inflation, some of the leading Virginians began to have second thoughts about the state Constitution. Jefferson was induced to waver in the direction of orthodox Whig thought about 'interests', and, taking up the new-found dogma about 'persons and property', he expressed the opinion that the two legislative Houses ought to represent these separate elements. Jefferson did not cease to believe in the ultimate right of the majority to control the destiny of the state. Madison made it clear, however, that he did not share this belief. One of the objects of the system of representation should be to keep the state virtuous by keeping its existing agrarian character. It would be not merely permissible, but necessary, to draw the lines of electoral districts in such a way as to prevent any future urban majority from coming to power. Neither Jefferson nor Madison changed his mind; and these opposing views were to come into mighty conflict when the time came to reform the state Constitution.

WITHIN a few years, the two great Virginians who were later to be associated in the founding of the Republican Party were firmly convinced of the urgent need for reform of their new state Constitution. Jefferson had the opportunity to examine the working of Virginia's version of government by consent when he drew up his answers to the enquiries of Barbé-Marbois,

[1] Max Farrand (ed.), *Records of the Federal Convention*, 4 vols. (New Haven, 1957), ii. 218 (hereafter referred to as *Records*).

which — his only self-attributed publication — appeared as the *Notes on Virginia*. Later he formulated a draft for a new Constitution, on which Madison made some instructive comments. But the two men gained much less support than their contemporaries, the British parliamentary reformers, were able to enlist in the ill-fated movement of the same period. The observations of Jefferson and Madison made up an intellectual critique of very great interest for their differing ideas of the meaning of representation, but of little political consequence at the time.

A first reading of Jefferson's strictures might cause the impression that the Revolution had been for no purpose. Having found that the majority of the men of the state who fought and paid taxes had no vote, he went on to the most grievous conclusions about the state of representation. These were guided by a clear conception of the fundamental geographic regions of the state. 'Below the falls', as he said, lived 19,000 electors, whose representation gave them control of half of the Senate, and only four short of half the members of the House of Delegates. The rest of the state contained some 30,000 voters who received their laws in effect from these 19,000.[1]

Jefferson was not wholly exempt from special pleading; in at least one Piedmont county, Powhatan, each voter had as much influence as four in the Northern Neck county of Fairfax.[2] Given Jefferson's belief in numerically scaled representation, however, the theme of his argument was undoubtedly correct; and his analysis grew constantly more correct as time went on and population moved into the western sections.

It is interesting to observe the influence of sections on Jefferson's method. It did not occur to him to doubt that the people living below the fall line formed a community in which they had a common political interest. Within that division, internal differences were not mentioned, and rivalries were presumably held to the level of personal ambitions. But major political conflicts might arise from the divergences of interest between the sections.

Jefferson was also severely critical of the concentration of powers in the legislature. This concentration he called 'the definition of despotism'.[3] The fact that the people chose the legislators did not make it any better; 'an elective despotism', he remarked, 'was not the government we fought for'.[4]

[1] Thomas Jefferson, *Notes on Virginia* (London, 1787), 192–4.
[2] Hilldrup, 'Convention', 138–9.
[3] Ford, *Notes*, 195.
[4] Cf. 'It may happen, that the majority may by a law, not in a confusion, destroy property; there may be a law enacted, that there shall be an equality of goods and estate....
If we strain too far to avoid monarchy in kings [let us take heed] that we do not call for

Allowing that he was giving a critical analysis in which theoretical possibilities were raised to the stature of facts and for the distinctly American tendency of that period to see unbearable oppression in minor constitutional defects, one may still ask what Jefferson can have meant by calling the elective system which he had helped to create a 'despotism'. The answer must lie partly in the intellectual tendencies which have been suggested. But no understanding of the thought that followed the early Constitutions can be achieved without taking in the terrific impact of the money inflation during the Revolutionary War.

A much more inflexible Virginian than Jefferson, Charles Lee, raging against the abuses of popular government reached significantly similar conclusions. After four years of self-government, he declared that it would be better that America were conquered (or rather to accept the terms Britain was then believed ready to offer)

than to endure any longer such an odious tyranny as the capricious arbitrary government of an unlimited uncontrollable assembly. . . . Your favourite Junius says, after Lock, [sic] that there cannot be a more fatal doctrine to Liberty establish'd than the omnipotence of Parliament — and this doctrine is certainly still less dangerous in G. Britain where the Parliament consists of three distinct branches than in America where it consists of only one, for from the constitution of the Senate, (as it is ludicrously calld) they must be made up of the self-same clay — for God's sake then do not talk of Liberty until you have established the fundamental points, the limitation of the power of the Assembly and the full freedom of the Press.

The abuses of the government were tyranny, injustice, and violence; America's 'free system' had been ornamented with the law making paper money legal tender, the confiscation law which stripped Tories and Whigs, friends and foes, women and children of their property for no crime ever pretended, and the tearing from the clergy of their lawfully owned freeholds.[1]

A violent outburst, no doubt, and not from a reliable source; but there is no reason to suppose that Jefferson was influenced by Charles Lee. Yet Jefferson writes in 1781 of 'an elective despotism'. The fact seems to be that Jefferson's thinking had begun to take a distinct turn in the direction of more orthodox Whig conventions.

This view was manifested in the remark, noticeably similar to Charles Lee's, that the Senate was 'by its constitution too homogeneous with the

emperors to deliver us from more than one tyrant.' Colonel Rich, 29 October 1647. Hill and Dell, *Good Old Cause*, 356.

[1] C. Lee to R. H. Lee, 12 April 1780; Lee Papers, University of Virginia.

House of Delegates'; it was chosen by the same people at the same time. The purpose of establishing different Houses of legislation, Jefferson continued, was to introduce the influence of different interests or principles. Some states provided for representation of persons in the House and of property in the Senate, but Virginia did not do so.

Jefferson had obviously been influenced by the 'persons and property' doctrine which, having been propounded in the *Essex Result*, had penetrated the Massachusetts Constitution of 1780 and had entered deeply into the grain of American Whig ideas. That the influence of 'different interests or principles' should be accommodated in the structure of the constitution was a doctrine which could be found in Montesquieu's defence of the separate representation of the nobility; but Jefferson did not go on to specify the manner in which he would have chosen to bring it about in Virginia.

Madison was more explicit. The lessons of experience ought, in his opinion, to be mixed with the theory of free government, and he advocated differential property qualifications for electors of House and Senate. This method would safeguard 'persons and property'. It was a distinction which had not been attended to in the commencement of the Revolution, when 'in the existing state of American population and American property the two classes of rights were so little discriminated that a provision for the rights of persons was supposed to include of itself those of property, and it was natural to infer from the tendency of republican laws, that these different interests would be more and more identified. Experience and investigation have however produced more correct ideas on this subject. It is now observed that in all populous countries, the smaller part only can be interested in preserving the rights of property'.[1] An interested majority could work injustice; and in advising on the making of a constitution for Kentucky he warned that if all power were put in the hands of those who were not interested in property rights it would lead either to the majority becoming the dupes of ambition or to their poverty rendering them 'mercenary servants of wealth'. The first case would subvert liberty by despotism growing out of anarchy, the second by an oligarchy founded on corruption.[2]

Madison thus soon came to share the anxieties which had produced such

---

[1] Madison and his contemporaries used 'experience' to mean the evidence of history, both recent and general; 'experience shows' and 'history proves' were almost interchangeable expressions in the Constitutional Convention of 1787 — Douglass Adair, 'The Use of History by the Founding Fathers: The Historical Pessimism of A. Hamilton', cyclostyled pamphlet. Madison's statement quoted above is a clear example of the same usage.

[2] 'Observations on Jefferson's Draft for a Constitution of Virginia', Hunt (ed.), *Writings of Madison*, v. 284–9.

tracts as the *Essex Result*, and Carter Braxton's pamphlet of 1776, and with more acumen than most he grasped the nature of the problem of combining majority rule with republican rights. The opinions which he formed when reviewing the Virginia Constitution in the 1780s remained unchanged until the end of his life. In the famous Convention of 1829, at the age of seventy-eight, he said:

It would be happy if a state of society could be found or framed, in which an equal voice in making the laws could be allowed to every individual bound to obey them. But this is a theory, which like most theories, confessedly requires limitations and modifications.

Persons and property were the two great objects on which government was to act. The rights of persons and the rights of property were the objects which government was instituted to protect. But Madison, who was never the servant of cliché, added that these rights could not well be separated;

the personal right to acquire property, which is a natural right, gives to property, when acquired, a right to protection, which is a social right.

The great danger in a republic was that the majority might not respect the rights of the minority — and he went on to advocate the use by Virginia of the federal ratio in the basis of representation in order to give the necessary protection to their property to the owners of slaves.[1]

Slavery indeed introduced one of those distinctions of interest which gave to the debate on the representation of interests and persons a hard and material urgency. This was never a debate about unsubstantial theories but always about the substance of power.

Jefferson, on the other hand, never moved firmly over into the position which he seemed to advocate in his *Notes on Virginia*, and those remarks should be regarded as representing a view either less clearly seen or less deeply held. In drafting a new Constitution, on which Madison's comments have been noted, he showed how far he would be prepared to go. Proportional representation was to determine the basis of the House, which was to be elected triennially — an early break with annual elections. No county was ever to go unrepresented (as could happen to small towns in Massachusetts), because counties whose populations were too small for one representative were to be annexed to the adjoining county. The crucial problem was to

---

[1] Hunt, *Writings of Madison*, ix. 359–63. See also *Federalist*, no. 54 (Madison). Farrand, *Records*, iii. 450–5, where Madison (in 1820) gives a more detailed explanation of the same general view.

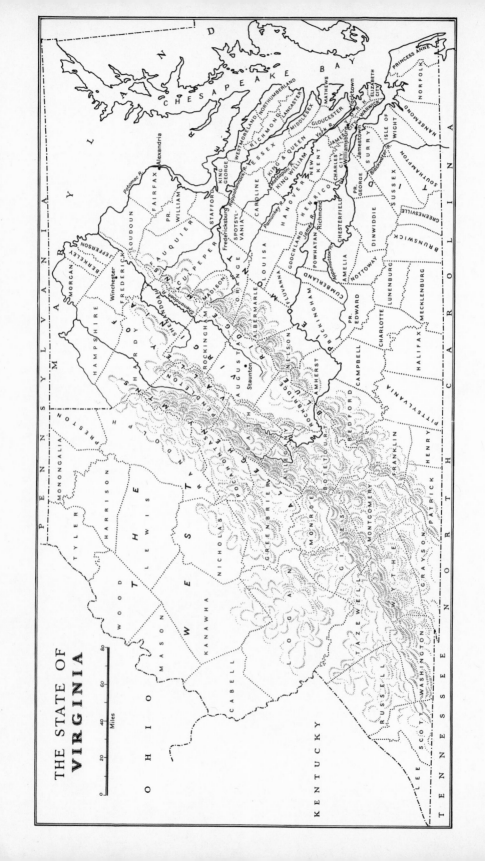

THE STATE OF
VIRGINIA

find a different basis for the Senate. Jefferson shied away from the idea of a higher property qualification, though he tried to achieve a sifting machinery by proposing a sort of electoral college. In each Senate district, each county was to elect four members for every one representative to which the county was entitled in the House; these electors from the several counties were to meet in their districts and to choose by ballot one Senator for every six delegates to which each county was entitled in the House. The Senate was to be of two classes, to retire at alternating periods of three years, so that (except for the first half in the first session) there would be a six-year term.[1]

The suffrage was to be extensive, covering all free male citizens of full age and sane mind, having one year's residence in the county, or having possessed real property (to a value not filled in), or having been enrolled in the militia; the same qualifications would apply for electors to the senatorial system. Jefferson did not say that the voters must be white. This was the furthest that he would go towards a systematic structure of balanced interests in the Whig tradition, though it was clear that when he wrote his *Notes on Virginia* he was prepared to lean towards property differentials, and seemed to have repented of some of his revolutionary egalitarianism.

Long afterwards, when the reform of the Constitution was again being urged, Jefferson offered his reflections in reply to a questioner. At that period, when he had drafted the Constitution annexed to the *Notes*, 'the infancy of the subject at that moment, and our inexperience of self-government', he observed,

occasioned gross departures in that draught, from genuine republican canons. The abuses of monarchy had so filled our minds that we imagined everything republican that was not monarchy. We had not yet penetrated to the mother principle that governments are republican only in proportion as they embodied the will of their people, and execute it. Hence, our first constitutions had really no leading principle in them, but experience and reflection.

A government would embody the will of the people in proportion as every member had an equal voice through his representative. He would approve amendments giving a general suffrage (not including women, infants, or slaves), equal representation in the legislature, and an executive chosen by the people. He did not approve of privileged representation for slave-owners by the federal ratio. He would have liked to divide the counties into wards, 'pure, elementary republics — all together making the State a democracy'.[2]

[1] Boyd (ed.), *Papers of Jefferson*, vi. 294–317.

[2] Richmond, *Constitutional Whig*, 1 December 1826, quoting a letter of Jefferson to S. Kercheval, Monticello, 12 July 1816. To what draft Jefferson referred is a little obscure,

A democracy! It was a far cry from the old orthodoxy of the Whig republic. It was also a far cry from the facts or conventions of Virginian political life in Jefferson's lifetime. Jefferson refused to adulterate his principles with that profound distrust of human motives which permeated the political mind of the American Whigs. There was no need, he declared in the same letter, to fear the people: 'they and not the rich are our dependence for continued freedom'.

Though his views may have wavered under the stress of the Revolutionary War, his thoughts were held together by a deep continuity. In 1776 Jefferson had already seen a connection between the equality of men in their inalienable rights, and the numerical apportionment of their representatives in the government. Under the Federal Constitution, the struggle against Hamilton and the Federalists was a struggle to defend all he believed in; and it does not seem extravagant to guess that his victory in 1800 restored his faith in the ultimate rightness of democratic decisions. There are, at any rate, few public men who have been able to reject this faith immediately after winning an election.

Jefferson's views of political right were connected with the sense of grievance which expressed itself in the swelling demand for constitutional reform before 1829 — as he showed by his sympathetic answer to enquiries in 1816. But those of Madison were not, and the reasons for reform urged by Madison in the 1780s would have given little support to the later movement. He agreed with Jefferson about giving the Senate a six-year term, but his anxiety to establish differential property qualifications and every practicable safeguard against the perils of popular government expressed his desire to make mixed government permanently safe against any risk of destruction by public feeling. His comments on Jefferson's proposals for putting the Senate on a basis of districts indicate the depth of the difference between their thoughts.

Madison rejected the idea. This system, he argued, encouraged local interests and discouraged attention to the 'aggregate interests of the Com-

since his own proposed new constitution hardly deserved (from his own viewpoint) the strictures he now made; one wonders whether he was confusing it with the actual state Constitution of 1776. In attacking the principle of a permanent national debt, he went on to sound an authentic note from the early years; there was a choice, he said, between economy and liberty and profusion and servitude. Some people attributed superhuman wisdom to the age of the Revolution, but, 'I knew that age well: I belonged to it, and labored with it; it deserved well of its country; it was very like the present, but without the experience of the present: and 40 years of experience in government is worth a century of book reading; and this they would say themselves, were they to rise from the dead . . .'.

munity'. Each Senator should be the choice of the whole society. He quickly anticipated the objection that would be raised — and always was raised when general systems of election were advanced against local elections — that the people would not know their representatives, stating in reply that merit was usually known.

No doubt Madison revealed here the greater awareness of the general or national scale of the problems of government which in the Federal Convention showed him as a vigorous and fearless nationalist; but he went on to reveal an even deeper strain of thought on the one point on which, contemplating the future population, he accepted Jefferson's scheme: where large towns that might unite their votes had grown up, the precaution suggested by Jefferson, of dividing the state into electoral districts, would be necessary after all, in order to secure 'an immediate choice of the people at large'.[1]

The growth of large cities was not an immediate prospect in Virginia, but Madison was aware of industrial trends elsewhere and his general principles took account of a possibly remote state of future facts; the future might put his principles to the test. Where 'large towns which might unite their votes', were actually big enough to form majorities, it becomes difficult to justify his anxiety to safeguard 'the immediate choice of the people at large'. Who, after all, were 'the people at large'?

The explanation is that Madison's view of the American social order, like that of his Whig contemporaries, was strongly prescriptive. His design for a Constitution was a design for the maintenance of an order whose substance already existed and whose outlines were in general clear. In this his position was entirely conventional, though his insight into the political aspect of the problem was, as always, acute. For it must be recognised that any system of representation acquires through its normal functioning an institutional life which naturally tends to reproduce the conditions which brought it into being, and the attitudes, the proprieties, and the values which justify its existence to those whom it governs. To achieve this kind of end, to form political society into an intended mould, was the design of the early state constitutions. The representation of persons and property was an object less grandiose than the representation of nobility and commoners, yet it corresponded to the American conception of an ordered society.

In the case hinted by Madison, the basis of the Senate meant more than the protection of property against a mob animated by the rage for paper money and the example of Shays's Rebellion (for his *Observations* were written in 1788 and were as much directed to the making of a constitution

1 Hunt (ed.), *Madison*, v. 284–94.

for Kentucky as towards Virginia).[1] It meant preserving the fundamentally agrarian character of the state, or of American society, against the rise of industrial cities. It was a problem of which Madison showed himself aware, in the debates at Philadelphia.[2] A system of representation viewed in this light and for these purposes became something more than a means of reaching the people and finding out their will: it became a means of prescribing their will for the purpose, and by this process defining the character of the whole society.

When the State of Virginia in the revolutionary period is taken as a whole, the absence of acute conflicts on economic issues, and the relative acquiescence of the humbler orders in the structure of a society which gave the leadership to the gentry, tend to reduce such deep designs to relative unimportance. But Madison was looking beyond Virginia, and he was looking beyond his own time. Jefferson's outlook, by contrast, was far more flexible. Though he notoriously disliked towns and industrial concentrations he did not seek to prescribe a system of representation in which their political influence would be restrained. But though he had reached through to proportional or numerical representation, he could not carry his countrymen with him. Massachusetts arrived at the same position, despite its engrained loyalty to the integrity of the towns, by the more direct route. The strongest towns could best secure their own interests through the adoption of the numerical principle.

11. Constitutional Reform and the Defence of the Whig Republic

Jefferson and Madison could not both have succeeded in reforming their state Constitution because their strictures sprang from differing views and pointed to divergent conclusions. The point may be considered academic, since neither of them

[1] Boyd (ed.), *Papers of Jefferson*, vi. 283.

[2] Farrand, *Records*, ii. 203–4. He also mentioned Virginia as an example of an unjust system of representation due to the unwillingness of minorities to relinquish residual power, i. 584.

got his way. If Jefferson's ideas had been adopted, the political mechanism would have been capable of adapting itself to changes in the social character of the population, if not without strain then without the threat of serious political convulsion; Madison's proposals, on the other hand, might well have accentuated the conflicts which soon began to grow.

These conflicts arose in the immediate sense from changes in the distribution and wealth of the population. The movement into the western regions, unaccompanied by redistribution of seats in the House of Delegates or Senate, brought about a marked inequality in representation; while the increase in the number of non-freeholding farmers and townsmen of various crafts and occupations threw into sharp focus the fact that the constitution-makers had aspired to build an orthodox Whig system embodying carefully planned controls against popular power. But it was not only physical movement that gave rise to the new discontent: movement itself was accompanied by restlessness, and deprivation turned to grievance when the country called on the services of the militia in the War of 1812, and a high proportion of the men found themselves without the right to vote.

The two rising streams of discontent effected an uneasy and suspicious conjunction. The newer gentry of the more recent settlements would have been satisfied by a reapportionment of legislative seats that did not alter the internal basis of power by extending the suffrage — a reform the threat of which struck fear into the hearts of the Republican leaders. These leaders — Archibald Stuart, Chapman Johnson, Benjamin Watkins Leigh — who fought against a democratic franchise, and who feared that even a moderate reapportionment of seats might upset the balance of power on which the security of property depended, were the legitimate heirs of George Mason and his Whig colleagues of 1776.

For fifty-three years after 1776 the electoral process was carried on under the prescribed forms. Yet those forms could be interpreted in a startling variety of ways. A formal guide is provided by the election laws; but the laws record only what the legislators intended, not what actually happened at elections; and a valuable commentary on electoral realities appears in the records of disputed elections. These varieties reflected the tension between the settled order and the restless, resentful ambition that would drive the under-represented population to threats of revolt or secession.

The House of Delegates had long made a practice of deputing the hearing of petitions alleging electoral irregularities to its important committee on elections and grievances. In 1804 the House adopted a new set of rules for the adjudication of such cases.[1] These rules suggest at least a hint that the rigid maintenance of the suffrage qualifications may have been an unpopular policy; for when a case of illegal voting was alleged, the burden of proof was to be placed on the plaintiff, who was required to show the land book or provide other proof to disqualify the voter. The rules also laid down that the voter would be held to be duly qualified if he had held his land for six months on the day of election, a step which was an outright amendment to the existing law, taken under the form of a private procedural arrangement in the House. The rules reaffirmed the law of 1736 on the point that a citizen might vote in any county in which he owned the required freehold, even though a non-resident of the county.

The commonest grievance was that a candidate had been returned on the votes of unqualified persons. In May 1799 the members returned for West Liberty, Ohio County, were unseated after a lengthy hearing in which it was shown that votes had been cast by non-freeholders, non-residents, and aliens.[2] In 1800 two remonstrants from Wood County were seated when they claimed that they had originally been returned but that the sheriff had given the certificate to their opponents after a counter-claim. Twenty-five names were listed in this case as 'bad voters' because they had no freehold.[3] A voter in Monroe County in 1804 was held to have been ineligible to vote because, although he had lived on and improved the holding of one hundred acres given him by his father eight or ten years earlier, the transaction had remained unrecorded.[4] The scale of illegal practices was often more generous. In one dispute, in 1824, 114 votes were challenged; while in another, four years later, the remonstrant objected to 195 votes — to which his rival retorted with objections to 127. To the large number of minors and non-freeholders were added the names of thirty-four persons whose existence was not otherwise recorded.[5]

A candidate who owed his election to fraud could reasonably expect to run the risk of challenge, despite the delays and expenses involved. The proportion of cases in which the plaintiff was upheld and the returned member unseated amounted to about one-third of the complaints. A proportion of this order indicates that despite frequent abuses the election laws were taken

---

[1] *Journal of the House of Delegates*, 1804, 46 (hereafter referred to as *JHD*).

[2] Ohio County petition, 1 May 1799, Virginia State Library (hereafter referred to as VSL); *JHD*, 1799–1800, 86–88.

[3] Wood County petition, 1800, VSL; *JHD*, 1800, 16–17.

[4] Monroe County, petition of John Woodward, 1804, VSL.

[5] Giles County petitions, 1824.

very seriously by the House of Delegates; and though it would be impossible to estimate the numbers who were deterred from frauds by this knowledge, the enforcement of the laws must certainly have had some such effect. The very frequency of the illegalities demonstrates that an appreciable section of the adult white male population was in fact disfranchised. In Massachusetts, by contrast, very high percentages of the adult male population frequently went to the polls, but complaints of voting by unqualified persons were extremely rare.

The fact that candidates might reach agreements not to challenge each other's illegal votes or that friendly sheriffs might occasionally change the rules, could not satisfy a people who claimed the right to vote as a republican heritage. The protest which had sounded so ineffectively from Jefferson began to acquire a more popular voice as the population, having moved steadily into the Valley and beyond, into the Trans-Allegheny west of the state, left thickening patches of labourers and tenants. From Frederick County, on the eastern flank of the Alleghenies, which in Washington's youth had been a distant outpost, the legislature received in 1796 a petition demanding a constitutional convention and complaining that the system deprived the people of representation in proportion to their numbers; it also objected to the mode of electing Senators.[1] About 200 freeholders and others of Patrick County petitioned against the suffrage qualification in 1806.[2] The fullest protest of this early phase of the reform movement came from western Pittsylvania, whose 'sundry Citizens, Inhabitants of the County' — not freeholders, be it noted — advanced a forceful if repetitive argument. Other states had profited by experience, and

... it is a matter of surprise, that, Virginia, who stood foremost in the late Revolution, both in the Declaration of her rights and Independence, who, we trust has kept pace with the knowledge of those rights with other parts of America, should so long have acquiesced under the imperfections of her first essay on the subject. — We are well aware that it is the interest of part of the community to oppose any reform; — and have expressed fears lest a Government should be obtained equal to the present — in plain terms they are afraid to trust the people — This has been and ever will be the language of Aristocracy; — the object of which is — to degrade the mass of the people and sacrifice *Public Rights* to private *Interest*....[3]

This demand for suffrage extension was grounded on the rights of those who paid taxes and were called on to fight for their country. The petition

[1] Frederick County petition, no. 3576 A, 18 November 1796, VSL.
[2] Patrick County petition, no. 5033, 12 December 1806, VSL.
[3] Pittsylvania County, petition of 24 December 1807, VSL.

also demanded that sheriffs and other county officers be made elective by popular suffrage and that militia officers up to the rank of captain be elected by their companies.

The War of 1812 gave the greatest single stimulus to the movement for suffrage extension, and by contrast these previous petitions were merely random outbursts. The War, both by calling out large bodies of men for militia service and by mustering them where they could easily be counted, created conditions which could have been expected to give rise to a new protest. Methods of petition became more advanced, and by 1815 the organisers had learnt to work on a general basis, using militia musters to circulate a printed form which showed that only a certain proportion of those on duty were able to vote. A space was left for the actual figure in each case. In a Shenandoah muster of 1,000, only 300 men claimed to be voters; in Rockingham not more than one-third of 800 could vote; only 200 out of 1,200 could vote in Loudoun[1] — and so it went on.

Despite the force of these demands, however, they were backed by little political power. It was not the reform of the suffrage, but the reapportionment of representatives which commanded effective support and threatened the stability of the old system. This demand was characteristic, a normal product of regional development. It proceeded from a populace rapidly changing both in geographical distribution and social character. Virginia's west was no longer the outward edge of the United States; the whole state was settled, and at the Convention of 1829 delegates were armed with the information that slavery, the surest indication of wealth, was moving into the Valley and penetrating beyond.[2] Moreover, as slavery spread in the interior it came to be adopted by a larger number of farmers working average-sized farms, while the general prosperity of the Tidewater diminished.[3] It was altogether natural that new men of substance in these more recently settled regions should demand a representation in the legislature, commensurate with the numbers in their counties; it was natural, too, that they should resent the political power of what seemed to them a Tidewater aristocracy owing its superiority solely to the corruption of the old system. The demand for reform in Virginia was thus somewhat analogous to the contemporary

---

[1] Shenandoah County Petition, 1816, Rockingham County petition, 1816, Loudoun County petition, no. 6563, 1815 (handwritten), VSL. Cf. Saxby in 1647. Hill and Dell, *Good Old Cause*, 357.

[2] *Convention 1829*, 280–1.

[3] Jackson T. Main, 'Distribution of Property in Post-Revolutionary Virginia', Mississippi Valley Historical Review, 253–6.

reform movement in Britain, where the rise of new centres of population had long previously rendered the distribution of seats wholly anachronistic.

The demand for suffrage reform was not a regional development. In the Tidewater, the poorer classes were increasing in numbers as slavery moved westwards. In the Piedmont, the Valley, and the west, and in the growing city populations of Richmond, Norfolk, Alexandria, and Petersburg, a large, increasing, and resentful aggregation of tenants, leaseholders, and artisans began to demand the right to vote. From about 1815 onwards these two strands converged to produce a formidable, at times a threatening, volume of protest. But they were not made of the same stuff. The movement for reapportionment included elements that were afraid of and hostile to the extension of the suffrage.

The antagonism between the two branches appeared when an unofficial reform Convention assembled at Staunton in 1816. The Convention adopted resolutions calling for a state Convention armed with unlimited powers to reform the Constitution. The provision for unlimited powers, and the demand that the question of whether to call a Convention or not should be put straight to the people, as against the proposal to let the legislature issue the call, occasioned heated debate. The two points were related. If the legislature were to issue the call, it could regulate the subjects to be dealt with and might have excluded consideration of the suffrage; a convention with unlimited powers would be free to take up all subjects of discontent.[1]

Archibald Stuart, a member of the Virginian ratifying Convention of 1788, judge, presidential elector, and influential state politician who had been associated with the *Richmond Enquirer*, gave William Wirt a revealing account of the clash of interests:

Johnson [Chapman Johnson of Augusta, who was to have a great part in the Convention of 1829] used his whole efforts to recommend a Convention whose powers should be limited to equalize the representation — he was powerfully aided by Tucker — their efforts were herculean but the question was lost by a considerable majority — The public feeling on this subject has become too strong to be resisted, the people appear determined that the minority in the state shall not continue to hold the reins of government....

My wish is that the senatorial districts should be perfectly equalized, let the counties remain as they are & have no Convention — I think this may be done constitutionally, but the objection to this is not only on constitutional grounds but because the representation in the house of delegates would be too large as well as unequal

[1] Fredericksburg *Virginia Herald*, 31 August 1816 (hereafter referred to as *VH*); *Richmond Enquirer*, 31 August 1816 (hereafter referred to as *R.Enq.*).

depend upon it something must be done — if the people cannot be satisfied with reform in the Senate then the next stand must be made for a Convention with limited powers — if we lose this I fear the right of suffrage will be extented [*sic*] this would be to sow the seeds of destruction in our country, I view this subject with horror — if we look forward but a few years we must see that for one land holder there will be many who have none, the rights then of those who own the country will be invaded by those who have no part of it and it will become in the progress to [of?] that state of things an objection to a candidate to be either a man of talents or property, the darkness and confusion which would ensue would even reach the counsels of the U States

Experience has taught us how even free holders who are in a state of dependence may be influenced to commit foolish acts what then might be expected if the idle and vicious and worthless are to have an agency in carrying on our government?[1]

The author of these dark warnings was not a Federalist anticipating the Jacobin terror, but a respected supporter of Jefferson's administration who had been an elector for both Jefferson and Madison.[2] Federalism was declining in Virginia, and divisions on the lines of the national political parties were conspicuously absent from the influences at work in the question of constitutional reform in the state.

The principal problems of the later and more famous debate were present and clearly understood in the Staunton Convention and the subsequent legislative session. The problem of representation was connected with that of taxation. The deeper fears of the Tidewater on this subject remained, to govern the course of its leaders in 1829; the power to tax had always, in American minds, meant the power to rule, and no teaching had been more clearly vindicated by the history of the Revolution itself. The taxing power had also lain at the heart of the problems besetting the Articles of Confederation; a government lacking this power lacked all adequate authority, but at the slightest sign of an excess of the power to tax, Americans habitually sensed imminent tyranny. The stubborn resistance of the Tidewater to a reform that would give the west a legislative majority was based on the fear that the taxing power would be used as an instrument of an attack on Tidewater property in slaves.

As early as 1816 the Tidewater itself felt a grievance in the existing distribution of the land tax, which was based on a law of 1782. One proposal, emanating from a Tidewater source, admitted the justice of the western

[1] Archibald Stuart to Wm. Wirt, 25 August 1816, photostat in William and Mary College Library; printed in *William and Mary College Quarterly* (Williamsburg, 1892–), 2nd series, vi (1926), 340–2.

[2] Grigsby, *Convention of 1788*, ii. 9–16.

demand for a reform of representation, but demanded a complete reassessment of land on the ground that values had swung towards the Piedmont and Valley while low country values had declined.[1] This was not a subject on which spokesmen of the Tidewater could be in complete agreement. If the property of that region were really in decline, then one of the principal shafts of the argument for the special representation of special interests would be weakened; and it remained more conventional to assert that the yield of lowland taxes was higher and the property greater and more stable.[2] It was not difficult to prove in 1816 that the yield from the lowland district was very much higher than from all the others combined; but in the movement of property, more perhaps than in the course of republican argument, the trend of events was on the side of those who spoke for the newer settlements.

The efforts of Chapman Johnson and his colleagues to check the demand for a convention, thwarted in the Staunton meeting, were successful in the legislature. The conservatives had an ally in the Governor, Wilson Cary Nicholas, whose address to the Assembly at its next session listed the points requiring their attention without mentioning the Constitution.[3] The old guard had several lines of defence, and were able to recover in the Senate what they lost in the House. The main task was to prevent the question from going out to the people: and to this end Tazewell, Mercer, and Smythe argued that the legislature had no right to call a Convention; and when that had been lost, that a special commission be appointed; and then that a Convention, if called, be bound by limiting conditions enforced by an oath.[4]

The latter proposal raised difficulties on two grave counts. One speaker objected that an oath binding members of a Convention would imply that the legislature had power to bind a delegate to disobey the instructions of his constituents, should they lie in the contrary sense. A still deeper objection[5] would have been one of basic constitutional theory. Once a constituent assembly has been called, it is by definition superior to the legislature which has convened it; it is the people in the exercise of their original sovereign power; it is supreme. No legislative conditions could control a constituent body.[6]

---

[1] *VH* (from *R.Enq.*), 31 July 1816.   [2] *R.Enq.*, 'A Lowlander', 14 August 1816.
[3] *VH*, 16 November 1816.   [4] *VH*, 18 December, 25, 29 January, 5 February 1817.
[5] Which does not appear to have been raised, though it may have been missed.

[6] Professor McCormick has pointed out to me that American experience shows several instances of 'limited' constitutional conventions, that of New Jersey in 1947 being one. This must be taken to represent a departure from the eighteenth-century view of the constituent character of a genuine constitutional convention.

The conservatives failed to prevent the passage of the Convention Bill in the House of Delegates, but rallied their strength in the Senate. That body defeated the House Bill, but proceeded to fob off discontent by passing a Bill to reapportion the senatorial districts. The west received, on a full count, nine Senators instead of four; but the eastern representation dropped from twenty to fifteen. A new land valuation measure more acceptable in the east was passed at the same time, so that the Tidewater had gained an important point by the struggle without giving up any effective power.[1]

The cause of reform had been scotched, not killed, but it took a long time to recover. It was not until 1825 that a new Convention met at Staunton to rally the supporters of the movement. Thirty-five counties and two cities sent 107 delegates to this meeting, which adopted resolutions demanding a reduction of the numbers in the House of Delegates, representation throughout the General Assembly based on free white numbers, and an extension of the right of suffrage. But the legislature still resisted, twice more rejecting Bills to call a Convention.[2] The *Enquirer*'s rival, the *Constitutional Whig*, which later supported Clay and bitterly opposed Jackson, declared that the action of the House would 'strike the whole country with just and indignant surprize'. The freeholders were the owners of the soil, the lords of the country, the masters of the government — and yet the House told them that they were not to be trusted. In denying that it had opposed suffrage extension, the *Whig* later asserted that it would defend the right of the non-freeholders to vote even if their votes were given to Jackson. It continued to give ardent support to the convention movement.[3]

The *Enquirer* was more cautious than the *Whig* on reform. Throughout both the preliminaries to the Convention of 1829 and the debates, the *Enquirer*, while insisting on justice for the west, emphasised the necessity of compromise in a manner unmistakably soft towards the east. 'The only question', it stated editorially, after six weeks of debate, 'is how the great and immortal principle of the majority, the cornerstone of Republican government, ought to be modified.' The east asked protection for its peculiar form of property; and the only question was, whether one House organised on its own rules would give this security?[4]

---

[1] *VH*, 15, 22 February 1817; Chandler, *Representation*, 26. The apportionment in the House of Delegates could not be changed without revising the Constitution; but the lawyers, having previously given the same opinion about the Senate, changed their minds in 1816.

[2] Chandler, *Representation*, 27–29; Richmond, *Constitutional Whig*, 27 January 1826.

[3] *Whig*, 18 August 1826.   [4] 3 December 1829.

Some Republican principles were evidently more immortal than others. Although the editorial went on to advocate suffrage extension it rejected the abolition of the county court system or the putting of all the executive power in the hands of one man. This came unusually close to a fresh admission of the preoccupation with slavery which conservatives several times in the Convention explicitly denied. The *Enquirer*, which supported Jackson for the presidency, advocated no reform that would threaten the existing structure of power.

One weapon of electors which now came into use was that of exacting pledges from candidates, and a great many such pledges were exacted before the elections of 1827. The result was the passage of a Bill for putting the question of a convention to the people. The response was a majority of more than 5,000 in favour — not as great a majority as the reformers may have expected.[1]

The conservatives were not beaten. They well knew that the crucial question, perhaps even more important than whether a convention was to be held, was that of the basis on which it was to be elected. The legislature thenceforward became the scene of a fierce struggle over the question of the basis, a struggle whose outcome was known by both sides to be of decisive importance for the meaning of the forthcoming Convention. Equality could not spring from inequality, and a Convention which resembled the unreformed legislature would offer little threat to the Constitution.

The position of the reformers was simple. They wanted the Convention to be elected on what they called the 'white basis' — a straight enumeration of the white population. This demand was countered by various proposals for a 'mixed' basis, in which either slaves or other forms of property would be enumerated in order to strengthen the representation of their owners. The conservatives were assisted by the fact that different reformers had differing degrees of warmth for their cause, and by the fact that they had formed an alliance in which some of the most powerful men for redistribution were half-hearted about the suffrage.[2]

The outcome was a Convention based on the senatorial districts.[3] This basis had already been overtaken by the movement of population since 1817, and was deeply disappointing to the reformers. At the end of it all, the

[1] Chandler, *Representation*, 30. The popular vote was: for holding a Convention, 21,896; against, 16,637.
[2] Edward Campbell to David Campbell, 11 October 1829; David Campbell Papers, Duke University Library.
[3] Chandler, *Representation*, 31.

Enquirer printed a long and bitter letter from Philip Doddridge, the most outspoken of the reform leaders, asserting that the basis of four members from each senatorial district was forced on them by the east and that the Convention had thus been organised by those who opposed it.[1]

12. The Issues Debated:
Persons, Property and Power

The enemies of reform in Virginia developed a case which combined Locke's conception of the natural right of property with an American version of interest representation. They wanted to base representation on persons plus taxable property. The real fear underlying this desperate fight against reform was that a hostile legislature might impose crippling taxes on slave property. The most powerful of the reformers were anxious for a redistribution of seats but, significantly, shared the conservatives' fear of universal white male suffrage. The suffrage reformers, appealing to the Declaration of Rights in the Constitution of 1776, argued that the principles adopted then could be fully implemented only by white manhood suffrage.

If the intentions of the men of 1776 and 1787 were to be the criterion, it is probable that the conservatives had the better of the argument. Madison, whose life spanned the whole period, had never changed his mind; and Jefferson, whose thought was more consistent with that of the suffrage reformers, had been in a small minority in 1776. What had happened in the interval to strengthen the hand of the suffrage reformers? The answer was in historical development, not in theory. The population, the occupations, the distribution of wealth in the State had changed; and a large unenfranchised and unrepresented class bitterly resented its unmerited exclusion from political liberty.

The struggle ended in an unsatisfactory compromise. It was not until the rise of a sharp two-party struggle in the 1840s that the final steps towards universal white male suffrage were taken. When the Virginians debated political rights, they meant rights for the white population only. The economy and the whole

[1] *Richmond Enquirer*, 26 March 1830.

social system were supported by agricultural workers who because they were Negro slaves never entered the discussion. Nevertheless, they were there all the time. Ultimately the doctrine of interests proved a clue to the deeply divided character of the State. It was the failure of an effective representation of interests that led to the partition of Virginia in 1861.

THE Convention of 1829–30 was the greatest assembly of notables in the history of Virginia, reinforced by the presence of two ex-Presidents of the United States.[1] It gave rise to a mercifully rare demonstration of rhetoric; there was hardly a speaker who, on rising for the first time — and it was generally the first of several times — did not spend some five or ten minutes in apologising for his deficiencies before so great an audience and throwing himself on the generosity of his hearers. But although the more than three months of debate were very largely a waste of time, they were not, from the conservative standpoint, a waste of energy: for when it was all over and both sides sank back in a common degree of exhaustion, the gains of the reformers were trivial by comparison with their aims or their exertions. Over the crested waves of oratory fluttered the first pennants of the Southern filibuster.

To defend the institutions of 1776, the opponents of reform were obliged to develop their argument; and what they arrived at was in fact a native American doctrine which looked singularly like an English one of the same vintage: interest representation. The reformists, scouring the same sources, refined from them the principle of political individualism — the basic principle of numerical representation. Both sets of arguments were extracted from the Whig precepts of the revolutionary era; neither had a logical claim to exclude the other; each could be reached by following one rather than another emphasis in the ideas of 1776; but on the whole the men of that generation were closer in sympathy and in purpose with the conservatives than with the reformists of 1829.

In pursuit of their thesis the conservatives returned to the distinction between persons and property. The interests at stake in Virginia were complex and intertwined; there was property on all sides. But constitutional debate in the Old Dominion had been surprisingly little concerned with this

[1] One of whom, Monroe, was too vain to refuse the honour of presidency of the Convention, in which place his deafness and ignorance of procedure and 'well known slowness of comprehension' caused much embarrassment, delay, and confusion. — G. C. Dromgoole to Rev. Edward Dromgoole, 6 October 1829, Edward Dromgoole Papers. E. Campbell to David Campbell, 6 October 1829, David Campbell Papers.

distinction, which weighed so heavily (for example) in Massachusetts; and the reason was that the conditions of 1776 had given to the interests of property a power and an authority too great and self-confident to need, at that time, the protection of detailed constitutional arrangements. A challenge of which John Adams and his contemporaries in several other states had been conscious in the Revolution had at last forced the Virginia Old Whigs to choose their weapons; and if the muskets were somewhat rusty, the passion with which they manned the ramparts was hardly less compelling than that of their forebears.

It is only necessary to read the debates of 1829, and the innumerable newspaper columns surrounding and preceding them, to recognise a profound change in the political climate since 1776. This change was to the advantage of the reformers. More than that — it was the condition of their existence as a major political force.

It is a mistake to think of the basic demographic condition as a steady and relentless increase of the western population compared with that of the east. For statistical, and to a large extent for political, purposes the state was considered to comprise four districts; the Tidewater, the Piedmont, the Valley, and the West, the last region being west of the Alleghenies. As Chapman Johnson showed, in a speech which occupies twenty-eight pages of fine print and took him two full days to deliver — at the end of which he gave way 'being much fatigued' — the movement of population had been highly irregular and was difficult to predict. But he felt safe in saying that 'the period is not distant when the majority of the white population will probably be West of the Blue Ridge' (which did not of course mean west of the Alleghenies); and in arguing from the tables that the demand for the labour of slaves would diminish in the middle districts and increase in the West. One reason for this estimate was that for the past ten years the price of tobacco had been better than that of other agricultural products, which tended to encourage that crop. These observations gave him confidence that a white basis could be introduced for representation without threatening the interests of slavery, since a substantial proportion of the farming population of the West would soon acquire an economic interest in its preservation.[1]

The increase and spread of population had all taken place under the aegis of those republican institutions which the men of the Revolution had devised for the State. It is no cause for surprise that this population should have come

[1] *Convention 1829*, 280–2. Johnson introduced into his speech detailed tables of population growth and slave-holding which it has not been thought necessary to reproduce here.

to resent the system which excluded them from the privilege of participating in the government, especially after the War of 1812 had called on men of all ranks to serve the country. The history of Virginia in this period, like that of other states, took on an increasingly non-agrarian complexity. The issue of greatest interest in the West was that of internal improvements; the legislature of Virginia could, by action or inaction, affect the future of the whole of the western section; and the failure of the legislature to provide adequate commercial channels between the West and the Virginian outlets not only caused deep dissatisfaction but also prompted western producers to divert their traffic to Baltimore; a development which had the gradual and incidental effect of reducing their sense of loyalty and attachment to Virginia. The West had also long demanded the advantages of state banks able to provide credit to expanding localities. Some of these demands were appeased, though not permanently satisfied, by state action in 1819; and this policy must be given some of the credit for the decline in agitation after the reapportionment of 1817.[1]

A business and manufacturing population came to dominate the life of the leading towns, and bank politics played an important part in state affairs. The people were affected by a wider variety of public issues, and felt themselves involved in the consequences of decisions taken by the legislature; and all the while the increase both of tenantry and of an artisan class brought into existence an increasing proportion of disfranchisement. As early as 1816 the Staunton Convention recommended the adoption of petitions requesting the restoration of rights and privileges of which the memorialists claimed to have been deprived 'by the early adoption of principles which, if not originally wrong, have become so by the subsequent operation of natural and accidental causes'. It was generally agreed, in this view, that in a republican government, the will of the majority should be the law of the land.[2]

Thomas Jefferson himself and his party both by doctrine and example offered further encouragement to the growth of reformist principles in Virginia. It was Jefferson who, almost alone in 1776, had advanced the view that republican government meant representation by numbers. And although Jefferson's Republican party had not been conspicuously devoted to the reform of domestic institutions, the necessities of political opposition to the Federalists, the practical problems of organisation, and finally the

---

[1] C. H. Ambler, *Sectionalism in Virginia* (Chicago, 1910), 94, 105–7. Chandler, *Representation*, 45. Compare these trends with those of Pennsylvania in the 1760s. In both cases Baltimore gained from the diversion of trade. See pp. 261–2.

[2] *VH*, 31 August 1816.

acceptance of their opprobrious designation as 'democrats', had all gradually given greater emphasis to the democratic aspects of the old Whiggery. This example lost much of its force when the party struggle died down in Virginia. The easy ascendancy of the Republicans reduced the need to seek votes or converts and left the leadership comparatively undisturbed. It is true that personal ambitions sought satisfaction in the electoral process; yet it was not personal ambition but political organisation which forced the older school, Federalists and Republicans alike (and each with about the same amount of reluctance), to seek the sweaty applause of the common people.

It is instructive to compare the tortuous advance of the more democratic principles in Virginia with their rapid and tumultuous victory in the equally conservative sister State of Maryland. The principles embodied in the Maryland Constitution of 1776 were essentially similar to those of Virginia, but in the elaborate pyramid of property qualifications and in the electoral college for the choice of senators they were actually applied with more care and elaboration.[1]

Long before the rise of political parties the course of Maryland politics had begun to reflect the influence of the overwhelming economic and demographic fact in the state — the growth of Baltimore. No other state, with the possible exception of Rhode Island, was so dominated by the growth of a single town. By 1798 Baltimore was the nation's third city, and between 1790 and 1810 its population increased by 244 per cent.[2] The social conditions of reform were brought into existence, largely through the growth of the American share in international trade, at the expense of many of the agricultural counties and without the benefit of parties; but party strife quickly led in the later 1790s to a contest for popularity which, in the prevailing conditions, was instrumental in bringing about a radical reform of the suffrage as early as 1801. At this point the Republicans stopped short. Within a few years, however, both parties realised that more strength could be drawn by enlisting popular support throughout the government than by maintaining the old graduated restrictions, and in 1809 all property qualifications for appointive or elective office were abolished.[3] The great seaport city of Baltimore had been chiefly instrumental in bringing down the

---

[1] Philip A. Crowl, *Maryland during and after the Revolution* (Baltimore, 1943), 86–87; Thorpe, *Federal and State Constitutions*, iii, 1691–1701.

[2] Thomas J. Scharf, *History of Maryland* 2 vols. (Baltimore, 1879), ii. 604–5; *Census of the United States*, 1850 (Washington, 1853), 222; and *Census of 1790* (Philadelphia, 1791), 47.

[3] Thorpe, *Federal and State Constitutions*, iii, 1705–12. Williamson, *American Suffrage*, 138–51.

guarded fortress of Whig orthodoxy, a full generation before the breaches were sprung in the defences of the old order in the agricultural Old Dominion.

The reformers in Virginia took the initiative when they asserted as a republican tenet the doctrine of simple majority rule. This principle was admitted by the opposition minority at the Staunton Convention of 1816, which agreed that the inequality of representation in the legislature was politically wrong and practically evil, but which claimed to tremble before the Constitution and was unwilling to call a Convention with unlimited powers.[1] The point was rejected by the eminent Littleton W. Tazewell, who declared in the subsequent legislative debate that if numbers were to be represented Richmond would govern the senatorial district to which it was attached. It was the natural tendency of towns to grow — Philadelphia doubled in ten years; Richmond would continue to grow, and on this principle would obtain a great share in the representation of the whole State. The true principle was that every interest should be represented. A numerical standard would throw power into the towns.[2] He was answered in the same debate by Charles Fenton Mercer,[3] who denied that Richmond would dominate, on the ground that the many navigable rivers would give many vents for exports and sites for commerce. If this simply meant more towns, it would hardly meet the anxieties of those who wanted to avoid a city-dominated system; but he turned Tazewell's argument by pointing out ironically that if property were to control the system of representation, then the value of property in Richmond and other towns would indeed give them 'undue influence'. Both sides were defending interests connected with property; but the logic of Tazewell's argument opposed the representation of interests to that of numbers.

This debate revealed that one trend expected in Virginia was the growth of population in the lower country through the rise of commercial towns. It was a prospect that might well have divided the Tidewater leadership. Why should not the rising merchants have planned to harness both population and property to their 'interest', and why should not the planters with whom they had so many ties of business — and often of family — have entered into the partnership? Yet they did not. Leigh, Tazewell, Stuart, and other legislative leaders, fought on for the restriction of the suffrage and

---

[1] *VH*, 4 September 1816.   [2] *VH*, 8 February 1817.

[3] Mercer was described by the *VH* (19 March 1817), as the most prominent speaker in the House of Delegates, 'whose sincerity, though a federalist, is doubted by no man in the House'. He deserved a seat in Congress.

the maintenance of their regional privileges under the old apportionment rather than take the risk of courting an enlarged electorate. They showed their colours when in 1829 they pressed the federal ratio — the enumeration of slaves. They may have sensed a threat to slavery in the growth of cities no less than in the rise of freeholds in the West; but in face of the complex if gradual challenge to their ascendancy they also seem to have stuck to a simplified vision of their interest, a sign of weakness and even failure of nerve.

Yet Leigh was reduced to the curious shift, while attacking the proposed Convention at Staunton in 1825, of asserting that he had enough 'pure democracy' in his principles not to let Mercer have the chief hand in framing a Constitution for him and his children.[1] A small point, but it illustrates the diffusion of the idea that 'democracy' was a normal principle in what had once been a 'republican' polity. The tendency of the day was for opening all the main offices of state to the elective principle, a line that was expected to influence the Convention to the consternation of older Whigs. 'I discover', wrote one to a member of the Convention, 'there is a growing tendency in this country to make everything depend on popular suffrage. In promoting this sentiment the father of our political church Thos Jefferson has not a little contributed. His works will just have been published and read when your Convention meets, and in these as I understand the opinion is expressed that the judges ought to be elected periodically by the people.'[2]

The only basis for the Convention that could eventually be agreed in the legislature was a mixed basis which gave official representation to both property and numbers. It was a direct implementation of the ancient Whig idea that political equality itself required the computing of taxation as a factor in representation. Analysis shows that one delegate was elected to represent every 13,151 white persons or by every $7,000.24; so that in the Convention each white inhabitant weighed, on the average, a little more than half a dollar in taxes.[3]

None of the reform advocates in the Convention spoke more eloquently than the petition of the non-freeholders of Richmond, presented without comment by Chief Justice Marshall.[4] They described themselves as 'a very

[1] *R.Enq.* 20 May 1825. Leigh wrote privately in 1825 that the majority in the Staunton convention were driving at a radical change in the executive 'and the abrogation of the freehold qualification of suffrage (which alone is everything).' Leigh to Tazewell, 22 August 1825, Tazewell Papers.

[2] Jas. Campbell to David Campbell, 28 March 1829; David Campbell Papers. The same experiment in Alabama was leading, in the writer's opinion, to 'a general prostitution of morals'.

[3] Chandler, *Representation*, 56–7.   [4] *Convention 1829*, 25–31.

large part, probably a majority, of the male citizens of mature age'. The burden of their plea was that the non-freeholders were responsible persons, fully the equals of the freeholders in civic capacity, but unable to call themselves free while they were denied the right to participate in the government. Attachment to property, often a sordid sentiment, was not to be confused with patriotism. If the landless citizens were ignominiously driven from the polls in times of peace, they had at least been generally summoned to the battlefield in time of war. The generality of mankind, argued the petitioners, desired to become property owners; there was no danger that they might attack the rights of property. They ridiculed the idea that moral or intellectual endowments could be ascribed to a landed possession — and many cultivators were not proprietors. Conservatives often expressed a horror of the development of large manufactures which would bring into existence a large, dependent proletariat who would merely vote at their masters' bidding; but the answer to this was that such establishments must for a long time remain at the mercy of those who affected to dread them. For how many centuries must unenfranchised citizens be deprived of their rights because a remote posterity might abuse them? The petitioners agreed that suffrage was a social (as distinct from a natural) right, but denied that the existing social limitations were proper. It was said to be expedient to exclude non-freeholders — but expedient to whom? Society was not composed only of the holders of certain portions of land. The Convention did not consist of the representatives of the people; it was the organ of a privileged order.

The authors of this powerful statement had anticipated all the main theses of the conservatives. The debates proved that some of the leading advocates of reform were either unwilling to accept the view which saw all citizens as equals in their membership and rights in society, or willing to give up that claim for compromise.

Reform gained an early advantage when the committee on the Bill of Rights reported resolutions accepting the principle of numerical representation; the suffrage of one qualified voter should avail equally with that of another whatever the disparity of their fortunes; neither should the aggregate fortunes of one group weigh more heavily than those of another.[1] It was also to be resolved that taxes ought to be laid according to the ability of the individual to contribute; a literally equal burden of taxation would be oppressive.

In the early phases of the debate, the question of taxation emerged to full prominence as almost the chief object of representation itself. Leigh asked

[1] *Convention 1829, 39.*

to know the reason for the proposal that the property of the State should be placed at the disposal of those who did not own it; reasons, he claimed, must lie, not in mathematics or abstractions, but in the actual condition of the Commonwealth.[1] The conservatives, facing an adverse report from the committee on the legislature, moved an amendment to base representation on 'the white population and taxation combined'.[2] This whole position was attacked by Samuel Taylor of Chesterfield, who distinguished two objects of the resolutions before the Houses, the elective franchise and the principles of taxation; both of which bore on the question of the apportionment of representatives.

'Our institutions are republican', said Taylor, 'in that they repose sovereignty solely in the people.' Representation he defined as sovereignty exercised through the agency of representatives, or agents. A compound of numbers and taxation would be nothing but a graduated franchise, and therefore unequal. The argument that property must have special safeguards introduced an oligarchic principle: representation was the effect of suffrage; it was the mirror which threw back the image of the voters. Property could not vote. 'When you look to representation,' he declared, turning to the problem of taxation, 'you look to men. When you look to taxation, you look to the ability to pay, to property.'[3]

The reformers had taken an important initiative. It was their keynote now that the peculiar character of republican institutions lay precisely in the fact that sovereignty was in the people and that therefore the immediate determination of the majority was the essential rule of republican government.

This claim they buttressed with a cogent argument as to the social ambitions of the disfranchised classes. The desire for property, said John R. Cooke of Frederick County, implied the desire to possess it securely. Men would not tear down the safeguards of the institutions to which they aspired. Representation based on numbers in fifteen other states, he added, had not led to any invasion of the rights of the wealthy by the poor. A further point to assuage the fears of the slave-owners was that the majority of the population were slaveholders (a doubtful claim) and that slaveholding already extended west of the Blue Ridge.[4]

---

[1] *Convention 1829*, 53.

[2] *Convention 1829*, 53. Motion of John W. Green of Culpeper.

[3] *Convention 1829*, 46–51. This speech preceded the amendment moved by Green; the reformers knew, of course, what the conservatives meant to do.

[4] *Convention 1829*, 54–62.

What the reformers had done was to extract from the Declaration of Rights of 1776 the pronouncement about equality and to expand it until it absorbed all the other concepts which controlled the thinking of the revolutionary generation. They were thus happy to agree with the proposal to readopt the Declaration of Rights without amendment. The 'Jus majoris', in the words of Philip Doddridge, was written into the third article of that document; it was the 'majority of the community' which was there endowed with the right to abolish or alter an inadequate government. But the Constitution itself he treated with scant respect. Doddridge used a favourite reformist line when he said that the Constitution was a temporary expedient got up in times of danger — elsewhere it was said to have been hastily drawn up in the heat of revolution, when harmony was above all imperative.[1]

This argument was, unfortunately, reversible. If the Constitution of 1776 had been adopted in haste, then so had the Declaration of Rights. The reformers had no obvious reason to claim that the latter document rather than the Constitution had expressed the true intentions of the fathers. As Richard Morris of Hanover pointed out in a thoughtfully reasoned speech, the Constitution had been carefully debated at the time; and — what was most unpalatable to the reformers — the principle of representation by numbers was new. It had not been affixed to the Constitution of 1776. The Constitution had been designed to protect not only personal rights but property also. He pointed to the United States Senate to confirm his view that in the judgment of Virginia mere numbers did not constitute a fit basis for representation.[2]

The truth was that the reformers' case was historically thin. Experience of self-government, though under certain British restrictions, was deep rooted by 1776. The weakness of Jefferson's initiative for the numerical principle and the extension of the suffrage lay in the lack of popular support.

---

[1] *Convention 1829*, 79, 85, 413.

[2] *Convention 1829*, 109–12. A more interesting argument on similar lines was that the original draft of the Constitution of 1776 had been closer to the demands of the reformers of 1829. This draft, as recommended by the reporting committee, 'was free of three of the objections which have been most vehemently urged against it in its present form: very narrow restrictions on the right of suffrage, the union of legislative, executive and judicial powers; the utter insignificance of the governor'. — Norfolk, *American Beacon* 3 October 1829, quoting *The Virginia Literary Museum* 25 September 1829.

But the early draft of 1776 had high property qualifications for both Houses, and did nothing to meet reformist objections on apportionment. It is doubtful whether the reformers would really have liked it any better; the suggestion that they would have done so certainly assumes that they adhered firmly to the Whig traditions about property.

Whatever the merits of the conservative case, they had the better of the argument when their enemies chose, as they insistently did, to pitch it on historical ground.

Doddridge was right in saying that the Declaration of Rights named the 'majority of the community' as the authority over the form of government; but what was the community? In Mason's opinion it was clearly related to the electorate. 'Those having a permanent common interest with and attachment to the community' were given the right to vote. The community to which they were attached presumably extended to all of their families, including their heirs and successors and perhaps their immediate dependants. It is doubtful whether Mason would have agreed for practical purposes of participation in government that 'consent' reached beyond those who were constitutionally empowered to represent the community understood in this sense. If he had thought so then he would have been prepared to extend the suffrage. 'The majority of the community' was a phrase no more to be taken literally than the many similar expressions which claimed that every single subject of the English realm was deemed to have given consent to laws enacted by duly chosen representatives. Locke, too, had spoken loosely of the majority, but it was obvious that his purpose was confined to the politically competent.

In the Convention of 1829 the poor found their voice in Philip Doddridge, the uncouth but able defender of the unprivileged.[1] The poor man in the West, Doddridge told the members, who was required to labour on the roads, often had to walk fifteen miles with his spade and axe. In many places ten or twenty days' work was required from journeymen who had not yet enough stock to commence for themselves.[2]

Although Doddridge relied on the majority principle in the Declaration of Rights, he also attempted to discredit the Constitution because it had been

---

[1] 'Dodridge is an old disepated dog of whom you have often heard me speak. He was once dead and his wife brought him back to life by pouring brandy into his throat. He is from Brook County, a little narrow neck of land in the extreme north western part of Va running up into Pennsylvania. He has none of the bland and polished manner belonging to the South. He is a low thick broad shoulder'd uncouth looking man having an uncommonly large head and a face with cheaks overloaded with flesh. . . . He speaks in the broad Scotch-Irish dialect although he is an excellent scholar & a man of extensive and profound research.' He was gifted with an excellent memory and powers of argument (John Campbell to James Campbell, 1 February 1829; David Campbell Papers). Grigsby reported that Doddridge was 'as busy as a bee, and as dirty as a hog' (to John N. Tazewell, 6 October 1829, Tazewell Papers).

[2] *Convention 1829, 425.*

based on consultation of only the fifty-acre freeholders; it had been made by a part of society for the benefit of that part. He asserted that slave representation lay at the bottom of the appeal for a combined ratio. He also replied to the argument that he who enters a partnership with the greater capital enjoys the greater share of influence — which the conservatives applied to government. It was not true of the law of partnery; it had to be agreed in the articles of co-operation. Would gentlemen press the logic of results, he enquired ironically, and give the greatest capitalists the greatest suffrage? Green was stung to jump up and state that he had not been concerned only to protect slave property and would have moved his amendment if there had not been a slave in Virginia. Two-thirds of the taxable property, he said, was owned east of the Blue Ridge.[1]

Doddridge, of all the reform leaders, stuck closest to the original demands and he ended by denouncing the eventual compromise.

John Locke did not desert the conservatives in their hour of need — though at least one of them deserted him. Abel P. Upshur, in a competent but theoretically rather alarming speech, announced that there were no original principles of government at all. 'Principles do not precede but spring out of government,' he said. He admitted nevertheless — and it was an admission which showed how much ground the reformers had gained by stealth — the general proposition that in free governments power ought to be given to the majority; however, he would not go so far as to say that majority government was necessarily free government. Differences of interest, according to Upshur, arose from property alone — a curious thesis, in view of the acute religious differences which had so often impinged on American politics. They did not propose to represent money, but the rights and interests that sprang from its possession: was protection to be withdrawn from the interests that had grown up in fifty-four years of government in Virginia? The taxation of slaves was oppressive because it taxed labour; and he came to the east's real fear when he warned that the west, once in power, would place the public burdens on the slaveholders. But in all the fifty-four years, the east with its advantages had never abused the taxing power; it was a benevolent, a paternal, government.[2]

If the reformers could serve themselves with appeals to first principles, so could the conservatives. The old line of persons and property was threaded through the bright but often ponderous beads of their argument. The venerable Madison stated it in one of his few utterances; it gave coherence to the insistent demand for the retention of a property qualification for the

[1] *Convention 1829*, 79–89.   [2] *Convention 1829*, 66–78.

suffrage and for the weighting of representation by mixing property with population. Madison himself came out in favour of applying the federal ratio, the kind of suggestion that from the reformist viewpoint justified all their fears. Philip P. Barbour also stated flatly that, as government acted on persons, they should be represented; and that as it acted on property, so it should be represented.

Barbour signified the American adaptation of the Lockian thinking of his predecessors when he said that, in the forming of society, some brought in their persons, others their property. It was a proposition that might suggest two lines of reply. One of these was offered by a speaker who said simply that each individual brings his all.[1] The rich, given greater political powers, could use them to the detriment of the poor. Another attack would have been to dismiss the hypothesis of an original compact and to argue from observable facts. But this approach did not appeal to the reformers, and it is interesting to note that it was Upshur, the conservative, who dared to deny the force of pre-social rights. In effect, the force of observable facts was what gave the reformers their strength; the theoretical arguments for numerical equality alone had not had any political influence at any earlier date.

The conservatives were also pragmatists. They needed to be able to argue that the existing arrangements met a practical need, and that their superiority had never been abused. Barbour, after some thought, observed that suffrage must anyway be unequal. If it was founded on universal natural rights it must in justice be made universal; if not, then it was for society to decide who should have it. (He also paused to dismiss the commonplace idea that women were politically incapable — their disfranchisement was merely a social decision.) There were many cases in which a majority of numbers did not rule, as in the relations between the Senate and President of the United States, or in elections where no candidate had an overall majority, or in juries. Only a general ticket — a single ticket for the whole state — could really express the will of the majority; they did not rule in practice. The best test of propriety, in morals as in politics, was practical utility.

When conservative speakers said that the majority in which they believed was one based on persons and property, they consistently failed to explain precisely in what way the interests which stood out in contrast to persons could be enumerated. These interests were no mere fiction. They did not in truth lie in property alone. The differences between the sections were not merely in amounts or types of property owned, but in national origins, to some extent in religion, and in manners. The West and the Valley had been

[1] *Convention 1829*, 95, 106. Alfred H. Powell.

peopled not so much by migration from the east as by movements of Scotch-Irish and Germans from further North; Doddridge was a far more natural leader in Trans-Allegheny Virginia than he could have been had he lived in the Tidewater. The Tuckahoes of the east and the Cohees of the west looked on each other as different types of people, who had been brought by history to co-operate in the same political institutions. But the demands of the west were thrust forward against a background of discontent so profound as to portend a division of the state. Had the eastern sections rejected all compromise, the representatives of the Valley and the West would probably have withdrawn from the Convention and a separatist western convention would have ensued. What was one day to become West Virginia (more than the Valley) already felt itself to have some of the character of a new state.

The theme of interests was applied both to property and to districts by Chapman Johnson. He said he would divide the state into districts consisting of contiguous counties having interests in common, give each district a number of delegates according to its white population, and to each county one delegate if the number of members for the district were equal to the number of counties in it. He seems not to have intended that the districts should be equal; it was a formula under which the legislature could arrange the representation according to the 'interests' of each district, giving, in Johnson's words, not a mathematical equality but 'a rational practical equality, assuring due weight and just protection to every local interest'.[1]

But Johnson still strongly favoured a landed qualification for the suffrage.[2] He began his immense speech with a refreshing, if somewhat brutal, note of realism:

We are engaged, Mr Chairman, in a contest for power — disguise it as you will — call it a discussion of the rights of man, natural or social — call it an enquiry into political expediency — imagine yourself, if you please, presiding over a school of philosophers, discoursing on the doctrines of political law, for the instruction of mankind, and the improvement of all human institutions — bring the question to the test of principle, or of practical utility — still, Sir, all our metaphysical reasoning and our practical rules, all our scholastic learning and political wisdom, are but the arms employed in a contest, which involves the great and agitating question, whether the sceptre shall pass away from Judah, or a lawgiver from between her feet.[3]

---

[1] *Convention 1829*, 265. J. A. C. Chandler, who wrote a history of Virginian representation in 1896, gave it as his own belief that each county should be represented because each county had its own interests. This view reminds one of the town tradition of New England. Chandler, *Representation*, 83.

[2] *Convention 1829*, 284.   [3] *Convention 1829*, 257.

Johnson's thinking exhibits all the principal characteristics of the true Whigs who had not given up the ideals of the eighteenth century and were determined to resist the advance of popular democracy. In 1816 he had strenuously defended the freehold suffrage while manœuvring for a palliative reapportionment of representatives. In 1829 he had not abandoned his basic belief that property in land was the only security that could safely be exacted against the liberty to vote.

In defending this view he put the point which had been common when the revolutionary constitutions were made. Let the qualification be so low, he explained, that the industrious of all classes, professions, and callings may acquire it in a few years of persevering labour; and so high as to be out of reach of the habitually idle. 'I should prefer real to personal property.'[1] But the Whig thesis that anyone could earn his freehold by a few years' hard work — that anyone who had the qualities required of a citizen would show them by his industry and so earn his title — was becoming badly out of date. The whole case had been answered in advance by the petitioners from Richmond, who pointed out that freeholds were not easy for those not already engaged in agriculture to acquire. Leigh made the same point as Johnson (for no one in this debate was deterred by the fact that his argument had already been made, or refuted), when he said that a freehold was easy to buy.[2] In arguing thus, Johnson, Leigh, and their supporters overlooked the fact that an artisan whose business had been built up in a city would simply not have an economic interest in purchasing a freehold in the country. Freeholds in the city were not the same matter at all; and the growth of the cities had rendered the old city franchise anachronistic.

Johnson, whose views were more moderate and more subtle than Leigh's, had a different position to propound. He wanted, under the limitations that have been noticed, to put representation on a white basis; and he was very alarmed by the suggestion which had been made in more than one quarter that the actual distribution of representatives ought to be tied to taxation. Despite the preponderance of taxable property in the Tidewater and Piedmont, Johnson anticipated that the long-term effects of making this connection a part of the system would be to throw the weight of property into the same scale with that of numbers in the rising cities of the Tidewater. Virginia would eventually be ruled by its city populations. A separation of property from numbers, though not very reassuring, was at least a defence against this threat, especially as the agricultural population was so extensive; and it is this analysis that explains his desire to retain the freehold, or at least

---

[1] *Convention 1829*, 284. [2] *Convention 1829*, 401–2.

the landed, qualification. It would attract industrious men out into the country.

Johnson went so far as to advocate that the franchise of the cities should be subject to limitations; by holding their representation to a prescribed number it would be possible to check the advance of their influence.[1] He agreed with those who saw the political rise of Boston, New York, and Baltimore as an evil; and he wanted to devise a system that would curb the menace in Virginia.

It was an interesting position. In Massachusetts, the numerical principle had been grafted on to the Constitution during the Revolution, as a result of precisely the type of combination of the interests of numbers and property which Johnson now dreaded; wherever large cities had sprung up, as in Boston, New York, and Baltimore, they had gained a domination over the political process, which had had a direct outcome in suffrage extension and some measure of redistribution in their respective states. Yet Johnson, both reformer and conservative, was fighting for a redistribution of seats that would correspond with the great movement of agrarian population; while hoping at the same time to maintain a mode of distribution and a set of suffrage qualifications that would prevent the reform of the Constitution from playing into the hands of the rising cities.

It is relevant to note the unsympathetic orthodoxy with which he regarded the disfranchisement of those whom he styled 'the imprudent and unfortunate'. They, in his view, had no right to complain; if they had lost their property they had no right to manage the affairs of others. This was virtually what the *Address* of the Massachusetts Convention of 1780 had said about the suffrage, and one of the assumptions on which it was based was that the normal conditions of economic life in America would never stand in the way of the self-advancement of the hard-working individual. A very few years later the economy of the Bay State had collapsed; and by 1786 the system of representation itself seemed for the time being unequal to the problem of government. Latterly, in Virginia as elsewhere, economic troubles had cut deep into the lives of numerous hard-working people through no fault of their own. Bank questions, internal improvements, marketing, and the market for different agricultural products, all posed problems beyond the powers of the individual farmer, and all required government attention. The handling of these matters could affect the fortunes of the people, rich and poor; and a man might lose the very possessions which qualified him to vote, by the operation of economic forces over

[1] *Convention 1829*, 274.

which his government had at least some measure of control. Others could make their fortunes through the same agency. In nothing was this more vitally true than in the much agitated question of internal improvements.

Chapman Johnson's view of suffrage and representation was essentially prescriptive. 'It is to the qualifications of suffrage . . . that we must look for the essential character of our government, for the security of all our rights, and for the protection of our property', he said.[1] This was little more than an amplification of the justification for any property qualifications at all; but it fell into line with his views on representation, which lay directly in the tradition of those which Madison had given to Jefferson when the two men had discussed the Virginia Constitution in its earlier years.

Watkins Leigh, by contrast, stood out as a romantic conservative. His major contribution was a long, and at times moving, speech in favour of the old landed order. He was dismayed to see the lack of regret with which young men deserted the lands of their forebears for the unknown west — though it did not occur to him that discrimination and poor opportunities at home might have had anything to do with it. He warned repeatedly that any extension of the suffrage would lead directly to the universal suffrage which he assumed all reasonable men opposed. That system, he declared, did not lead to real popular elections but to the nomination and control by the caucus — for which 'convention' was merely a new and more popular name.[2]

The opposing forces did not succeed in reaching agreement in principle. One of the central points insisted on by the reformers was that of future reapportionments at fixed intervals; the attempt of William F. Gordon, of Jefferson's county of Albemarle, to lay down a permanent distribution was condemned by Leigh as futile. Leigh instead subtly proposed to give the legislature discretion to create new counties — which could result in the making of new eastern counties by the subdivision of old ones. Leigh also tried to play on sectional fears, hinting that the aggressive spirit of the West should be as alarming to the Valley as it was to the east — and it was in the Valley that he expected the greatest increase of population.[3]

The full demands of both sides having failed, the Valley leadership became willing to recede and accommodate itself to an arrangement that was reached behind the scenes. After nearly eleven weeks of the struggle, on 19 December, Leigh offered his support to a plan of Gordon's by which specific numbers of seats in each House were ascribed to the various sections. As soon as Doddridge saw what was happening he knew he had lost, though

[1] *Convention 1829*, 284.
[2] *Convention 1829*, 394–407.   [3] *Convention 1829*, 675–6, 678–9.

he once more put his motion for the white basis in the House. The Valley had joined the Tidewater in compromise and the out-and-out reformers were defeated. The arrangement on the count would give the eastern sections a majority of twenty-seven seats in the joint ballot of the two Houses. Even reapportionments, in 1841 and thence at ten-year intervals, though provided for, were placed at the discretion of a two-thirds' majority of the legislature.[1]

The compromise led to a bitter public dispute between Cooke and Doddridge. Cooke had maintained that much had been gained and that he had agreed to Gordon's plan only when he saw that a fuller success was hopeless.[2] He later told his constituents that the conservatives had repudiated Locke's theory of natural rights and had taken their stand on what they called 'enlarged expediency'. He picked out Upshur's remark that there were no original principles of government, but he advocated the adoption of the Constitution. The new plan gave, in his opinion, the nearest approximation to the white basis that could be obtained. He released the startling statistic that in Frederick County alone the unenfranchised citizens outnumbered the freeholders by 2,200 — a proportion of nearly nine to five — and warned of threats that if they were not given representation they would refuse to pay taxes and would resist collection by force.[3] Doddridge would have none of this willingness to compromise. He told his constituents that their equal and just claims had been betrayed and lost. The traitor was Cooke, who had decided to vote for Gordon's scheme if the West's plan was lost. Leigh, having learnt of this, announced Gordon's plan as a practical basis which he would accept. Doddridge held that the east would have submitted if the west had not been betrayed by disunity in its leadership; but then, he used 'the West' in the general sense often adopted by the reformers, when in fact the Valley was generally regarded as a separate section. Doddridge advised the voters to reject the Constitution, and later warned them that its adoption would lead to the dismemberment of the state.[4]

The floodgates of reform were thrown open to admit a trickle of democracy. In the 1827 referendum on whether to hold a Convention, 38,533 or 28 per cent of the adult white males in the state participated. Doddridge said later in debate that the total number entitled to vote was 44,320 and that only one-seventh of the qualified voters had failed to turn out, which as

---

[1] The manœuvres and motions of this phase can be followed in *Convention 1829*, 674–90; Thorpe, *Federal and State Constitutions*, vii. 3821–3. Chandler, *Representation*, 44.

[2] *Convention 1829*, 691.

[3] *R.Enq.* 13 February 1830.   [4] *R.Enq.* 26 March, 20 April 1830.

a round figure was not far wrong. (His own proposals, incidentally, would have enfranchised another 30,236.)[1] The new Constitution was ratified in an election, open to all who were prospectively enfranchised by it, but attended by only 29 per cent of the adult white males. In the election of Jackson in 1832, only 31 per cent appear to have voted. It was not until 1840 that a major leap was recorded in the voting figures. The pressure for suffrage extension seems to have come in 1829 from a comparatively small element of the disfranchised. Its power sprang from political consciousness and leadership. It was the achievement of this group which opened the way for the multitudes who voted in 1840.

If suffrage extension had not been linked with the discontent over representation it would not have been achieved before the Civil War. The failure of the two sides to agree to a set of principles is a matter of more than theoretical interest. In the issue, the suffrage was extended to leaseholders and to tax-paying householders, but not to tax-payers in general;[2] and it was made subject to a list of reservations so tortuous as to baffle successive attempts at elucidation for many years. As to the basis of representation, the compromise was a mere declaration of numbers — a sad decline from the high claims of both sides to speak for rights and principles. The voters decided, by ratifying the Constitution, to go on working the political institutions of Virginia: the rights that had been betrayed, the interests that had been sacrificed, proved not to be so inalienable as to demand secession by the West or resistance by the remaining sections. The struggle had been intense; and the distrust exhibited by both sides, considered in the light of the interests at stake, would have been enough to bring violent secession in slightly different times and circumstances. The Convention of Republican Virginia exhibited scarcely more agreement over political principles than did the Parliament of the Reform Bill.

One of the great obstacles to reform in Virginia was a negative factor: the comparative absence of party rivalry. The Federalists, despite their strength in the west, petered out in the Era of Good Feelings; and although the later Whig Party was represented by the *Constitutional Whig* in Richmond, Virginia was not an early centre of Whig strength. Where — as in Maryland and New Jersey, to take two cases only — the Federalists and Republicans of the Jeffersonian era were in close competition, it was not the idealism of the Republicans, but the necessity of both parties to seek votes

[1] See table, p. 560. *Convention 1829*, 423–4.

[2] Between 25,000 and 30,000 adult white males appear still to have been excluded from the suffrage. Ambler, *Sectionalism*, 168; Williamson, *American Suffrage*, 234.

that put suffrage extension on the political programme. In Virginia the unsatisfactory nature of the compromise of 1830 made further agitation inevitable; it was like a peace treaty which leaves an irredentist problem threatening future war. The appropriate time for renewed activity came after the census of 1840 had shown a great increase in the western population making the two sections almost equal.[1] There seems also to have been a decline in the internal sectional complexity and a stronger tendency to see trans-Alleghany Virginia as a potentially separate society.

The tenacity of the conservatives in resisting both suffrage extension and redistribution was revealed, in the Convention of 1829, in their shrewd refusal to be drawn into new avowals of principle. That the situation could pose problems in view of their own republican principles is evident from the reflections of the young Hugh Blair Grigsby, who observed that a political theorist might expect revolution to spring from an equal distribution of power between so many unequal and dissimilar sections. 'But I must say' he added,

that I have lived long enough to find out that political magnanimity is but an empty thing; and all societies ought to ponder well before they surrender from abstract considerations that which may well nigh ruin them.

Chief Justice Marshall, entertaining the leaders of both parties to dinner, impressed his guests with practical reasoning and eschewed abstract political theory as a ground for constitutional revision.[2] It was part of a consistent conservative attitude which regarded the principles of the Revolution as a dignified but distant penumbra beneath which the proper task of politics was to maintain the order of society. At heart the attitude was not much different from that of the leading British Whig families in the era of the American Revolution, or that of the Quakers of Pennsylvania in their own time of crisis.

Had they agreed to accept the doctrine that the majority shall govern both in making the Constitution and in ordinary legislation; and the corollary, of such intense importance to the reformers, that political representation ought to be nothing more than a mechanism for discovering the will of that majority on a purely numerical basis, they would have deprived themselves of all ground for opposing the advance of those regional and political forces which they believed to threaten their property and system. But they held out,

[1] Ambler, *Sectionalism*, 253.
[2] H. B. Grigsby to John N. Tazewell, 3 February 1829, John Wickham to L. W. Tazewell, 21 December 1828. Tazewell Papers.

agreeing to a substantial modification of practice in both sectors but not to any modification of theory. For them, the Declaration of Rights which had announced the principles of 1776 was a safe guide in adversity; and their title to it was assuredly as fair as that of their reforming enemies.

When the issue of distribution arose again in due course after the census of 1840, the conservatives of the east showed the same rugged persistence. A legislative committee, appointed to examine petitions from western communities, reported firmly in favour of reapportionment in both branches of the legislature 'according to the numbers of qualified voters in their several constituent bodies'.[1] Why, asked the committee majority, should not one citizen's vote weigh equally against another's? The matter, in a republican community, seemed to be a mere exercise of convenience. This quiet remark contained a basic assumption about the nature of a 'republican community' which the conservatives completely rejected. And it is an error to suppose that, because both sides in these debates agreed that they were discussing republican principles, they were therefore in basic agreement about the meaning and proper application of such principles. The committee minority, in a separate report, described the idea that a law of nature gave to the majority a right to control the minority as an 'exploded notion'.[2]

This conservative minority on the committee spoke for a majority in the House. Once more Virginians were reminded that government operated separately on persons and property, and that property ought to be considered in fixing the basis of representation. 'No system of representation can be just, equal and safe,' they declared, 'which does not recognise taxation as one of its elements.' In this view they were supported by the example of several sister states and, more important, by the Federal Constitution. The majority report admitted the damaging truth that the history of representation in Virginia was not favourable to 'correct principles'.

The suffrage was not under discussion. Once again suffrage extension had to await the rise of a powerful movement for reapportionment, now effectively delayed by the eastern majority. When new demands for a state Convention came forward, about 1845, western leaders objected to any assembly that was not convened on a white basis.[3]

The emergence of a well organised Whig party assisted the cause of suffrage extension. The Whig leadership in the east, lacking control of election machinery and finding itself in a permanent disadvantage, began to see new hope in an appeal to the unenfranchised. But when at length a

[1] *R.Enq.* 27 January 1842.   [2] *R.Enq.* 27 January 1842.
[3] Chandler, *Representation*, 51–53.

Convention Bill passed the General Assembly, it was the mixed basis that prevailed and it was the sectional issue that took first place.[1] The demand for suffrage reform would have lacked effective institutional representation without the patronage of party, but once the Convention had assembled, the force of the demand became irresistible.

Constitutional conventions, held at intervals of approximately twenty years, had to serve as a substitute for wars; another five months of debate must at least have exhausted a great quantity of energy. By this time there were eastern members who were ready to risk a division of the state; but they settled instead for another practical compromise. The western sections at last gained their majority in the House; the east retained control of the Senate, the west having a fractional advantage in the joint ballot. Once again the east refused to commit itself to a declaration of principles; and most of the arguments on both sides had been heard before.[2]

The difficulty of reaching an agreement on the principles of representation led to another makeshift plan for reapportionment. It was decided that in 1865 the legislature should take the matter up, but if it failed to reach a decision the Governor was to submit four plans to the people: (1) The white suffrage basis for both houses; (2) the mixed basis for both; (3) a taxation basis for the Senate with a suffrage basis for the House; and (4) the mixed basis for the Senate with the suffrage basis for the House. This complex plan, which would have been difficult to implement without intense controversy, was a measure of the internal hostilities of Virginia politics. Nor could it any longer be said with certainty that the leaders on all sides considered the working of common institutions a satisfactory system where disagreement on policy, and on the interests to be governed, was so charged with foreboding. The new Constitution met with strong opposition in the east, where some at least would have preferred to divide the state.[3]

The new suffrage basis extended to all adult white males except paupers; the Governor, the judges, and the county officials were to be elected by the voters; even the ancient system of county government had, technically at least, been breached at length.[4]

The old principle that all the people should share in the constituent power, which had never been put into practice in Virginia, could be invoked to explain the device by which the new suffrage was used for purposes of ratification. But the vote in percentage was actually lower than in any of the

[1] Ambler, *Sectionalism*, 259; Chandler, *Representation*, 56–59.
[2] Chandler, *Representation*, 61–71.   [3] Chandler, *Representation*, 67–70.
[4] Thorpe, *Federal and State Constitutions*, vii. 3832–7.

three previous presidential elections.[1] The Constitution itself, however, received the immense majority of 75,748 votes over 11,063.

The year 1865, in the sense imagined by the Convention, never arrived. Not only had the Old Dominion been ravaged by Civil War, but the long-threatened separation had taken place; and the creation of the separate state of West Virginia, though immediately an outcome of the secession crisis, was no adventitious accident. The debate over constitutional reform was, as Chapman Johnson had said in 1829, a struggle for power. The men who based their defences on the doctrine of interest representation may indeed have been making a mistake about the nature of the challenge, and may have over-estimated the danger to their system: but they firmly believed that they were fighting for both economic and political life. It was their side which began to urge the division of the state in preference to submission when the whole issue arose again in the 1840s.

The best that can be said for the republican principles on which all parties agreed, was that each of the pre-Civil War conventions led to an agreement to go on working the machinery rather than to break up the state. Yet it was a reluctant and embittered agreement, constantly threatened by disruptive discontent. The truth was that a high degree of abstract consensus on republican principles was not enough to provide for harmony in the clash of the vested interests of pride and property.

Virginians, nevertheless, did make use of the traditions and machinery of consultation to achieve a large measure of reform, which by 1850 included both the distribution of representatives on a basis roughly — though not strictly, and not even in principle — that of population; and the extension of the suffrage till it came near to admitting the principle that each adult white male had a stake in society.

Despite great differences of history and geography, these achievements represented the combined action of the same forces that had come together to establish the numerical principle in Massachusetts, in Pennsylvania, in the Continental Congress and Convention, and — within the limits imposed by its different history and institutions — in Great Britain. In Virginia the movement of population and the rise of new centres of property took the form both of the growth of Richmond and other cities and the settlement and cultivation of the West. The rise of a settled western population, with its own stake in the social order and the security of property, was certainly the most powerful force in the demand for redistribution; and although it was an agricultural development, its demands were similar in principle to

[1] See Appendix, p. 560.

those of the industrial middle classes of the cities of Britain — fair and equitable representation for their own interests within the system that in general acknowledged the rights of the major 'interests' to have representation. There was in truth no more cogent or persuasive argument than that put in 1829, that slavery was moving in to the west, and that western farmers would soon have an interest similar to the planters of the east.

As in the other states, the demand for numerical representation in the form of suffrage extension derived much of its strategic strength from its conjunction with the demands for the representation of new property on the old basis of interests: a 'legitimate' demand which could be held within the principles of the older system, but one which was not easy to argue without recourse to the numerical doctrine.

In Britain, the new manufacturers could safely argue for representation for Manchester and Birmingham without calling for universal suffrage; though even in Britain, such advances as were made in the suffrage were dependent on the stronger pressure of the manufacturers in their own interests. But in Virginia, the drive for redistribution to give equitable representation to the western regions in its very nature tended to sweep into its fold a larger and more generous following of suffrage extensionists. The reason lay in the nature of a society of relatively independent farmers; a much more substantial proportion of the actual population was engaged in both sides of the movement than could be the case in Britain.

Yet it was never a movement of full co-operation or entirely united interests. If the conservatives had been shrewder they would have granted a more general redistribution long before 1829 without touching the suffrage; such a move would have exposed the frailty of the movement for the suffrage extension and the impotence of demands based on an individualist interpretation of the words of 1776.

The painful slowness of the progress of reform in Virginia, when contrasted with other states and regions, was largely due to the fact that the political leadership was not compelled to meet the challenge offered by the chief agencies of reform elsewhere. Virginia was extremely slow to develop a strong two-party system; although the Federalists made ground under John Marshall, they never threatened to take the state away from Jefferson and the Republicans, whose ascendancy after 1800 was nearly complete. The splintering faction of the Tertium Quids under John Randolph of Roanoke did not in any way affect the general character of political society. It is significant that when at last suffrage reform made real progress it was under the aegis of the Whig party — not the Republicans or Democrats —

when two parties were driven to compete for votes, and when a larger proportion of the voters could be found in the towns.

The towns were the second absent element. Virginia had no Philadelphia or Boston or Baltimore. It lacked that great agency of democracy. The political progress wrought by the settlement and cultivation of the west resembled the heavy movement of the plough through the furrow. It was no rival for the dynamo of the city.

CONTINENTAL REPRESENTATION

13. The Case Against Parliament and the Radical Tradition in America

JUST as the English conflict of the seventeenth century compelled the antagonists to consider the state as a whole, so the rise of the great American controversy with Britain brought about a similar concentration of thought and expansion of vision among the contenders. For the conventions that governed the British official mind the issues did not pose problems of any great complexity. Apologists for Parliament could stand safely on the ground taken in 1765 by Thomas Whately, when he explained that the colonists were 'virtually represented' in Parliament.[1] The idea was not entirely novel, since the notion of 'tacit consent' had been used by Locke, but it was a new justification for parliamentary rule of the colonies.

This argument even offered the colonists a modicum of unintended encouragement. For the doctrine of 'virtual representation' clearly implied that some kind of representation was indeed required to give the law its authority; so that when the leading exponents of the rapidly developing school of colonial political thought had satisfied themselves that the colonies were in fact not represented in Parliament, and when tentative proposals for the election of American members had fallen flat on both sides of the Atlantic, the issue of representation was ruled out, and Americans were relieved of their nagging residue of obligation to Parliament. This phase of the argument was completed by James Wilson in his famous pamphlet, *Considerations on the Nature and Extent of the Legislative Authority of the British Parliament,*

---

[1] *The Regulations Lately Made Concerning the Colonies and the Taxes Imposed upon Them, Considered* (London, 1765).

which appeared in Philadelphia in 1774. Wilson, against his own earlier expectations, was led to conclude that Parliament had no authority at all in the colonies. It was clear that the issue between Britain and her American colonies was not one of representation but of sovereignty.

It was not to be expected that this intense debate, to which American leaders devoted an increasing degree of their moral and mental energies, would be without repercussions within the colonies themselves. The progress of the American cause had American consequences in both the theory and practice of representation. Some of the more evident practical consequences included the erection of a public gallery in the Massachusetts Assembly chamber in Boston, the grant of increased representation to the more populous and wealthier counties of Pennsylvania, and the intensification of interest in politics that produced the hotly contested elections of 1776 in Virginia.

The need of the colonial leadership to be sure that the cause was understood, to rally the people in its support, brought about a closer *rapport* between the Assemblies and the electorate. The clearest local demonstration of the success of the Assembly policies of resistance came with the formation of the committees of correspondence, which harnessed effective powers of local government to the service of the provincial and Continental Congresses. When, in each province separately, a provincial Congress had superseded the old Assembly, then the system of representation had been locked into the colonial machinery of resistance, and Independence was not far away.

Independence had certainly seemed very far away when the debate had begun, at the end of the Seven Years War. And it is one of the sweetest temptations, as it is one of the most serious errors, in the interpretation of American development after 1763, to suppose that all the more significant movements were tending in the same direction.

The disputes with Britain tended to consolidate American sentiment and to help the colonists towards the discovery of a collectively 'American' identity. By forcing the leaders of opinion among the merchants, planters, and lawyers who were also in general the leaders of the Assemblies to seek popular support, the imperial controversy also brought about some popularisation of the political process within the colonies. Yet it would be a mistake to attribute these developments entirely to the force of the major controversy. A drift towards popular suffrage has been noticed as something which was quietly overtaking the politics of Virginia in the 1760s, and the reasons for this tendency appear to lie within the borders of the Old Dominion. At that period, the advance of popular participation had not yet begun to threaten the grip of the gentry. The sad affair of Matthew Marrable, disqualified after election to the House of Burgesses for making promises to the electorate, at least demonstrated that such promises could have political effects: there would be more of them in the future!

Virginian society was badly shaken by the exposure of the Robinson scandal after the Speaker's death in 1766. It is hard to believe that these revelations left the traditional leaders of society and politics feeling quite as self-assured as they had been used to feel, and the incident may reasonably be supposed to have weakened the deference of some of the humbler planters and tenants. At all events, when the time eventually arrived for electing a provincial Convention, the elections were more keenly fought than ever before, and some of the dominant men were turned out, or hard-pressed, in their own counties.

In Massachusetts the towns, especially those of the seaboard, seethed with an intermittent ferment of libertarian defiance. In 1766 the Council virtually collapsed as a pillar of the traditional order. While it would be an inversion of the political system to argue that the townspeople were themselves formulating the principles of policy, the more significant point is that the policy of defiance could never have been sustained without their participation. In Philadelphia, on the other hand, the rise of popular discontent against the prevailing order was primarily an indigenous movement, owing its strength only incidentally to the larger conflict. But that discontent brought out very large bodies of voters without the licence of any change in the election laws.

All of these eruptions suggest a powerful undercurrent towards more popular government. Yet they might never have been strong enough to dictate the future of American politics if the Revolution had not played into their hands. There is no evidence that the Radicals in Pennsylvania would have been able to seize power but for the peculiar exigencies of the revolutionary crisis, which brought to their aid, among other things, the influence of the Massachusetts members of the Continental Congress. The artisans of Philadelphia were up in political revolt against the power and pretensions of the merchant gentry of the city; but the very nature of their protest — not to mention the copious evidence from the domestic life of eastern Pennsylvania itself — makes clear that a distinct, and politically very powerful, social and economic hierarchy effectively governed the province. When new constitutions were made in Virginia and in Massachusetts it soon transpired that the surge towards more popular government was under control. All of the new state Constitutions, except that of Pennsylvania, where the Radicals had won a somewhat inconclusive victory, were deeply imbued with the idea of property. The individual right to property was universally regarded as an attribute of political liberty, so that the constitutional defence of property was to be expected. But the idea of property as a political attribute might, at the same time, have been cut down to the same size as the individual voter. Only in a formalistic sense can this be said to have happened in Virginia, because in Virginia the new Constitution left the prevailing leadership assured of the substance of power; and even the most radical proposals put forward in 1776 drew a clear line between the political rights of those with property and those without. In Pennsylvania the furthest advance was made by the adoption of a tax-payer suffrage, a step at once vitiated by the qualifying oath of loyalty. Most significant of all, in Massachusetts (as in most of the other states) an elaborate system of economic differentials was introduced into the new form of government.

Compared with England, the American states were all 'Radical'. They were Radical in the sense that Cartwright and Jebb, Christopher Wyvill and the Yorkshire reformers were Radical. There were differences between the views of these Radicals, but they were due largely to differences of local situation: in principle the similarities, not the differences, mattered. The American Revolution, and the early phase of state constitution-making, demonstrated one point of outstanding importance. The Radical tradition, to which the Americans owed so much, and which was to give energy to the new moves for parliamentary reform in Britain, was wholly compatible with the persistence of the political theory of social differentiation.

The pure logic of a drive towards popular power, conceived in the tradition of personal equality, might have been expected to result in the establishment of the unicameral legislature in each of the states. Such a result would have recognised that in America, as John Adams had remarked, there was only one 'order' — that of the people; it would have swept away the relics of separate 'estates', which had never borne much relevance to American conditions. Yet it was only in Pennsylvania, and there for special reasons, that this distinctively 'Radical' object was attained — to be reversed in favour of a more conventional frame of 'mixed' government in 1790. The truth was that hardly any of the American leaders wanted to establish an 'undifferentiated' republic in America. The old and feeble idea of estates had crumbled away. But property had risen in its place. Property, in this sense, was not a mere attribute of individual ownership, but was an ingredient of the social order. Property emerged from the confusion as a sort of independent 'estate'.

The logic of unicameralism was set forth very clearly by the anonymous author of a Philadelphia pamphlet, *Four Letters on Interesting Subjects*.[1] The whole object of holding annual and equal elections should be to bring the rival interests into one House where they could hear each other's arguments; to separate them into two Houses would keep them in 'dangerous opposition'. A distinct part of the interest of this argument lies in the very use of the word 'interests', which was eventually to supersede 'orders' and 'estates' in the vocabulary of politics. American political thought, like that of Britain, was groping towards a more realistic language, while American leaders grappled with local realities.

There is further significance in the fact that the 'interests' discerned by the author were the landed and the merchant interests. What worried him was not the antagonism of upper and lower elements on the economic scale, but that of propertied elements whose interests might conflict. There is an underlying assumption that all those with a basic commitment to the land, whether independent farmers, tenants, or labourers, were united in a single interest; while much the same might be said of the whole community of commerce, comprising as it did the range of a civic economy that gave employment to the great merchant, the domestic retailer, and the journeyman. The social assumptions behind these usages were closely comparable to those current in Britain, where the concept of 'interests' was coming into use in political discourse.

The use of the word 'interest' did not resolve the problems that would face American leaders but it did free them to tackle those problems in a more realistic way. It furnished a concept that would survive to describe social conflicts long after those which agitated the eighteenth century had passed away. Americans also owed a significant debt to the word 'consent', which was made to bear a new burden of meaning in the course of the internal, as well as the external, debate arising from the conflict with Britain.

In 1774 Samuel Seabury, an Anglican minister and a Tory, declared that 'The position that we are bound by no laws to which we have not consented either by ourselves or by our representatives is a novel position unsupported by any authoritative record of the British constitution, ancient or modern'.[2] In this he was wrong. Some notion of consent was evident in numerous earlier records of parliamentary procedure. But 'consent' was being turned into something far more active than the tacit acceptance of the law which it

[1] See Bernard Bailyn, *Pamphlets of the American Revolution*, vol. i (Cambridge, Mass., 1965), 187–8.
[2] Bailyn, *Pamphlets*, 99.

had meant to Locke, and which it had usually meant even in the American colonies. The right of 'instruction', which, if not undisputed by clear-headed critics, was extremely popular in America, did seem to imply that the voters themselves were continuously 'present' in the actual making of the laws. A representative Assembly, it was repeatedly asserted, was nothing less than the whole people in miniature. If this were true, then the whole people were giving the law, not merely accepting it.[1]

The case would have been sounder if its advocates had frankly said 'the whole electorate' rather than 'the whole people'. As a theory for the justification of law, it came nearest to actual practice in Massachusetts in 1779, with the enfranchisement of all adult males for the election of a constitutional Convention. The transformation of passive consent into something resembling active, even continuous participation, was a direct result of the galvanic action of the debate with Britain. Americans had been forced to examine the meaning of their own language, and, in conditions which gave them an unusual opportunity to apply meaning to action, they had charged the old notion of 'consent' with a more democratic connotation than it had ever borne before. The results at the time were limited; but this was a strand of thought thrown up by the Revolution, legitimate, even essential to the logic of the cause, which future Radicals and future reformers could rightly claim for their own. It was a decisive step in the history of the 'good old cause'.

14. Representation as a Test of Sovereignty

The problem of organising a government for the American continent provided a severe test for Whig theory. All the unresolved issues seemed to converge. The states had wrestled individually with the question of whether persons or property, or a mixture of both, should be sovereign within the State. But how were the states to be weighed against each other? The question arose at the very beginning. The states first came together as virtual sovereignties and voted as equals; but as they were unequal in population and in wealth, that system could not permanently endure. In default of a more accurate standard, population came to be

[1] The point is discussed by Professor Bailyn, *Pamphlets*, 98.

accepted as the measure of a state's wealth, first for purposes of taxation, and eventually for determining the scale of representation. In 1787 the language of state sovereignty was still spoken and states retained their equality in the Senate. In reality, however, the independent sovereignty of the states had been displaced by an American version of interest representation. At the same time the House of Representatives was placed on the new and national basis of proportional, or numerical, representation. The Constitution incorporated, but it also profoundly modified, not only the Whig doctrines which the Americans had inherited from Britain, but even those which they had tried and developed for themselves.

EACH of the several American provinces had a practical ground for claiming to constitute a legal sovereignty; for each had a government whose writ ran to the boundaries of the province: but there it stopped. The great problem of the Continental Congress was to make its writ run across the borders of the provinces which, after 2 July 1776, collectively comprised the United States of America.

The central issue, which tested the competing claims of provinces and Congress, was that of representation. This question had to be decided at the beginning. The smaller provinces claimed equality with the greater; but the greater ones asserted that the very factors which made them greater were the factors which required to be counted as a basis of representation. For urgent practical reasons it had to be agreed to give each province one vote; but this decision was highly unsatisfactory. On theoretical grounds, of the kind that might translate themselves at any moment into matters of policy, it was unsatisfactory because it failed to give due weight to the interests of property. On practical grounds it would not work because when the Articles of Confederation were formed the principle was extended to require unanimity for changes in the. Constitution — a virtual imitation of the Polish *liberum veto*, which obstructed and nearly throttled the entire system.

The necessary minimum of reform therefore affected the Articles, and when reforms could no longer be avoided, representation was still the central and unresolved problem.

No royal writ summoned the Assembly at Philadelphia in September 1774, which was to be called the Continental Congress. It was called forth by the initiative of the representative Conventions of the provinces; it consisted of delegations of unequal numbers, appointed by the several Conventions of the provinces; and by its mere existence it posed a problem of representation.

Until the Congress met, there was no Assembly of America; but as soon as it was in being, it was the sole body competent either to speak for America to the outside world or to establish standards and procedures to govern the continent. It quickly got to work by drafting the Articles of Association that were circulated to, and approved by, the provincial Conventions. The Declaration of Independence in due course was an act of the Continental Congress, which alone could speak with authority for the colonies collectively. There were therefore strong logical grounds for regarding it as having the attributes of a government. But with equal certainty its members were delegates of state (or provincial) governments. The issue was confronted immediately: were the several delegations to vote in accordance with the wealth and scale represented by their proportion of the whole of America, or were they, being the delegates of sovereigns, to vote as equals?

Under the Crown the provinces, though separate units of government, were obviously not sovereigns; they could not claim to be independent sovereignties until after the Declaration of Independence. That was the work of the Congress, only to be reaffirmed by the individual state Congresses — but just as the Congress begins to get the better of the argument, one is reminded that it had absolutely no power of coercion over any province or state and could in fact have done nothing to prevent any one of them from withdrawing from the whole concern.

The problem of representation could have been solved at once, in spite of its legal difficulties, by an act of will. Had all the delegates agreed with the pronouncement of Patrick Henry that government was dissolved and the distinctions between Virginians, Pennsylvanians, New Yorkers, and New Englanders were no more; had they wanted to sink themselves into a nation, there would have been an end to the argument. But no sooner were the provincial delegations confronted with this choice than they discovered the potency of their provincial loyalties.

One of the delegates from a small state, probably Ward of Rhode Island, observed that they had come if necessary to make a sacrifice of their all; the weakest colony by such a sacrifice would suffer as much as the greatest.[1] This was intended as an argument for equality; actually there is no logical reason why it should be considered to extend beyond a claim for representation proportional to the interest of each province, for it was no less true that Virginia or Massachusetts risked a sacrifice of their 'all'. The Congress was up against the irreducible fact of the corporate selfconsciousness of the separate colonies.

[1] Edmund C. Burnett (ed.), *Letters of Members of the Continental Congress* 8 vols. (Washington, 1921–6), i. 12–15.

John Adams, in a speech on the first day, reviewed the extent of the problem with a clarity that deserves full quotation from his own notes:

This [he said] is a question of great importance. — If we vote by Colonies, this method will be liable to great inequality and injustice, for 5 small colonies, with 100,000 people in each may outvote 4 large ones, each of which has 500,000 inhabitants. If we vote by the poll [i.e. by poll of the individual delegates present] some colonies have more than their proportion of members, and others have less. If we vote by interests, it will be attended by insuperable difficulties to ascertain the true importance of each colony. — Is the weight of a colony to be ascertained by the number of inhabitants merely — or by the amount of their trade, the quantity of their exports and imports, or by the compound ratio of both. This will lead us into such a field of controversy as will greatly perplex us. Besides I question whether it is possible to ascertain, at this time, the numbers of our people or the value of our trade. It will not do in such a case, to take each other's words. It ought to be ascertained by authentic evidence, from records.[1]

One difficulty here mentioned could easily enough be disposed of in principle: if a proportional voting system could have been agreed, then the mere fact that each colony had decided for itself how many delegates to send, leading to inequalities in the delegations, need not have stood in the way. Each delegation could then have cast the number of votes allotted to its colony in terms of population, wealth, or whatever basis was accepted. But this would have underlined the fact that each delegation voted as a unit. It would have needed a more strict apportionment of numbers to colonies before individual voting became possible. As it was, differences within delegations appeared from the outset. Patrick Henry's plea for a purely numerical scale encountered practical objections among his own Virginian colleagues. Richard Henry Lee and Richard Bland seem to have opposed the appointment of a committee, as desired by Henry, to try to find a basis for some form of proportional representation, as neither of them could believe that the necessary information was available. Edmund Pendleton, looking beyond this objection, suggested that a committee could at least 'lay the foundation for the Congress to take some other steps to procure evidence of numbers and property at some future time'.[2]

The argument was settled by the practical consideration that the material for any differentiated system was simply not available, but in order to avoid prejudicing future discussion the Congress recorded this difficulty, stating that the decision to give each colony one vote was taken because it was

[1] *Adams Papers*, ii. 123–4.
[2] *Adams Papers*, ii. 125–6.

unable at the moment to 'procure proper materials for ascertaining the importance of each Colony'.[1]

What was the 'importance' of a colony, province, or state? The decision on equality of voting was of great prospective significance because, despite the disavowal, it established a practice. When the different elements mentioned by Adams were available for evaluation, there was inevitably to be a more searching enquiry into the value given to this vague but significant notion designated as 'importance' or 'weight'. The debate was resumed in 1776 when the committee of the Congress, delegated to draw up Articles of Confederation, reported on the question of the quota of money to be made over by each state to the common treasury and the 'manner of voting in Congress'.

The report proposed that requisitions should be in proportion to the number of inhabitants, except Indians; that a census should be taken every three years; but that 'In determining questions each colony shall have one vote'.[2]

This gave rise to two closely related discussions, the first about the basis of taxation and the second about the basis of representation. The first brought out strong arguments in favour of treating population as the measure of the wealth by which a state was to be assessed for requisitions; taxation, it was admitted by Samuel Chase of Maryland, should always be in proportion to property, but although this was the true rule, it could not be adopted in practice and a simpler standard was needed. The number of inhabitants was 'a tolerably good criterion of property'. John Adams agreed that numbers were 'a fair index of wealth'. But difficulties were already arising over slavery, and James Wilson urged it as the duty of the Congress to lay every discouragement on the importation of slaves. Were slaves, then, to be counted as among the population for purposes of assessments? Adams had, in this debate, no apparent objection to enumerating slaves, on the ground that as labourers they helped to produce the wealth which was to be assessed. But if slaves were going to be enumerated as persons for any purposes whatever, it would be easier, when the time came, to claim them as persons for the basis of representation; an opening had been made for the principle of the partial enumeration of slaves, as subsequently adopted in the Federal Constitution. For the present, the proposal of Chase that white inhabitants form the basis for taxation was rejected; and the Articles of Confederation

[1] *Adams Papers*, ii. 126, n. 4, *Journals of the Continental Congress*, i. 25 (hereafter referred to as *J.C.C.*).

[2] *J.C.C.*, vi. 1098, 1101. The references to the debates are from 1098–1105.

settled on the rule that each state was to be assessed according to the value of its land.[1]

The question of representation ranged further and reached deeper. It was here that the special character of the smaller states made its appearance. Already they expressed their fears of being dominated by the larger ones. If an equal vote were refused, said the Reverend John Witherspoon,[2] 'the small states will become the vassals of the large'. He warned the Congress that foreign powers would make this a handle for disengaging the smaller states from the confederacy (a threat to be repeated eleven years later by Gunning Bedford of Delaware) and stated that colonies should 'in fact be regarded as individuals; and that as such in all disputes they should have an equal vote'. He remarked that in the East India Company they voted by persons and not by the proportion of stock held. Nothing relating to individuals would ever come before Congress — nothing but what would respect colonies. He also answered Franklin, who had alluded to the fact that Scotland had expressed the same fears about union with England as the small states did now, yet had never been subjected to any unfairness, by distinguishing between a federal and an incorporating union; it was to the latter class that the Union between England and Scotland belonged.

Franklin's speech drew on experience in Pennsylvania where, he said, the representation had originally been equal but had become unequal by time and accident; to this he might submit, rather than disturb the government (thus disarming any criticism of Pennsylvania that might weaken his case), but it was very wrong to set out in this practice when they had it in their power to establish what was right. He was for proportioning the representation according to population in all cases.

So was John Adams. His argument succeeded in integrating wealth and numbers into a concept of interest but at the same time defining interest for practical purposes in terms of numbers. The feat was made possible by a strongly nationalist assertion of the basic character of the Congress. 'We stand here', he declared, 'as representatives of the people. In some states the

[1] But it should be noted that this rule was never effectively operated. For the duration of the war, when a land valuation was impracticable, Congress adopted the population standard; when the intended land valuation scheme came into effect it raised such great difficulties that an amendment to the Articles was actually proposed by the Congress, to adopt the population basis. This was never ratified. It remained doubtful whether population or land value was to remain the standard. E. James Ferguson, *The Power of the Purse* (Chapel Hill, 1961), 209.

[2] President of Princeton and a delegate of New Jersey, which was to oppose the nationalising tendencies of the Virginia Plan at Philadelphia in 1787.

people are many, in some they are few.' Reason, justice, and equity never had weight enough to govern the councils of men — interest alone did it. (None the less, these three virtues were noticeably on the side of the majority; it was only the interests of minorities, or perhaps small states, which appeared by implication to threaten reason, justice, and equity.) Interest alone could be trusted and therefore the interests within doors should be the mathematical representatives of the interests without doors. The bent of this argument was now clear, and he proceeded to make it clearer: 'The individuality of a colony is a mere sound'. He then illustrated from one of those simple business propositions that they all understood. A had £50, B £500, and C £1,000, in partnership: was it just that they should dispose equally of the moneys of the partnership?

Adams then came down on the central point at issue in the whole debate, though no other speaker appears to have grasped it so firmly or put it so clearly. Suppose it was said in reply that the bargain was made by independent individuals? (Witherspoon in effect had said so.) 'The question', replied Adams, 'is not what we are now but what we ought to be when the bargain is made. The confederacy is to make us one individual only.'

Here then, for the American confederation, was a clear statement of the prescriptive purpose of representation. It was instinctively understood by the small states when they fought the individual basis; it was groped for by many of the speakers for numerical representation. Adams also anticipated some of the leading arguments to be heard eleven years later in the same place. He pointed out — as Madison was to do later — that Virginia, Pennsylvania, and Massachusetts, the three great states, could never have an inclination to combine for the oppression of the smaller; the smaller would combine on specific issues with different larger states. If a proportional vote would endanger the small states, an equal vote would endanger the large.

Earlier the same year, the numerical principle had been seized in Massachusetts by the Seaboard spokesmen as the instrument of their combined weight of property and numbers. It is of the highest significance that when the great debate on the principles of representation was transferred to the continental scheme, it was the delegates of the great states — Adams for Massachusetts, Wilson and Franklin for Pennsylvania, Henry and Pendleton for Virginia (with doubts expressed by their colleagues for practical rather than theoretical reasons), who declared fearlessly and energetically for the basis of numerical representation, at the heart of which lay the coiled, slow spring of the far-reaching doctrine of majority rule.

The idea that property ought of right to have its representation in the political system had not been ousted. On the contrary, it was brought under the protection of the majority principle. Chase, who rightly described the provision on representation as 'the most divisive article in the draft', said that the smaller states should be secured in all matters concerning life and liberty, the greater ones in all respecting property. To supply this need he proposed that in votes relating to money the voice of each colony be proportioned according to the number of its inhabitants.

But already, as later, the small states had a deep sense of their political identity and would not give it up. They had more — a power of veto. The large states were not so situated as to be able to threaten to form a separate confederation; the debates of the existing or prospective one were complicated by the numerous exigencies of war, of finance, of the problem of disposing of western lands, of foreign policies, and domestic intrigues. No inroads were made on the ground taken by the small states from the very beginning; and the Articles of Confederation incorporated the principle that each state, being sovereign, had an equal vote with every other.

The constitutional history of the Articles of Confederation was controlled in the last resort by the provision that any alteration in the Articles required the unanimous consent of the contracting parties. Congress was preoccupied with those questions that had already identified themselves as the themes of controversy if not as issues for urgent decisions. The war was brought successfully to a conclusion and the western lands were provided for in the famous land ordinances of the 1780s; but in foreign policy and in public finance the Congress found itself crippled by the weakness of its own constitution. The decline of force in the central authority of the Confederation caused alarm to those who, for whatever reasons, viewed American affairs on a continental scale; but to those elements who were doing well out of the extensive liberties allowed to state action, it seemed tolerable enough. The difficulties of Congress led to a weakening of its calibre as it ceased to be attractive to men of the first abilities, and state legislatures made the first and strongest claims. States which had failed in meeting the requisitions of the Congress could defy it with impunity. 'As unanimity is now necessary upon the most trivial questions,' wrote Nathaniel Gorham to James Warren in 1786, 'we feel the inconveniences of the liberum veto of the Polish Diet.'[1] The delinquent legislature of New Jersey received a visitation from the Congress, from which it heard strong and menacing language. The present principles, they were told by Charles Pinckney, were unequal and oppressive. If a new Confederation were formed to render government firm and

[1] Burnett, *Letters of Continental Congress*, viii. 317–18.

energetic, the large states would contend for and insist on greater influence. They would not agree to unite on principles giving states which did not contribute one-tenth of their quota an equal vote. 'A new confederation', threatened Grayson of Virginia, 'will put you in your proper place.'[1]

The failure, for want of unanimous consent, of the two plans to reform the financial structure of the Confederation by strengthening certain congressional powers served to deepen the feeling among several well-placed observers that the whole American experiment faced a crisis. One possibility, often mentioned but not seriously promoted in open politics, was that of monarchy; but what really looked probable was the splitting up of the Confederation into as many as three separate confederate republics. Madison felt certain that if this were to be prevented the existing polity must be reformed, or even refounded, upon different principles of representation.

He put his views to Edmund Randolph shortly before the opening of the Federal Convention in Philadelphia. After noticing the need to reform the representation and the danger of partition, he went on:

I hold it a fundamental point that an individual independence of the States is utterly irreconcileable to the idea of an aggregate sovereignty. I think at the same time that a consolidation of the States into one simple republic is not less unattainable than it would be inexpedient. [This view he was to modify after three weeks or so of struggle in the forthcoming Convention.] Let it be tried then whether any middle ground can be taken which will at once support a due supremacy of the national authority, and leave in force the local authorities so far as they can be subordinately useful.

The first step to be taken, is I think a change in the principle of representation. According to the present form of the Union, an equality of suffrage if not just towards the larger members of it, is at least safe to them, as the liberty they exercise of rejecting or executing the acts of Congress, is uncontrollable by the nominal sovereignty of Congress. Under a system which would operate without the intervention of the States, the case would be materially altered. A vote [i.e. of one elector] from Delaware would have the same weight with one from Massts. or Virga.[2]

---

[1] Burnett, *Letters of Continental Congress*, viii. 321–30, 330, n. 49.

[2] 'An equality of suffrage' here means equal representation, based, that is, on population. Hence if the 'intervention of the states' as sovereigns with equal votes were withdrawn, the vote of one elector in Delaware would be reduced to the same proportions as that of one elector in Massachusetts or Virginia. Equal voting in Congress of course meant that one voter in a small state had powers equal to many times the number in a large state. Thus Madison argues that the power of Congress should be strengthened at the expense of the states; and that the unit voting rule should be abolished in Congress, where representation should be made proportional to population. It meant majority rule over the whole Union. As before, this proposition comes from a large state.

Madison went on to examine the bearing of these proposals on the different sections.

The change in the principle of representation [he continued] will be relished by a majority of the States, and those too of the most influence. The Northern States will be reconciled to it by the *actual* superiority of their populousness: the Southern by their *expected* superiority in this point. This principle established, the repugnance of the large states to part with power will in great degree subside, and the smaller states must ultimately yield to the predominant will. It is also already seen by many and must by degrees be seen by all that unless the Union be organised efficiently on Republican principles, innovations of a much more objectionable form may be obtruded, or in the most favorable event, the partition of the Empire into rival and hostile confederacies will ensue.[1]

Madison, before the Convention assembled, had thought his way through the major problems that were to confront it.

15. At Philadelphia Again

The nationalists were quick to see that a genuinely national government required a national legislature based on a representation according to population — on a purely numerical scale. Failing this — which they could not impose — they insisted on a numerical basis for the House of Representatives while conceding the equality of the states in the Senate. In providing for a national executive, they applied the same principle: in order to make him a completely national officer they must give him a national constituency. Their first thought was of election by the legislature; but later they turned to an electoral college based on the several states. It was to be a filtering process for a nation-wide electorate.

Meanwhile the executive office was separated from the legislature and given considerable independent power and influence. The consequence was a distinct impairment of that grand concept of the supremacy of the legislative power which American Whigs had received from Locke. During the controversy with Great Britain American Whigs had developed the theory that statute law, even when

[1] Madison to Randolph, 8 April 1787; Madison Papers.

made by Parliament, was subordinate to the 'fundamental' law of the kingdom. In principle this doctrine challenged the prevailing and historic Whig view of the supremacy of the legislative power. The Constitution of the United States took the distinction still further; in it, the legislative power was dethroned, and the Constitution declared itself to be 'the supreme law of the land'.

These arrangements also impaired another Whig principle, the separate interest of property, by which it was entitled to separate representation. But this principle had not been surrendered. What was done, rather, was to melt property and persons into a single concept for the purpose of ascertaining the 'weight' of a community for political representation. The idea of property as a political interest was incorporated into that of numbers, but numbers became the sole instrument of measurement. The compromise gave deep uneasiness to some of those concerned, but was the only workable solution in view of the difficulties of assessment and of application that would have been encountered in trying to maintain a distinct representation of property.

The special character of interests other than those of numbers gained permanent recognition in the Senate. The English Whig idea that certain corporate interests required representation for their protection, and that their place in the state entitled them to that privilege, had thus emerged in American conditions under the somewhat inappropriate aegis of state sovereignty. The interests of slavery, and the shadowy future interests of the great geo-economic sections, were not provided for in the structure devised at Philadelphia — but within that structure they would have to work out their accommodation with the Union.

I. 'THE GREAT DIFFICULTY LIES IN THE AFFAIR OF REPRESENTATION'

WHEN all allowances have been made for spring freshets and laborious communications, the unpunctuality of the delegates appointed to the Federal Convention in Philadelphia seems to contain a residue of political significance. Scepticism as to the outcome is implied by indifference about the beginning; the more so when contrasted with the early arrival and purposeful activity of the delegation from Virginia.

The Virginia delegates occupied the interval between the first meeting on 14 May and the formal opening of the Convention on 25 May by drafting a plan for a new Constitution. There being no formal agenda, the Virginia Plan, when presented by Governor Edmund Randolph, became the basis of discussion. Thus do matters of procedure transmute themselves into matters of substance.

In one major respect the Virginia Plan was revolutionary: it proposed to convert the United States confederacy into a nation. This intention was implicit in the fact that the new legislature was to consist of two chambers, a characteristic of British — and state — sovereignty.[1] The members of the first, or lower, House were to be elected by the people of the several states; the members of the second, by those of the first. This proposal recalled the old Massachusetts Council, except that the upper House was to hold office 'for a term sufficient to ensure their independency', for the concept of the separation of powers, now much advanced, was seen to imply separation between the two branches of the legislature itself, not merely between the different functional departments of government — legislative, executive, and judicial. The new national legislature was to enjoy all the power needed to govern the nation as a whole; power to legislate 'in all cases in which the separate States are incompetent, or in which the harmony of the United States may be interrupted by the exercise of individual legislations; to negative all laws passed by the several States, contravening in the opinion of the National Legislature the articles of Union; and to call forth the force of the Union against any member failing to fulfill its duty under the articles thereof'.

The Plan went further in defining the national character of the new government by proposing a national executive — an institution for which the existing Confederation had no place. The executive was to be chosen by the legislature, and was to take over the executive rights so far exercised by the Congress. As an outcome of strenuous debates, the executive was later to be dissociated from the legislature on the ground that the proposed method of election would make it subservient. This step went far to establish the separation of powers as it has since been known in America. It is therefore significant that the Virginia delegation did not at first see any danger in making the executive into a legislative appointment. The truth was that legislative power was understood as the great instrument of government — a point repeated by Madison in *The Federalist* when he wrote, 'In a republican government, the Legislative authority necessarily predominates'.[2] It was the traditional Whig view, to which an alternative did not seem logically possible. It had been modified by the shocks administered in the Confederation by several of the state legislatures, and stern objections were raised against the idea of giving the legislature the power of appointment. It was

[1] Farrand, *Records,* i. 20–23.
[2] *Federalist* no. 51.

Madison who later introduced the plan, finally adopted, for an intermediate electoral college.

Though the Virginia Plan broke with convention in its nationalising propensities, it did so in a very conventional manner. It conceived of the new nation as an enlarged and, geographically and administratively, somewhat complicated version of an existing state — say, the state of Virginia. The new Constitution was to incorporate some of the reforms that Madison and Jefferson (who of course was not present) would have liked to see in the Old Dominion. The Plan projected on to a national scale the conventional Whig concepts, tempered as they had been by recent legislative experience, of the proper objects of political representation.

Behind the Virginia Plan lay the formal scheme of persons and property, each represented in a separate chamber. But for those who wanted to give property this separate institutional character the difficulty was to find a method of election which would really effect the purpose. This problem brought out some sharp differences between advocates of what were basically similar views of society. The debate was brought into focus by John Dickinson, who moved that the members of the second branch be chosen, not by the members of the first as in the Virginia Plan, but by state legislatures.[1] Dickinson was certainly no less anxious than Madison to preserve the rights of property in the second chamber; he actually compared the two houses with the Lords and Commons, arguing that the powers in the American legislature ought to resemble them in flowing from different sources and thus checking each other;[2] yet Madison at once saw in this a threat to the indispensable principle of proportional representation in the allocation of legislative seats. A departure from this was 'inadmissible'; but the alternative was to give the senate (as it was already being called) excessive numbers, which would disable it from proceeding 'with more coolness, more system and more wisdom than the popular branch'. The difference between the two men is interesting since Dickinson, a true spokesman of upper class interests, represented the diminutive state of Delaware and was therefore friendly to the idea of the continued influence of state legislatures while Madison had the characteristically more national viewpoint of the greater states.

That viewpoint was taken perhaps even more definitely by James Wilson of Pennsylvania. Wilson objected to the idea that the two Houses should rest on different foundations, which he thought would lead to dissensions, and was for election of the Senate by the people, in constituencies formed of

[1] Farrand, *Records*, i. 150.   [2] Farrand, *Records*, i. 156–7 (Yates's notes).

population districts. Wilson emerged as one of the most fearless nationalists of the Convention, and significantly as one who had least fear of the dangers of popular elections. A variant view was advanced by Elbridge Gerry, who stood for the great state of Massachusetts, but agreed with Dickinson that the appointments to the Senate should be made by the state legislatures.[1]

Both in the debates about the Senate, and in the division over the representation in the lower House, it was clear that a strong element in the Convention was convinced of the urgent need to erect special safeguards for the interests of property. Gouverneur Morris affirmed that the upper House was to protect the aristocratic and propertied interests, and again that property was the chief object of society.[2] This came in a discussion of the subordinate question of the exact ratio of population to each member; and Rufus King of New York concurred with Morris in almost the same words.

With these sentiments the delegates from South Carolina and Georgia were in wholehearted agreement. They intervened several times to assert that the second branch ought to represent the people according to their property, that property was the principal object of society and that it was the only just measure for representation.[3] These statements did not however introduce harmony with opinions held to the north of them, for the property which the South Carolinians were concerned to protect was held in Negro slaves.

The two leading schools of advocates for property rights, those of the eastern merchants and of the southern planters, collided over slavery. The issue arose when the Convention reached the problem of a basis of representation for the lower House; it came up again over the apportionment of taxation; and indirectly when the taxation and representation of the populations of the future western states had to be determined. It was no part of the doctrines of Gouverneur Morris that the rights of men to security in the property they had inherited or earned included a right to property in other men, particularly in a government which claimed to have been founded in defence of liberty. He waxed eloquent and bitter in his denunciations of slavery, of the slave trade, and of any compromise that would give countenance to either.[4] The Southerners meanwhile insisted on a method of apportioning representatives that would allow the enumeration of their slave population. It was not difficult to reply that as the slaves were denied civil attributes in all other respects it would be inconsistent to count them for representation. Yet it was admitted that they were property, and Morris, among others,

---

[1] Farrand, *Records*, i. 152, 154–5.   [2] Farrand, *Records*, i. 511, 533.

[3] Farrand, *Records*, i. 528, 533, 542.   [4] Farrand, *Records*, i. 588, 593, ii. 221–3.

held strong views on property. It was also true that Morris's views concurred with those of the South Carolinians in another point: both sensed danger in the rise of the new West.

The west was expected to develop a numerous population. But it was also generally thought that compared with the prosperous east, with its trans-Atlantic commerce and its rich plantations, the west would long remain poor; so that the rise of a western population presented the ominous spectre of a sort of agrarian proletariat, which appeared to both these parties to offer a threat to the property and security of the east extremely similar to that which Madison and others feared from the rise of towns.

In both cases the reaction was a policy of prescriptive discrimination. The west, declared Gouverneur Morris, would not be able to furnish enlightened men; the busy haunts of men, not the remote wilderness, was the proper school of political talents, and if the westerners got power into their hands they would ruin the Atlantic interests. He pointed to the history of Pennsylvania to bear him out, that the members from the back country were always averse to the best measures.[1]

Madison, whatever he might say about city populations, had no undue fears of the new population of farmers rising in the west, and attacked Morris's argument with some acerbity. His reasoning, Madison told him, was not only inconsistent with that of his own past arguments but with itself. At the same time as urging the South to rest implicit confidence in a northern majority, he was still more zealous in exhorting all to jealousy of a western majority. 'Does he determine human character by the points of the compass?' All those who possessed power were to be mistrusted to a certain degree. No unfavourable distinctions against the west were admissible, either on grounds of justice or of policy: but in any case Madison countered the fear of a poor and greedy west by anticipating much bigger western exports and revenues, especially when, as it must be, the Mississippi was opened.[2]

Fittingly, it was Morris who found a way of compromise. It was eventually agreed that representation in the lower House was to be apportioned by population; but direct taxation, whenever the Federal government should apply it, would be assessed in the same ratio; that is according to the numbers of representatives allotted to each state. The west would be represented according to population but would be taxed on the same basis. As it was expected to be more populous than wealthy, this was meant as a disadvantage that would in some way compensate the east. The south was to be permitted to count three-fifths of its slave population for purposes of representation;

[1] Farrand, *Records*, i. 582.　　　[2] Farrand, *Records*, i. 582 ff.

but as it would be subject to direct taxation in the same proportions it could claim this liability as a counterweight to the obvious charge that it had gained an unfair advantage in congressional representation — and representation, too, in the college of presidential electors. Meanwhile the deep South agreed to a clause permitting the Congress to prohibit the importation of slaves after twenty years. This decision was no afterthought, but implemented an indispensable condition of northern acceptance. As Rufus King declared in a strong speech, it was wholly unacceptable to the North that the slave states should first enumerate their slaves for representation and then proceed with indefinite future slave importations. Even so the compromise was distasteful; as late as 8 August he was not sure whether he could assent to it in any circumstances.[1]

The whole concept of separate representation for persons and property implied the threat of a clash between these two sets of interest. This threat appeared again in the demand of some of the now familiar leaders of the high property interests for a property qualification on the suffrage franchise.

Gouverneur Morris, whose interventions were becoming so frequent as to diminish his influence, appropriately moved that the national congressional suffrage be limited to freeholders.[2] Morris unconvincingly warned the Convention that the Constitution as it then stood threatened the country with aristocracy. It would grow out of the House of Representatives. People with no money, having the vote, would sell their suffrages to the rich; the future would see an increase in mechanics and manufacturers dependent on their employers. The man who does not give his vote freely, remarked Morris, is not represented — and he denounced as meaningless the formula about taxation and representation. Nine-tenths of the people being freeholders would be pleased with his proposal.

All this was to be expected from Morris. He was trying to provide, not for the present, but against the future; and what is significant in this outlook is the support he got from Madison.

Madison's views, however, were entirely consistent with those which he offered soon afterwards to Jefferson on the Constitution of Virginia. Viewing the matter on its merits alone, Madison remarked, the freeholders of the country would be the safest depositories of republican liberty. The right of suffrage was certainly one of the fundamental articles of republican government and ought not to be left to be regulated by the legislature. In Madison's view the question of a freehold qualification would depend on the probable reception such a change would meet with in the states where the suffrage

---

[1] Farrand, *Records*, ii. 220.   [2] Farrand, *Records*; this debate occupies ii. 201–5.

was already more extensive. This point was taken by several other speakers who emphasised the insuperable objections that would arise in the several states which already allowed a more general suffrage; Mason, Madison's colleague, opposed him on this ground. The South Carolinians, Butler and Rutledge, though staunch guardians of the rights of property, both severely condemned the idea of restricting the suffrage to freeholders.

But Madison, like Morris, was looking to the future.

In future times [he argued] a great majority of people will not only be without landed, but any other sort of, property. These will either combine under the influence of their common situation; in which case the rights of property and the public liberty will not be secure in their hands: or which is more probable, they will become the tools of opulence and ambition, in which case there will be equal danger on another side.[1]

He also remarked that the corruption which prevailed in Britain was rife in the cities and boroughs,

in many of which the qualification of suffrage is as low as it is in any of the U.S. and it was in the boroughs and cities rather than in the Counties, that bribery most prevailed, and the influence of the Crown on elections was most dangerously exerted.

It is instructive to see Madison drawing on the House of Commons in order to warn the United States of the dangers inherent in a mass franchise. It is instructive also to note the sharp differences between him and Mason, who adhered firmly to his belief in 'attachment and permanent common interest with society'. Mason would no doubt still place the standard of attachment pretty high, but he could see no reason why it should not be widespread; he asked whether the merchant, the moneyed man, the parent of a number of children who would pursue their fortunes in their own country, ought to be viewed as suspicious characters, unworthy to be trusted with the common rights of their fellow citizens?

Madison's speech becomes easier to understand in the light of what we know about his views on the Constitution of Virginia. It was remarked in that connection, that he was looking beyond Virginia and stating a general objective for American Society. There is a remarkable consistency between this outlook and that of the entrenched opponents of Virginian suffrage reform a long generation later. For Madison, like them, was opposed to admitting into the Constitution the instruments by which the structure of society could, however gradually, be altered. His stand was in a distinct

[1] Farrand, *Records*, ii. 203–4.

sense doctrinaire. But although his thought differed so sharply from Mason's, they both stood by the Whig principles of their time; though they gave to them certain differences of quality. The key to these principles was responsibility. Mason simply did not discuss the prospective problem of the urban proletariat, but believed that a desired level of social responsibility could be attained as well by the merchants and others as by the farming freeholder; but as Morris's and Madison's city masses were presumably not expected to acquire such property qualifications as would be the urban equivalent of the freehold (for Mason confined himself to defending persons of obvious substance), it is reasonable to suppose that he would have agreed with Madison on this important matter of legislating to prescribe the future. What Madison did was to offer a view of American society. It was to remain agrarian; and this agrarian character was intended to predominate in its political counsels. Madison knew full well that great manufacturing cities had grown up in England and, as he showed by his illustration, he deeply distrusted the political consequences. It did not occur to him — or at any rate he did not advance the view — that the business of the Convention might include the devising of a political scheme in which the rights of a mass city populace could be included and given political protection; that such a populace would arise he deemed certain, and it is profoundly interesting that he did not hold the view that the advance of the economy would take them forward into prosperity. On the contrary, he seems to have expected that European conditions would soon prevail in American cities. His concern was to establish safeguards against this future American population, not to provide for its protection.

It was a sensible decision to leave each state to determine its own suffrage and to place the elections to Congress on the same footing. The members who objected to a freehold suffrage were certainly right in holding that the strongest opposition would meet any plan to restrict the suffrage for Congress in states where it was already more widely exercised in local elections; and Madison himself had remarked that the reception of the plan in such states would have to decide the question. But that did not prevent him from airing his own true feelings on the subject.

The numerical majority had no such terrors for Madison when it came to establishing a basis for the representation of the people in Congress. There were two separate objectives of battle in which this issue was involved. The first and by far the more important concerned the Senate; when that struggle had been ended by unwilling compromise, there remained the problem, already mentioned, of whether representation in the lower House should be apportioned on numbers alone or on numbers combined with some measure of wealth.

The Virginia Plan, in its nationalising character, attempted to leap over the central fact of the confederation system and to carry on the argument about the details of government when safely landed on the other side. For a couple of weeks the strategy seemed to be working. But by that time the smaller states had caught their breath, and on 15 June William Paterson of New Jersey laid before the Convention a complete alternative plan of government.[1]

The central object of the New Jersey Plan was to strengthen the powers of Congress while retaining the sovereignty of the states. The purpose was implied by the form in which the Congress was envisaged. The reference throughout was simply to 'the U. States in Congress', a style which meant that the existing single-chamber Congress would continue to meet. A Congress of state delegations was of course different in principle from a legislature composed of representatives from a single political entity, and although the New Jersey Plan would have brought into existence a new executive, elected by the Congress, there was no room in it for a bicameral legislature. The executive was intended to be plural, and to be largely dependent on Congress.

A short contest, during which Hamilton arose to offer his own plan of government in a speech lasting five hours, ensued; and on 19 June the Convention, sitting in committee of the whole House, rejected Paterson's plan by a vote of seven to three, one state divided. From that time forth the struggle of the small states for their political survival centred on the structure of the Senate.

It was on that day that Madison remarked, 'The great difficulty lies in the affair of Representation; if this could be adjusted, all others would be surmountable.'

The Virginia Plan had envisaged as the principal objects of representation the same interests that were seen to exist within the state — broadly given the now classical definition of persons and property. But its designers had overlooked, or rather they had attempted to suppress, the political fact of the states. It was very difficult for Madison, King, Wilson, and other energetic nationalists, to comprehend what it was that the small states so fervently desired to retain. The nationalists wanted to convert the United States into a single whole, and Madison, his temper surely near breaking point, once remarked that the small states would have nothing to fear from a Union in

[1] Farrand, *Records*, i. 242 ff.

which they would be mere counties of one entire republic; in attacking the compromise by which the deadlock was finally broken, he threateningly declared that if the large states confederated on their own they would have nothing to fear from the small, which would be unable to remain outside.

To a number of delegates, the basis of this compromise seemed increasingly tolerable as the struggle wore down the determination of the less headstrong nationalists. The states could retain their sovereignty in the Senate, while the people of the states were to be represented numerically in the House. This proposal, formally placed before the Convention after a grand committee, from which the nationalist leaders were excluded, had been anticipated in debate. It became the basis of the federal structure on which the new Constitution was raised. But it was fiercely repudiated by the nationalists, who saw in it the defeat of their concept of the new Union.

The states individually, large or small, did not embody specific economic interests. Their citizens would enjoy the protection of a more powerful government under the Virginia design, and as Madison pointed out at some length, there was no reason to suppose that Massachusetts, Pennsylvania, and Virginia, which had entirely different products, were distant from each other in geography, and had differences of manners and religion, were likely to combine to oppress the smaller states.[1] What, then, did the small states fear? What did they want to defend?

An answer was difficult to find. The spokesmen of the small states repeated their vague fears of oppression and pleaded that their existence was threatened. Dr Samuel Johnson of Connecticut came nearest to an explanation when he observed that the controversy would be endless while one side considered the states as districts of people composing one political society and the other considered them as so many political societies. The fact was, he said, that the states did exist as political societies; and as such they must be armed with some power of self-defence. He thought that Mason had seen to the bottom of the matter; aristocratic and other interests ought to have a means of defending themselves, and states had their interests as such and were equally entitled to a like means.[2] What Johnson had tried to pin down was the corporate interest of the states in their own political existence. His remarks, however, did not go far to explain the nature of this interest, which can best be understood as the force of institutional habit. These political entities had, after all, endured for some one hundred and fifty years; they had not been created by the Revolution, but had survived it. The generations of connection with familiar places and procedures, the intimate networks of

[1] Farrand, *Records*, i. 447.   [2] Farrand, *Records*, i. 461.

family and friendship in the management of institutions, the sense of locality, the knowledge of the keys to control on the domestic stage — all these formed collectively a social and political fabric dear to the managers of the smaller states and in all likelihood dear to the peoples. The nationalists, though many of them were loyal to their states, were conspicuously less committed to local interests. Their leading spokesmen had worked for many years on the continental stage, and by serving the Congress and the army had acquired a strong sense of nationhood. Some of them had business interests of interstate ramifications and prospects that would depend on the force of a central government and would owe nothing to that of the states. Whether through character or interest, they were men who had the gift of a continental imagination.

It was in determining the basis of the House of Representatives that the main battle was pitched between the advocates of property and numbers, and in this the guardians of high property found themselves outflanked. The main burden was again assumed by Gouverneur Morris, though he was supported, perhaps to his discomfort, by the slave advocate Rutledge. Morris insisted that the number of inhabitants could never be relied on to give a proper standard of wealth. He opposed a resolution for taking a periodic census as a basis for apportioning representatives; there were, he averred, amazing differences between the comparative numbers and wealth of different countries.

Madison, however, had no fear of numbers, provided they were freeholders. In his reply to Morris he volunteered economic predictions which were less dismal than those he applied to the towns. Admitting that numbers of inhabitants were not an accurate measure of wealth, Madison held that in the United States 'it was sufficiently so for the object in contemplation'. Under the similarity of governments, laws, and manners, and the intercourse between the parts of the United States, he believed that population, industry, the arts, and the value of labour, would tend to equalise themselves.[1]

Many delegates accepted the doctrine that wealth ought on principle to be weighed in the apportionment of representation. It was a perfectly orthodox view; to reject it would have let in an extreme dependence on the people; but it had to be agreed that no new property qualifications could be imposed by the Constitution, and the only remaining possibility was to work out some system by which the tax assessments would be included in the calculation of population on which the apportionment was to be based. It has already been seen that direct taxation was eventually attached to repre-

[1] Farrand, *Records*, i. 578–85.

sentation; but in this procedure it was the representation which came first, and that representation was (except for the three-fifths ratio of slaves) firmly based on population. Several members, including Franklin and Wilson, argued earnestly for numbers on pure principle.[1] But the decisive argument, advanced in different connections by many speakers, was simply that, in the United States, numbers of population would be as good a rough guide to the wealth of a community as could be obtained by an investigation of property. Land valuations had proved extremely difficult to obtain and unreliable under the Confederation; it was widely felt that the differences likely to be disclosed by a laborious investigation of wealth would not lead to significant differences from a count of population.

It was thus agreed that representation in the House of Representatives should be based on electoral districts within the states, these districts to be drawn by the state governments in equal proportions. The exact numbers to be included in each constituency gave rise to further debate before being fixed at thirty thousand for each representative in Congress.

It was more on grounds of expediency than principle that this flat numerical ratio found favour with the Convention. The difficulties and disputes that would arise over the investigation and adjustment of apportionment on a mixed basis of numbers and wealth, added to the uncertainty as to whether differences of any significant political value would result, swung most members to the numerical side. In practice, the method adopted was bound to strengthen the interests of 'persons' and weaken that of 'property'. For property had lost almost its last institutional safeguard in the electoral system. Not quite its last, however: slave property, under the Federal ratio, was specially protected. Nevertheless the persons who were to vote under the Federal Constitution were to do so as persons, not as the owners of specified amounts or types of property; their state governments might, and usually did, impose property qualifications, but these were, so to speak, not known to the Federal government. Once the Federal government was in operation, its electoral system gave a possibly unintentional but nevertheless an unmistakable impetus to the idea of political democracy.

[1] Farrand, *Records*, i. 197–201; Franklin, not for the first time, alluded to the history of the Union of Scotland with England, and quoted from the Records of the Continental Congress the Resolution of 6 September 1774: '. . . that in determining questions in this Congress each colony or province shall have one vote: the Congress not being possessed of or at present able to procure materials for ascertaining the importance of each colony.' Wilson's speech was one of his most powerful. Ibid., i. 605.

II. DARKER INTERESTS, PRESENT AND FUTURE

The great clash between large and small states overshadowed all other issues and, until resolved by the famous compromise over representation in the Senate, threatened to ruin the whole enterprise. The tenacity of the small states proved irreducible; the persuasions of Wilson, the patient reasoning of Madison, the force of Morris, proved powerless. The small states could insist on their sovereignty because it already existed. Yet their struggle for survival carried larger implications. The whole state system was threatened by the Virginia Plan, a possibility which had been seen and challenged at the outset by Charles Pinckney of South Carolina.[1]

In a sense, then, the small states were bent on resisting a drive towards the kind of nationhood that would supersede the old idea of the individual state. It was unavoidable that the struggle should take the form provided by existing institutions. Yet behind these institutions new formations were beginning to emerge, formations that were to be of greater weight than the original states, to which they bore only an arbitrary and incidental connection.

It has been customary to attribute perspicacity to Madison and King for drawing the attention of the Convention to the fact that a division had appeared along the boundaries of slavery. It was Madison who introduced the subject on 29 June and again on 30 June, in divining this 'great division of interests'. 'It did not lie [said Madison] between the large and small states: it lay between the Northern and Southern; and if any defensive power were given it ought mutually to be given to these two interests.' He was so strongly impressed with this important truth that he had been casting about in his mind for some expedient that would answer the purpose. The one which had occurred was that, instead of proportioning the votes of the States in both branches to their respective numbers of inhabitants computing the slaves in the ratio of five to three, they should be represented in one branch according to the number of free inhabitants only, and in the other according to the whole number, counting the slaves as if free. (This was before the compromise giving the states equal representation in the Senate.) By this arrangement the southern scale would have the advantage in one House, and the Northern in the other. He had been restrained from proposing this expedient by two considerations: one was his unwillingness to urge any diversity of interests on an occasion when it was too apt to arise of itself; the

[1] Farrand, *Records*, i. 33–34.

other was the inequality of powers that must be vested in the two branches, and which would destroy the equilibrium of interests.[1]

It was not so much percipience as realism that prompted Madison and King to raise this ominous question — and as Madison hinted, tactless realism at that. Madison's introduction of the idea that what the new Constitution would need was an arrangement for the representation of the major sectional interests of North and South shows, however, that he had looked further into the future than his colleagues, and it stands as the only attempt to think out an institutional means of providing for this problem. Another attempt was to be made in the Virginia and Kentucky Resolutions of 1798 and 1799, when the acts of the Federal government seemed to Madison and Jefferson to threaten the liberties which the Constitution had been erected to defend. But by that time it was necessary to take the existing state structure as the frame in which a reply was to be developed. The next attempt came from the Northern side, with the attack on the Federal ratio that gave to the south its permanent over-representation in the counsels of the Union. The attack was mounted at the Hartford Convention of 1814, and although it failed then it was renewed in the movement of opposition to the admission of Missouri as a slave state. The next phase saw the constitutional revisionism of John C. Calhoun, whose schemes for a permanent procedure for the representation of southern interests under what threatened to become a northern majority followed, not directly, but logically, from the tentative suggestions offered by Madison to the Philadelphia Convention.

As Madison saw, there was no practicable machinery to answer the problem. The South got its three-fifths slave enumeration, itself a tangible gain for the representation of special interests. For the rest, the geo-economic sections of the growing Union had to find their representation through the old state structure, and by means of the many and flexible possibilities for groupings between states and alliances between sections which came into existence under the new Constitution.

III. A MIXED EXECUTIVE — PRIME MINISTER AND KING

When the great crisis over the Senate had been resolved the delegates were to discover that other obstacles, almost as difficult, still divided them. One of these lay in the question of the relationship of representation to the interests

[1] Farrand, *Records,* i. 486–7.

of population and wealth; another, connected with it, in the special interests of slave owners; yet another, in the nature and manner of election of the executive. All of these problems involved the relationship in a republican society under the rule of law, between the rights of numerical majorities and the other interests which Whig theory recognised as 'legitimate' and which it was therefore the specific duty of a republican form of government to protect.

None of these problems proved more intractable than that of the national executive. To decide that the executive power should reside in a single individual rather than a board was easy compared with the questions of his length of tenure, re-eligibility, and mode of appointment. Experience had taught that the true qualities of the small number of men whose integrity and powers of leadership might qualify them for this high office would be known only to the higher circles of continental political life. Within the several states, the common people had no personal knowledge of any but the leading men of their own communities and perhaps of a few outstanding public figures; and the Virginia Plan proposed what must at first have seemed the most practical solution, by placing the election of the national executive in the hands of the national legislature.

Almost the only strength of this suggestion lay in the extraordinary difficulty of finding any better method. When the matter was eventually passed to the Committee of Eleven with sundry other questions, the resolution of the Convention stood in favour of the Virginia proposal; and it was only with the report of that committee, as late as 4 September, that the appointment of the President was finally taken out of the legislature and given to the electoral college, to be called into existence quadrennially for the exclusive purpose of making the election.

In contrast to the idea of giving the presidential appointment to a small and select group, or to a larger select group such as the national legislature, stood that of holding a popular national election. This, however, brought out the strongest objections of two men who in the end refused to put their signatures to the Constitution — George Mason and Elbridge Gerry. Mason, an honest descendant of the Old Whig cause, who more than once spoke of the necessity of frequent elections to let the representative lose himself in the mass of the people from which he came, stated that 'He conceived it would be as unnatural to refer the choice of a proper character for chief Magistrate to the people, as it would, to refer the trial of colours to a blind man. The extent of the Country renders it impossible that the people can have the requisite capacity to judge the respective pretensions of the

Candidates.'[1] Gerry 'feared that the people would be misled by a few designing men... The popular mode of electing the chief Magistrate would
certainly be the worst of all.'[2] The real danger here was that a general election
would be preceded by just that type of interstate political organisation which
lay in the power of the commercial community, with its intricate network of
business connections, but which lay beyond the control of the mass of the
farmers and apparently most of the planters. Both Mason and Gerry preferred election by the legislature — a view reiterated by Mason as late as
26 July after the whole matter had been thrashed out several times.

The idea of legislative appointment had the disadvantage that it contra-
vened the dogma of the separation of powers. The trouble was that the
delegates wanted the new head of state to have some of the attributes of a
prime minister but some of the attributes of a king; and they allowed
themselves to be confused by their own terminology. When they spoke of
the 'executive' they thought of the Crown; when they spoke of the 'national
legislature' their minds reverted to the House of Commons. But in this
scheme they believed, on the basis of all too recent but not very closely
observed experience, that the 'minister' was the Crown's servant, exerting
an improper influence over the representative branch of government. There
is little sign of their having appreciated the importance of the fact that,
although the minister was truly appointed by the Crown, and had to enjoy
the royal confidence, he was also obliged to command the confidence of the
Commons. It is true that both Lord North and the younger Pitt were
George III's servants and avoided contravening his major wishes. But their
great value to the king lay in the very fact that they were able to lead the
House of Commons where other men could not. The subtle transition
which was gradually taking place in British constitutional procedure did not
lean entirely towards the Crown.

Had the Crown been completely separated from the legislative process, as
was later to happen, it would also have ceased to be the 'executive'. The real
executive lay in the Civil Service and its whole administrative system, which
fell under the authority of the ministry, not the Crown. The Philadelphia
Convention attempted to withdraw the executive as far as possible from the
legislative process while investing it with genuine executive powers. They
were trying to establish a branch of government, not a mere head of state.

The result was a decided weakening of the legislature. This step, which
must be considered one of the most distinctive American contributions to
the Whig theory of the republic, was the practical consequence of the

[1] Farrand, *Records*, ii. 31.   [2] Farrand, *Records*, ii. 57.

insistence on the doctrine of the separation of powers, and it was the achievement, in high degree, of James Madison.

It was Madison who repeatedly intervened to insist that the separation of powers was essential to free government and that separation meant the independent exercise of the separate powers.[1] In a long speech on 25 July he argued the point which was independently held by John Adams and applied by him (unsuccessfully) in Massachusetts in 1780, that the importance of the executive was its power to control the legislature. Thus Madison helped to break the back of the provision in the Virginia Plan itself by which the legislature would have controlled the appointment of the President. (Which was, ironically, to happen when Jefferson was elected President in 1800: but then because no candidate had the requisite majority of electoral votes.)

When they faced away from legislative appointment of the Executive, the delegates confronted the alarming prospect of an election by the people. An election by state legislatures or governors was unacceptable to the nationalists for obvious reasons; yet if the legislature was not to be trusted with this election, why should it be referred to the people who elected that legislature?

It is a significant indication of the nationalists' political character that they showed so little anxiety at the prospect of a popular election. An important point in favour of this method was that it made the national executive independent of the states, as observed (perhaps tactlessly) by Wilson in an early discussion on 1 June. He repeated the point the next day, his preference for election by the people apparently gaining strength as he thought about it. Madison agreed with him from the beginning, repeating his conviction when the matter was more fully debated nearly two months later; with all its imperfections, he liked the idea of popular election best.[2]

The idea of a specially elected college of presidential electors, meeting in each state separately, which seemed through most of the summer to be unlikely to be adopted, found favour with the nationalists as a practical means of implementing popular election. It had the further advantage of sifting the popular vote through the strainer of a narrower group of distinguished men in each state, a procedure shown by other examples to be soothing to the anxieties of the American Whig mind. Rufus King, another of the strongest nationalists, declared early in the discussion for election by electors chosen by the people,[3] but the Convention decided to permit each state legislature to form its state electoral college in its own way — by

[1] Farrand, *Records*, ii. 34, 56, 109–10.
[2] Farrand, *Records*, ii. 56, 111.   [3] Farrand, *Records*, ii. 55–6.

popular vote or by legislative appointment. A further protection for the states was thus introduced into the mesh of the Whig filter — and uniformity was made almost impossible.

The question of how to elect a President was closely connected in principle with that of representation in Congress. The nationalists, who were ardent for proportional representation in both houses, were also strongest for popular election of the executive. Hamilton, who in general took little part because of his dislike of the whole scheme as being too weak, and who had good claims to be considered the strongest believer in strong national government in the Convention, advocated proportional representation in both Houses;[1] it was a procedure that served to attach the common people directly to the central government without the intervention of the states. The position of Paterson, guardian of the rights of small states — and by implication, of states as forms of government — is extremely significant. Paterson also chimed in with endorsement of the electoral college, but on the basis of giving to the smallest state one vote and to the largest only three;[2] a proviso which, in view of the vast disparities of population, would virtually have served to convert the electoral college into a secondary instrument of states' rights.

The nationalists — or National Whigs as they might better be called — showed no fear or hesitation about the wholesomeness of the popular will. They had received and had undertaken to model a government based on the consent of the governed. Though in some form or phrase such consent had long stood as a principle of English constitutional doctrine, it was a distinctively American contribution to insist that consent could no longer rest on legal fiction. American whiggery required some much more explicit procedure for the implementation of consent.

There was, however, some disagreement about the proper extent of the political basis — the suffrage. As has been seen, the Convention decided to avoid the problem by putting the suffrage for the House of Representatives on the same footing as that for the lower House in each several state; so that each state would determine for itself. Once this had been agreed, there was no impediment to the National Whigs' claim for both representation and the election of the President on the numerical principle.

The validity of this principle was contributed to by two factors: it was supremely practicable, and appeared to many speakers as the only basis that would prove so; and it conformed in an adequate, if imperfect, degree to the ideological criteria that American Whigs held in common. A popular basis

[1] Farrand, *Records*, i. 36, 193. [2] Farrand, *Records*, ii. 56.

alone would not have done this; some means of assessing property, in order that it should be fairly represented, was earnestly sought; but what eventually satisfied the Convention was the conviction that under American conditions, numbers themselves provided an adequate guide to the distribution of property. There were, as has been noted, certain exceptions and provisions: the west was expected to be poor, and as a punishment for equal representation of its numbers was to be subjected to direct taxes on the same basis; the south wanted special protection for its slave property and was given the federal ratio, three-fifths of the slaves to be enumerated for representation. Nor was there agreement as to the future of American economic development; but those who wanted special safeguards for property did not ask for the representation of property by itself but rather for some method of mixing property with persons.

It was this sort of mixture that gave to a state, or district, what was called 'weight', or 'importance'. And a decisive step had been measured in the forming of modern institutions when it was decided that this great element of political authority was adequately determined by the principle of proportional representation; by, in short, the majority.

In Massachusetts, the majority principle made its decisive advance through the conjunction of the interests of mercantile wealth and the city populations of the seaboard. Something similar happened in Maryland, under the dominating influence of the rise of Baltimore, and in New York. It was not population alone that carried the day, but population allied to the leading interests of the most influential form of property. In Virginia, it was only when the interests of under-represented regions demanding reapportionment of legislative seats, combined with the unenfranchised non-freeholders, that the demand for suffrage reform gathered any momentum.

On the continental scene the operative principle, though not simply identical, was similar in character. The National Whigs, for a variety of reasons, saw the United States as a nation. The allegiance of every citizen, then, had to be drawn towards the national authority, and that authority had to draw its strength from the people of the Union, not from a congeries of unequal units claiming equality with each other in the Union. There is every reason to believe that the national vision of Wilson, Madison, Hamilton, King, Washington, Gouverneur Morris, Robert Morris, and their many comrades, superseded and transcended the private or local interests that compelled their attention to the urgent problem of strengthening the Union. The most powerful of the interests making for a stronger and more national type of government were in general (though not without exceptions) connected with the larger states, or with the business interests more intimately allied to the leadership in those states.

The majority principle thus emerged as the one which would give a proper representation to 'weight' in the Union much as it had done in the states where, sooner or later, it was to gain a leading place in the Constitution. But in spite of this victory, the principle of majority rule emerged from the Philadelphia Convention with an ambiguous authority in American government.

IV. THE ANATOMY OF A FEDERAL MAJORITY

Some of the discordant strains which had sounded in the Convention emerged again, louder and with numerous subtle variations, in the state ratifying Conventions which followed. The most serious objections to the formula of the proposed Constitution were levelled, not against the representative aspects of the new government, but against the omission of a Bill of Rights. Had a declaration such as that of Virginia, of Massachusetts, or that which was in fact added by the first ten amendments, actually been offered with the original instrument, it is probable that the whole anti-federalist movement would from the beginning have been much weaker and would never seriously have threatened the adoption of the Constitution.

That the effect of a Bill of Rights would have limited the powers of the Congress was significant, for the separation of the executive, invested as it was with a power of veto, already stood out as a marked move in that direction. Much anti-federalist feeling was based on the ingrained impression that government was always safest in local hands; and the deep fear that any form of government which created a legislative body remote from the habitations of the people would become an independent power, was accentuated by the suspicion that the great commercial interests, who so dominated affairs in the north-east and whose influence seemed to depend on inner channels of communications and to blossom in such societies as that of the Cincinatti — the officers' club of the Revolutionary army — would swiftly gain control of the approaches and occupy the citadel of the continental government.[1]

---

[1] The best account of the anti-federalists is that left by their own speeches, in the ratifying Conventions, and pamphlets. See, for example, S. B. Harding, *The Contest over the Ratification of the Federal Constitution in the State of Massachusetts* (New York, 1896); H. B. Grigsby, *The History of the Virginia Federal Convention of 1788* 2 vols. (Richmond, 1890 and 1891). And see Cecelia M. Kenyon, 'Men of Little Faith: The Anti-Federalists

These anxieties the authors of *The Federalist* endeavoured to assuage. In that great work, the disharmonies of the Convention were submerged, as, indeed, were the deep misgivings of Hamilton himself. *The Federalist* cannot be understood simply as a text designed to elucidate the meaning of the Constitution: its object was to elucidate the major implications of the Constitution in the light of the urgent need to obtain electoral support. While many themes which have become familiar in the study of Whig ideas of representation reappeared in the successive numbers of the papers of *Publius*, they were shaped and pointed for popular approval and in some instances stood in sharp contrast to the emphasis they had received in the Philadelphia Convention.

The old theme of persons and property played a much diminished part; principally, no doubt, because it had been overclouded in the Constitution itself by the issue of state sovereignty. Madison used it, however, in a skilful but specious defence of the Federal ratio. He observed that some states, including New York (to whose citizens his remarks were immediately addressed), made separate provision for the representation of persons and property; but the Federal Constitution did not do this. 'The rights of property are committed into the same hands with personal rights.' This was an argument for the special representation of property in the choice of those hands.[1]

Madison had earlier developed his ideas about interests in far greater detail. In that analysis of the causes of faction which has become familiar to every properly educated undergraduate, he distinguished principally the interests of those who held, and those who were without, property. But he also discerned 'a landed interest, a manufacturing interest, a mercantile interest, a monied interest, with many lesser interests. . . .'[2] Had he chosen to pursue the point he could easily have referred to the interests of the law and of other professions — that of Harvard College, for example, was specially noticed in the Constitution of Massachusetts; an army interest was painfully noticeable in American civil affairs at the end of the Revolutionary War, and its officers had grouped themselves conspicuously if not discreetly into the Society of the Cincinatti; a banking interest was already becoming a specialised branch of the more general 'mercantile' denomination; and

on the Nature of Representative Government', *William and Mary Quarterly* (January 1955), 3–43. For a general account, see J. T. Main, *The Anti-Federalists Critics of the Constitution 1781–8* (Chapel Hill, 1961).

[1] Jacob E. Cooke (ed.), *The Federalist* (Middletown, Conn., 1961), 370.

[2] *Federalist*, 59 (No. 10). He seems to have been reading Burke!

although it was customary to treat the landed classes as being unanimous in character and sentiment, there were in reality distinctions between planters, freehold farmers, and tenants that were to have deep political repercussions in certain states. 'Manufacturers' probably meant individual craftsmen; but the omission of a labouring or 'mechanical' interest is perhaps more symptomatic of Whig thinking.

Hamilton, in a later number, offered to soothe the fears of the landed interests in a manner clearly reflecting some of the arguments recently heard inside the Convention. 'In a country consisting chiefly of the cultivators of land where the rules[1] of an equal representation obtain the landed interest must upon the whole preponderate in the government. As long as this interest prevails in most of the state legislatures, so long it must maintain a corresponding superiority in the national senate, which will generally be a faithful copy of the majorities of those assemblies. It cannot therefore be presumed that a sacrifice of the landed to the mercantile class will ever be a favorite object of this branch of the federal legislature. . . .'[2]

All these interests could never have been represented of themselves. It was therefore safest so to distribute the representation that all would have a voice, the preponderant interest in any one constituency quite naturally predominating there while yielding in others.

The theme was rounded off by Hamilton, who observed that 'The idea of an actual representation of all classes of the people by persons of each class is altogether visionary. Unless it were expressly provided in the Constitution that each different occupation should send one or more members the thing would never take place in practice.'[3] Hamilton continued with an illuminating account of the political unity of interests in a society governed by deferential respect for leadership. 'Mechanics and manufacturers', he remarked, 'will always be inclined with few exceptions to give their votes to merchants in preference to persons of their own profession or trades'; in addition to the fact that they had good economic reasons for doing so, they knew that the merchant was 'their natural patron and friend. They are sensible that their habits of life have not been such as to give them those acquired endowments, without which in a deliberative assembly the greatest natural abilities are for the most part useless. . . .'[4]

---

[1] Cooke has 'rulers', presumably a misprint. [2] Cooke, *Federalist*, 406–7.

[3] Cooke, *Federalist*, 219 (No. 35).

[4] Cf. Amos Singletary in the Massachusetts ratifying Convention: 'These lawyers, and men of learning and moneyed men, that talk so finely, and gloss over matters so smoothly, to make us poor illiterate people swallow down the pill, expect to get into Congress

A number of incidents in the recent history of such cities as New York and Philadelphia suggested that not all mechanics and manufacturers shared Hamilton's impression of the deference that was due from them to their social superiors; yet, on the whole, these remained only incidents, even though they could be significant ones in a revolutionary situation; another forty years were to pass, and much was to change in the economic life of the eastern cities, before the working men took the initiative of forming a party of their own, held their own conventions, or nominated their own members for public office.

In view of the fear, so widely shared by anti-federalists of different regions, classes, and interests, that the new institution of government would pass into the control of their enemies and would somehow prove beyond their own political reach, it was essential to the authors of *The Federalist* to persuade them of the truly representative character of the new Congress. They therefore devoted no fewer than seven essays, numbers Fifty-two to Fifty-nine, to defending and explaining the character of the House of Representatives. The first six of these were written by Madison, as was an important discussion of the democratic nature of the Constitution in essay Fourteen. The arguments of these essays are linked, and that of number Fourteen might well have been used to summarise and conclude the thesis, had the opportunity existed for a more deliberate preparation of the whole series.

The representative character of the House was not difficult to defend. With the exception of his defence of the Federal ratio, which does not carry conviction, he was able to deal with all the main objections with masterly strength. The key to the argument was provided in number Fifty-seven, where Madison dwelt on the fact that the electors of the House would be the electors of the popular House in their own several states.

> Who are to be the electors of the Federal Representatives? [he asked] Not the rich more than the poor; not the learned more than the ignorant; not the haughty heirs of distinguished names, more than the humble sons of obscure and unpropitious fortune. The electors are to be the great body of the people of the United States. They are to be the same who exercise the right in every state of electing the correspondent branch of the Legislature of the State.[1]

themselves; they expect to be the managers of this Constitution, and get all the power and all the money into their own hands, and then they will swallow up all us little folks like the great *Leviathan*; yes, just as the whale swallowed up Jonah!'

Cecelia Kenyon, 'Men of Little Faith', 5–6, n. 4.

[1] *Federalist*, 385.

The force of this argument — and not only that, but the need of it as a Federalist weapon — is enough to demonstrate the extreme tactical wisdom of the Convention in rejecting any sort of special qualification for voters for the Congress; and the danger of rejection to which Gouverneur Morris would have subjected the Constitution by his insistence on a property qualification.

It was in number Fourteen that Madison took up the problem presented by the widespread reception of Montesquieu's doctrine that republican government could not be sustained over an extensive territory. This belief caused deep and genuine misgivings. It seemed only too clear that any government extending over so great an area as that of the United States, even in 1787, let alone what it would become, would require more power than was healthy for individual liberty. The American people had succeeded through a long and bitter struggle in ridding themselves of such power when exercised from across the sea, and many of them had no desire to risk setting up a similar centre of power to be exercised on their own shores. The fact that the government would be by Americans made it no better; philosophical doubts about human nature were reinforced by deep internal suspicions and hostilities.

On the part of an influential section of the American public, these attitudes were directed against what was known as 'democracy'. In its strict sense, the word 'democracy' was used as by Aristotle, to refer to a small republic in which the mass of the people ruled themselves directly. Madison, who was keenly aware of the importance of clear definitions, told readers of *The Federalist* that he meant by 'a pure Democracy' 'a Society, consisting of a small number of citizens, who assemble and administer the Government in person'.[1] It was thus quite possible for a democracy to possess different ranks of society and degrees of wealth, and the term did not necessarily imply social or economic equality; it defined the constitution, and to some extent the procedure, of government. But most Americans who spoke on the subject feared that in such a system the poor would use their majority to dominate the rich and seize their goods.[2] In a more complex or extended society, the democracy — the definite article was often used — was simply the mass of the people, those especially with little or no property of their own. Speakers

---

[1] *Federalist*, 61.

[2] Contrast, however, the ideas of John Adams, who believed that the rich would always find a means of influencing the whole system. He thus showed himself a true disciple of Harrington. Those who held that the political system would determine the economic character of society were in a sense reversing Harrington.

in the Convention frequently used 'the people' interchangeably with 'the democracy'.

It is an unmistakable indication of the temper in which the Convention opened that early references to 'democracy' were generally hostile. Shays's Rebellion and the rampages of the paper money school were fresh in the minds of the representatives of credit and property — more particularly of commercial property; though new issues of paper money had in fact received the powerful support of merchants in Pennsylvania, South Carolina, Maryland, and Rhode Island, where it had also been supported by upper class landed interests. But when Gerry, Randolph, and others inveighed against the excesses of democracy, what they meant was not so much 'pure democracy' as the strength of the 'democratic' element in the supposedly mixed Constitutions of the states.

Yet, as the Convention debates went on, a subtle, significant change crept into the tone with which this subject was discussed. The more intemperate remarks belonged, on the whole, and with the splendid exception of Gouverneur Morris, to the earlier phases; references to 'the people' became increasingly respectful; the nationalists, as has been observed, dwelt heavily on their trust in the popular judgment for purposes of national elections. This process was completed in *The Federalist*, by James Madison.

It would have been too much to expect of Hamilton or Jay. But Madison offered the American people a highly democratic definition of a republic, though he noticed two great points of difference between a republic and a democracy. The first, 'the delegation of Government . . . to a small number of citizens elected by the rest: secondly, the greater number of citizens, and greater sphere of country, over which [a republic] may extend'.[1] Madison had by no means shed his whiggism; he went on at once to expatiate on the advantages of the filtering process prescribed by representation, explaining that 'Under such a regulation, it may well happen that the public voice pronounced by the representatives of the people, will be more consonant to the public good, than if pronounced by the people themselves convened for the purpose'. The opposite danger was that factions might gain popular favour for private purposes — and the great advantage of an extensive republic was that its area rendered such combinations improbable. Hence an extensive republic would preserve the fundamental purposes of a democracy while being less liable to its defects.

[1] *Federalist*, 62. Be it noted that this signal advance occurred in no. 10, which has become famous for entirely other reasons. Surely one of the most original essays in the history of political pamphleteering!

Familiarity ought not to render the reader impervious to the brilliance of this argument. For Madison was not arguing abstract questions. He was engaged in refuting one of the most serious convictions of the day, and his method was an appeal from the popular basis of the system of representation in the Constitution to the common sense of the people.

A few days later, in number Fourteen, he developed the point that the 'great mechanical principle' of representation, which had been discovered in Europe, was to be made the basis, in America, of 'unmixed and extensive republics'. Unmixed: the government derived all its powers from the people whom it represented, owing nothing to monarchy, hereditary nobility, or any other 'estate' of the realm. Representation, then, was propounded as nothing more than the machinery by which democracy was to be extended, with safety for all interests, over the face of the whole republic.[1]

Madison was able to achieve this transition at the cost of comparatively little sacrifice of the older Whig ideas of the purpose of the republic. In his own state, forty-two years later, he proclaimed once more that government operates principally on persons and property; he did not give up the defence of the Federal ratio, but actually advocated its adoption in Virginia. We know too, that only next year Madison was to apply very orthodox Whig principles in his recommendations for Kentucky. One reason for his Whig consistency was that the early history of the American government under Federalist control taught him to look once more into the problem of the protection of special, local, or individual interests — which, being under attack, had of course to be redefined as 'rights'. There were two lines of defence, both of profound consequence for American history, though when followed out into counter-attack they did not lead towards entirely the same objectives. One was the Virginia Resolutions, pointing toward local protective action by state governments against the legislative majority in Congress — and this would one day be developed, without Madison's authority, into secession. The other was the foundation of the Republican

---

[1] This argument is not wholly compatible with the doctrine of judicial review. The interpretation of constitutional law is, in the nature of the case, partly a legislative process; and when judges who owe nothing to the elective process render decisions which affect statutes passed by the legislature, they introduce into the actual working of the system a modifying, sometimes a controlling, element which lies beyond the reach of representation. The dilemma was inherent in the Constitution — a point of which Madison, unlike some of his later critics, was keenly aware. See Hunt, *Writings of Madison*, v. 294. At this period Madison leaned strongly towards legislative power as the cardinal republican principle, and was inclined to vest the necessary 'checks' in the executive branch. Since the executive was elective his argument was wholly consistent.

party. And this achieved gratifying success in the election of Jefferson in 1800.

The second reason for Madison's ability to expound democracy from a whiggish base lay in the political structure of states and nation. The truth was that the Federal government was newly democratic in its relationship with the state governments, and thus, indirectly, with the people in the states. It granted more liberties to the states than did some of the state governments to their own peoples. By resting upon the suffrage qualifications obtaining in each state, and by leaving each state legislature to determine the method of appointment of presidential electors, and by vesting the appointment of senators in those legislatures, the Constitution left vast areas of constitutional development entirely within the province of the states. The states themselves, by their mere existence, came to represent the persistence of the idea of indestructible special interests, and special interests duly came to take refuge under the sovereign protection of State governments and their associated rights.

The United States Constitution thus left it to each state separately, through its choice of senators, through its mode of appointing electors, and through the suffrage qualifications it imposed for its own popular House, to determine the relationship of its citizens to the Federal government; although the Federal government, by acting directly upon the person of each citizen, exerted a powerful influence in making that relationship direct, immediate, and, in the long run, democratic. The closer the Federal government came to the person and the property, not to mention the liberty or the ideals, of the citizen, the more likely it was that the citizen would reciprocate by taking a direct interest in the composition of the Federal government. This the Federalists learnt to their cost when discontent over a land tax, antagonism to the Alien and Sedition laws, preparations for war, and a military establishment prepared the ground for their general defeat in the elections of 1800.

The existence and operation of the Federal system thus exerted a gradual influence by example on the political ethos of the states. It was a process of which the nationally organised Republican party was probably the most potent single instrument.

When, in his first Inaugural, Jefferson exalted the principle of majority rule, he expounded the republican principles to which his defeated opponents must conform. Yet they might well have asked, sardonically, the majority of what? The variety of procedures adopted in the sixteen states which took part in the elections of 1800 renders it difficult, perhaps impossible, to classify them as an expression of public opinion.

Only four states permitted popular election of their presidential electors:

Rhode Island, Maryland, Virginia, and North Carolina. Of these, Virginia changed from a district system under which a number of electors would have been returned for each of several districts (used in 1796), to a general system under which all the candidates stood throughout the state; a deliberate manœuvre by Jefferson's supporters in the state legislature in order to give their candidate the unanimous vote of the state. All twenty-one Virginian electors were Jeffersonians; the district system would have returned two or three Federalists. Massachusetts, conversely, restored nomination of electors by the General Court in order to exclude Republicans who would, by current indications, have gained votes. New Hampshire and Pennsylvania also reverted from popular to legislative appointment, and in Pennsylvania (where a compromise eventually provided eight Republican and seven Federalist electors after it had seemed possible that the state would achieve its own disfranchisement), it was the old and not the new legislature which made the appointments. Alexander Hamilton proposed the same procedure to Governor Jay of New York, in order to avert the danger of Republican successes when it became clear that his enemies were winning in his own state — a letter to which Jay appears not to have replied. There were other manœuvres in other states, notably South Carolina. Until a late stage in the autumn, the Federalists could reasonably anticipate success.[1]

Another factor, not usually noticed since it was inherent in the Constitution, was the operation of the Federal ratio. Since the Republicans gained much of their support in the South, and New England tended to remain loyal to Adams, it is worth noting that the Federal ratio gave them a far larger number of electors (the number in each state being equal to the number of members of the House of Representatives and Senate) than would have been due to the white or voting population alone. In 1796 Adams had won by three electoral votes; now Jefferson was to win by eight. Not surprisingly, the Federalists began, after four such defeats, to attack the Federal ratio as a fundamental inequity of the Constitution.

All one can say with confidence about Jefferson's majority is that it was a majority of electoral votes. A tide of opinion was clearly running with him — the congressional elections made that certain. Whether it would have prevailed to unseat Adams under a completely uniform system of popular voting, or a uniform system of legislative appointment, or a uniform system of representation only of citizens, is a question which may be impossible to answer but not profitless to ask.

[1] Edward Stanwood, *History of the Presidency* 2 vols. (Boston and New York, 1898), i. 60–61.

It was appropriate that this ambiguity should remain. The Constitution had not given America majority rule, as Jefferson only two years earlier had himself dared to proclaim in the Kentucky Resolutions. In the variety of state governments, as in the United States Senate, a complex variety of special interests remained entrenched — enough to illustrate John Adams's remark of 1776 that the variety of types of republican government was infinite. Truly, a consensus of the highest importance had been brought into being, under which a majority decision arrived at by an agreed procedure must be respected. That alone was a major achievement of American government. But the essential problem of the composition of that majority remained in large measure under the determination of the governments of individual states. The state, as an embodiment of regional interests or controlled by its own system of electoral gerrymander, was the political unit with which the national party itself had to make terms.

PART FOUR

Interest Representation in Britain and the Slow Birth of the Political Individual

1 . Representation in English Practice: Politics versus Principles

The great achievement of the English Revolution, which was not really complete until the Act of Settlement, was to establish the security and independence of the Houses of Parliament. Since the days of the Tudors seats in the House of Commons had grown more desirable and had been sought with increasing eagerness. The pressure caused the old rule that members should be resident in their constituencies to fall into disuse; there was no 'locality rule' in England after the middle of Elizabeth I's reign. The communities which sent members up to Parliament very gradually came to be identified as the 'Commons'. But representation was based on a wide variety of local rights and special histories: there were practically no uniform election procedures but early in the reign of James I the House of Commons gained the important right to determine the credentials of its own members.

The independence gained by Parliament was greatly strengthened by the essenttial privacy of its own debates. The struggle with the Crown had brought about a high degree of identification between Parliament and the politically conscious elements among the people, but the nature of that struggle concentrated most of the attention on the liberty of Parliament. The events of 1688–9 gave rise to very little discussion of Parliament as a representative institution. From that point of view it was riddled with anachronism and anomaly. But these things did not cause widespread discontent: they were not yet political material. Parliament did not use its new security to open itself to more popular influence. Instead it moved in the direction of oligarchy.

EXCEPT for the slender band of Commonwealthmen who claimed to be the only true heirs of the Puritan Revolution, the critics of British government in the eighteenth century agreed with its defenders in holding that its true style was that of a limited monarchy. Both these terms — monarchy and limitation — were essential to the character of the Constitution. Hereditary monarchy was essential to give continuity and thence strength — or 'energy', as it was called — and to avert the collapse of government in disputes about the succession. It also gave the system legitimacy. The limitations were essential because they prevented tyranny, and because, through institutions of political representation, they expressed the consent and embodied the interests of the people.

Limitations on the Crown were not confined to statutory restraints on the prerogative. The confidence of the king was indispensable to the formation of a ministry — but the ministry had in practice to be led in the House of Commons. It was the subtle interweaving of the leadership in the Commons with the support of the great men and their clans in the Lords, that produced a combination which could always prove more powerful than the Crown; and it was to a Parliament of these interests that the Hanoverians owed their succession. When the same combination, in collusion with the Crown, was supported by overt patronage and invisible influence, it gave to the government an increasingly oligarchic appearance. The whole system might without distortion have been styled a 'limited oligarchy'.

The quiet building up of a social oligarchy, reflected in political power, was fortified by the growth of great estates. The effect during the eighteenth century was not so much to introduce new principles as to cement an existing structure.[1]

It was certainly not a narrow oligarchy. The House of Commons constantly recruited men of recent wealth and personal ambition, while successive administrations found it necessary to make room for members with sufficient administrative ability to carry on the business of government. But the increasing stability of government, the chief aim and achievement of Walpole, permitted — and even encouraged — a degree of stultification. It is difficult to feel that the talent available to George III for appointment to the highest offices was as various or as vigorous as that which had been at the disposal of William III or Anne. The House of Commons was strengthened in its relations with both the Crown and the Lords by the Septennial Act of 1716, which gave each parliament a life of seven years instead of three. But the first object of this famous Act was to withdraw the Commons from the control of the electors. The House became decreasingly representative of what was in any case a very small electorate; and even this electorate enjoyed only a sketchy and fortuitous relationship with the people of the kingdom.

Towards the middle of the eighteenth century, great problems of war and empire fell within the responsibilities of Parliament; but they did little to alter its composition, or even its working methods. William Pitt kept the Newcastle system in being by a transfusion of energy — but did not change

[1] G. E. Mingay, *English Landed Society in the Eighteenth Century* (London, 1963), 15 (hereafter referred to as *Landed Society*).

that system. Even the baser but electorally important sphere of borough freemanship recruitment became increasingly narrow.[1]

Had Chatham's mental health enabled him to lead the administration that he formed in 1766, it is possible that the subsequent humiliating exposure of the frailties of the British parliamentary system might have been averted, at least until some moderate improvement had been effected. But even this point is debatable;[2] and no system is sound when any one man proves indispensable. Long before the American troubles reached the crisis of Revolution, discontent with various aspects of the system had cut new channels of criticism which flowed from many quarters to Westminster. The Wilkes case, arising from the refusal of the House of Commons to seat John Wilkes after his election for Middlesex in 1768, fanned the existing discontent and supplied radicals and other critics with evidence to satisfy them that the House was indeed an oligarchy, answerable not to the electors but only to itself.

It was from this episode that a revived Radical movement began to set its sights on a far more thoroughgoing constitutional reform than had been proposed by the earlier Place Bills and grumblings from the counties and the City. The American War sharpened these differences, but as it was a popular war engaging national pride, it might have done much to restore confidence had it been properly conducted. Failure was disastrous; and in the end the minister, Lord North, fell because of the failure of his policies and the consequent loss of sufficient parliamentary support to enable him to carry on the government. That, in the eighteenth century, was a very rare event. The reformers meanwhile insistently demanded the restoration of a constitutional balance which was alleged to have been distorted by Crown and ministerial influence.

This political reformation was to be directed principally at the system of representation in Parliament. For different groups of reformers the word 'representation' connoted different ideas, and the history of representation in England had different meanings. But in general they agreed that the balance of the Constitution established at the Revolution of 1688–9 was right, had been subverted, and ought to be restored.

---

[1] J. H. Plumb, *Sir Robert Walpole:* i. *The Making of a Statesman* (London, 1956), 12–13 (hereafter referred to as *Walpole*). Mingay, *Landed Society*, 36. This stiffening had an economic base. The possibility of entering the landed class was limited by the growth in the eighteenth century of great family settlements, which diminished the amount of land that might otherwise have been available for purchase.

[2] And in more than one sense. A stronger government might have made the same mistakes of general policy with more skill and determination in execution!

I. THE POLITICAL REPRESENTATION
OF LIMITED OLIGARCHY

None of the upheavals of the seventeenth century made more than a temporary impression on either the formal arrangement of English society, or the fundamental right of private property. The great forces released by the Puritan Revolution showed a curious willingness to reassemble themselves, after a short interval of experiment, in the familiar forms of the social order. The Restoration, by returning to the old establishment of Crown, Lords, and Commons, confirmed the system to which Cromwell's own government had groped its way with stubborn unwillingness. The struggle for domestic power did not cease; but it was waged, as in the main it had been under Charles I, between elements which found their representation within these forms. Although the Revolution of 1688–9 had all the appearance of a victory for that constitutional anomaly, Parliament-without-the-king, it soon afterwards became clear that King William III had brought to the throne a high sense of the prerogative, combined with a strong determination to lead the nation in his own policy.

Considered logically, the Constitution was a sort of usable tautology. As all British subjects owed allegiance to, and received protection from the Crown, so all were present, or represented in, the legislature. To have denied that one was represented in Parliament would have been tantamount to a denial of obligation to obey the laws, which was sedition. It would have been like denying that one received protection from the Crown, and declaring therefore that one owed no allegiance.

The rhetoric of this elemental composition of the kingdom would far outlive, if not its usefulness, then certainly any relation it might ever have had to the actual distribution of property or political influence. If, in the seventeenth or eighteenth centuries, a traveller from a distant country, exceptionally well equipped with linguistic and technical information but lacking all knowledge of the forms of the Constitution, had set himself to draw a map of the distribution of land, of wealth, of trades and manufactures, and of authority ecclesiastical and civil, one may imagine him going a long way before he found it necessary to infer the existence of a House of Commons and a House of Lords. 'To describe the England of those days', says the historian of Elizabethan parliaments, 'as a federation of counties would be legally ridiculous, yet such a misnomer contains a valuable truth.'[1] Such a misnomer would have continued to contain valuable truth some two hundred years after the death of Elizabeth I, and some truth for a much longer time. Throughout the eighteenth century the county, under the judicial and administrative domination and the social authority of the squires, continued to be the unit of government which impinged most directly and intimately upon the individual. A county member who was also a borough patron once spoke in Parliament as though his county were a separate state, 'declaring that, if certain proposals became law, they would reserve their position'.[2]

The county was not the only unit to which an individual might belong, or in which he might find security or representation. The realm — to reverse the approach by looking from the centre — was subdivided into a multiplicity of groups, most of them having strong ties of locality but each with its own special character. The merchant companies, operating under royal charters, and the trade guilds which conferred on their members economic privileges and a valuable form of corporate identity, represented those ties of interest and affinity that had sprung from economic activities. The borough corporations, deriving their rights from royal charters, maintained in town local government all the privileged peculiarities of the counties. These rights were brought under fire by Charles II and by James II, who proceeded to withdraw the charters of corporations by process of writs of *quo warranto*. When these had been restored, and the local families whose authority had been undermined had regained their former positions, the Revolution of 1688–9 had achieved all that was required at the level of local government. There was no further programme. The society and order of the country had been disrupted, traditional authority endangered; once order had been restored and the danger removed, the gentry became watchful and obstinate defenders of their local liberties, which meant their local powers.[3]

Freehold in land remained the most nearly inalienable of property rights and, therefore, of personal liberties. Freehold, however, could also subsist in other properties, including the tenure of office and the suffrage franchise.

---

[1] J. E. Neale, *The Elizabethan House of Commons* (London, 1950), 21.

[2] J. Steven Watson, *The Reign of George III* (Oxford, 1960), (hereafter referred to as *Geo. III*), 51, n. 2 (admittedly the county was Cumberland!). See in general 42–57 and the author's observation, 'It is an error to think of local government in 1760 as a subordinate authority operating within defined limits. On the contrary the effective government of England was, as far as concerned everyday things, conducted on a county or a borough basis with little interference from London', etc.

[3] Plumb, *Walpole*, i. 39–42.

Dr Hough, the President of Magdalen College, Oxford, when dismissed by James II,[1] asserted that he had been deprived of his freehold. Judicial offices, other than those of judges, were also held to have a freehold character,[2] making the claim to tenure not unlike that which incumbents enjoyed under the contemporaneous system in France.

The liberties recognised and protected under the Constitution were those of guilds, corporations, and other bodies enjoying official status, including the Houses of Parliament themselves; and these liberties naturally included the rights of such bodies to their property as well as the rights of individuals to the security of their freeholds. The liberty of the House of Commons meant, essentially, its independence: of threats from the Crown, of improper influence from the Lords, and of pressure from public opinion too, except when exerted during elections. The long period of consolidation under the earlier Hanoverians produced very little by way of serious political challenge to this complex array of vested privileges, franchises, and interests. When, in 1771, certain Radicals were infringing the privileges of Parliament by advancing the profoundly subversive doctrine of the liberty of the Press to publish parliamentary proceedings, they devised a tactic which in itself symbolised how deeply this new claim to liberty was rooted in old claims to privilege. The publishers of three journals were summoned to answer at the bar of the House of Commons for breach of privilege in publishing debates; they failed to appear. The Speaker then issued his warrant for their arrest and sent the messenger of the House into the City to find them. This, however, was an invasion of the privileges of the City of London; and it was the Commons' messenger who found himself under arrest. To procure his release, the deputy-serjeant of the House had to go bail for him.[3] The incongruous suggestion of the northern M.P., that his county might consider itself a state, hardly seems immoderate compared with the privileges and immunities which every lawyer recognised as inhering in the City of London!

When, in this later phase, the state of representation in Parliament aroused angry expostulations, the defenders of the *status quo* began to explain that in fact (if not in theory) the great merit of the House of Commons lay in the representation which it gave to all the various 'interests' of the

---

[1] Plumb, *Walpole*, i. 38; Sir Charles Grant Robertson, *Select Statutes, Cases and Documents* (London, 1947) (hereafter referred to as *Select Statutes*), 408–20. (Ashby *v.* White, 1704.)

[2] David Ogg, *England in the Reigns of James II and William III* (Oxford, 1955), (hereafter referred to as *James II and William III*), 62. For development of this point see pp. 458–62, 468–9.

[3] The incident is recounted by Watson, *Geo. III*, 141.

kingdom. The rhetoric of the tripartite division between Crown, Lords, and Commons began to break down as a newer and more realistic assessment took shape in debate. But a full century earlier, and certainly in the reign of William and Mary, the active economic, religious, legal, and political life of England, involving much also of its social life, was already separated into multitudinous nodules of corporate power. The greatest interest group among them was no doubt that of the London merchants, long a powerful and largely self-sufficient oligarchy. It was of these knots of interests that the realm was compounded, and they were already various and important enough in the later seventeenth century to suggest the applicability of the later theory that the function of the Commons was to represent the significant interests of the nation.

Yet each had its internally hierarchic structure, reproducing in microcosm the detailed and engrained sense of order and deference which held the whole nation — and was thought to hold the whole universe — together. No great legal absurdity would be risked in explaining that the House of Commons represented a federation of oligarchies.

The history of the reigns of the later Stuarts taught the Whigs no new lessons but confirmed all that they already knew about the limitation of the prerogative. When they and their eighteenth-century successors spoke of the 'Liberty' of Parliament they meant the independence of Parliament from corruption or coercion by the Crown. The Tories — other than those who became Jacobites — had learnt rather more. It was impossible to deny that if any form of constitutional monarchy was to work, the Crown must keep to the rules. It must be held by someone fundamentally loyal to English interests, and honestly determined to make the system of divided sovereignty — or to put it more positively, of the collective sovereignty of the Crown, Lords, and Commons — work more successfully than it had recently done.

The Revolution of 1688–9 was a Tory, no less than a Whig, achievement. It was in historiography, not history, that the Whigs carried it away as their own. Yet it was the Tories whom Charles and James had disappointed, and the ambiguity of the later Stuarts' attitude to the interest of England accentuated the Tory embarrassment. It was not without irony that under the new settlement surprisingly similar protests should soon be repeated as a result of the anti-French policy pursued by William III. The Roman Catholic James, like his elder brother, maintained a pecuniary as well as a sentimental liaison with the French court; but the Protestant William actually continued to be Stadholder of the United Provinces. Foreign advisors in London and foreign influences in English policy were considerably more manifest under William than under his dispossessed predecessor, and although William's policies lay closer to the general conception of the national interest, the more unpopular aspects of his conduct provoked strangely similar sounding opposition.

English history cannot be traced in national isolation. The foreign commitments of the later Stuarts, of William III, and of the earlier Hanoverians necessarily involved the executive in the affairs of Europe and made foreign affairs a domestic interest. The English nation had showed itself a great deal more permanent than its successive royal families; and the events of these reigns suggested the solidification of an idea of the national interest that might at times be distinct from, even at odds with, that of the Crown. The independence of Parliament became an expression of the Englishness of Parliament.[1] This idea took its strongest formulation in terms of religious identity: it had been found by experience, according to the Declaration of Rights, to be 'inconsistent with the Safety and Welfare of this Protestant Kingdome to be governed by a Popish Prince or by any King or Queene marrying a Papist. . . .'

Despite the assumption by this English and Protestant Parliament of its right to declare the throne 'vacant', and to settle the succession both in 1688 and again in 1701, it is necessary to recognise the limits as well as the extent of the powers claimed by Parliament in the actual administration of the Constitution. Parliament wanted to place certain distinct limitations on the prerogative, on the freedom with which the Crown might exercise its own independence. The Commons had already, under Charles II, asserted their right to originate money bills and began, under William, to wield power over the disposal of national finances. By insisting on shorter parliaments through the Triennial Act of 1694, Parliament curtailed the royal prerogative of determining when new elections were to be held, and thus of maintaining any one parliament in a long life debilitated by corruption. William III was under no illusions about this and accepted the Bill only after having killed an earlier one with his veto. The Act of Settlement provided a channel for the expression of the bitter resentments against William's foreign advisors while legislating against a repetition of these experiences under the future foreign succession that was already envisaged. It was enacted that no person born out of the kingdoms of England, Scotland, and Ireland, or the dominions belonging to them, might be a member

---

[1] An analogous position developed in the American colonies. The colonial Assemblies came to represent the local, territorial 'interest' in contradistinction to that of the superior British authority present in the royal governor.

of the Privy Council or of either House of Parliament or 'enjoy any Office or Place of Trust either Civil or Military or . . . have any Grant of Lands Tenements or Heriditaments from the Crown to himself or to any other . . . in trust for him'. Persons born abroad of English parents (the Act does not say Scottish or Irish) were exempt; but naturalised foreigners were not. A foreign-born subject might be made a peer but would have no seat in the Lords. The strongest 'place' clause of all such efforts in England was included by the provision that no holder of any place or office of profit, or any pensioner under the Crown, might sit in the Commons. This unworkable exclusion was soon modified by the provision that such persons might sit in the Commons on being re-elected after the appointment. No future monarch was to be allowed to leave the kingdom without the consent of Parliament; and no future monarch who should be of foreign birth might engage his British realm in war for the defence of his foreign possessions without the consent of Parliament.[1]

These measures went far beyond the desires of the ministry; and the limitation on the monarch's freedom to leave the country was a personal reflection on the king; but the Act relied on a singular degree of parliamentary support. This support was primarily due to mutual mistrust. The country groups, merging with that by no means extinct species who thought of themselves as Tories, were obliged to ask themselves what would happen if the monarchy were captured by the Whigs. This danger taught them the wisdom of placing restraints on the prerogative. Parliament was likely to exert much greater influence over the Hanoverian monarchy than it had usually been able to do in the past; and this enabled Tories to see the advantage of excluding placemen from the Commons and thus removing one means by which this form of parliamentary influence could be exercised. These considerations all helped the Tories to appreciate the merits of established Whig views. Hence the attitudes of both Whigs and Tories in supporting the Act of Settlement were consistent with their past records, but consistent in a way that led to agreement on these provisions.[2]

[1] 1 W. and M. s. 2, c. 2 (The Declaration of Rights); 6 & 7 W. and M. c. 2; 2 & 13 W. III c. 2; 6 Anne, c. 2.41. From Robertson, *Select Statutes*.

[2] Keith Feiling, *A History of the Tory Party, 1640–1714* (Oxford, 1924) (hereafter referred to as *Tory Party*), 343–5; Ogg, *James II and William III*, 466 ff. Robert Walcott, *English Politics in the Early Eighteenth Century* (Oxford, 1956) (hereafter referred to as *English Politics*), 89. Both Feiling and Ogg lean to Tory origins of the Act of Settlement's clauses in restraint of the prerogative, Ogg being the more emphatic. It is a little difficult not to think that this point is over-emphasised. Although he observed that the Act 'represented a Tory view of the constitution', and restored the Commons to the primal functions of

There was no doubt another reason for the single-mindedness of the House of Commons. Institutions develop their own inner cohesion, an *esprit de corps* which always makes itself known when the institution is thrown into sharp juxtaposition with some other body exercising power in the same field. The point is illustrated by the frequent failure — or refusal — of the separate chambers of bicameral legislatures to agree with each other when virtually no issue other than self-esteem is at stake; and more sharply still by the incessant disputes between the White House and Capitol Hill (regardless of the incumbents) on questions of imagined indignities. The House of Commons, after the reign of James II and the record of William III, could not but be acutely conscious of its importance and its dignity.

These curtailments of its freedom, however, did not deprive the Crown of the major prerogative power over war and peace for the British realm, nor did they stake any new claim for the area of parliamentary authority. It is obvious that Parliament was not an administrative body. The place clauses of the Act of Settlement were intended (ineffectively, as it turned out) to widen the separation between Parliament and the executive, not to strengthen any control that Parliament might possess of that department. The deliberative branches, in fact, were making no claim to take over the responsibility for the day-to-day running of the country, for the execution of laws or the application of policy. The legislative power had not yet emerged as a permanent arm of government, making, amending, and supervising an endless stream of statute law. In the law-making procedure, the weight was indeed gradually shifting over to Parliament, and, in Parliament, towards the House of Commons. But the 'legislative power', constitutionally understood, included the Crown with the chambers, and there was no constitutional warrant for asserting that the right to formulate and pass laws lay particularly with the representatives of the people. When that great change came about, it was not because of any logic or popular sovereignty implicit in the doctrine of the Constitution; it was through changes of substance in the distribution of power and property under the Constitution.

advising and petitioning the Crown, this is difficult to reconcile with his other observations, that the limitation on the movements of future monarchs represents the first encroachment by the House of Commons into the royal prerogative in foreign affairs, and further that the provision forbidding a plea of royal pardon as a bar against impeachment 'removed the last obstacle to ministerial responsibility'.

II. SEATS AND SUFFRAGE

It seems natural that the Crown should have maintained a more than paternal interest in the composition of a House of Commons with which it had so sensitive a relationship. Yet a retrospect over this field, going back to the period of the most marked increase in borough incorporations under the Tudors, does not reveal the Crown as having been in control of the composition of the Commons.

It was the Tudor gentry who exerted the greatest pressure for seats in Parliament; and Elizabeth I's grants of incorporation, given with increasing reluctance, indicated a persistent necessity to yield to this pressing demand from so many of her subjects, particularly when they had strong agents in the great men at court. The great phase of political advance, which will always be known by the famous phrase, 'The Winning of the Initiative by the House of Commons',[1] was made possible by the authority gained by that House in the previous century, an authority based on the fact that the majority of M.P.s were gentry of considerable responsibility and influence in their counties — and not less so if they happened to be country gentry sitting for boroughs. There was little opportunity for the Crown to exert influence by designating the extent of the franchise; in the large majority of Elizabethan borough incorporations, the electorate and the corporation were coextensive.[2] The last conflict to occur before 1832 between the Crown and Parliament over the representation of a new corporation was settled in 1673, when Charles II was permitted to grant a charter to Newark, but not to decree the extent of its suffrage franchise.[3] It would in any case seem unlikely, except in such special cases as those where a large number of customs officers were voters of the borough, that the Crown would have been able to exert much direct influence on the choice made by the boroughs, and hence on the political disposition of the Commons. It was the great borough patron who emerged as the really significant new figure in the parliamentary politics of the constituencies under Elizabeth I;[4] the Crown and the ministry, under Charles II and Carmarthen (earlier Danby), encroached on the electoral freedom of certain areas; but it was not until the eighteenth

[1] Wallace Notestein, *The Winning of the Initiative by the House of Commons*, British Academy Raleigh Lecture (London, 1924).

[2] Neale, *Elizabethan House of Commons*, 246–7.

[3] Betty Kemp, *King and Commons* (London, 1957), 10–13.

[4] Neale, *Elizabethan House of Commons*, 146.

century, after the passing of the Septennial Act and of an Act in 1729 which confirmed the ownership rights of borough patrons, that the Crown, with appropriate ministerial assistance, and means provided by the civil list, assumed a permanent share in the electoral system. The Crown then sought to be represented among the other interests in Parliament.

The crisis of 1688 was a repetition of the conflict between Crown and Parliament caused by the inability of the Stuarts to accept the conventions of limited monarchy: but there was no repetition of the debate between Parliament and the people. There were no 'Putney debates' of 1688. That is the unacknowledged reason why the Whig historians were pleased to call the events which caused the overthrow of James II a 'glorious revolution'.

The primary reason for the absence of any popular leadership was practical. The Revolution was bloodless, there was no civil war, and no freshly recruited army of the people. The Tory and Whig leaders in both Houses of Parliament who managed the whole affair were perfectly confident of their right and power to speak for 'this Protestant Kingdome', even though the Protestant Church with which they identified the kingdom had endorsed the most vindictive persecution of Protestant dissenters, whose cause had been befriended by a Catholic king.

The assumption that the parliamentary leaders represented the people had to be inferred from their declarations rather than from the actual distribution and state of representation in the country. There is a strange contrast between the activity of the House of Commons both before and after the Triennial Act, but especially in the light of the closer touch with the electors which that Act required, and the quiet, ancestral drift which had gradually separated the parliamentary constituencies from the population. The depopulation of the medieval Cornish villages and the decay of ancient parliamentary boroughs, which became so familiar in the publications of the parliamentary reformers in the later eighteenth century, had long since produced an incongruous discontinuity between that curiously assorted national *élite*, the electors, and the common people as a whole. As early as 1653 Cromwell's Instrument of Government gave representation to some northern towns that were not to be represented again until 1832; but the rise of the midland and northern cities as centres of mass population lay in the future. The gross disproportion between the few who chanced to enjoy the occasional benefit of representation and the mass who knew nothing of such exotic privileges had not yet begun to assume the shading that would come with the rise of the industrial cities with their industrial working classes. Though the decline of the south-west, the rise of London and other mercantile centres, notably Bristol, and the increase of a number of small manufacturing cities, all hinted at major movements of population, the process of drift had not taken on any peculiar political significance. Each shire always elected its two knights, and there were no great cities wholly unrepresented. The greatest peculiarities lay rather in the continued representation of almost deserted villages than in the complete non-representation of new concentrations. It occurred to the first Earl of Shaftesbury that the decayed boroughs ought to be deprived of their representation, but he never pursued the point in public.[1]

According to Locke, the following of custom without reason led to 'gross absurdities'; as when 'we see the bare name of a town, of which there remains not so much as the ruins, where scarce so much housing as a sheepcote or more inhabitants than a shepherd is to be found, sends as many representatives to the great assembly of lawmakers as a whole county numerous in people and powerful in riches'.[2] Locke here complained of the under-representation of populous counties. It is significant (at least in the light of later development in the same abuse) that he chose to mention counties rather than cities, and that he did not make what would have been had it been evident, the much more striking contrast with wholly unrepresented areas. Locke hinted, with his usual reticence as to particulars, that the situation caused much dissatisfaction; but he despaired of a remedy, because under the English government the constitution of the legislature made it supreme as long as the government stood, leaving the people without power to act. That the legislature might reform its own basis evidently seemed to him too implausible to be worth discussion.

For 402 years of the history of the English suffrage franchise the best-known date was 1429. It was then that the privilege of voting in county elections for representatives in Parliament was limited to the holders of freehold property (land or tenements) worth — i.e. bringing an income of — 40s. a year clear of all charges. These persons were to be resident in the county; and an Act of 1432 added that the property also was to be situated

---

[1] P. A. Gibbons, *Ideas of Representation*, 14–15. A paper recommending the reform of decayed boroughs, and the ballot, was found in Shaftesbury's papers after his death. But it is to be noted that he also thought it advisable to bring the 40s. county freehold suffrage up to date, which meant restoring the value represented by 40s. in 1430 — a sharp raising of the property qualification; and he anticipated the country M.P.s under William and Anne by advocating property qualifications for candidates — and higher ones than for the suffrage.

[2] Locke, *Second Treatise*, para. 157.

in the county. The preamble to the Act of 1430 recited that the purpose was to prevent riotous and disorderly elections. 'Very great, outrageous and excessive number of people, of which most part was people of small substance and of no value, whereof every of them pretended a voice equivalent as to such election with the most worthy knights and esquires', had disturbed recent elections, it declared.[1] In 1429 the New World was unknown to the Old; and 40s. was a sum worth much more than it became after the discovery of American silver and the money inflation of the sixteenth century. In later centuries not only opponents of popular suffrage, but persons who wanted to see a general rectification of the election laws, frequently adverted to the point that the franchise had actually grown far more popular than had originally been intended, and demanded the raising of the property qualification to put it back on the level of 1430. When the desire of small property owners to enjoy the perquisites of the franchise was encouraged by the needs of candidates in search of voters, the trend towards popularisation was impossible to reverse. In the earlier seventeenth century the subdivision of freeholds coupled with increasingly flexible interpretations of the legal definition of the term brought about a pronounced increase in what were called 'faggot voters'. Men were permitted to vote in respect of annuities and rents, as trustees and mortgagees of property to the qualifying amount, as holders of leases for life and in respect of their wives' dowers. At a later date church pews sometimes qualified the incumbent to vote.[2]

Ever since 1444, when borough elections were severed from any connection with the county court, the boroughs of England had developed their several franchises with singular disregard for any consistent principle. In the later middle ages the new boroughs gaining charters entitling them to representation in Parliament acquired much more oligarchic Constitutions than the earlier ones. English history had never known a period in which the common people, considered as a mass, or, with more dignity, as an estate, had been formally represented as a matter of right. That view of society was a possible inference from the concept that the commons were present in Parliament through representatives while the peers were present in person, but it was not one that members of Parliament were anxious to take. Even the later eighteenth-century parliamentary reformers had exceedingly mixed feelings about reducing the several privileged corporations to one common mass, and in general preferred to advocate the extension of such privileges

---

[1] 8 Henry VI, c. 7.

[2] E. and A. Porritt, *The Unreformed House of Commons* 2 vols. (Cambridge, 1909), (hereafter referred to as *House of Commons*), i. 22.

to a few more corporations, or their transfer from decayed boroughs to newer and more populous centres.

The transition by which the various local communities, or communes, came imperceptibly to be merged into *the commons* or common people of the kingdom, governed by and entitled to uniform political rights, seems to have taken longer than the corresponding development in etymology. The question interested Sir Edward Coke, who noted that the word appeared in the statute 28 Elizabeth cap. 3, providing that Coroners of counties should be chosen in full county 'per les Commons de mesure counties'. Legally, he observed, these commons were the free tenants or free holders of the counties.[1]

The phrase 'the common people' was already familiar in Shakespeare's time: Coriolanus, for example, was reproached for not having loved them.[2] But the representatives of the communes, summoned to sit in the lower House of Parliament, were deputies of specified districts; not representatives of the general mass of common people. It would be difficult to fix a date by which the commons in Parliament had become assimilated to the common people as a whole; the process was obviously spurred by the conflicts of the seventeenth century, but it was gradual, and may not have been complete even in the eighteenth.

That process was assisted by the ancient duty of the deputies, once arrived at the High Court of Parliament. Although authorised to commit their communities, they were assembled to consult 'for the common good of the whole realm'. There was nothing new in the theory propounded by Burke in 1774 that Parliament, once assembled, transcended its constituencies and represented the 'whole nation'; it was probably as old as Parliament itself.

The increasing demand for seats in the later sixteenth century made the right of representation a valuable possession for a borough and the franchise an advantageous privilege for the individual. In some boroughs, the corporations exercised their powers to limit the number of freemen, enhancing the value of the small number of potentially lucrative votes; but in others they responded to the needs of eager candidates by willingly creating new honorary freemen. It was also possible to confer freemanship on non-residents, a practice dating from James I's reign; and freemen going to live elsewhere retained their privilege of voting in the borough. As prospective candidates were expected to pay a tribute to the borough according to the number of freemen, the practice raised the expenses of elections without any inconvenience to the boroughs.

[1] Sir Edward Coke, *Institutes of the Laws of England*, Pt. IV (London, 1669), 2–3.
[2] They were also simply 'the commons', as in, *Henry vi, Pt. II*, Act III, Sceneii.

Every borough had its own electoral history and each its own peculiar distribution of the franchise. The right to vote was often derived from burgage tenure, which meant the possession of title to some ancient property. The acquisition of such a tenure might give the landlord the control of the votes of all the persons dwelling in his houses. Even large boroughs sometimes had very small electorates because the parliamentary borough had not always been allowed to keep pace with the growth of population. Yet by the beginning of the eighteenth century, one-fourth of the parliamentary boroughs of England had a franchise large enough to satisfy the requirements enacted in 1832.

In some boroughs a qualification to vote was acquired by residence, usually qualified in some way. The basic qualification, where no other authority existed, was generally that of being an 'inhabitant householder', and Maitland remarked that if any qualification could be spoken of as the common law qualification, it was this.[1] Residents who shared the ancient local obligations of paying 'scot' — local taxes — and bearing 'lot' — obligation to fill local offices — were frequently allowed to vote; and in some very libertarian communities, every man who had a hearth of his own to boil a pot on — and who therefore came to be accidentally known as a potwalloper — had the accompanying privilege of voting. The terms of the municipal charter entered the picture where they conferred the right on the freemen, the members of the corporation. There were many different ways of acquiring freemenship, which might be earned by apprenticeship, served really or nominally, or might be bought or gained by marriage, or received as a gift. Some, as Maitland characteristically remarks, were born free. Where the royal charter restricted the franchise to the governing body, who appointed successors to vacancies, the corporation was known as a close borough. It was these places which, because of their compact size and the possibility of negotiating with a small group of men, frequently slipped into the pockets of great landowners or wealthy patrons, who thereafter treated them as personal property and either sat for them in person or filled them like ecclesiastical livings. In these cases, the process of the selection of the candidate being perhaps the most tightly closed of all primaries, the member was expected to allow his vote in the House to be controlled by the wishes of his patron whenever the latter expressed himself on an issue. To renege on this obligation was at least as serious a breach of convention as that of refusing instructions from a constituency, and there were many who would have regarded it as worse.

[1] F. W. Maitland, *The Constitutional History of England* (Cambridge, 1919) (hereafter referred to as *Constitutional History*), 356.

The drift towards a parliamentary oligarchy in the eighteenth century was given a distinct push in 1729 by the Act which had the effect of confirming the claims of the owners of parliamentary boroughs and the traditional controllers of borough nominations.[1] The previous effort of Parliament in this direction had been the Last Determinations Act of 1696, which confirmed the permanence in each case of the last determination of the rights of elections in a borough. The latter measure made a sturdy contribution to the impenetrable stability of British political life, already raised on the foundations of the Septennial Act. Borough owners were protected from the importunities of unenfranchised members of the borough community within, and from outsiders wanting to gain a foothold.[2] The value of seats was inevitably enhanced.

III. RESIDENCE OF M.P.s

The parliaments of the seventeenth and eighteenth centuries constituted a full legal representation of the several shires and boroughs whose members were authorised to commit them to the decisions taken. The logic of this authority strongly suggests that the members ought themselves to have been inhabitants dwelling among those communities, and so in principle they were; a residence qualification had been laid down by statute in 1413.[3] But the practice of residence dropped into disuse in the reign of Elizabeth I and was never resumed. It is true that election writs called for residence, but the limited nature of the role expected of the representatives, who were closer in theory to attorneys exercising a defined delegated power on behalf of their constituent-clients, made it easy for some of the communities to appoint strangers to act for them. It could also be a saving of expense.

The Elizabethan gentry crowded into the boroughs in their search for seats. Parliament attempted in 1571 to stop the process and to insist on the rule of residence. The House of Commons sustained the traditional law, after hearing a strong warning that the liberty of each town to elect from outside its own members could easily lead to their loss of liberty through the domination of great men. But social pressure was much too strong for ancient legality, and the Commons' vote failed to check the drift.[4]

---

[1] See p. 412–13.   [2] Porritt, *House of Commons*, i. 9–11.

[3] May McKisack, *The Parliamentary Representation of the English Boroughs during the Middle Ages* (London, 1962), 47.

[4] Neale, *Elizabethan House of Commons*, 146–8, 158–61. Neale calls this 'practical wisdom', a typically British comment.

This development was of tremendous importance in the history of English representation. If the rule of residence, or 'locality rule' as it came to be called in America, had been insisted on it would have been almost impossible for an upper class leadership to find seats in the House of Commons as a matter of legitimate reward for the attainment of a certain social or economic eminence. It must also be recognised that, if the Commons had come to consist largely of petty burgesses with little or no weight outside their own towns, it is hard to imagine that they could have played the strenuous part in contests with the Crown which transformed the constitutional history of the seventeenth century. At a later epoch much of the great talent in the House entered through proprietary boroughs — a point which the opponents of reform were particularly fond of making in debate; and of course they could hardly have been eligible for these places if a year's residence before election had been required. Later still, the great political parties needed the system to enable them to seat their leading personages in Parliament. The neglect of this rule has certainly greatly facilitated the entry of ability into the House of Commons.

So clear is the force of the demand for seats that one can see no way in which it could have been resisted. Had the rule of residence been enforced, it would have been circumvented by an amendment permitting the possession of property in the constituency to qualify the candidate, and gentlemen seeking these seats would have added some small purchase to their outlay. However, if the whole picture be reversed, and one imagines the rule of residence strictly maintained, it becomes hard to see how Old Sarum, which had no inhabitants at all in the eighteenth century, could have been represented in Parliament. This in turn suggests that strict adherence to the rule would have been the instrument for enforcing an earlier reform of the system of representation.

IV. PRIVATE DEBATES: PUBLIC INTEREST

The liberty of Parliament included its privacy. The freedom of the Commons in their debates was one of the oldest and most honoured of their liberties, and therefore of the constitutional liberties of England. This freedom had originally to be fought for against the Crown. But it was never thought of as being a popular liberty. In the same sense that the liberty of Parliament was its privilege, so did parliamentary privilege include the secrecy of the debates.

If debates were made public, the liberty of Parliament would be impaired — strictly, it would be a breach of privilege; even the publication of division lists was held to be a breach of privilege.[1] Members of the Commons were elected by their shires and boroughs and entrusted by them with great duties; but, once elected, the whole of the responsibility fell on the Commons; none of it remained in the constituencies. A member might be held accountable when he stood for re-election, but even in this case his relationship with his own constituents was a special, in a sense a privileged, relationship; and it could plausibly have been maintained that he was not obliged to tell them how he had voted in divisions.

But as Parliament's business was the nation's, public interest could never be stifled. Tension had arisen in the reign of Elizabeth I, who herself warned the House in 1585 'that she heard how parliament matters were the common table-talk at ordinaries, which was a thing against the dignity of the House'. In 1589 the Speaker, in response to a member's request, admonished the House that as they were the Common Council of the Realm, their speeches were not to be relayed for table-talk. The clearest statement of this view came in a shocked utterance of Sir Robert Cecil during the Monopolies excitement: 'Then I must needs give you this for a future caution', he warned them — 'that whatsoever is subject to a public exposition, cannot be good. Why! Parliament matters are ordinarily talked of in the streets. I have heard myself, being in my coach, these words spoken aloud: "God prosper those that further the overthrow of these monopolies. God send the prerogative touch not our liberty." '[2]

The doctrine of instruction cuts across the privacy of debate. There is no reconciliation between the two. If a constituency can lawfully instruct its representative, then it must logically have access to his record to know whether he has kept his trust.

The eighteenth-century electors who took an active interest in the conduct of their members were not necessarily Radicals. Burke's constituents at Bristol took it as a matter of course that their local economic interests were the special province of their representative, on which they were fully entitled to instruct him: they would not otherwise have elected him. But clearly the Radical agitation for the opening of parliamentary proceedings to the public was consistent with the principle of instruction as practised by a number of urban constituencies at times of political excitement. Both these arguments insisted on the accountability of members to the country. In face of the intense interest generated by the public issues of the age of the American

[1] Walcott, *English Politics*, 34.   [2] Neale, *Elizabethan House of Commons*, 417.

Revolution (though not all of them American issues), the doctrine of privacy collapsed. Too many members were themselves interested in public support to make secrecy possible. The newspapers both fed and throve on the interest of members and of the public. The old arguments for privacy of debate rapidly ceased to carry conviction, and after a few years of uncertainty and resistance by the administration of Lord North, the newspapers of the 1770s were able to carry to the reading public the full story of parliamentary debates.

Between the Stuart Restoration and the American Revolution, electoral politics in England presented their managers with many practical problems. By contrast, the theoretical problems such as the duration of parliaments and the relationship between constituents and representatives, though large in outline, obtruded only rarely into political life and were kept under the control of the parliamentary leadership with comparatively little difficulty. With the operation of the representative arm of government there was on the whole not much discontent. It is significant that when William Penn appealed to the electorate in his pamphlets of 1674 and 1679[1] he invoked the Gothic tradition, proving himself a disciple of the Commonwealth circle, but did not suggest that Parliament itself was in any need of reform. On the contrary, he assumed that the electors already had in their own hands a satisfactory instrument for the promotion of all the reform that was needed.

The Triennial Act, and the Septennial Act which repealed it, may be considered major measures in controlling the fundamentals of representation. They did much to define the sort of relationship that was to obtain between Parliament and people. But in the Act of Settlement and again in a very large amount of the parliamentary debate of the eighteenth century, the interest of all parties lay principally in defining or limiting the relationship between Parliament and the prerogative. The dangers that Parliament might control the Crown and that the Crown threatened to corrupt Parliament were the themes in a recurring dialogue. It was a debate which reached the deepest problems of the nature of the Constitution, and it was revived by every breath that seemed at any moment to endanger the precarious and rarefied balance of that almost perfect machine.

The avowed Commonwealthmen, Neville and Sidney in the earlier days, Toland (Harrington's editor), Trenchard, Gordon, and Robert Molesworth, never accepted fully the normal convention that the representative part of the system was truly representative. The random nature of the electorate was to them an offence against Whig principles: the electorate was not the

[1] See pp. 79, 81.

people and even the existing electorate was corruptly and improperly represented. In this attitude — in which they were joined by an occasional rogue Tory, such as Swift, who scorned to compromise with sham — they stood outside the conventions to which Court or Country party, Whig and Tory, agreed to conform. For this independence of mind they deserve to be remembered, and for much trenchant analysis of political realities which those conventions concealed.[1]

It must be recognised that they were always a small, perhaps a tiny minority, and were entirely without influence on the course of government. Under the régime of Walpole the oligarchy of Parliament reflected the character of social life, and the people of England showed very little desire to question or disturb the social order in which they lived.[2] All this is not to say that English representation was wholly lacking in theoretical justifiability. To say that would almost have been to say that it could not be rationally, or at any rate legally, explained. However, in the eighteenth century a serious interest in theory was generally connected, rather as a consequence than a cause, with serious interest in reform.

2. Whig Government, Tory Criticism

The position which Parliament gained by the Revolution of 1689 was rocked by the crises of William III's reign. After the end of the prolonged wars against France, and with the Hanoverian succession, Parliament rebuilt its strength on the basis of the existing conventions of privacy of debate and independence from outside scrutiny. Three major statutes helped to strengthen this security. The first of these was the Last Determinations Act (1696) and the third was an Act of 1729, both of which tended to confirm the rights of the existing owners of borough franchises; the other was the more famous Septennial Act of 1716, which prolonged the life of each Parliament from three to seven years.

The credit for making English liberty secure was now claimed exclusively by the Whigs, who ceased to be constitutional revisionists and became the men of

[1] Caroline Robbins, *The Eighteenth Century Commonwealthman* (Cambridge, Mass., 1959).
[2] Plumb, *Walpole*, i. 34.

power. Consequently, the critics of the system were those who stood outside the complacent Whig establishment. On the more radical wing the descendants of the 'True', or 'Old' Whigs carried on the seventeenth-century tradition, handed down by Harrington and his disciples. On the other side, the keenest critics were Tories, or their political heirs. The most distinguished of these was Viscount Bolingbroke, who accepted the principles of 1688 and attacked Walpole — for subverting the foundations of the Revolution Settlement! These criticisms helped to ensure that the men who ran the government did not go to sleep. The economic developments of the eighteenth century also helped to keep the system alive and to prevent the oligarchic tendencies in Parliament and society from suffocating political liberty. The 'nabobs' from the East India trade forced their way into the Commons, and new wealth raised the price of seats. Discontent in the City of London also ensured that the system would not pass without criticism. In the crisis of the great wars of the mid-century the House of Commons could once more produce, in William Pitt, a leader who could unleash the energies of the nation. These things ensured that the system of representation would remain open to change.

ANY hope that the revolution of 1688–9 might 'settle' the kingdom in a prolonged stability was doomed by the very interest which William himself had in accepting the English throne. The throne of England meant the alliance of England against France; the accession of William and Mary aligned England and prepared it for its role in the next round of the long struggle. Europe was involved in England, and English political development was shaped by the relationship to Europe.

The reigns of William and Mary and Queen Anne were marked by frequent changes of ministry. These changes did not result from general elections. Ministerial reconstructions depended on the court and on the arrangements, alliances, and enmities of the great nobles who led the parliamentary parties. Elections did, however, affect the composition of the House of Commons; and opinion was free to operate in enough of the constituencies to affect the strengths of parties in that House. It was often not so much public as private, or constituency, opinion — turning on the efforts of the local member in the interests of the district, or on local questions. But members also recognised loyalties, the outline of which was not blurred by the smaller groups into which they could be broken down. The Parliament of 1702 was understood to have a Tory majority; the elections of 1707 gave a majority to the Whigs in the Commons while they suffered heavy losses in 1710. Public opinion may seldom have been national, but sometimes it could make up in concentration what it lacked in extent, especially when it was concentrated in London; as, for instance the Commons votes on the South Sea Bubble, which reflected public indignation outside.[1]

The debates on the Septennial Act showed a very real appreciation of public opinion. If the explanations offered in defence of the Bill are to be believed, opinion in the country could have affected the House of Commons seriously enough to weaken the ministry and, by implication, the newly established Hanoverian succession. There need be no doubt that the Septennial Act diminished the effectiveness of outside opinion as a check to the ministry, thus contributing to what was known as the 'liberty' of the Commons — since liberty meant independence, and independence of popular control, though not quite as respectable an object as independence of the Crown, was certainly to be valued. Opinion did not die out under Walpole — much of it was grateful and supported him. But eruptions of opposition disturbed his régime, forcing him to withdraw the Excise Bill in 1733 and even provoking him to impose the stage censorship in 1737. What happened was that the opposition came to be contained within the framework of parliamentary politics; though it challenged a ministry it ceased to endanger the throne. Though the Rebellion of 1745 showed that this development could not be taken for granted, the manner of its failure showed how far the parliamentary system had assumed control in British politics: power was exercised through the system, opposition was contained in it.

I. THE STATUTORY BASIS OF STABILITY

Political stability was founded on certain statutes. In the Act of Settlement, the restraints upon the prerogative looked forward to a further period under a foreign ruler; and although the connection with Hanover continued to be a source of anxiety and distrust until the accession of George III, the British Parliament was certainly a stronger institution than it had been in the seventeenth century. The attempt to exclude all royal officers from the Commons had soon proved impracticable; the Court had a part to play in policy as well as appointments, and the real need was for a close liaison between it and the Commons. Complete separation would have worked only if either the Crown had been reduced to a sinecure, or the Commons to a merely consultative function. With the amendment by which ministers were

[1] Walcott, *English Politics*, 109; Plumb, *Walpole*, ii, *The Kings Minister*, 138, 163–4, chapter 9.

allowed to sit in the House of Commons on re-election by their constituents, the basis was established for the growth of a flexible relationship between Court and Commons, influenced by factors as various as public opinion, the personality of the monarch, and the quality of the Commons leadership. The clue to the development of the system was that there existed among all the leading members a common interest in making it work, but at the same time there were very few hard and fast rules. The Constitution may be thought of as an organism, but not as a machine.

In 1710 the Tory squires in Parliament had enough strength to pass the Act requiring a landed qualification for members: knights of the shire were to possess estates to the value of £600 per annum, burgesses one worth £300.[1] The squires might have felt twenty years before that their position had been threatened by the Revolution, but the wars had weakened them again; they were threatened by the power of the landed and military nobility and by rising merchant wealth, itself increased by war-time contracts; they hoped to fortify the parliamentary defences of the gentry against the claims of contractors, the sons of peers, and the merchants. But there is little sign that the Act was closely observed, and in any case rich men could buy land.[2] It does not seem probable that this measure had much effect on the composition of the House of Commons in the eighteenth century, though no doubt it helped to maintain the conventions about the superiority of landed property.

The Septennial Act of 1716 repealed the Triennial Act of 1693 and made parliaments with a life of seven years the rule in Britain for almost two centuries. The importance of the measure was fully apprehended at the time, as well as revealing the principal views as to the place and manner of representation in British political life.

The first point about the Septennial Act is that it was prescriptive. Though this may be self-evident, it is not necessarily obvious. All election laws are prescriptive; many of them in some way seek to influence the outcome of elections, and some are promoted with a view to altering the balance of parties or interests within the Constitution. The Septennial Act sought to limit the part played by the representation of the electorate in the

---

[1] 9 Anne cap. 5. Maitland, *Constitutional History*, 292.

[2] Though very few could amass in one lifetime a large enough quantity to put them above the gentry, there was nevertheless, even in the second half of the eighteenth century when land prices were higher than ever before, 'a constant infusion of new landed proprietors from trade, industry and the professions'. G. E. Mingay, *Landed Society*, chapter II, 47.

working of the Constitution, with a view to producing certain far-reaching alterations in the character of political life. Unlike measures which seek to open the political process to the people, to enlarge the opportunity for the expression of public opinion as an influence in the making of laws, and which have behind them the question, 'What do the people want?', the Septennial Act laid out the limits within which the people might be permitted to speak, and determined, with pronounced success, the future political character of the electorate itself.

Speakers for the Bill did not hesitate to declare that the temper of the nation was too dangerous to permit an election, that the people were highly disaffected, the Protestant succession was in danger, and even that, owing to the ruinous expense of elections occurring every three years, French money and directions were actually controlling English elections. The fact that this measure for controlling elections to the Commons had been introduced in the Lords did not escape censure; but on the whole there was not much difference in the arguments used in the two Houses. One peer expressed the view that the forty shilling franchise was now too low and that the electorate consisted of the dregs of the people; the Bill would end the dependence of the government on the caprice of the multitude.[1]

The objections of the landed gentlemen were also aired in a style which was to become familiar. Frequent elections caused turmoil as well as dividing neighbours, friends, and nearest relations. They ruined gentlemen's estates, and made them not only beggars, but slaves to the meanest of the people. At the level of higher policy, it was alleged that triennial parliaments had made a triennial king, a triennial ministry, and a triennial alliance; they had led to continual contention. In rejecting the argument that it was illegal for Parliament to lengthen its own life, ministerial speakers replied that Parliament could make or unmake any law 'on consideration of necessity'. And in any case, they said, there was no evidence of annual or frequent elections as a matter of right or custom in the early records.[2]

The opposition ranged from questions of constitutionality to those of expediency but dwelt more on matters of principle. Shippen warned the Commons that continuation of this Parliament would not quell discontent but would give the malcontents a new handle in telling the people they were not represented; then, using the opposite assumptions, he denied that dangerous discontent existed — it was odious to imply that his Majesty had not evoked the loyalty of the people. By the time this Parliament was due to

---

[1] *Parliamentary Debates* (London, 1741), vi. 291–2, 378, 402–4, 417–24.
[2] *Parliamentary Debates*, v. 417, vi. 424–6, 449–52.

dissolve, in eighteen months, the present heats would have subsided; why, then, prolong its life now? The member hinted at darker designs — that the ministry intended to revoke the Act of Settlement's restrictions on aliens. He also cited early writs to prove the practice of holding frequent elections, and told the House that they had no legislative capacity save what they derived from the elections. Another member observed that the legislative power could not revert to the people during the life of the legislature, but must revert to them at the end of the period for which it was given. The Bill was an open violation of the people's liberties, or at least a breach of trust; a standing force would be required to make it last.[1]

The opponents denied that the Triennial Act had caused danger or inconvenience, and pointed out that ten parliaments had been elected without difficulty, some of them in war-time. They dwelt on the popularity of that Act and warned that serious discontent would result from depriving the people of their share in the legislature. In the Lords one peer remarked with foresight that if the Bill passed, it would become necessary to pass a Bill for limiting the number of offices in the House of Commons; long sittings would give the Crown the temptation to multiply the number of offices. (In 1721, the Lords rejected a Commons Bill against bribery in elections.)[2]

The prognostications of the opponents of the Septennial Act were speedily fulfilled. By 1733, opposition had come to concentrate on two measures meant to undo the evil: a Place Bill, and a new Bill to repeal the Septennial Act and restore triennial parliaments. The Place Bill was very popular, and the ministry's determination to have it thrown out caused anxiety to some honest supporters of Administration who could not deny to themselves that the growth of patronage was threatening to become a serious breach of the constitutional liberties of the Commons.[3] The opponents of the Court, as Walpole had feared, soon afterwards mounted a powerful attack on the Septennial Act, the basis of the whole ministerial system. William Bromley, M.P. for Warwick, moved the repeal. He began his speech with Henry VIII's long parliaments, glanced menacingly at Charles II's, and then plunged into the sorry record of the recent administration. His case was based on an explicit connection between the constitutional position and the enactment of bad laws. In addition to the burdens imposed on the gentry and on honest representatives who could not afford to serve for seven years (a dubious proposition), the system had filled the

[1] *Parliamentary Debates*, vi. 404, 426–32.

[2] *Parliamentary Debates*, vi. 381, 384, 391–2, 439–6, viii. 13 February 1721.

[3] Earl of Egmont, *Diary* Hist. MSS. Comm. (London, 1923), ii. 37–38.

House with placemen and given the Crown too great an influence over their debates and resolutions. Septennial parliaments fixed bad ministers in office for seven years and had produced a long series of bad Acts; the Treason Law, the Riot Act, a multitude of taxes, the heavy national debt, standing armies in time of peace, a permanent salt duty, the sinking fund passed that very session to pay the Navy debt — all these were due to the septennial system. Moreover, it prevented many young gentlemen of great family and fortune from serving their country in Parliament, for if at the time of the election they were one month short of twenty-one, they could not expect to gain a seat for seven years. Lord Bacon, he remarked, had compared parliaments to a pack of cards — long parliaments had too many court cards in them.

Another speaker reproached the ministry for its breach of Whig principles.

Such labour to increase the power of the Crown over the Parliament is very contrary to the honest principles of the Whigs, who value themselves on being friends to the liberty of their country, and it is very unfortunate that to please the Court the Whigs must desert their principles and turn Tories, whose principle is to advance the power of the Crown. But though some Ministeries disallow the Tory principles of government to be *de jure*, yet all ministeries like the exercise of it *de facto*, for what they want is power, by which they please their Princes and secure themselves.[1]

The *status quo* was ably defended. To an unusual extent it may be said that both sides were right; opponents of the Septennial Bill had feared precisely what had come to pass, while the ministry had intended to gain those benefits of stability and ministerial advantage which the working of the Act had in fact given them. For this reason, the debate, which repeated many of the arguments heard in 1716, searched into the differing concepts of the Constitution. The triennialists held that representation had a far weightier place in the proper balance of the Constitution than was allowed by septennial elections, that the House of Commons should be compelled to return frequently to its source in the electorate, and should be reminded that it exercised power as a trust. Walpole and the supporters of the ministry did not, of course, for one moment deny the importance of the representative part of the government; but they saw it only as a part, as an element which had to be provided for at decent intervals and which ought normally to enjoy a distinct independence of any external control. One ministerial speaker put this view of government with great clarity:

Members of Parliament when chosen [he said] must be as independent of their electors as of the Crown, otherwise they will be under an influence that may be pre-

[1] Egmont, *Diary*, ii. 38; 55–57.

judicial to the general good of the nation, for the desires of a Corporation may thwart the good of the whole, and contending particular interests would be an eternal discord to measures of Parliament. Septennial Parliaments in great measure prevent that influence, for he who is not to return under an obligation to ask the favour of his voters to be speedily chosen again will act more freely for the general good than if he is, and the common people will not ride the gentry.[1]

The difference between the two sides was deep. Opponents of the ministry — those at any rate who opposed on principle and not out of malice or disappointment — believed that the government should be so constructed as to seek the will of the people and be guided — and in the last resort controlled — by their will. The fact that this duty did not apply to the whole system made it all the more obligatory on the representative branch; and some of them were in fact Commonwealthmen who saw little merit in the Crown or peers. The view of Walpole and his majority, when generalised beyond a mere gloss on the politics of staying in power, was that the country needed government, and government of a certain type and force; that the House of Commons, as the most important single unit in the system, was a corporate entity, to be reconstituted or refreshed from time to time — but armed with the fullest legislative authority without regard to outside opinion. All doctrines of the right of instruction were abhorrent to this view. Local corporation interests were merely 'discordant'; and all members of Parliament were representatives of the whole nation.

Parliament, in this light, was not created in order to express the will of the variety of shires or corporations; it did not exist to find the desires of the different constituencies and translate them into legislative action. Certainly the representatives of individual constituencies had the right and duty to inform the Commons of their local interests when they happened to be touched, and might initiate legislation for the sake of those interests; but Parliament existed because the nation needed government; the duty of the House of Commons was to take its share in the burden of providing good government, entirely regardless of popularity or local opposition. Parliament alone could judge national issues and provide for the national interest.

Another measure that went to consolidate political life was the Last Determinations Act of 1696, which militated against change in the rights of borough electors by declaring that the last determination by the House of Commons on such disputes was to be definitive. Significantly, this Act was amended in 1729 in a manner that greatly strengthened the rights of the owners of boroughs and the controllers of borough nominations. In effect,

[1] Egmont, *Diary*, 58.

according to Porritt, it confirmed property in boroughs and had vast importance in delaying parliamentary reform, because it made borough owners safe against any agitation by unenfranchised groups within the borough, or against those outside wanting to break down their domination. Naturally, the measure enhanced the value of borough ownership.[1]

II. THE IMPORTANCE OF BEING WHIG

As a natural result of their appropriation of power, the self-styled Whigs grew away from the older Whig tradition of constitutional criticism. That role fell to the varied factions of opposition. Among these were those 'Old Whigs', or Commonwealthmen, who carried on the bright but somewhat lonely banner handed down from the circle of Harrington; they were vigorous polemicists and their presence was known even if it was not felt. In addition there were the highly independent and often anti-ministerial merchants of the City of London, who contributed a streak of radical opposition and in the process not infrequently attached themselves in the House of Commons to the Tories. The Tories themselves, nearly all of them descended from Tory stock, generally opposed the ministry both under Walpole and the Pelhams, without being a prey to the ambition for office which so clearly consumed the fringe of opposition Whigs.[2]

In the (now normal) circumstances of Whig power, it was the Tories who came forward most consistently with the demand for a Place Bill. The curious assortment of elements pressing for this limitation on the power of ministerial patronage actually caused Viscount Perceval — a potential sympathiser with the measure — to withhold his support, not wishing to join with a collection, 'some of whose principles tend to a Commonwealth and others more than suspected to be Jacobites'.[3]

Tory criticism of Whig doctrines was no new thing; it was conducted with poise and intellectual self-confidence under the later Stuarts, and long before the political establishment of the Whig ascendancy it had fully exposed the more vulnerable frailties in the doctrines of social contract and tacit consent.[4] As early as the Act of Settlement, the Tories claimed — or

[1] Porritt, *House of Commons*, i. 8–11.
[2] John B. Owen, *The Rise of the Pelhams* (London, 1957), 66–75.
[3] Egmont, *Diary*, ii. 38.　　　　[4] Feiling, *Tory Party*, chapter xvii.

may be credited with — the clauses placing restrictions on the prerogative; after 1715 it virtually became their constitutional duty to insist on the importance of restraining Court influence over Parliament, which in practice meant ministerial influence. It was more than a duty, it was a pleasure to draw attention to the importance of the right of representation, and of free and frequent elections; by the time of the Septennial Bill, the Tories were masters of Whig doctrine.[1]

Swift, in an unusually sweeping attack on the corruption of institutions, called for the abolition of rotten boroughs and the representation of the populations of large towns. This view was a perfectly logical development from the now accepted position that the people ought to be genuinely represented in their own branch of the legislature; Swift, characteristically, was not content merely to accept the House of Commons as it stood and call for its liberty and independence — he saw that representation in the Commons needed reform. He also demanded the reduction of election expenses and supported annual parliaments. He accepted the unlimited, absolute nature of the legislative power, saying that the supreme power in a State could do no wrong, because whatever it did was the action of all; but within that power, the whole body of the people must be fairly represented, under a duly limited executive. These were the political principles he recommended to a Church of England man.[2] On the whole, however, it remained the convention of politics that the existing arrangements of town and county constituencies would give the people an adequate share in the representation, provided only that elections were kept free and corruption were checked.

This assumption was implicit in the work of Viscount Bolingbroke. In a tract published in 1733, he adopted as his own the leading principle of legislative power and the Whig doctrine that the king could do no wrong. It was therefore his officers who were accountable. Liberty consisted in laws made by the people; they were free not from the law but by the law.[3] In his later and better known work, the *Dissertation upon Parties*, Bolingbroke based himself equally firmly on the principles of the Revolution Settlement but rejected both Whiggism and Toryism as being out of date and incompatible with the real necessity, a national union. It is worth emphasising the extent

---

[1] *Parliamentary Debates*, vi; Gibbons, *Ideas of Representation*, 24.

[2] Jonathan Swift, *Sentiments of a Church of England Man with Respect to Religion and Government* (1708); *Essay on Public Absurdities*; Gibbons, *Ideas of Representation*, 24.

[3] Henry St. John, Viscount Bolingbroke, *The Freeholder's Political Catechism* (London, 1733).

to which the Whig principles of the era of the Revolution had been taken over as essential to an informed critique of eighteenth-century politics. The king, he said again, could do no wrong; it was the ministers who were responsible for everything done to the prejudice of the Constitution. But Bolingbroke declined to admit that all the ends of the Revolution had been achieved — they were subverted by the corruption of Parliament and its consequent dependence on the Crown.

Bolingbroke claimed that his opposition paper, *The Craftsman*, had attempted 'to arouse the spirit of old Whiggism'; and asked sardonically why this should cause alarm to men who professed to call themselves Whigs and pretended a zeal for the government founded on the Revolution?[1] The truth, he asserted, was that there was now no longer either Whig or Tory, only Court party and Country — and it was the Country party which accepted the faith of the Old Whigs. Bolingbroke dwelt very emphatically on the claims of Parliament within the Constitution as left by the Revolution. In order to accomplish the designs of the Revolution, the freedom of elections, the frequency, integrity, and independency of parliaments must be provided for — these were the essentials of British liberty. He even advocated a restoration of annual, or at least triennial, parliaments. 'Frequent *elections*', he stated, 'are as necessary to control parliament, as *frequent sittings of parliament* are to control the King.' In the British Constitution, the House of Commons represented the democracy; but in rejecting the contention that Walpole's practices of corruption were necessary in order to preserve the Constitution, he added that the combined Lords and Crown would prevent a democratic tyranny by the Commons.[2]

Bolingbroke was more than ordinarily perceptive about the distribution of property and its constitutional significance. It is true that he stuck to the convention that the government was a mixture, a constitution of three simple forms, but he said this mainly to give weight to the claims of the 'democratical power' in the House of Commons. More important was his observation that the property of the Commons had in fact become, on the whole, much greater than that of the Lords — very few shares of private property were greater among the Lords than the Commons. 'Peers are in some points commoners with coronets on their coats of arms.' The interests of these two estates concerning property were the same; these two orders had no temptation or means to invade each other. The peers were accountable only to God

---

[1] Henry St. John, Viscount Bolingbroke, *A Dissertation upon Parties* (London, 1744), (hereafter referred to as *Dissertation*), vii–xii.

[2] Bolingbroke, *Dissertation*, 9, 124–5, 130–1, 202.

and their consciences; but the Commons, sitting by a delegated right, were accountable to their constituents. The only danger to the Constitution was corruption. It could not be endangered by triennial parliaments.[1]

Bolingbroke, so often considered a representative Tory, had in fact adopted most of the principles of the Old Whigs — though he stopped short of the republican brand — and chastised his Whig enemies for their betrayal of the Revolution. As he appeared, for political reasons, as an opponent of the Whig establishment, his writings were not scrutinised by the American heirs of that tradition with the same care as those of Sidney, Milton, and Locke, to say nothing of the natural law theorists of continental Europe. Had they taken that trouble they might have been spared some errors. For Bolingbroke was able to point out the basic homogeneity of property interest present in both chambers of the bicameral British legislature, from which it followed quite clearly that the interests of the two 'estates' were basically the same. Americans of the Revolutionary and constitution-making era were permeated with the notion that these estates stood for fundamentally different, even divergent, interests, and that the outlines of the pure British model (when cleared of a corruption that appeared to be entirely of royal origin) provided the example on which their own institutions must be built.

Bolingbroke played within safe limits. He indulged in much discussion of the rights and claims of the Commons, he called them 'the democracy', he traced the historical rise of their properties, and he adverted to the need to protect their constitutional freedom by free and frequent elections. But he never questioned the assumption that the House of Commons, as constituted, did represent the whole body of the people. He made no criticism of the distribution of seats, of burgage tenures, or the strange inconsistencies in the rights of suffrage. The disposition to question the basis of the House of Commons itself represented a profoundly different point of view, one which emerged once or twice in this period but was in very large measure a new departure when taken up, towards the end of the American War, by the movers for parliamentary reform.

There was very little disposition, even among the most vociferous opponents of particular ministers or policies, to attack the social order or to question the assumption that the Constitution itself, whether considered as an organism, or as a fabric, or as a pile, ought to be shaped upon and fitted to preserve and defend that order. No one could have made this clearer than Bolingbroke, who took his stand on the Revolution Settlement and proceeded to blame the Whigs for subverting it.

[1] Bolingbroke, *Dissertation*, 207–14.

The conventional belief that Lords and Commons being different estates had different interests, and that therefore their separate Houses stood as checks on each other in the structure of the legislature, continued to be repeated year after year and generation after generation. Bolingbroke's acute criticism, though it must have been widely read, seems not to have disturbed the even tenor of constitutional rhetoric. The reason may have been that he did not offer a sufficiently clear alternative theory of the Constitution as a whole. His powers of practical observation were applied to a general view which looked back, with a kind of radical conservatism, to the principles of the Revolution.

Much of the most vigorous political pamphleteering under the earlier Hanoverians was directed against the Test Acts; and, being mainly concerned with questions of religious liberty, touched only incidentally on the place of representation in the Constitution. The implication of the arguments of John Trenchard and Thomas Gordon, the authors of the *Independent Whig* and of *Cato's Letters*, which were widely read and often reprinted from the early 1720s, was that the admission of the middle-class Dissenters to complete religious equality and normal political life, with a commensurate reduction in the authority of the Church of England, would make the country safe against Popery, High Church dogmatism and politics, and any possible Tory revival. These writers believed in independent criticism of all the measures of government, rejected claims based on authority, and affirmed the basic similarity of the people in all ranks of society. It was chance and education, not nature, that made the difference between a slave and a lord; the people nearly always judged right except when misled by wicked men. These flourishes should not be taken for a programme. No one in fact believed in such things as universal suffrage, and when polemical writers alluded to the people, they were not likely to be understood to include the mob. Gordon cleared the point up by saying that when he spoke of the people he did not mean 'the idle and indigent rabble', but 'all who have property without the privileges of nobility'. The nobility were those who by reason of property and education possessed social privileges denied to the people.[1] A generation later, Alderman William Beckford, M.P. for the City of London, who was later to emerge as one of the parliamentary reformers, continued the same line of thought when he demanded recognition for 'the middling people', declaring that the scum were as mean as the dregs and that the nobility, 'about 1200 men of quality', received more

[1] Caroline Robbins, *Eighteenth Century Commonwealthman*, 115–25.

from the body politic than they paid to it.[1] The Commonwealthmen of the eighteenth century certainly agreed with the Dissenters that British liberties ought to extend to individual liberty of religious conscience; and the fear of popery, so widely expressed and so evidently a state of active alarm, was not merely religious, but was a mode for the statement of opposition to all of the more authoritative acts and claims of government. When religious conformity limited political liberty and at the same time a minister in close understanding with the court was able to control Parliament, diverse elements were discontented and prepared to say that the Constitution was being undermined, and each element demanded liberty.

When the Constitution consisted of institutions for the reconciling and working together of different estates, it seemed natural to say that each of these estates had a liberty which the Constitution was meant to defend. Some of the clearest and most significant remarks on these lines were those of Montesquieu. The success of his book, *De l'Esprit des lois*, as an appraisal of British government, seems somewhat startling in view of the brevity of his observations. No doubt it was due in part to his lavish praise of England, whose people he described as the freest there had ever been on earth; but it may also have been due to the acceptability of what he said to the various different interests with some liberty to defend.

In writing of the British Constitution Montesquieu distinguished between the interest of the nobility and that of the commons. If the nobles were mixed up with the people, the common liberty would be their slavery. Their share in legislation ought to be in proportion to their other advantages in the state — which would be achieved if they had the power to check the enterprise of the people as the people had the power to check that of the nobles. Thus the legislative power should be confined to the nobles as a body, and to a body chosen to represent the people, each to meet and deliberate separately. Montesquieu saw the two legislative chambers as the whole legislative power of the state. The executive, as he saw it, was divided into two sections, neither of which influenced the making of laws. War and peace, foreign negotiations, and defence belonged to the monarch; the administration and enforcement of justice belonged to the judges, or to a department which he called that of civil jurisdiction. But when talking of the legislative power he said that this 'power of judging' was nugatory, leaving the two chambers in full authority. And as a ruling power was necessary, for the purpose of moderating the whole, he was in favour of confiding this to the house of the nobility.

[1] Lucy Sutherland, 'City of London' in *Essays to Namier*, Pares and Taylor (eds.), 66.

Montesquieu affirmed that the nobles' house must be hereditary. That was its nature; and it must have a great interest in conserving its prerogatives, which in themselves were odious, and would always be in danger in a free state.[1]

The tenor of Montesquieu's discourse was strongly favourable, not only to liberty, but to individual participation in the representative part of the government. He held that all citizens in the several districts should have the vote, except those who were so low as to have no will of their own, a concept developed one hundred years earlier by the Levellers and later reiterated by Blackstone in the famous *Commentaries*. The secret ballot could later be advocated as a protection for the 'dependent' votes by Radicals who wanted universal male suffrage.[2] Blackstone agreed that representatives should be chosen from among the inhabitants of each district and not from the nation at large, because each member would know the needs of his own town. But he objected to the doctrine of instruction on each question that might confront the legislature. It would lead to interminable discussions and would render each deputy the master of all the others, so that in moments of urgency the force of the nation might be checked by mere caprice. He also opposed the secret ballot. Popular suffrage he accepted — but it must be public; for he did not regard the ordinary citizen as a very reliable repository of political trust. He felt that the lesser people ought to be enlightened by the principles and held in check by the gravity of higher personages. The voting practices current in the North American colonies would probably have struck Blackstone as eminently satisfactory.[3]

Montesquieu devoted a chapter to the Constitution of Britain, but his references to actual institutions are elusive; nor does he seem to have been a close observer of political life. However, much of the chapter may be read as a discourse on the vital importance of keeping a separation between the branch of government that makes permanent laws and that which enforces the laws — the executive. In order to maintain their separate existence, they must have power to check each other; in order to maintain liberty, they must act independently of each other. Liberty would be lost when these two branches, or powers, were merged in the same hands; and he observed that if there were no monarch, the executive power must never be entrusted to a group of men drawn from the legislative body.[4]

[1] Charles de Secondat, baron de Montesquieu, *De l'Esprit des lois* (Revised edition, London, 1757), 320–1.

[2] J. H. Burns, 'J. S. Mill and Democracy, 1829–1861' *Political Studies*, v. 2, 162.

[3] *De l'Esprit des lois*, 24; 317–18, Sir Wm. Blackstone, *Commentaries on the Laws of England* 4 vols. (Oxford, 1765); Macpherson, *Possessive Individualism*, chap. iii.

[4] *De l'Esprit des lois*, 322.

This is a curious observation. For it could reasonably be argued that the British Constitution, which he extolled, was developing just these characteristics, which he deplored, at about the time of his investigations. Certainly (though he noted the importance of the legislative power to punish ministers), he missed the vital nature of the connection, in the persons of the king's ministers, between the Court, which he seems to have thought of as the real embodiment of executive power, and the Parliament, which he seems to have regarded as having a limited form of legislative function. To a large extent it would have been accurate to say that administration, the larger responsibilities of policy, and even war, peace, and foreign affairs were in the hands of 'a group of men drawn from the ranks of the legislative body' — though 'checked' by needing to retain a relationship of special confidence with the monarch. This odd discrepancy between observation and theory has led to the traditional criticism that what Montesquieu praised was not the British Constitution but his own misinterpretation of it: was he under the impression that the exclusive place clauses of the Act of Settlement were actually in operation? He did not entirely clear up this question by his own qualifying remark that English liberty was established by law — it was not for him to examine whether the English really enjoyed this liberty or not.[1]

The emphasis placed by Montesquieu on the separation of the executive and legislative powers entered into the canons of American doctrines of constitutional liberty, appearing in written form in most of the state Constitutions in and after 1776, even when the body of those documents concentrated most of the effective power in the legislature and made the Governor its servant. This doctrine rose from irreproachability towards sanctity during the years between the first state constitutions and the Federal Convention of 1787, not through any additional reading of Montesquieu but by reason of events in the complex history of the American states. It gave a theoretical sanction to a set of arrangements which would probably have been arrived at for political reasons. The libertarianism of his general opinions, the high value he placed on individual security, seem to comport strangely with his insistence on special safeguards for aristocratic privilege. But in fact this was another liberty. The nobles, with their estates, their high birth and heritage, had their liberties no less valuable to them than those of the commons; Montesquieu's view that the property of the peerage, together with their special interests, ought to be represented in a separate legislative chamber might be considered as a slight twist of the theory of Locke. For Locke had argued that people freely brought their property with them into

[1] *De l'Esprit des lois*, 333-4.

society. And whether or not he was indebted to Locke, his views seem to have formed a bridge to the doctrine announced by the American, Theophilus Parsons, in 1778 in the *Essex Result*, according to which the two great and separate interests on which government acts were those of persons and of property. Since the protection of property was the original purpose of the social contract, its special character required special protection; and the two types of interest were accordingly to be represented in two separate legislative chambers. This explanation of the necessity for bicameral legislatures rapidly became a standard element in American republican theory, both because of its great importance to the practical protection of the more conservative interests in the states, and further, as a development of the grand theory of the separation of powers.

If the British Constitution had really been as it was made to appear, either by its exponents or by its occasional and angular critics, it would probably not have worked at all. Though the critics all saw through the outward forms to genuine flaws of both scheme and detail, none of them was able to do full justice to the flexibility and subtlety of the actual working of political representation.

In the eighteenth-century social and economic structure, the non-representation of the lower classes — a concept that had not yet even come into use — did not matter. Neither from above or below was there any appreciable movement against it. When the time came for the effective downward extension of representation and eventually of suffrage, it would be through profound alterations in the distribution of population and economic power, not through any unravelling of tendencies inherent in the Constitution. What did matter was the imperfect representation of the Dissenters.

It would have been impossible to exclude Dissenters entirely from political power in either local or national government, and the Toleration Act of 1688, followed (after a reaction towards persecution which produced the Occasional Conformity Act and the Schism Act of 1713) by the annual Indemnity Acts, beginning in 1728, permitted Protestant Dissenters an increasing measure of effective political liberty. The Indemnity Acts did not permit Dissenters to stand for offices barred to them under the various tests; they simply exonerated them from prosecution for having done so, and permitted them to remain in office. It would be a mistake, somewhat characteristic of the more unctuous sort of English history, to suppose that this beneficence filled the large numbers of Protestant nonconformists with grateful satisfaction; what it did was to take the sting out of what might otherwise have become a really alienated and bitter opposition.

The Quakers obtained some relief by the Act of 1696, which permitted them to make affirmations rather than swearing oaths. There was no legal obstacle to Dissenters voting for Parliament or even being elected if they were otherwise qualified, though social factors made the election of a Dissenter extremely improbable. In the early years after 1688, a minority with a special interest to defend or promote did not confine itself to Parliament, and the Quakers attached at least equal importance to their influence with William III. But it was the Quakers who developed the earliest techniques for systematically keeping their claims before both ministers and members of the House of Commons, and who, during Walpole's régime, brought the art of lobbying to a pitch that left little room for further sophistication until the advent of modern means of communication, and the use of the public meeting.[1]

The Quakers kept up close correspondence with each other throughout the country, aiming among other things to inform outlying districts of the passage of measures which favoured them, and thereby helping, incidentally, to advance the uniform enforcement of the laws. They discovered when Walpole was in power that in order to get anything done in Parliament they must first have the sympathy of the minister, and an interview with 'a Person or Persons in Power' became, from 1721, the normal preliminary to a parliamentary campaign. They also learnt the value of approaching M.P.s in their homes, before leaving their counties to go up to Parliament; they would follow up, after extracting promises, by bombarding their members with letters, and county constituents would then come up to town to watch the performance of their representatives.[2]

The organisation developed by the Quakers gave an example to the other nonconformist denominations — the Presbyterians, Independents, and Baptists. When, after several years of faltering activity usually characterised at its best by approaches to the Throne, these sects decided in 1727 to set up a permanent political committee, to be known as the Protestant Dissenting Deputies, it was gradually coming to be seen that the aggregation known to the Constitution as 'the commons' was developing depths and subtleties that no administration could afford to ignore. Walpole certainly saw this. The famous general election of 1734, coming as it did after his severe handling in Parliament over the Excise Bill, was a time to rally all possible sources of support, and Walpole made use of his connections with the Dissenting

[1] N. C. Hunt, *Two Early Political Associations* (Oxford, 1961), (hereafter referred to as *Political Associations*), 41, 83, 110–12.
[2] Hunt, *Political Associations*, chapters iv, v.

Deputies. Dissenters throughout the country were urged by their Deputies to give support to 'the Interest of Friends of Civil and Religious Liberty in the ensuing Elections of Members of Parliament'.[1]

It must be admitted that the organised Dissenters did not achieve their ambition of the repeal of the Test and Corporation Acts and the complete recognition of their religious equality. Statutes always lagged behind social custom — as was also the case with the far more formidable restrictions on the liberty of Roman Catholics and Jews. They did, however, achieve a very remarkable success with the Privy Council in a prolonged litigation, lasting some ten years, over the possession of a piece of glebe in Rhode Island. The Deputies persisted in the support of their American co-religionists until the Privy Council finally handed down a favourable decision. It was not itself a parliamentary lobby, but it proved the power of organised action in a common interest — action of a type which could also be brought to bear in elections and in parliamentary debates. They achieved more; for it fell very heavily to the Dissenting Deputies in London to carry on the fight against the Anglican plan to found a bishopric in the American colonies, and their conduct of this prolonged struggle to keep the colonies free of an English establishment constantly revealed their domestic political influence. It was influence, rather than power; but it was a force with which ministries had to reckon. The Deputies could always see members of the ministry and could exert the dangerous threat that unfriendly actions might set the Dissenting interests of the country in political opposition. According to one highly qualified observer, 'They had great influence in elections to parliament.'[2]

III. UNEXPECTED SOURCES OF VITALITY

The parliamentary stability established by the system of Walpole and New-castle was never allowed to become a mere inert oligarchy; it was constantly subjected to an enfilade of contrary and splintering movements, which prevented the stultification of British political life beneath the suffocating bulk of a small group of great lords. The drift appeared hard to resist as boroughs containing a small number of burgages were swallowed up and those with manageable numbers of voters were brought under the control of pecuniary

[1] Carl Bridenbaugh, *Mitre and Sceptre* (New York, 1962), 39–42.

[2] Bridenbaugh, *Mitre and Sceptre*, 44–45, 286–7 (quoting Bishop Wm. White (1748–1831), who was acquainted with the members of the committee in 1771–2).

temptation or threat. To enter the system certainly required great wealth if not great patronage. Yet new men did enter it. For the greatest wealth actually being generated, other than that which the landlords drew from rents, came in from overseas trade: from the Indies and from the American Empire, which after 1763 reached from Canada to the Caribbean. The influx of wealth from the exploits of the East India Company, and from West Indian sugar, had the effect of forcing up the price of seats in the House of Commons. It was a matter of endless lamentation; and it was often denounced by those who were driven out of the market and despoiled of their political hopes, as a form of corruption. What they meant was that they could no longer afford the price. From these critics the nabobs — the new rich men from the Indies — came in for all the scorn that is traditionally earned along with the acquisition, rather than the mere inheritance, of wealth.

Yet the ability of the parliamentary system to retain a certain flexibility, a vital accessibility to movements from below, was due in no small part to the nabobs. It was they, more than any other class, who kept the system open, and who, by forcing their way into seats reserved for the sons or favourites of those who were born great, checked the gradual advance of oligarchy on the one hand and the equally stultifying grip of mediocrity on the other. The nabobs, though they did not themselves form or represent a unified interest, contributed more than their contemporaries to making the House of Commons a chamber in which interests could be identified by their presence — and thus into making the representation of interests a specific, recognised function of Parliament. They contributed rather more than their share to maintaining in the House of Commons an element of really representative character, and thus to keeping it open to eventual reform without revolution.

The political presence of the nabobs was felt in the House of Commons, and by all those with an interest in seats there. As such it served to emphasise the increasing weight of that House in contrast to the Lords and to the Crown. This development, by no means obvious in the days of William and Mary, or of Anne, later owed much to the stabilising effects of the Septennial Act. The great Speaker, Onslow, looked back on his parliamentary experience to observe that 'the passing of the septennial bill formed the era of the emancipation of the British house of commons from its dependence on the crown and the house of lords'.[1] Not quite the argument offered by proponents of the Bill at the time of its passage; but it shows how, freed also from frequent reduction to its electoral base, the House was able to develop a sort of corporate life of great solidity and long expectation. The strengthening of the

[1] Betty Kemp, *King and Commons*, 42–43.

House of Commons, if it were to come about, would demand great leader-ship, and for this it was clearly indebted to Walpole — who, not because he opposed the Crown, or for that matter the peers; but because of the subtlety, the almost tactile sense of political reality, with which he worked in con-junction with them, brought to the service of the Commons the most powerful leadership that could have been found. The career, as a commoner, of William Pitt would have been impossible but for the foundation work of his detested enemy, the 'prime minister'.

The failure of Carteret, Walpole's brilliant successor, only served to underline the principle that an administration must command the support of the Commons — a principle that had been made clear enough by the ultimate fall of Walpole himself. No administration could take the Commons for granted. Ministerial majorities there had to be earned. Although the body of independent country gentlemen in the House might generally be expected to rally to the ministerial side in a division on the general ground that the king's government had to be supported, their support might be questionable at the very moments when it was most required — moments when seriously divisive issues such as the Excise Bill had come for determination to the floor of the House. A marked disposition to oppose the administration affected so large a number of M.P.s — no fewer than 267 were so listed after the general elections of 1741 — and so many seats had also to be found for those 'men of business' who for sheer knowledge and competence were deemed essential to the success of the ministry, that the openings for the exploitation of patronage as a purely political lever were greatly diminished.[1]

The Pelhams, Henry and his brother, the Duke of Newcastle, took the business of concentrating power in the Commons an important step further by going far to advance — if not finally to establish — the interest of the House in appointments that came under the Crown. The House, to be sure, could not presume to dictate such appointments, but it might suggest them; and the threat of a veto of the Crown's nominees had an obvious force of persuasion. That the Pelhams had to drop Cartaret before his unpopularity impaired their authority was evidence of the grasp which the brothers had established — a grasp which owed much to their appreciation of House of Commons politics.

These various factors, diverse in themselves, combined in one thing — to keep the system alive. The tremendous costs of the great general election contests, the exertions of the ministry in 1734, 1741, 1748, 1754, and 1761, and the strain they placed on both public and private resources, were causes

[1] Owen, *The Pelhams*, 6; Plumb, *Walpole*, ii. 244.

of intense anxiety and of a rising political bitterness among the lesser gentry and the merchants who could not pay the price. But they were at least not signs of a moribund political system.

The most potent single centre of discontent with the system was the City of London. The City, though absurdly under-represented in Parliament in terms of numbers or wealth, was of great importance to all administrations for financial reasons; many of its ordinary merchants, however, did not even consider themselves truly represented by the great merchants and men of finance who could afford to sit in Parliament. It was to be expected that the rise in the importance and war-gained wealth of the City under William Pitt's ministry should have led to demands for an increase in the City's share in parliamentary representation. Although the City's peculiar brand of separateness tended to isolate it from the main forces in Parliament, its opposition-minded brand of radicalism made it a natural seed-bed of demands for various measures of political reform.[1] The issues arising from the conduct and termination of the Imperial wars, the Stamp Act agitation, and perhaps above all the question of the East India Company, breathed new life into Parliament as a forum of debating and determining national policies. It was inevitable that its performance should be watched with intense vigilance by those who had begun to doubt its representative competence.

Not only were the wealth and importance of the City enhanced by the Great War for the Empire, but so also was the political character of the House of Commons. William Pitt was, to use a later phrase, a superb House of Commons man. That he could be called 'the Great Commoner' distinguished him from the run of noblemen; but he did more than mobilise the House behind his war effort — his career galvanised it, for the first time since the Septennial Act and perhaps as never before, into a nationally representative institution.

The early years of George III's reign neither strengthened the intrinsic claims of the House of Commons, nor satisfied any of the discontented elements that the existing state of representation would be likely to admit of any prospect of better policies. What was needed to rally the people (especially in the London area) was a touch of drama and a flash of leadership; the grass was dry, and the firebrand appeared in the person of John Wilkes. The outcry that went up over the refusal of the House of Commons to recognise Wilkes's election as Member for Middlesex, though very much a local affair, was quickly linked with more general issues. Societies were formed; Old Whigs and new Radicals converged in a new impulse; political excite-

[1] Sutherland, *City of London*, 60–61, 66–67.

ment rose, a widening reading public insisted on being fed with reports of the debates in Parliament; and members, sensing the changing climate, sought outside support by supplying the printers with copies of their speeches.

The excitement might have been kept mainly to the City and the more democratic constituencies, had it not been for the American War. Being a popular war, that conflict tended to strengthen both the Commons and the ministry. It was not the debating of the issues of representation between the Colonies and the mother country that impelled the new reformist wave in Britain; America had few sympathisers, and the American arguments had little bearing on British political arrangements. What really affected the domestic politics of representation was not American reasoning but American resistance. The miscarriage of the War, the entry of France, the incompetence of soldiers and ministers, the rise of taxation, and in the end the dreary prospect of failure — these things excited a discontent that looked beyond the composition of the ministry of Lord North to the fundamental relations between Crown and Parliament, and to the character and composition of the House of Commons itself.

3. Old Whigs in New Battles

The upheavals of the 1760s, added to the discontent with the ineffectiveness of parliamentary representation, portended a new wave of unrest. The issues surrounding the East India Company, the Wilkes affair, and the American Colonies gave rise not merely to a new opposition but to a new criticism of the working of the Constitution.

It was never in any sense a united opposition. Representatives of the counties felt aggrieved by the use of Treasury funds to fight county elections and influence M.P.s; they also resented the competition of new wealth which they could not match; and many of them were jealous of the aristocracy. Another branch of the reform movement, tracing their descent to the Old Whigs, demanded much more radical extension of suffrage and redistribution of parliamentary seats. The difference between the moderate reformers and the Old Whigs could be traced in their attitudes to English history. The moderates looked back to 1689 and wanted only to purge away the corruption that had eaten into the system in the eighteenth century. The more radical forces looked back to a supposed Gothic Constitution which had been overthrown by the Normans. These different reformist elements might agree on certain points — both for example wanted to increase the representation of the counties. But they really belonged to different schools of thought, and the differences would grow more distinct as all their efforts were frustrated.

IN 1769, on the merits of three expulsions from the House of Commons in rapid succession, John Wilkes achieved the strange confluence of his own disorderly career with the history of British liberties. The Commons, as a kind of corollary to their right, gained in 1603, to determine the qualifications of their members, had also occasionally exercised the power of expelling a member for misconduct. Colonial Assemblies did the same thing often enough to make it clear that they regarded the right as a normal attribute of legislative independence.[1] Wilkes, three times returned for Middlesex, was expelled from the House of Commons, the seat being awarded after the third election to his rival candidate. He got back into the Commons in 1774 and after persistent efforts he persuaded them in 1782 to expunge the resolution declaring his 'incapacity' from their records, 'as being subversive of the rights of the whole body of electors in this Kingdom'.[2]

If the administration did not deserve the charges of tyranny, it had a title to some of the opprobrium to which it was subjected by the opposition both in and out of Parliament. No section of constitutional theory could be made to defend the exercise by the House of Commons of a proscriptive veto on the choice of the electors.

I. OPPOSITION

The Wilkes affair brought a new factor into the smouldering, eruptive fires of radical opposition. It was the force of sustained, purposeful organisation. While Wilkes remained in prison, his friends, led by the inflammatory parson John Horne (later Horne Tooke), founded the Society of Supporters

---

[1] Mary P. Clarke, *Parliamentary Privilege in the American Colonies* (New Haven, Conn., 1943), 268. As recently as 1920 the Assembly of New York refused to seat six duly elected representatives because they were Socialists.

[2] George Rudé, *Wilkes and Liberty* (Oxford, 1962); Ian R. Christie, *Wilkes, Wyvill and Reform* (London, 1962), chapter 2.

of the Bill of Rights. The Society was split by Wilkes's return and the discovery of his adherents that his own interest in liberty was that of filling his own purse. But as early as June 1771 the residue of the Society announced its policy of requiring candidates at elections to give pledges, signed and confirmed on oath, that if elected they would work to shorten the duration of parliaments, reduce the number of placemen in the House of Commons 'and endeavour to obtain a more fair and equal representation of the people'.[1] Reformers came to sit in Parliament regularly for the London constituencies and made a practice of putting reform motions into the agenda of parliamentary debates. Through these debates, through the writings of Junius and of other political controversialists such as Almon, Mrs Catherine Macaulay, and James Burgh, the ideas of the Old Whigs were given new spirit.

The more radical reformers had no expectations of power. Their ideas had had little appeal for the Rockingham group, who still hoped to form a ministry. Yet if any progress were to be made, some sort of alliance, or convergence of these forces was required. The practical possibilities of an alliance between reformist forces inside and outside Parliament actually strengthened after the death of Rockingham (1 July 1782) with the advent, after the failure of the Fox-North coalition, of the younger Pitt. The Yorkshire Association movement, which rose in 1780 to develop an impressive show of strength for the next few years, was a product of the organising zest of Christopher Wyvill. It is not difficult to see in the light of history that the movement had little chance of achieving any fundamental reform, that its appeal was limited and its immediate force derived from discontent over transient rather than permanent grievances. Assuredly, however, the movement gathered up the various strands of contemporary criticism of the system of representation, so that the theoretical suppositions, the characteristics and extent of that criticism can be examined in its records.

Pitt, the movement's main hope, had lost interest before the French Revolution. But the line did not die out. The young Charles Grey reintroduced the issue of parliamentary reform with a motion in the Commons in May 1793. The newly formed and somewhat aristocratic Society of the Friends of the People joined John Cartwright's Society for Constitutional Information (founded in 1780) in the work of disseminating theories and developing the habit of discussion of constitutional rights as a prelude to

[1] Christie, *Wilkes, Wyvill and Reform*, 48. The idea was advanced earlier by Mrs Macaulay in her attack on Burke, *Observations on a Pamphlet entitled Thoughts on the Cause of the Present Discontents* (London, 1770).

political action. But the French Revolution had a complex effect on British politics. All the supporters of the government contracted their muscles in horror and readied themselves politically as for the defence of a fortress. But not so the Foxite Whigs, who never confessed to the same fears and continued with startling liberty to attack the entire policy of the government. Meanwhile, the artisans in some of the older centres of craft manufactures began to get the idea of political action. They were rallied by the French example, corresponded with Jacobin clubs, and addressed each other as 'citizen'. From this side sprang the London Corresponding Society and the societies which kept in touch with it in the manufacturing north.

All of these groups claimed some strand of descent from the old English Whig tradition, though they differed widely as to the proper ingredients of true contemporary whiggery. But it would be a mistake and a misunderstanding to suppose that all ideas about representative government were the property of one or another branch of reformers. The reformist campaigns, though they failed in their political objects, achieved two broad and interesting types of result. In the first place they forced the opponents of reform, from Lord North onwards, to define their views of the Constitution, to offer an intelligible defence of practices that were attacked as abuses, and even to examine their own assumptions as to the meaning of representation. This process led to the second gain, which was a marked, if gradual, increase in the House of Commons' sense of public accountability for its own conduct. To a certain extent, Parliament reformed itself. Moreover, although it suited Burke and the Rockinghams to call the King's Friends 'Tories', Lord North and his successors were defending a system which they had inherited from the undisputed Whigs of the earlier eighteenth century. Might not Lord North, that charming and witty debater, have replied to his critics, 'We are all Whigs now'?[1]

---

[1] The best-informed account of the political reform movements between the Wilkes affair and the decline of the Yorkshire Association is in Christie, *Wilkes, Wyvill and Reform*. G. S. Veitch, *The Genesis of Parliamentary Reform*, first published 1913, reprinted with an introduction by Ian R. Christie (London, 1964), was an admirable pioneer work which retains much of its quality. Herbert Butterfield, *George III, Lord North and the People* (Cambridge, 1949), also examines the Yorkshire movement. The course of political events as chronicled in these works must be assumed as the ground of the present discussion, which is mainly concerned with opinion.

II. GOOD GOVERNMENT: HOW IT WAS FOUND
AND LOST AGAIN

Except in moments of self-congratulation, persons in power seldom speculate on the objects of government. That type of enquiry is a privilege reserved for the leisure of opposition, but eighteenth-century politics produced enough opposition to make sure that the question would not be lost sight of.

No Whig could deny that government was in some sense a trust. That fundamental tenet had been stated by Locke[1] in reply to Filmer's reassertion of the principle that government was based on authority derived from a divine right. Good government, therefore, fulfilled the conditions of the trust by acting for the general good. The Scottish philosopher Francis Hutcheson, who anticipated the more formal doctrines of the Utilitarians and was a teacher of Adam Smith, maintained that the prosperity of the whole community was the criterion of whether the trust of power was properly exercised, and he did not shrink from asserting the right of resistance to tyranny and the right of ill-treated colonies to separate themselves from their mother country.[2] An important feature of this view was that the colonies were to be the judges of the case. Dr Joseph Priestley, directing his attention to kindred problems, also observed that the object of government was 'the happiness of the whole community',[3] a view which implied that each member of the community should be made as happy as government could help him to be. But these general statements, though not so platitudinous in their time as they came to appear, could hardly strike fear into the hearts of a powerful oligarchy ruling to its own satisfaction. Locke himself had not taken the case beyond general terms.

An abuse of the fiduciary character of government, sufficient to cause dissatisfaction or even revolt, would bring the question of representation back into the discussion; but only by degrees. Locke's general aims could in

---

[1] Locke, *Second Treatise*, sections 141–2; also implied in 110–12 and 149.

[2] Robbins, *Eighteenth Century Commonwealthman*, 186–95. Francis Hutcheson, *System of Moral Philosophy*, 2 vols. (London, 1755), and *Enquiry Concerning Moral Good and Evil* (1738).

[3] Joseph Priestley, *An Essay on the First Principles of Government* (London, 1768), 56.

Jeremy Bentham considered himself indebted to this expression for the origin of the phrase 'the greatest happiness of the greatest number'. See Joseph Priestley in *Dictionary of National Biography*.

fact be achieved to a measure that the people would tolerate without treating the reform of representation as an urgent matter.

Many of the objects of government, particularly in times of peace, would seem to have been attainable without recourse to a detailed application of first principles; but when political power was exercised as an attribute of private privilege, or even as a right of property, the fiduciary principle could be reshaped into a weapon of attack on government. By the time of the discrediting of the North administration, it could be given a renewed practical meaning. But it could also draw forth some sophisticated re-formulations of the opposite view. From the American War, the full range of issues involving political representation was threshed out on the floor of the House of Commons in a recurring debate that may be said to have lasted until the enfranchisement of women in the twentieth century.

'Did freedom depend on every individual being represented in that House?' (the Commons) asked Lord North, in one of the debates on Alderman Sawbridge's annual motion to shorten the duration of parliaments; 'certainly not; for that House, constituted as it was, represented the whole Kingdom. Freedom depended on a very different circumstance. He was free, because he lived in a country governed by equal laws.' He questioned whether reform was really desired by the people, and in an attack on the doctrine of instruction he nicely turned the fiduciary argument on the reformers. Members were not sent there to represent a province, as in the States-General of the Netherlands, but were sent there 'as trustees to act for the benefit and ajudge for the whole kingdom'. The minute a member took his seat as member for Banbury, Helleston, or Old Sarum he was to consider himself a representative of all England.[1] The acrimonious debate on the measure to disfranchise the borough of Cricklade for corruption called forth some very frank statements on the rights of property in the suffrage franchise. The franchise, said Lord Loughborough, 'was daily bought and sold', and instead of observing that it ought not to be bought and sold he concluded that it was 'consequently a species of property'. He agreed with Lord Mansfield, who argued for the same reason that a disfranchisement Bill was therefore a Bill of pains and penalties. The interesting point about this argument is that it was directed at the question, not of the right to exercise the vote, but of the value — the cash value — of that right. Cricklade was to be merged into a larger constituency, taking away its right to be represented as a corporation without depriving its inhabitants of their votes as individuals. Lord Mansfield 'would

[1] *Cobbett's Parliamentary History of England, 1066–1803* 36 vols. (London, 1806–20), xxiv (16 June 1784), 987–91.

never bear to be seriously told, that the property within the borough would not be seriously affected by the franchise being multiplied'. Crewe's bill to disfranchise revenue officers — intended as a blow at the influence of the Crown — was opposed in 1782 on the ground that it would deprive men of a property right arising from freehold tenure; one member said this went against Magna Charta, according to which no man was to be disseized of his freehold without the judgment of his peers. The Tory argument here came very close to that of Wilkes, who had cited the opinion of Lord Chief Justice Holt in the case of *Ashby* v. *White* (1704): a man's freehold was a common law right and the right of voting was annexed by law to the freehold. It was 'of the nature of his freehold and must depend on it'.[1] But Fox, putting on true Whig colours, declared in answer to North that charters and governments alike were no form of property, but were trusts for the public good; and the Duke of Richmond, speaking after Mansfield in the Lords, asserted that 'that very public who delegated the trust for the benefit of the whole community, were at all times, and as often as occasion presented itself, fully competent to new model and frame the extent of the trust; or in the event of abuse, totally to withdraw it, either by transferring that right to others, to participate with them, or finally, if necessity should call for the measure, to annihilate the franchise.'[2] Yet in the Revenue Officers Bill, Mansfield himself of all people flashed the sword of true whiggery. Place Bills, he declared, said who could not sit in Parliament; but this Bill 'takes away at one stroke what every Englishman is entitled to consider as his inalienable birthright'.[3] Every Englishman! Inalienable birthright! Whom had Mansfield been reading?

Crewe's Act was one of three, the others being Burke's Act for the Reform of the Establishment and Clerke's Act for the Exclusion of Government Contractors (from seats in the Commons), which the Rockingham Whigs, now back in office in alliance with Shelburne, after the fall of North, passed through Parliament in the spring of 1782. These measures implemented the programme of Economical Reform. Their passage in turn exposed

[1] The same view has a curiously different aspect when it appears in America. The right of the Assistants in Massachusetts Bay to their office, declared John Cotton in a sermon, was 'as inviolable as that of a private citizen to his freehold' (Haynes, *Representation and Suffrage*, 23). Yet, though this statement refers to office rather than to the suffrage, it is unmistakably from the same standpoint. Public position is a branch of private right.

[2] Cobbett, *Parliamentary History*, xxii (13 May 1782), 1389; xxii (17 April 1782), 1336–43; xviii (22 February 1775), 358–67; xxii. 761–3, 1391–3. Robertson, *Select Statutes*, 408–20.

[3] Cobbett, *Parliamentary History*, xxiii. 96. For debate on bribery see (ibid.) xxiv. 765–8.

the weakness of the field for parliamentary reform, to which Shelburne — the disciple of Chatham — was favourable, but which encountered the hostility of Rockingham and the Cavendish connection.[1]

The three Acts were more pragmatic, less doctrinaire, than was the programme for reform of representation. Nevertheless they represented a doctrine. It was that of the Rockingham Party, as developed in opposition to the King's Friends, and which burgeoned into a concerted attack on the influence of the Crown in Parliament. The principle was that of restoring the due weight of the Commons; but what the new administration did not admit was the charge that the Commons as constituted gave a defective representation of the people. They suffered no doctrinal pangs about disfranchising a large number of subjects who happened to make their livings as employees of the Crown, or about extending the practice of exclusion from Parliament to merchants who happened to have government contracts. It would be difficult to find an action that brings out more clearly the contrast between the ideas of the different branches of reformers. Yorkshire and Westminster reformers might be willing to disfranchise as a punishment for corruption, but their interest pointed to a genuine extension of the representative character of the Commons, while the Rockinghams sacrificed 'rights' in the interest of 'balance' and the people called Tories indignantly defended the right of suffrage. Those Tories who did so because they believed in maintaining the market value of the property could be confuted out of Locke; but when their spokesmen defended the individual franchise as a right inhering in freehold property they were better Whigs than their opponents.

All demands for any type of reform had in common the assumption that Britain was badly governed. By 1780 that was not a difficult view to maintain, but it was symptomatic of the deep and grudging discontent rumbling through the country that so much of the opposition carried its charges far beyond the persons and mistakes of the ministry and asserted that the reforms needed were of a constitutional, not merely a political, order. The correct defence against these charges was to claim that the country already enjoyed good government and that recent failures were not blameable on disorders in the Constitution.

Lord North took the floor to oppose Pitt's motion for reform in 1783. No proof had been offered that the Constitution was defective, he said, and turning to criticisms of the disasters of recent history he offered a remarkable piece of evidence of a strange disjunction that was still possible in eighteenth-

[1] Christie, *Wilkes, Wyvill and Reform*, 142–3.

century political thought. Disasters there had been, but '. . . these evils, these misfortunes, these calamities, were as little imputable to any defect in the constitution, as the earthquake in Lisbon had to do with the frame of government in that country'.[1]

Both defence and attack relied upon constitutional aesthetics. Pitt wanted to remove defects which threatened to destroy 'the most beautiful fabric of government in the world'. North wanted to preserve it as being 'the most beautiful fabric that had ever existed perhaps from the beginning of time'.[2] Beauty was discovered in order, in the harmonious relationships of the elements of a grand composition, or design; and not least important, beauty belonged in the happiness these things could produce. The rumblings of a new Romantic movement could no doubt be detected in a few works of art; perhaps there were hints of it in Burke; but it had not begun to disturb the platitudes of parliamentary discourse.

The Conservatives — as they deserve to be called — in due course worked out a full theory of representation, or rather, refashioned the material which lay to hand, in justification of existing institutions. But the initiative lay with the reformers. There were moments at which some of them may even have thought they could win.

III. HISTORY AS A WITNESS: SAXONS AND PLANTAGENETS VIEW THE EIGHTEENTH CENTURY

Everyone who believed in the necessity for reform believed, by definition, that things had got worse. But when had they started to get worse, and what had they been like before? On those questions the more radical reformers diverged sharply from the stately Whig peers with their parliamentary followers. Few subjects are more interesting or more revealing than the views of history entertained by reformers in politics; it was by their views of English history that the groups under discussion defined their relationship to contemporary problems.

The claim of reformers that what they aimed to do was not to innovate but to restore the Constitution was no mere point of tactics. It is clear that they deeply believed in the validity of this view of the past and that their belief that the Constitution had been corrupted from an earlier and purer form gave

---

[1] Cobbett, *Parliamentary History*, xxiii. 848–53.
[2] Cobbett, *Parliamentary History*, xxii (7 May 1782), 1416, xxv. 456.

passion to their denunciations of the wicked men who had corrupted it. One of the leading essays on the whole subject was Burke's *Thoughts on the Cause of the Present Discontents*, which has coloured generations of historical writing on the dark designs of the King's Friends. The supplanting of the enlightened ministry of his patron, the Marquess of Rockingham, by the administrations of Chatham, of Grafton, and finally of North — the worst, because his régime showed signs of stability — amounted for Burke to something like an unconstitutional usurpation of power. Burke was, however, very far from admitting that the system of representation needed any reform: speaking against Pitt's first motion for a committee to enquire into the representation of the commons, in May 1782, he asserted that the House had remained essentially the same — an aggregate collection of three parts; knights, burgesses, and citizens — 'for at least five hundred years'. Pursuing his convictions round a persuasive intellectual circuit, he then deduced the original principles on which the House of Commons stood from its present condition and argued from its present condition that there could have been no serious departure from its original principle.[1] But in the more radical or truer Old Whig view, corruption had been eating into the system for so long a time that one might have wondered that any of it had survived.

The Anglo-Saxons, it must be admitted, had by this period begun to lose their grip on the Old Whig imagination. The main emphasis now fell on the fidelity with which certain Plantagenet kings had adhered to the principle of annual parliaments and equal representation. Major Cartwright, in his first important controversial pamphlet, *Take your Choice!*[2] praised the British Constitution as being, in its genuine spirit and purity, harmonious with the law of nature, while he called the common law the perfection of human reason; innovations, he admitted, could improve, but should be watched carefully. But then he came to the point: making parliaments annual and representation equal would be no innovation; they were the ancient practice of the Constitution. Granville Sharp, whose pamphlets on reform were printing many times as the movement gathered, emphasised the need to enforce the ancient law (which was being reintroduced in America in the new state Constitutions, though he may not have known the fact) that both electors and elected must be residents of their districts. 'In eodem comitatu commorantes et residentes' appeared in a writ which Sharp quoted on the authority of Prynne. That annual parliaments were 'the most ancient and

[1] *Works of the Rt. Hon. Edmund Burke* (London, 1834), ii. 486–90.
[2] London, 1776. The name reminds one of Paine's *Common Sense* in its refreshing brevity.

salutary right of the commons of Great Britain' was the argument contained in the title of another pamphlet, and supported by much reference to the statutes and parliamentary writs of Edward III, in almost every year of whose reign writs had been issued to the sheriffs for new elections. Against Blackstone, who said that these statutes empowered the king to hold annual parliaments only 'if need be', Sharp argued from the writs that the phrase 'if need be' permitted the king to hold them oftener than once a year. The order to hold annual parliaments was absolute.[1] These authorities constituted the respectable stock-in-trade of the Old Whigs or new Radical reformers whenever they came to their theme of annual parliaments. There is every reason to think that they were right. The Acts of Edward III, passed in 1330 and 1362, enjoin the holding of annual parliaments at a period when the calling of a new parliament invariably meant new elections; the practice of keeping a parliament in being through prorogation had not been invented. But from the reign of Edward IV, and especially under the Tudors, parliaments were held with less regularity and were often kept in being for more than one year.[2] There could, however, be little foundation in the documents for the view that these early parliaments represented the people on a basis of numerical equality. The shires and communes were not required to send representatives in numbers proportionate to their populations, nor were their parliamentary votes weighted on that principle.

The Edwardian statutes had in fact been superseded by later statutes. A Triennial Act was passed in 1641, and though it was repealed as being contrary to the king's just rights in 1664, it was then made the king's duty to ensure the holding of a parliament at least every three years — a duty which Charles II ignored towards the end of his reign. There followed the Triennial Act under William and Mary, and of course the Septennial Act under George I.

It is hardly surprising that even those reformers who were most certain that the ancient Constitution had been subverted by villainous conspiracy rather than by the infiltrations of historical change should have been a little vague as to the precise time and place of its downfall. The venerable Saxon myth had laid all the blame on the Norman Conquest. But then the Saxon type of liberty had been partially regained between the reigns of Henry II and Edward III. The wicked law of 1430 restricting the suffrage to forty shilling freeholders was obviously another point of downward departure,

[1] Granville Sharp, *The Legal Means of Political Reformation*, 7th edition (London, 1780), 23-29, 46-52.

[2] Maitland, *Constitutional History*, 177, 182, 248, 250-1, 295, 373.

but did not appear to be matched by corresponding acts of usurpation until parliaments were made the instruments of the Tudors. This line of interpretation could be maintained without holding on to the Saxons at the far end. But it is significant that Thomas Jefferson, nursed on the oldest of whiggery in his Virginian cradle of republican principles, went on believing in them to the end. In 1824, only two years before his death, he affirmed to Cartwright that the Tories were descended from the Normans, the Whigs from the Saxons. The American constitutional system, he declared, had only restored the long-lost polity of Anglo-Saxon England.[1]

The victory of the Parliament in the Civil Wars had clearly created the best conditions for a return to true Whig principles. It was from here that the Old or True Whigs traced their own direct ancestry. It was of that phase that James Burgh observed that England had enjoyed a republic 'one of the most unmixed ever known — a true government by representation' before it was 'destroyed by the villainous Cromwell'.[2] It took Lord Mansfield to point out in one of the later debates that Cromwell had been forced to create the Protectorship, not by vanity, but by the need for executive power.[3]

The appeal to ancient history had an emotional force that the Conservatives found hard to resist. They could, one may feel, have replied to the reformers with the perfectly valid affirmation that all of the statutes altering the electoral system had been just as constitutional as the earlier ones, and might further have argued that they were, in their times, actual improvements. But it was almost as important to them as to their opponents to be able to claim consistency with the intentions of their ancestors. Thus Blackstone had stated that parliaments were to be held every year but not necessarily elected afresh every year, and North, replying to one of Sawbridge's extensive but not very entertaining surveys of the historical evidence, said 'What our ancestors had in view was that parliaments should *sit* annually', and this had now been attained.[4] He could also make the point that, owing to the depreciation of the currency since the forty shilling statute of 1430, the suffrage had in fact been re-extended to something like its original scope.[5] Though he incorrectly attributed the statute to Henry VII, he argued

---

[1] To Major Cartwright, 5 June 1824, H. A. Washington (ed.), *Writings of Thos. Jefferson* 9 vols. (Washington, N.Y., 1854), vii. 355; quoted by E. S. Corwin, 'The Higher Law Background of American Constitutional Law' (reprinted from Harvard *Law Review*, 1928–9), (Ithaca, N.Y., 1957), 24–25, n. 66.

[2] James Burgh, *Political Disquisitions* (London, 1774), i. 9.

[3] Cobbett, *Parliamentary History*, xxiii. 96–97.

[4] *Parliamentary History*, xxi (8 May 1780), 600–1.

[5] *Parliamentary History*, xxiv (16 June 1784), 987–91.

shrewdly that to 'renovate' the Constitution 'would *lessen* the power of democracy'.

That the government had been corrupted by Crown influence was common reformist ground. But even the Glorious Revolution gave scant satisfaction to so pungent a critic as Catherine Macaulay, who was contemptuous of the self-congratulatory lamentations of the great Whigs. The government, she argued, had been corrupt ever since the Revolution Settlement; but that Settlement had been no popular victory, no success for True Whig principles or the old constitution. 'Had anything more than a mode of tyranny more agreeable to the interests of the Aristocratic faction, who took the lead in the opposition to the arbitrary administration of king James, been the probable consequence of the Revolution, that important circumstance in the annals of our country had never taken place.'[1] This cruel attack on everything the Rockingham Whigs held dear marked the sharp line of distinction between the radical reformers and the moderates. For the most part, the Settlement made in 1688–9 was held as sacred as that of 1787 came to be later in America. Mansfield was on a good Whig wicket when he stated that, at the Revolution, the government was divided equally into three estates, under which arrangement the people had an essential part of the power lodged in them.[2] This difference in the constructions of the past had a distinct bearing on the reconstruction of the present. It marked the distinction between the moderate Whigs who wished to restore the balance of 1689 and the Radical Reformers who wanted to return to what they believed had been the 'ancient constitution'.

It was over more recent history that the bitterest disputes flared up. The event which had given rise to the recent movements for economic and parliamentary reform was the American War of Independence.

The parliamentary reformers would have been better placed to take advantage of the failure of the government over America if they had revealed their superior wisdom at an earlier date. In fact only a few of them could point to records of opposition to the whole tenor of administration policy towards the Colonies — Fox not being one. North plainly had the better of the argument when he said, in a moving speech soon after his fall, 'They say that the American war was the war of the crown, against the wishes of the people. I say it was the war of parliament; not one step was taken without the sanction of parliament. It was the war of the people', and had been popular at its commencement. 'I was the creature of parliament in

[1] *Observations on . . . Present Discontents*, 13–15. *Parliamentary History*, xxx. 827–33.
[2] *Parliamentary History*, xxiii. 96–97. However, he was mistaken in regarding the Crown

my rise; when I fell I was its victim.'[1] Fox was compelled to admit that the war had been begun with the wishes of the people. The fault in the system of representation, however, had prevented the House of Commons from responding quickly enough to the wishes of the people when they wanted the war to end.[2] It is true that Wilkes had claimed, in a speech on reform in 1776, that in view of the unrepresentative composition of the House of Commons it was absurd to justify 'all the iniquitous, cruel, arbitrary, and mad proceedings of administration, because they had the approbation of the majority of this House'.[3] Erskine varied the grip, while trying to keep his hold on the government's throat, by admitting that the American war had been popular, 'because the people felt it was their war, and the people unfortunately connected the House with themselves, though there was no substantial connection'.[4] The truth, he explained, was that the House was merely an executive government, not a representative body; had the people seen that point, they would never have given their support to its policies. 'If the House of Commons had then in substance represented the people', he went on, 'America would still have been an affectionate colony.' He concluded by attributing not only the separation of America but the consequent convulsions all over Europe to the corruption in the House. Grey had stressed the same theme: a reform of representation in 1763 would have averted the American war.[5] The review of history had by that time begun to merge into the question of whether the current policies of the administration corresponded with the wishes of the people — an issue that was to reappear continually until reform was eventually achieved, and beyond.

The Whig reformers did not on the whole make out a very convincing case on historical points. They laboured under an unspoken inhibition. For they had no interest in attacking the successful and glorious wars of the century, which had been carried forward under substantially the same system as that which they blamed for the one that had failed. Of the wars under the Hanoverians, Jenkinson pointed out in reply to Grey, only the American war had become unpopular — and in that case the minister had been forced to quit only eighteen months after a general election which had placed complete confidence in him.[6] It seemed a convincing sign that deep changes in public feeling really were reflected in the balance of forces within the Commons. Yet the reformers in general showed little taste for deepening the historical side of their case even when they brought history in on their

---

[1] *Parliamentary History*, xxiii. 848–53.   [2] *Parliamentary History*, xiii. 861–2.

[3] Christie, *Wilkes, Wyvill and Reform*, 65.   [4] *Parliamentary History*, xxx. 827–33.

[5] *Parliamentary History*, xxx. 802.   [6] *Parliamentary History*, xxx. 817.

side, a fact which remains as significant evidence of the limited character of their intentions. They offered little comment on the social or economic consequences of the defective representation. Their interests and the remedies proposed were riveted on to political effects, political methods, and forms.

This is not to say that the reformist Whigs, either moderate or radical, lacked an idea of national interest. Far from it. Differences of opinion about the nature of the national interest and the way it was to be discovered added to differences of opinion about history, to differentiate between the moderates and the Radicals. Burke gave the matter a formulation that was to become classical when, on his election for Bristol in 1774, he delivered the speech in which he repudiated the doctrine of instruction as arising from 'a fundamental mistake of the whole order and tenor of our constitution'.[1] Parliament, declared Burke, was not a Congress of ambassadors from different and hostile interests (and the word Congress was being used at that time for the meeting of delegations from the different American colonies in Philadelphia); 'but parliament', he went on, 'is a *deliberative* assembly of *one* nation, with *one* interest, that of the whole; where, not local purposes, local prejudices, ought to guide, but the general good, resulting from the general reason of the whole.' He had already stated that government was a matter not of will but of reason and judgment.

Parliament, because of its composition, would give due consideration to all of the legitimate special or local interests within the nation. Parliament, 'the grand inquest of the nation', was precisely the place where this consultation of interests took place; and it was through that process that the one national interest would be arrived at. This was not by any means Burke's private view — its importance lies in the fact that it was orthodox. Lord North, no ally of Burke, put the matter in almost the same way when opposing reform ten years later.[2]

In this view, a rather subtle relationship existed between Parliament and public opinion. Orthodox Whig opinion certainly did not assume the existence of a unified or standing body of public opinion outside the Houses of Parliament. It recognised rather the variety and variability of the interests which moved the many parts of the kingdom in their ways and preoccupations. Duly constituted, Parliament, though always bound to consider these interests, needed no prompting or controlling by instructions or pledges. To admit that doctrine was to put, as Burke said, the wills of local interests

[1] *Burke's Speeches and Letters on American Affairs* (London, 1908); Everyman edition, 68–75.
[2] *Parliamentary History*, xxiv. 987–91.

above the reason of the nation. The separateness of Parliament was no mere convenient gloss on the Septennial Act, but was one of the pre-conditions of its proper ability to do its work.

The Radical reformers, with their demands for annual parliaments, their use of instruction of representatives, and election pledges both as doctrine and instrument, also believed in a national interest. But they attributed to the people a sort of unified political consciousness so different from anything seen in the orthodox Whig view as to stand for a significantly different political philosophy. They did not believe in the separateness of Parliament — that doctrine was to them nothing but the jargon of a court junta; they wanted the House of Commons to be attached to the people in the constituencies. They conceived of the will of the people as acting directly on the government; and the government as giving form to and executing the people's decisions.

4. The Representation of Interests

The glory of the settlement of 1689 lay partly in the fact that it was bloodless, and partly in that it resolved the constitutional crisis without disturbing the structure of English society and its relationship to Parliament. According to an ancient convention, the realm of England was composed of three estates. These estates were the peers spiritual, the peers temporal, and the commons. The peers were present in person in the House of Lords and were excluded from taking part in elections to the House of Commons. The commons were present by representation in their own chamber of Parliament.

This venerable theory bore no relation to political reality, nor were its prescriptions faithfully observed. Peers often took a hand in elections, and the consolidation of the parliamentary oligarchy in the eighteenth century brought into existence a structure of politics for which an expression such as 'estates of the realm' was merely an inapplicable metaphor. Even 'mixed government' failed to describe the facts.

The changing character of English government plainly required a new description and new explanation. Yet it was not until 1769 that Burke threw out the observation that the true purpose of the House of Commons was to represent the great interests that had gradually formed in the kingdom. The leading interests were those of land, commerce, the armed services, and the professions. None of these interests was in fact as unified or as coherent as Burke's theory implied; but this theory was closer to the facts than the anachronistic language of 'estates'.

In the face of insistent demands for reform, Conservatives began to see the merits of the theory of 'interest representation' as a weapon of defence. If it could be shown that, despite the anomalies of the system of representation, the leading interests of the nation really were represented in Parliament, there was plainly no need for reform. The interest theory therefore entered into orthodox constitutional discourse.

The most formidable demands for reform in the later eighteenth century sprang from the discontent of the landed interest, especially the gentry of Yorkshire. Their main demand was to restore their strength in the House of Commons. They were almost as suspicious of the aristocracy as of the Crown; but they offered only limited support to the more radical reformers in London. The Yorkshire movement under the leadership of Christopher Wyvill became the centre of a national but short-lived Association. It gained the support of the younger Pitt, but lost him again soon after he came to power. The movement had died away before the French Revolution.

T H E idea that the House of Commons ought to represent, not the consent of every man individually, nor the estates of the realm, so much as the great and legitimate interests of the State was first formulated by Burke.[1] He developed the thesis in the process of explaining his objections to large-scale reforms aimed at removing all forms of influence from the government. This problem brought him to consider the nature of influence. 'A great official, a great professional, a great military and naval interest, all necessarily comprehending many people of the first weight, ability, wealth, and spirit, has been gradually formed in the kingdom. These new interests must be let into the share of representation, else possibly they may be inclined to destroy those institutions of which they are not permitted to partake.' Then, having waved distant recognition of the respectable view that no influence at all ought to affect the mind of a member of Parliament, he went on to affirm the contrary opinion. So far from fearing the effects of having office-holders in the Commons, he said that 'a place under the government is the least disgraceful to the man who holds it, and by far the most safe to the country.'

[1] *Thoughts on the Cause of the Present Discontents* (1770). *Works* (London, 1834), i. 148.

Burke's solutions to the problems of the day were purely political — return the Rockingham party to power. But in the progress of the argument he had marked the outlines of the general doctrine of interest representation, which was to grow shortly into a new Whig orthodoxy. Forty years later Sir Francis Burdett, speaking in the Commons on Curwen's Reform Bill, incorrectly described these doctrines as 'Novel and extraordinary'. The mere admission that interests were represented as such appeared to Burdett as a thing to be denounced as corruption; but the situation by that time had become very confused, because the penetration of the doctrine of interest representation offered to almost every form of interest the cloak of legitimacy.

I. THE LANDED INTEREST

As the theory that the House of Commons not only represented, but of right ought to represent, an agglomeration of interests was to gain credence as an almost official explanation of its true constitutional function, it becomes necessary to ask in what measure those great interests did regard themselves as protected in that House.

Without doubt the fundamental interest of the kingdom was that of land. There was scarcely a blade of grass which was not represented, said Chatham.[1] And in advocating the addition of one knight for each shire he explained that they represented the soil. It seems indeed that the land itself led a political existence independently of the people who lived on it. This view, romantic though it may now seem, was maintained wholly without mysticism. It may have owed its origins to the feudal theory that all the land of the realm was owned — as common land, if not that of king or barons. If so, the political identity of the land did at least arise from a connection with people. But that reason for the connection does not appear in the text of remarks to the effect that soil and blades of grass were represented in Parliament. It seems to have been intolerable to the eighteenth-century political mind to imagine that there might be stretches of land belonging to the realm which were not in any way represented, even if they were not populated.

So much was the supremacy of the landed interest taken for granted that Burke felt required (in a speech in connection with Grenville's Bill of 1770 for establishing an impartial committee to hear and determine election disputes) to deny its claims. Parliament, he said, was not intended to represent landed property only: and then, pursuing the Rockingham party's attach-

[1] Veitch, *Genesis of Parliamentary Reform*, 37.

ment to the merchants, he reversed the emphasis by claiming that it was meant to represent the commercial interest chiefly, as appeared from the ancient establishment of the boroughs.[1] But the very grandeur, the unimpeachable respectability of the landed interest, was an impediment to intelligent enquiry into precisely what interests were involved. As usually happens, however, they identified themselves when things began to go wrong. The incursion into Parliament of the nabobs, the other rich merchants, and the successful lawyers, and the use of treasury funds in elections, produced a minor stream of laments to the effect that the landed interest was losing its proper influence. The long duration and eventual failure of the conduct of the American war stirred the gentry of Yorkshire and some other districts to a high pitch of discontent. But the truth was complicated. The competition of these powerful commercial figures, added of course to that of the Treasury, certainly placed a great strain on those landed elements who were least able to bear the cost. It was not the great landlords, but the weaker members of the gentry and tenantry, who went down in the struggle.

A practical organiser of a parliamentary reform movement, such as Wyvill, could not afford to work with the assumption that what he had to do was to arouse a united protest from the 'landed interest'. One of Wyvill's more acute difficulties arose from the fact that he had to steer clear of the Rockinghams because the violent prejudice of the Yorkshire gentry against the great lords would seriously have impaired his chances of winning the support of the gentry in the county. It was a particularly tricky situation because Wyvill was convinced that he needed the Rockinghams on his side in order to gain enough influence in Parliament.[2]

These painful internal conflicts were unknown to theory; and there were reasons for holding that a somewhat diffused but very effective notion of the interests of the middle range of landowners had some weight in policy. It was after all the desire to reduce the burden of the land tax that induced George Grenville to plan the taxation of the American Colonies. The numerous Enclosure Acts of the eighteenth century meant the giving of parliamentary time and goodwill to the landed interests involved in each case. Until these policies began, at the turn of the century, to bring out bad will between rival local forces, they did little to detract from the comfortable, if inexact, view of a prevalent agricultural harmony.

[1] *Parliamentary History*, xvi (30 March 1770), 920–1. For the Rockingham dependence on the merchant interest see also Burke's *Short Account of a Late Short Administration* (1766).

[2] Christie, *Wilkes, Wyvill and Reform*, 75.

Considered in this general light the landed interest had little to complain of. By common consent it was represented not merely in Parliament, but as an estate by the House of Lords itself. But that did not end the matter. Land had its share, along with the other interests, in the Commons. Lord North, opposing an addition of knights, observed that the House of Commons resembled the whole legislature in providing for and preserving the due balance between the great interests, landed, commercial, moneyed. To add county members would give the landed interest superiority, which would amount to undue influence.[1] If the landed interest were considered as a homogeneous whole, North was certainly right. Great landowners among the nobility, supplemented by commoners of almost equal weight, directly controlled the return of 205 seats in the general election of 1761; but such factors as personal influence, local traditions, and the deference of tenants indubitably raised the figure. Though great changes came over British society between the accession of George III and the passing of the Great Reform Act, the powerful grip of the great landlords remained unbroken. According to Dr Thompson, 'The best opinion seems to be ... that in the final decade of the unreformed Commons 177 individuals influenced the return of 355 Members, just over two-thirds of the representatives of England and Wales. Within this total, 87 peers were credited with the return of 213 Members, and 90 commoners with that of 137 Members.'[2]

In the light of all this, one may ask why so much of the burden of the grievances from 1780 onwards was expressed in demands for an increase in the representation of the shires? The answer, however, divides the reformers. The Rockinghams, it must be remembered, did not support the demand. Their grudge was the control of corrupt boroughs by the Crown, and the economic reform programme to cut back Crown influence substantially satisfied their ideas as to what needed to be done. Burke, the chief spokesman of the group, was passionate and insistent in his denunciations of any move whatever to alter the structure of the Commons. The main body of parliamentary reformers, however, did believe in the need for a change in the composition of the Commons. Their attitudes can best be seen in Yorkshire.

---

[1] *Parliamentary History*, xxiii. 848–53.

[2] F. M. L. Thompson, *English Landed Society in the Nineteenth Century* (London, 1963) (hereafter referred to as *Landed Society*), 45–47. He begins with Namier's figures for 1761 but, noting that Namier was concerned to identify only those cases where the return could, if necessary, be enforced by compulsion, Dr Thompson goes on to discuss other means of influence. T. H. B. Oldfield, *Representative History of Great Britain and Ireland* (London, 1816), provides a vast compendium of information for use by reformers, giving much statistical detail on the control of seats and the proportion of voters to inhabitants.

They were far from being real political radicals, and Wyvill found that he had carefully to avoid sponsoring extreme doctrines that might alarm the gentry. The doctrines they accepted were safe Whig fare: the history of the corruption of the well balanced Constitution of 1689 by the Septennial Act and the use of Crown patronage. What is fairly clear is that, in a large and populous county with a highly independent gentry, the alterations demanded would have brought about a strengthening of the gentry, not of the great nobles and landlords.

The bitter grievances of the Yorkshire gentry were not due primarily to an unfair weight of taxation. On the contrary, they were let off rather lightly compared with the freeholders of the southern counties.[1] But it remains possible that they considered themselves grievously under-represented for the taxes they did pay, and this grievance grew more pressing as the government's commitments increased the likelihood of a reassessment of taxes. It is significant that in October 1782 the *York Chronicle* carried two successive articles, presumably by Wyvill, advocating schemes for the redistribution of seats in Parliament among the counties in accordance with the distribution of the weight of taxes. The plans under discussion also involved merging the parliamentary boroughs into constituencies made up of county districts.[2]

The vitality of the Yorkshire Association movement cannot be explained by any one factor, much though it undoubtedly owed to its leader, Wyvill. Some of the explanation must lie in the history of the county itself, with its hints of an independence amounting almost to a kind of political separatism. But the Yorkshire movement was pre-eminently a landed movement, the cities of Sheffield and Leeds taking no exceptional part, and it can be understood only with an understanding of the character of the gentry and tenantry. The size and populousness of the county gave its people a feeling of collectively possessing a certain political weight.[3] One essential inducement to political activity was the feeling of effectiveness. It was a general rule in English and American politics before the emergence of party-political democracy, that spontaneous widespread interest was a function of freedom — or, to be more precise, of the conviction that individual participation could have a visible effect on the result of an election. Neither in the counties nor in the boroughs where the result was controlled by outside powers was there more than a flicker of interest in politics. But a numerous and sub-

---

[1] As shown by Christie, *Wilkes, Wyvill and Reform*, 229.

[2] Christie, *Wilkes, Wyvill and Reform*, 158.

[3] Populous counties with a large tenantry were the most inclined to opposition. Thompson, *Landed Society*, 118.

stantial agricultural middle class in the form of freeholders and favourably placed tenants were politically free; and they had it in their power to determine the elections to the House of Commons. These features prevailed in Yorkshire just as they did, changing the terms for the circumstances, in the city electorates of Middlesex, Southwark, Westminster, and the City. Nor is it to be overlooked that a similar movement of great power and much greater success arose in Ireland, where 'Grattan's Parliament' was established in 1782, and where a substantial measure of legislative independence was achieved. Though it was not to last beyond 1801, that achievement was a tribute to the force that could be generated by a proud and independent landed class exerting itself under able leadership at a time which, for external reasons, was politically propitious.

Landed society was changing in the later eighteenth century. The heavy burdens of the three long wars, beginning with 1756, accentuated the pressure on the weaker or less efficient or simply less fortunate landowners; while men of new wealth from commerce and the law moved in, and the more powerful and efficient increased their gains. The rise of the men of commerce began to alarm the representatives of the land in the Commons. 'Were it not for burgage tenure boroughs and others that were bought,' declared Sir William Young in 1793 — and then, replying to the ironic 'hear, hear!' — 'he had declared he intended to speak out, and would therefore repeat, that boroughs that were bought and controlled by men of property formed the only balance to the commercial influence, which was increasing by rapid strides and ought to be checked.'[1] It is clear that he feared the reforms proposed by Grey would swing more power to commerce and possibly, by enfranchising the cities, to industry, at the expense of agriculture. 'What chance have we', asked the Earl of Sheffield in a slightly different vein, 'when the House of Commons is filled with moneyed men, speculators, and underlings in office? Must not the landed interest — must not men like me, who have uniformly opposed a reform in Parliament, acknowledge the necessity of it, and join in a cry that will be heard?'[2] Though his specific, harking back to the addition of knights, was the opposite of Young's, and was probably the more correct, his apprehension of the evils of society was much the same. The landlords could see the change coming over the House of Commons: between 1761 and the early years of the nineteenth century the proportion of merchants in the House rose from one-ninth to one-quarter. What they failed to see was the overwhelming continued pre-

[1] *Parliamentary History*, xxx. 839.
[2] Mingay, *Landed Society*, 265–6.

ponderance of land, with which three-quarters of all M.P.s still had some concern as late as 1832.[1]

The old story of the Crown versus the representatives of the people was wearing thin. The representatives of the people — the political nation — were sharply divided among themselves. Measures introduced during the wars with France revealed an increasing conflict of interests within the landed classes. Over the attempts to introduce a general Enclosure Act that would provide uniform, swift, and economical procedure for enclosures, over the prohibition of wool exports, and over tithes, the smaller farmers were defeated in Parliament by the great lords who now increasingly claimed the name of the 'landed interest'.[2]

If these divisions made the House of Commons the scene of conflict between interests which had much to lose in the struggle, they made it a place of decision. They sharpened the necessity for an effective representation, the understanding of the fact that actual numbers would count. The idea of the 'national interest' could not survive as a pious gloss on the fraternal agreements of an oligarchic ruling class. Meanwhile the concept of the 'landed interest', though it was to sustain a long and honoured life, had been exposed to the searching suspicion of being a sham, whose placid continuity concealed a variety of elements, sometimes in harmony but sometimes in vital conflict.

II. THE COMMERCIAL INTEREST

The soil of England and the grass that grew in it would have remained, and for the most part would have yielded crops to the same tillers and have grazed the same herds even if they had not been represented in Parliament. Not so with commerce. Britain was a great trading nation. The Navigation Act of 1651 and the whole of the mercantile system founded upon it and elaborated by further Acts in the succeeding century, together with the establishment in 1696 of the Board of Trade, connoted the mutual involvement of the interests of commerce with the policies of government. As industrial manufacture began to take its place in the scheme of the national economy, the northern centres of that manufacture had an undisputed claim on the attention of the Commons. 'Did Manchester, Leeds, Birmingham, desire to send members?' asked Lord North in one of his most persuasive speeches

---

[1] Mingay, *Landed Society*, 113.   [2] Mingay, *Landed Society*, 261.

against reform; 'Would sending members be an advantage to these towns? Did any believe that a petition from Manchester, Leeds or Birmingham would be less attended to than a petition from Helleston or Old Sarum? Petitions from Manchester, and the others, always received as much attention as petitions from boroughs that were represented.'[1]

Both commercial and industrial interests had reason to feel satisfied with their influences. There could be little ground to fear that either antagonism or neglect might endanger their prosperity. The main political questions of the 1760s turned on the East India Company, which was of such public importance as to produce an entertaining reversal of the usual direction of interest representation: the national administration felt bound to maintain its interest in the government of the Company. Whig lords took up voting qualifications and went down to India House to vote for one side while Paymaster Henry Fox put departmental funds at the service of the rival party. The complex negotiations of 1766–7 ended with a permanent government interest in the Company's profit. After reforms in the structure of the Company in 1773, the management of it became one of the normal ministerial activities.[2] It must, from the American point of view, have appeared a decisive comment on the meaning of 'virtual representation' that in 1773 the North administration felt obliged to save the Company by granting it a monopoly of tea distribution in the Colonies, without so much as pausing to discover whether the Colonies might have a different view.

At the end of the American war, Shelburne bequeathed to the younger Pitt a broad-minded plan for reciprocal trade with the former Colonies. Pitt also worked out a plan for liberal trading concessions to Ireland, which country occupied a very disadvantageous position under the restrictions of the British navigation system. Opposition to these schemes mounted both inside and outside Parliament; Manchester raised 55,000 signatures for a petition against the Irish concessions. Pitt, though First Lord of the Treasury, was compelled to abandon them both.[3] Pitt and his successors developed the complicated blend of strategic and mercantile policies that dominated British conduct during the long French wars after 1793; and although the justification offered was military, the fact was that the system of blockade, combined with licensed exemptions issued by the Board of Trade,

---

[1] *Parliamentary History*, xxiv. 987–91.

[2] Lucy Sutherland, *The East India Company in Eighteenth Century Politics* (Oxford, 1952) (hereafter referred to as *East India Co.*), 103–4, chapter vi, 267.

[3] Watson, *Geo. III*, 276–8; Palmer, *Democratic Revolution*, 307.

was always inspired by considerations of self-interested commercial policy as well as economic warfare.[1]

All of this, however, did not prove the existence in the British economy of a single, unified, commercial interest. One of the most familiar of all the features of the rise of English overseas trade was the rivalry between London and the so-called 'out-ports', notably Bristol and, in the eighteenth century, Liverpool. When to this is added the diversity of interests of companies trading with different and distant parts of the world, the notion of a general commercial interest becomes only a little more precise than that of the 'middle class'. Both the East India and the West India traders were always present in the Commons, the latter in much greater strength; as many as fifty or fifty-one of those business men generically designated as 'merchants' were returned in the general election of 1761.[2] It is true that much of the rivalry was for government contracts,[3] and that most of the rivals could therefore be reasonably designated as being connected by a similarity of interests. A major exception occurred in the great debate as to whether, after the Seven Years War, Britain ought to acquire Canada or retain the rich sugar island of Guadaloupe. In that case it transpired that the West India interest did not control the course of empire.

Still only rich men could enter Parliament, and the lesser trading classes in the City were far from satisfied. The City was the seat of a sharp streak of resentment against the pretensions of the upper landed classes, which, when worked out in terms of the absurd under-representation of London against its tax payments and population, gave rise to the demand for an increase in the representation in the Commons. Although commerce generally received so much attention, inequalities could cause violent resentment. The big merchant whose position in Parliament and confident connections with the administration resulted in an opulent contract to supply the army or navy in some overseas base would thereby rise higher, but his good fortune would give no satisfaction to the small trader outside.[4] They did not consider him their representative.

James Burgh, in his *Political Disquisitions*, pointed out, rightly enough,

[1] Bradford Perkins, *Prologue to War: England and the United States, 1805–1812* (Berkeley and Los Angeles, 1961), 304–6. The same point may be made about the 'Rule of 1756', a British invention which barred neutral trade in war-time with the colonies of belligerents against Britain with whom the same trade had not been carried on before the war.

[2] Sutherland, *East India Co.*, 19; Namier, *Structure*, i. 61.

[3] Namier, *Structure*, i. 56–72.

[4] Sutherland, 'City of London', 61. Christie, *Wilkes, Wyvill and Reform*, 16–17.

that trade and manufactures had increased the value of land. Burgh laid great stress on the importance of merchant representation in strengthening British trade against foreign competition: he also made a point which, though difficult to test, certainly touched an important issue, when he remarked that the Bill for restraining paper credit in America (1764) was brought in 'owing to a want of merchants in the house'. The London merchants, he added, 'always vote on the side of liberty'.[1]

Much of the material for the City radicalism came from elements discontented with their inadequate voice in Parliament. The demand these forces had to contribute to the reform movement was principally for a reapportionment of representatives. They showed no interest in an extension of the suffrage. It was an emphasis to be expected where a populous electorate was frustrated by gross inequalities of representation.

In face of rapid but unequal economic development and of accompanying social stresses, the old system was remarkable chiefly for its flexibility. Had new merchants been unable to get into Parliament, the Constitution would have cracked. But here, it was the perverse merit of the rotten boroughs and burgage tenures that they came to the rescue; they stood, in all their fusty rural charm, as glittering prizes on the road to the House of Commons.

III. INTEREST REPRESENTATION: THE NEW ORTHODOXY

Burke had also named 'a great official, a great professional, a great military and naval interest'. The 'official' interest was presumably that of the 'civil servants' — those departmental servants of individual ministers who would now hold career posts in the Civil Service but were, in the eighteenth century, quite often members of Parliament. The professional men were for the most part lawyers. Many senior and some junior officers of the services were also members of Parliament.

It may not be too frivolous to suggest that Burke's method of enumerating the great interests which ought to be represented in the House of Commons was to look round the House of Commons to see who was actually there. It was not the interest of the profession, but the advancement of the individual, that was normally the motive for seeking entrance to the House. Years of loyal support for Administration were frequently cited as reasons for service promotions, while promotions were sometimes conferred — or sought —

[1] *Political Disquisitions*, i. 51–54.

by the Duke of Newcastle in order to give a good administration supporter the standing he needed for a particular election. Because patronage was almost essential for getting a start in life, almost all had to secure it. There were certain merciful exceptions.[1]

Unfortunately neither Burke nor other exponents of the theory of interest representation explained exactly what benefits these professions and services were to obtain, or why they stood in need of actual parliamentary representation rather than access to government departments. The argument could be reversed: because these men were senior officers the country was entitled to the benefit of their counsel in Parliament. But this did not mean that they were consulted in order to speak for the interests of their professions.

Nevertheless the great interests of the kingdom gathered periodic additions. It was important to keep a proper balance: a short list simply lacked weight and conviction; an excessively long one would begin to smack of universal suffrage.

The theory of interest representation contained very little to frighten the established order. By the time of the new wave of parliamentary reform, begun in the Commons by Grey in 1793, it was open to such a pure Conservative as Charles Jenkinson to adopt the interest thesis. His speech has a certain importance in the iconography of representation not only because of the fullness of his treatment but also because it was taken as being a model for the theory by James Mill, in his Utilitarian tract, *An Essay on Government*.[2]

'We ought not to begin', Jenkinson declared, 'by considering who ought to be the electors and who ought to be elected but ought to begin by considering who ought to be elected and then constitute such electors as would be likely to produce the best elected.' (This view of representation, incidentally, would have gratified the restored Bourbon monarchy in France after 1815, under which members were virtually nominated.) Jenkinson set himself three questions: 1. What is the best House of Commons? 2. How would it be best composed to answer its object? 3. What is the way of so composing it? He answered the first with a general statement of the constitutional principle that the legislature was 'representative of all descriptions of men in the country'. Secondly, he came to actual membership. All agreed that the landed interest should have preponderant weight; manufacturing and

---

[1] Namier, *Structure*, i. 31–72. Promotion to senior service rank, especially in the navy, could not normally be secured without some signs of ability; and lawyers very largely made their own careers, sometimes from fairly modest beginnings.

[2] *Parliamentary History*, xxx. 808–20.

commercial interests came second; 'in a manufacturing country like this, they ought to have great weight', he said. Then he mentioned the need for professional men, the army, the navy, and the law. Finally, with startling frankness, he came to the members who 'wished to raise themselves to the great offices of state'. He failed to say whether this important element in the legislature was to be recruited from some completely other source than those enumerated, but he seems to have meant all the men of high ambition and ability who could manage to get into Parliament without representing interests. It was the professional people, he said, who made the House the representatives of the people. This led to his third question and to the advantages of the 'rotten boroughs', which gave entry for the professions. The House of Commons, Jenkinson affirmed, was the democratic part of the Constitution, 'the virtual representatives of the people'. It ought to be affected by public opinion; but public opinion ought not to have such great weight as to prevent the exercise of the deliberative function.

This exposition brought a very caustic reply from Samuel Whitbread,[1] who observed that the texture imagined by Jenkinson never had existed and never would exist. The expedient of settling who should be elected before going in search of electors made it a matter of small importance who should perform the farce of electing nominated representatives. He took note also of the defence of rotten boroughs on the ground that they furnished members of distinguished ability who could not otherwise afford election. But if elections were conducted as they ought to be, Whitbread replied, representation would be accessible in all places to persons of moderate fortune.

Yet Jenkinson's doctrine, ominous though it might seem to the Old Whig tradition, was merely an echo of the new Whig orthodoxy, which had been adumbrated by the philosopher William Paley, in his *Principles of Moral and Political Philosophy*. Under a republic, Paley had admitted, without king or lords, it was true that the present state of representation in the Commons would produce a confused and ill-digested oligarchy; but 'if the properest persons be elected, what matters it by whom they are elected?' The House of Commons in fact contained the most considerable landlords and merchants, the heads of the army, the navy, and the law; the occupiers of the great offices of state, and many private individuals of eloquence, knowledge, and activity. 'If the country is not safe in these hands,' he asked, 'in whose hands would it be?'[2] He stated with the frankness that was coming

---

[1] *Parliamentary History*, xxx. 882.

[2] W. Paley, *Essay on the British Constitution* (being chapter 7 of *Principles of Moral and Political Philosophy*, reprinted separately) (London, 1792), 36–37.

to characterise the defence of burgage tenures that the sale of small borough seats helped to bring talent into the House of Commons. He stoutly defended the ownership by peers of seats in the Commons; it helped to maintain the alliance between the two branches, which was good for the Constitution. The House of Commons would be in danger if the Lords had no influence over it; but there was no danger in the Crown having control of a few seats. He found the existing state of representation eminently satisfactory. The members were so connected with the mass of the community 'by a society of interests and passions', that 'the will of the people, when it is determined, permanent, and general, almost always at length prevails'.[1]

Paley may possibly have been right. These statements, and the arguments of the opponents of reform who always asserted that the Commons were faithful to the will and desires of the people, were very difficult either to prove or refute. The argument, in fact, had a circular inclination, since the House of Commons was firmly upheld as the only place where public opinion — in its 'determined, permanent and general' form — could find its ultimate expression.

To satisfy the labouring classes that they received fair treatment under the system, Paley addressed to them a few observations of magisterial complacency in a separate pamphlet.[2] The fixed rules of property were the defence of the poor; the laws which accidentally cast enormous estates into one man's possession, he explained, were, after all, the selfsame laws which protected and guarded the poor man. The labouring man had advantages over the rich — regular occupation and the satisfaction of practising frugality. The rich, unfortunately, were often satiated, tired of luxury, and subject to feelings of disgust. The more obvious remedies for this disquieting state of affairs escaped Paley's attention; but he did not think the poor needed representation in Parliament. In listing the trades and professions who obtained seats, he made no mention of artisans or of the more lowly labourers, but he did maintain that a virtual representation was obtained by the existing variety of qualifications, by the mixing of members with their electors and of the electors with the rest of the population.[3]

While Paley's thoughts do not make exciting reading, his lack of originality has its importance. His work was widely read as a text book. He wrote

[1] Paley, *British Constitution*, 39–41 (hereafter referred to as *BC*). The use of the word 'society' in this sense has disappeared.

[2] W. Paley, *Reasons for Contentment Addressed to the Labouring Part of the British Public* (2nd edition, London, 1793).

[3] *B.C.*, 13–16.

sensibly about the constitutional tradition, dismissing the notion of 'original principles' of which radical reformers were so fond, and pointing out that the Constitution was not founded, or remade, at any one time, but was the result of historical growth and occasional remedies for needs; the power of patronage, of such obvious importance, was not to be found in it. He owed much to the Whig tradition, into which he incorporated the recent advance made by the reporting of parliamentary debates — an important part, he said, of effective representation. He also affirmed the basic Lockian tenet that the true representative must be affected by the laws he makes; taxation by the Commons was taxation of themselves.[1] (This of course meant taking seriously the virtual representation of the poor, who paid taxes on basic commodities.) In discussing the provisions required for the perpetuation of the Constitution, Paley expounded a doctrine of balance that corresponded happily with the existing institutions. Parliament's power over supplies acted as a check on the king's power to declare war; each order of interests was balanced against the others, and the Lords would check the vulgar passions and prejudices of the voters (a precaution that would not, however, be right or necessary if the common people were in the habit of thinking coolly before deciding). Some of these remarks bring him surprisingly close to Madison on American Federalism. Not least, Paley's position remains significant because he mixed in his thinking two general concepts belonging to Whig tradition. The government of England, he began by stating, was a combination of kingdom, aristocracy, and republic — that is, of the Crown and the ancient 'estates'. This was no different from saying 'King, Lords and Commons'. But in discussing the 'republican' element — or the 'democratic', as the House of Commons was technically called by the language of the day — he adopted a fully digested theory of interest representation. The two theories, first of the estates of the realm, and secondly of the interests, were capable of living comfortably side by side, as they did in the mind of Burke; and the monarchy itself seems to have been regarded as an 'estate'.[2] But the language of 'estates', though still in rhetorical use, belonged to the past — it was not connected with realities. The language of 'interests', on the other hand, despite its own lacunae and vagueness, could be seen to connect with the way men behaved, with what they had at stake on particular issues, with how they voted. It was a usable political language. Most of all it could be used, even by parliamentary reformers, without threatening to undermine the order of Britain's *ancien régime*.

The theory of interest representation as it was developed before the Re-

[1] *B.C.*, 1–13, 18.   [2] *Parliamentary History*, xxiii. 96 (Mansfield).

form Act gave an account of only a limited number of the social or economic interests of the nation. Yet it was a flexible instrument. Its scope could be enlarged to include new interests as they emerged into political significance; and despite the obvious inconsistencies and conflicts even within some of the groups so described, it offered a more adaptable and usable method for analysing the composition of the political nation than the vague and tendentious theory of class structure was later to do. Interests could offer some share of representation to individuals who obtained no other share. An element of interest representation survives in any effectively working system.

5. Great Oaks and Grass Roots

The parliamentary reform movement of the later eighteenth century did not achieve parliamentary reform. What it did bring about was a searching examination and clarification, the first for nearly a century, of the theory and practice of representation. One interesting result was that Parliament, forced to defend its right to govern a country of which the vast majority of subjects were only nominally represented, became more conscientious. To some extent it reformed itself. Another result was that Conservatives ceased to apologise for the influence of property in the government. Practices which had once been regarded as corrupt came to be defended as legitimate. Debate, on both sides, was informed by a greater sense of reality.

The reform movements gave rise to a ferment of discussion. Major Cartwright led the demand for universal manhood suffrage. Both this and many more modest proposals were pressed by men who insisted on the right of the commons to full representation in their share of the national legislature: they did not demand an abolition of the Lords or the Crown. Even the most limited reforms, such as measures to disfranchise boroughs which had been guilty of gross electoral corruption, met stiff opposition. The franchise was generally admitted to be a form of public trust; but it was also regarded as a legitimate and valuable form of private property.

In the wake of the French Revolution, and in the teeth of bitter hostility from the Pitt administration, a new wave of Radical reformism sprang up and it was from this phase that the word 'Radical' derived. While the reformist Whigs renewed their fruitless pressure in Parliament, the artisans of London and the North country began their own independent movement. Their ultimate object was to secure political representation, not for estates or for interests, but for individuals. They therefore represented, in British politics, a view which had already entered into American constitutional practice.

I. IN DEFENCE OF CORRUPTION

ONE word united all reformers in anger: 'corruption'. Yet Whigs generally agreed with each other that property had a natural and proper place in the political system and that its influence in politics was in a sense correct and legitimate. The attack on corruption brought, in reply, a defence of the systematic influence of property: and a generation after the American War of Independence, after the Rockingham programme of Economic Reform and the wider Association Movement, the effects of this debate had been not to purge corrupt practices out of the body politic but, on the contrary, to reveal the profound extent to which the House of Commons depended upon and accepted methods which would once have been regarded as corrupt.

Wherever it was agreed that the electoral system had been corrupted, then reform, by definition, was required. As early as 1770, the House of Commons had become convinced that its method of settling disputed elections was as discreditable as it was inefficient. The liberty of the House to determine the qualifications of its own members had been turned into an opportunity for the trial of party or factional strength; cases were not decided on the merits of the evidence. Grenville's Controverted Elections Act (1770) handed these disputes over to select committees, and though the earlier abuses were not entirely eliminated, the intention was defined. The debate on the Bill had shown a stirring of conscience on the question of the relationship of Members of Parliament to their constituents.[1] The use of Civil List money to buy up parliamentary boroughs was also held to be corrupt, for the dual reasons that bought votes were not free votes, and that the Crown had no legitimate business in the Commons. Yet in face of all this, one of the most profoundly significant changes in the eighteenth

---

[1] *Parliamentary History*, xvi. 902–27.

century was the growth, first of tolerance, then of defence, of electoral corruption.

Complaints about the high cost of elections began to be made early in the century.[1] Corruption was generalised into a political issue by the enemies of Walpole; but the fall of the minister had little or no effect on the system by which he had ruled. Probably the Imperial and American wars did more than any commercial or domestic force to bring money into the reckoning of politics. The influence of the Crown, said Shelburne in an angry speech on the Civil List arrears in 1777, was not the only influence tending to bring the nation to destruction, ruin, and slavery; nor were the effects of corruption confined to Parliament. Scarcely any man possessed a political right which he did not wish to sell for as much money as it would bring on the market. The nation was composed of buyers and sellers; purchase was always made with the intention to dispose; each of their lordships wanted to bring local boroughs over to their influence; where was there a borough not to be bought or influenced? (One sees why Shelburne was unpopular.) Contracts, he went on, were an inexhaustible source of influence and the great contractors divided the fruits among themselves; Shelburne charged them with having a property influence in the prolongation of the war.[2] These accusations and the charges of parliamentary reformers made it necessary to construct a system of defence. At first it may have been a little sheepish, but later, after the deaths of Pitt and Fox, it became open and avowed. On one hand, corruption was explained as an incidental and unimportant product of a sound and successful system. Lord North had connived at this method by dismissing Wilkes's Motion for a More Equal Representation of the People in Parliament with ridicule. 'Lord North was very jocular,' says the report; 'he supposed Wilkes was not serious, because he must be well pleased with his success in London and Middlesex. It would not be easy', he added, 'to prevail on those who had an interest in the boroughs, on whom he bestowed so many hard names, to sacrifice to ideal schemes so beneficial a species of property'.[3] The motion was negatived without a division. When Lord Mahon brought in a Bill in 1782 to prevent bribery at elections, he ran into difficulties as soon as he tried to give his measures teeth by disfranchising voters who broke the law and by incapacitating such candidates from sitting in the present Parliament. Fox opposed the Bill, saying that the Grenville committees were not courts, were not called upon to pronounce on bribery

---

[1] For example in the debate on the Septennial Act.
[2] *Parliamentary History*, xix. 183–6 (6 April 1777).
[3] *Parliamentary History*, xviii. 1297–8.

except incidentally, and should therefore not have the power to impose incapacities; he was for putting the whole thing off for one year. When the incapacitating clause was rejected, Mahon withdrew his Bill.[1]

Under the Portland ministry, in 1808 and 1809, the luxurious squalor of upper aristocratic life infiltrated the army and the government. A parliamentary investigation confirmed the truth of rumours that the mistress of the Duke of York, Commander-in-Chief of the army, had taken money from persons seeking military promotions or War Office favours; though a division in the House exonerated the Duke from personal corruption, he was obliged to resign (to be reinstated two years later). At once, Lord Castlereagh was charged with illegal use of an appointment in the India Office, the proceeds of which had been put to paying the costs of the election of a protégé; and when the government secured a not very convincing majority to defeat the motion of censure on Castlereagh, both he and Spencer Perceval, Chancellor of the Exchequer, were accused of corrupt use of treasury funds to control elections in Ireland. To the Whigs in opposition as well as to Radicals, the apparent increase in the influence of government was tantamount to a renewal of the old menace, the influence of the Crown.[2]

Reformers seized on specific ills as evidence that the whole system was in decay; with the result that William Windham,[3] who had long been one of the most energetic opponents of reform in Parliament (though he introduced some reforms in army recruiting when secretary at war) in defending Castlereagh and Perceval against censure, found himself engaged in a defence of the existing system of representation. Corruption, he admitted, existed from top to bottom — 'but he believed more would be found at the bottom than at the top'.[4] The Government, however, could not resist the demand for legislation against corruption in elections. In 1809 John Christian Curwen, M.P. for Carlisle, a solid example of the independent gentry, introduced a Bill to prevent the sale of seats. The Speaker, Charles Abbot, supported the Bill. The Government were not happy; they obtained amendments, under which, though 'express' bargains by the Treasury were made illegal, 'implied' bargains were permitted to continue; thus softened, the Bill was allowed to become law.[5] But the debates had been revealing.

Corruption — as the reformers called it — was now explained, not

---

[1] *Parliamentary History*, xxiii. 101–9 (21 June 1782). Pitt observed that Fox's speech showed that he had not read the Bill, which provided that the Grenville committee must expressly declare that bribery had taken place before imposing its judgment.

[2] Watson, *Geo. III*, 447–51.   [3] M.P. for the Borough of Higham Ferrers.

[4] *Hansard*, xiv, 521–2.   [5] Watson, *Geo. III*, 449.

merely (as earlier) as a subsidiary effect of a good system, but as being the legitimate mechanism by which the rightful influence of property was secured. There was, said Davies Giddy[1] — a frequent speaker in these debates — a necessary connection between property and power. Formerly, taking money at interest was called usury and condemned; but it was needed by a commercial nation; and now the same mistake seemed to be made about influence and money. Property must necessarily give a person influence, he pointed out, and that influence would tend to procure the return of members to Parliament. George Johnstone[2] made the same point with particular reference to the small boroughs. The danger, if the Bill passed, was that the agent and manager, who was best known to the electors and managed all their affairs, would become their choice as member of Parliament; 'then indeed our constitution would be destroyed', he told the House, 'because the representatives of the nation would no longer represent its property.' And the experience of France showed that if power and property were disunited, the possessors of power would soon wrest the property. Windham spoke powerfully on the same side, denying that the transactions in question were corrupt. Going painstakingly over the whole list of influences — the landlord's over his tenants, the manufacturer's over his workers, that of the opulent man dropping hints to the butcher and baker in a borough town — which reformers denounced as wrong, Windham declared that property might be the means of giving virtue the means of acting, and asked how the influence of property was to continue, if such means were not lawful? Coming back to a favourite point he rounded on the reformers by telling them that the great mass of abuses began and ended with the people.[3]

The passage of the Act, after vigorous denunciations of Treasury peddling and warnings that if relief were not granted the people, driven to despair, would seek other means, proved that a gesture was required to allay the anxiety of the country; but it was possible largely because the Act did not really strike at the roots of the influence of property. Even Wharton,[4] in supporting the Bill, had affirmed that the possession of property ought to have a predominant influence in the election of members; what he wanted to eliminate was the open market. They should not sell their friends, neighbours, and dependants for sordid gain. Certainly, there were voices warning

---

[1] M.P. for the Borough of Bodmin. [2] M.P. for Heydon Borough.

[3] *Hansard*, xiv. 665, 723, 737–68. Windham's long speech is a mine of source material for electoral practices and morals in his time.

[4] Richard Wharton, M.P. for Durham City.

of the dangers of cutting out monetary bribery while leaving to the government the power of influence by offers of office, which Burdett described as being more dangerous than bribes.[1] It seems probable that Curwen's Act did, however, diminish the power of the government through direct interventions;[2] what it left was the pervasive influence of the great landlords and the big employers.

Nor did it effectively destroy bribery. In 1812 the *Edinburgh Review* published an article examining the methods of evasion then in practice. It alleged that an election dinner might cost £500; but the grand item was travelling charges. A large number of persons, whose freemanship entitled them to votes in boroughs containing 300 to 400 electors, actually lived in London, spent dissolute lives trading their votes and influence over the candidates, and had to be conveyed to the elections at the candidates' expense. The *Review* advocated a residence qualification for voters and supported Lord Tavistock's Bill for moving county polls from place to place. Election expenses should be reduced by establishing certain standard requirements, and procedure should be simplified. The defence of the present system would be more consistent in the form of a property qualification of £50,000 for a county and £10,000 for a borough; but the Westminster electors had shown how to solve the problem in 1807, when in support of Sir Francis Burdett they opened a subscription, paid everything themselves, and kept the whole expense down to £2,000.[3]

II. THE GENTRY AND PARLIAMENTARY REFORM

Much of this electoral luxuriance had flourished for over a century in the shade of the 'great oaks' whose pastures Burke so richly manured.[4] The high aristocracy conducted themselves as though they were contractors for government; such advantages as might be expected from political reform are rather comparable to those of superior estate management. There was little

[1] *Parliamentary History*, xiv. 370, 838–49, 978.   [2] Watson, *Geo. III*, 449.

[3] *Edinburgh Review*, xx. 1812, 127–43. The cost of contesting Liverpool or Bristol was stated as £12,000; the great Westminster contest — fought by Fox in 1785 — was supposed, with committee hearings, to have mounted to £80,000; Wilberforce's committee in Yorkshire in 1807 gave their expenses as £58,000.

[4] Richard Pares, *George III and the Politicians* (Oxford, 1953), 60, n. 2. In a letter of 7 November 1772 Burke compared himself to a melon, the Duke of Richmond and his patron, the Marquess of Rockingham, to 'great oaks'.

common ground between those who believed that the Constitution provided for representation of the people only in one branch, and those who believed that the whole authority of the government was based on representation.

Yet it was logical to hold the first view, which was that of an overwhelming majority of those who left any record of their opinions, and still to entertain radical ideas on the subject of representation. If the people had a legitimate share in one House only, it became all the more important that they should enjoy a full and free voice there. Granville Sharp actually stated this in the first half of the lengthy title of his best-known pamphlet, *A Declaration of the People's Natural Right to a Share in the Legislature*; an emphasis which he perhaps redressed by adding, *Which is the fundamental principle of the British Constitution of State*. Sharp attacked Pufendorf and other continental civil lawyers for attempting to substitute will for reason as the foundation of law; the maxim, 'the law to bind all must be approved by all' struck Sharp as being a principle of natural equity, which led him to affirm that a share in the legislature was not only a British right, but a natural right. The doctrine of the omnipotence of Parliament he denounced as 'a kind of popery in politics'. Sharp thus ranged himself with the natural rights school in America, and expressed the sincerest sympathy with the Colonists in their resistance to parliamentary tyranny; representation being an essential element in maintaining the equilibrium of power, or mixed government limited by law, whenever British government ceased to be limited in any part of the dominions it ceased to be lawful. Yet Sharp was devotedly loyal to the Empire, and pointed out elsewhere that reform at home would convince the Americans of the sincerity of the sovereign and would thus promote the recovery of the Empire.[1] But when this was written, in 1777, it was too late for such gestures even if they had been possible. When the young Pitt put forward his first reform plan in 1782 he stated the same view: that of a balanced Constitution in which the people had their share through the House of Commons; it was that House only which had become corrupt and was to be reformed. Even the radical Duke of Richmond, who as early as 1780 introduced a Bill for annual parliaments and universal suffrage, held the same general view of the Constitution. The restoration of a genuine representative system in the Commons was a basic step to the re-establishment of the Constitution on its true principles. Richmond, moreover, wanted to cut through the jumble of boroughs and counties and establish equal electoral districts, to be called boroughs, thus introducing into the

[1] Granville Sharp, *The Legal Means of Political Reformation* (7th edition, London 1780), 19.

House of Commons the pure principle of numerical representation: but only in the House of Commons. His scheme would have left the House of Lords free to pursue its own interests.[1]

It would have been extremely difficult for any reformer, however bent on the rights of individuals, to separate the idea of representation from that of property. 'I talk not of *boroughs* — I talk of *men*', avowed the dauntless Major Cartwright; but that did not prevent him for connecting men politically with their property. His political thought admitted no inconsistency in advocating universal manhood suffrage in the most forthright egalitarian terms and proceeding to establish property qualifications for Members of Parliament. For a county Member, he thought that a landed estate of £400 'might be sufficient'; for London, the same, or otherwise property in the kingdom worth £12,000; for other cities, £300 in land or £9,000 in other property — clear of all debts and demands.[2] In Cartwright's House of Commons, the interests of property would be in very safe hands.

Cartwright's conception of the good Whig society, however, was consistent and remarkably complete. He proceeded from the rationality of man, without which freedom of choice, and thence virtue and vice, would have no meaning. In this view, both law and religion presupposed freedom of choice, and happiness appears to have been the result of freely chosen good actions. Moreover he supposed that all men shared equally in the attributes of sense, feeling, and affection, were guided by the same reason, and restrained by the same moral sense. 'It is liberty, not dominion, which is held by divine right,' he declared. Special talents and virtues might elevate men; and he admitted that large states, being incapable of pure democracy, had found hereditary distinctions useful. But ultimately all these depended on the will of the people.

Cartwright did not want to tear down the existing Constitution. The legislative power was reposed in king, nobles, and in delegates to represent the commons, and he asserted that in its genuine spirit and purity the British Constitution was harmonious with the laws of nature. But the manifold evils of the time — in which he included not only great political disasters such as the revolt of the Colonies, but the national debt, the prevalence of cruel statutes and punishments, the distress of the poor, the multitudes of beggars, the vice of the cities, and the gaming and adultery of the higher ranks — could be remedied by a true representation of the people in their own branch.

---

[1] *Parliamentary History*, xxii. 1417; xxi. 686–8. Alison Gilbert Olson, *The Radical Duke* (Oxford, 1961), 48–60.

[2] John Cartwright, *Take Your Choice!* (London, 1776), 58–9, 69.

That would of course necessitate annual parliaments and equal representation. And equal representation meant the numerical principle of equal electoral districts applied in minute detail. He gave close attention to his central theme of universal manhood suffrage, arguing against Blackstone that personality was 'the *sole right* of being represented, property has in reality nothing to do with the case. The property of any one is totally involved in the *man*'; it was worthy of the attention of his Member of Parliament, but contributed nothing to his right of having that representative. Cutting below the conventional complacency of moderate reformers, he observed that the poor had an interest in the Constitution and in representation — a poor man had a wife and children and, as Locke had said, every man had a property in his own person; the labouring man paid taxes on his food and clothes and no man ought to be taxed without his consent. According, therefore, to the received doctrine of property, no man could be without a right to vote for the legislature.[1]

Cartwright's view on property would be easy to misunderstand, and still easier to misrepresent, perhaps because the issue seemed to him so plain. He fully adhered to the philosophy, derived from Locke and set out at some length by James Burgh in his recently published volumes, that every man owned an inalienable property in his life, personal liberty, his character, and his right to earnings.[2] This, then, was the legitimate property which was entitled to representation; but its representation was fully achieved by the numerical representation of individuals; there was no property beyond the individual to be weighed in the scale of political rights. This is not to imply any doctrine of communal or equal property. The ownership of estates and personal possessions was clearly a legitimate right too — and Cartwright, as has been seen, laid down property qualifications, high ones at that, for Members of Parliament. The difficulty would be resolved through the connection between rationality, virtue, liberty and property. Cartwright, like Jefferson (but unlike Madison), was an optimistic Whig. He never doubted that the people, once properly enfranchised, would promote right actions, and that right actions could remedy the grievances from which they suffered. Their own rights being protected, they would lay no claim to the property of others, and the high property qualifications, while standing as a decent safeguard against improper or mobbish elements, would presumably be agreed as reflecting the common people's natural respect for their social superiors. He was an extremely outspoken and courageous man who seems

[1] Cartwright, *Take your Choice!*, 2, 3, 4–6, 8–10, 15, 19–20, 22, 58–62.
[2] *Political Disquisitions*, i. 37.

unlikely to have put the point in merely to make his other arguments more acceptable; that seats in Parliament should be filled by gentry and merchants seemed to him to be a matter of course; he did not even think the point needed explanation. Neither did he pause to consider why, in that case, such qualifications should have appeared necessary.

One of the most revealing touches in the pamphlet, following the exposition of the division of the kingdom into equal electoral districts, came in the observation that the proportions of representatives (for different sections of the country) could be made perpetual, 'as no alteration, in point of numbers, could possibly be so considerable, as to give the people either cause or inclination to demand a new proportional division throughout the kingdom'.[1] It was, then, a pre-industrial, an essentially domesticated rural nation that Cartwright had in mind, as static as the Oceana of Harrington! And yet he was to live into the era when the reform of Parliament would be imminent for precisely the reasons of which he denied the possibility — a vast alteration in the distribution of population; and would become imminent, moreover, upon the grounds that took very little account of the supposed rationality and equality which he urged as the most cogent reasons!

Burgh, whose compendium provided much of the source information used by parliamentary reformers in this period, had been responsible for some confusion about the representation of property. Although he gave space to the individualist view adopted by Cartwright, he also complained that one of the chief grievances requiring redress in Parliament was that 'they are not a representation of the property of the British people'; and he elaborated the point by a comparison with stockholding in the East India Company. His other chief grievances were length of parliaments and the corruption both of elections and of members in their voting in the House.[2] These were typical City views. Wilkes, advocating parliamentary reform in 1776, developed Burgh's thesis about the interest of the poor in the making of laws for their protection and in the taxation of commodities they had to live on, and mentioned the importance of laws protecting mechanics and labourers in contracts and agreements with 'rapacious masters'.[3]

Once natural rights had been postulated as the basis for civil society, it became difficult to stop short of universal suffrage — including women, as opponents of reform were fond of pointing out. The strongest centre of this school was in Westminster, where the sub-committee of the Association produced, on 27 May 1780, a model report for the extreme principles of

[1] Cartwright, *Take Your Choice!*, 63–64.
[2] *Political Disquisitions*, i. 24–26.   [3] *Parliamentary History*, xviii. 1295–6.

radical reform. The ground that was becoming familiar about the rights of individuals was re-covered; the argument led straight to universal male suffrage exercised in equal electoral districts, payment of members, annual parliaments, the abolition of property qualifications for members, the use of the secret ballot, the total exclusion of placemen. Not least important as a consequence of the setting up of equal districts was the point that each of these new constituencies was to elect a single member.[1] When this aim was achieved a century later, it greatly facilitated the organisation of nation-wide political parties. These views, which had no prospect of practical adoption, reflected the rational purism of Dr John Jebb, a former Fellow of Peterhouse who, after having resigned his fellowship owing to the onset of Unitarian convictions which of course conflicted with the Thirty-nine Articles, had become a physician and an energetic reformer.[2]

The contributions of religious dissent were also reflected in the dedication to the reform movement of Dr Richard Price, who — like Dr Joseph Priestley — gave it both intellectual force and a socially permissible kind of moral fervour. Price, whose pamphlet on civil liberty appeared in the year of American Independence, separated civil from other forms of liberty and emphasised the community's right to self-government by universal suffrage.[3]

But universal suffrage was a wholly academic ideal. So absurd did it appear to nearly all ordinary and practical people that the extremism of the Westminster sub-committee could only embarrass men like Wyvill, who had some hopes of obtaining support in Parliament for more moderate measures. It gave aid and comfort to the enemies of all reform, such as Soame Jenyns, whose influential tract, *Thoughts on a Parliamentary Reform*, was published in 1784. The great object, he said, was to secure a parliament totally independent of the Crown and its ministers; and universal suffrage with annual parliaments was the most uniform, consistent, and effective scheme of reform proposed; the only objection to it being that it was absolutely and utterly impracticable. He then invited readers to imagine the riot and confusion of letting loose the multitudes of labourers and 'manufacturers' of every kind, 'of soldiers and sailors, thieves, smugglers, rogues and vagabonds'. Since London had gone through the terrifying ordeal of the Gordon riots, it did not take a great deal of imagination to picture the mob in action at

[1] Christopher Wyvill, *Political Papers, Chiefly Respecting the Attempt of the County of York . . . to Effect a Reformation of the Parliament of Great Britain*, 6 vols. (1794–1808), i. 228–43.

[2] Similar views were advanced by other ardent Radicals, such as Brand Hollis and the printer, John Almon, publisher of *The Annual Register*.

[3] Richard Price, *The Nature of Civil Liberty* (London, 1776).

elections, nor did the sober citizenry need much exhortation to steel them against giving the suffrage to people without property to defend.

Property, in fact, was the only basis on which any extension could be hoped for or, in the opinion of practical reformers, even desired. Christopher Wyvill went as far as wishing to extend the suffrage to copyholders. This, in view of the complexity of the land tenures in England, meant taking in more small tenants — many of whom already enjoyed the privilege owing to slightly different terms of tenure; it would increase the weight of the lesser gentry without in any way threatening to bring in the city mobs. Wyvill never departed from the convention that the ownership of some measure of property must be the criterion of that kind of social responsibility which made the suffrage franchise safe. In his only theoretical publication — which, significantly, was a letter of advice to the Volunteer movement in Ulster, and not a proposal to be adopted in England — he considered the more radical principles, only to reject them. Society, he thought, had a right to exclude from the exercise of the rights of citizens such persons as could not hold them without danger to the public.[1] The public, then, the political nation, consisted of the owners of its land and property. At the ebb tide of the reform movement, in 1797, Charles Grey was ready to go almost as far on the qualifications of M.P.s. He introduced in that year another motion for an enquiry into parliamentary reform, arguing that seats should be distributed on a basis, not of universal suffrage indeed, but of universal representation; the qualifications should be such that no man, however mean, might not hope by honest industry and exertions to obtain a seat in the House of Commons. He advocated single-member constituencies, which by implication were to be composed of equal electorates. The only men he wished to exclude from Parliament were those who had neither landed property, nor were engaged in any commercial enterprise, nor were professors of any science — men without property, industry, or talents, who obtained seats through the influence of great men. Grey revealed the character of a Whig with a great stake in that landed interest when he remarked the great towns should have a larger number of electors per representative than the counties — otherwise 'the populous towns would acquire a too great local ascendancy'. (In the great towns he wanted to extend the suffrage to householders.) Grey also gave it as his view that a father, having given a hostage to society, was 'not unworthy of a share in the legislation'.[2]

[1] Wyvill, *Papers*, iii. 49–55, 58–76.
[2] *Parliamentary History*, xxxiii, 644–53. Cf. Madison's views, see 303. Grey's argument had been put by another moderate reform essayist two years earlier, who maintained that

Down to the Reform Bill, the idea of suffrage extension, as a right or an expedient, had to do battle with the old concept of property in suffrage. The disfranchisement of places found guilty of electoral corruption, or their absorption into larger constituencies, thereby diminishing the value of the votes owned by the original electorate, continued to provoke remonstrances on the grounds urged by Lord North. Sir William Grant, Master of the Rolls, called the principle 'monstrous' when bribery at Aylesbury was debated in 1804; if all the houses in Aylesbury were to fall down except six, the six householders would undoubtedly be the voters of Aylesbury, he declared; those burgers who had not taken bribes ought to be the electors, 'and should not have their franchise deteriorated by letting in a number of strangers to share them'. The same issue was raised when Lord John Russell's Motion for Reform was introduced in 1819 — once again supporters had to urge that the privilege of voting was not a property but a public trust. By 1827 Canning, fighting a rearguard action, was clearly aware that the defence of a distinct propertied right in the suffrage was no longer tenable. But still, in cases where corruption called for parliamentary action — this time in Grampound and Penryn — 'the most constitutional mode was, not to adopt an entirely new representation, but to confine, as much as possible, the franchise — which though strictly a public privilege was still in an innocent sense a valuable private possession — to the same description of interest as that from which it was taken'. The forces against reform, overwhelming in the eighteenth century, thus proved resilient into the nineteenth; and part of their strength lay in their ability, whether they were replying to reformers such as Burgh and Cartwright, or to Fox or Grey in Parliament, to appeal to a fundamental belief in the relation of property to the social structure which moderate reformers shared with them.

Burgh's own principal intention was to build up a force of public opinion that would compel Parliament to reform itself. He had no intention of threatening it with rebellion nor of subverting the social order. Neither had the gentry who lent themselves to Wyvill's movement. Wyvill and Granville Sharp urged and exercised caution; and the history of the movement is at least as remarkable for the reticence and opposition of the gentry of several of the

the nation was made up of a collection of families, and that therefore householders should be permitted to vote, as they did in America. John Longley, *An Essay toward forming a more complete Representation of the Commons of Great Britain* (London, 1795). This writer, who was under the mistaken impression that American elections were free from riots, was a follower of the Gothic tradition; he wanted a restoration of King Alfred's division of the kingdom, the Saxon Constitution, and the laws of Edward the Confessor.

counties approached, and for their tendency to withdraw after an initial response, as it is for forthright indignation against the Government. It was the Radicals in Westminster, notably Jebb, who took the most revolutionary view; and Jebb in fact held that as Parliament was not a true representative body, an association that truly represented the people would have a higher constitutional power; it would actually supersede Parliament if it failed to act.[1] He was ready to look on the Association, acting nationally through a meeting of delegations of county freeholders as a sort of convention parliament. This view was chimerical. There was no hiatus in the continuous exercise of government power, no collapse of the executive, and no failure of the Civil Service through which such a Convention could stride to power — even if it had wanted to, which it did not. But no account of the development of opinion can overlook the fright of the Gordon Riots, which gripped London in June 1780. What began as a sordid but frivolous demonstration against Roman Catholics turned into an orgy of fire and loot. The house of the good Sir George Savile, M.P. for Yorkshire and one of the most distinguished friends of moderate reform, was attacked; members of the Government were roughly handled; no person to whom the mob took a passing dislike could feel safe; prisons were stormed, and brigades of ruffians rampaged in the streets. This, then, was the mob. It was this episode, coupled with the recollection of the Wilkite demonstrations, that so powerfully reinforced the conservative convictions of the parliamentary majority against any radical extension of the political nation. Members of Parliament must have felt that they had witnessed a living demonstration of the meaning of the often repeated phrases about property and responsibility. It is true that the argument could be made to cut the other way: reform might forestall worse disasters; and a strengthening of the landed interest would be reform with restoration. But this argument lacked urgency because the discontents upon which the landed movement was based were transient. They held no threat to the peace of the country. Worse disaster did strike, soon afterwards, as though in dark confirmation of the suspicions of the conservative majority — in France in 1789.

[1] Christie, *Wilkes, Wyvill and Reform*, 73; Granville Sharp, *Circular Letter to the Petitioning Counties* (London, 1780); Pares, *George III*; Oscar and Mary Handlin, 'James Burgh and American Revolutionary Theory', Massachusetts Historical Society *Proceedings* vol. 73 (1961). 38–57.

III. RADICAL REFORM

The logic of the Association arguments for parliamentary reform cut somewhat deeper than the intentions of the gentry. The political life of the country was arranged in a variety of shires, of corporations, or of the newly respectable 'interests'; but the reform arguments implied the existence of the political personality of individuals. As a philosophical proposition the political individual had existed at least since Hobbes and had developed a distinct strength of character from the inspiration of the Levellers and their True Whig successors.[1] But as a component of any real political movement he did not exist: he was an idea in the mind of his masters. That idea, infused with life by the events of the American revolutionary era, began to acquire form and substance in Britain with the aid of another revolution.

The influence of the French Revolution on British politics was profound, but gradual. The Reform movement of the 1780s had already receded and Wyvill's chief hope, Pitt, whom Jebb had never trusted as a reformer, had lost interest. In March 1790, when the Irishman, Flood, introduced a carefully thought out plan of reform in a motion in the Commons, Fox laid the matter to rest by observing that he considered this 'a sleeping question, for the present'.[2]

The execution of the king and queen of France and the entry of Britain into the continental war divided the country bitterly. The Foxite Whigs affirmed their basic satisfaction with the course of the Revolution and denounced the warlike policy of the administration; in doing so they placed themselves at the front of a movement that was springing from new sources in English society. Both in London and in the industrial north, tradesmen and skilled workers, invigorated by the French example, began to take an interest in parliamentary reform. In May 1792 a group from Sheffield,

---

[1] For an interesting discussion of the economic mechanism which helped to liberate this view, see Macpherson, *Political Theory*.

[2] For Jebb's opinion, *Life and Correspondence of Cartwright*, 159–80. Decline of Pitt's interest, *Wyvill Papers*, iv. 31–32 n. 61. *Parliamentary History*, xxviii. 452, 471. Flood said that unless the people were actually represented, they were not represented at all. 'In what does actual representation consist? In this, that as, by the general law of the Constitution, the majority is to decide for the whole, the representative must be chosen by a body of constituents, whereof the elective franchise may extend to the majority of the people.' Fox remarked that the outline of these proposals was the best that had been suggested, which anticipates his later inclination towards more radical reforms: but he did not agree with Flood that the representation ought always to be founded on a majority.

calling themselves 'mostly tradesmen and artificers dispossessed of freehold land' sent a significant petition to the House of Commons. They advanced, on their own behalf, the old arguments that 'their all is at stake', that they paid their full share of taxes, and so on; but such arguments had come previously only from the ranks of the gentry or the educated persons already of parliamentary class. '[We] think men are the objects of representation,' declared the petitioners, 'and not the land of the freeholder, or the houses of the borough-monger.'[1] A few days later, reform petitions were presented from no fewer than twenty-three places, most of them in Scotland.[2] The major debate was opened by Grey's motion for reform.

Grey, supported by Erskine, an able recruit to the debating ranks of the reformers, pleaded for a restoration of the principles of the English Revolution, a moderate extension of the franchise and a simplification of electoral procedure together with some redistribution of seats. Pitt, goaded by reminders of his reformist past, turned fiercely on the reformist Whigs and, in a furious attack on the French Revolution and all its works, linked their objects with the 'equalised anarchy announced in the code of French legislation'. He 'perceived the formation of a small but not contemptible party who wished to introduce those French principles which he could not but regard with horror'.[3]

The debate of 1793 has already been mentioned because of the adoption of the fully-fledged theory of interest representation into the canons of parliamentary conservatism by Jenkinson and Mornington. It was notable also for a new streak of radical doctrine in the parliamentary Whigs. Sheridan and Fox spoke with new and unusual force in favour of the principle of representation. Sheridan took up the point that opponents of reform had stressed that the principle of the constitution was selective; but that, he replied, was confusing the means with the principle. 'The principle of our Constitution was representation; the means was selection and distribution.' According to a Bill of James I's reign, the whole of the Commons were supposed to be present when a Bill passed their House.[4] He was laying

---

[1] *Parliamentary History*, xxx. 776. Compare the petition of the non-freeholders of Richmond, Virginia, in 1829; and Virginia reform petitions of 1796. The principles are the same, and the language not far different.

[2] *Parliamentary History*, xxx. 786. And including a printed petition from Norwich; the Speaker pointed out that by a resolution of 23 September 1656, private petitions were not to be printed; and despite the objections of Fox, the latter was withdrawn.

[3] *Parliamentary History*, xxx. 234, 800–8, 890–902.

[4] There was an ancient custom that when a division led to the passing of a Bill, the whole House, opponents as well as supporters of the Bill, must go out with it and bring it in

a new and significant emphasis on representation. Fox took the same theme at great length and with considerable eloquence. He insisted — probably for the first time in his career — that the majority principle was right, and even said that his objection to universal suffrage was not due to mistrust of the majority, but because there was no certain mode of collecting such a suffrage; and that owing to illegitimate influences, an appeal to a limited number would give a better guide to the desire of the majority. In 1797 he was to say 'The system should satisfy the prejudices and the pride, as well as the reason of the people'. The House of Commons should not only be, but appear to be, the representatives of the people. Good men, he admitted, sat for close boroughs; but that was not the whole issue — it was not representation. 'If a man comes here as a proprietor of a burgage tenure, he does not come here as a representative of the people.' And in the earlier debate, he flourished the incendiary issue of the peerage and the monarchy. A House of Commons chosen to be a complete representation of the people would be too powerful for the House of Lords and even the king; the people were not made for them, but they for the people. But he was sure that the people felt and believed the Lords and the king to be useful and essential parts of the Constitution, and as such a freely chosen House of Commons would cherish and protect them both — 'within', he added, 'the bounds that the Constitution had assigned to them'.[1]

Fox, Grey, Whitbread, Sheridan, Flood, and the other speakers for reform had always disclaimed any intention of altering the system of the Constitution. But in this debate, Fox and Sheridan imparted a more radical inclination to their standard doctrines. The Conservatives had always spoken, and even though they had come to adopt the colours of the interest principle, they still spoke of the Constitution as consisting of King, Lords, and Commons; the House of Commons providing 'the representation'. This definite article can tell us a long story. For it was significant in the speeches of the Whigs by its quiet disappearance. They had ceased to speak of 'the representation'. And in the same period they ceased to speak, as reformers had always done in the past, of 'a reform in Parliament', and began to speak of 'a reform of Parliament'. When the definite article had gone, it left representation standing alone as the leading principle, no longer merely an ingredient, of the Constitution. Briefly, to Fox and Sheridan and to their

---

again. 'The practice clearly had its origin in the twin medieval ideas that law-making involved the consent of the whole community and that members were attorneys for their constituencies.' Neale, *Elizabethan House of Commons*, 397–8.

[1] *Parliamentary History*, xxx. 921. *Debrett*, ii. 642–7.

successors in the long struggle for parliamentary reform, the true merit of the Constitution was that it was based on representation.

Too much should not be made of this. Political divisions had become intensely bitter and were to get even worse. Fox eventually protested against Pitt's repressive policies by the misguided step of refusing to attend Parliament at all. The Foxite Whigs were speaking out of their hatred for the administration and under no danger of being called to exemplify their words; Grey himself was never so radical again, certainly not when he was Prime Minister. But the discussion retains its significance, because it exposed the cargo which lay in the hold of the stately Whig galleon; a cargo which helped to give it ballast and perhaps, in the end, to give point to its voyage.

The parliamentary reformers had to tread with particular care round the skirts of the monarchy and peerage. Their enemies always enjoyed the tactical advantage of being able to point out that the logic of reforming the system of representation led straight to an exclusively representative government and would therefore end in a pure republic. Such risks proved no inhibition to the rough intellectual energies of Thomas Paine, whose pamphlet, *Common Sense*, had helped to release the urge for American independence from the doubts imposed by habitual loyalties. Paine did not hesitate to derive pure republican principles from the basic standard of representative government; and his manner of arguing had a brusque simplicity calculated to appeal to all those who wanted to feel that the whole complex subject lay fully within their grasp. Consequently he gave considerable anxiety to those who were promoting measures for practical reform. Cartwright, working in two societies formed in the 1790s — the Friends of the People and the Friends of the Liberty of the Press — made it part of his task to counteract the efforts of Paine towards pure republicanism.[1] But Paine, who bitterly attacked the economic privileges vested in the legislative power of the Lords, had also seen that certain redistributive economic principles could be enforced as a result of a reform of representation, and probably exerted some influence on the new Radical movement by urging a humane plan of tax reimbursements to the poor, and of taxation graded according to ability to pay.[2]

The Friends of the People, as the name hinted, were not too intimately connected with the people themselves. The Society was founded in April 1792 to promote parliamentary reform and restore freedom of elections, by Charles Grey, Erskine, and others, and had twenty-three members of

[1] *Life and Correspondence of Cartwright*, 192.
[2] Thomas Paine, *Rights of Man* (London, 1792), ii. 56–59, 76–81.

Parliament among its founders. Its social composition is indicated by its subscription: two and a half guineas on joining, and two and a half guineas a year thereafter. The Society ceased to meet after the prosecutions against reformers started by the Pitt administration in 1794.[1] By contrast, the London Corresponding Society, which held a first meeting of eight persons in January 1792, asked for a subscription of one penny a week.

The revived Society for Constitutional Information was also in the field adding its efforts to those of the Friends of the People in collecting and diffusing knowledge about political practices. The Friends made a most useful contribution when, after investigation, they made public a report on the state of representation, giving much detail of the contrast between the distribution of parliamentary seats and of centres of population, and of the actual control of close boroughs, which formed the basis for Grey's campaign in the Commons. But the London Corresponding Society regarded them with distrust, Francis Place noting that one of the Friends' earliest acts was to disclaim all connection with the Society for Constitutional Information 'and with every society that did not adopt their vague and general declaration'.[2]

The London Corresponding Society began, like the others, with a simple interest in the reform of Parliament. By the end of 1794, however, the drafting of a Constitution brought out some of the social views underlying its concrete political aims. This Constitution went through two drafts, the second being revised, abridged, and printed by order of the general committee.[3] According to this document, individuals need not relinquish any more of their natural independence than was necessary to preserve the weak against the strong, and to enable the whole body to act with union and concert, for the general good and against common enemies. All government abstractly considered was an evil; the question was, not how much government the people would bear, but how little was required to secure the grand object of general happiness. Taxes ought to be levied impartially on the whole body according to capability. (These passages seem to reflect Paine's influence.) There should be no privileges and no violence (as in the impressing of seamen). The statement went on to declare what were the civil rights to the enjoyment of which all persons in society were equally entitled.

These began with the elements: of protection for liberty, life, and property, and in the redress of grievances; but they were then elaborated to include 'equality of enjoyment of bodily and mental faculties', and equality

---

[1] Francis Place papers, British Museum add. mss. 27808.
[2] Add. MS. 27808.　　　　　[3] Add. MS. 27813.

of encouragement for the exercise of talents, and consequently 'the free enjoyment of the advantages thereby obtained'. Freedom of publication and worship, and the unrestrained exercise of private judgment not involving trespass on the equal rights of fellow citizens, concluded the list. The method advocated for securing these rights was equality in the choice of representatives; every officer and magistrate should be made responsible to 'the great body of the people'.

The individual emerged from this declaration, not merely as an atomic politic unit, but as a person capable of growth and cultivation; and in spite of the lightness with which government was supposed to rest on the citizens, society was clearly intended to be responsible to every one of its component members for the protection and encouragement of those latent talents. It was a by no means unsophisticated view of the obligations of society in the eighteenth century. The earlier draft, which was much longer and more detailed, listed the specific grievances which a true representation of the people was expected to redress. The first of these was the Corn Act, 'a grievance immediately resulting from the restriction of representatives to men of landed property'. The price of bread had more than doubled, while good seasons led to exports in order to advance prices. The game laws, enforced by a 'Bashaw in the form of a country justice' from whom there was no appeal; the excise laws and stamp duties, and the consequent system of spies and informers; the Mutiny Act; the impress service; the system by which army and navy promotions resulted from parliamentary connections — all these evils had grown up under the protection of a corrupt and unfair representation and could be rectified by reform. The statement demanded that all partial corporations be abolished and the whole land be considered as one corporation. It called for an equal division of the country into electoral districts, for the residential requirement for voters, universal and annual suffrage, residence of representatives, and payment for their services. Votes should if necessary be brought in writing, to prevent riots and, significantly, to prevent voting in party groups — but the secret ballot was not recommended. It appears that the opinions of the Duke of Richmond, who regarded the ballot as degrading to Englishmen, may have influenced this decision.[1]

Two years earlier, the founders of the Society, Thomas Hardy and Maurice Margarot, had issued an Address to the Inhabitants of Great Britain[2] which claimed that an honest parliament could cut its meetings

---

[1] Add. MS. 27808. However, the ballot was adopted for elections in the Society.
[2] Add. MS. 27812.

down to sixty-four days in the year. There would be no party debates, 'the interest of the people being one'. (Long speeches would also diminish, 'the people seeking reason not oratory', a well-taken point.) A Declaration adopted in November 1792 expressly repudiated the charge that the Society was hostile to king or Parliament; 'we wish only to *restore* the lost liberties of the constitution', and had no intention of invading the property of others. This led to an important explanation of the social views of the Society.

We know and are sensible [they said] that the wages of every man are his right; *that differences of strength of talents, and of industry, do and ought to afford proportional distinctions of property*, which when acquired and confirmed by the laws, is sacred and inviolable.

And on the explosive question of France, they observed that as Britain had never sunk so low at the foot of despotism 'so it is not requisite that we should appeal to the same awful Tribunal as our brethren on the Continent'.

We desire [they continued] to overthrow no property, but what has been raised on the ruins of our liberty! We look with reverence on the landed and commercial interests of our country; but we view with abhorrence that monopoly of burgage tenures, unwarranted by law or reason in this or any other nation in Europe.

Though the House of Commons was the source of their calamities it might also be that of their deliverance.

When these assumptions, and the demands growing from them, are brought into relation with one another and viewed as a whole, they reveal an analysis of English society, both actual and desired, that compares favourably with those of philosopher Paley (who thought these people ought to be content with their lot) or those of eminent parliamentarians expounding the theory of interest representation. All the ills of the people were held to be due to faults in the electoral system. The bitterly attacked corn and game laws were seen as products of the over-representation of the landed interest; the vast tangle of privileges and abuses was attributed to the chronic corruption of the system over the last century. A state of warfare between the productive classes of the nation was nowhere held to be a necessary condition; rather it was a *malaise* to be cured. Their desire was to reduce the country to one harmonious whole, with the result that the really necessary business of Parliament could be transacted in a session of two months; and in this whole, the majority that would rule in Parliament would clearly reflect the wishes of the majority of the country. Inequalities of wealth were the natural products of inequalities of talent and sheer willingness to work; the great wrong arose when the poor were taxed to support unnatural inequalities that were the products of privilege and abuse. These economic inequalities were plainly seen as harmful to the development of the individual personality, to which each person was entitled as a civil right.[1] But once the principle of equality had been restored to the representative system, and burgage tenures had been cut away, the disease would be cured, the elements would spring back into their natural, harmonious relations with each other, and the nation, to use the significant phrase excised from the final draft of the Constitution, would form 'one corporation', whose majority would move it as a whole.

The Pitt administration chose to persecute and destroy the London Corresponding Society and to try Thomas Hardy for treason. (He was acquitted by a London jury.)[2] They might have taken the view that the philosophy of the Society was remarkably flattering to the Constitution. The new Radicals sought no remedies of the French type, nor did they admit that their social superiors were enemies to their own interests; they stoutly maintained, on the contrary, that the Constitution contained all the principles necessary for the happiness of the country. They were children still of the pre-industrial order of English reform, and in spite of the fact that they were townsmen, catering for an increasingly urban type of society, their whole attitude to politics reveals a great confidence in the integrity of the individual. But it would not need a great deal to tilt this movement into a more revolutionary channel. It was, however, only one of the forces at work in British politics, and one which had no hope of success without the alliance of the entrenched powers in Parliament. Francis Place, who took over the leadership from Hardy, was to live into the era when industry had assembled the new forces of a working-class proletariat. That body could exert effective pressure on the political system only by bridging the gap

---

[1] Cf. Joseph Priestley, *An Essay on the First Principles of Government* (London, 1768), 55–59: 'The more political liberty the people have, the safer is their civil liberty'. And, 'A sense of political and civil slavery makes a man think meanly of himself. . . .' It had the effect of debasing his mind and making him abject; a sense of political and civil liberty, even if not exerted, gave a feeling of power and importance. These remarks made in 1768 may be compared with the sociological arguments in favour of equal rights for Negroes in the United States, as advanced before the Supreme Court in 1954.

[2] On 5 November 1794. A signal date in the history of British liberties, in commemoration of which it might be considered appropriate to let off a few fireworks.

between Whigs and Radicals, already marked out in 1794 by the London Corresponding Society:[1] and this could be achieved only by an alliance between the workers and the employers of their labour.

6. The Debate Continues, but History Goes a Little Faster

Political individualism received a new injection of vitality and an addition of intellectual respectability from the Utilitarians, whose system reduced all political decisions to an individual basis. When Utilitarian logic was applied to politics it led to universal suffrage. However, the Utilitarians, like the more limited Whig reformers in Parliament, continued to attach great importance to a socially reliable, economically substantial, and educated leadership.

Parliament, which stood in ever-increasing need of reform, and which on a variety of issues was demonstrably out of touch with public opinion, was no longer governed by the conventions of the eighteenth century. The recognised accountability of Parliament to public opinion was one of the principal changes. The rise of Press reporting had forced Parliament to abandon its earlier privacy, a development which amounted to a profound modification in the Constitution.

This improvement did not check the impetus to reform: on the contrary it made it more urgent. The power of the drive for reform came from the combination of two separate forces. The Radicals, supporters of the principle of political individualism, were leaders of the movement for manhood suffrage. The greater parliamentary Whigs, who in due course formed a government under Grey, were mainly interested in a moderate extension of suffrage and a wide redistribution of parliamentary seats. The impetus for this reform came from the newer centres of industrial wealth and population.

When the Whig view of politics is examined in detail it proves to be a new and sophisticated version of the respectable doctrine of interest representation. The chief difference between them and the Tories was over what interests ought to be

[1] The London Corresponding Society spoke of being 'united for a Radical Reform in Parliament'. Add. MS. 27814. This early use of the word gives the movement its new designation.

represented. The Radicals were keenly aware of this but were hopelessly out-numbered, even in the reformed House of Commons.

The principle of individualism made a slight advance in 1832. That limited advance was not due to Radical strength. It was due to the alliance with property, which demanded seats even more than votes. Yet it was only through the operation of this alliance that political individualism could work towards majority rule, either in Britain or America.

THE political activists who resumed the drive for parliamentary reform while Napoleon still dominated Europe continued to insist that their aim was to restore the old Constitution. The first object, Burdett proclaimed, was to reunite king and people by a common bond of allegiance and protection; the balance of the Constitution would be restored by defending both the prerogative and the rights of the people. Ponsonby, speaking in the Commons on Thomas Brand's motion for reform in 1812, tried to disarm the apprehension that a truly representative House of Commons would prove too powerful for the Lords and Crown. But it was precisely that fear which the Hon. J. W. Ward,[1] who was to become one of the most eloquent opponents of reform, dwelt on in this debate, the Commons was an assembly which had 'in a manner absorbed the whole power of the state'; he therefore made no pretence that the House, as constituted, was already a perfect representation; and he defended the influence in it of Crown and Lords.[2] There was some truth in this account of the power of the Commons, and the fear behind it was that after an effective reform, it would become the whole truth. Grey, though he affirmed himself a friend to 'temperate, intelligible, and definite reform' — by which he meant a limited measure which would not lead on to more — had become tepid;[3] the Whigs in Parliament would lend themselves to a cleaning-up measure like Curwen's, and 115 of them voted for Brand's much more radical Bill which called for triennial parliaments, but there was no practical hope for such gestures. Cartwright, returning to the attack, asserted that political liberty and parliamentary representation were convertible terms; he was coming down with increased emphasis on the character of the House of Commons as the only 'vital organ' of the nation — the only branch, he said, which was *essential* to LIBERTY — (the

[1] John William Ward, M.P. for the Borough of Wareham; George Ponsonby, who led the Whigs in the Commons after the elevation of Grey to the Lords, sat for Tavistock; Thomas Brand, M.P. for Hertford County.

[2] *Hansard*, xiii. 116.

[3] Watson, *Geo. III*, 450; G. M. Trevelyan, *Lord Grey of the Reform Bill* (London, 1920), 169–70.

emphasis was his own). Aristocracy and royalty now were merely 'useful alloys which may wear well and durably'. The Commons were the pure gold.[1] It was just this sort of tendency in the reformist argument that the Conservatives most feared. And its implications were yet to pose for the Whig reformers some of their most taxing dialectical problems.

I. ENTER THE UTILITARIANS

Meanwhile the Radicals found that their cause had recruited the formidable energies of the legal philosopher, Jeremy Bentham, who had developed the principle of utility into a systematic philosophy. In 1809, after his arguments for applying the hard test of utility as the method of procuring the greatest happiness of the greatest number had run up against consistent political frustration, he turned his attention to the problem of parliamentary representation. It was clear, from the atomistic character of the principle of the greatest happiness, that whatever political system Bentham approved would have to provide for a majority of individual units of happiness; and once Bentham had decided that these units could best judge their own interests, he was quickly led to conclude that they could provide for their own satisfaction by possession of the vote. It followed that they must each exercise equal weight, and that the electoral districts should be equally divided. The essay in which he announced these conclusions, his *Catechism*, was circulated privately and was not published until 1817. A few years later James Mill composed, as a contribution to the *Encyclopaedia Britannica*, his *Essay on Government*,[2] which was separately reprinted several times and was soon established as the full — to use a word they would have detested, the orthodox — exposition of the Utilitarians in that field.

Both the vigour and the weakness of Mill's exercise lay in the *a priori* manner of his reasoning. His conclusions were presented with clean and uncluttered simplicity because they were reached from first principles without any pause for the collection or examination of historical evidence. This attitude, which was made possible by the one-sidedness and finality of the Utilitarian assumptions about human nature, was exposed to its not very profound depths by Macaulay in his shattering review, published, on the occasion of a reprint, in the *Edinburgh Review*.[3]

[1] John Cartwright, *Reasons for Reformation* (London, 1809).

[2] Ernest Barker (ed.), James Mill, *Essay on Government* (Cambridge, 1937). Jeremy Bentham, *Plan of Parliamentary Reform in the form of a Catechism* (London, 1817).

[3] *Edinburgh Review*, 1829. The identification (which in any case would hardly be mis-

We have here [said Macaulay] an elaborate treatise on government, from which, but for two or three passing allusions, it would not appear that the author was aware that any governments actually existed among men. Certain propensities of human nature are assumed; and from these premises, the whole science of Politics is synthetically deduced!

Mill, however, despite his adoption of certain arguments that Macaulay exposed as being reversible, did confront the problem of how to bring about a community of interest between the government and the governed, which he answered with 'the grand discovery of modern times, the system of representation'.[1] In order to prevent the representative body from developing a corporate interest of its own, Mill advocated frequent elections. He made a pointed examination of the claims of interests, and it was here that he took up Jenkinson's defence of interest representation made in answer to Grey in 1793.[2] He argued that there would be nothing to prevent the various

takable!) is given by Barker in his Introduction to the *Essay*. Macaulay begins with a tribute to the Utilitarians as 'these smatterers . . . whose attainments just suffice to elevate them from the insignificance of dunces to the dignity of bores, and to spread dismay among their pious aunts and grandmothers . . .' Macaulay made nonsense of Mill's patronising treatment of the rights of women and exposed the shallowness of his thinking about the supposed propensity of people to oppress each other as though oppressive and cruel exploitation were the only manner of achieving personal satisfaction. He seemed particularly keen to ridicule the chiselled precision of Mill's style — which he no doubt felt as an implicit rebuke to just that kind of rounded eloquence which Macaulay himself practised so grandly.

[1] This curious attribution suffers least from being read to mean that effective, enforceable representation was a 'discovery of modern times'. Nevertheless, it certainly exposes Mill to the criticism that he was ignorant of history; it also shows that he arrived at his views by a completely separate route from the whole school of Whig and Radical reformers, who, despite a tendency to get lost in the mists of antiquity, were keenly aware of the representative element in the early constitutional history of England. Mill, a Scot, no doubt brought Scottish democratic ideas to bear on the political application of Bentham's Utilitarianism; until about 1808, Bentham expected the upper classes to apply his principles, which he had not regarded as politically democratic. (Barker's Introduction, xii–xiii.) James Madison had also attributed 'the great principle of representation' to 'Modern Europe', but he was well aware of the presence of the principle in ancient societies as a component if not a determinant element of government. *The Federalist*, nos. 14 and 63.

[2] Jenkinson, of course, as Lord Liverpool, was now Prime Minister. Barker suggests that Mill may really have been replying to an article in the *Edinburgh Review* of December 1818 by Sir James Mackintosh, who there expounded a theory of varied or functional representation as an alternative to Bentham's; however, it was Liverpool's speech that he cited, perhaps feeling that the political ideas of the reigning Prime Minister made a serviceable target.

interests which were represented in the House of Commons from forming into combinations powerful enough to dominate the whole of the un-represented part of the country; and the fact that he refrained from using specific issues in recent history, but preferred to allow the general implications of the argument to sink in as a point of principle, may well have added to the gradual effect on public opinion.

Macaulay, whose attack was in places somewhat overdrawn, had reason to be concerned; for Mill's reasoning was dangerous to the Whig reformers. They themselves were exponents of interest representation. Their difference with the Tories concerned the identity and extent of the great interests of the nation which ought to have members in Parliament; it was not, at root, a difference of principle.

Mill's thought was akin to that of the Radicals, in one distinctive difference from both Whigs and Tories. When he insisted on universal manhood suffrage and electoral equality, he accepted the implication that everything was to be determined by numbers.[1]

Nevertheless, a practical problem confronted the Utilitarians when they reached the end of the chain of reasoning leading from the greatest happiness of the greatest number to universal suffrage: how to ensure that the right people were elected? It was no less important that Mill should be able to answer this question satisfactorily than it had been to Charles Jenkinson to do so from the opposite point of view, in 1793. Mill was confident that the wisdom of the community lay in what he called 'the middle rank'; and equally, that the people below them, who were in the habit of seeking their advice, teaching their children to look up to them and depending on their assistance in every difficulty, would choose their political representatives from these social leaders.[2] He therefore felt safe in dismissing the fears aroused by occasional disturbances, pointing out that these occurred at times in manufacturing towns where there were a few rich, many poor, and a scarcity of the establishing force made up of the virtuous middle rank.

---

[1] And he carried this method to peculiar lengths. In discussing the dangers from majority rule, he argued that the interest of each member of the majority in oppressing the minority would not be very great, because 'Each man of the majority, if the majority were constituted the governing body, would have something less than the benefit of oppressing a single man'; but if voting qualifications 'did not admit a body of electors so large as the majority, in that case . . . we shall see again that each man would have a benefit equal to that derived from the oppression of more than one man' — and so on progressively as the elective body grew smaller. It was a curiously desiccated way of describing either the temptations or the methods of oppression, which certainly owed little to the observation of politics. *Essay on Government*, 50.   [2] Mill, *Essay on Government*, 70–73.

II. THE PROBLEM OF LEADERSHIP

The economic distresses arising from the shortages before and after the end of the Napoleonic Wars led to widespread violence. Unemployed machine wrecking in the industrial north and midlands, and sporadic rick-burning and acts of destruction in the countryside, must have helped to foster among innumerable owners of property the feeling of belonging to the 'middle rank', soon to become identified in the loose but prevalent term as the 'middle class', distinct from the propertyless urban and rural masses below, and the small but powerful aristocracy above. The ancient ritual of closing ranks against the mob would no longer work: the ranks were too thin and too many of those who belonged to the recognised propertied classes were themselves trying to get in. All the supporters of parliamentary reform were faced with the problem of assuring themselves, as well as their opponents, that neither redistribution of seats nor suffrage extension would result in the actual exercise of power by the labouring orders. On the dangers of admitting Bentham's plans for reform, the *Edinburgh Review* cautioned its readers that it all depended on what opinions were taken up by the majority: if the 'laborious classes' adopted the principle of universal suffrage then 'a permanent animosity between opinion and property must be the consequence'.[1]

When Whigs admitted to these anxieties, the Tories had the better of the tactical argument. J. W. Ward, speaking in the Commons in 1817, drew a vivid picture of the horrid consequences of democracy.

We are to imagine to ourselves five or six hundred persons, each with twenty or thirty thousand constituents at his back — no indolent, no contemplative, no retired persons among them; no persons that thought, and dared to act as if they thought, that the people can be better served, than by immediate compliance with the popular wish; all active, and enterprising — able, or making up the want of ability by those parts that so commonly supply their place in a democracy — without a single moment for pause, or reflection; dividing their feverish years betwixt debate and canvass — without dignity, without security — constantly catching at a trust that escaped too fast from their hands to be exercised with firmness, or wisdom, — bidding away at a perpetual auction of popularity, the happiness of the very people, whose favour they were to court. And this in an assembly ... that would be content to take one third of the power of the state, and leave the other two to be peaceably enjoyed by an hereditary monarch, and a privileged order![2]

[1] *Edinburgh Review*, no. 31, 1818–19, 172.
[2] *Hansard*, 36, 764–5 (20 May 1817).

Reformers undoubtedly had an obligation to counter this type of attack. James Mill had affirmed that the people would respect the monarchy and nobility because they would recognise them as beneficial to good government.[1] Lord John Russell, introducing his Reform Motion in 1821, took up Mill's line; disturbances in the rich and populous communities of Birmingham and Manchester were linked with the absence from those towns of the political leadership conferred by the habit of parliamentary representation. Consequently when such men as the Radical agitators Hunt and Knight came among them, 'the people knew not what to make of them or their doctrines'. On the other hand, in towns which were represented there were candidates for seats who handed on their opinions to those they wished to represent.[2] It was at least a debating point of some shrewdness, since it reversed the argument of his opponents. Nearly ten years later, Whig reformers were still hammering at the same point. The best reform, said Hobhouse, would not change the class of individuals who would sit in the Commons. The principal gentry and merchants would still be selected to represent the people, but — and the emphasis was important — 'a Reform would send them there on a different principle, and with different motives; and so assembled, they would act on different principles'.[3]

The prediction that a reformed parliament would still be a safe one for the existing order was substantiated by the general election of 1832, following the passage of the Reform Act. The new House of Commons was so similar in social composition to the old that even the banking, merchant, and industrial elements were no stronger, in comparison to the country gentry and aristocracy, than before.[4] The Radicals won a number of seats, their strength being enhanced by the energy and intellectual ability of their leading members, but they could make no lasting impression on policy except in alliance with the Whigs. It was a cause of acute dissatisfaction to them that, although they felt they would lose their identity and fail their constituents if they allowed themselves to be taken in tow by the Whigs, and although they regarded the Whigs and Tories as belonging to essentially the same classes and interests, they could never hope to gain a majority over them. Emotionally they wanted to drive the Whigs and Tories together to expose their similarities; tactically, it could mean only defeat for Radical purposes to do so. Nothing could make clearer the comfortable ascendancy enjoyed by the great propertied and landed interests who had divided over Reform, but had

---

[1] Mill, *Essay on Government*, 60–62.   [2] *Hansard*, N.S. v. 615 (9 May 1821).

[3] *Hansard*, N.S., xxii, 703 (18 February 1830).

[4] Elie Halévy, *History of the English People* (London, 1927), iii. 63; Gash, *Politics*, 106.

proved able to treat the distribution of political advantages as very much a family matter.[1]

From about 1821, when Canning had first admitted in the Commons his apprehension that eventual reform was probable,[2] that probability was increasingly influenced by the force of public opinion. The debate was not parliamentary but national. That fact alone represented a profound alteration in the texture of British politics, and one that had come about within the space of some sixty or seventy years.

III. PUBLIC OPINION AND PARLIAMENT

In 1601 Sir Robert Cecil had warned the House of Commons against allowing 'parliament matters' to be discussed outside the House. In 1771 the North administration tacitly agreed to permit the reporting of debates. By about 1810, and from that time until the Reform, the failure of the House of Commons to represent and comply with the demands of public opinion was the principal ground of attack on the whole system of representation, and proved the most penetrating instrument in the armoury of reform. 'Sixty years ago', remarked the *Edinburgh Review* in 1818, 'the opinion of Parliamentary parties might be said to represent all the opinions of the nation. The case is now materially different. The numbers of those who take an interest in public affairs, has increased with a rapidity formerly unknown. The Political Public has become not only far more numerous, but more intelligent, more bold, more active.' It went on by way of explanation to speak of the pressure of public distress and the magnitude of the revolutions during the past thirty years. The recent general election had not produced changes in the House of Commons to match the change of opinion; those who had canvassed the counties had found that political opinions had penetrated into places where they had never reached before.[3]

The chief agent of this process was a free Press.[4] In 1781, a Member had

---

[1] See the interesting conversation of Alexis de Tocqueville with Roebuck and John Stuart Mill in J. P. Mayer (ed.), Alexis de Tocqueville, *Journeys to England and Ireland* (London, 1958), 84–87. Tocqueville's analysis of politics led him to predict the return of Peel to power by 1836 — prematurely (Peel came back in 1841), but a right reading of the direction, with which Roebuck and Mill agreed.

[2] *Hansard*, vii. 136.

[3] *Edinburgh Review*, no. 31, 1818–19, 171–2.

[4] A. Aspinall, *Politics and the Press* (London, 1949), in general and especially 33 ff.

denounced the delegate meeting of the counties associated for reform as 'dangerous and unconstitutional'; by 1830 it was generally conceded by Whigs and Tories alike that the Press exercised a power that could challenge and weaken the government; 'This', said Inglis, of public opinion expressed in petitions but chiefly in the Press, when he replied to Russell in the debate on the first Reform Bill, 'is the real control, to which we all look more or less.'[1] It can be no exaggeration to consider this development as a profound modification in the British Constitution.

Parliament's official disapproval of the publication of its proceedings for the purpose of influencing opinion, though a standard attitude, was challenged occasionally even in the seventeenth century. ' 'Tis a *brave world* when *private men* shall take *their liberty* with transactions of Parliament', declared L'Estrange in opposition to a motion to print the votes in 1685. 'It is a sort of appeal to the People', added another speaker; to which Coventry rejoined, 'The *weight* of England is the People'.[2] But the House of Commons itself had appealed to public opinion by printing the Grand Remonstrance in 1641. Andrew Marvell, M.P. for Hull, kept in constant touch with his constituents, and wrote accounts of parliamentary debates intended for use as propaganda against the Court; his *Growth of Popery* was frequently used in eighteenth-century histories.

Any question of the propriety of the general public entertaining opinions about parliamentary proceedings was really foreclosed, before the rise of a widespread Press, by the impossibility of knowing the information available to Parliament; a point that was not unnaturally reinforced by the conviction of many members that the complex and weighty matters they had to discuss would be beyond the comprehension of the common people. Local people knew the details of local questions; they could not be expected to grasp affairs of state. The view was expressed, without the slightest disrespect to the electors, by a Mr Bramston in 1735, when moving an amendment to an Election Bill, with the object of strengthening the last determination of the House in disputed elections: it was important to establish among the people a good opinion of the impartiality, integrity, and justice of the House in its proceedings on state affairs, 'especially such as relate to foreign transactions, the facts are not publicly known, nor can the motives or arguments for and against any question be understood by the vulgar; and therefore in

[1] Gash, *Politics*, 26–27; Sir Robert Inglis was M.P. for Oxford University.

[2] *The Observator*, iii. no. 24, 1 April 1685; A. Grey, *Debates* (1763), viii. 293. Professor Caroline Robbins has kindly supplied me with these references and the subsequent ones relating to Marvell.

such questions, it is not easy for the people to comprehend the debates'; but they did know and comprehend what went on at elections in their own neighbourhoods — and so would suspect the operation of private interest or party zeal if they discerned inconsistency or contradiction in the determination of such issues by the House.[1]

These uncertainties could not check the rise of waves of public opinion on issues of urgent importance — the Excise Bill, the cider tax, and the war with Spain, to mention only three under Walpole. The truth, or an important part of it, was that a better informed and more active public opinion existed in many constituencies than the official complacencies of Parliament admitted. Moreover there were certain points, particularly in Middlesex and the Metropolis, where the doctrine of instruction was kept alive, a decided rebuke to the claim of parliamentary privacy; for if constituents could instruct their members they could certainly claim to hear of their proceedings.

On specific local issues, constituencies might be allowed the right to exercise a close influence over their members, however, without admitting the more general implication of instruction — that local electors had the right to shut off all discussion of national issues. Public opinion, in the eighteenth century, was not a clearly defined entity; and when it was conceived of as being national in scope of object, it was not in the country, but inside Parliament, that public opinion was discovered.

That was the meaning of Burke's famous statement to the Bristol electors, and of similar pronouncements by men as far at variance with Burke in political affairs as Lord North. A large assortment of local impulses of feeling or opinion were imparted by the constituencies — particularly the alert ones, like Bristol or Yorkshire — along lines of communication leading to the House of Commons. It was the function of the Commons not merely to receive but to evaluate, to inform themselves of all available intelligence and to transform all these local impulses into an opinion as to the national interest. In the same sense, the various 'interests' discovered by Burke were not to dictate policy to Parliament but to supply information upon which the national interest could be determined. They had a right to do so, because the nation itself had an interest in the prosperity of the 'interests'. That in a sense was what was meant by calling them the legitimate interests, by invoking their greatness as an element in that of the State. It was in this sense that Parliament could be called 'the great inquest of the nation'; and it was Parliament's virtue that, while representing the interests of the nation, it was itself disinterested.

[1] Chandler's *Commons Debates* (London, 1742), ix. 94–99.

No single cause can be adduced to explain the rapid blossoming of news-papers and the public addiction to the reading of parliamentary reports that led in 1771 to the dropping of formal restrictions on the reporting of debates. The large and intelligent populations of the leading British commercial cities had long regarded parliamentary affairs as their own business, and the accretions of wealth brought in from the Empire had added substantially to the prosperity and self-importance of those cities. They also added to the class of persons with enough leisure to seek election to Parliament and to interest themselves in public affairs. Walpole's peace had begun the process, but there can be little doubt that Pitt's conduct of the Seven Years' War did much to stimulate a sense of emotional communication between the country at large and its leadership in the House of Commons. To all this must be added the wealth, growth, and sophistication of the capital. London with its great population was far too close to the actual conduct of events to be kept for long at a distance by the assumed remoteness of Parliament; and members, during the sessions, were Londoners. The big debates in Parliament, at the close of the Seven Years' War, over the East India Company, over Wilkes, over the series of American crises, were intrinsically so important as to provoke this populace to intense interest; and Wilkes himself supplied the brand that inflamed that interest with a sense of outrage. Members for constituencies with large electorates could see the value of appealing to the multitude; they built up their own strength while supplying the rapidly increasing demand for reports of speeches. Discussion centred on politics, and politics were influenced by discussion. Before long the newspapers were devoted in large part to parliamentary reports and the appetite of the public seemed insatiable;[1] an appetite that was eager to consume the output of political literature in the form of pamphlets, tracts, and volumes such as those of Burke, Mrs Macaulay, Allan Ramsay, James Burgh, Granville Sharp, and Cartwright. It was London which provided the great market and centre for this ferment. If Lord North and his ministers had really been as bad as Burke painted them, they could have struck a real blow for Toryism by removing the capital to York!

The dreary debates about the responsibility for the American War, which the parliamentary reformers began as a method of attacking the system of representation, brought little credit to either side. The most the reformers could establish, even to their own satisfaction, was that public opinion had turned against the war some eighteen months or two years before the administration had been forced from power; it was not an overwhelming

[1] Aspinall, *Politics*, 33–37.

dialectical victory. But the constant reiteration of the theme did have one important effect. It placed on administration spokesmen the burden of proving that they had in fact been faithful to public opinion. When North said that he was the creature of Parliament in his rise and in his fall, he clearly implied the view that parliamentary opinion was that of the public. When defenders of the existing order fought back against the charges of the opposition, they insisted again and again that Parliament never failed, in the long run, to represent the true sense of the nation; and by so doing they accepted the doctrine that Parliament was in fact accountable to public opinion. This was the more important because the discussion ran through a period when that opinion was becoming more and more distinct, self-conscious and sensitive; the debate itself helped to bring about the existence of a continuous political mind in the country, watching and judging the performance of Parliament.

In their political struggle against Pitt, the Foxite Whigs in 1791 received an unusual fillip from a short-lived incident in foreign policy. The administration, worried about the aims of Russia in a war against the Turks, issued an ultimatum and put the navy into a state of preparation for war. The action came to be called 'the Russian armament'. Pitt got the necessary votes in the Commons, but only against stiff opposition, and soon afterwards he withdrew the ultimatum. The opposition claimed that Pitt's climb-down was a victory for public opinion, a humiliation for the administration, and a proof that votes in the House could cut across the feeling of the country. public opinion, declared Fox, when Grey's first notice of a reform motion was debated next year, had forced Pitt to give up his plan despite his great majority; on this matter the people were not represented in Parliament. The House, added Sheridan, did not go against the measure; but the people forced the minister to abandon it. It was certainly a sharp debating thrust, but Jenkinson countered it with some analysis of the actual voting. If it could be shown, he said, that the members from the close boroughs (those corrupted by the government) had occasioned the decision to arm, and then disarm without success, then the objection might be sustained: but the reverse was the fact. The members for counties and populous boroughs voted for the administration in large numbers; as many members from close boroughs voted against, as those who voted for it. 'The defect is not in the representation,' he continued, 'it is in human nature.' He added that he had always thought public opinion should have a certain weight in the Constitution, but was fearful lest the government should become too democratic. It cannot be concluded that Pitt was swayed by public opinion but he may well have noted that, in view of the extent of the opposition, he might have difficulty in maintaining supplies if he went to war.[1]

To this process of formal criticism, agitated periodically into a sense of outraged indignation, the governments of Pitt in the 1790s and Liverpool between 1816 and 1819 reacted with severe repression aimed directly against the freedom of the Press and of public association. The most effective — though not the most violent — measures were the stamp duties that drove William Cobbett's *Political Register* out of circulation. The Six Acts of Liverpool's government were the more serious in that, unlike Pitt's, they were passed in time of peace. Yet the Government always knew they were fighting a losing battle and that, however they might hope to suppress the diffusion of violent and subversive ideas among town and country labourers (who made a practice of organising reading sessions, usually held in taverns, for the benefit of the illiterate), they could not hope to check the spread of intelligence among the professional and business classes.[2]

Radical reformers charged not only the governments but the House of Commons with complete failure to respond to public opinion. 'The petitioners', declared a petition from Reading for the reform of Parliament (no longer merely 'in' Parliament) 'have observed, of late years, and especially during the present administration, an entire difference of opinion between the people and their representatives in parliament on almost every question of general feeling and national importance.'[3] Public opinion was of course present, a factor to be weighed by governments, but that did not satisfy the fiercely Radical but well-informed newspaper, *The Black Dwarf*, that opinion really exercised a sufficient check on 'the present governing class in England'; even the parliamentary Whigs, whom the paper held in contempt, had expatiated on ministerial defiance of public opinion.[4]

The assumption behind these attacks was, of course, that all public opinion was united with the Radicals; and despite the evident diversity of different sectors of opinion among different professions, classes, and regions, the Tories were frightened enough to give the impression that they shared that assumption. Ward insisted, in discussing abuses, that Parliament had 'completely gone along with the improvement that had taken place in the public feeling on this subject'; he admitted that a reformed House of Commons would be directly affected by public opinion, and expressed his fear of

[1] *Parliamentary History*, xxix. 1313–14; 1335. Watson, *Geo. III*, 296–7. *Parliamentary History*, xxx. 817–19.

[2] Aspinall, *Politics*, 369 ff.

[3] *Hansard*, xvi. 954–55.   [4] *Black Dwarf*, vi. 18, 2 May 1821.

mob passions; he wanted Parliament to represent public opinion 'not from day to day but from period to period'; it was the duty of public men to oppose vulgar prejudice flowing in a direction contrary to reason and justice.[1] In 1822 Canning, while asserting as a merit of the House of Commons that it was susceptible to public opinion, argued persuasively that the independence of the House from an immediate popular control gave it the necessary freedom to adopt salutary measures when they were unpopular, as with certain currency measures, and even to go ahead of public opinion — as with the removal of disabilities upon Catholic peers. The Commons could be more liberal than the public.[2] Sir John Nicholl in 1817, though not advocating reform, indicated the development that Whig thinking was to pursue, when he treated the freedom of the Press, the growth of public opinion, and above all the reporting of parliamentary debates, as a broadening of the effective representation of interests. The happenings in both Houses were submitted to public opinion throughout the kingdom; 'No grievance, real or imaginary, is felt by any body of men, however small, or any individual, however low or obscure, that is not here subjected to discussion.'[3] Rather a complacent picture, in a country that was soon to experience the Peterloo massacre; but an indication of extreme sensitivity to the newly risen force of the popular interest in and the public sense of responsibility for political policy.

When Lord John Russell moved for a Reform of Parliament in 1819, he described the 'separation on some occasions between the opinions of the people and the declared will of the House of Commons' as the most difficult part of his subject. The historical survey he then offered showed a new departure in Whig thinking, one that no longer owed any debt to the old polemics about the American War. He did not claim that reform would incline the Government less to war; he recognised the popularity of the American and French wars, and he admitted that Walpole's long rule would not have passed in peace in a popular assembly. He took up the history of Dunning's famous resolution about the influence of the Crown in 1780, and then analysed the voting on the subsequent motion — not to dissolve the House until the influence of the Crown had diminished — which had been defeated. A heavy majority of English, Scottish, and Cornish boroughs helped to defeat that motion; the county members supported the motion,

---

[1] *Hansard*, xxiii. 113–42. Those who witnessed the influence of McCarthyism on American legislatures will recognise that Ward's position was not one of blind reaction.
[2] *Hansard*, vii. 106–36.   [3] *Hansard*, xxxvi. 751–2.

two to one.[1] His examination of other issues led him to the opinion that the House did not act as a faithful representative of public opinion on domestic questions. Moderate Whig views of this stamp did not claim to seek what Ward and other Tories feared — a direct dictation of the public to the House; rather a greater degree of that indirect influence which everyone acknowledged to exist, but which governments could still ignore and frustrate.

Despite all the hardships, riots, and threats of these turbulent years of economic depression, one issue dominated the nation above all others. It was the prosecution of Queen Caroline. In order to get rid of his detested wife, King George IV asked the ministry to introduce a Bill to dissolve his marriage; the Queen, whose wanderings in Italy would not have given her much more claim to public sympathy than her husband had earned as Prince Regent, was suddenly paraded as another innocent but gallant victim of the vicious persecution of the ministry. She became a popular heroine, the centre of great demonstrations of enthusiasm. The Government, having got the Bill — for which they had no great liking — through the Lords, decided to drop it because of the danger of defeat in the Commons. However, in January 1821 that House voted to remove the Queen's name from the liturgy. The indignation of the public seemed more conclusive of the gap between public opinion and Parliament than in previous issues on which more material interests depended. One member of twenty years standing, who had opposed every motion for reform in that period, told the Commons that he had at last changed his mind because he was convinced that the House, on that vote, was acting not under but against public opinion.[2]

The new policies to which the Liverpool government turned after 1822, with the introduction of Peel, Huskisson, and Canning into the ministry, could go some way to alleviate specific problems but could not redress the sense of grievance which now arose from non-representation as a fact in itself. Moreover, as Lord Melbourne observed in an eloquent, reflective speech on the first Reform Bill in 1831, every public calamity or distress, no matter what its cause, gave rise to a renewed demand for reform of representation — a call 'accompanied by a rankling sense of injustice

[1] *Hansard*, xli. 1091–107. Note the acceptance of the Cornish view that Cornwall does not belong to England!

[2] *Black Dwarf*, vi. 3, 17 January 1821; *Hansard*, N.S. iv. 223–4 (31 January 1821); a summary of the affair of the Queen will be found in Sir E. L. Woodward, *The Age of Reform* (Oxford, 1949), 64–66. Shelley's satirical verse drama *Oedipus Tyrannus, or Swellfoot the Tyrant* is a virulent and highly entertaining attack on the conduct of the king and his ministers which catches the popular mood.

suffered, and of rights withheld'.[1] Yet when reform came, its limits soon proved as grievous to the Radicals as its extent was infuriating to the Tories.

IV. THE GREAT REFORM ACT AND THE NEW BALANCE OF INTERESTS

The actual timing of the Reform Act owed much to the preoccupation of Parliament with the previous crisis resulting in Catholic emancipation in 1829. Even when the Reform Bill had been introduced, the inordinate time taken by the debates in both Houses, the general election in the spring of 1831 following the defeat of the Government in committee, the defeat of the second Bill in the Lords, and the prorogation of Parliament in October, followed by the introduction of the third Bill in December 1831, sustained and protracted the proceedings far beyond the point at which the country had grasped the fact that reform was the real policy of the Grey government. Excitement was high during much of the time, rising in ominous waves and outbursts of violence at moments of exasperation. The original Bill, as Russell introduced it amid bitter laughter from some of the Tory benches, underwent some amendments during this lengthy process, but emerged without much modification in principle.

The borough franchise was made uniform at last, being extended to all householders rated at £10 or more; the county franchise was given to £10 copyholders, holders of £50 leases for a term of years, and £50 tenants-at-will, the latter a concession to landlords, who were expected to be able to control these tenants' votes. Fifty-six boroughs were disfranchised. Their representation was redistributed, mainly among the industrial towns, while the old Whig demand for an increase in knights of the shire was reflected in the doubling of the seats for twenty-six of the counties.[2] Separate provisions were made for Scotland and Ireland.

Radicals felt little cause for gratitude. The common law right of voting in England was by payment of scot and lot, which made the actual value of the property immaterial, whereas the Whig Bill required that £10 worth of taxes must be paid up; the registration proceedings were likely to disfranchise some people for as much as thirty-two months after moving house. Three-quarters of the artisans of England, said one bitter pamphleteer, would be disfranchised by this Whig sleight-of-hand.[3] The Tory John

[1] Gash, *Politics*, 11.   [2] Woodward, *Age of Reform*, 77–83.
[3] Anon. pamphlet, *Whig Fraud and English Folly!* (London, 1831).

Wilson Croker's analysis showed from the other side that the counties of Durham, Northumberland, and Cumberland, in which he accused the leading ministers of having family interests, would gain disproportionate increases of representation.[1]

Russell gave three reasons for the enfranchisement of the new boroughs.[2] First, to give representation to the centres of trade and manufacture; secondly, to bind a large class of people to the institutions of the country, teaching them to look to the House of Commons as the tribunal where their grievances could be discussed and remedied; thirdly, to improve the House, as a representative body, by bringing in men qualified to take part in the discussion of new problems.

The concept of interest representation had by this time entered so deeply into the context of political debate that it was rarely adverted to as a specific idea. Nevertheless it was assumed in Russell's and the Whigs' case; and Huskisson, shortly before his death in 1830, had made an interesting attempt to redefine the problem in order to limit the necessary extent of reform. Debating the representation of the northern cities, he pointed out that Leeds was the capital of the woollen manufacture 'and therefore might justly be taken as the Representative of their interest; that Sheffield, though with a large population and an extensive hardware manufacture, would be fully represented by Birmingham, which was the head of that manufacture; and that Manchester was, in a certain degree, justly regarded as the capital of the cotton manufacture. Thus, by giving the franchise to these three great towns, all the different interests would be represented in that House.'[3] This, a compromise which would have limited the redistribution, revealed an attempt to refashion the interest idea to economic elements that were also regional in character. Yet it is clear that a very pronounced degree of the old notion of 'virtual representation' had really to be conceded if one were to believe that the whole of the interest of Sheffield would be perfectly safe in the hands of a couple of members for Birmingham. As far as the Tory leader Sir Robert Inglis was concerned, virtual representation was still a valid principle. The wishes of Manchester, he said, were as much consulted as those of any town which sent members to Parliament. To this argument Macaulay made a formidable reply. 'Now, Sir, I do not understand', he said, 'how a power which is salutary when exercised virtually can be noxious when exercised directly. . . . A virtual representative is, I presume, a man

---

[1] John Wilson Croker's *Speech in the House of Commons, 21 September 1831* (London, 1831).

[2] Gash, *Politics*, 16.   [3] *Hansard*, N.S. xxii. 893.

who acts as a direct representative would act: for surely it would be absurd to say, that a man virtually represents the people of property in Manchester, who is in the habit of saying No, when a man directly representing the people of property in Manchester, would say Aye. . . .'¹ A cogent argument.

It is instructive, in the light of this speech, to recall Macaulay's attack on James Mill for advocating a plan that would unmistakably have yielded a direct representation for every numerical constituency.² The Radical partisans of *The Black Dwarf* had offered their readers no illusions about the reforming ambitions of the Whigs. The Whigs, they insisted, proposed a class system as a remedy for Tory mis-government; they wanted to introduce the representation of interests — which it would supposedly be the object of legislation to render subservient to the one common interest of society. 'It is absurdly represented that the common interest is composed of "local and professional interests" when a child can see that these local and professional interests must be *opposed* to the general interest.' The *Edinburgh Review* (which was here under fire) was wrong in saying that the general interest was composed of different local and professional interests: the reverse was the case — the general interest forming a minute component of every local and professional interest. 'The joint stake varies in an inverse ratio with the number combined.' The *Review* was also mistaken in assuming that the mere return of representatives would protect the interests of the returning class: the power of government was vested in a majority of the assembly.³

Here the writer struck on a crucial difference between the philosophy of the Radicals and that of the Whigs. When equal electoral districts, made up of all (or the very great majority) of adult men, sent members to Parliament by majority votes, then the majority inside the House of Commons would be expected to represent the opinion of the majority outside. Quite naturally, at this early stage, before such a contingency seemed a practical possibility, Radical thought was concerned with justifying majority rule, and had hardly even envisaged the possibility that the majority in the country might not really share one single interest and on most issues of any complexity would actually speak with an uncertain or divided mind. Thus John Stuart Mill, reviewing Bailey's *Rationale of Political Representation* in 1835, rejected as a fallacy the doctrine of the representation of interests and laid down that the only interest to be consulted and represented was 'the general interest'.⁴

---

¹ *Hansard* 3rd series, ii. 1197.   ² See above, pp. 481–3.
³ *Black Dwarf*, vi. 18, 2 May 1821.
⁴ Burns, 'Mill and Democracy', v. 2–3, June and October 1957, 166. Mill later became critical of this attitude and observed that complex notions such as 'general interest' must

The immediate point, which had descended from the work of Cartwright and had been powerfully supplemented by the contributions of Bentham and Mill — who enjoyed a standing among intellectuals that Cartwright and his associates had never attained — was that when men were considered to be equal in their political rights, that equality rendered superior weight to the numerical majority.[1] The principle, disarmingly enough, was present in Locke's *Second Treatise*, a work which seems to have been neglected by all parties to the debate.

No representation of interests, however subtle or subdivided, could work on that principle. The Whigs, whose limited but practical mode of political thought was far more consistent with the past, were even now not completely alienated from the ancient usage by which the whole House of Commons had once brought in a Bill after it had been passed over opposition. Arthur Onslow, generally held to have been the greatest Speaker of the Commons in the eighteenth century, deplored divisions because they emphasised differences, whereas the object of debates should be to provide ministers with the consensus of the House.[2] The sole justification for the representation of frankly sectional, business, or professional interests must be that each of them was subordinate to the general interest of the nation as developed and revealed in the House of Commons.

In spite of obvious vagueness in points of detail, this was a mode of thinking that worked. This was particularly true in the days before the organisation of political parties as national bodies outside the Houses of Parliament created a standing majority from which the Government of the day could claim to have received a mandate.[3] The gravamen of the Radical charge against the Whigs was that, in the name of 'interest representation',

be broken down into these elements (Burns, 173). He agreed with Bailey that M.P.s ought to be paid a salary so that government could become the life-work of a hard-working profession.

[1] A view which progressively carried less and less weight with John Stuart Mill himself. After receiving an impetus from Toqueville, Mill became deeply preoccupied with the problem of balancing the votes of the masses by giving extra weight to those of the educated classes. He also abandoned his belief in the ballot (Burns, 'Mill and Democracy', 288). Also see Mill, *Representative Government*.

[2] Watson, *Geo. III*, 64.

[3] Another specious theory, of course. Political parties long remained essentially internal parliamentary arrangements, without national machinery. Until the Reform Act of 1867, party organisations formed into existence only for the purpose of fighting constituency elections, and dissolved again afterwards. The idea of maintaining a network of constituency organisations developed after 1867. H. J. Hanham, *Elections and Party Management* (London, 1959), 92–93.

they were really foisting a slightly enlarged form of mere class government on the majority of the nation.

This was largely true. The Whigs were attaching the competent commercial, industrial, and professional middle classes, and a section of the skilled artisans, to the old Constitution. Not surprisingly, the mass of the workers who had demonstrated for Reform and the Radicals who had led them were scathing about the deceitful methods of the Whig aristocracy and continued to agitate for the reforms of which they felt cheated.

Yet the Whigs had accepted a widened version of 'interest'; one whose structure had been modified to admit of the legitimacy and permanence of the force of public opinion. As early as 1792 Paley, in expounding the correct Whig doctrines as received at that time, had incorporated the accountability of Parliament to public opinion into the rationale of the existing order. In an earlier age, all the interests spoke to Parliament expressly through their representatives in it; but with the rise of the newspapers — supplemented by a vast burgeoning of the use of the right to petition, which went into decline only after the final Chartist fiasco in 1848[1] — the content as well as the style of political expression had changed. Interests as various as the entire range of occupations or minorities in the country could bring their needs to the notice of the public. Not one of these would be likely to command a majority for itself, but each could command a hearing. The inclusion of additional interests had the further advantage of representing individuals who might otherwise not have been represented in their constituencies; moreover it did so by a method which offered some check to the pressure of the majority, of which Whigs and Conservatives were equally nervous.

The Tories, insistently pointing out that the Whigs were opening a door they could never shut, warning about the ultimate democratic consequences of admitting the least modicum of reform, had in a limited sense got the better of the argument.[2] They said the Reform Act would destroy the balance of the Constitution; the Whigs claimed that it would restore the balance. The great significance of the Whig argument was that the Constitution had got out of balance, not because of encroachments by the Crown, not, as of old, because of corrupt use of Treasury funds and patronage; but because the economic and demographic structure of the nation had changed. It was to that structure that the Constitution had to be related, and it was

[1] Peter Fraser, 'Public Petitioning and Parliament before 1832', *History* (October, 1961), 195–211.
[2] Gash, *Politics*, 3.

with respect to these forces that it required to be balanced. When Macaulay appealed to the sense of the past by invoking this ancient expression,[1] so long out of date in its old connotation of a balance between the Crown and the estates of the realm, he bore witness to that fact.

When universal suffrage had been achieved, and an electoral system nearer to the Radicals' hearts' desire had been moulded, it would remain true that in much of its political life the House of Commons would remain loyal to the ideas of interest representation. When disciplined majorities came to prevail over divisions in the House, each of the parties would become a little House of Commons, both sounding out opinion and in turn receiving — often through efficiently organised lobbying — the demands of a variety of social, religious, regional, professional, and economic interests. The notion of a purified, disinterested majority rule was in truth an illusion, further from reality and far less pliable than that of a representation of competing, but roughly organised, roughly disciplined interests under the aegis of a national interest, dimly perceived but never wholly absent.

That lesson was hardly to be learnt by a majority which felt cheated of its rights. 'To property and good order, we attach numbers', said Durham in a phrase of deep historical significance.[2] Not very large numbers, as yet — but this attachment was their only hope. The rights of suffrage had been compelled to follow through the gap driven into the defences of the old order by the wedge of property.

[1] Gash, *Politics*, 15.   [2] Gash, *Politics*, 16.

PART FIVE

The Comparative Dimension

I. THE FULFILMENT OF LEGISLATIVE POWER

T w o American revolutions converged in 1776 and ran in a mingled stream until the final achievement of Independence. The first of these, announced to the world by the Declaration of Independence and carried out by the ensuing war, would not have been possible without the character that colonial politics had taken from the second, inner revolution, which had developed according to an entirely different rhythm, in time far more gradual, and in temperament essentially civilian.

This civilian process was nothing less than the American fulfilment of the great Whig tradition, which had once, not inappropriately, been known as 'the good old cause'. The American Whigs of the revolutionary era and their British contemporaries were fellow-citizens of a Whig Republic. They not only spoke the same language and appealed to the same heritage but to an almost disarming extent they tended to approve and deprecate the same things. This very similarity accounts for some of the difficulty of interpreting the principles that were involved in the conflict; and it also tends to conceal the nature of the particular emphasis and quality that American experience had given to the leading Whig doctrine to have emerged from the English struggles of the seventeenth century.

Those struggles were pitched over the question of lawful power, which in its nature meant the authority to give laws; and Locke here made judicious use of Hooker to affirm the supreme authority of the legislative power. The argument supposed, as Locke stated, that all rightful government was in some way fiduciary, sanctioned by the consent of the people and containing an element of representation. The notion that every man in England was virtually present in Parliament to consent to the passing of laws and taxes never, of course, had much to do with the facts; the consent of all was a legal fiction. Yet it was a significant fiction, for it was the persistence of some such justification in the minds of lawyers that made them consider the laws lawful.

In England after the Restoration the legislative power could never mean less than the Crown, Lords, and Commons in Parliament assembled. Yet the Stuart monarchs, at odds with their subjects as represented in Parliament, showed a marked propensity for relying on foreign aid; an attitude that became more compromising when their foreign associations and private convictions connected them with the Roman Catholic religion. From the constitutional view it became curiously beside the point that many ordinary English people still shared that religion with their monarchs. Given the Protestantism of the major interests represented in Parliament, the effect was to give a particularly sharp edge to the claims made by Parliament as the spokesman of the estates of the realm against the Crown: it led to a deep implicit emphasis on the Englishness of Parliament. Even the later adoptive monarchy of the Whigs, first in the persons of William and Mary, then in the Hanoverians, was saddled with the implication of alien connections which might cut across the interests of England; and against which specific statutory precautions were held to be necessary. For the Whigs, as for the Tories, of the Convention Parliament it was enough that the legislative power be lodged in the constituted Houses of Parliament. There was no disposition to ask searching questions about the precise meaning of the representation in those houses of the people outside.

In the American colonies, the tension between the Crown and the Parliament had an ironical reflection. Representative Assemblies had been called to assist in the work of government; and when issues arose on which royal or proprietary Governors, armed with instructions from England, clashed with the demands of those colonial interests which had attained representation in the Assemblies, then it was the British Governor who stood out as the representative of a kind of alien interest. In a system of divided powers the different branches show an almost unavoidable tendency to suspect slights on their own dignity and to develop a strong sense of institutional identity. The actual composition of the Assemblies combined with these factors, during recurrent clashes with the Governors, to build in colonial minds a deep and abiding feeling for the *Americanness* of the Assemblies.

American colonists absorbed the doctrine of legislative supremacy, but they also received the theory, as well as the institutional forms, of mixed government. The men who ran colonial affairs had good reasons to believe in it. For one thing, that form bore a flattering resemblance to the Aristotelian prescription for stability in the state; and for another, since both classical and English education taught them that the executive power, the nobility, and the commons or 'democracy' were all permanent and necessary ingredients of society, and since mixed government on the Whig model meant a popular power that could check the prerogative while assuring representation to the commons, neither history nor contemporary politics could show them any better prescription for political liberty.

For a period of about fifty years, before the American Revolution, the forms and the theory of mixed government came under gruelling and cumulative pressure. During this time the Assemblies, by a variety of means but in ways that produced the same general result, came to absorb the largest share of that very legislative power which all regarded as supreme.

Each colonial Assembly made itself in the image of the British House of Commons. It quickly established control over that vital factor, its own composition, claiming as the Commons had done under James I the power to judge the credentials of its own members. In addition to electing their own speakers, the Assemblies also asserted the familiar privileges during the duration of their sessions — freedom of speech, freedom of members from arrest, and the articles of parliamentary privilege. Privileges in fact could be used in a high-handed way to restrain the liberty of the Press and even the liberty of citizens to criticise the Assembly or to impugn the honour of the members.

Colonial Assemblies were not normally the scenes of any single-minded unity of purpose or the agencies of any one movement. There is little reason to suppose that in their clashes with governors they felt themselves driving relentlessly on towards ultimate independence; nor were colonial politics perpetually dominated by such conflicts. There were, however, certain specific issues in whose determination lay a significant shift of real power. The most obvious was the question of governors' salaries, in which the northern colonies had won, by the middle of the 1730s, an ascendancy that was to prove enduring. The power claimed by the Assembly of Massachusetts to control the disbursement of funds raised by its own vote was a gain from which there would be no subsequent retreat. Massachusetts and Pennsylvania had enjoyed from early years the advantages of annual elections; in Virginia, the attempt of the House of Burgesses to place the Assembly on a septennial basis, though no more than a move to adopt British practices, stood forth as an unmistakable assertion of legislative power over constitutional matters and as such was disallowed by the Crown. When — as in 1767 — the Crown intervened to prevent the formation of new constituencies it thereby limited the power of the Assembly to control its representative character and function. These issues, the regularity of elections and the representative base, were understood on both sides to involve the full meaning of constitutional authority. They were conflicts about real power; they were also conflicts about the location of rightful power — of power centred on consent. The Crown could not afford to yield to colonial Assemblies the whole of the ground on which, even by British theory, the right to govern was based.

The fact that the colonial governor came over armed with royal instructions which he was not obliged to reveal, or portions of which he could reveal as suited his own timing, and the further fact that his gestures summoned up the huge shadow of the British Crown, did not free him from the need to negotiate constantly to maintain his position. It was his natural policy to ally himself with groups whom he thought capable of controlling the legislature; some, notably Spotswood in Virginia, sought to build an extensive party in the Assembly; while all governors could be expected to deploy their powers of patronage to secure the loyalty of influential colonists. But even the strongest found fatal flaws in their armoury. Their financial weaknesses were due partly to the permanent refusal of British governments to put colonial salaries on the Civil List; and even where these questions were not paramount, governors could never get things done for long without winning the collaboration of the Assemblies; they were chronically weakened, in terms of the kind of influence which governments normally exerted in the period, by the simple fact that colonial government never developed the intricacy and complexity that might have given rise to extensive patronage and consequent power.

The most potent, though not the most pliable instrument available to the Governor was his Council. The Council usually combined both judicial and legislative with an element of executive power. In Pennsylvania it was a frail thing, almost withering after 1701, so that some people were left with the impression that the province had a unicameral government. In Massachusetts, under the Charter of 1691, the Council was elected by the Assembly, but even so it did not materially differ in style from that of Virginia or other provinces in which it was composed of men of acknowledged rank and wealth.

Colonial electors in general and on most occasions agreed as to the right of such men to hold commanding positions in government. Moreover the bicameral system had not been imposed on the colonies by British command; colonial bicameralism was an indigenous growth. The emergence of an upper chamber corresponded both to the needs of government and more particularly under that government to the needs of the high and mighty propertied interests of a profoundly property-conscious society. Since the possession of property was itself the chief manifestation of liberty the existence of an upper chamber, not only before the Revolution but subsequently as a direct result of it, was a natural and proper consequence of the determination of the colonists to defend their liberties.

At the end of the seventeenth century the Council stood as one of the strongest institutions in the colonies, fully equal to holding its own with the other branches of government. It would have been hard to predict that within some twenty-five years it would begin to lose its grip in face of the competition of the Assembly. Yet, in spite of that, the decline in the influence of the colonial Council was in turn an indigenous process, owing nothing to British example and resulting from a gradual, but on the whole deliberate, alteration in the choices of the leading colonists, and from changes in the character of their society. It is no less fascinating, for that reason, to observe the remarkable correspondence of this process with the relative decline of the House of Lords. This is not, of course, to say that the House of Lords lost its influence over British life and social values; it is rather to say that as the embodiment of an estate, as a branch of government, it became more and more homogeneous with the House of Commons. An almost identical trend was noted by Jefferson as a reason for criticism of the Virginia Senate soon after the Revolution; and Jefferson, a loyal Whig, was complaining that the two Houses ought to stand for separate interests!

Comparisons often prove more striking for the contrasts than the similarities they reveal, and the significance of these similar developments in British and American institutions lay in the enormous difference of pace. The House of Lords continued to fascinate the British mind — and some American minds, too — deep into the twentieth century; the name alone reverberated with a feudal grandeur that was wholly absent from the history and could have little effect on the ambitions of Americans thinking of their own Upper Houses. (Some of this sentiment clung to the United States Senate; but it had other interests to represent and other values to defend.) Moreover, and this difference was of overwhelming importance, the House of Lords was always more than the representation of the nobility: it consisted of the nobility in their persons; and if Americans, or British governments planning American institutions, had really meant to lay down the aristocratic principle as the basis for American politics, they should have conferred the right to a personal seat in the Upper House on all men above a certain definable status. To select a small minority for this distinction, especially when it ceased even to be a representative minority, was a policy that directed the ambitions of the remainder towards the honours and rewards of the elective chamber.

The decline of the Council — and the process was analogous if not actually parallel to that of the Lords — took place as the leading men came to appreciate that they could exert more influence in the elective Assemblies than in an appointive upper House. It was in their Assemblies that Americans found the legitimate, American expression of that great instrument of the Whig purposes — the legislative power. Some significance must also attach to the size of the Assemblies, which were much larger than the Councils. Precisely because the colonists looked on themselves as English, their Assemblies became in their minds the agencies of all rightful power over taxation and local government.

The consequences were of incalculable importance not only in bringing on the American Revolution of separation from Britain but in forming the character of the new state governments and eventually that of the American Constitution. In the final colonial phase, with the Council unable — or unwilling — to oppose the will of the Assembly, the colonial governor was reduced to a position not much above that of a rather strong negotiator in a foreign country. What had happened, after some half-century of gradual accretion of power by the popular House, was that notwithstanding the theory of mixed government to which nearly all still officially subscribed, the real and effective legislative power — that of making laws which would be obeyed — had been gathered up in a single branch, and that branch rested directly on the electorate. The rise of the representative arm of government had converged with the domestic drive towards legislative power.

The American Revolution was not brought about as a defence of a stable or static democratic form of government against the encroaching tyranny of Crown or Parliament. It was not fought in order to inaugurate sweeping advances towards more democratic forms of government. It developed, point by point, out of the policies of British administrations and the interpretations given by leading colonists to those policies. It was a struggle between British initiative and colonial resistance; but neither the timing nor the methods nor the strength of that resistance were mere accidents of response to British policies. It may truly be said that the final stages in the Americanisation of the colonial legislatures were forced by unwanted British measures — that the meeting of the streams of full legislative power and of American political representation was compelled by the structure of British dykes. But these were streams which sprang from American sources; and their confluence — and thus the American Revolution itself — were the culmination of some half-century's momentum. In that very significant sense the American Revolution was not a beginning but an end.

The old Assemblies, the new and revolutionary provincial Congresses, contained their fair and politically respectable proportion of members who would have been content to have averted that culmination. Many more were concerned to moderate its implications for domestic government. But whatever their preferences, the Americans could not escape (and many of them of course embraced) the consequences of having made an independent Confederation from the base provided by a long cycle of domestic development. The fact now was that the whole responsibility for government in the former colonies rested solely in American hands and that the whole was therefore based squarely on American representation.

Formerly the theory of mixed government had always provided that a portion — which in America had necessarily meant the major portion — of the general legislative power was to belong to the representative branch. In Britain that branch was the House of Commons; in the American colonies, the Assemblies. The merit of the colonial Council lay in the very fact that, not being subject to the electorate, it stood for certain more stable interests, could perform more specialist duties, and by its mere existence provided a check or balance to the popular House. The Council, however, did not govern by any hereditary right; it stood on shaky foundations, especially as the great weight of opinion in America was against such things as hereditary political power. The effect of the assumption of legislative power by the representative branch, carried forward into actual independent sovereignty, was to deprive the interests in the Councils of the last vestige of a claim to a place in government on any appointive or privileged basis. Councils were in truth very soon to be reconstituted under the name of Senates. But they could never be reconstituted on the former ground; the whole legislature, including the Governor — the whole of the old and venerable 'legislative power' — was henceforth to be in some form representative; all future legislative chambers were to draw their powers and owe their membership to elections.

This turn of events meant that America had arrived by 1776, not as a matter of some pugnaciously abstract theorising but as a matter of plain, unavoidable fact, at a position which only the most violent Radicals would have affirmed in Britain. By 1797, driven almost to despair by the Pitt régime, seeing no hope of power for themselves, and therefore perhaps willing to risk the more, the parliamentary Whigs led by Fox and Grey began to make a similar assertion about the British Constitution. They began to declare that the fundamental principle of the Constitution was representation: the institutions, including even the Lords and the Crown, were merely instruments. That high-water mark of radicalism at least revealed the direction in which the tide would flow. It was not a point to which any of them, least of all Grey, would return when the twist of politics gave them the power to act.

So complete was the assumption of legislative power by the Assemblies that their immediate successors, the provincial conventions based on the same electorates, exercised their authority to form new, independent Constitutions for their states. Only in Massachusetts (and later in New Hampshire) were these instruments of government even submitted to the people for ratification. In Massachusetts, however, the force of the popular belief in the theory of compact took the unprecedented course of converting that theory into something closely resembling fact; and in the elections for the Constitutional Convention to meet in 1779–80, every adult man in the state was given the vote; a franchise whose extraordinary and fundamental nature was to be underlined by the ensuing Constitution, which actually narrowed the suffrage for Assembly elections.

The idea of the constituent power of the people took root. When the great Convention of Philadelphia came at last to consider the problem of ratification, the tactical acumen of the leaders of that body perceived the advantage of what the theory of compact already taught: that a constitution ratified by popular conventions would have the strongest possible case to call itself 'the supreme law of the land'. The subsequent state ratifying conventions were not in fact as universally based as had been that of Massachusetts; but the principle of the constituent power of the people (soon afterwards to be adopted in France) was, in intention, of the same origin.

Written Constitutions offered a welcome opportunity to affirm undying principles. One of the principles which had come down to the Americans, though somewhat tangled in the teachings of Montesquieu and the inferences to be drawn from the British Constitution, was that of the separation of powers. The powers which were supposed to be separated had a tendency to shift their identity from time to time. Once they had been mainly the executive and the deliberative branches of government; the separation of powers could at times mean little more than a prohibition against plural office-holding. It was a doctrine which gained much prestige in America from the dark lessons inculcated by British history in the eighteenth century; the corruption of the Commons by the Crown was a stark warning about the perils that could attend the merging of such powers. State constitutions tended to affirm the principle of separation while reposing most of the power in the elective Assemblies; and the troubles of state histories in the next few years helped to convince the men who met at Philadelphia in 1787 that the representative accumulation of legislative power had gone too far for the public good — too far for the safety of the very interests that government had been instituted to protect.

This great store-house of the legislative power was invaded by the makers of the Constitution. The entire building was taken down and laboriously rebuilt. The rich and treasured contents in due course were divided up and parcelled out between separate branches of the new government, each of which was given a separate constitutional base, each of which was equal in its own sphere to the others.

When James Madison, in the brilliant essay forming the fifty-first of *The Federalist Papers*, observed that in a republican government the legislative authority necessarily predominated, he was no longer engaged in affirming the truths of the past; his business now was to explain and justify the elaborate steps that had been taken to keep that power under restraint. A significant section of the whole work was devoted to the task of convincing the earnest but often rather simple adherents of that great prescription for liberty, the separation of powers, that the new Constitution did in fact adequately conform to their demands.

Madison and his generation owed more to Locke, the American, than they could reasonably hope to repay. But two of his principles, which had served so well in the past, were now finally repealed. The grand Whig doctrine of legislative supremacy disappeared from the law of the American Constitution; the written instrument itself acquired the supremacy. As of old in Britain and in the separate states, the law-making power was divided between the two Houses, each planted securely on different foundations. Locke, however, had also claimed that the legislative power must remain 'sacred and unalterable in the hands where the community have once placed it', a depository where it would be as safe from the predatory designs of the multitude as it would from the king. The makers of the Constitution rejected that doctrine too, advancing in turn an even higher claim: henceforth the legislative power would cease to be supreme, and the supreme power itself would be alterable.

After 1787 constitutional government in America developed on lines so different from those of Britain as to suggest the working of different principles, even the defence of different values. Yet the contrasts between forms of government were wider and more striking than the different objects those forms were meant to represent. In Britain nothing happened to interfere with the political sovereignty of Parliament. No new crisis, no internal conflict, posed any challenge to the government that could not be dealt with within the framework of the existing system. When the long-delayed movement towards parliamentary reform achieved its limited aims in 1832 the sting could be drawn from the resentment of the more influential sections of the disfranchised and unrepresented by extending the suffrage and redrawing the map of the constituencies — by amending the system of representation; and further reforms would simply carry the same demands further forward. It was perfectly natural that the ministers of the Crown should remain members of Parliament answerable, as they had been since the Glorious Revolution, to a manageable majority in the House of Commons. To have defined them as the 'executive' and to have separated them from the Commons, so far from being a safeguard to liberty, would have taken them beyond the control of the representatives of the people. Nothing would have been more dangerous; no one who understood English liberty would have suggested it.

It was not so in America. The engrossment of legislative power by the colonial legislature actually culminated in the Revolution, which in turn meant the final separation between the representative government and the 'executive' office of the royal Governor, who had become the symbol of an alien and hostile power.

In the new state constitutions both power and sentiment weighed overwhelmingly in favour of the legislatures, and governors were retained as vestigial emblems of sovereignty, so weakened as to appear in some cases merely as emblems of political impotence. Yet the Governor was still the 'executive', charged with certain duties and set aside, in accordance with the dogma of the separation of powers, in his separate compartment. Never could a governor be trusted with power over the Assembly — to do that would be to risk a repetition of all the corruption to which the British Constitution had succumbed in the eighteenth century.

It was the direct result of this situation that when the makers of the Federal Constitution created a national executive, a headship of the Union which was also to be an active department of government, they separated that department from the legislature. Technically speaking it would still have been possible to place the President and the secretaries of departments in the Senate — greater difficulties than that were surmounted in the Convention; a form of government responsible to a congressional majority could have been brought into being as the foundation of the new Constitution. But this was a technical rather than a true historical possibility. It was far from clear at the time that the cabinet system of responsible government was to develop as the leading principle of the British parliamentary system, and much of the contemporary evidence suggested the advisability of avoiding rather than imitating the British method. Beyond this, in any case, the history of representative government in America had already, and very effectively, brought about the separation between representative and executive branches; that state of affairs had not been recently proposed, but had been reached as a result of a long process; and the experience of that process, accentuated by the legislative sovereignty tried out in most of the states, had confirmed in American minds the truth of the doctrine to which in theory they already subscribed. The executive was thus separated from the genuinely legislative functions of government in America as a result of the American engrossment of those functions. Thence the executive was driven upwards into a separate department. This was the final stage in the long cycle, marking the end of the doctrine of legislative supremacy and the beginning of the national phase of American government.

The guardianship of the law of the Constitution fell, eventually and logically, to the Supreme Court. The fact that the Court has interpreted that law in different ways under the influence of differing kinds of pressure or persuasion does nothing to detract from its duty, or its authority, to judge the constitutional issues that involve the meaning of republican government. Republican government, in whatever form, unquestionably involves political representation, and when political representation is impaired or denied then the resulting grievance is by its very nature a constitutional grievance which lies with the Supreme Court. When the suffrage franchise is denied the Constitution is expressly violated; and when a section of the electorate maintains that it is impaired by an unrepresentative apportionment of seats in the legislature, then (whether the plaintiffs are right or wrong in the case) the principle of representation, on which all republican forms of government are founded, is affected. Both kinds of case call equally for the justice that, in the last resort, only the Supreme Court can give: both kinds, to use its own language, are 'justiciable'. The determination of the Supreme Court in *Baker* v. *Carr*, which arose from the grievance of mal-apportionment in Tennessee in 1962 and in which the Court accepted this responsibility to preside over the representative character of republican government, was fully consistent with its historic guardianship.

II. AN AGE OF POLITICAL CAPABILITY

American colonists acquired the legal right to representative forms of government from the Crown but in practice they discovered those forms for themselves. The enterprise of founding a commercial company involved a high degree of participation among the adventurers, and when, as was bound to happen, political institutions were unpacked on dry land from the corded bales of commerce, this form of organisation translated itself into a broader diffusion of political rights than the settlers themselves had been used to. In Rhode Island, at the early date of 1647, a small group of four towns, fired by radically republican views, declared themselves a 'democracy', and proclaimed the separation of Church and State; but that was neither the intention nor the tendency of the rest of New England or of the remaining colonies.

Colonial soil, however, refused to nourish ancient feudal forms of government. That discovery was made, ironically enough, by John Locke, who gave the Americans two cuttings, apparently from different trees of political thought. The one was the *Second Treatise of Civil Government*, which flourished mightily but produced flowers of a distinctly American colouration; and the other was his stillborn plan to export a feudal system of tenures and dignities to Carolina. The American colonies could adopt, and transform, a variety of frames of government, but nothing could flourish there without the power to attract settlement and reward enterprise, which feudal rights had conspicuously failed to do in England.

The rise of the House of Commons and the founding of representative institutions in the colonies were contemporaneous developments. The liberties of Englishmen came to be indissolubly connected with the privileges of the Commons, a lesson that was never lost on the leaders of colonial Assemblies. Benefiting partly from the stimulus of parliamentary example, but also in large part from long periods of English weakness and English indifference, the Americans staked out with extraordinary rapidity the ground on which to build their own self-government.

These gains, these conquered worlds of self-determination, were largely illusions. The world order did not exist in which a small, defenceless people could protect themselves in isolation; nor did the Americans seek isolation. They wanted to live by the profits of trade and the products of their lands, and they took pride in the growth of their population and economy, to which they sought to attract capital and for the exploitation of which they needed labour. By the end of the seventeenth century their several societies, though differing from each other, had acquired the contours of social order, of political stability. In Virginia, after the upheaval of Bacon's rising in 1676, the larger planters entrenched themselves in control of their counties and also, by representation, of the House of Burgesses. Pennsylvania wrested a new Charter from its Founder in 1701 — the most liberal document of the era, but one which recognised the implicit power of the older settlements and of the greater accumulations of property. Massachusetts received a new Charter from William and Mary in 1691 and with it a conventional order of Whig government. The navigation and mercantile system had grown to imperial proportions, and the foundation of the Board of Trade indicated a permanent English interest in the regulation of overseas affairs. There are good grounds for regarding the end of the seventeenth century as marking a new beginning in colonial politics.

Those politics grew up in a constantly intriguing contrast to those of the mother country. Even the widest differences served, when viewed comparatively as part of a larger spectrum, to illuminate the beliefs and processes on each side; contemporaries on both sides were keenly aware of the more significant differences and were not infrequently critical of their significance.

The various colonial institutions could be taken to illustrate the varieties of republican government. They could also be taken, with or without approval, to illustrate the characteristics of popular government as advocated by Old Whigs in England.

Whenever British governors in the eighteenth century found the Assemblies unmanageable, they heaped abuse on them for their low character. The power of the electorate, exerted in New England and Pennsylvania in annual elections, sometimes appeared to the governors to be reflected in the poor quality of the members elected. In later years Hutchinson generalised these observations, and denounced the Boston town government as 'an absolute democracy'. By prevailing British standards the style of government was certainly popular, though it did not depart in principle from recognised and legitimate English forms. The popular content of colonial government meant that disputes flared up about the true location of the legislative power — the point was questioned in Virginia as early as 1701 — but the principles to which colonial government was committed remained, like the forms, legitimate principles which British government was also supposed to maintain.

Colonial legislators owed their election to a very much wider franchise than usually obtained in Britain. This franchise was so firmly grounded in the ownership of property that practically no one could have been found to argue that a right to vote existed without the qualification of an 'interest' in the form of visible freehold or of personal property of sufficient quantity and value to give the owner a certain degree of personal independence. The orthodox English view was exactly reproduced by the argument that the voter must be, by his property, independent enough to have 'a will of his own'. The rapidity of colonial economic development, the shortage and consequent high wages of labour, cheap land, and a commensurately generous scale of opportunity for personal advancement had the effect of bringing a high proportion of the community into the pale of active citizenship at some time in their lives. Of these, a great many would have begun without political rights, and some would not have acquired enough property until middle life, so that the voting age of twenty-one probably represented a lower proportion of the potential electorate than would exercise the suffrage upwards of the age of thirty. The colonists, however, rediscovered through experience the truth of Harrington's dictum that power follows the distribution of property, to such a point that in many areas the property in question, following his prescription, was property in land; and the inference, which Harrington himself would have approved, was that where property was diffused, so was power. So important, however, was the safeguard of property ownership that in Massachusetts the elections to town offices, which really affected the daily lives of the people, were controlled by higher qualifications than those for the more distant provincial Assembly. In Virginia local government, safe in the hands of the county courts, was not entrusted to the indiscretions of popular elections.

When colonial Assemblies first began to meet, it was natural that their members should be drawn straight from the several districts, towns, or counties that formed the constituencies. However, the physical difficulties and the costs of this direct representation sometimes led to the adoption of the expedient of deputing the responsibility to a gentleman who resided nearer to the capital; there was no hard and fast rule that representatives must be residents of their constituencies. In England that rule, though derived from early practices, had fought a losing battle under Elizabeth I, for it stood in the way of the ambitions of the merchants and gentry striving for seats in Parliament. In the colonies, on the other hand, residence was always very much the rule, non-resident representation the exception. When the rule of residence was first enforced, it was not as a matter of principle but rather as a means of keeping certain individuals out of the legislature. Politics had not become a profession and the competition for seats did not reach the stage where non-residents could contribute materially either to private ambition or public service; the notion that a representative should be a member of his own constituency, sharing its interests because they were his own, certainly belonged in the old, uncomplicated catalogue of republican virtues; and it is not surprising that when American state constitutions came to be drawn up, the rule of residence should have been written into them.

When Burke, rejecting the obligation to obey the instruction of his electorate, reminded them that a Member of Parliament was a representative of the whole nation, he implicitly confirmed the basic British feeling for the unity of the State. It was appropriate that this idea should have been given its classical statement by Burke, who had dashed down to Bristol for the election of 1774 after chasing constituencies in other parts of the country. This characteristically British practice, by which any constituency could be represented by any candidate it chose, regardless of his residence, might be called 'voluntary representation'. After 1776, the American custom finally lost this 'voluntary' character, which had in fact never been strong in the colonies. The result was that the compulsory representation of each locality by one of its own residents reinforced the diversity of American politics and made a virtue of particularism.

By the time the Constitution was framed, it was clear that public service at the Federal level must be remunerated from public funds. There might otherwise be no way to secure public servants. Massachusetts, with its very strong tradition of town government, might have saved itself some trouble if it had taken the opportunity in 1780 to make the costs of representative government a charge on the State treasury; but it had always been a town charge, and in times of poverty, which recurred in 1786, some towns preferred to risk the fine for non-representation rather than bear the expenses of sending a member. Virginia, on the other hand, did pay her members from the public chest. The scale was not generous and would not furnish an independent living. Only men whose economic affairs were in good order could be expected to maintain themselves on a member's salary away from home. But the principle was of great value. In Britain it was the Chartists who, in their time, put forward the demand for payment of members of Parliament, that humble men with no private subsistence might seek election; but it was not until 1911, as a result of the difficulties of Labour Party members, that the principle of payment was adopted in Britain.

When colonial legislators arrived at the capital they elected their speaker and other officers, heard an address by the Governor, and proceeded to arrange themselves under the direction of the Speaker into appropriate committees. What did they do next? The Governor might present specific proposals for legislative action which would form a sort of agenda; but except in moments of crisis, when these points had been used up, the bulk of the subject matter for attention came up to them from the constituencies.

Massachusetts assemblymen would receive either instructions, or a homily on the interests of the town, from the town meeting. Virginian members were apprised of the grievances and demands of their counties by the county courts, which had been canvassed for that purpose by the sheriff; and these different procedures were characteristic of the colonial legislative process. Another major source of legislative material was the private or public petition. The Assemblies dutifully attended to huge quantities of information and passed laws, after three readings each, on the pleas of innumerable townships, merchants, farmers, planters, clam-diggers, husbands, or wives. It must all have seemed, to the more reflective members, a curious terminal to have reached on the road to power; and one can hardly be surprised that men with large estates to look after sometimes preferred to abjure the splendours of public life. Yet these humdrum matters occasionally gave place to graver issues. The extraordinary alacrity with which colonial legislators scented tyranny on every breath of parliamentary wind, and sprang to the defence of their liberties before the British ministry was conscious of threatening them, may perhaps have been due in part to that great instigator of public activity — boredom. They knew, however, where the interests of their people lay, for they attended to them in every session of detailed and painstaking work; they knew the value of the ancient right of petition through which they derived so much of their information, and they knew also that if they did not defend their own interests, no one else would do it for them.

In neither Britain nor the colonies had the idea expressed by the word 'government' yet taken hold. What the king's ministers collectively formed was called an 'administration', and it is perhaps significant that the usage of the eighteenth century did not afford that institution the benefit of a definite article. Administration acted or as often refrained from acting, but it did not become the administration; and 'government' is a nineteenth-century word. Much of Parliament's time was taken up with local and private questions, and it may be remarked that in the first place every single Act of Enclosure came in response to a private motion. Nevertheless the preoccupations of the eighteenth century produced a marked increase in what would later be called 'government business'; and a substantial amount of it was prepared under the authority of the Secretaries of State. The colonies had hardly succeeded even to the notion of a permanent 'administration', and much of the continuing importance of the Council lay in its power to meet the Governor for administrative and judicial business. Colonial government never depended for day-to-day management on a majority in the Assembly, although of course a determined majority there could on occasions make great difficulties for a Governor.

When great issues of state disturbed the equanimity of all responsible people, it was the legislature which had to debate and act. Legislatures became instruments of decision, and their records provided for posterity a documentary history of self-government. These great debates and high resolves, however, were comparatively and mercifully rare. Colonial legislatures seldom met for as much as half the year, often for much less. Such a group could not consider itself the nucleus of a permanent administration. At the height of the imperial crisis, Assemblies were disabled by the fact that they could not lawfully meet without the authority of the Governor, and it was in part for that reason that they had to be superseded by the provincial congresses, which, though unknown to the charters, were elected on the same franchises as the old Assemblies, thereby retaining a strong semblance of legality.

Colonial Assemblies seldom convened to debate a previously known agenda. What happened was that the leading men of the several communities were elected to meet their equals, to hear from the Governor whether any particular problems faced them, to hear from the constituencies what grievances needed redress, to resolve on these points, go home again and tell their electors what they had done. Those electors could, and occasionally did, make their will felt. The Pennsylvania election of 1710 remains the most extraordinary of all, the landslide beside which most later ones appear as the merest ripples. The infancy of the province perhaps detracts a little from its more general significance, but Pennsylvania electors showed a sense of public policy in later years over the proprietary question; the Virginia voters rebuked Spotswood over his patronage policy in 1715 and pronounced on the Tobacco Inspection law in 1735; several governors of Massachusetts confronted hostile electorates, the most clearly identified issue of policy arising over the Land Bank. These election issues demonstrated that popular representation was no mere façade but was a force with which legislators and governors might have to reckon. That force was implicit in the fact that constituencies were small in numbers, so that representatives could be expected to know, and be known to, a much larger proportion of their electorate than in Britain — except, of course, in the case of the close boroughs, where the point made no difference because the elections were not free.

The popular side of colonial representation was subject, however, to distinct restraints. The Assemblies themselves, adept as they were at dogging their governors with assertions based on parliamentary precedents, and in creating — as in Virginia — their own committee systems, and everywhere in defending their versions of House of Commons liberties, also fortified themselves with the characteristic privileges of Parliament. They brooked no interference with their dignity or privacy by individual citizens; they could, by majority vote, expel elected members whose conduct gave offence; they could discipline and restrain the Press; and until the outbreak of the quarrel with Britain, they had been showing an increasing tendency to reproduce the oligarchic autonomy of the House of Commons. The fact that the tendency was more pronounced in Virginia where new elections took place about every three years, than in Massachusetts or Pennsylvania which enjoyed the benefit of the extreme Whig doctrine of annual parliaments, suggests that under the then prevailing conditions the Radicals had the better of the argument.

The strong and growing sense of Assembly privilege was challenged from time to time by the claim of constituents to instruct their representatives on specific issues. These issues, however, were usually local; they tended to arise on points where the member would already know and share the feelings of his electors, especially in Massachusetts and Pennsylvania, where they might otherwise be expected not to have elected him. The threat of instruction therefore seldom laid on members a claim to any sort of continuous responsibility, still less of a duty to communicate with their constituents during the session. There were notable exceptions in Pennsylvania, where the Quaker party majority appealed from the proprietor to the people, a move that was at once honest and shrewd. But in the normal course of their deliberations the colonial Assemblies shared with the parent House of Commons a most valuable protection against public interference in the form of the privacy of their business. No medium existed to communicate the doings of the legislature to the electorate; and although a returning member might be expected to tell about the events of the session when he got home, no convention of a dialogue between members and constituents had been established, nor were members usually held accountable on seeking re-election.

It was in the dispute with the mother country in the 1760s that the immediate political advantages of publicity began to open doors in these legislative walls. Yet, although public galleries were erected, the newspapers were slow to carry the debates to their readers. In Massachusetts the first step, though formally in response to a petition, may well have been taken as an initiative by the Assembly to rally public opinion — or perhaps to impress on country members the force of feeling in Boston.

Every detail of the dispute with Britain bore home to the Assemblies the vital importance of informing the populace of the issues — in a sense, of reversing the process of instruction by arousing popular determination to back the colonial legislatures in their resistance. The consequences were of great and increasing significance for the character of American representation, for they counteracted the tendencies towards oligarchy, the incipient resemblance of the native institutions to the 'constituted bodies' which, standing between monarchs and people, exercised so much quietly effective power throughout Europe; the imperial crisis brought the Assemblies back to the people.

In Britain the initiative towards parliamentary publicity did not spring from the ministry: but it did arise at the same time and it did win support inside the Commons. The interest of members wanting to connect themselves with public opinion coincided with an insistent demand from the reading public, and after a few gestures of official resistance, the regular reporting of debates became normal practice. Long before Parliament was reformed, Conservatives had learnt to acknowledge the force of public opinion, and actually to claim it as a merit of the system that the House of Commons could never escape the vigilance nor ignore the grievances of an informed populace.

Elections are to politics what a trial for murder is to law: in them is concentrated the intelligence and morality of the entire system. The contrast between elections in the more popular constituencies in England and the American colonies was of style rather than substance. They were governed on both sides not only by similar laws but often by distressingly similar morals. The most pronounced differences tended to be of the sort that served, by the deployment of strong light and shade, to bring out the underlying similarities of principle.

American elections often presented a curious mixture, difficult to understand at its face value, of local turbulence and basic order, of jocular familiarity and implicit deference. Colonial society was truly represented — was truly present — on these occasions. For colonial conditions had given rise to splendid opportunities for rapid self-aggrandisement — that was a large part of their attraction: yet the colonists strove to maintain themselves in an orderly manner in accordance with the laws and customs they had inherited. They knew none better and had no wish to aspire to anything different. The periodic eruptions of vigorous independence by colonial electorates may be considered the equivalent, within republican norms, of peasant revolts, all the safer and more decorous for being legal and peaceful and of limited effect. These manifestations arose in large part from a limited, but valid, a felt independence of economic and personal stature. In the country, this independence was closely connected with the important fact that the voting freeholders and tenants were numerous. The cities, especially the seaports, also often proved themselves the seed-beds of a numerous and often rowdy electorate. The behaviour of the comparable English constituencies was strikingly similar. In Middlesex, in Westminster, and in some other represented city areas an active, independent electorate jostled its social superiors and made them fight for their places. Those same characteristics of independence and numbers which gave so much vitality to Virginia were equally vigorous among the freeholders and gentry of Yorkshire, and go a long way to explain the strength of that county's political protest. Virginians and Yorkshiremen had much in common.

When these facts are comprehended in their comparative dimension they do more than illuminate the variety, or similarity, of local politics. They do much more: for they explain the American Revolution. The great force of the argument on which Americans were so quickly able to agree was that the rights they enjoyed were English rights — that they, the Americans, were Englishmen. This was no mere theory of convenience. They felt as they did because they were genuinely, and from the domestic point of view legally, accustomed to English liberties. The English character of all that was most republican — all that was most Old Whig — in American elections did not prove this as a matter of constitutional law: it merely showed it to be a fact.

The electoral system of the colonies was capable of giving a very real representation to a multiplicity of local interests. It is not, for that reason, to be considered as the kind of system that would in later centuries be called a 'democracy'. The election laws, the customs that controlled eligibility and even the relationship of the legislature to the electorate disqualified it from such a description, which, significantly, the colonists themselves would have indignantly rejected. To the (rather limited) extent that the colonies needed to be governed, the system was capable of giving adequate government; when their interests, upon the consensus of colonial opinion, required opposition or resistance to Britain, the same system was capable of formulating that resistance. It was an age, not of democracy, but of political capability.

The later democracy of equal political rights and equal access or eligibility, at all levels of the State, could not have developed without this foundation of capable self-government. The capacity for responsible self-government requires a subtle fusion of laws and habits — of respect for law with respect for custom. Societies can acquire these characteristics and learn these values gradually, by diffused experience and in all probability not otherwise. That is the fundamental significance of the history of the Anglo-American Whig republic. The contrast between the transformation of American government from capability to democracy and the transformations which followed the overthrow of the *ancien régime* in France and revolutionary Europe, is infinitely greater and more impassable than the contrast between the comparable processes in America and Britain.

Americans, building for the future after 1776, were committed to the belief that their heirs ought to be under republican forms of government. They were not committed to any belief in the advent of democracy. The sense in which the men specifically charged with the making of constitutions in the new states understood their own words committed them to giving permanent security to the interests of property, when necessary at the expense of those persons, be their numbers large or small, who owned no property or too little. Their doctrines, and the political facts they rested on, were also capable of yielding a different and more democratic emphasis under the pressure that was later to be exerted by changes in economics and society. The facts of population and the distribution of wealth would then press back the defences of the orthodox Whigs, and the advancing forces of popular democracy were strengthened by their alliance of conscience inside the Whig stockade. For in the next wave of discontent, the unenfranchised and the unrepresented could claim to be deprived of their rights, and it was one of the legacies of the eighteenth century that, in America, rights were facts too.

Such rights were of ancient vintage. Natural, inherent, and inalienable they may have been — no one can disprove it; but for all that, their development into practical politics was certainly not inevitable. Colonial politics did not result from the unfolding of tendencies that were present in England at a given phase of colonisation; in fact they could, and did, develop in different ways according to different conditions and resistances. In the south, under colour of similar forms, a profoundly different type of society from that of the middle areas and the north took root, flourished, and spread westwards. Moreover, civil government in the colonies in North America owed a great deal of its native liberty to the relative weakness of its continental enemies. When military conflict occurred its theatre was always distant from the centres of civilisation: in this it was like Britain, but utterly and most significantly unlike the continent of Europe.

According to the Whig view of the origins of society, to which Americans were intellectual heirs, these rights were guaranteed by an original compact. During the struggles with the Stuarts, this compact among the people was duplicated into a slightly more formal notion of 'an original contract between King and People' — to use the language of the Declaration of Rights — but after being invoked to justify the overthrow of King James II, it played a diminishing part in English history. Recourse to contract theory is usually a sign that government is breaking down. The Declaration of Independence in due course turned the same accusation against King George III.

In America, notions of compact were to have a much longer life. They survived as positive ingredients of political thought, at two loosely connected levels. The more enduring of these concerned the Federal Constitution, which — mainly in the basis of the Senate — bore traces of the earlier Confederation. A Constitution which provided for a unified executive and judiciary and for representation in the popular House on a basis of numbers was both logically and legally incompatible with the principle of a compact between separate and equal states; but under the threat to constitutional liberties that was posed by the Alien and Sedition Acts of Adams's administration, even Madison was prepared to turn back to the superseded idea of such a compact and to affirm, through the famous Resolutions passed in 1798 by the legislature of Virginia, that the Constitution bore that character. A generation later, these resolutions furnished ammunition for the defence of sectional interests through the medium of states rights. It took four years of civil war to make the meaning of the Constitution more precise.

The other level was that of state government. The constitutions formed in the Revolution derived much of their authority from the idea of compact, however obscurely it might be conveyed, for it was a recurrence to compact that seemed to give governments their just powers by assuring them of the consent of the governed.

Consent was not in itself a very active concept. In Harrington's Oceana, the common people were to be entitled at the best to be consulted and to render their affirmative or negative vote to propositions handed down from above; while Locke's version was little more than a concrete statement of a legal fiction. William Penn had intended to put the Harringtonian idea into practice in his province, but was surprised by the independence of his people. Colonists, many of whom were voluntary settlers or soon earned a sufficiency of their own, showed a capacity for participating in local government; from their activity, the vague ideas about the meaning and expression of consent that could be read in the Old Whig and the more orthodox books, began to take a slightly more positive meaning. The onset of the Revolution itself helped to advance and define that meaning, to make of consent an act of participation rather than an act of submission.

Consent was closely connected with compact, since it was the social compact that people were supposed originally to have consented to. The idea had a deep history in America, not owing exclusively to the mythological preconceptions of Old Whigs, for Puritan thought had been engrossed with the contractual nature of the connection between Man and God. This relationship appeared to have an analogy in government. Men had brought their persons and their property into society for protection, and it was the liberty to own and dispose freely of that property that gave force to their resistance to parliamentary taxation. The doctrine died hard. It was brought back into battle in the great Virginia debate of 1829–30 when the representatives of the slave-owning interest, supported by the venerable James Madison, fought with such tenacity against a constitutional reform, which they feared because of its power to deprive them of their defence against taxation by their own state government. The case had worn thin by repetition. Individuals had come singly and voluntarily into society, bringing their property, and they were therefore entitled to a share in that society's government commensurate with the property they had brought — or, to be more practical, with the amount they now owned. The notion of an original compact confirming the sanctity of private property was thus woven tightly into the fabric of the case for the protection of special interests. The argument had been shaped by Theophilus Parsons in 1778 in the *Essex Result*. It led to the conclusion that the principle of the equality of persons would violate the more important principle of the equality of rights. By the time Virginians used it in the years that led up to the Reform of Parliament, it had become a very American argument; the ancestry was English, but the English line had died out.

The difference is revealing. Great debates about political representation took place in Parliament, and in these debates the safety of society was balanced against the expression of minority interests, and the redress of personal grievances. Inside and outside Parliament, it was agreed that Parliament owed good government to the whole nation and was responsible for the interest of the whole of society; and that agreement had superseded the ancient idea that the rights protected by Parliament were guaranteed by the unalterable moral and legal force of an unwritten, unrecorded original compact.

Virginians, debating closely related issues at almost the same time, were not in the least embarrassed by the *naïveté* of these arguments, which many of them plainly understood in a literal sense. This quaint, stubborn political fundamentalism, which in altered contexts was to appear and reappear at much later periods in American history, was among other things an expression of a peculiarly American resentment against the necessity of government. 'Your *aristoi*', John Adams had once observed to Jefferson,

'... will not suffer themselves to be governed.' Had he lived in a later generation he might have chosen to extend his observation to a wider section of the people.

III. ESTATES, INTERESTS, AND THE BEGINNINGS OF POLITICAL INDIVIDUALISM

The rhetoric of political discourse changes very slowly. Because people continue, with disarming simplicity, to believe the words they utter, they frequently imagine themselves to be governed by the forms described by a rhetoric belonging to the past. What is more, they believe in those forms. English political discourse in the eighteenth century recurred to the ideal of a realm comprising concrete and separate estates, each of which was properly represented in Parliament; and this rhetoric persisted long after Bolingbroke had pointed out that the Lords and Commons had become homogeneous with one another — that peers were often commoners with coronets.

One of the long unquestioned assumptions about this political order was that of its coherence with the social order of which it was the political representation. The bedrock of that social order was the equally unquestioned unity of the landed interest. The peers, being great landlords, not only sat in the House of Lords in their own right but evidently represented the undivided interest of the land; but this theory was not strictly compatible with the simultaneously held view that the county knights also held a stake in the landed interest which they defended in the Commons. The truth was that the interpenetration of the two Houses, the ownership of so many seats in the Commons by peers, the presence of peers-to-be in the Commons — these realities, developed with great subtlety by the politicians of the eighteenth century, bore no practical relationship to the grand theory of the estates of the realm.

The interests of the kingdom were far more various and more flexible in their relationships than any theory to be worked out until the arrival of Burke. When Burke propounded the theory of interest representation, suggested perhaps by a glance round at the actual composition of the House of Commons, it was little more than a hint. Burke was particularly concerned to advance the claims of the merchant interest, on whom the Rockingham party leant so heavily, but this concern necessitated a stock-taking of the landed interest, admitted by all to be the most fundamental and permanent. It was from the idea of a permanent landed interest that the bridge could be built from the estates of the realm to the more complex, and incomparably more interesting and realistic, theory that the function of Parliament was to represent the several legitimate interests of the realm.

The idea of interest representation soon became popular in Parliament. Its attraction lay in the fact that it could be used on all sides; and it did little to detract from the claims of those county reformers who would have been fully satisfied with an increase in the representation of the landed interest. Before very long, Lord North's successors as defenders of the old régime took up the principle of interest representation. Supported by the recently emerged agreement that Parliament was accountable to the people through the reporting of debates and subject to the publicity of the press, the new Tories were able to demonstrate that the argument between themselves and the bulk of the reformers was not so much a difference of principle as merely of the precise balance to be desired in a system of assorted interests.

At the height of the Association movement for parliamentary reform, the House of Commons was reminded that public office was not a form of property but a trust. It was a respectable view, but one which made little impression on a system that had long been permeated with the implicit assumption that political rights, like freeholds, were forms of property. Blackstone indeed had observed that a rich man whose property was diffused had a right to vote in more than one place 'and therefore has many representations' — a provision that was incorporated into the election laws of colonial Virginia but, significantly, was abolished there after Independence. In face of renewed attacks which carried the odious charge of corruption, Conservatives began to regroup their arguments. The sentimentalism of the past had lost its utility. What they now claimed — the argument was implicit in the speeches of the 1790s and avowed when the attack was resumed, about 1809 — was that the influence of property accorded with the normal and intentional working of the parliamentary system. That influence, when exerted in elections, was not corrupt but legitimate. The reform movement had by that time at least succeeded in purging much jaded rhetoric from the defence of the old régime.

The progress of reformist arguments, however, was painfully slow. At the time of the Association, and for perhaps a generation thereafter, even the newer industrialists appear to have had little use for reform. They could buy borough seats for themselves instead. Their petitions had great weight with the Commons. It was only when the industrial cities grew big with the new working masses, when the owners and employers themselves grew so numerous that the old system no longer gave them any feeling of representation, and when its gross incongruities offended their dignity even more cruelly than it failed their interests, and when Bentham and James Mill scorched the swollen mass with intellectual acid, that reform became inevitable.

The Whigs under Grey and Russell were the victors in the Great Reform Act. Yet in face of the criticism advanced by Radicals and Utilitarians, their views had come to look surprisingly like those of the Tories whom they so bitterly opposed. The Tories had adopted the principle of interest representation for the House of Commons — to which the reply of the Whigs was that the interests accepted by the Tories were too narrow and exclusive. The problem, then, was to redefine the legitimate interests for purposes of representation. The debate was not between rival concepts of the fundamental purposes of political representation, but over the adequacy and adaptability of a system whose general principles were acknowledged by both sides.

With these views, these relative (if embattled) complacencies, the Radicals and Utilitarians had little patience. Since the founding of the London Corresponding Society the politically minded artisans had moved towards the full doctrine and the full implications of universal manhood suffrage. Both they and the more philosophical Utilitarians rejected the concept of multiple-interest representation and asserted instead that the State, made up of however many interests, was one nation; a nation composed of morally and politically equal individuals. It followed that parliamentary constituencies should be composed of equal numbers of voters and that all adult men should possess the right to vote. The forming of parliamentary majorities would then follow from the numerical majorities in the electorate. The ultimate consequence of this new and radical individualism would be a single state, owing nothing to estates or interests, and governed by the direct application to parliamentary institutions of majority rule.

The advance of these doctrines was destined to be even slower than that of parliamentary reform. The logic of democracy was at best a debatable issue, as John Stuart Mill discovered when faced with its fuller implications: and logic is in any case the least impressive of political weapons. In the long run the only hope lay in an almost indefinite extension of the interests entitled to representation. That process could come about only with the alliance of the more powerful interests which the old system had deprived of representation; and it was this alliance, not the force of numbers, that brought about the limited advance of 1832.

The British doctrine of a realm made up of discrete estates did not have an easy passage across the Atlantic. Locke's attempt to impose upon Carolina an unnatural aristocracy was, by virtue of its failure, a significant contribution to American institutional thought. But Americans were fully committed to the principles of what in the eighteenth century was called 'mixed government'. The monarchical element was provided by the presence and very real power of the royal Governor — or the proprietary one, in Pennsylvania; the Council assisted the Governor in the discharge of his business and in sitting as a court of appeal; but it also acted as an upper House of legislation. The lower House represented the people, which came to mean the whole of the colonial interest in contradistinction to that of Britain.

American criticism of Britain in the era of the Revolution was directed against the corruption of the Commons by the Crown. It did not involve any objections to the principles or existence of the House of Lords or of the bicameral principle of government. When American critics asserted that the legislative power ought to be in the colonies they included the Council, which had in any case arisen as a native colonial institution, in that designation; what they repudiated was the British element, not the concept of an upper chamber. Mixed government was admired for its stability, that great Aristotelian virtue, and for its superior ability to ensure justice to all social orders.

Although the free part of American society did not fit itself comfortably into the model of estates — hardly a surprising matter in view of the fact that its meaning in Britain was ancestral rather than real — American political thought agreed that government operated on the two entities of persons and property. The formalisation of that view in 1778 in the *Essex Result* gave Americans an explanation of the institutional policy to which they were committed by history and prudence. Moreover, there were practical reasons for ensuring the continuity of the upper chambers, for the whole system stood committed to the protection of property, some of the larger accumulations of which might not seem wholly secure in the power of Assemblies that were highly susceptible to popular feeling. Very large fortunes had been made in the colonies; and in view of the expected advance of the country, still larger ones lay in prospect; the Revolution certainly appeared to be no time to dismantle the institutions in which they might be expected to exert their proper influence. John Adams put the matter the other way round: he expected that influence to be so powerful that in the public interest it ought to be contained. The result, a senate based on property, was the same.

The doctrine of persons and property was all that remained of an attenuated American version of estates of the realm. In fact it stood closer to the idea of interests, and as such it maintained a flourishing institutional life in the new state constitutions. These considerations explain the re-establishment, in those constitutions, of the upper Houses; without taking them into account, the domestic history of the American Revolution can never be more than partially understood; but when they are seen in the full context of American institutional thought, they resolve those ambiguities which have sometimes been held out as paradoxical, or even as contradictory, to the purposes of the Revolution.

Estates had multiplied into interests. But the idea of persons and property came forward into Federal affairs at the Philadelphia Convention, in the shape of the Virginia Plan. In the course of the debates, the United States Senate was converted from the embodiment of the interests of property into that of the separate states — the visible sign of their residual sovereignty. In this capacity it came in later years to stand out as the main forum for the most important and divisive of all the aspects of the particular American history of special interests.

It was the Senate which preserved the principle that certain kinds of distinct, corporate interest, other than those of population, were entitled to political representation. In the long run it was the great geographical sections, not individual states, which made use of that principle; and this development was extremely momentous because such sections could grow to control powers and attract loyalties to rival those more properly belonging to the Federal government. A generation before the Civil War, John C. Calhoun of South Carolina began to expound doctrines by which the special interests of his state, and of the South, might be maintained within the Federal structure. His basic problem was one that Madison, concerned as he had so often been with the protection of constitutional minorities, would certainly have understood. Calhoun was attempting to deal with the problem on a large scale, and the interest he had at heart was of great complexity, since it involved the political as well as the economic structure of a large area of the Union; but none of this need conceal the fact that he was engaged in an attempt to adapt and develop the old and honoured theory of interest representation. A peculiar danger presented itself, however, when such an interest occupied a distinct geographical section, and when, further, it possessed the institutional means of separate action.

Madison had anticipated these grave sectional divisions. But when he discussed the problem of interests in the tenth number of *The Federalist*, he was occupied immediately with the problem of so dividing the government as to resist the formation of political parties. No doubt influenced by his great Irish fellow-Whig, Burke, Madison anticipated the division of the country into conflicting and competing economic and professional interests, and maintained that the chief cause of conflict would be between those with and those without property. The political organisation of these interests he called factions, a disparaging name for parties — but he hoped that parties would merely come and go as their temporary objects dictated. By an irony which he cannot have either anticipated or enjoyed, Madison himself soon became one of the leading agents in the process by which interests were consolidated into parties; and after parties, with their own loyalties and values, had come into being, interests moved between and among them in their urgent, private pursuits. The history of state legislation in the nineteenth century was largely that of the pressures of competing business enterprises seeking incorporation or advancement, while in Congress the complex history of tariff legislation reflected, at one time or another, the demands of almost every impulse of economic interest.

The advance of interests into the arena of legitimised representation meant the decline of one force that had never been voted for: virtue. When Montesquieu wrote about the spirit of laws, it seemed perfectly correct to dwell emphatically on the power of abstractions. The essential principle of a democracy, the quality which made it workable, was virtue. Similarly the principle of monarchy was honour. Neither princes nor people found virtue easy to maintain, and laws were required to give it support. An aristocracy needed to be guided by a spirit of moderation. The English and American exponents of the law of the Constitution, without speaking strictly this language, would have found corresponding values: when Coke had said that deputies were summoned to Parliament to consult for the good of the whole realm, when Burke affirmed that each member, once elected, must represent the general interest of the nation, they declared the importance of virtue to a republic. Americans of the era of the Revolution insistently returned to the theme of republican virtue, a Roman characteristic of which they rightly feared the imminent loss. The explicit representation of interests, however, let in a different principle. The representatives of interests were not obliged even in theory to consult for the public good. The best that a theorist such as Madison could do, when faced with the inevitability of some form of interest representation, was to argue that the public good would be served by the balancing of interests.

In an expanding nation, the doctrine of interest representation, adaptable to the purposes of sections, had a disintegrating effect — an effect that was advanced by long periods of inertia at the centre. How amusing it would have been, and how apposite, if James Madison had contemplated the work of the Federal Convention and remarked, 'The state will wither away'!

The decline of virtue could also be traced in the decline of the older idea of free elections. A free election as understood in the eighteenth century was one in which no influence of any sort was brought to bear on the electors; but when candidates began to appeal to the material interests of the voters, that convention crumbled beneath a welter of competing boasts and promises. The fading of the venerable concept of the public good was concealed for a time by the fact that, under conditions of Roman simplicity and virtue, the whole people were expected to become guardians of the public good. But when the loyalties of the people were divided between parties, when rival claimants went straight for the pride or pockets of a vast electorate, then the idea of a disinterested Assembly of their representatives, consulting with a sole view to the good of the whole, became almost as archaic as the royal prerogative. In the several states, it was recollected again from time to time by Constitutional Conventions. In the Federal government, failing an effective President, it became a ward of the Supreme Court.

British reformers, Whig or Radical, were always aware of the problem. John Stuart Mill returned after his Radical interlude to make the problem of responsible leadership in a democracy one of his gravest anxieties; his father had complacently anticipated the continuation of educated leadership as a result of the natural deference of the masses towards their superiors. What they heard from America tended to confirm their opinion about the need for prudence in the advance of democracy in Britain.

Britain was never threatened by the disintegrating tendencies that seemed to spring up with such alarming spontaneity where Americans brandished Whig rights. In the seventeenth century British government, whether royal or parliamentary, was made strong by the ancient spirit of authority. The unity of the State certainly cracked during the Civil War, but not fatally, and not for long. Peers, spiritual and temporal, and commons, whether standing as estates or representing interests, never questioned the authority of Parliament to speak for the whole realm. Even the most extreme Radicals proposed nothing that could undermine the unity of the State. On the contrary, their theories made it necessary to view the State as a more unified and single entity, with its population of equals, than did the more differentiated views of either Whigs or Tories. In America, the men who stuck most firmly to the virtue of small and local government and who resisted the nationalising direction of the Federalists were those whose views carried the most implacable tendencies to centrifugal force. But extreme particularism did not imply personal equality or majority rule as a matter of principle — such matters would depend on the character of each local society. It is of the highest significance that the advance of the political individualism which yields majority rule came under the protection of the strongest nationalists in the Philadelphia Convention.

Sectional or state particularism could shield special inequalities beneath the patronage of general rights. The liberty of the medieval baron was presumably not synonymous with the liberty of his serfs; and the liberty of freeholders in the Southern colonies and states was not that of the slaves. Negro slavery is sometimes dismissed from discussions of republican institutions as though it were some adventitious or even extraneous factor to which the liberties enjoyed by the bulk of the white population were only incidentally related. This is a fundamental error. Political liberty in the South was based on the relative economic independence of citizens, whether they were large planters or small freeholders. That independence, together with prospects of economic growth and prosperity, was built on the enslavement of the mass of the ordinary working people, whose labour was indispensable but whose interests remained, in the nature of their case, wholly unrepresented.

Political representation stopped short at the white population; that white population contained persons of a variety of different origins and religions. The borderline of republican institutions was marked along a borderline of skin pigmentation, and the granting of the electoral franchise to the mass of coloured labourers was not on the agenda of Whig republicans. (It is remarkable that in North Carolina, free Negroes were permitted to vote until 1835, when their liberties fell victim to the advance of Jacksonian democracy.)

The importance of this point should not be mistaken. It not only helps to define the limits of representative institutions in Virginia: it helps to explain those institutions, and thereby to establish their character. This character has been concealed from students of those institutions, as it was concealed from contemporaries, by the deception of colour, and consequently by irrelevant considerations of race relations. If the slave labour force had happened to be white, such considerations would never have intruded into the argument. Yet the social and economic interests of the planters would have rendered the political enfranchisement of their labour force as intolerable if they had been white as when they were black. No one proposed the enfranchisement of the landless agricultural labourer, and Jefferson's offer of a grant of fifty acres would obviously not have been conceivable if slaves could have obtained their manumission by taking it up. Not even by the most fanciful stretch of imagination can one envisage a House of Delegates extending the suffrage to the labour force save on one condition only:

that each planter should absolutely have controlled the votes of his own men. This would have been analogous to the control of factory workers by their employers, an eventuality greatly feared by Whig, and even by Radical, thinkers. It would, of course, have made the great planters into baronial lords.

In the British political mind the idea that the Constitution was formed of estates of the realm under the Crown showed a tenacity that was due in part to the endurance, in both name and form, of the historical legislative chambers, and in part also to the fascination exerted by coronets (or the aspiration to them) over commoners — a fascination which is said not to have wholly disappeared in the twentieth century. When the concept of interest representation, which was both a description and an attempt to justify the observable facts, began to gain credence, it did not have the effect of displacing the older idea but grew up and flourished beside it. The two ideas, as attempts to explain the Constitution, were not wholly compatible, not wholly contradictory, but the inconsistencies of view which caused different members of Parliament to see different values and purposes in what they took to be the same institutions did not impair the working of the Constitution while those institutions themselves still worked.

As the industrial cities brought forth a huge force of unskilled labourers, political critics tried to find a new set of terms to describe the social order that seemed to be coming into being. The word 'order' gave way to the word 'class'. The persisting structure of British government gave some colour of validity to the notion that the realm was now divided, both socially and politically, into three classes; upper or aristocratic, middle, and working. The subsequent history of the advance of democracy was largely a history of the gradual extension of political representation to the working classes. When first identified they were almost entirely without official recognition, except in places where they qualified as pot-wallopers, and it was a large and gravely discontented section of the newer middle classes who were struggling to get into the system. Later in the nineteenth century, political parties began to form themselves on lines roughly suggested by the inexact but rugged notion of a class system, while social theory and much subsequent historical explanation were fired by the desperate doctrine of class conflict.

The idea of the class system and the doctrines of class conflict served as a useful shorthand for analysis and no doubt as an indispensable expression of the emotions necessary to sustain great political purposes. An abbreviated method of notation is as necessary for organisation as it is for theory. The truth, however, was more complicated. No one who had to deal with political realities in the middle nineteenth century would have mistaken the skilled crafts whose leaders joined in forming the London Trades Council for un-skilled industrial labourers: certainly the crafts would not have done so! The amorphous sectors of population who found themselves described as 'middle' or 'working' class were actually divided into far more numerous interests, each of them more compact than 'classes', and internally more coherent.

The personal representation of private individuals could on rare occasions serve to defend a personal right, but could mean little to the general work of Parliament. What could and did count was the fact that, as long as the individual possessed the right to vote, his interests could be consulted through forms of collective representation. Party organisation did not supersede interest representation; but parties arranged the interests, consulted them, interested themselves in them. The system helped in large measure to resolve the problems of leadership which had so disquieted the worthy, well-educated Radicals of Utilitarian convictions. Neither the antique estates of the realm nor the recent and tendentious idea of a class system gave an account of the economic and social order as accurate or politically as satisfactory as the interest analysis; but still more significant was the fact that the grouping of interests, whether within parties or independently of them, was a method of organisation for which the parliamentary system afforded effective means of institutional action.

The representation of the variety of economic, regional, and multifarious other interests survives and is bound to survive as a means of expression, of communication, and of action. But the need of interests, as interests, does not provide the theoretical basis for representative government. That basis can consist only of the equal representation of individuals, because equal and numerical representation is the only political foundation which provides that the demands of specific interests be measured according to a single standard. Interests which entrench themselves in the forms of government may be perfectly legitimate in themselves, but they are liable to be overtaken by other interests, equally legitimate, equally entitled on grounds of equity to effective representation.

Much the most striking examples of this type of inequity have arisen as a result of the assertion, made by certain kinds of entrenched interest in the United States, that one interest is more fundamental, more inherently entitled to claim the protection of the entire system, than another. The disproportion between the voting power of rural and urban districts resulting from the refusal by state legislatures to reapportion their constituent basis according to changes in population, stands out as the most obvious case of the conflict between the perpetual representation of special interests and the principle of majority rule.

The problem of equity can be stated as a problem of measurement. One interest cannot be the measure of another interest. Numbers alone, arranged in equal constituencies, can provide a means of measurement which remains consistent, can be seen to be consistent, and within the limits of human frailty, can therefore be seen to be just. The gerrymander is simply the rotten borough of democracy; its inventors and perpetuators have corrupted the American system of government quite as surely, as skilfully, and as willingly as the agents of the Crown corrupted the British Constitution in the eighteenth century.

It has been noted that the control of representation falls properly under the aegis of the Supreme Court — that, as decided in *Baker* v. *Carr*, disputes about representation are 'justiciable'. It emerges from these observations that judgments in favour of the principle of the numerical majority enforce the logic of political representation and are therefore acts of political justice.[1]

Constitutional development, however, does not grow out of logic, and constitutional reasoning is meaningless unless it applies to conditions. The Whigs who made the American constitutions held different opinions about the nature and extent of representative government. By their actions they admitted political individualism, not as a leading, but as a collateral principle, into constitutional law and therefore into political practice. The institutional context in which these steps were taken was one in which it was generally agreed that property as well as persons ought to be weighed when assessing the 'importance' of a state for purposes of representation — a procedure that was eventually discarded, reluctantly, on grounds of technical difficulty, not of principle; this was one of many examples of the political evaluation of material property that were fully in keeping with Whig-republican principles both in America and Britain: Wyvill's Yorkshiremen spoke the same language as John Adams of Massachusetts. Nothing in the historical context of the American Revolution committed the holders of such doctrines as these to a belief in the necessity of equalitarian political democracy. On the contrary: some of the most characteristic leaders of Whig-republican politics, when they looked forward to the rise of industrial cities, urged the need to arrange the system of representation so as to exclude or limit the influence of the industrial workers. James Madison, who was soon afterwards to found the Jeffersonian Republican Party and to write the Virginia

[1] They have also been found to conform to the logic of the Constitution in *Wesberry* v. *Sanders* and *Reynolds* v. *Sims*, both decided in 1964.

Resolutions, put this argument to Thomas Jefferson. A generation later, their successors in the Old Dominion, still true Republicans, fought a long, tough defence of these same principles. The same theme, almost the same proposals, were heard in the House of Commons in the gloomy year 1797 from the young but despondent Whig reformer, Charles Grey.

The identifiable political individual who nevertheless emerged with such undoubted increase of standing from the state and Federal Constitutions was understood to be a taxpayer and an owner of property. In theory it was perfectly correct to follow this reasoning to the conclusion that if non-taxpayers or owners of insufficient property became a majority, then that majority would be excluded from politics. It was, then, the trend of events and the distribution of property, as well as the massing and movement of population, that gradually extracted the democratic threads from the dense but somewhat tangled fabric of Whig theory.

What mattered most of all for that time — the time of Revolution and the making of Constitutions — was the fact that individuals came to be counted as the basic units of representation. That they might be fewer in number than the whole population, that they might even constitute some sort of privileged *élite*, was less significant for the moment than the fact that they were now counted as individuals. Americans did not yet say 'One man — one vote', but they did say, 'One elector — one vote', and that by itself was a major breach in the inherited texture of corporate representation; it was a breach which many people in Massachusetts, devoted to their towns, did not much like. Yet it was carried forward in other states. For there were already a great many of these enfranchised individuals, and history was going to make more of them.

Political individualism, though not yet capable of being fully implemented, emerged as a practical theory — a theory capable of practical development — in the era of the American Revolution. That fact alone gives to the events of that period a primary character in the subsequent development of political representation in both America and Britain. The course of those developments, however, depended on other forces; if, for example, America had continued, as Madison and those contemporaries who soon joined him in the Jeffersonian-Republican Party had originally hoped, to grow into a large agricultural nation undivided by political parties and trading mainly in the produce of its farms, there would have been no particular reason to expect the rise of the more modern kind of democracy — not, at least, for a much longer period. Foreseeing the growth of great cities, Madison also, as a necessity of his convictions, foresaw ways of blocking an equalitarian representation of their inhabitants.

What emerged was not a single system understood in the same sense by all those who participated in the same forms of government; many men with different ideas of what an institution is or ought to be can work together, accepting the consensus imposed by that institution, yet using it and even changing it for their own ends. Successive generations do not deposit geological layers on top of each other, for history is not like geology; the ideas of former generations survive in the teachings, habits, and buildings of their successors. A new form of government encapsules those which survive from the past. Thus neither America nor Britain was to be governed in the next era by any one clear and dominant theory of representation. The truth was far more complicated, even under the written, explicit forms of American Constitutions. Within the compass of the majority principle there survived the threads of interests, economic, geographic, ecclesiastic, and dogmatic. Corporations and classes, minorities aggressive and defensive, could better serve themselves by collaborating to work within the system than by repudiating it.

The American system was to be splintered by secession, but even if secession had been victorious in battle it would not have solved the problem of minority representation in the state. The agreement on which nineteenth-century forms of representative government emerged was not by any means an agreement as to any single unifying method or even purpose; it was rather a willingness to keep representative institutions going, with all their conflicts of interests and aims, all their competing and overlapping committees and claims — claims to seniority, claims to inalienable right, claims to mandates, claims to privilege, claims to efficiency — than to renounce the stability that representative government was able to combine with its principled offer of political justice. That offer could never have been held out, in the long run, to the rising populations of America and Britain without the ultimate recognition of the equality of individuals. Only by this assessment of the individual as the basic unit of political representation could the foundations of majority rule be laid down. The single-minded, disinterested majority, concerned only for the 'national interest', as imagined by the British Radicals, would rarely if ever exist except in war-time; but the principle that legislative majorities stood for majorities of free and independent voters, though it was not to stand alone in constitutional law, was to remain indispensable to legitimate government: to its continuity and its authority. That principle was to be the nearest successor to the royal prerogative.

The wealth and economic power that lay massed in the great states of

Massachusetts, Pennsylvania, and Virginia also harboured the larger populations. These states were those which had the highest interest in the constitutional application of majority principles and the least to fear from them. Those states which owed their greatness to the seaport cities, Boston, New York, Philadelphia, Baltimore, reproduced the same association of forces. The concentrated wealth of the merchant and manufacturing interests could keep its grip on political power only through a numerical apportionment representing the vast numbers who made up the city populations. In an attenuated form it was basically a similar alliance which helped to edge forward the interest of a more popular representation in Britain.

This alliance transformed political individualism from a lawyer's theory, or a romance with an unbelievable future into a turbulent and gritty reality. The great transformation owed more to the cities than to the countryside, to seaports and international commerce, than to the farm and the plough. And this was something which Aristotle, from whom English and American Whigs had learnt so much, could also have foretold.

Appendix I

A FALLACY IN THE THEORY OF INSTRUCTION

THE right of constituents to instruct their representatives was a favourite doctrine in America. It seemed very natural in such provinces as Massachusetts, where each town had a distinct corporate identity, met once a year to elect a representative to go to the General Court, and discussed the town interests. It appeared less frequently in southern provinces where the voters were rather meeker towards their social superiors. But one of the central arguments for the right to instruct was advanced in a discussion in the Virginia House of Burgesses in 1754, and as this argument runs straight back to the tradition of the Old Whigs and Commonwealthmen, whose beliefs also inspired so much of the early frames of government in Pennsylvania and led to the provision that delegates in that province should come to the Assembly armed with instructions from their electors, it is worth examining the reasoning on which it was based.

In 1754 Speaker Robinson and the 'favourers of popularity' in their debate with Landon Carter had upheld the right to instruct. Their argument was based on the Old Whig thesis that the whole people had once been able to meet in a single assembly, and that the practice of representation had been instituted simply to avoid confusion as numbers grew too large — 'to avoid the confusion of those mighty numbers', in Penn's own phrase.

Although the problem of collecting the sense of the people became technically more complicated, the principle did not undergo any essential change while the doctrine of instruction lasted. Opponents of the theory always pointed out that binding instructions forestalled the possibility of debate; that they might be suitable to a congress of separate sovereignties but were incompatible with that of a single state. But they failed to expose a logical fallacy in the reasoning that connected the supposedly historical origin of the assembly with the right to instruct.

This historical origin was, of course, taken seriously. Taking it, then, at that valuation, and supposing that the method of representation had been evolved to retain the exact purpose of that assembly after the growth and dispersal of population had rendered the primal meeting physically impossible, no equivalent of the primal meeting remained in the system.

What the instruction school claimed for each separate constituency was an indefeasible right to instruct its own delegate deriving from the original right of all the people to meet together without delegates. This theory therefore assumed that each separate constituency had inherited all of that original power. But this was impossible. No one constituency could ever logically hold more of the original power than would belong to a section of the original members.

The right of instruction was indissolubly connected with the principle of representation which asserted that the legislature was neither more nor less than 'the whole people in miniature'. But if so, then the legislature derived from that fact an authority superior to that of any one constituency; and its reasoning and decisions were the nearest attainable approach to those of the whole people. Which authority, being present in the legislature but absent from the separate constituencies must deprive those constituencies of the right to instruct.

Appendix II

VOTING STATISTICS IN AMERICA

THE basic sources for these tables are population statistics and election returns. Before 1790, population statistics are based on Greene and Harrington,[1] while those of 1790 and after are based on the United States census returns. Estimates for the years between census years have been obtained by subtracting the total in the earlier from that in the later census year; the difference has been divided by ten, and one-tenth has been added for each succeeding year down to the end of the decade. The estimates of the adult white male population and the adult male population of free coloured persons (which have been added to the totals in a separate column when figures are available) have been obtained by use of a similar principle. Where the census breaks the returns at age groups sixteen and twenty-six, the total number in that age group has been divided by two, and half the remainder (representing the total over twenty-one) has been added to the rest of the total over twenty-six. This method has varied slightly according to the type of information given in the census returns.

The election returns before 1780 are too fragmentary to be of much significance. But from 1780 onwards the figures were systematically recorded. Those for Massachusetts are to be found in the Massachusetts Archives, those for Connecticut in the Office of the Secretary of State at Hartford, Connecticut, in the Connecticut State Library, and in the *Connecticut Courant*, and the returns for New Hampshire in the New Hampshire Law Library, Concord, New Hampshire.

The Pennsylvania voting statistics are taken from *The Pennsylvania Manual, 1949–50*, 91 and 96; the voting particulars for Maryland have been taken from returns in Executive Papers, Hall of Records, Annapolis. The figures for Virginia are derived from the county returns in the Archives of the Virginia State Library. Where necessary, and in Virginia from 1824 to 1832, figures were taken from Stanwood's *History of the Presidency* and in Virginia, 1836–60, from W. Dean Burnham, *Presidential Ballots, 1836–1892*. North Carolina figures are from *The Manual of North Carolina*, 1913, and from the State Archives.

These tabulations have appeared severally in *The William and Mary Quarterly*, *The Pennsylvania Magazine of History and Biography*, *The Maryland Historical Quarterly* and *The Journal of Southern History*, and are reproduced by courtesy of those journals.

[1] Evarts B. Greene and Virginia D. Harrington, *American Population before the Federal Census of 1790* (New York, 1932).

MASSACHUSETTS, CONNECTICUT AND NEW HAMPSHIRE ELECTION STATISTICS, 1780–1860

Year		Free adult white males	Free adult males	Election	Votes	Percentage adult white males voting	Percentage adult males voting
1780	Mass.	70,000		Const. of 1780	16,235	23	
1781	Mass.	72,386		Gov. and Lt. Gov.	12,281	17	
1782	Mass.	74,772		Governor	8,585	12	
1783	Mass.	77,158		"	7,744	10	
1784	Mass.	79,544		"	9,108	11	
1785	Mass.	81,930		"	7,631	9	
	N.H.	19,000		"	7,079	37	
1786	Mass.	84,316		"	9,065	11	
				"	8,231	9	
	Conn.	45,000 (approx.)		"	5,823	13	
	N.H.	19,000		"	8,567	45	
1787	Mass.	86,702		"	24,588	28	
	N.H.	20,400		"	9,285	45	
1788	Mass.	89,088		"	22,157	24	
	N.H.	23,665*		"	8,838	37	
1789	Mass.	91,474		"	21,384	23	
	N.H.	26,930*		"	8,534	31	
1790	Mass.	93,865		"	16,518	17	
	Conn.	47,400	48,100	Congress	1,320	2	2
	N.H.	31,196		Governor	7,762	24	
1791	Mass.	96,509		"	17,038	17	
	N.H.	31,826		"	8,967	28	

Year	State	Total	Total	Office	Vote		
1792	Mass.	99,153		"	16,894	17	
	N.H.	32,456		"	8,389	27	
1793	Mass.	101,797		"	18,266	18	
	N.H.	33,086		"	9,854	29	
1794	Mass.	104,441		"	23,454	22	
	Conn.	49,640	50580	Congress	3,766	7	7
	N.H.	33,716		Governor	10,470	31	
1795	Mass.	107,085		"	17,710	16	
	N.H.	34,346		"	9,440	27	
1796	Mass.	109,729		Gov./Pres.	26,493/16,112	24/14	15
	Conn.	50,760	51,820	Governor	7,773	15	
	N.H.	34,976		"	10,775	30	
1797	Mass.	112,373		"	25,658	22	9
	Conn.	51,320	52,440	Cong. (special)	4,896	9	
	N.H.	35,606		Governor	10,823	30	
1798	Mass.	115,017		"	21,259	18	9
	Conn.	51,880	53,060	Congress	5,298	10	
	N.H.	36,236		Governor	12,151	33	
1799	Mass.	117,661		"	33,013	28	
	N.H.	36,866		"	11,738	32	
1800	Mass.	120,304		"	37,059	31	
	Conn.	53,000	54,300	Congress	7,806	14	14
	N.H.		37,706	Governor	16,732	37	44
1801	Mass.	123,065		"	45,816	24	
	Conn.	53,312	54,644	"	13,307		24
	N.H.		38,402	"	15,639		40

Year	Free adult white males	Free adult males	Election	Votes	Percentage adult white males voting	Percentage adult males voting
1802	Mass. 126,026		Governor	49,583	39	
	Conn. 53,624	54,988	"	16,314	30	29
	N.H.	39,098	"	19,166		48
1803	Mass. 128,887		"	43,409	33	
	Conn. 53,936	55,332	"	22,446	41	40
	N.H.	39,794	"	21,317†		53
1804	Mass. 131,748		Gov./Pres.†	54,499/55,282	41/42	
	Conn. 54,248	55,676	Governor	17,979	33	32
	N.H.	40,490	"	24,282		60
1805	Mass. 134,609		"	64,100	47	
	Conn. 54,560	56,020	"	20,660	38	36
	N.H.	41,186	"	28,443		68
1806	Mass. 137,470		"	75,171	55	
	N.H.	41,882	"	20,573		49
1807	Mass. 140,331		"	81,500	58	
	N.H.	42,578	"	16,861		39
1808	Mass. 143,192		"	81,147	56	
	N.H.	43,272	"	15,899		36
1809	Mass. 146,053		"	93,322	64	
	N.H.	43,968	"	30,983		70
1810	Mass. 148,918	150,836	"	90,813	61	59
	Conn. 56,123	57,736	"			
	N.H.	44,667	"	31,575		71
1811	Mass. 151,428	153,336	"	83,917	55	54
	N.H.	45,496	"	32,094		70

Year							
1812	Mass. 153,938	155,836	Gov./Pres.	104,156/78,135	68/50	67/50	
	N.H.	46,325	Governor	31,982		69	
1813	Mass. 156,448	158,336	"	100,223	64	63	
	N.H.	47,154	"	35,729		75	
1814	Mass. 158,958	160,836	"	102,477	64	63	
	N.H.	47,983	"	38,542		81	
1815	Mass. 161,468	163,336	"	95,017	59	58	
	N.H.	48,812	"	36,198		74	
1816	Mass. 163,978	165,836	"	97,084	59	58	
	Conn. 58,667	60,442	Gov./Assistants	21,659/17,063 (approx.)	37/29	35/28	
	N.H.	49,641	Governor	38,407		77	
1817	Mass. 166,488	168,336	"	84,496	50	50	
	Conn. 59,091	60,893	Gov./Cong./Council nom.	26,976/9,101/23,100	45/15/39	44/15/38	
	N.H.	50,470	Governor	35,375		70	
1818	Mass. 168,998	170,836	"	70,927	41	41	
	Conn. 59,515	61,344	Gov./Const. ratif.	17,878/26,282	30/44	29/42	
	N.H.	51,299	Governor	31,465		61	
1819	Mass. 171,508	173,336	"	79,885	46	46	
	Conn. 59,939	61,795	"	25,975	43	42	
	N.H.	52,128	"	24,265		45	
1820	Mass. 112,833‡	114,656	"	53,297	47	46	
	Conn. 60,361	62,245	"	20,671	34	33	
	N.H.	52,955	"	24,771		45	
1821	Mass. 115,996	117,824	"	49,086*	42	41	
	Conn. 61,206	63,098	"	11,618	19	18	
	N.H.	53,711	"	24,448		45	

Year	Free adult white males	Free adult males	Election	Votes	Percentage adult white males voting	Percentage adult males voting
1822	Mass. 119,159	120,992	Governor	49,849	41	45
	Conn. 62,051	63,951	"	10,016	16	15
	N.H.	54,467	"	23,980		44
1823	Mass. 122,322	124,160	"	65,330	53	52
	Conn. 62,896	64,804	"	10,230	16	15
	N.H.	55,223	"	29,943		54
1824	Mass. 125,485	127,328	Cong./Gov./Pres.	27,882/73,051/37,303	22/58/29	21/57/29
	Conn. 63,741	65,657	Gov./Pres.	7,572/9,565	11/15	11/14
	N.H.	55,979	President	10,032		18
	N.H.		Governor	30,348		54
1825	Mass. 128,648	130,496	"	37,426	29	28
	Conn. 64,586	66,510	"	10,431	16	15
	N.H.	56,735	"	29,729		52
1826	Mass. 131,811	133,664	"	39,992	30	29
	Conn. 65,431	67,363	"	11,971	18	17
	N.H.	57,491	"	30,251		52
1827	Mass. 134,974	136,832	"	39,119	29	28
	Conn. 66,276	68,216	"	13,603	20	20
	N.H.	58,247	"	27,411		46
1828	Mass. 138,137	140,000	Cong./Gov./Pres.†	35,526/34,318/35,892	25/24/24	25/24/25
	Conn. 67,121	69,069	Gov./Pres.	9,560/18,286	14/27	13/26
	N.H.	59,003	Gov./Pres.	39,897/45,056		67/76
1829	Mass. 141,300	143,168	Governor	35,203	25	24
	Conn. 67,966	69,922	"	10,038	15	14
	N.H.	59,759	"	42,246		70

Year	State			Type			
1830	Mass.	144,459	146,335	,,	47,173	32	32
	Conn.	68,815	70,773	,,	13,588	19	19
	N.H.		60,515	,,	42,441		70
1831	Mass.	149,055	151,030	,,	53,415	36	35
	Conn.	69,460	71,426	,,	18,866	27	26
	N.H.		61,589	,,	42,294		69
1832	Mass.	153,647	155,723	Gov./Pres.	64,225/60,585	41/39	40/39
	Conn.	70,105	72,079	Gov./Pres.	17,050/32,341	24/46	23/45
	N.H.		62,663	Gov./Pres.	39,233/44,496		63/71
1833	Mass.	158,241	160,416	Governor	62,474	39	38
	Conn.	70,750	72,732	,,	21,778	30	29
	N.H.		63,737	,,	33,476		52
1834	Mass.	162,835	165,109	,,	75,180	46	45
	Conn.	71,395	73,385	,,	36,948	51	50
	N.H.		64,811	,,	30,173		46
1835	Mass.	167,430	169,802	,,	64,903	38	38
	Conn.	72,040	74,038	,,	42,710	59	57
	N.H.		65,885	,,	40,900		62
1836	Mass.	172,025	174,495	Gov./Pres.	78,389/77,721	45/45	43/44
	Conn.	72,685	74,691	Gov./Pres.	37,988/38,040	52/52	51/50
	N.H.		66,959	Gov./Pres.	30,925/24,925		46/37
1837	Mass.	176,619	179,188	Governor	83,838	47	47
	Conn.	73,330	75,344	,,	45,325	62	60
	N.H.		68,033	,,	24,532		35
1838	Mass.	181,213	183,881	,,	93,941	51	51
	Conn.	73,975	75,997	,,	50,040	68	66
	N.H.		69,107	,,	54,570		78

Year	Free adult white males	Free adult males	Election	Votes	Percentage adult white males voting	Percentage adult males voting
1839	Mass. 185,807	188,574	Governor	102,066	55	54
	Conn. 74,620	76,650	"	51,226	68	67
	N.H.	70,181	"	54,601		78
1840	Mass. 190,401	190,673	Gov./Pres.	127,315/126,439	66/65	65/65
	Conn. 75,261	77,301	Gov./Pres.	55,424/56,938	73/75	71/73
	N.H.	71,251	Gov./Pres.	50,799/59,098		71/83
1841	Mass. 198,144	198,645	Governor	111,062	55	55
	Conn. 77,648	79,696	"	48,837	62	61
	N.H.	72,609	"	51,689		71
1842	Mass. 205,887	206,617	"	117,992	57	56
	Conn. 80,035	82,091	"	51,253	64	62
	N.H.	73,967	"	48,104		65
1843	Mass. 213,630	214,589	"	121,288	56	56
	Conn. 82,422	84,486	"	54,928	66	64
	N.H.	75,325	"	44,583		59
1844	Mass. 221,373	222,561	Gov./Pres.	134,225/131,124	60/59	59/59
	Conn. 84,809	86,881	Gov./Pres.	60,929/64,616	71/76	70/74
	N.H.	76,683	Gov./Pres.	48,692/49,187		63/64
1845	Mass. 229,116	230,533	Governor	105,924	46	45
	Conn. 87,196	89,276	"	57,908	66	64
	N.H.	78,041	"	45,765		58
1846	Mass. 236,859	238,505	"	101,916	43	42
	Conn. 89,583	91,671	"	57,265	64	62
	N.H.	79,399	"	55,194		69

Year	State			Office			
1847	Mass.	244,602	246,477	"	105,443	43	43
	Conn.	91,970	94,066	"	59,674	65	63
	N.H.		80,757	"	60,500		75
1848	Mass.	252,345	254,449	Gov./Pres.	124,055/134,409	49/53	49/53
	Conn.	94,357	96,461	Gov./Pres.	61,015/62,398	65/66	63/64
	N.H.		82,115	Gov./Pres.	61,542/50,104		75/61
1849	Mass.	260,088	262,421	Governor	109,497	42	41
	Conn.	96,744	98,856	"	56,466	58	57
	N.H.		83,471	"	56,033		67
1850	Mass.	267,830	270,398	"	121,372	45	44
	Conn.	99,127	101,250	"	60,006	60	59
	N.H.		84,836	"	55,789		66
1851	Mass.	273,839	276,403	"	137,187	50	49
	Conn.	101,605	103,739	"	61,480	60	59
	N.H.		85,291	"			
1852	Mass.	279,848	282,408	Gov./Pres.	138,450/125,275	49/44	49/44
	Conn.	104,083	106,228	Gov./Pres.	12,385/64,768	11/63	11/62
	N.H.		85,746	Gov./Pres.	60,405/50,545		70/59
1853	Mass.	285,857	288,413	Governor	129,006	45	45
	Conn.	106,561	108,717	"	12,163	11	11
	N.H.		86,201	"	56,556		64
1854	Mass.	291,866	294,418	"	129,981	44	44
	Conn.	109,039	111,206	"	61,041	56	55
	N.H.		86,656	"	57,931		66
1855	Mass.	297,875	300,423	"	136,582	46	45
	Conn.	111,517	113,695	"	64,551	58	57
	N.H.		87,111	"	64,690		64

Year	Free adult white males	Free adult males	Election	Votes	Percentage adult white males voting	Percentage adult males voting
1856	Mass. 303,884	306,428	Gov./Pres.	156,925/167,056	51/55	51/54
	Conn. 113,995	116,184	Gov./Pres.	66,715/80,720	58/71	57/69
	N.H.	87,566	Gov./Pres.	66,703/69,775		76/79
1857	Mass. 309,893	312,433	Governor	130,536	42	41
	Conn. 116,473	118,673	"	13,039	12	12
	N.H.	88,021	"	65,882		75
1858	Mass. 315,902	318,438	"	119,249	38	37
	Conn. 118,951	121,162	"	79,127	58	57
	N.H.	88,476	"	67,963		76
1859	Mass. 321,911	324,443	"	109,051	34	33
	Conn. 121,429	123,651	"	78,789	59	58
	N.H.	88,931	"	69,156		78
1860	Mass. 327,921	330,448	Gov./Pres.	169,609/169,175	51/52	51/51
	Conn. 123,908	126,142	Gov./Pres.	88,385/80,457	71/66	70/64
	N.H.	89,384	Gov./Pres.	71,603/65,943		80/73

* My estimate. † Certain rejected returns omitted. ‡ After separating from Maine.

PENNSYLVANIA ELECTION STATISTICS,
1790–1840

Year	Free adult males	Election	Votes	Percentage of free adult males voting
1790	98,680	Gov.	30,527	31
1793	107,698	Gov.	29,296	27
1796	116,716	Pres.	22,932	19
		Gov.	31,031	26
1799	125,734	Gov.	70,677	56
1802	136,786	Gov.	65,010	47
1804	144,834	Pres.	23,740	16
1805	148,858	Gov.	82,477	55
1808	160,930	Pres.	54,253	32
		Gov.	111,564	70
1811	172,158	Gov.	57,603	33
1812	175,338	Pres.	78,853	44
1814	189,449	Gov.	81,593	43
1816	199,665	Pres.	43,066	21
1817	204,773	Gov.	125,614	61
1820	220,097	Pres.	32,206	15
		Gov.	134,226	64
1823	241,904	Gov.	154,007	64
1824	249,173	Pres.	47,252	19
1826	263,711	Gov.	75,059	28
1828	278,249	Pres.	152,500	58
1829	285,518	Gov.	140,007	49
1832	310,952	Pres.	158,638	51
		Gov.	129,500	41
1835	338,192	Gov.	200,413	59
1836	347,272	Pres.	128,538	37
1838	365,432	Gov.	250,146	68
1840	382,973	Pres.	288,026	75

MARYLAND ELECTION STATISTICS,
1790–1814

Year	County	Free adult white males	Total free adult male popn	Election	Votes	Per-centage F.A.W.M.	Per-centage Total
1790	Allegheny	886	..	Congress	408	46	..
	Anne Arundel	2,336	..	,,	166	7	..
	Baltimore Town	3,072	..	,,	3,048	99	..
	Baltimore County	4,214	..	,,	2,486	57	..
	Calvert	880	..	,,	238	27	..
	Caroline	1,365	..	,,	690	50	..
	Cecil	2,236	..	,,	901	40	..
	Charles	2,184	..	,,	1,018	46	..
	Dorchester	2,087	..	,,	549	26	..
	Frederick	5,610	..	,,	688	12	..
	Harford	2,352	..	,,	1,285	54	..
	Kent	1,428	..	,,	635	44	..
	Montgomery	2,592	..	,,	1,419	54	..
	Prince George's	2,113	..	,,	975	46	..
	Queen Anne's	1,681	..	,,	499	29	..
	St Mary's	1,819	..	,,	380	20	..
	Somerset	1,760	..	,,	181	10	..
	Talbot	1,512	..	,,	297	19	..
	Washington	3,040	..	,,	1,152	37	..
	Worcester	1,600	..	,,	280	17	..
1792	Allegheny	1,021	..	,,	148	14	..
	Anne Arundel	2,350	..	,,	1,275	54	..
	Baltimore Town	3,422	..	,,	1,209	35	..
	Baltimore County	4,500	..	,,	1,433	31	..
	Calvert	858	..	,,	493	57	..
	Caroline	1,370	..	,,	497	36	..
	Cecil	2,094	..	,,	1,204	57	..
	Charles	2,128	..	,,	1,166	55	..
	Dorchester	2,041	..	,,	582	28	..
	Frederick	5,611	..	,,	438	7	..
	Harford	2,390	..	,,	1,166	49	..
	Kent	1,388	..	,,	765	55	..

MARYLAND ELECTION STATISTICS, 1790–1814 (cont.)

Year	County	Free adult white males	Total free adult male popn.	Election	Votes	Percentage F.A.W.M.	Percentage Total
1792	Montgomery	2,432	..	Con.	1,119	46	..
	Prince George's	2,069	..	"	1,192	57	..
	Queen Anne's	1,655	..	"	1,119	67	..
	St Mary's	1,739	..	"	514	29	..
	Somerset	1,784	..	"	256	14	..
	Talbot	1,516	..	"	1,066	71	..
	Washington	3,126	..	"	321	10	..
	Worcester	1,756	..	"	778	44	..
1794	Allegheny	978	..	"	679	69	..
	Anne Arundel	2,364	..	"	1,141	48	..
	Baltimore Town	3,772	..	"	160	4	..
	Baltimore County	4,786	..	"	43	1	..
	Calvert	836	..	"	578	69	..
	Caroline	1,377	..	"	530	38	..
	Cecil	1,952	..	"	1,289	66	..
	Charles	2,072	..	"	1,264	61	..
	Dorchester	1,995	..	"	1,176	59	..
	Frederick	5,612	..	"	924	16	..
	Harford	2,428	..	"	1,256	51	..
	Kent	1,348	..	"	695	51	..
	Montgomery	2,272	..	"	1,102	48	..
	Prince George's	2,025	..	"	635	31	..
	Queen Anne's	1,629	..	"	1,004	61	..
	St Mary's	1,659	..	"	525	31	..
	Somerset	1,808	..	"	468	25	..
	Talbot	1,520	..	"	651	42	..
	Washington	3,212	..	"	1,211	37	..
	Worcester	1,912	..	"	699	36	..
1796	Allegheny	1,024	..	Pres.	649	63	..
	Anne Arundel	2,378	..	"	390	16	..
	Baltimore Town	4,122	..	"	765	18	..
	Baltimore County	5,072	..	"	731	14	..
	Calvert	814	..	"	266	32	..
	Caroline	1,383	..	"	162	11	..
	Cecil	1,810	..	"	392	21	..
	Charles	2,016	..	"	442	21	..

MARYLAND ELECTION STATISTICS, *1790–1814* (*cont.*)

Year	County	Free adult white males	Total free adult male popn.	Election	Votes	Percentage F.A.W.M.	Percentage Total
1796	Dorchester	1,949	..	Pres.	583	29	..
	Frederick	5,613	..	„	1,917	34	..
	Harford	2,460	..	„	618	25	..
	Kent	1,308	..	„	774	59	..
	Montgomery	2,112	..	„	1,310	62	..
	Prince George's	1,981	..	„	1,226	62	..
	Queen Anne's	1,603	..	„	538	33	..
	St Mary's	1,579	..	„	419	25	..
	Somerset	1,832	..	„	24	1	..
	Talbot	1,524	..	„	581	38	..
	Washington	3,298	..	„	2,035	61	..
	Worcester	2,068	..	„	133	6	..
1800	Allegheny	1,115	1,140	„	571	51	50
	Anne Arundel	2,406	2,796	„	1,218	50	43
	Baltimore Town	4,820	5,512	„	1,935	40	35
	Baltimore County	5,641	6,014	„	1,077	19	17
	Calvert	768	844	„	221	28	26
	Caroline	1,392	1,542	„	560	40	36
	Cecil	1,524	1,617	„	1,015	66	62
	Charles	1,904	2,046	„	621	32	30
	Dorchester	1,858	2,449	„	850	45	30
	Frederick	5,614	5,732	„	3,808	68	66
	Harford	2,539	2,875	„	808	31	28
	Kent	1,230	1,676	„	758	61	45
	Montgomery	1,788	1,853	„	1,267	71	68
	Prince George's	1,893	2,055	„	1,192	63	58
	Queen Anne's	1,555	1,811	„	824	53	45
	Somerset	1,881	2,027	„	302	16	14
	St Mary's	1,421	1,576	„	340	24	21
	Talbot	1,536	1,933	„	689	44	35
	Washington	3,471	3,556	„	2,122	61	59
	Worcester	2,379	2,491	„	530	22	21
1801	Allegheny	1,130	1,155	Con.	641	56	55
	Anne Arundel	2,421	2,854	„	1,189	49	41
	Baltimore Town	5,253	6,013	„	1,254	23	20
	Baltimore County	5,538	5,912	„	460	8	7

MARYLAND ELECTION STATISTICS, 1790–1814 (cont.)

Year	County	Free adult white males	Total free adult male popn.	Election	Votes	Per- centage F.A.W.M.	Per- centage Total
1801	Calvert	768	847	Con.	387	50	45
	Caroline	1,392	1,552	"	261	18	16
	Cecil	1,599	1,706	"	407	25	23
	Charles	1,871	2,009	"	805	43	40
	Dorchester	1,876	2,474	"	343	18	13
	Frederick	5,652	5,777	"	2,561	45	44
	Harford	2,585	2,943	"	909	35	30
	Kent	1,230	1,681	"	286	23	17
	Montgomery	1,819	1,894	"	850	47	45
	Prince George's	1,846	2,115	"	954	51	45
	Queen Anne's	1,567	1,860	"	405	25	21
	St Mary's	1,407	1,562	"	339	24	21
	Somerset	1,928	2,040	"	285	14	14
	Talbot	1,540	1,948	"	220	14	11
	Washington	3,462	3,551	"	2,052	59	57
	Worcester	2,383	2,510	"	269	11	10
1803	Allegheny	1,160	1,185	"	952	82	80
	Anne Arundel Baltimore Town and County	11,453	11,925	"	8,284	72	69
	Calvert	769	853	"	607	79	71
	Caroline	1,392	1,572	"	653	47	41
	Cecil	1,748	1,884	"	782	44	41
	Charles	1,804	1,935	"	1,063	59	55
	Dorchester	1,912	2,524	"	681	35	27
	Frederick	5,728	5,867	"	4,728	82	80
	Harford	2,676	3,079	"	1,821	68	59
	Kent	1,230	1,691	"	625	50	36
	Montgomery	1,880	1,976	"	1,369	72	69
	Prince George's	1,752	2,235	"	940	53	42
	Queen Anne's	1,592	1,976	"	892	56	45
	St Mary's	1,379	1,534	"	509	36	33
	Somerset	1,921	2,066	"	580	30	28
	Talbot	1,548	1,978	"	595	38	30
	Washington	3,444	3,541	"	2,505	73	71
	Worcester	2,390	2,548	"	584	24	23

MARYLAND ELECTION STATISTICS, 1790–1814 (cont.)

Year	County	Free adult white males	Total free adult male popn.	Election	Votes	Per-centage F.A.W.M.	Per-centage Total
1804	Allegheny	1,175	1,200	Con.	341	29	28
	Anne Arundel	2,527	3,208	,,	900	35	28
	Baltimore Town and County	11,784	13,122	,,	2,888	24	22
	Calvert	770	856	,,	322	41	37
	Caroline	1,393	1,582	,,			
	Cecil	1,823	1,973	,,	382	21	19
	Charles	1,770	1,898	,,	304	17	16
	Dorchester	1,930	2,549	,,	1,002	52	39
	Frederick	5,765	5,912	,,			
	Harford	2,721	3,147	,,	1,272	46	40
	Kent	1,230	1,696	,,	389	31	22
	Montgomery	1,911	2,017	,,	918	48	45
	Prince George's	1,705	2,295	,,	704	41	30
	Queen Anne's	1,604	2,031	,,	341	21	16
	St Mary's	1,365	1,520	,,	631	46	41
	Somerset	1,918	2,079	,,	1,217	63	58
	Talbot	1,553	1,993	,,	862	55	43
	Washington	3,435	3,536	,,	502	14	14
	Worcester	2,394	2,567	,,	2,014	84	78
1806	Allegheny	1,206	1,230	,,	496	41	40
	Anne Arundel	2,597	3,144	,,	1,820	70	57
	Baltimore Town and County	12,446					
	Calvert	771	862	,,	368	47	42
	Caroline	1,393	1,602	,,	1,014	72	63
	Cecil	1,973	2,151	,,	1,155	59	58
	Charles	1,703	1,822	,,	818	48	44
	Dorchester	1,966	2,599	,,	1,841	94	71
	Frederick	5,839	6,002	,,	3,519	60	58
	Harford	2,813	3,281	,,	1,868	66	57
	Kent	1,230	1,706	,,	729	59	42
	Montgomery	1,972	2,100	,,	1,712	86	81
	Prince George's	1,611	2,414	,,	1,432	89	59
	Queen Anne's	1,630	2,140	,,	1,009	61	46
	St Mary's	1,337	1,493	,,	529	39	35

MARYLAND ELECTION STATISTICS, 1790–1814 *(cont.)*

Year	County	Free adult white males	Total free adult male popn.	Election	Votes	Per- centage F.A.W.M.	Per- centage Total
1806	Somerset	1,910	2,105	Con.	1,203	63	57
	Talbot	1,562	2,021	„	1,200	77	59
	Washington	3,417	3,526	„	2,012	59	57
	Worcester	2,401	2,604	„	1,771	73	68
1808	Allegheny	1,235	1,260	„	892	72	70
				Pres.	843	*34	33
	Anne Arundel	2,670	3,260	Con.	1,557	58	47
				Pres.	636	*12	10
	Baltimore Town	8,292	9,523	C.	3,952	47	41
				P.	2,848	*17	15
	Baltimore County	4,811	5,195	C.	3,706	77	71
				P.	1,780	37	34
	Calvert	772	865	C.	783	100 +	91
				P.	728	94	84
	Caroline	1,393	1,622	C.	1,099	78	67
				P.	898	64	55
	Cecil	2,122	2,330	C.	1,919	90	82
				P.	881	41	37
	Charles	1,640	1,746	C.	1,111	67	63
				P.	398	24	22
	Dorchester	2,003	2,655	C.	1,047	52	39
				P.	1,014	50	38
				(incomplete)			
	Frederick	5,914	6,095	C.	4,983	84	81
				P.	4,809	*41	40
	Harford	2,905	3,419	C.	1,919	66	56
				P.	1,158	39	33
	Kent	1,229	1,713	C.	1,154	93	67
				P.	467	37	27
	†Montgomery	2,034	2,185	C.	1,559	77	71
	Prince George's	1,516	2,534	C.	1,396	92	55
				P.	1,154	76	45
	Queen Anne's	1,651	2,251	C.	1,344	81	59
				P.	431	26	19

*
} See notes to 1812.
†

MARYLAND ELECTION STATISTICS, 1790–1814 (cont.)

Year	County	Free adult white males	Total free adult male popn.	Election	Votes	Percentage F.A.W.M.	Percentage Total
1808	St Mary's	1,308	1,465	C.	713	54	48
				P.	321	24	21
	Somerset	1,890	2,131	C.	1,001	52	46
				P.	741	39	34
	Talbot	1,572	2,050	C.	1,281	81	62
				P.	1,057	67	51
	Washington	3,400	3,516	C.	2,568	75	73
				P.	2,590	*38	37
	Worcester	2,410	2,641	C.	1,460	60	55
				P.	864	35	32
1810	Allegheny	1,266	1,294	Con.	317	25	24
	Anne Arundel	2,738	3,376	„	1,669	61	49
	Baltimore Town }	9,158	10,525	„	} 5,075	36	32
	Baltimore County }	4,611	4,995	„			
	Calvert	773	870	„	386	50	44
	Caroline	1,394	1,644	„	893	64	54
	Cecil	2,272	2,508	„	1,022	45	40
	Charles	1,569	1,672	„	567	41	39
	Dorchester	2,038	2,704	„	938	46	34
	Harford	2,997	3,552	„	1,401	47	39
	Kent	1,229	1,723	„	511	41	29
	Montgomery	2,096	2,265	„	374	17	16
	Prince George's	1,423	2,654	„	1,369	96	51
	Queen Anne's	1,681	2,365	„	665	39	28
	St Mary's	1,279	1,438	„	457	35	31
	Somerset	1,894	2,158	„	572	30	26
	Talbot	1,580	2,080	„	781	49	37
	Washington	3,382	3,502	„	757	22	21
	Worcester	2,416	2,679	„	1,890	78	71
1812	Allegheny	1,344	1,372	Con.	1,085	80	79
				Pres.	950	*35	34
	Anne Arundel	2,816	3,474	C.	2,127	75	61
				P.	1,266	*23	18

* Under the election law of 1806, ch. xcvii, these counties were arranged in districts each of which chose two electors, so that each voter was entitled to cast two votes. The percentage figures have accordingly been halved.

MARYLAND ELECTION STATISTICS, 1790–1814 (cont.)

Year	County	Free adult white males	Total free adult male popn.	Election	Votes	Percentage F.A.W.M.	Percentage Total
1812	Baltimore Town	9,576	11,105	P.	3,467	*18	16
				C.	4,273	44	38
	Baltimore County	4,793	5,211	C.		‡61	
				P.	2,394	50	45
	Calvert	780	888	P.	599	76	67
				C.	367	47	41
	Caroline	1,406	1,664	P.	1,111	79	66
				C.	1,245	88	75
	Cecil	2,346	2,620	P.	1,549	66	59
				C.	972	41	37
	Charles	1,596	1,650	P.	451	28	27
				C.	1,189	74	72
	Dorchester	2,061	2,704	P.	1,113	54	41
				C.	1,927	93	71
	Frederick	6,242	6,509	P.	4,717	*38	36
				C.	5,500	88	84
	Harford	2,917	3,424	P.	1,410	48	41
				C.	1,602	55	46
	Kent	1,219	1,709	P.	984	80	57
				C.	576	47	33
	†Montgomery	2,010	2,255	C.	1,564	77	69
	Prince George's	1,512	2,544	P.	1,109	73	43
				C.	1,539	100+	60
	Queen Anne's	1,719	2,293	P.	1,127	65	49
				C.	1,182	68	51
	St Mary's	1,287	1,448	P.	311	24	21
				C.	517	40	35
	Somerset	1,942	2,252	P.	766	39	33
				C.	1,545	79	68
	Talbot	1,596	2,076	P.	1,392	87	67
				C.	1,446	90	69

* See notes to 1812.

† Under the election law of 1806, Montgomery County was divided between a district electing one, and a district electing two electors, making it impossible to infer the number of voters from the number of votes cast.

‡ See David Hackett Fischer, *The Revolution of American Conservatism* (N.Y., 1965) 189.

MARYLAND ELECTION STATISTICS, 1790–1814 (cont.)

Year	County	Free adult white males	Total free adult male popn.	Election	Votes	Percentage F.A.W.M.	Percentage Total
1812	Washington	3,554	3,676	P.	2,304	*32	31
				C.	2,910	81	79
	Worcester	2,396	2,681	P.	988	41	35
				C.	1,930	80	71

* See notes to 1812.

VIRGINIA ELECTION STATISTICS, 1800–60

Year	Free adult white males	Total free adult males	Election	Votes	Percentage white males	Percentage all
1800	104,837	109,868	P	27,177	25	24
1804	108,345	114,420	P	12,843	11	11
1808	111,853	118,972	P	19,914	17	16
1812	115,999	123,471	P	20,803	18	17
1816	120,787	127,919	P	6,956*	6	5
1820	125,575	132,366	P	4,321*	3	3
1824	132,931	140,734	P	15,335†	12	11
1827	138,448	147,010	Conv. ref.	38,533	28	26
1828	140,287	149,102	P	38,719	28	26
1829	142,126	151,194	ratif.	41,618	29	28
1832	146,768	156,264	P	45,325‡	31	29
1836	152,376	162,228	P	53,629	35	33
1840	157,984	168,192	P	86,394	55	51
1844	174,913	185,546	P	95,539	55	51
1848	191,837	202,902	P	92,004	48	45
1850	200,299	211,580	ratif.	86,811	43	41
1851	203,990	215,319	G	124,571	61	58
1852	207,677	219,055	P	132,604	64	61
1855	218,738	230,263	G	156,629	72	68
1856	222,425	233,999	P	150,233	68	64
1859	233,486	245,207	G	148,656	64	61
1860	237,176	248,944	P	166,891	70	67

* A few counties may have been missed in these returns.
† No return for Grayson County.
‡ No returns for Giles, Hardy, Prince Edward, and Floyd counties.

SAMPLE STATISTICS IN NORTH CAROLINA,
1804 and 1808

County	Free adult white males	Total free adult males	Election	Votes	Percentage free adult white males	Percentage free adult males
Year 1804						
Beaufort	842	900	Cong.	719	85	80
Washington	361	374	Cong.	316	88	84
Pitt	1,099		Cong.	700	64	
Franklin	918		Commons	649	71	
Hyde	682		Cong.	565	83	
Warren	1,002	1,020	Commons	633	63	62
Iredell	1,563		Cong.	663	42	
Ashe	496		Cong.	441	89	
Edgecombe	1,232		Cong.	979	79	
Year 1808						
Burke	1,719	1,734	Cong.	1,118	65	64
Lincoln	2,415	2,416	Cong.	1,169	48	48
Buncombe	1,462	1,467	Cong.	1,108	76	76
Rutherford	2,099	2,100	Cong.	1,438	68	68
Chatham	1,697		Cong.	1,351	80	
Edgecombe	1,418	1,477	Cong.	1,200 +	85	81
Randolph	1,640		Cong.	1,090	66	
Person	785		Cong.	698	89	
Rockingham	1,504		Cong.	1,090	72	
Guilford	1,970		Cong.	1,395	71	
Caswell	1,326		Cong.	937	71	
Cumberland	1,334		Cong.	906	68	
Robeson	1,135		Cong.	859	76	
Richmond	1,006		Cong.	829	82	
Anson	1,236	1,258	Cong.	1,087	88	86
Montgomery	1,219	1,227	Cong.	934	77	76
Moore	1,019		Cong.	772	76	
Orange	2,711		Cong.	2,930	100 +	

NORTH CAROLINA ELECTION STATISTICS,
1816–61*

Year	Free adult white males	Total free adult males	Election	Votes cast	Percentage free adult white males	Percentage free adult males
1816	78,072	78,192	?	9,549	12	12
1824	86,032	90,012	P	36,036	42	40
1828	90,584	95,572	P	51,775	57	54
1832	93,499	98,779	P	29,425	31	30
1835	94,456	99,421	Call of Conv.	49,244	52	50
			Amendments	48,377	51	49
1836	94,775	99,635	Gov.	63,943	67	64
			P	50,453	53	51
1838	95,413	100,063	Gov.	54,584	57	55
1840	96,053	100,493	Gov.	80,387	84	80
			P	79,486	83	79
1842	99,943	104,547	Gov.	72,354	72	69
1844	103,833	108,628	Gov.	82,019	79	76
			P	82,149	79	76
1846	107,723	112,655	Gov.	79,113	73	70
1848	111,613	116,709	Gov.	84,218	75	72
			P	79,905	72	68
1850	115,506	120,768	Gov.	87,417	76	72
1852	119,932	125,326	Gov.	91,570	76	73
			P	78,772	66	63
1854	124,358	129,884	Gov.	95,349	77	73
1856	128,784	134,442	Gov.	102,568	80	76
			P	85,212	66	63
1857	132,106	136,721	Free Suff. Amendt.	69,386	53	51
1858	133,210	139,000	Gov.	96,475	72	69
1860	137,640	143,554	Gov.	112,586	82	78
			P	96,112	70	67
1861	139,853	145,833	Conv. question	94,005	67	64

* The voting figures have been taken from the *Manual of North Carolina, 1913*; and I have received additional information from Mr W. Frank Burton, the State Archivist.

Method and Bibliography

EACH of the five territorial areas examined in this book was subject to an acknowledged government, even though the power was usually incomplete and was sometimes contested by more than one authority. Governments have long been in the habit of leaving ample and reasonably continuous records of the more legitimate side of their activities; and these official records therefore provide a series of columns, each supporting its particular local study.

It should be admitted that *Cobbett's Parliamentary History of England ... 1066–1803* (36 vols., London, 1806–20) later continued by T. C. Hansard as *The Parliamentary Debates* (1st and 2nd series) which have been depended on as the most satisfactory compilation, do not strictly conform to the definition of an 'official' record. Part, in fact, of the theme of this book lies in the struggle to gain a recognised position for the published reports of debates, and their fragmentary and incomplete nature is itself a product of the difficulties experienced by the early reporters. A very full reading of these debates wherever they touch on issues of representation has revealed that despite all their shortcomings, the reports do show that every point of view that was to develop serious constitutional significance was expressed at some time in Parliament. For the earlier phases, *Parliamentary Debates* (London, 1741), Chandler's *Commons Debates* (London, 1742), and A. Grey, *Debates*, vol. viii (London, 1763), have provided some materials for parliamentary opinion touching on the principal constitutional issues. *Statutes of the Realm* constitute the full official record of the laws, but, for purposes of reference, Sir Charles Grant Robertson's *Select Statutes, Cases and Documents* (London, 1947) is still a serviceable compilation on constitutional and electoral history since 1660. The vast body of commentaries on the laws and constitution of England ranges from works which acquired a virtually official status, such as those of Coke and Blackstone, to opposition tracts which claimed that the 'official' view was itself a distortion of the true intent of the laws. The works which have contributed to this study are listed below with alphabetical impartiality.

An introduction to the use of American colonial, state and local records, which form an indispensable part of the material used in the American side of this work, will be found in the *Harvard Guide to American History* (Cambridge, Mass., 1960), especially pp. 125–39 and 217–37.

There are one or two additional points which may be worth the attention of those who intend to embark on research in the public records of the states. In American states, as elsewhere, statutes and ordinances sometimes represent intentions rather than achievements. When using colonial laws, it is particularly important to ascertain whether a statute passed by the Assembly was passed or negatived by the Privy Council in London. The *Harvard Guide*, p. 274, lists certain works dealing with the general question of the review of colonial legislation. The safest procedure is to trace colonial statutes in the *Journals of the Commissioners of Trade and Plantations*, 11 vols. (London, 1920–35). Even that is not the last word on the subject, because there is some reason to suspect that a law which was vetoed by the Crown but was the obvious wish and interest of an American province whose Assembly had passed it, may well have been practised by general consent. On this sort of question the researcher must dig into whatever local records he can find.

An important case in point is that of the election laws. These, moreover, were frequently violated by a large variety of local election practices. The best evidence crops up when the defeated candidate disputes the election return, leading to an enquiry by the Assembly's committee on elections. These hearings can often be traced through the legislative records; those of Virginia print the evidence in full. State archives sometimes retain the original depositions from these cases, the Hall of Records in Annapolis having a very good collection. Court records can also be used to discover whether a statute was seriously enforced. The foregoing study has shown, for example, that the interesting Virginia statute for compulsory voting was a dead letter — a point made all the clearer by the obviously extraordinary nature of the charges when a prosecution against non-voters was instigated.

The public legislative record does not give a full account of a Bill's birth and struggle for life. One of the most fruitful sources of early legislation being the petition, those state archives which have good collections of petitions contain rich information about the real origins of the legislation which got on to the books. The date and demands on a petition can sometimes be usefully compared with the actual wording and timing of a Bill on the same subject. Not all Bills are passed into law. Where rejected Bills survive, they may bear handwritten endorsements that help to explain their fate.

Every well-organised state archive, library, or historical society contains at least one immensely valuable storehouse of information: the archivist or librarian.

The main purpose of the list which follows is to provide a simple bibliography of works cited, together with a small selection which lie in the immediate background or have exercised some influence over the development of the present study. Several of the specialist works cited contain their own bibliographical essays. On the English side, each of the Oxford histories is equipped with an ample exploratory guide; a useful example on the American side is Greene's *Quest for Power* (see p. 578 below). It does not seem necessary to use this note as yet another introduction to methods and techniques in the study of English history.

LIST OF SOURCES

MANUSCRIPT COLLECTIONS

BRITISH

British Museum
Francis Place Papers. Records of the London Corresponding Society.
Public Record Office. CO 5: vols. 1372, 1330.

MASSACHUSETTS

Massachusetts Archives, State House, Boston
Town meeting returns on constitutions of 1778 and 1780: vols. 156, 160, 276, 277.
House of Representatives, Journals, 1788–89; 1811–12.
House Documents (petitions).
Senate Documents.
Acts, 1811, 1813; original papers.
Return of votes for Governor and Lieutenant Governor.

Massachusetts Historical Society
Hutchinson Papers (transcripts).
Hutchinson Letterbooks.
Bowdoin-Temple Papers.
James Bowdoin Papers.
Cushing Papers.
Mellen Chamberlain Papers.
Israel Williams Letterbooks.
John Hancock Papers.
Sedgwick Papers (including George Minot's Journal).
Harrison Gray Otis Papers.
Timothy Pickering Papers.

NEW YORK

New York Public Library
Samuel Adams Papers.

New-York Historical Society
Rufus King Papers.

PENNSYLVANIA

Historical Society of Pennsylvania
Pemberton Papers
Isaac Norris Letterbooks.

Presbyterian Historical Society
Francis Alison Sermons.

MARYLAND

Hall of Records
Executive Papers.

VIRGINIA

Virginia State Library
Bruce-Randolph Collection.
Petitions.
Tazewell Papers.

University of Virginia, Alderman Library
Landon Carter Diary.
Landon Carter Papers.
Lee Papers.

Virginia Historical Society
Lee Family Papers.

Colonial Williamsburg
Tucker-Coleman Papers.
Robert Wormeley Carter Diary.

NORTH CAROLINA

University of North Carolina. Southern Historical Collection
Edward Dromgoole Papers.
Goldsborough-Wirt Papers.

Duke University Library
John Clopton Papers.
David Campbell Papers.

Library of Congress. Manuscript Division
James Madison Papers.

ORIGINAL PRINTED SOURCES
OFFICIAL OR PUBLIC DOCUMENTS

GENERAL AND CONTINENTAL

Thorpe, Francis Newton, *Federal and State Constitutions, Colonial Charters and Other Organic Laws*, 7 vols. (Washington, D.C., 1909).
Journals of the Continental Congress, ed. Worthington Chauncy Ford, 34 vols. (Washington, 1904–1937).
Records of the Federal Convention, ed. Max Farrand, 4 vols. (New Haven, 1937).
United States Census, 1850 (Washington, D.C., 1853).

STATE AND LOCAL

Acts and Resolves of the Province of Massachusetts Bay (Boston, 1869–1922).
Massachusetts Charter, Laws and Resolves (Boston, 1726).
A Collection of the Proceedings of the Great and General Court on the Salary Question (Boston, 1729).
Journals of the House of Representatives (Massachusetts) (Boston, 1919–).
Journal of the Convention ... of 1780 (Boston, 1832).
Journal of the Debates and Proceedings in the Convention ... to Revise the Constitution of Massachusetts ... 1820–1821 (Boston, 1853).
Cushing, Luther S., Storey, Chas. W., and Josselyn, Lewis, *Reports of Controverted Elections in the House of Representatives in the Commonwealth of Massachusetts, from 1780 to 1852* (Boston, 1853).
Boston Town Records in *Report of the Record Commissioners of the City of Boston* (Boston, 1895).
Cambridge Town Records.
The Early Records of the Town of Dedham, Massachusetts, 1602–1706, ed. D. G. Hill. (Dedham, 1819).
Historical Records of Dedham, 1635–1847 (Dedham, 1847).
Town Records of Dudley, Massachusetts, 1732–1794 (*Pawtucket, R.I., 1893*)
Watertown Records (Newton, Mass., 1893).
New Jersey Archives, First and Second Series (various places; 1880–).
Pennsylvania Archives, Eighth Series (Harrisburg, 1931–5).
Statutes at Large of Pennsylvania (collection of 1896).
The Statutes at Large: Being a Collection of all the Laws of Virginia, 1619–1792, ed. W. W. Hening, 13 vols. (Richmond, 1809–23).

Journals of the House of Burgesses, ed. H. R. McIlwaine (Richmond, 1909).

Calendar of Virginia State Papers.

Proceedings and Debates of the Virginia State Convention of 1829–1830 (Richmond, 1830).

Accounts and Papers, 39 vols., Vol. 17, Pt. II, *Members of Parliament* (London, 1878).

PRIMARY PRINTED SOURCES

Adams Family Correspondence, ed. L. H. Butterfield, 2 vols. (Cambridge, Mass., 1963).

Adams, John, *Defence of the Constitutions of Government of the United States of America*, 3 vols. (Philadelphia, 1797).

— *Works*, ed. Charles Francis Adams, 4 vols. (Boston, 1852).

Diary and Autobiography of John Adams, ed. L. H. Butterfield, 4 vols. (Cambridge, Mass., 1961).

Adams, John Quincy, *Life in a New England Town: 1787–1788* (Boston, 1903).

Alexander, James W., *Forty Years Familiar Letters*, ed. John Hall, D.D. (New York, 1870).

Bentham, Jeremy, *Plan of Parliamentary Reform in the Form of a Catechism* (London, 1817).

Beverley, Robert (attributed), *An Essay upon the Government of the English Plantations on the Continent of America* (London, 1701), ed. Louis B. Wright (San Marino, 1945).

— *The History and Present State of Virginia* (London, 1705), ed. Louis B. Wright (Chapel Hill, 1947).

Blackstone, Sir William, *Commentaries on the Laws of England*, 4 vols. (Oxford, 1765).

Braxton, Carter, *An Address to the Convention of Virginia on the Subject of Government in General etc. By a Native of the Colony* (Philadelphia, 1776). (A copy is in Library Company of Philadelphia.)

Bulkeley, Gershom, *Will and Doom: The Miseries of Connecticut* ... (1692) (reprinted Hartford, 1895).

Burgh, James, *Political Disquisitions*, 3 vols. (London, 1774).

Burke, Edmund, *Works* (London, 1834).

— *Speeches and Letters on American Affairs*, Everyman edition (London, 1908).

— *A Short Account of a Late Short Administration* (London, 1766).

Burnett, Edmund C. (ed.), *Letters of Members of the Continental Congress*, 8 vols. (Washington, 1921–6).

Cartwright, John, *Take Your Choice!* (London, 1776).

— *Reasons for Reformation* (London, 1809).

— *Life and Correspondence*, ed. F. D. Cartwright, 2 vols. (London, 1826).

Chamberlayne's *Present State of Great Britain* (London, 1735).

Coke, Sir Edward, *Institutes of the Laws of England*, Fourth Part (London, 1669).

Croker, John Wilson, *Speech in the House of Commons, 21 September 1831* (London, 1831).

Dudley, Paul, *Objections to the Bank of Credit Lately Projected at Boston* (Boston, 1714).

Egmont, Earl of, *Diary*, Hist. MSS. Comm. (London, 1923).

Franklin, Benjamin, *Cool Thoughts on the Present Situation of our Public Affairs* (Philadelphia, 1764).

Galloway, Joseph, *An Answer to an Invidious Pamphlet, intituled, A Brief State . . .* (London, 1755).

[—] *A True and Impartial State of the Province of Pennsylvania* (Philadelphia, 1759).

Speech of Joseph Galloway Esq. . . . in answer to John Dickinson Esq., delivered in the House of Assembly May 24, 1764 (Philadelphia, 1764).

Grigsby, Hugh Blair, *History of the Virginia Federal Convention of 1788*, ed. R. A. Brock, 2 vols. (Richmond, 1890–1).

Harding, S. B., *The Contest over the Ratification of the Federal Constitution in the State of Massachusetts* (New York, 1896).

Harrington, James, *Works*, ed. John Toland (London, 1700).

Hutcheson, Francis, *Enquiry Concerning Moral Good and Evil* (1738).

— *System of Moral Philosophy*, 2 vols. (London, 1755).

Hutchinson, Thomas, *History of Massachusetts Bay*, ed. L. S. Mayo, 3 vols. (Cambridge, Mass., 1936).

Jay, John, Hamilton, Alexander, and Madison, James, *The Federalist*, ed. Jacob E. Cooke (Middletown, Conn., 1961).

Jefferson, Thomas, *Notes on Virginia* (London, 1787).

— *Writings*, ed. H. A. Washington, 9 vols. (New York, 1854).

— *Works*, ed. Worthington Chauncy Ford (New York, 1894).

Jefferson, Thomas, The Papers of, ed. Julian P. Boyd and others (Princeton, 1950–).

Lee, Richard Henry, The Letters of, ed. James Curtis Ballagh, 2 vols. (New York, 1912).

Leigh, Benjamin Watkins, *Substitute . . . Proposed by Mr Leigh, of Dinwiddie . . . on the Right to Instruct . . . Senators . . .* (N.P., N.D. [1812]).

— *Substitute Intended to be Offered to the Next Meeting of the Citizens of Richmond . . . in lieu of the Report of the Committee* (Richmond, 1824). (Copy in Library of Congress.)

Lloyd, David, *A Vindication of the Legislative Power* (Philadelphia, 1725).

Locke, John, *Locke's Two Treatises of Government*, ed. Peter Laslett (Cambridge, 1964).

Logan, James, *The Antidote: Some Remarks on a Paper of David Lloyd's* (Philadelphia, 1725).

Longley, John, *An Essay Toward Forming a more Complete Representation of the Commons of Great Britain* (London, 1795).

Lynde, Samuel, and others, *A Vindication of the Bank of Credit Lately Projected at Boston* (Boston, 1714).

Macaulay, Catherine, *Observations on a Pamphlet entitled Thoughts on the Cause of the Present Discontents* (London, 1770).

Madison, James, *Writings*, ed. Gaillard Hunt, 9 vols. (New York, 1910).

Marshall, Benjamin, 'Extracts from the Letter-book of 1763–1766', Stewardson, Thos., *Pennsylvania Magazine of History and Biography*, 1896.

Mill, James, *Essay on Government*, ed. Ernest Barker (Cambridge, 1937).

Mill, John Stuart, *Utilitarianism, Liberty and Representative Government*, Everyman edition (London, 1947).

Munford, Robert, *The Candidates: or, the Humours of a Virginia Election*, ed. Jay B. Hubbell and Douglass Adair (Williamsburg, 1948).

Oldfield, T. H. B., *Representative History of Great Britain and Ireland*, 6 vols. (London, 1816).

Paine, Thomas, *Common Sense* (Philadelphia, 1776).

— *The Rights of Man* (London, 1792).

Paley, William, *Essay on the British Constitution* (London, 1792).

— *Reasons for Contentment addressed to the Labouring Part of the British Public*, 2nd edition (London, 1793).

Parsons, Theophilus, *Result of the Convention of Delegates Holden at Ipswich in the County of Essex* (Newburyport, Mass., 1778).

Penn, William, *England's Present Interest Discover'd* (London, 1675).

— *England's Great Interest in the Choice of this New Parliament* (London, 1679).

— *An Essay towards the Present and Future Peace of Europe* (1693) (reprinted Philadelphia, 1944).

Penn and Logan Correspondence (Philadelphia, 1872).

Pownall, Thomas, *The Administration of the Colonies*, 3rd edition (London, 1765).

Price, Richard, *The Nature of Civil Liberty* (London, 1776).

Priestley, Joseph, *Essay on the First Principles of Government* (London, 1768).

St John, Henry, Viscount Bolingbroke, *The Freeholder's Political Catechism* (London, 1733).

— *A Dissertation upon Parties* (London, 1744).

Secondat, Charles de, baron de Montesquieu, *De l'Esprit des Lois* (revised edition, London, 1757).

Sharp, Granville, *A Declaration of the People's Natural Right to a Share in the Legislature* (London, 1775).

— *The Legal Means of Political Reformation*, 7th edition (London, 1780).

— *Circular Letter to the Petitioning Counties* (London, 1780).

Shelley, Percy Bysshe, *Poetical Works*.

Sidney, Algernon, *Discourses Concerning Government* (London, 1704).

Smith, Sir Thomas, *De Republica Anglorum* (London, 1600).
Smith, William, *A Brief State of the Province of Pennsylvania* (London, 1755).
— *An Answer to Mr. Franklin's Remarks on a Late Protest* (Philadelphia, 1764).
Swift, Jonathan, *Sentiments of a Church of England Man with Respect to Religion and Government* (1708).
— *Essay on Public Absurdities* (date doubtful).
Tocqueville, Alexis de, *Journeys to England and Ireland*, ed. J. P. Mayer (London, 1958).
Whately, Thomas, *The Regulations Lately Made Concerning the Colonies and the Taxes Imposed upon Them, Considered* (London, 1765).
Wilson, Thomas, *The State of England*, A.D. *1600*, ed. F. J. Fisher (Camden Misc.) (London, 1936).
Wyvill, Christopher, *Political Papers, Chiefly Respecting the Attempt of the County of York . . . to Effect a Reformation of the Parliament of Great Britain*, 6 vols. (1794–1808).

ANONYMOUS OR UNATTRIBUTED PAMPHLETS

Houghton Library, Harvard

The Houghton Library contains a large collection of New England election sermons on which certain statements in the text have been based.

Massachusetts Historical Society

The Present Melancholy Circumstances of the Province Considered, and Methods for Redress Humbly Proposed (Boston, 1719).
The Distressed State of the Town of Boston once more Considered . . . with a Scheme for a Land Bank Laid Down (Boston, 1720).
Americanus, *A Letter to the Freeholders, and other Inhabitants, qualified by Law to vote in the Election of Representatives* (Boston, 1739).
A Letter to the Freeholders and other Inhabitants . . . qualified to vote . . . (Boston, 1742).
To the Freeholders of the Town of Boston (Boston, 1760).
A New England Man, *Letter to the Freeholders and Qualified Voters relating to the Ensuing Election* (Boston, 1749).

Historical Society of Pennsylvania

To the Freeholders and Freeman Electors of Representatives for . . . Philadelphia (1727).
To the Freeholders and Freemen. A Further Information, 2 Oct. 1727.
'J.H.', *To the Freeholders, to Prevent Mistakes*, Philadelphia, 1727.
To the Freeholders of the Province of Pennsylvania, 1743.

'Philadelphus', *To the Freemen of Pennsylvania and more especially those of the City and County of Philadelphia*, 1755/2.

A Letter from a Gentleman in Philadelphia, to a Freeholder in the County of Northampton, 1757.

'Pennsylvanicus', *To the Freeholders of the County of Philadelphia*, 1757.

To the Freeholders and Electors of the City and County of Philadelphia, 1764/4.

Election broadsides nos. 1764/4, 5.

A Looking Glass for Presbyterians (Philadelphia, 1764).

A True and Faithful Narrative of the Modes and Measures Pursued at the Anniversary Election, 1770 (Philadelphia, 1771).

Library Company of Philadelphia

To the Freeholders and Other Electors of Assemblymen for Pennsylvania, 1 Oct. 1765.

Address to the Freeholders and Inhabitants of Philadelphia, in answer to ... the Plain Dealer.

Private

Whig Fraud and English Folly! (London, 1831).

NEWSPAPERS AND PERIODICALS

Black Dwarf (London).
The Edinburgh Review

American Beacon (Norfolk, Virginia).
Constitutional Whig (Richmond, Virginia).
Essex Journal (Massachusetts).
Hampshire Gazette (Massachusetts).
Independent Chronicle (Boston).
Massachusetts Spy
Pennsylvania Packet
Pennsylvania Gazette
Pennsylvania Chronicle
Raleigh Register
Raleigh Star
Virginia Herald (Fredericksburg).
The Virginia Literary Museum
Worcester Magazine (Massachusetts).

SECONDARY WORKS

ARTICLES AND OTHER ESSAYS

Adair, Douglass, 'The Use of History by the Founding Fathers: The Historical Pessimism of A. Hamilton', privately circulated.

Andrews, C. M., 'The Boston Merchants and the Non-Importation Movement', Colonial Society of Massachusetts *Publications*, vol. xix, 1917.

Bailyn, Bernard, 'Politics and Social Structure in Virginia' in James M. Smith (ed.) *Seventeenth Century America* (Chapel Hill, 1959).

Bridenbaugh, Carl, 'The New England Town: A Way of Life', *Proceedings* of the American Antiquarian Society, vol. 56, for April 1946 (Worcester, Mass., 1947).

Brown, Robert E., 'Democracy in Colonial Massachusetts', *New England Quarterly*, 1952.

— 'Rebuttal' of critique by John Cary, *William and Mary Quarterly*, April 1963.

Burns, J. H., 'J. S. Mill and Democracy, 1829–1861', *Political Studies*, June and October 1957.

Brown, B. Katherine, 'Freemanship in Puritan Massachusetts', *American Historical Review*, July 1954.

Corwin, E. S., 'The Higher Law Background of American Constitutional Law', *Harvard Law Review*, 1928–9. Reprinted, Ithaca, New York, 1957.

Colbourn, H. Trevor, 'Thomas Jefferson's Use of the Past', *William and Mary Quarterly*, January 1958

East, Robert A., 'Massachusetts Conservatives in the Critical Period' in Richard B. Morris (ed.), *The Era of the American Revolution* (New York, 1939).

Fraser, Peter, 'Public Petitioning and Parliament before 1832', *History*, October 1961.

Greene, Jack P., 'Foundations of Political Power in the Virginia House of Burgesses, 1720–1766', *William and Mary Quarterly*, October 1959.

Handlin, Oscar and Mary F., 'Revolutionary Economic Policy in Massachusetts', *William and Mary Quarterly*, January 1947.

— 'James Burgh and American Revolutionary Theory', Massachusetts Historical Society *Proceedings*, vol. 73 (1961).

Hindle, Brook, 'The March of the Paxton Boys', *William and Mary Quarterly*, October 1946.

Jameson, James Franklin, 'Did the Fathers Vote?', *New England Magazine*, 1890.

— 'Virginia Voting in the Colonial Period, 1744–1774', *The Nation*, 27 April 1893.

Kenyon, Cecelia M., 'Men of Little Faith: the Anti-Federalists on the Nature of Representative Government', *William and Mary Quarterly*, January 1955.

Macaulay, T. B. (Lord Macaulay), unsigned review of James Mill's *Essay on Government* in *Edinburgh Review*, 1829.

Main, Jackson T., 'The Distribution of Property in Post-Revolutionary Virginia', *Mississippi Valley Historical Review*, September 1954.

Morison, Samuel Eliot, 'The Struggle over the Adoption of the Massachusetts Constitution of 1780', *Proceedings* of the Massachusetts Historical Society, vol. 50, 1917.

Morris, Richard B., 'Insurrection in Massachusetts' in Daniel Aaron (ed.), *America in Crisis* (New York, 1952).

Notestein, Wallace, *The Winning of the Initiative by the House of Commons*, British Academy Raleigh Lecture (London, 1924).

Rothermund, Dietmar, 'The German Problem of Colonial Pennsylvania', *Pennsylvania Magazine of History and Biography*, January 1960.

Simmons, Richard C., 'Freemanship in Early Massachusetts: Some Suggestions and a Case Study', *William and Mary Quarterly*, July 1962.

Snow, Vernon F., 'Parliamentary Reapportionment Proposals in the Puritan Revolution', *English Historical Review*, July 1959.

Sutherland, Lucy, 'The City of London in Eighteenth Century Politics' in Richard Pares and A. J. P. Taylor (eds.), *Essays Presented to Sir Lewis Namier* (London, 1956).

Tawney, R. H., *Harrington's Interpretation of his Age*, British Academy Raleigh Lecture (London, 1941).

Thayer, Theodore, 'The Quaker Party in Pennsylvania, 1755–1765', *Pennsylvania Magazine of History and Biography*, January 1947.

Trevor-Roper, H. R., 'Oliver Cromwell and His Parliaments' in *Essays Presented to Sir Lewis Namier*.

Zimmerman, John J., 'Charles Thomson, the Sam Adams of Philadelphia', *Mississippi Valley Historical Review*, December 1958.

FULL-LENGTH WORKS

Akagi, R. H., *The Town Proprietors of the New England Colonies* (Philadelphia, 1924).

Ambler, C. H., *Sectionalism in Virginia* (Chicago, 1910).

Ammon, Harry, 'The Republican Party in Virginia, 1789–1824', unpublished Ph.D. thesis, University of Virginia, 1948.

Aspinall, A., *Politics and the Press* (London, 1949).

Bailyn, Bernard, ed. with Intro. *Pamphlets of the American Revolution 1750–1765* (Cambridge, Mass., 1965).

Barry, J. S., *History of Massachusetts*, 3 vols. (Boston, 1855–6–7).

Beveridge, Albert, *Life of John Marshall* (Boston, 1916).

Becker, Carl L., *The Declaration of Independence* (New York, 1922; reprinted New York, 1959).

Bezanson, Anne, *Prices and Inflation during the American Revolution: Pennsylvania 1770–1790* (Philadelphia, 1951).

Black, J. D., *The Reign of Queen Elizabeth* (Oxford, 1959).

Blitzer, Charles, *An Immortal Commonwealth: The Political Theory of James Harrington* (New Haven, 1960).

Bradford, Alden, *History of Massachusetts from 1775 to 1789* (Boston, 1825).

Brennan, Ellen, *Plural Office-Holding in Massachusetts 1760–1780* (Chapel Hill, 1945).

Bridenbaugh, Carl and Jessica, *Rebels and Gentlemen, Philadelphia in the Age of Franklin* (New York, 1942).

— *Cities in Revolt* (New York, 1955).

Bridenbaugh, Carl, *Myths and Realities: Societies of the Colonial South* (Baton Rouge, 1952).

— *Mitre and Sceptre* (New York, 1962).

Bronner, Edwin B., *William Penn's 'Holy Experiment'* (New York, 1962).

Brown, Robert E., *Middle-Class Democracy and the Revolution in Massachusetts* (Ithaca, 1955).

— and B. Katherine, *Virginia 1705–1786: Democracy or Aristocracy?* (E. Lansing, Michigan, 1964).

Bruce, Philip Alexander, *The Institutional History of Virginia in the Seventeenth Century*, 2 vols. (New York, 1910).

Brunhouse, Robert L., *Counter-Revolution in Pennsylvania 1776–1790* (Harrisburg, 1942).

Butterfield, Herbert, *George III, Lord North and the People* (Cambridge, 1949).

Chamberlain, Mellen, *A Documentary History of Chelsea [Massachusetts] 1624–1824*, 2 vols. (Boston, 1908).

Chandler, J. A. C., *History of Representation in Virginia* (Baltimore, 1896).

— *History of Suffrage in Virginia* (Baltimore, 1901).

Channing, Edward, *Town and County Government in the English Colonies of North America* (Baltimore, 1889).

Clarke, Mary P., *Parliamentary Privilege in the American Colonies* (New Haven, Conn., 1943).

Craven, Wesley Frank, *The Southern Colonies in the Seventeenth Century, 1607–1689* (Baton Rouge, 1949).

Christie, Ian R., *Wilkes, Wyvill and Reform* (London, 1962).

Crowl, Philip A., *Maryland during and after the Revolution* (Baltimore, 1943).

Cushing, Harry A., *The Transition in Massachusetts from Province to Commonwealth*, Columbia Univ. Studies in History, Economics and Public Law, VII (New York, 1896).

De Grazia, Alfred, *Public and Republic: Political Representation in America* (New York, 1951).

Dodson, Leonidas, *Alexander Spotswood* (Philadelphia, 1932).

Douglass, Elisha P., *Rebels and Democrats* (Chapel Hill, 1953).

Dunaway, Weyland F., *The Scotch-Irish of Colonial Pennsylvania* (Chapel Hill, 1944).

Feiling, Keith, *A History of the Tory Party, 1640–1714* (Oxford, 1924).

Ferguson, E. James, *The Power of the Purse* (Chapel Hill, 1961).

Flippin, Percy Scott, *The Royal Government in Virginia, 1624–1775* (New York, 1919).

Gash, Norman, *Politics in the Age of Peel* (London, 1953).

Gibbons, P. A., *Ideas of Representation in Parliament 1651–1832* (Oxford, 1914).

Greene, Jack P., *The Quest for Power: The Lower Houses of Assembly in the Southern Royal Colonies, 1689–1776* (Chapel Hill, 1963).

Griffith, Elmer C., *The Rise and Development of the Gerrymander* (Chicago, 1907).

Griffith, E. S., *History of American City Government, Colonial Period* (New York, 1938).

Griffith, Lucille Blanche, 'The Virginia House of Burgesses, 1750–1774', unpublished Ph.D. thesis, Brown University, 1957.

Guttridge, G. H., *English Whiggism and the American Revolution* (Berkeley and Los Angeles, 1963).

Handler, Edward, *America and Europe in the Political Thought of John Adams* (Cambridge, Mass., 1964).

Halévy, Elie, *History of the English People*, vol. iii (London, 1927).

Hanham, H. J., *Elections and Party Management* (London, 1959).

Harlow, Ralph V., *History of Legislative Methods before 1825* (New Haven, Conn., 1917).

Hart, F. H., *The Valley of Virginia in the American Revolution* (Chapel Hill, 1942).

Hawke, David, *In the Midst of a Revolution* (London, 1961).

Haynes, G. H., *Representation and Suffrage in Massachusetts, 1620–1891* (Baltimore, 1894).

Hill, Christopher, and Dell, Edmund, *The Good Old Cause* (London, 1949).

Hilldrup, Robert LeRoy, 'The Virginia Convention of 1776', unpublished Ph.D. thesis, University of Virginia, 1935.

Howard, G. E., *Introduction to the Local Constitutional History of the United States*, vol. i (Baltimore, 1889).

Hunt, N. C., *Two Early Political Associations* (Oxford, 1961).

Jacobson, David L., 'John Dickinson and Joseph Galloway', unpublished Ph.D. thesis, Princeton University, 1959.

Jensen, Merrill, *The New Nation* (New York, 1950).

Keith, Charles P., *Chronicles of Pennsylvania* (Philadelphia, 1917).

Kemp, Betty, *King and Commons* (London, 1957).

Kendall, Willmoore, *John Locke and the Doctrine of Majority Rule* (Urbana, Ill., 1941).

Klein, Philip S., *Pennsylvania Politics, 1817–1832: A Game Without Rules* (Philadelphia, 1940).

Klett, Guy Soulliard, *Presbyterians in Colonial Pennsylvania* (Philadelphia, 1937).

Kurtz, Stephen G., *The Presidency of John Adams* (Philadelphia, 1957).

Labaree, Benjamin W., *Patriots and Partisans: The Merchants of Newburyport, 1764–1815* (Cambridge, Mass., 1962).

Labaree, Leonard W., *Conservatism in Early America* (New Haven, 1948).

Lincoln, Charles H., *The Revolutionary Movement in Pennsylvania, 1760–1776* (Philadelphia, 1901).

Lingley, Charles R., *The Transition in Virginia from Colony to Commonwealth* (New York, 1910).

Lokken, Roy N., *David Lloyd, Colonial Lawmaker* (Seattle, 1959).

Maccoby, S., *English Radicalism 1762–1785* (London, 1955).

McCormick, Richard P., *The History of Voting in New Jersey . . . 1664–1911* (New Brunswick, 1953).

McKinley, A. E., *The Suffrage Franchise in the Thirteen American Colonies* (Philadelphia, 1903).

McKisack, May, *The Parliamentary Representation of the English Boroughs during the Middle Ages* (London, 1962).

Macpherson, C. B., *The Political Theory of Possessive Individualism* (Oxford, 1962).

Maitland, F. W., *The Constitutional History of England* (Cambridge, 1919).

Malone, Dumas, *Jefferson the Virginian* (Boston, 1948).

Mays, David J., *Edmund Pendleton, 1721–1803*, 2 vols. (Cambridge, Mass., 1952).

Miller, John C., *Sam Adams, Pioneer in Propaganda* (Boston, 1936).

Mingay, G. E., *English Landed Society in the Eighteenth Century* (London, 1963).

Morris, Richard B., *Government and Labor in Early America* (New York, 1946).

Morison, Samuel Eliot, *The Life and Letters of Harrison Gray Otis, Federalist, 1765–1848* (Boston, 1913).

— *Three Centuries of Harvard, 1636–1936* (Cambridge, Mass., 1942).

Morse, Anson Eli, *The Federalist Party in Massachusetts to 1800* (Princeton, 1909).

Morton, Richard L., *Colonial Virginia*, 2 vols. (Chapel Hill, 1960).

Namier, Sir Lewis, *The Structure of Politics at the Accession of George III*, 2 vols. (London, 1929).

— *England in the Age of the American Revolution* (London, 1961).

Neale, Sir John E., *The Elizabethan House of Commons* (London, 1949).

Nettels, Curtis B., *The Money Supply of the American Colonies before 1720* (Madison, 1934).

Newcomer, L. N., *The Embattled Farmers* (New York, 1953).

Ogg, David, *England in the Reigns of James II and William III* (Oxford, 1955).

Olson, Alison Gilbert, *The Radical Duke* (Oxford, 1961).

Osgood, Herbert L., *The American Colonies in the Eighteenth Century*, 4 vols. (New York, 1924–5; reprinted Gloucester, Mass., 1958).

Owen, John B., *The Rise of the Pelhams* (London, 1957).

Paige, Lucius R., *A History of Cambridge, Massachusetts, 1630–1877* (New York, 1883).

Palmer, R. R., *The Age of the Democratic Revolution: I, The Challenge* (Princeton, 1959).

Pares, Richard, *George III and the Politicians* (Oxford, 1953).

Perkins, Bradford, *Prologue to War: England and the United States 1805–1812* (Berkeley and Los Angeles, 1961).

Plumb, J. H., *Sir Robert Walpole*, 2 vols.: i, *The Making of a Statesman*; ii, *The King's Minister* (London, 1956).

Pocock, J. G. A., *The Ancient Constitution and the Feudal Law* (Cambridge, 1957).

Porritt, E., and A., *The Unreformed House of Commons* (Cambridge, 1909).

Proud, Robert, *The History of Pennsylvania* (Philadelphia, 1797).

Robbins, Caroline, *The Eighteenth Century Commonwealthman* (Cambridge, Mass., 1959).

Rudé, George, *Wilkes and Liberty* (Oxford, 1962).

Scharf, Thomas J., *History of Maryland*, 2 vols. (Baltimore, 1879).

Selsam, J. Paul, *The Pennsylvania Constitution of 1776* (Philadelphia, 1936).

Sharpless, Isaac, *A Quaker Experiment in Government* (Philadelphia, 1898).

Shepherd, W. R., *History of Proprietary Government in Pennsylvania* (New York, 1896).

Shipton, Clifford K., *Sibley's Harvard Graduates* (Cambridge, Mass., 1933 — in continuation).

Sly, J. F., *Town Government in Massachusetts 1620–1930* (Cambridge, Mass., 1930).

Smith, J. E. A., *History of Pittsfield, Massachusetts*, 2 vols. (Boston, 1869 and 1876).

Spencer, Henry Russell, *Constitutional Conflict in Provincial Massachusetts* (Columbus, Ohio, 1905).

Stanwood, Edward, *History of the Presidency*, 2 vols. (Boston and New York, 1898).

Sutherland, Lucy, *The East India Company in Eighteenth Century Politics* (Oxford, 1952).

Sydnor, Charles S., *The Development of Southern Sectionalism* (Baton Rouge, 1948).

— *Gentlemen Freeholders: Political Practices in Washington's Virginia* (Chapel Hill, 1952).

Taylor, Robert J., *Western Massachusetts in the Revolution* (Providence, 1954).

Thayer, Theodore, *Pennsylvania Politics and the Growth of Democracy, 1740–1776* (Harrisburg, 1953).

Tinkom, H. M., *Republicans and Federalists in Pennsylvania, 1790–1800* (Harrisburg, 1940).

Tolles, Frederick B., *Meeting House and Counting House* (Chapel Hill, 1948).

Thompson, F. M. L., *English Landed Society in the Nineteenth Century* (London, 1963).

Trevelyan, G. M., *Lord Grey of the Reform Bill* (London, 1920).

Veitch, George, *The Genesis of Parliamentary Reform* (1913), reprinted, ed. Ian R. Christie (London, 1964).

Walcott, Robert, *English Politics in the Early Eighteenth Century* (Oxford, 1956).

Washburn, Wilcomb E., *The Governor and the Rebel* (Chapel Hill, 1957).

Watson, J. Steven, *The Reign of George III* (Oxford, 1960).

Wells, W. V., *The Life and Public Services of Samuel Adams*, 3 vols. (Boston, 1865).

Williams, David Alan, 'Political Alignments in Colonial Virginia 1698–1750', unpublished Ph.D. thesis, Northwestern University, 1959.

Williamson, Chilton, *American Suffrage from Property to Democracy* (Princeton, 1960).

Woodward, Sir E. L., *The Age of Reform* (Oxford, 1949).

Index

Abbot, Charles, Speaker of H. of Commons, 460

Acton, Lord, 23

Adams, John, influence of Harrington on, 11–12, 13; on aristocracy, 12, 51, 216–23, 290, 525; on Otis, 65 n; diary of, 66–7, 68; *Thoughts on Government* by, 135, 186, 220, 221, 290; and Mass. Constitution, (draft) 179 n, (1780) 191, 192, 208, 217; and 'orders' of society, 186, 214, 216–17, 223, 342; *Defence of the Constitutions* by, 216; and Continental Congress, 252, 261, 347, 349–50; and property, 266, 273 n, 529; and Pa. Constitution (1776), 273, 291; *see also*: xvi, 23, 316, 370, 381, 382

Adams, John Quincy, 231

Adams, Samuel, and Stamp Act, 66, 67; and Mass. Constitution (1780), 191, 195, 199, 210; *see also*: 252, 258

Address, The, accompanying Mass. 1780 Constitution, 195–8, 205, 209, 210, 329

Address to the People, by General Court, Mass. (1786), on public finance, 232

administration, use of word, 518

'Advice' of Mass. Assembly (1728), on control of finance, 59, 60

aesthetics, constitutional, 435

age qualification for suffrage, (Mass.) for non-churchmen, 36; (Va.) for senators, 284, proposed for electors, 287

agrarian character, of Va. and of U.S., Madison's desire to preserve, 296, 304, 361

Agrarian (Law), in Harrington's *Oceana*, 9, 13; lacking in Pa., 77

agricultural interest (Mass.), 176, 200, 201

Alabama, election of judges in, 320 n

Albany, Congress at (1754), 143

Albemarle county, Va., under-represented, 289

Alexandria, Va., growth of, 288, 309; voting in (1795), 151

Alien and Sedition Acts (U.S.), 380, 524

Alison, Rev. Francis, Presbyterian leader (Pa.), 269

Allen, William, anti-Franklin representative, Pa., 278

Almon, John, political controversialist, 429

amateur tradition (Va.), 150

American War of Independence, xvi; in Mass., 201; in Pa., 280; and constitutional reform (Britain), 387, 427, 439–40; debates in Parliament on, 489–90

Anabaptists (Pa.), 123

Andros, Edmund, Governor of Mass. (1686–9), 37, 55, 218; Governor of Va., 133

Anglican Church, disestablishment of (Va.), 282

Anglicans, in Mass., 36–7, 47, 55, 205; in Pa., 104, 123; plan of, to establish American bishopric, 423

Anti-Federalists, 373, 376

appointments, *see* patronage

apprentices, excluded from suffrage, (Mass.) 245, (Pa.) 84; and freemanship of boroughs, 400

aristocracy, in Harrington's *Oceana*, 10, 11, 12; John Adams on, 12, 51, 216–23, 290, 525; Sidney and, 14; Va. leadership regarded as, 154–5; property as a substitute for the 'estate' of, 170, 342; virtues of, in a republic, 183–4; in Pa., 261; 'afraid to trust the people', 307; Gordon and Beckford on, 417–18; Montesquieu on, 418–19, 420

Aristotle, 192, 377, 504, 539; influence of, on Harrington, 8, 11, and Sidney, 14

army, Putney debates of, 6; 'beast with a great belly' (Harrington), 8; British, in Mass., 68

army and navy interest, in H. of Commons, 452

army interest (U.S., after War of Independence), 374

Articles of Association, proposed and circulated by Continental Congress, 346

Articles of Confederation, 310, 345, 348, 351

artisans

   in Britain, Radical movement among, 430, 458, 471–2

   in Mass., 210

   in Pa., excluded from suffrage, 84; position in society of, 268, 269; Paine and, 269–70; in Philadelphia, 250, 259, 260, 265, 267, 341

   in Va., 142, 317, 328

Assemblies, colonial, xv, 30–2, 215; modelled on H. of Commons, 31, 128, 142, 156, 505; 'cannot be partial or corrupted', 120, 121; reasons for attempting entry to, 158–9; in revolutionary crisis, 282, 340, 518; powers and privileges of, 428, 505, 508; and Governors, 504, 505, 515, 518; susceptible to popular feeling, 529

Assembly, Mass., composed of elected representatives of towns, 39, 52, 73; gains leadership over Council, 30, 54, 63–4; favours proprietors of land in disputes with townsmen, 43, 56; claims power to disburse funds raised by its own vote, 57–8, 505; public gallery for,

Ipswich, Mass., seaboard town, 64, 182
Ireland, landed interest in, 448; trade with, 450
Ireland, Northern, immigrants to Pa. from, *see* Scotch-Irish
Ireton, Henry, on suffrage, 286 n

Jackson, Andrew, Presidential election of, 312, 313
Jacobin clubs, British artisans correspond with, 430
James II, 14, 389, 390, 391; overthrow of, 396, 523
Jay, John, Governor of New York, 381
Jay's Treaty (1794), 149; instructions to representatives on, 163
Jebb, Dr John, Radical, 342, 467, 470, 471
Jefferson, Thomas, and Locke, 17, 25; and reform in Va., 126, 282; *Notes on Virginia* by, 146, 289, 297, 300, 301; and majority rule, 281, 304, 317, 323, 380; on similarity of two houses of legislature in Va., 284, 507; on suffrage, 286–7, 288–9, 320; and Va. Constitution (1776), 296–9, 300–2, 304–5, 314; an optimistic Whig, 302, 465; and Virginia and Kentucky Resolutions, 367, 382; as President, 370, 380, 381; and Saxon myth, 438; *see also* 152, 154, 356
Jefferson's Embargo (1807), 245, 246
Jefferson's Republican Party, 148, 155, 294, 317–18, 337, 536, 537
Jenkinson, Charles (later Lord Liverpool), 440, 483, 490, 491; and interest representation, 453–4, 472, 482
Jennings, Edward, President of Va. Council, 130
Jenyns, Soame, on reform, 467
Johnson, Chapman, Va. Republican leader, 305, 309, 311; speech of, at 1829 Convention, 316, 327–30, 336
Johnson, Dr Samuel, representative of Conn. at Philadelphia Convention, 363
Johnstone, George, M.P., on property and power, 461
judges, in Mass., 49, 193, 211; in Pa., 106; in Va., 335; Federal, 320, 379 n; as subordinate branch of executive (Montesquieu), 418
judicial system, Va., attempt of Governor Spotswood to reform, 131–2
Julius Caesar, Penn on, 81
Junius, 298, 429
justice, in Harrington's *Oceana*, 10, 84; a fruit of government (Penn), 79
Justices of the Peace, in New England, 47, 51, 218; in Pa., elected (1776 Constitution), 272; in Va., co-opted, 156
Justices of the Supreme Court, 53 n

Keith, Sir William, Governor of Pa., 91, 97, 98–101, 116
Keithians, Quaker sect, 88 n
Keithians, supporters of Governor Keith, 100, 103
Kent, Benjamin, on Mass. Assembly, 176 n
Kentucky, Constitution of, suffrage in, 153; Madison and, 299, 303
Kentucky Resolutions (1798, 1799), 367, 382
Keppele, Heinrich, German elected to Pa. Assembly, 111
King, Rufus, of New York, at Philadelphia Convention, 242, 357, 362, 370; and slavery, 359, 366, 367
king can do no wrong (Bolingbroke), 414, 415
King's Friends, 430, 434, 436
Kinsey, John, Chief Justice and Speaker, Pa., 109, 110

labourers, non-representation of, (Mass.), 210, (Pa.), 84; (Va.), 315, 533; (Britain), 421; Paley on, 455
Lamb, Sir Matthew, Counsel of Board of Trade, 145
Lancaster county, Pa., as constituency, 103, 110, 123
land, in Harrington's *Oceana*, 8–9, 13, 17; represented in Parliament, rather than people, 25–6; policy of Governor Nicholson on (Va.), 130, 131, speculation in (colonies), 56, 144; as most permanent and excellent kind of property, 266; scheme for assessing states for taxation by value of, 348–9, 365; proprietors of (Mass. and Pa.), *see* proprietors
Land Bank, Mass., 62–3, 64; legislature elected on issue of, 69, 519
land ordinances, on western lands of U.S. (1780s), 351
land tax, (Pa.), 113; (Va.), 310, 312; (Federal), 380; (Britain), 445
landed gentry, *see* gentry
landed interest, in Mass., 169, 177–8; in Pa., 82, 169, 266, 343; in Va., 125, 286; in H. of Commons, 266, 443, 444–9, 453, 468, and H. of Lords, 526; London Corresponding Society on over-representation of, 476, 477
landed qualification, for M.P.s (1710), 408; *for suffrage see* freeholders
Last Determinations Act (1696), 401, 405, 412–13
law, distinction between permanent or constitutional, and statute law of Parliament, 3, 17, 18–19, 26, 353–4; natural, 10, 20; codification of (Va.), 282; reason as foundation of (Sharp), 463
lawyers and others, interest of, 374, 452
leadership, in Sidney's version of Gothic myth, 14; Utilitarians and, 479, 483; problem of,

Nicholas, Wilson Cary, Governor of Va., 311

Nicholl, Sir John, on broadening representation of interests (1817), 492

Nicholson, Sir Francis, Governor of Va., 130, 131

nobility, the, *see* aristocracy

nominations for candidates for Assembly, protest at method of making (Pa., 1770), 267

non-freeholders (Va.), votes cast by, 306; demand for suffrage by, 320–1, 372

non-residents (Va.), votes cast by, 306

Norfolk, Va., suffrage in, 142, 293–4; letter from citizens of, 162; representative of, 285; growth of, 309

Norman Conquest, in Gothic myth, 80, 437

Norris, Isaac, Speaker of Pa. Assembly, 256 n; pamphlet by, 96; correspondence of, 103, 105–6, 111, 120, 122, 123

North, Lord, and George III, 369; fall from office of, 387; and representation, 430, 432; opposes reform, 435, 438, 446, 449–50, 469; and American War of Independence, 439–40; on Wilkes, 459; *see also* xvi, 404

North, the, of U.S., division of interests between South and, 366–7

North Carolina, property qualifications for voting in, 208, 282, 292; presidential elections in 381; free Negroes vote in (until 1835), 533; voting statistics for, 563–4

Northampton, Mass., gentry of, 177; objections of, to 1780 Constitution, 212–13, 225

Northampton county, Pa., representation of, 264, 279

Northern Neck district of Va., representation of, 288, 297

Nott, Edward, Governor of Va., 130

numbers, representation as a solution of the problem of, (Sidney) 15, (Penn) 80, 81, 87, 539, (*Essex Result*) 184; and property, combined power of, 76, 92, 248, 264, 275, 276, 320, 329, 350; as opposed to 'weight', 207, 260, 263; 'n., or property, or both' (Mass.), 173–8, 202; 'attached to property and good order' (Durham), 499; *see also* numerical representation

numerical representation, principle of, xvii, 92, 110, 190; in Locke, 24, 25; shift towards (Mass.), 52, 170, 175, 180, 190, 203, 205, 248, 329, 350; Boston and, 213–14; Gerry Administration and, 247–8; in Pa., 92, 262–5, 274–5, 276; Jefferson and, 289, 297, 302, 304; political individualism the basic principle of, 315; Va. reformers and, 315, 319, 321; at Continental Congress, 347, 348, 349, 350, 352 n; in election of President, 371; proposed for H. of Commons by Duke of Richmond, 463–4, by Cartwright, 465, accepted by Mill, 483; political justice and, 535–6

Occasional Conformity Act (1713), 421

Oceana, Commonwealth devised by Harrington, 8–13, 78, 524; resemblance of Pa. Constitution to that of, 76, 77, 83

officials, British, in Mass., 68; (civil service) interest of, 452

Ohio county, Va., election petition from, 306

Old Sarum, borough of, 402

oligarchy, in Va., 125; system in 18th-century Britain as a limited, 385, 386, 387, 391, 401, 405, 406; movements opposing, 423–7

Onslow, Arthur, Speaker of H. of Commons, 424, 497

opposition, political, county conventions, Mass., as, 226, 229, 242; to policy of majority, not to Constitution, a delicate distinction, 242–3; contained within frame of parliamentary politics (Britain, 18th-century), 407; to Whigs, 428–30

optimists, political, Locke, 23; Jefferson, 302, 465

'orders' of society, 12, 169, 186, 342; bi-cameralism and, 214–26; *see also* estates of the realm

'ostracism' of aristocracy in Upper Chamber (J. Adams), 12, 219 n, 220, 221, 290

Otis, James, jun., representative of Boston, 65; and Stamp Act, 16, 67, 71

Otis, James, sen., 65

pacifism, of Quakers, 78, 102, 104, 108, 112

Paine, Tom, *Common Sense* by, 258, 269, 474; on suffrage in Pa., 265

Paley, William, on British Constitution, 454–6, 477, 498

Palmer, Mass., asks for paper money, 228–9

pamphlets and broadsides, (Mass.), on 'Bank of Credit', 61; (Pa.), Penn's, 80, to electors, 94, 97, 99–101, Quaker, against Governor, 107, in proprietary interest, against Quakers, 109; (Va.), 135; (U.S.) on instruction of representatives, 163; (Britain), on Test Acts, 417, on reform, 489

paper money, (Mass.) 62, 228, 233–4, 240–1; (Pa.) 98, 100, 102, 108; (Va.) scandal of disposal of, 154 n; (U.S.) merchants and, 378; (Britain) Bill for restraining issue of in America (1764), 452

Parliament, xv, 3, 4–5, 15–16, 36; proposals for American members of, 339; independence of, 392, 411–12, 442; as 'the whole nation' (Burke), 399, 441, 531; liberty of, 390, 391, 402–3, 407, 519; Englishness of, 392, 504; stability of, established by Walpole and Newcastle, 407–13; reforms itself (slightly), 430, 457; 'the grand inquest of the nation', 441, 488, 525; accountable to public opinion, 479, 490, 498, 527; duration of, *see* elections,

342; for legislators and Governor, 179 n,
197, 212, 225, 226, 248
in N.C., for electors, 208, 282, 292
in Pa., for electors, 84, 88, 256, 259, 261;
abolished (other than tax payment), 271
in Va., for electors, 136, 138, 143, 146–7;
proposed in draft Constitution, 287, 323 n;
demand for retention of, 325–6
U.S., proposed differential, for different
Houses, 299, 302; proposed for electors
to Congress, 359, but not adopted, 364, 377
proprietors of land
in Mass., 39–40; town meetings originate
with, 43; disputes between townsmen and,
43, 56
in Pa., Penn family as, 76, 82, 87, 94; strife
between Quakers and, 87, 98, 105–6, 108,
118, 250, 254, 255; claim of, to exemption
from taxation, 90, 108, 113, 114, 118, 120,
121; Scotch-Irish as allies of, 93, 94, 104,
105, 112, 124, 250, 263, 269; right to
purchase land from Indians confined to,
113; patronage by, 98, 106, 113, 118–19,
251; as hereditary rulers, 116
Protestant Dissenting Deputies, 422–3
Protestantism, Parliament and, 392, 504
Proud, Robert, historian of Pa., 105 n
public gallery, for Mass. House of Representatives, 69–70, 340
public opinion
in Britain, freedom of H. of Commons from
pressure of, 390, 407; H. of Commons and,
406–7, 441, 454, 455, 469, 486–94, 520–
1; Whigs and, 498
in U.S., Mass. Assembly as agent of, 70;
mobilised by Republican Party, 161;
permeated with doctrine of consent, 191
Puritan Church, Mass., electorate confined to
members of, 34; disestablished, 40
Putney debates (1647), 6; none in 1688, 396
Pym, John, 6

Quaker interest, Pa., 105
Quaker meetings, 101–2, 103, 122
Quakers, in Pa., 76–7, 93, 101, 250, 254;
religion of, 78, 96; strife between Penn
family and, 76, 77, 87, 98, 105–6, 108, 118;
appeal to Crown to depose Penns, 57, 77, 98,
116, 120, 250, 251; represent merchant
interest, 94, 105; claim to speak for the
people, 101–2, 109, 112, 118, 121–2, 520;
end of system of, 109–24; and Indians, 112;
permitted to vote in Va., 139; in 1764
election, 257, 258; affirmations by, 274, 422;
in British politics, 422
qualifications, for electors and representatives,
see age, birth, landed, naturalisation, property,
racial, religious, *and* residence qualifications

Quietists, among Germans in Pa., 109
quorum, size of, in Mass. H. of Representatives,
199–200, 239, 242; Pa. Assembly deprived
of a, 253

racial qualifications for suffrage, 533; in Mass.
(1778), 179; in Va. (1723), 140
Radicalism, in American thought, 196, 342
Radicals
in Britain, and Wilkes case, 267, 367, 387,
426; and publication of debates, 390, 403;
of City of London, 426, 452; convergence
of Old Whigs and, 426, 437; and Gothic
myth, 428; and the people, 442, 465;
movement of, among artisans, to secure
representation of individuals, 458, 471–9;
in 1832 H. of Commons, 485; alliance of,
with Whigs, 479, 480, 485; reject interest
representation, 497–8, 528
in Pa., plan of, in action (1776 Constitution),
77, 270–80, 341–2; in Philadelphia, 250,
253, 258, 260
Ramsay, Allan, political writer, 489
Randolph, Edmund, Governor of Va., 163 n,
352, 354, 378
Randolph, John, of Roanoke, 151–2, 337
Randolph, Peyton, Speaker of Va. Assembly,
154
Randolphs, leaders in Va. Assembly, 154
rank, social, in New England, 44–6, 56; in Pa.,
105, 260–70
Reading (England), reform petition from,
491
rebellions, in Va., 1676 (Bacon's), 128, 139,
514; in Mass., 1786 (Shays's), 226–44; in
Britain (1745), 407
recusants, in Va., 139
referendum (Va., 1827), on whether to hold a
Convention, 313, 331–2
reform
economical, Rockingham programme of, 433,
458
Locke on impossibility of, 19–20
Parliamentary, American War of Independence and, 387, 416; and theory of
representation, 405, 457; Swift and, 414;
Old Whigs and Radicals converge in, 426,
437; the gentry and, 462–70; Radical,
471–8; Lord Melbourne on, 493–4
of suffrage, Va., demands for, 307–14;
opponents of, 315–16; Conventions to
effect, *see* Conventions, Reform
Reform Act (1832), 494–9, 512, 528
Reform of the Establishment, Burke's Act for,
433
religion, question of public support for, (Va.)
163, (Mass.) 195; of Crown, Parliament and,
392

tea, monopoly of distribution of, in colonies, given to E. India Co., 450
tenants of land, treated as freeholders for suffrage (Va.), 147; increase in number of (Va.), 317; interests of, 375
Tennessee, case of *Baker* v. *Carr* on malapportionment in, 513, 536
Tertium Quids (Va.), 337
Test Acts, opposition to, 417, 423
theocratic state, Mass. as, 34, 37
Thomas, George, Governor of Pa., 101, 102, 103
Thomson, Charles, leader of Philadelphia artisans, 367
'ticket', use of the expression, 103, 107; (Mass.), electoral, 70; (Pa.), 'the Old' (Quaker), 110, 238, 256, 257, 263; 'the New' (proprietary party), 256, 257, 263
Tidewater, district of Va., 144, 151, 154 n, 155, 316; over-represented, 288, 289; diminishing prosperity of, 308, 309; and taxation, 310–11, 312, 328; allied with Valley district, 331
tithes, landed interest and, 449
tobacco, inspection of crops of (Va.), 131, 132, 134, 140, 152, 519; price of (1820s), 316
Toland, John, Commonwealthman, 8, 404
Toleration Act (1688), 421
Tories, 391, 393; as critics of government, 406, 413, 414; King's Friends as, 430; defend right of suffrage as property, 434; 'descended from Normans' (Jefferson), 438; differ from Whigs on identity and extent of interests to be represented in Parliament, 483, 526–8
town meetings, New England, 43–53, 190; property qualifications for voting in, 36, 48, 50, 515–16; forbidden by Governor Andros, 37; business of, 49–50; and election of representatives, 51–2; of Boston, 50, 60, 67–8, 71, 181, 202, 206, 515; instruction of representatives by, 72, 517, 539; declared illegal by Britain, 74; reject 1777 draft Constitution, 179; election of delegates to county conventions by, 236; Federalist leaders and, 244
towns
pure democracy only possible in small (Sidney), 14; interests of large, secured by numerical representation, 304, 319
in New England, 38–54
in Mass., as political constituencies, 38, 50, 51, 52, 180, 190, 193, 204, 248; representation of, 63, 172, 173–4, 180, 230; constitutional rights of, 73; struggle between representation of individuals and of, 199, 200, 213–14, 537; incorporation of new, without representation, 173; smaller and poorer, under-represented, 230, 234–5; participate in defiance of Britain, 341

corporate interest of (Mass.), 39, 52, 53, 181, 200, 203, 207, 213, 275, 286 n; allied with agricultural interest, 200; offended by gerrymandering, 247
in Va., representation of, 142, 285, 294, 338
see also individual towns
Townshend duties, 66, 206, 266
Trade Acts, 65
trade guilds, 389, 390
Treasurer, election of (Mass.), 57–8
Treasury funds, use of, in elections (Britain), 427, 445, 498
Trenchard, John, Commonwealthman, 404, 417
Triennial Act, (1641–64), 437; (1694), 392, 396, 404, 437; repeal of, 408, 410
trust, power of government as a, 411, 431, 432, 527
Tuckahoes, of eastern Va., 327

unicameralism, pamphlet on, 343. *See also* legislature, unicameral
union, federal or incorporating, 349, 355
Upshur, Abel P., Va. conservative, 325, 326, 351
Upton, Mass., on 1777 draft Constitution, 203
Utilitarians, 479, 481–3; reject interest representation, 527–8

Valley district of Va., 155, 307, 316, 331; movement of slavery into, 308; demand for reform in, 309, 311; representatives of, at reform Convention, 327, 330–1
Van Schaack, Henry, representative of Berkshire county, Mass., 241, 243, 244
Vermont, suffrage in Constitution of, 153
veto, of Privy Council, circumvented by colonial Assemblies, 31, 57; of colonial Governors, 55, 59; of Penn, 85; proposed for Governor and Council in *Essex Result*, 187 n; proposed for Governor in J. Adams's draft Constitution for Mass., 220; of small states, 351; of President, 373; of Crown, 392; threat of, from H. of Commons, to Crown patronage, 425
Virginia, taken as representative of the South, xvi–xvii; Assembly and Council in, 30; identification of legislative power in, 125–35; electorate in, 136–48; elections in, 148–65, 381; voting statistics for, 150, 560; instructs delegates to Continental Congress for independence, 253; planter aristocracy of, 261; 1776 Constitution of, 181, 281–96, 296–304; constitutional reform in, 304–14; Madison advocates Federal ratio for, 379
Virginia Company, 127, 132
Virginia Gazette, 134